MORNEAU SHEPELL HANDBOOK OF CANADIAN PENSION AND BENEFIT PLANS

16TH EDITION

Morneau Shepell Handbook of Canadian Pension and Benefit Plans, Sixteenth Edition

© LexisNexis Canada Inc. 2016

November 2016

Library and Archives Canada Cataloguing in Publication

Morneau Shepell Handbook of Canadian Pension and Benefit Plans,
    Previously published under title: The Handbook of Canadian Pension and Benefit Plans.

Includes index.
ISBN 978-0-433-48981-8 (paperback)

1. Old Age Pensions--Canada. 2. Employee Fringe Benefits--Canada. 3. Social Security--Canada. I. Whiston, Bethune A. II. Gottlieb, Lois C. III. Morneau Shepell (Firm) IV. Title: Handbook of Canadian Pension and Benefit Plans.

HD7106.C2M4   658.3'25'0971   C2008-905183-3
KF755.S66 2012

Published by LexisNexis Canada, a member of the LexisNexis Group
LexisNexis Canada Inc.
111 Gordon Baker Rd., Suite 900
Toronto, Ontario
M2H 3R1

Customer Service
Telephone: (905) 479-2665 • Fax: (905) 479-2826
Toll-Free Phone: 1-800-668-6481 • Toll-Free Fax: 1-800-461-3275
Email: customerservice@lexisnexis.ca
Website: www.lexisnexis.ca

Printed and bound in Canada.

PREFACE

Morneau Shepell is the only human resources consulting and technology company that takes an integrative approach to employee assistance, health, benefits, and retirement needs. The Company is the leading provider of Employee and Family Assistance Programs, the largest administrator of pension and benefits plans and the largest provider of integrated absence management solutions in Canada. Through health and productivity, administrative, and retirement solutions, Morneau Shepell helps clients reduce costs, increase employee productivity, and improve their competitive position.

Established in 1966, Morneau Shepell serves approximately 20,000 organizations, ranging from small businesses to some of the largest corporations and associations in North America. With almost 4,000 employees globally, Morneau Shepell provides services to organizations across Canada, the United States, and around the globe. Morneau Shepell is a publicly-traded company on the Toronto Stock Exchange (TSX: MSI). For more information, visit morneaushepell.com.

The 16th Edition is the result of the efforts of the following professionals employed with or seconded to Morneau Shepell:

Alexandra Russell
Alison Coelho
Andrea Bassett
Andrew Fung
Andrew Rivers
Andrew Zur
Audia Bacchas
Bethune Whiston
Charles-Antoine Villeneuve
Cheryl Kane
Conrad Ferguson
Daniel Dumas
Dany Vignola
Darren Klorfine
David Krieger
David White
Debbie Gallagher
Deborah Wisteard
Diana Munteanu

Doug Stafford
Ed Lee
François Turgeon
Fred Vettese
Geneviève Henry
Gianna Marks
Glorie Alfred
Gregory Clooney
Gregory Yap
Hamish Dunlop
Hubert Lum
Idan Shlesinger
Jamie Johnson
Jan Robinson
Jay Desai
Jean Bergeron
Jean Demers
Jean Valois
Jennifer Del Vecchio

Jennifer West
Jessica Wolfraim
JJ Lee
John Trieu
Joy Sloane
Julie Vandal-Lemoyne
Kayee Ng
Kelly Beaudoin
Kristen Coady
Kristina Percy
Linda Evans
Luke Moran
Marc Drouin
Maria Zaharia
Marlene Taylor
Maryse Gagnon-Ouellette
Maude Trudeau-Morin
Meghan Vallis

Mélanie Dupont
Michael Devos
Michelle Loder
Nichola Peterson
Nicolas Bérubé
Nisha Modi
Paul Winnett
Paula Allen
Peter Nicolopoulos
Richard Béliveau
Riza Sychangco
Stephanie Knox
Susan French
Tejash Modi
Terry Chan
Tyler Scott

We would also like to thank the individuals at LexisNexis Canada Inc. who assisted with the preparation of this book, namely Gian-Luca Di Rocco, Manager, Content Development and Acquisition, Victoria Wood, Content Development Associate, Tina Eng, Editorial Manager, and Bana Moulhem, Editor.

Bethune Whiston and Gregory Clooney, Co-ordinators

July 31, 2016

LIST OF ACRONYMS

The following are acronyms in this publication:

ACPM	Association of Canadian Pension Management
AcSB	Accounting Standards Board
AD&D	Accidental Death and Dismemberment
AIMCO	Alberta Investment Management Corporation
AIR	Annual Information Return
APS	Alberta Pensions Services Corporation
ASC	Accounting Standards Codification
ASO	Administrative Services Only
ASP	Application Service Provider
AVC	Additional Voluntary Contributions
AWCBC	Association of Workers' Compensation Boards of Canada
AWI	Average Weekly Income
bcIMC	British Columbia Investment Management Corporation
BPO	Business Process Outsourcing
CANSIM	Canadian Socio-economic Information Management database. Statistics Canada, the Bank of Canada and Canada Mortgage and Housing Corporation maintain information contained in this database.
CAP	Capital Accumulation Plan
CAAT	Colleges of Applied Arts and Technology
CAPSA	Canadian Association of Pension Supervisory Authorities
CCAA	*Companies' Creditors Arrangement Act*
CDPC	Canadian Drug Insurance Pooling Corporation
CDPQ	Caisse de dépôt et placement du Québec
CEIC	Canada Employment Insurance Commission
CFR	Claims Fluctuation Reserve
CHST	Canada Health and Social Transfer
CI	Critical Illness
CIA	Canadian Institute of Actuaries
CICA	Canadian Institute of Chartered Accountants
CLHIA	Canadian Life and Health Insurance Association
COA	Council on Accreditation

COB	Coordination of Benefits
CPA	Chartered Professional Accountants (Canada)
CPI	Consumer Price Index
CPP	Canada Pension Plan
CRA	Canada Revenue Agency
CSA	Canadian Securities Administration
DB	Defined Benefit
DC	Defined Contribution
DGL	Dependent Group Life
DICO	Deposit Insurance Corporation of Ontario
DIN	Drug Identification Number
DIP	Debtor-in-possession
DLR	Disabled Life Reserves
DPSP	Deferred Profit Sharing Plan
DSU	Deferred Share Unit
EAP	Employee Assistance Program
EASNA	Employee Assistance Society of North America
EFAP	Employee and Family Assistance Program
EDI	Electronic Data Interchange
EHC	Extended Health Care
EI	Employment Insurance
ELHT	Employee Life and Health Trust
EPPA	*Employment Pension Plans Act* (Alberta)
EPSP	Employees Profit Sharing Plan
ERISA	*Employee Retirement Income Security Act of 1974* (U.S.)
ESG	Environmental, Social and Governance
FAQ	Frequently Asked Questions
FASB	Financial Accounting Standards Board (U.S.)
FPP	Flexible Pension Plan
FPR	Foreign Property Rule
FSCO	Financial Services Commission of Ontario
FSRA	Financial Services Regulatory Authority
FST	Finanical Services Tribunal
GAINS	Guaranteed Annual Income System (Ontario)
GDP	Gross Domestic Product

GIC	Guaranteed Investment Certificate
GIPS	Global Investment Performance Standards
GIS	Guaranteed Income Supplement
GST	*General Sales Tax*
HCSA	Health Care Spending Account
HRA	Health Risk Assessment
HRSDC	Human Resources and Social Development Canada
IAS	International Accounting Standard
IBNR	Incurred But Not Reported
IFRS	International Financial Reporting Standards
IMCO	Investment Management Corporation of Ontario
IPP	Individual Pension Plan
IFRIC	International Financial Reporting Interpretation Committee
ITA	*Income Tax Act* (Federal)
IVR	Interactive Voice Response
JSPP	Jointly Sponsored Pension Plans
LAP	Large Amount Pooling
LDI	Liability Driven Investing
LIF	Life Income Fund
LIRA	Locked-In Retirement Account
LLP	Lifelong Learning Plan
LRIF	Locked-In Retirement Income Fund
LTC	Long-Term Care
LTD	Long-Term Disability
MCCSR	Minimum Continuing Capital and Surplus Requirements
MDI-10	Major Depression Inventory
MEPP	Multi-Employer Pension Plans
MESSQ	Ministry of Employment and Social Solidarity of Quebec
MIE	Maximum Insurable Earning
MJPP	Multi Jurisdictional Pension Plan
MS	Morneau Shepell
MUPP	Multi Unit Pension Plans
NBIMC	New Brunswick Investment Management Corporation
NCDB	Negotiated Cost Defined Benefits
NEO	Named Executive Officers

OAS	Old Age Security
ODB	Ontario Drug Benefit
OECD	Organisation for Economic Cooperation and Development
OL	Optional Life
OMERS	Ontario Municipal Employees Retirement System
ORPP	Ontario Retirement Pension Plan
OSC	Ontario Securities Commission
OSFI	Office of the Superintendent of Financial Services
OTC	Over-the-counter
PA	Pension Adjustment
PAR	Pension Adjustment Reversal
PBGF	Pension Benefits Guarantee Fund (Ontario)
PBM	Pharmacy Benefit Manager
PBSA	*Pension Benefits Standards Act* (Federal)
PBSR	*Pension Benefits Standards Regulations, 1985* (Federal)
PCIC	Parents of Critically Ill Children
pCPA	Pan-Canadian Phamaceutical Alliance
PEBD	Pensions and Employee Benefits Division
PHS	Psychological Health and Safety, National Standard of Canada for
PHSP	Private Health Services Plan
PIAC	Pension Investment Association of Canada
PIPEDA	*Personal Information Protection and Electronic Documents Act* (Federal)
PPN	Preferred Provider Network
PRB	Post Retirement Benefit
PRI	Principles of Responsible Investing Association
PRIF	Prescribed Registered Retirement Income Fund
PRPP	Pooled Registered Pension Plan
PSA	Personal Spending Account
PSAB	Public Sector Accounting Board
PSPA	Past Service Pension Adjustment
PSP Investments	Public Sector Investment Board
PSPP	Public Service Pension Plan
Q&A	Questions and Answers

QPIP	Quebec Parental Insurance Plan
QPP	Quebec Pension Plan
QSPPA	Quebec *Supplemental Pension Plans Act*
RAMQ	Régie d'assurance-maladie du Quebec
RCA	Retirement Compensation Arrangement
RFP	Request For Proposal
RIA	Responsible Investment Association (Canada)
RIF	Retirement Income Fund
RLIF	Restricted Life Income Fund
ROM	Royal Ontario Museum
ROR Clause	Reservation of Rights Clause
RQ	Retraite Québec
RRQ	Régie des rentes du Québec
RRP	Registered Pension Plan
RRIF	Registered Retirement Income Fund
RRSP	Registered Retirement Savings Plan
RSF	Rate Stabilization Fund
SDA	Salary Deferral Arrangement
SEB	Subsequent Entry Biologics
SEM	Search Engine Marketing
SEPP	Single Employer Pension Plans
SERP	Supplemental Executive Retirement Plan or Supplementary Employee Retirement Plan, depending on the circumstances.
SIN	Social Insurance Number
SIPP/G	Statement of Investment Policies, often referred to as a Statement of Investment Policies and Procedures or Statement of Investment Policies and Goals
SMEPP	Specified Multi-Employer Pension Plans
SOMEPP	Specified Ontario Multi-Employer Pension Plan
SPLC	Morneau Shepell Summary of Pension Legislation in Canada
SRI	Socially Responsible Investing
SRPP	Shared Risk Pension Plan
STD	Short-Term Disability
STRP	Saskatchewan Teachers' Retirement Plan

SUB	Supplemental Unemployment Benefits
TAQ	Tribunal administratif du Québec
TBP	Target Benefit Pension Plan
TFSA	Tax-Free Savings Account
THI	Total Health Index
TPA	Third Party Administrator
TTY	Text Telephone
UI	Unemployment Insurance
VRSP	Voluntary Retirement Savings Plan
WC	Workers' Compensation
WCB	Workers' Compensation Board
WLRP	Wage Loss Replacement Plan
YBE	Year's Basic Exemption
YMPE	Year's Maximum Pensionable Earnings, as defined under the Canada Pension Plan. Similarly, "MPE" refers to Maximum Pensionable Earnings under the Quebec Pension Plan.

TABLE OF CONTENTS

Chapter 3
Employer Pension Plans — Terms and Conditions

Chapter 15
Winding Up a Pension Plan 443

PART II: EMPLOYEE BENEFITS

Chapter 16
Overview of Employee Benefits

Chapter 17
Provincial Hospital and Medical Insurance Plans

Chapter 21
Disability Benefits and Income Programs

Chapter 24
Post-Retirement and Post-Employment Benefits

Chapter 26

Chapter 27

PART III: DEVELOPING AREAS

PART I

RETIREMENT INCOME ARRANGEMENTS

Chapter 1

OVERVIEW OF RETIREMENT INCOME ARRANGEMENTS

Executive Summary

More than ever before, governments, employers, and employees are concerned about pension planning.

This chapter describes the changing environment within which pension arrangements operate, and looks at how governments, employers, and employees view pension arrangements. The different types of government and employer pension arrangements are described, as are the issues that an employer might consider in choosing a pension arrangement that best meets its needs and the needs of its workforce.

The balance of the chapters in Part I describe the pension programs sponsored by government and the variety of plans sponsored by employers in more detail. The typical terms and conditions found in employer plans are described, as are the considerations, including legislation that an employer will take into account when deciding on these terms and conditions. While the focus is on registered pension plans, Part I also reviews other supplementary plans for executives and other retirement income and savings arrangements.

Part I also looks at governance issues generally — the administration and financial management of pension plans and the investment of pension fund assets. A specific chapter in Part I, Chapter 4, *Governance of Retirement, Savings, and Other Benefit Plans*, is devoted to the recent development of governance guidelines in Canada and compliance with those guidelines. Finally, because pension arrangements operate in a complex legislative environment, separate chapters in Part I are devoted to the taxation system in which retirement arrangements operate and to pension standards legislation.

History

Informal pension arrangements existed in Canada as early as the late 1800s to provide benefits to employees who were no longer able to work or to widows of former employees. In 1887, the federal government passed the *Pension Fund Societies Act*, which enabled employees to establish pension funds to which an employer might or might not contribute. A few of these societies still exist. The federal government further encouraged the implementation of pension plans through income tax legislation introduced in 1919. This legislation allowed an employee to deduct from taxable income the contributions made to a pension plan. Further changes to income tax legislation, in later years, allowed employers to deduct their contributions to pension plans on behalf of their employees.

Pension arrangements were originally provided on a pay-as-you-go basis. In 1908, the federal government passed the *Government Annuities Act*, which provided a means of pre-funding pension benefits. Government annuities were discontinued in 1975. Canadian insurance companies introduced group annuity contracts for pension plans during the 1930s as an alternative to government annuities. In 1961, insurance companies were authorized to establish segregated pension funds, and since that time, group annuity contracts have largely been replaced by segregated fund and deposit administration contracts. Today, while almost 50%[1] of pension plans are funded through insurance company contracts, these plans tend to be small (in terms of numbers of members) and account for only 17% of the total membership of all Canadian employer-sponsored pension plans. Large employers favour trusteed arrangements under which they assume responsibility for the investment of pension fund assets. Assets are generally held by a trust company or individual trustees and investment of these assets is typically delegated to one or more investment managers.

Canadian governments have also actively implemented broad-based retirement programs. Old Age Security (OAS) pensions were first introduced by the federal government in 1952. The Canada and Quebec Pension Plans (CPP/QPP) were established in 1966 and the Guaranteed Income Supplement (GIS) was introduced in 1967. In recent years, these arrangements have been subjected to intensive scrutiny due to concerns over their long-term financial viability. In 1989, OAS ceased to be a universal arrangement when benefits became subject to a clawback for high income earners. The future of the CPP/QPP was somewhat uncertain in light of escalating contribution requirements and the changing demographics of the Canadian workforce. This prompted the government to review proposals for reform of the CPP/QPP to ensure it would be sustainable in the long-run, without placing too much of a financial burden on future generations. Since 1998, a variety of amendments have been made to the CPP/QPP to ensure both plans' financial sustainability,

---

[1]   See Statistics Canada, *CANSIM, table 280-0014* (for fee), http://www5.statcan. gc.ca/cansim/a26?lang=eng&id=2800014.

including a new schedule of contribution rates and incentives to postpone retirement. In June 2016, an agreement in principle was reached to expand the Canada Pension Plan.[2]

The first of the provincial pension benefits Acts was introduced in Ontario in 1965, and it provided improved vesting and funding of benefits under employer-sponsored pension plans. Today, nine provinces plus the federal government have comparable legislation (referred to throughout this Handbook as pension standards legislation) in place.

Major reform of pension standards legislation took place in the 1980s and early 1990s. Revisions were made to the minimum standards for employer-sponsored arrangements, covering such items as eligibility for plan membership, vesting of pensions for terminated employees, benefits for spouses of plan members, plan administration, and governance. While all provinces continue to adjust their pension standards legislation on a fairly regular basis, most provinces have since adopted a third set of reform-type legislation. Further initiatives for reform have come from the Canadian Association of Pension Supervisory Authorities (CAPSA) in the form of pension governance guidelines and proposed principles for a model pension law.

In the early 1990s, the federal government introduced major changes to the *Income Tax Act* (ITA), which significantly altered the tax treatment of retirement savings arrangements. The government's stated purpose of this "tax reform" was to put members of all types of retirement arrangements on a "level playing field" and to eliminate the more favourable treatment previously enjoyed by members of employer-sponsored pension arrangements. In the 1997 federal Budget, an adjustment known as a Pension Adjustment Reversal (PAR) was introduced to deal with concerns that some of these "equality" provisions introduced in 1992 were actually creating inequitable results for some plan members.[3]

In the province of Quebec, legislation was adopted in 1997 to provide phased retirement provisions, permitting employees to receive an annual lump-sum payment from their pensions while continuing employment. Alberta subsequently enacted similar legislation.

The federal government is likewise promoting the concept of "phased retirement".

---

[2]   Further details on government-sponsored arrangements can be found in Chapter 2.

[3]   Chapter 8 provides additional information on the taxation of retirement savings arrangements.

Shifts in demographic patterns have brought about a reduction in the working-age population coupled with a reduction in the number of years worked by this group. There has been a constant reduction of the number of people in the 15-65 age group and an increase in the post-65 age group. While, between 1970 and 2005, the median retirement age dropped from 65 to just below age 61, it subsequently increased reaching 64 in 2015.[4] In an effort to address the looming labour shortage as the baby boomers start to retire, proposed changes to the ITA were introduced in the 2007 federal Budget to allow defined benefit pension plan members who have met certain age and benefit entitlement tests (but at age 60 in any event) to receive a partial payment of their accrued pensions while concurrently accruing pension credits should their employment continue during this "phased retirement" period.

Employers are not obligated to offer phased retirement. Furthermore, employers are likely to favour offering this program to selected individuals rather than to a whole class of employees, but this may not be allowed by law. Nonetheless, some provinces have already made changes to their respective pension laws to accommodate phased retirement.[5]

In 2011, in an effort to increase pension coverage among Canadians, the federal government introduced the Pooled Registered Pension Plan (PRPP). A PRPP is a large-scale and low-cost defined contribution pension plan intended for small to medium employers, employees whose employer does not provide a pension plan, or for self-employed individuals to participate in a registered pension plan (RPP). Although PRPPs are intended to be simple and straightforward, provinces will have to modify existing pension legislation in order to allow PRPPs.

Present Position

Canadians typically receive retirement income from three key sources: government-administered pension programs, employer-sponsored retirement savings programs, and personal savings. Each of these sources is sometimes referred to as one leg of a three-legged stool.

Government Pension Programs

Government-administered pension programs include two distinctly different programs:

---

[4]   See Statistics Canada, CANSIM, table 280-0051, http://www5.statcan. gc.ca/cansim/a26?lang=eng&id=2820051.

[5]   Phased retirement is discussed in more detail in Chapters 3 and 9.

- OAS and GIS, which supply the base of the retirement income system and are financed out of general tax revenues; and
- CPP/QPP, which are work-related arrangements with earnings-based benefits financed solely by employee and employer contributions.

Currently, all persons who have resided in Canada for a sufficient period are entitled to the OAS benefit commencing at age 65. For those with sufficiently high individual incomes, however, OAS benefits will be entirely taxed back. For individuals with small incomes, the GIS and an Allowance (paid to spouses and common-law partners of pensioners) may also be payable. OAS benefits are now taxable; in contrast, the benefits from the GIS and the Allowance are tax-free.

In addition to these federally administered social security programs, some provincial programs, such as Ontario's Guaranteed Annual Income System (GAINS), also provide pension supplements, subject to an income test.

The CPP/QPP provides a basic level of earnings replacement on earnings up to the Year's Maximum Pensionable Earnings, which is linked to the average Canadian wage and indexed annually. Virtually all employees and self-employed persons in Canada, other than those with very small earnings, must contribute to one of these plans. Unlike the social security programs, which are income-tested, the CPP/QPP are universal and are financed solely by contributions from employees, employers, and the self-employed, without any government subsidy. The benefits are payable in addition to OAS and benefits from other income-tested programs. Benefits from the CPP/QPP are subject to income tax. In June 2016, an agreement in principle was reached to expand the Canada Pension Plan by increasing the maximum earnings subject to the CPP, the replacement rate and the required contributions.[6]

Employer-Sponsored Pension Plans

On January 1, 2014, there were 17,757 employer-sponsored pension plans in operation, covering nearly 6.2 million employee members.[7] These included 1,224 plans covering nearly 3.2 million federal, provincial, and municipal government employees, and a great variety of individual and multi-employer plans maintained by commercial, industrial, and other private sector organizations of all sizes. The assets of these employer-

---

[6] Chapter 2 provides more details on government pension programs.
[7] See Statistics Canada, *CANSIM, table 280-0014* (for fee).

sponsored pension plans have grown to total nearly $1.5 trillion over the last few decades.

Personal Savings

Some people continue to earn income after they have reached normal retirement ages. Personal savings through Registered Retirement Savings Plans (RRSPs), profit sharing plans, and savings plans are often important sources of retirement income for older individuals. Others rely on personal resources in addition to pension income, such as investment income, personal savings, and home ownership.

In the 2008 federal Budget, the government introduced a new savings vehicle, the Tax-Free Savings Account (TFSA), which allows individuals additional tax-advantaged savings in addition to their RRSPs. While TFSAs have been available since 2009, it is anticipated that they will not play a significant role in saving for retirement.[8]

All Sources Needed

Except for lower income earners and the self-employed, all legs of the three-legged stool are necessary to accumulate sufficient retirement savings to maintain a comparable standard of living after retirement. However, the ability of individuals to accumulate adequate overall retirement savings is obviously influenced by certain variables beyond the individual's control (i.e., government cutbacks such as the implementation of the OAS clawback, the OAS and GIS increased age eligibility, and an employer's desire to reduce pension costs and risks).

There has been increasing responsibility placed on individuals to save for their own retirement. Tax sheltering for retirement savings has been constrained somewhat by the federal government's actions. High personal income taxes have also reduced the amount individuals can divert to personal savings. These constraints have been alleviated somewhat by the recent increases in the defined benefit, money purchase, and RRSP dollar limits under the ITA.

The changing nature of the three-legged stool has caused, and will continue to cause, the government, employers, and financial institutions to increase their focus on educating individuals on their role in saving for a secure retirement and making them aware of the relevant issues. Chapter 5

---

[8]   See Chapters 8 and 14 for further discussion of TFSAs.

includes a more detailed discussion of the tools that can be used to educate employees about their retirement programs.

Establishing Pension Plans

An employer may pay pensions out of current revenue without setting up a pension plan. As long as retirement payments out of current revenue are reasonable, the employer may deduct them as an expense for income tax purposes, as if they were salary or wages.

However, if an employer formally commits to paying a group of employees a pension when they ultimately retire, and this commitment is sufficiently defined, the pension plan regulators may consider the arrangement to be a formal pension plan; that is, a plan "organized and administered to provide a pension benefit for employees". Implicit in this definition is that the primary purpose of a formal pension plan is to provide retirement income in the form of a lifetime annuity. So far, the authorities have not considered group RRSPs or supplementary arrangements for employees as falling within the definition of a pension plan.

A formal pension plan has two main features:

- The plan contains provisions stating how the pension and other benefits are determined, together with the terms and conditions under which the benefits will be payable; and
- Financial arrangements are made to provide the funds needed when benefits fall due, usually by building up assets in a trust fund or under an insurance contract.

As with most contracts, the employer and employees have latitude in negotiating the terms of the pension plan, subject to applicable legislation.

In addition to deciding on the level of benefits, the employer will need to decide what group or groups of employees to cover. A small employer will typically have only one pension plan applying to all of its employees. A large employer may have a variety of pension plans — perhaps one plan for salaried staff and different plans for unionized groups. A large employer may also have special retirement arrangements for its executive group. A pension plan may also be established by a group of unrelated employers for their employees. Multi-employer plans are often established by trade unions or trade associations in certain industries.

Pension legislation does not mandate that an employer establish a pension plan; nor does it require that, if a pension plan is established, the plan cover all of the employer's employees. However, if an RPP is established, all employees within a similar class must be eligible to join the plan. On the other hand, if pension benefits are being provided outside an RPP, the employer has complete freedom to tailor the benefit structure to suit its needs.

The pension contract can be terminated by the employer if sufficient notice is provided to its employees. The termination of a pension plan can be precipitated by many different types of business events, including divestiture, merger, insolvency, or a change in the corporation's philosophy towards the provision of pension benefits. Sometimes, the termination of one type of pension plan may be followed by employee participation in a new type of retirement savings vehicle, which may or may not be an RPP. Complex provincial rules and administrative policies govern the treatment of employees' accrued benefit entitlements when a plan is wound up, when a company or division is sold, or when a pension plan is converted to another type. Generally, these rules and policies establish minimum benefit levels that must be provided to employees in such situations.

Legislative Environment

Historically, the development of formal pension plans in Canada was encouraged by the favourable tax treatment that was provided under income tax legislation. In order for the employer and members of a formal pension plan to enjoy the tax shelter under the ITA, it is necessary to apply to the Canada Revenue Agency (CRA) for registration of the pension plan.

Subject to certain conditions and limits, registration under the ITA allows employees and employers to deduct their pension contributions from their respective incomes for tax purposes. Registration also exempts the pension fund's investment income from taxation. However, all benefits paid out of the plan are taxable to the recipient with the exception of certain transfers.[9]

In addition to registration under the ITA, a formal pension plan must be registered under pension standards legislation maintained by all provinces (except Prince Edward Island, which has prepared legislation but has not yet proclaimed it in force). A pension plan that covers employees in more than one province need only be registered in the province with the greatest number of employees. A pension plan must comply with the pension legislation of each province that has enacted

---

[9]   Details of legislation under the ITA are contained in Chapter 8.

pension benefits legislation with respect to any plan members who report for work in that province.

In 2016, representatives of the governments of British Columbia, Nova Scotia, Ontario, Quebec and Saskatchewan signed a new interim *Agreement Respecting Multi-Jurisdictional Pension Plans*, effective July 1, 2016. This agreement is intended to replace the existing multi-jurisdictional agreement previously signed by Ontario and Quebec in 2011, along with the *Memorandum of Reciprocal Agreement*, which was originally signed in 1968. The 2016 Agreement was negotiated as an interim measure while CAPSA coordinates amendments that will address the changing solvency funding regimes across Canadian pension jurisdictions.

The federal government has enacted similar legislation that governs pension plans for businesses under federal jurisdiction (i.e., transportation, communications, and banking). This legislation also applies to employees in the Yukon, Northwest Territories, and Nunavut.

Pension standards legislation governs the terms and conditions of the formal pension plan, minimum funding requirements, and the investment of plan assets. The intent is to protect the interests of plan members. The pension commitments must be funded by advance payments under an accepted method. This means that pay-as-you-go and terminal funding are not allowed under the legislation.[10]

Arguments For and Against Pension Plans

Government View

Private pension plans for employees are encouraged by governments because of their social utility. Government programs provide a reasonable minimum income for all seniors, but most employees look for more than the minimum and so are encouraged to save for their retirement. Pension plans are thought to foster the desirable qualities of independence and self-reliance. Employment pension plans reduce the pressure on government to increase income security benefits. Also, the contributions to pension funds, whether channelled through insurance companies or trust funds, generate large amounts of capital needed to develop Canada's resources and industry. Accordingly, the government encourages the development of pension plans by granting them special tax privileges.

---

[10]   Pension standards legislation is examined in detail in Chapter 9.

The tax privileges provided to pension plans lead, of course, to lost tax revenues. For this reason, the federal government places a limit on the tax assistance provided to pension plans.

Employer's View

As a rule, it is the employer who decides whether or not to establish a pension plan, and if so, what its conditions and benefits will be. Sometimes, an employer agrees to establish a pension plan as a result of collective bargaining, or because its competitors provide pension benefits.

If a company decides to provide pensions, an RPP delivers them at the lowest cost and in the most orderly manner for several reasons.

- An RPP allows for contributions of pre-tax dollars to be accumulated in a fund, with the earnings not subject to income tax until a benefit is paid to an employee.

  Consider a simple example where investments earn a before-tax return of 10% per year and the tax rate is always 50% (for employers and employees). For this illustration, we will ignore "bracket shifting", that is, any difference between the tax rates applicable when contributions are paid into the fund and when benefits are paid out.

  If the company were to place $1,000 into a registered fund, its cost would be the same as to set aside $500 in a non-registered fund. After one year, the registered fund would accumulate to $1,100, as interest is non-taxable. If the fund is then converted into a pension, the after-tax proceeds would be $550.

  The non-registered fund of $500 would earn $50 of investment income, on which $25 would be owed as tax. The after-tax proceeds would therefore be $525. Registration of the fund has effectively resulted in tax-free interest on the company's outlay. The results compound if the example were extended over several years.

- An RPP allows a company to expense its pension costs in the years in which the pensions were earned by and credited to its employees. It is sound accounting and business practice to recognize liabilities as they arise and allow for them in the costing of the product or service provided by the business.

- The existence of a pension plan makes it easier for a company to retire employees in an orderly fashion as employees reach retirement age or as part of business restructuring.

- A good pension plan improves the employer's competitive position in bidding for labour, particularly labour with specialized skills. This will become more important in the future if labour shortages occur as the baby boomers retire.

- Certain types of retirement savings plans can be designed to improve the employees' interest in the profit objectives of the company. For example, the employer's contribution can be tied to the level of company profit in a Deferred Profit Sharing Plan (DPSP), a group RRSP, or through innovative money purchase plan designs.

On the other hand, for valid reasons, some companies do not establish pension plans.

- Some employers may prefer to use these funds to reinvest in their own enterprises, where the potential return could be higher than in a pension fund.
- Some employers are discouraged by rising administration costs as well as the time and effort required to comply with federal and provincial legislation. Given the complex requirements of pension reform that have continued to emerge since the 1980s, smaller employers may prefer a DPSP or group RRSP.
- Some social security benefits are "selective"; that is, subject to various forms of income tests. The GIS and provincial pension supplements are examples. Income from company pension plans could reduce or eliminate social security benefits with the result that the employer is subsidizing the government rather than assisting the company's pensioners.
- Some employers feel that saving for retirement is the employee's responsibility and that RRSP limits and salaries are high enough for employees to accumulate adequate pensions through personal savings.

Employee's View

A formal pension plan can give an employee a retirement income which, together with government programs, is considered adequate. Funding of the plan gives the employee confidence that the promised pension will be paid because the pension assets are in the hands of a third party. Pensions should then be secure, even if the employer becomes unprofitable or the business is wound up.

A pension plan also permits an employee to save money on a tax-sheltered basis. While an employee could use a personal RRSP, this alternative is often less convenient and requires greater self-discipline.

The changing nature of the three-legged stool, changing demographics, and economic events have increased employee interest in pension plan issues and created a greater demand not only for employers to establish pension plans, but also to have pension plans designed to meet the employees' needs: tax-effective plans, plans with suitable termination as well as retirement benefits, and funded arrangements.

As the maximum earnings that can be pensionable under a registered pension plan have decreased from about six times the average wage in 1976 to approximately 2.5 times the average wage today, there has been a dramatic increase in the number of employees for whom adequate pensions cannot be provided through registered pension plans. As a result, there have been increased employee expectations and demands for employers to provide top-up arrangements.

Types of Employer-Sponsored Retirement Income Plans

An employer who has decided to provide a pension plan for its employees must decide whether to establish a registered or a non-registered arrangement. A registered arrangement is one that is registered with the provincial or federal pension authorities and with the CRA; it must comply with the requirements specified in the applicable pension standards legislation and with the ITA. Under a registered plan, employees are not taxed on employer contributions made on their behalf and investment earnings on plan funds accrue tax-free. In contrast, in a non-registered arrangement, employees are taxed on employer contributions made on their behalf and investment earnings on plan funds are generally taxed.

This chapter deals with registered plans. Non-registered, supplementary arrangements are discussed in Chapter 13.

The employer needs to decide on the type of plan to enact. In other words, the employer must decide how the plan will deliver benefits. Most pension plans will fall into one of the following broad categories:

- Defined benefit plans;
- Defined contribution plans; and
- Combination or hybrid plans.

The following table provides a summary of these types of plans.

TYPES OF PENSION PLANS
Registered Pension Plans

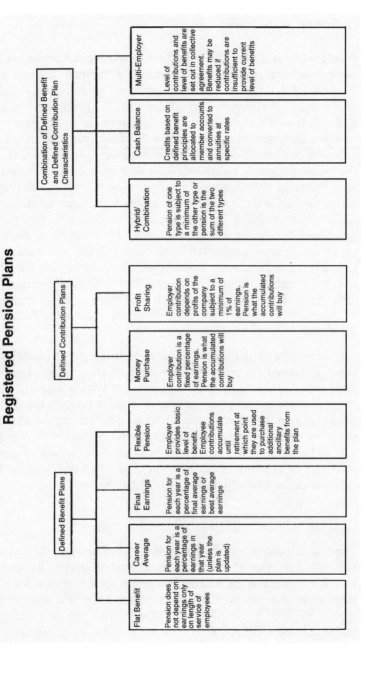

Defined Benefit Plans

Flat Benefit	Career Average	Final Earnings	Flexible Pension
Pension does not depend on earnings only on length of service of employees	Pension for each year is a percentage of earnings in that year (unless the plan is updated)	Pension for each year is a percentage of final average earnings or best average earnings	Employer provides basic level of benefit. Employee contributions accumulate until retirement at which point they are used to purchase additional ancillary benefits from the plan

Defined Contribution Plans

Money Purchase	Profit Sharing
Employer contribution is a fixed percentage of earnings. Pension is what the accumulated contributions will buy	Employer contribution depends on profits of the company subject to a minimum of 1% of earnings. Pension is what the accumulated contributions will buy

Combination of Defined Benefit and Defined Contribution Plan Characteristics

Hybrid/ Combination	Cash Balance	Multi-Employer
Pension of one type is subject to a minimum of the other type or pension is the sum of the two different types	Credits based on defined benefit principles are allocated to member accounts and converted to annuities at specific rates	Level of contributions and level of benefits are set out in collective agreement. Benefits may be reduced if contributions are insufficient to provide current level of benefits

Defined Benefit Plans

A defined benefit plan specifies the formula for determination of benefit entitlements and employees are promised a "defined" amount of pension. The cost of this type of plan is determined, on an actuarial basis, as the total amount of money required to provide the given level of benefit for all employees in the plan. Usually a regular or classic defined benefit plan specifies that employees contribute a fixed percentage of their earnings to help fund the benefit, while it is the employer who assumes the financial risk of the plan through contributions that are not fixed, but rather based upon actuarial calculations. However, a new breed of defined benefit plans emerged in the last few years, in which the financial risk is shared or shifted completely to the employees. For example, Ontario's Jointly Sponsored Pension Plans, New Brunswick's shared risk plans, and the target benefit plans introduced by recent legislation in Alberta and British Columbia, are plans in which financial risk is shared both the employer(s) and the members, while Quebec's Member-Funded Pension Plans are defined benefit plans in which the employer's contribution is predetermined and the members collectively assume the financial risk of the plan.

According to Statistics Canada, as of January 1, 2014, defined benefit plans accounted for approximately 59% of all pension plans, but these plans cover 71% of employees belonging to employer-sponsored pension plans. Defined benefit plans may be subdivided into two types: flat benefit plans that provide a fixed benefit under a formula that usually disregards the level of participants' earnings, and unit benefit plans that provide a unit of pension usually expressed as a fixed percentage of earnings for each year of credited service. Within these types of plans, the four most common defined benefit plans are described below.

Flat Benefit Pension Plan

The annual pension under a flat benefit or uniform benefit pension plan is a specified number of dollars for each year of service. For example, the benefit formula may be $20 per month for each year of service, so that a member of the plan with 10 years of service would receive an annual benefit of $20 X 10 X 12, or $2,400. The pensions are commonly integrated with CPP/QPP retirement benefits by providing bridge or supplemental benefits from retirement to age 65.

The flat benefit formula ignores differences in earnings. The flat amount of pension is established in terms of wage levels and dollar values at the time the benefit level is set, despite the fact that most of the pensions will not be paid until a future date when wage levels and dollar values are likely to have increased. For this reason, most flat benefit plans are subject to periodic upgrades in their benefit formula in an attempt to reflect increases in inflation and wage levels.

Approximately 15% of all defined benefit pension plans are flat benefit plans. These plans are prevalent in unionized environments, so part of the collective bargaining process often involves negotiating increases in the flat benefit accrual rate.

Flat benefit plans originally had the advantage of being simple and easily understood by employees. However, as a result of the collective bargaining process, many of these plans now contain complicated features, such as variable rates for different job classes or periods of service, minimum benefit levels, bridge benefits, and other special provisions.

Career Average Earnings Pension Plan

Under a career average earnings pension plan, the member's pension is calculated as a certain percentage of earnings in each year of plan membership. If a member earned $50,000 in 2015 and $55,000 in 2016, then under a 2% career average plan, the benefit accrued for 2015 would be 2% of $50,000 or $1,000 and the benefit accrued for 2016 would be 2% of $55,000 or $1,100 for a total accrued benefit of $2,100 at the end of 2016.

The career average earnings formula gives equal weight to employment earnings in each year of the employee's working lifetime, and therefore, may provide a low pension relative to employment earnings just prior to retirement. This is particularly evident in the case of an employee who has made significant advancements over his or her career, or for all members if inflation is high. This problem is often overcome by updating the earnings base that will produce results similar to those calculated under a final average earnings plan. (Final earnings plans are described below.) As an example, a plan may be improved such that, for all service accrued prior to 2016, the benefit is calculated as 2% of 2015 earnings times years of service up to 2015. Thus, earnings for each year prior to 2015 are deemed to be equivalent to the earnings in 2015 for benefit calculation purposes.

Career average plans are frequently integrated with the CPP/QPP by having a lower percentage benefit credit on earnings up to the CPP/QPP earnings ceiling and a higher percentage above the ceiling. If employees contribute to the plan, the contribution formula may also be integrated with CPP/QPP contributions.

Career average earnings plans account for approximately 46% of all defined benefit pension plans in 2014. Career average earnings plans are straightforward to administer and easily understood because the exact pension amount can be determined at any particular time. However, many such plans were converted to final average earnings plans because employers were constantly updating the plans due to high inflation in previous years. Nonetheless, they are still popular with certain employers because the cost is more manageable for them, as pensions already earned are not affected by an employee's future earnings, and the employer can choose the timing of any upgrade.

Final Average Earnings Pension Plan

Under final average earnings pension plans, the member's pension is based upon the length of service and average earnings for a stated period before retirement. For example, the plan formula may be 1.5% of average earnings in the five years immediately prior to retirement, multiplied by the years of service accrued. Thus, for a member with final average earnings of $50,000 and 25 years of service, the annual benefit would be calculated as 1.5% X $50,000 X 25, or $18,750. In order to protect employees whose earnings decline as they approach retirement, some plans may use a best average earnings base in the benefit calculation. An example of this would be the five consecutive years of highest earnings in the last 10 years before retirement.

A final average earnings pension plan best meets the basic objective of providing continuity of income after retirement, such that the pensioner may maintain a standard of living after retirement comparable to the one he or she enjoyed while in active employment. It recognizes the long-term changes in the value of the dollar, up to the employee's retirement age, and the fact that most employees receive promotions during their working lifetime.

Most final earnings plans are contributory. Benefits and employee contributions are often coordinated with government pensions in the same way as career average plans.

Approximately 49% of all defined benefit pension plans were final average earnings plans in 2014. These plans are popular for salaried employees and have been adopted by many large and well-established Canadian employers, including those in the public sector.

Flexible Pension Plans

Flexible pension plans represent a relatively new design alternative for plan sponsors. The first plan of this type was implemented in the early 1990s for a large private sector employer. Flexible pension plans offer a tax-effective means of providing enhanced retirement benefits to employees. A flexible pension plan is a defined benefit pension plan in which the employer pays for the basic pension benefit and the employees pay for additional ancillary benefits. This allows employees to enhance the value of their pensions without increasing their Pension Adjustments (PAs) (explained later in this chapter) or reducing the amount of allowable RRSP contributions.

A front-end flexible pension plan requires the employee to choose the ancillary benefits in advance in exchange for his or her contributions. Under a back-end flexible pension plan, the employee makes his or her contributions, which accumulate, and the employee may then choose the ancillary benefits he or she desires upon termination or retirement. Examples of ancillary benefits include post-retirement spousal benefits, an enhanced definition of final average earnings, enhanced early retirement benefits, and indexing.

Aside from the tax advantages, a major advantage of the flexible pension plan is that it is tailored to meet the needs of each individual employee. If an employee is satisfied with the current level of benefits provided, he or she need not contribute to the plan. On the other hand, an employee may contribute the maximum each year, and thus ensure more generous retirement benefits. From an employer's perspective, this type of plan is administratively more complex than a regular defined benefit plan. In addition, its success requires a higher level of understanding on the part of members.

Defined Contribution Plans

A defined contribution plan specifies the level of contributions to be made to the plan by both the employer and the employee. Contributions accumulate with investment earnings until retirement. Thus, the amount of retirement income that may be purchased with the account balance is unknown until the actual retirement date. Defined contribution plans account for 37% of all pension plans in Canada, but cover only 17% of all members belonging to pension plans. The two basic types of defined contribution pension plans are outlined below.

Money Purchase Pension Plan

This is an employer-sponsored arrangement where employer and employee contributions are defined. The plan may be fully employer-paid, or require employee contributions as well. Contributions may be a fixed percentage of earnings, a fixed dollar amount, or a specified amount per year of service or per hour worked. An employee becomes vested in employer contributions made on his or her behalf after being a member of the plan for a specified period, generally not more than two years. Vesting is subject to pension standards legislation. If an employee terminates prior to that date, the benefit received will be based on the employee's contributions only. (This is not applicable in some provinces such as Quebec, Manitoba, Ontario, and the federal jurisdiction, as members in these provinces vest immediately.)[11] The employer contributions that are forfeited in this situation are usually used to reduce the employer's cost.

Profit Sharing Pension Plan

A profit sharing pension plan is a type of defined contribution plan where employer contributions are linked to the profitability of the company. The employer's total annual contribution is determined using a formula related to profits. The CRA requires that employer contributions be at least 1% of employees' earnings, even in years of little or no profit. Allocation of profits among plan members may be based on a points system under which points are assigned based on service, earnings, or both. Investment earnings and forfeitures are allocated to employees in proportion to their account balances.

Although profit sharing plans are registered arrangements where employer contributions made on behalf of employees are not taxable to the employees, these arrangements have a significant drawback to employees if used for pension plan purposes. Contributions are linked to profit, and thus further increase the uncertainty associated with the level of retirement income provided by a defined contribution plan. From the employer's perspective, costs are linked to the company's ability to pay. In addition, this type of plan may act to motivate employees and lead to increased productivity.

---

[11]   See Chapter 9 for more details.

Plans with Defined Benefit and Defined Contribution Characteristics

Hybrid Plans

Hybrid pension plans have defined benefit and defined contribution components. The most common type of hybrid plan provides the greater of a defined benefit pension and the pension that may be purchased with the member's defined contribution account balance. For example, the defined benefit may be calculated as 1.5% of final average earnings for each year of service. The employee may be required to contribute 5% of earnings to a defined contribution account in the plan and these contributions may be matched by the employer. At retirement, the member's account balance is converted to a pension. If this defined contribution pension amount is less than the defined benefit pension amount, then the defined benefit pension amount is paid. If the defined contribution pension amount is greater than the defined benefit pension amount, then the defined contribution pension amount is paid.

This type of plan essentially operates as a defined contribution plan. Its major advantage is that it alleviates some of the employee uncertainty associated with a defined contribution plan, because it guarantees a minimum level of retirement income. However, like a defined benefit plan, an actuarial valuation is required to determine the adequacy of the fund to support the defined benefit guarantee.

Combination Plans

The combination plan offers a benefit that is the sum of the pension provided through the defined benefit component and the pension provided through the defined contribution component. Typically, the employer will provide a defined benefit of, for instance, 1% of final average earnings. Employees will contribute to the plan, and their contributions will be deposited in a defined contribution account that will accumulate until retirement. There may also be some employer matching of the employee contribution. At retirement, the member will receive the defined benefit pension in addition to the pension that can be purchased with his or her defined contribution account balance.

Hybrid and combination plans represent less than 2% of all pension plans in Canada. Most employers find these plans too complex to administer and too difficult to explain to employees.

Cash Balance Plans

A cash balance plan is another example of a plan that combines defined benefit and defined contribution characteristics. Like a defined contribution plan, the employer credits an amount based on a percentage of the employee's earnings (i.e., 5% of earnings), to a hypothetical account for each individual employee. This credited amount accumulates at a specified rate of interest until termination or retirement. The interest rate is a set rate and is frequently a rate linked to the Consumer Price Index. The fact, however, that the account is a "hypothetical" account is one of the reasons that a cash balance plan is a defined benefit plan. In a cash balance plan, it is the employer who makes the investment decision, takes the investment risk and ultimately is liable for a guaranteed benefit payment. Cash balance plans expose the employee to little investment risk and for the employer, as it is a defined benefit plan, a cash balance plan provides flexibility in setting the benefit level and also allows for a certain degree of funding flexibility. Cash balance plans provide higher benefits on termination than regular defined benefit pension plans. This is an attractive feature for a mobile workforce.

Cash balance plans became popular in the United States in 1980s. They have not, however, become as popular in Canada, and furthermore, they may not be permitted under the ITA provisions.

Multi-Employer Plans

A multi-employer pension plan is another example of a plan that combines characteristics of defined benefit and defined contribution plans. A multi-employer plan is usually established by union negotiation with two or more non-affiliated employers in a related industry. Typically, these plans are established in industries in which employees frequently move between employers but remain part of the same trade union. Although the employee may work for several of the employers, he or she will remain a member of the plan and earn credits as if employed by only one.

Multi-employer plans specify both the contribution level and the level of benefits. For example, employer contributions may be determined as a certain number of cents for each hour worked by each employee. The benefit is generally determined using a flat benefit formula.

The level of contributions to the plan is typically determined through the collective bargaining process. Actuarial valuations are required to determine if the level of benefits is supportable by the contribution rate. Unlike plans for single employers, benefits may be reduced if they cannot be supported by the current level of contributions and if employers are unable or unwilling to increase their contributions; however, a legislative modification following a recent legal case confirms Quebec as an exception to this rule.[12]

Target Benefit Plans

A target benefit plan is another example of a plan that combines characteristics of defined benefit and defined contribution plans. They are similar to defined benefit plans in that they pool longevity and investment risks, but are also similar to defined contribution plans in that contributions are fixed or variable within a narrow range. Target benefit plan design is similar to the design of multi-employer plans, except that they are established by a single employer.

Target benefit plans specify both the contribution level and the level of benefits. The level of contributions to the plan is typically determined through the collective bargaining process. Actuarial valuations are required to determine if the level of benefits is supportable by the contribution rate. Similar to multi-employer plans, benefits may be reduced if they cannot be supported by the current level of contributions. Ultimately, target benefit plans are designed to deliver a targeted benefit while giving administrators the flexibility to adjust benefits in response to the plan's funded position.

As of July 2016, the provinces that have specific target benefit plan provisions in their legislation are New Brunswick, Quebec, Alberta and British Columbia.[13]

Ontario and Nova Scotia have passed legislation (not yet in force as of the writing of this chapter) permitting target benefit plans in particular circumstances (i.e., collectively bargained or multi-employer plans). The Ontario government is expected to release details related to the proposed regulatory framework for target benefit multi-employer plans which will help inform the subsequent development of a framework for single-employer target benefit plans.

---

[12] Refer to Chapter 10 for a discussion of this case, *Multi-Marques Distribution Inc. v. Regie des rentes du Quebec*, [2008] J.Q. no 2587, 2008 QCCA 597 (Que. C.A.). Multi-employer pension plans are discussed in further detail in Chapter 11.

[13] Alberta and British Columbia also allow for the conversion of defined benefit plans into target benefit plans.

Other Retirement Income Arrangements

There are several other retirement income arrangements an employer can establish in place of or to supplement pension plans. These include RRSPs, DPSPs, and other Employee Profit Sharing Plans.[14]

Plan Design Considerations

There are a number of fundamental issues that need to be considered when designing retirement income arrangements. The issues and their relative significance have changed over time. As well, pension and tax reform have resulted in major review and redesign of existing arrangements.

Employers who established pension plans in the early 1900s generally had a paternalistic culture. They were concerned about the well-being of their employees and were intent on ensuring they were financially secure in retirement. Often employees spent their entire careers with one employer and the pension plans were viewed as a reward for long service.

Times have changed. Few employers can now afford to continue this paternalism. Although employers may be concerned about the well-being of their employees, the environment is such that many employers must do what is necessary to remain competitive.

The changing environment has changed the focus of plan design. If an employer does not expect employees to work their entire career for the enterprise, this is an important consideration when designing the plan. If an employee does not expect to retire from the plan, retirement benefits may not be perceived as valuable. Employees will focus instead on the level of termination benefits.

In addition, there has been a shift in responsibility for ensuring that an employee has adequate retirement income. Increasingly, employers are not prepared to assume sole responsibility and encourage employees to share in the responsibility. In fact, many employers are actively involved in educating employees about the importance of saving for retirement.

The following comments highlight some of the principal issues in plan design.

---

[14]   These arrangements are discussed in Chapter 14.

Adequacy

The major goal of retirement income arrangements is to ensure that employees will have an adequate level of retirement income. While earlier vesting and locking-in and increased frequency of job changes have shifted more attention to benefits for terminating employees, the primary focus remains the retiring employee.

Most plan sponsors aim to provide an adequate level of retirement income at normal retirement. Generous early retirement provisions can be quite expensive. Consequently, if funds are limited, it may be preferable for an employer to provide a generous benefit formula and less generous early retirement provisions.

Adequacy is often measured as the ratio of an employee's retirement income from all sources to the level of earnings just prior to retirement. The resulting "retirement replacement ratio" of after-tax pension to the after-tax rate of pay just before retirement is seldom 100%. Income needs in retirement are usually less than in working years, for a number of reasons. No longer are there work-related expenses (i.e., travel or meals away from home). By retirement, the house mortgage has generally been paid off and the care and education of children is usually complete. Many goods and services are reduced in price for senior citizens as well.

As a rough guide, taking into account standard expenses and income tax deductions, most individuals believe they need approximately 60-70% of pre-retirement income (the percentage will be higher at lower incomes) to enjoy the same standard of living as they enjoyed prior to retirement. A middle-income individual will receive approximately 30-35% replacement from CPP/QPP benefits and OAS as they currently exist.[15] Therefore, an employer plan that delivers 30-40% of pre-retirement earnings could be considered adequate by a middle-income employee.

Adequacy is a relative rather than an absolute concept. Therefore, many employers will measure the adequacy of their retirement income plan not only against some accepted norm but also by comparing them to the industry standard or to the plans offered by their major competitors. It is not uncommon for an employer who is considering a redesign of its plan to conduct a survey of the benefits offered by other employers in competing companies or related industries.

---

[15]   In June 2016 the Federal and Provincial Finance Ministers agreed to phase in the expansion of the CPP from 2019 to 2023, with the intention of increasing the replacement rate on pensionable income for service accrued after January 1, 2019.

Tax-Effectiveness

The current system of tax assistance for retirement savings is addressed in Chapter 8. The system of savings limits applies to all retirement income arrangements. This means that an individual's allowable RRSP contributions are reduced by the value of any benefits earned under registered pension plans or DPSPs. This value is known as a Pension Adjustment. For money purchase plans, the PA is the sum of employer and employee contributions. For defined benefit plans, the benefit is converted to a value using the system's prescribed formula. The PA is nine times the amount of pension accrued in the year, minus $600.

This factor of nine is based on some key assumptions:

- The employee will remain to retirement; and
- The plan provides some valuable ancillary benefits (such as unreduced retirement at age 63, survivor benefits, or indexing).

The factor of nine overvalues the pension accruals under all defined benefit pension plans, and particularly overvalues pension accruals for younger employees who most likely will not remain in the same pension plan for their full careers. Few plans other than those in the public sector provide all of the valuable ancillary benefits assumed in the PA calculation.

The 1997 federal Budget introduced an adjustment known as a Pension Adjustment Reversal to deal with concerns that the factor of nine was producing unfair results. The PAR effectively increases the RRSP contribution limit if an employee ceases (after 1996 and before retirement) to be entitled to a benefit under a DPSP or a benefit provision of an RPP, and does not have a sufficiently large termination benefit.

If an employer's objective is to maximize tax-effectiveness — and employers will be under pressure from at least some employees to do so — the employer will need to modify the design of the plan to optimize the PA and/or reduce the RRSP contribution room taken up by the plan's benefits. To do so, the employer can:

- Reduce the defined benefit credit and add ancillary benefits while maintaining the same cost;
- Introduce a defined contribution component;
- Introduce flexible plans where employees can buy ancillary benefits; or
- Allow employees to opt out of the plan.

Tax-effectiveness is a relatively new design issue and has been responsible for much of the plan review activity of the 1990s, as well as the search for new and innovative plan designs.

Changing Demographics

In the latter half of the 20th century, Canada experienced the baby boom followed by the baby bust. An extraordinary number of births occurred following the Second World War. Since then, birth rates have been declining. As a result, the Canadian population is aging.

What impact does an aging population have on pension plan design? To begin with, employees are probably more knowledgeable about pensions than they ever have been in the past. Baby boomers are concerned about their retirement income.

Employers are also concerned. Sponsors of defined benefit plans will see a definite increase in their annual cost as the workforce ages, and will need to consider cutting back benefit levels in order to control costs.

In addition to the aging population, another demographic change that has occurred is the diversity in the composition of the workforce — more two-income families and part-time employees, and increased frequency of job change — with accompanying diversity of needs. Employers face a greater challenge in defining plan objectives.

Equity

The pension plan should be equitable among members with different employment histories. The plan should also be seen to be equitable to employees in varying circumstances. Several different concepts of equity exist, sometimes in conflict. For instance, should pensions be equal in value or equal in amount? In defined benefit plans, pension standards legislation requires that the amount of pension to males and females with the same employment history be the same, although this treatment provides greater relative value to females who, on average, can be expected to live longer than males. On the other hand, in a defined contribution plan, the pensions of two individuals of different ages who are retiring now with identical work histories will not be of the same amount. These pensions, however, will have the same value.

While defined contribution plans provide equal value to all members regardless of age, defined benefit plans may provide equal pensions to two individuals of different ages, but the values will not be equal. This means that a young employee with the same years of service and earnings history as an older employee will have a pension of a lesser value. Many pension plans provide valuable ancillary benefits to employees who meet certain criteria. Plans may also impose constraints on service or earnings when calculating benefits. When these complications are introduced, equity can be an elusive ideal.

Pensions are frequently integrated with the CPP/QPP by providing a lower rate of benefits on earnings up to the CPP/QPP earnings ceiling, or by an offset of part of the government benefit. This integration may raise a question of equity between employees with high and low earnings, if the reduction to integrate is perceived to be excessive.

Cost and Cost Sharing

A fundamental question when establishing a pension plan is how much the employer is willing to spend. The employer needs to set cost parameters and examine alternative designs opposite these criteria. For example, a final earnings plan with a generous benefit formula and generous ancillary benefits will be very expensive relative to a modest career average plan.

For many employers, stability of cost is vitally important because of the nature of their businesses. Unforeseen cost increases or deficiencies could place the company in a precarious financial situation. These employers might prefer to implement a defined contribution plan where cost levels remain predictable and stable. On the other hand, defined benefit plans may offer funding flexibility not found in defined contribution plans.

Employers must also decide on the level of cost sharing. That is, do they want employees to contribute to the plan, and if so, at what level? This will depend, in part, on the employer's philosophy on who has responsibility for the delivery of retirement income. Also, employee contributions will help reduce employer cost, which in turn may allow the employer to offer a more generous plan. Pension standards legislation imposes limits on the extent that benefits may be funded through employee contributions.

Coordination with Government Pension Programs

When Canada's national pension system provided only a modest flat dollar benefit at age 70, government benefits were often ignored in designing the pension plan, although they may have influenced the amount of pensions. Today, CPP/QPP benefits are large enough that they cannot be ignored in the design of a pension plan. Employers with generous pension plans must coordinate or integrate the pension plan with these social security benefits.

A defined benefit pension plan can be integrated with the CPP/QPP in a number of ways:

- The "step rate" method, under which lower rates of benefits and contributions apply on annual earnings up to the CPP/QPP earnings ceiling (called the Year's Maximum Pensionable Earnings, or YMPE, this ceiling was \$54,900 in 2016);[16]
- The "direct offset" method, under which the calculated pension is reduced by all or part of the government pension;
- The "ineligible earnings" method, under which integration with government benefits is achieved by ignoring a slice of earnings for both contribution and pension purposes (the ineligible earnings may be a fixed amount of, for example, \$10,000, or may be a percentage of the YMPE of say, 30%).

Chapter 3 discusses alternative integration approaches in more detail. It should be noted that the ineligible earnings method is now rarely used.

Human Resource Planning

In choosing a plan design, the employer will want to consider its staff planning objectives. For example, a pension plan can be used to attract and retain employees. Where labour is scarce, the pension plan could be structured to discourage early retirements. Or, it may be used to support or even encourage early retirement programs through the provision of enhanced benefits to employees who voluntarily elect to retire early. An employer may also use the pension plan to facilitate the transfer of employees between locations or as a strategic element to the union negotiation process.

As described earlier, effective with the 2007 Budget, the federal government allows employees to start receiving a portion of the defined benefit pension they have earned without actually retiring. The regulations outline which employees may receive their pensions and when. While the legislation calls this phased retirement, the regulations do not actually require a reduction in employment hours by the employee. Employers are not required to provide this feature and should consider their staff

---

[16]   As part of the CPP expansion, the maximum earnings covered by CPP are expected to increase by 14% phased in over a two-year period from 2024 to 2025.

planning objectives and availability of employees before implementing this approach.

Compensation Philosophy

A pension benefit is only one part of an employee's total compensation. Some employers view pensions as a form of fixed compensation or deferred wage. These employers view pensions as a reward for long service and a way of providing employees with security. Other employers have a compensation philosophy geared more heavily towards variable compensation that rewards individual performance only; employees of these organizations may be expected to plan for their own retirement by saving through RRSPs. Other employers may combine elements of both compensation philosophies.

The key concept is that companies should look at the context in which pensions are designed and delivered. By examining and giving weight to each of the components of the total compensation package, with retirement income being just one of these components, companies are able to achieve an appropriate balance between providing incentives for individual and/or corporate performance, and providing employee security. Companies with different cultures and objectives will strike the balance differently.

Variations in Design for Different Groups

As mentioned earlier in this chapter, an employer may have different pension plans for different employee groups. This can be driven by a variety of factors — differences in the compensation structure (i.e., hourly, salaried, or executive), union associations, the distribution of employees by age and pay, the level and predictability of profits, competitors' plans, and the demand for labour.

Pension plans for salaried and hourly staff are often designed to replace a target level of retirement income for employees who put in a full working career with the employer. For example, under a 2% integrated final average plan, a retiring employee with 35 years of service can expect to receive 70% of his or her pre-retirement income in the form of a pension.

The objectives in designing a top-up arrangement for executives can be very different. Tenure with the company is likely shorter, benefits are limited by the CRA, and the relationship of pension benefits to other elements of compensation is likely of more significance for this group.[17]

Legislation

Pension plans must comply with pension standards legislation in the jurisdictions where the employer has employees, and they must also qualify for registration under the ITA. Plans must satisfy requirements of other related legislation as well, including human rights, employment standards, family property, and workers' compensation.

Location

As mentioned earlier, and subject to CAPSA's *Agreement Respecting Multi-Jurisdictional Pension Plans*, employers operating in different provinces must administer their pension plans subject to the provisions of pension standards legislation in several jurisdictions. In an attempt to minimize the administrative requirements, an employer can design a plan that, to the extent possible, meets the requirements of all jurisdictions instead of a plan with different provisions to satisfy each jurisdiction's minimum rules. While this increases the employer's cost of funding the plan, this cost is offset by lower administration costs.

A "uniform" plan is also perceived by some employers to be more equitable, because it treats all employees of the company in the same manner. Despite these advantages, it is important to realize that it is not possible to develop a common set of rules respecting the provincial variations with respect to all terms of the pension plan. The best that can be accomplished is uniformity in a large number of the plan terms.

Setting Objectives

The key point to keep in mind in the design of pension arrangements is that no two situations are identical and the design must be tailored to the specific circumstances of the various employee groups, the employer, and the industry in which the employer operates. Plan sponsors need to establish the criteria, define and evaluate their alternatives, and then select the arrangement and design that best meets their objectives.

---

[17]   Chapter 13 provides a more detailed review of executive retirement plans.

Chapter 2

GOVERNMENT PENSION PROGRAMS

Executive Summary

Canadians typically receive retirement income from three key sources: government-administered pension programs, employer-sponsored retirement savings programs, and personal savings. Each of these sources is sometimes referred to as one leg of a three-legged stool. This chapter focuses on the government-administered pension component of the Canadian retirement system, which includes:

- Old Age Security (OAS);
- Guaranteed Income Supplement (GIS) and Allowance benefits; and
- Canada and Quebec Pension Plans (CPP/QPP).

When the CPP/QPP were introduced, the aim was to provide, together with the OAS pension, a replacement ratio of approximately 40% of pre-retirement income up to the national average wage (15% from OAS and 25% from CPP/QPP). A recent announcement in June 2016 to expand the CPP is not only expected to increase this ratio by 8% but is also expected to increase the covered pensionable earnings of the CPP by 14%. A recent announcement by the Finance Minister of Quebec indicates reforms to the QPP may also be coming, however, it is expected that QPP changes, while similar, will not mirror those taking place for the CPP.

At January 1, 2016, the maximum possible basic pension was $19,956.24 annually ($6,846.24 from OAS and $13,110 from CPP/QPP). Government policy expects that individuals will make further savings for their retirement, either through personal or group arrangements.

OAS benefits are paid out of current tax revenues. Based on the actuarial valuation as at December 31, 2012, total OAS expenditures are projected to be 2.3% of Gross Domestic Product (GDP) in 2013 and is expected to reach a high of 2.8% in 2033. These projections included the effects of the aging population and the planned gradual increase in the age of benefit eligibility (which was subsequently reversed).

The CPP/QPP are funded solely out of the contributions of the participants and their employers, with reserves established to cover approximately two to three years of benefit payments. The latest actuarial valuation of the CPP projects that the current legislated total contribution rate of 9.9% of pensionable earnings is sufficient to meet its obligations and remain financially stable over the long term, despite the expected increase in benefits to be paid to an aging population. The June 2016 announcement to expand the CPP comes with the expected future increases in contributions, which are described in the section below "Canada and Quebec Pension Plans". The latest actuarial valuation of the QPP recognized that the maximum contribution rate of 10.8% that will come into effect in 2017 may not be sufficient to ensure a long-term stable ratio between the reserve and cash outflows for the following year, and that this contribution rate may need to be changed as early as in 2018.

Historical Overview

The OAS benefit provides a flat monthly pension for Canadians aged 65 and older who meet certain residency requirements. The OAS benefit was originally designed as a universal benefit available to all Canadians who qualified. The universality of the program has since been eroded by the implementation of a "clawback" tax in 1989, which requires pensioners earning an income over a specified threshold ($73,756 in 2016) to pay back part of their OAS pension. The full OAS pension is eliminated if a pensioner's net income exceeds a specified limit ($119,398 in 2016).

The GIS is an income-tested benefit that provides additional monies over and above the OAS benefit. The GIS provides a flat monthly benefit, which is reduced by $1 for every $2 of any other income received — other than the OAS pension and a few other excepted amounts — to maintain the needs-based approach to the benefit.

The Allowance provides an income-tested additional amount for 60- to 64-year-old spouses or common-law partners of OAS pensioners who are eligible to receive the GIS. A Survivor's Allowance may be paid to 60- to 64-year-old surviving spouses or common-law partners on the pensioner's death.

The CPP/QPP were introduced in 1966. They are earnings-related plans that are compulsory for nearly all employees and self-employed persons and are financed solely through employee and employer contributions and investment earnings on those contributions. The benefits available from the plans are designed to assist in providing retirement income for working Canadians, as well as disability, death, and survivor benefits. The aim of the CPP/QPP retirement benefit has been to provide a pension approximately equivalent to 25% of the worker's average annual lifetime earnings up to a yearly maximum, which is adjusted to reflect current wage levels.

In the 1990s, as the future financial sustainability of the CPP/QPP came into question, the government was forced to contemplate some new solutions. Due mainly to Canada's aging population, higher than expected disability benefit payments, and lower-than-expected economic growth, pay-as-you-go contribution rates to the CPP were projected to increase to 14.2% of earnings by the year 2030 unless changes were implemented. This prompted the government to review proposals for reform of the CPP/QPP to ensure that it would be sustainable, fair, and affordable in the long run, without placing too much of a financial burden on future generations.

In 1998, a variety of amendments were made to both the CPP and QPP. A new schedule of contribution rates for both plans was introduced, and the rate was structured to increase from the 1997 rate of 6.0% to an ultimate rate of 9.9% in 2003, which has remained unchanged for the CPP. The contribution rate for QPP increased to 10.65% in 2016. Additionally, as a result of the amendments, the Year's Basic Exemption (YBE) for both CPP and QPP has been frozen at $3,500 and is no longer indexed. Consequently, as the Year's Maximum Pensionable Earnings (YMPE) increases each year in line with increases to the Canadian average wage, contributors will be paying more into the CPP/QPP as a greater portion of their earnings are subject to compulsory contributions. Also, both plans effectively reduced the retirement benefits payable to future retirees by increasing the averaging period for calculating average pensionable earnings from three years to five. Furthermore, both plans lowered the maximum death benefit payout from $3,500 to $2,500, and it is has been frozen at that level.

The method for calculating combined benefits was also changed as a result of the 1998 amendments, lowering the combined survivor/disability benefits for all new beneficiaries and the combined survivor/retirement benefits for many new beneficiaries.

One very significant change brought about by the 1998 amendments to the CPP was the establishment of the CPP Investment Board — a Crown corporation that acts at arm's length from the government. The Board invests CPP funds in financial markets, broadly following the same investment rules as other pension plans.

In July 2000, Parliament enacted most of Bill C-23, *An Act to modernize the Statutes of Canada in relation to benefits and obligations.* Bill C-23 amended more than 60 federal Acts, including the CPP and OAS, to provide same-sex partners with the same benefits and coverage as those already provided to common-law partners of the opposite sex.

On June 7, 2002, the Quebec National Assembly passed Bill 84, *An Act instituting civil unions and establishing new rules of filiation.* The intent of the Act was to enable the solemnization of gay and lesbian civil unions, although it is equally applicable to opposite-sex couples. The legislation defines a civil union as "a commitment between two persons eighteen years of age or over who express their free and enlightened consent to live together and to uphold the rights and obligations that derive from that status". Among various pieces of other legislation, the Act amended the QPP. The legislation affects the definition of a surviving spouse, in that same-sex partners who have entered into a civil union now automatically qualify as a surviving spouse. Even prior to Bill 84, a same-sex partner could qualify as a surviving spouse, but he or she had to meet the cohabitation period time specifications set out in the QPP (and these rules continue to be applicable for those who choose not to enter into a civil union). The definition of former spouses with regards to the division of unadjusted pensionable earnings was also altered to reflect the new status of individuals who have entered into a civil union.

Bill C-36, which made several amendments to the CPP and the OAS program, was enacted by Parliament on May 3, 2007. Several of the amendments provided for simplification of the administration of the OAS program, both for the government and for the beneficiaries of the program. The CPP was amended to allow contributors to request a statement of the history of their contributions more than once a year, and former common-law partners to be able to apply for a division of CPP pension credits more than four years after the date of separation. Among other administrative changes, Bill C-36 provided for the creation of electronic services such as online applications for both the CPP and OAS.

Two key amendments to the CPP in Bill C-36 were based on recommendations made by federal, provincial, and territorial ministers of finance at the conclusion of the triennial review of the CPP in June of 2006. Effective January 1, 2008, applicants for disability benefits with 25 or more years of CPP contributions need to have valid contributions in only three of the last six years (reduced from four of the last six years). Also, the CPP's full funding provision was integrated into actuarial reporting and contribution rate setting. The full funding provision requires that changes in benefits are to be paid for in full so that their costs are not passed on to future generations. The results of the actuarial valuation of the CPP dated December 31, 2009, as well as the results of the latest actuarial valuation of the CPP dated December 31, 2012 (which are briefly summarized at the end of this chapter) reflected the full funding of the additional cost of the change in the eligibility requirements for disability benefits.

Bill C-51 (the *Economic Recovery Act*), which received Royal Assent on December 15, 2009, changed the adjustment factors to be applied to CPP benefits to more closely reflect actuarial equivalent values. Also under Bill C-51, effective January 1, 2012, contributors are able to start their pension as early as age 60 while still continuing to work. CPP contributions must continue under these circumstances and will serve to increase the individual's CPP benefit each year.

The latest actuarial valuation of the CPP projects that the current legislated total contribution rate of 9.9% of pensionable earnings is sufficient to meet its obligations and remain financially stable over the long term despite the expected increase in benefits to be paid to an aging population.

In its March 2011 Budget, Quebec introduced changes to the QPP designed to improve QPP funding, maintain intergenerational equity, and encourage experienced workers to continue working. These changes were designed and implemented primarily out of concerns about the long-term financial sustainability of the QPP arising from the results of the QPP's December 31, 2009 actuarial valuation.

Beginning in 2012, the QPP contribution rate was increased by 0.15% per year, and will continue to increase at this rate until it reaches 10.8% in 2017. Thereafter, an automatic mechanism will be implemented to align the QPP contribution rate with the QPP's steady-state rate. The steady-state rate is the minimum rate sufficient to maintain a steady ratio of assets to expenditures over the long term. This automatic mechanism will achieve a fairer intergenerational balance as it will achieve greater contribution and financial stability over the long term. The legislated QPP contribution rate is 10.65% in 2016.

Adjustments made to QPP pensions for early and postponed retirements were also changed in the Quebec government's March 2011 Budget. The adjustments have been designed to encourage experienced workers to stay in the labour market longer.

Despite the changes introduced in the Quebec government's March 2011 Budget, the latest actuarial valuation of the QPP recognized that the maximum contribution rate of 10.8% that will come into effect in 2017 may not be sufficient to ensure a long-term stable ratio between the reserve and cash outflows for the following year, and that this contribution rate may need to be changed as early as in 2018.

In 2011, Part 3 of Bill C-3, the *Supporting Vulnerable Seniors and Strengthening Canada's Economy Act*, amended the Old Age Security Act to provide top-up benefits for certain GIS and Survivor's Allowance recipients. Details of these top-up benefits are provided later in this chapter.

In 2012, the federal government introduced changes to OAS and GIS benefits in order to address concerns about the long-term sustainability of the programs and the increasing burden of future OAS payments on Canada's future working population. The government cited the following projections from the Chief Actuary in support of these changes: OAS expenditures are projected to increase from approximately $38 billion in 2011 (2.3% of GDP) to $108 billion by 2030 (about 3.1% of GDP). As the number of seniors doubles over the next 20 years, the number of working-age Canadians is expected to remain largely the same. In 2010, OAS benefits cost slightly over $2,100 per worker. By 2030, OAS benefits will cost $3,600 per worker (in 2010 dollars).

To address the foregoing concerns, the 2012 Federal Budget proposed a gradual increase in the age of eligibility for OAS and GIS from 65 to 67, and Allowance Benefits from 60 to 62, over the period from 2023 to 2029. As described below, this change was later cancelled in the 2016 Federal Budget.

Effective July 2013, individuals have been permitted to defer the commencement of their OAS pension past age 65 for up to five years. Those who choose to defer will receive a higher annual pension.

In the 2016 Federal Budget, the federal government proposed the cancellation of the provisions in the OAS Act which relates to the implementation of the gradual increases in the age of eligibility for OAS, GIS and Allowance benefits. The Budget cited that the cancellation of these changes was made against the background of the new government's commitment to strengthening the public pension system and improving the pension benefits for seniors. The Budget also mentioned that this move will place these benefits, which represent an important part of retirement income particularly for seniors with lower incomes, back in their hands.

On June 2, 2016, the Ontario Government passed the *Ontario Retirement Plan Act – Strengthening Retirement Security for Ontarians, 2016* (ORPP Act). The ORPP Act aimed to ensure that every eligible employee will become a member of the Ontario Retirement Pension Plan (ORPP) or a comparable workplace pension by 2020. The ORPP was designed to assist in addressing the retirement benefits gap amongst Ontario employees and thereby complement existing retirement plans.

However, at the time that the Ontario Government passed the ORPP Act, they acknowledged that they were still open to potential CPP enhancements as part of a national solution to strengthening the retirement security, provided this would target those who need it most and will result in substantial replacement benefits in retirement.

On June 20, 2016, the Federal and Provincial Finance Ministers agreed to expand the CPP and a decision was taken by the Ontario government to halt the implementation of the ORPP. This announcement to expand the CPP is a significant development in the debate of recent years regarding enhancing the Canadian retirement income system. The key features of this expansion announcement are described below in the section "Canada and Quebec Pension Plans".

This chapter describes in detail social security benefits as they currently exist and provides, as well, an overview of the key issues facing the government-administered retirement programs.

Old Age Security

The government-supported tier of Canada's income security system provides pensions through a combination of three programs:

- OAS, which provides monthly benefits to all who reach age 65 and meet certain residence requirements, but is subject to a special tax or "clawback", described in more detail in the section "Taxation";
- GIS, which provides monthly benefits to OAS recipients subject to an income test and residence requirements; and
- Allowance and Survivor's Allowance (formerly referred to as Spouse's Allowance and Widowed Spouse's Allowance), which provide monthly benefits to a living or deceased pensioner's spouse or common-law partner. These benefits are only paid out to those who are between the ages of 60 and 64, and they are subject to residence and income tests.

The Old Age Security Act

The federal *Old Age Security Act* came into force on January 1, 1952, and provided universal pensions as a right, without a means test. The original benefit of $40 per month pension payable from age 70 was raised several times, and the criteria for qualification was also made more favourable.

When the CPP was enacted in 1965, OAS benefits were changed in important respects:

- The Act was modified to provide a GIS effective January 1, 1967; and
- The commencement age for benefits was progressively reduced to age 65, and the amount of the benefit was gradually raised.

An income-tested Spouse's Allowance (now referred to as the Allowance) was introduced October 1, 1975, payable to eligible spouses of OAS recipients aged 60 to 64. In 1979 legislation was introduced to allow recipients who became widowed to continue to receive benefits to age 65, and in 1985 the Spouse's Allowance was first payable to all widows and widowers from age 60 to 64 and in need.

Since 1972, OAS and GIS benefits have been indexed to the increases in the CPI, the adjustments being made quarterly. The Allowance and the Survivor's Allowance have been indexed since inception.

The pension under the OAS is paid in addition to that payable from the CPP/QPP. The payment commences in the first month after the application has been approved. For those persons who are late applying for the OAS benefit, retroactive payments can be made for up to 12 missed monthly payments.

The 2012 Federal Budget introduced an enrolment process that will eliminate the need for many seniors to apply for OAS and GIS. Automatic enrollment was phased in over the period from 2013 to 2015.

Qualifications for OAS Benefits

To qualify for the pension benefit, a person must furnish proof of age and must have met a residence qualification.

Prior to July 1, 1977, the conditions were:

- 40 years of residence in Canada after age 18; or
- 10 years of continuous residence in Canada immediately prior to the date of application for the pension; or
- If the applicant did not have 10 years of Canadian residence between the ages of 55 and 65, the applicant could make up each missing year by three years of Canadian residence between ages 18 and 55, provided the applicant resided in Canada for the year immediately before applying for the pension.

All persons meeting one of the above conditions qualified for the full OAS pension.

New residence requirements were introduced for individuals who were under age 25 on July 1, 1977, and for people over age 25 who did not reside in Canada before July 1, 1977. A full OAS pension is payable for 40 years of residence in Canada after age 18. A proportionate pension is payable for those with 10 to 40 years of residence after age 18. If the person is residing in Canada as of the date of attainment of age 65, a proportionate pension is payable if they have at least 10 years of residence in Canada after age 18. For example, someone with 14 years of residence would receive 14/40 of the maximum amount. If the person is not residing in Canada at age 65, 20 years of residence after age 18 is required to be eligible for the proportionate pension.

A person who does not meet the Canadian residence requirements described in the previous paragraph may still qualify for a proportionate pension if he or she lives or has lived in a country that has a reciprocal social security agreement with Canada.

A person over age 25 on July 1, 1977 and previously resident in Canada can qualify under the pre- or post-July 1, 1977 rules, whichever provides the more favourable benefit.

Portability of OAS Benefit

Canada has negotiated reciprocal agreements with some countries so that social security benefits may be preserved when people emigrate or immigrate. Persons who have spent portions of their working lives in more than one country may receive partial social security benefits from each country.

Where there is no reciprocal agreement, the OAS pension is payable for six months after the pensioner leaves Canada and may be resumed if the pensioner returns. If, however, the pensioner had 20 years' residence in Canada after age 18, the pension is not affected by the pensioner's absence from Canada.

Universality

Until 1988, the OAS pension was universal; that is, it was paid to all qualifying applicants irrespective of their wealth or income. Beginning with the 1989 taxation year, however, a special tax or "clawback" on the OAS pension was imposed by the federal Income Tax Act (ITA).

The tax was phased in over three years, so that by 1991 it was fully implemented. More details on the effect of the clawback are given in the section "Taxation".

Financing

Pensions under the *Old Age Security Act*, including the GIS and the Allowance, are financed on a pay-as-you-go basis from Government of Canada general tax revenues.

An actuarial valuation report (Report) on the OAS program at December 31, 2012 indicated that the ratio of total annual expenditures to GDP is expected to increase from a level of 2.3% in 2013 to 2.8% in 2033, driven largely by the retirement of the baby boom generation. This was partly mitigated by the proposed gradual increases in the age for benefit eligibility. The proposed change to the age for benefit eligibility was subsequently reversed in 2016 (the resulting impact of which will be reflected in the next actuarial valuation of the OAS dated December 31, 2015). The Report cited a number of factors (which reflected the planned increases in the age of eligibility) that may contribute to a reduction in eligibility of new retirees for the programs and effectively reduce the cost of the OAS program.

It was determined that the annual expenditure of the OAS program relative to GDP over the long term is expected to fall to 2.4% by 2050, given that benefits are indexed to inflation as opposed to wages. The number of beneficiaries for the basic OAS pension is expected to grow from 5.3 million in 2013 to 8.4 million by 2033. The number of GIS and Allowance beneficiaries is expected to grow from 1.8 million to 2.9 million over the same period.

Total annual expenditures are expected to increase from $43 billion in 2013 to $96 billion in 2030 and to $181 billion by 2050.

For the period 2010 to 2012, OAS, GIS and Allowance payments totaling approximately $116 billion were made. In 2007-2009, $102 billion of benefit payments were made.

Given the cancellation of the proposed gradual increases in the age for benefits eligibility, the results and conclusions in the December 31, 2012 Report are likely to change materially in the next review.

Taxation

The OAS pension is included in the income of a taxpayer for the purposes of taxation, and regular income tax is paid on these amounts.

Beginning with the 1989 taxation year, a special tax, or "clawback", on OAS, GIS, and Allowance benefits was imposed by the ITA. The tax was phased in over three years and was fully implemented by 1991. The clawback is achieved by a 15% surtax of a taxpayer's net income in excess of a certain dollar amount ($73,756 in 2016) including benefits. Thus, the total amount of the OAS benefit is taxed away from taxpayers with high incomes (incomes above $119,398 in 2016).

Effective in July 1996, OAS benefits are paid on a net basis, after taking into account the anticipated clawback of benefits. The amount of benefits payable are estimated based on the individual's income for the prior year. The actual clawback is still based upon the individual's actual income for the year, and any differences are settled upon the filing of a tax return.

Non-residents are subject to the clawback based on their net world income, rather than only on income taxable in Canada, as had been the case. Non-residents are required to file a form containing relevant tax data to avoid having any of their OAS benefits withheld at source on account of the clawback tax liability.

Pension Commencement and Deferral Processing

Effective April 2013, seniors who are eligible to receive the OAS will automatically receive a notification letter the month after they turn age 64 from Service Canada.

Individuals who defer their pension will receive a higher annual pension. The adjustment will be a 0.6% increase in the OAS pension for each month of deferral beyond age 65 up to a maximum of 36% at age 70. Individuals who elect to defer receipt of their pension for this period will not be eligible for GIS and their spouses will not be eligible for Allowance benefits for the period OAS has been delayed.

Guaranteed Income Supplement

The GIS is available to all recipients of the OAS pension, subject to an income test. The supplement is reduced by $1 for each full $2 of other monthly income over and above the OAS pension. Income for this purpose is the individual's income for the previous calendar year as defined by the ITA, minus pension payments and allowances under the Old Age Security Act, payments under the Family Allowance Act, similar payments to either of these under provincial legislation, or death benefits under the CPP/QPP. For purposes of the GIS income test, income includes any income from the CPP/QPP (other than death benefits), private pension plans, earnings, and investments.

The GIS benefits are indexed quarterly in line with increases in the CPI.

Benefit payments from the GIS are not taxable income to the recipients.

The maximum amount of GIS is the same for a single person and for a married person/common-law partner whose spouse or common-law partner does not receive either the OAS pension or an Allowance. The GIS for a single person and for a person whose spouse or common-law partner does not receive an OAS pension or an Allowance is greater than the GIS received by a person whose spouse or common-law partner also receives an OAS pension or an Allowance.

Allowance and Survivor's Allowance

The Allowance and the Survivor's Allowance apply to pensioners' spouses and common-law partners, and to deceased pensioners' spouses and common-law partners. The applicant spouse or common-law partner of an OAS pensioner may receive the Allowance or Survivor's Allowance if he or she is between the ages of 60 and 64, and if the applicant qualifies under an income test as well as a residency test. The residency test requires that the spouse or common-law partner reside in Canada for at least 10 years after attaining age 18. If the applicant lives or has lived in a country that has a reciprocal social security agreement with Canada, he or she may still qualify for a partial benefit without meeting the aforementioned Canadian residency requirements.

The Allowance is reduced by $3 for every $4 of the couple's income from sources other than OAS, until the OAS pension is reduced to zero. After the OAS pension has been eliminated, for a couple, the reduction applied to the remaining GIS is then reduced by $1 for every $4 of the couple's monthly combined income. For a surviving spouse, the portion relating to the GIS is reduced by $1 for every $2 of monthly income.

The Allowance is payable to the month of death or the month preceding attainment of age 65, whichever comes first. Also, the Allowance ceases to be paid in the event of separation, or when the applicant ceases to be a spouse or common-law partner.

The Survivor's Allowance is payable to the month of death, the month preceding the attainment of age 65, the date of remarriage, or the date that is a year after entering into a common-law relationship, whichever comes first.

Top-Up Benefits for GIS and Allowance Recipients

In 2011, Part 3 of Bill C-3, the *Supporting Vulnerable Seniors and Strengthening Canada's Economy Act*, amended the *Old Age Security Act* to provide top-up benefits for certain GIS and Survivor's Allowance recipients.

Effective July 1, 2011, a GIS recipient who was single, or whose spouse or common-law partner was not a pensioner, was eligible to receive a top-up benefit of up to $50 per month. For couples that included two GIS recipients or couples that included one GIS recipient and one Allowance recipient, a top-up benefit of up to $70 per month was payable. Survivor Allowance recipients were also entitled to a top-up benefit of up to $50 per month. The maximum top-up benefit was reduced by $1 for every $4 of single income in excess of $2,000, or combined income in excess of $4,000. The maximum top-up benefits were set to increase each year in line with increases in the CPI.

In keeping with the government's commitment to increasing the quality of life for seniors, the 2016 Federal Budget improved upon the benefits to single seniors and couples who may be more vulnerable to the risk of poverty:

i.   Single seniors are considered three times more likely to live in poverty amongst seniors in general. Therefore, the Budget proposed an increase to the GIS top-up benefit of up to $947 per annum which is scheduled to commence in July 2016, for seniors who rely almost exclusively on OAS and GIS benefits. Vulnerable single seniors with income of $4,600 or less will receive the full benefit and the benefit will be eliminated for income above approximately $8,400. For incomes in between these two amounts, the top-up benefit will be gradually reduced; and

ii.   Couples who are in receipt of GIS and Allowance benefits and are living apart for reasons beyond their control, such as a requirement for long term care, will receive a higher benefit based on their individual incomes. It is the understanding that seniors who are living apart under such circumstances will be subject to a higher cost of living and therefore susceptible to increased risks of poverty. This proposal takes into account existing legislation which allows couples in which both individuals are GIS recipients to receive benefits based on their individual incomes.

As well, based on the 2016 Federal Budget, benefits for single seniors will be increased quarterly in line with the cost of living.

Recognizing that seniors experience cost-of-living increases which are based on a different set of goods and services than younger populations, in the 2016 Budget, the government stated that it is also exploring the development of a new Seniors Price Index that will reflect the cost of living being experienced by seniors and therefore ensure that the OAS and GIS will keep pace with inflation.

Maximum Monthly Pensions Under the Old Age Security Act

The following table shows maximum monthly pensions for the various components for selected years. For 2016, the GIS and Allowance pensions include the maximum top-up benefits mentioned above.

Date Effective	Basic OAS Pension	Guaranteed Income Supplement		Allowance	
		Single[1]	Spouse or Common-Law Partner of Pensioner (each)	Regular Allowance[2]	Survivor's Allowance
1/1/52	$40.00				
1/7/57	$46.00				
1/2/62	$65.00				
1/1/67	$75.00	$30.00	$30.00		
1/1/72	$82.88	$67.12	$59.62		
1/1/77	$141.34	$99.13	$88.03	$ 229.37(3)	
1/1/82	$227.73	$228.63	$176.27	$ 404.00	$ 404.00(4)
1/1/87	$297.37	$353.41	$230.17	$ 527.54	$ 582.42
1/1/92	$374.07	$444.54	$289.55	$ 663.62	$ 732.64
1/1/97	$400.71	$476.20	$310.18	$ 710.89	$ 784.82
1/1/02	$442.66	$526.08	$342.67	$ 785.33	$ 867.02
1/1/05	$471.76	$560.69	$365.21	$ 836.97	$ 924.04
1/1/06	$484.63	$593.97	$389.67	$ 874.30	$ 967.24
1/1/07	$491.93	$620.91	$410.04	$ 901.97	$ 999.81
1/1/08	$502.31	$634.02	$418.69	$ 921.00	$1,020.91
1/1/09	$516.96	$652.51	$430.90	$ 947.86	$1,050.68
1/1/10	$516.96	$652.51	$430.90	$ 947.86	$1,050.68
1/1/11	$524.23	$661.69	$436.95	$ 961.18	$1,065.45
1/1/12	$540.12	$732.36	$485.61	$1,025.73	$1,148.35
1/1/13	$546.07	$740.44	$490.96	$1,037.03	$1,161.01
1/1/14	$551.54	$747.86	$495.89	$1,047.43	$1,172.65
1/1/15	$563.74	$764.40	$506.86	$1,070.60	$1,198.58
1/1/16	$570.52	$773.60	$512.96	$1,083.48	$1,213.00

Source: Extracted from Service Canada Income Security Programs Information Card (Rate Card).

(1) spouse or common-law partner not receiving OAS or regular Allowance

(2) spouse or common-law partner must be a GIS recipient

(3) first paid in 1975

(4) first paid in 1979

The following table shows the maximum OAS, GIS, Allowance, and Survivor's Allowance amounts payable at January 1, 2016 for married or common-law partners, single individuals, and survivors of pensioners in the appropriate age categories. The table assumes:

- The pensioner is (or was) an OAS pension recipient over age 65;
- The spouse or common-law partner is the spouse, common-law partner, or survivor of the pensioner and is over age 60; and
- Neither the pensioner nor the spouse has any other income that would reduce these benefits.

| Benefit | Single Person over age 65 | Married Couple/ Common-Law Partners | | Survivor age 60-64 |
		Spouse/ Common-Law Partner age 60-64	Spouse/ Common-Law Partner over age 65	
OAS • Pensioner • Spouse	$570.52 n/a	$570.52 0	$570.52 $570.52	n/a 0
GIS • Pensioner • Spouse	$773.60 n/a	$512.96 0	$512.96 $512.96	n/a 0
Allowance or Survivor's Allowance • Spouse	n/a	$1,083.48	0	$1,213.00
Total:	**$1,344.12**	**$2,166.96**	**$2,166.96**	**$1,213.00**

The foregoing table excludes top up benefits, as discussed earlier, which will become effective in July 2016 to certain single seniors and couples who are in receipt GIS and Allowance benefits. Allowance benefits.

Provincial Supplements

Several of the provincial and territorial governments offer a variety of benefits to assist low-income seniors. These benefits range from income assistance to home heating subsidies. Examples of programs are:

- *Alberta* – Alberta Seniors Benefit;
- *British Columbia* – Seniors Supplement;
- *Manitoba* – 55 PLUS program;
- *New Brunswick* – New Brunswick Low-Income Seniors' Benefit;
- *Newfoundland and Labrador* – Low-Income Seniors' Benefit;
- *Northwest Territories* – Seniors' Home Heating Subsidy and Supplementary Benefit;
- *Nunavut* – (See N.W.T. above as many programs are currently the same);
- *Ontario* – Guaranteed Annual Income System (GAINS);
- *Saskatchewan* – Saskatchewan Income Plan; and
- *Yukon* – Yukon Income Supplement.

Canada and Quebec Pension Plans

Introduction

The CPP/QPP are government-sponsored plans designed to partially replace employment income in case of retirement, death, or disability. They came into effect on January 1, 1966. The province of Quebec exercised its constitutional right to opt out of the federal plan and established the QPP. The provincial statute applies to those who work in Quebec (regardless of where in Canada they live), while the CPP governs those who work in Canada outside Quebec. Members of the Canadian Forces and the RCMP stationed in Quebec belong to the CPP.

The CPP/QPP are compulsory and cover practically all employees and self-employed persons. The main exceptions are casual and migratory workers, and certain types of employment such as exchange teaching, employment as a member of certain religious groups (this exception was abolished under the QPP in 1998), the employment of a child by their parent without remuneration and, in the case of the CPP, employees of provincial governments, unless the province agrees to have its employees covered.

CPP/QPP benefits are funded by contributions from employers and employees and investment earnings on those contributions. There is no government subsidy. The benefits are earnings-related and indexed annually to increases in the CPI to offset the effects of inflation.

Historically, the level of retirement pension under the CPP/QPP was set to provide, together with the OAS pension, a replacement ratio of approximately 40% of income up to the national average wage (15% from OAS and 25% from CPP/QPP).

On June 20, 2016, with the exception of Quebec and Manitoba (which later agreed to the changes), the Canadian Federal and Provincial Finances Ministers agreed to expand the CPP. The following key developments were a result of this announcement:

1) The CPP replacement rate on pensionable income is set to increase from 25% to 33% on service accrued after January 1, 2019. This change will be phased-in over a five year period from 2019 to 2023. Over the same five year period, the basic CPP contribution rate on earnings up to the YMPE is to be increased by approximately 1% for both employers and employees;

2) A new tier of contributions will apply for earnings between the YMPE and a new maximum limit that is 14% higher than the current limit. This increase will be phased in over two-year period from 2024 to 2025. The contribution rate for this new tier of contributions will be approximately 4% of earnings for both employers and employees, and these contributions will be tax-deductible, as opposed to being eligible for tax credits;

3) The Working Income Tax Benefit is set to increase, which will help offset the effect of increased contributions for low-income earners; and

4) The Ontario Finance Minister stated that the Ontario Retirement Pension Plan (ORPP) will not go forward.

The Quebec Finance Minister stated that the proposed agreement is not sufficiently targeted. In response, the Quebec Government proposed a modified version of the expansion for public consultation in the summer of 2016.

The CPP/QPP are administered by the Minister of National Revenue and the Quebec Minister of Revenue, respectively, for that part of the plan that relates to coverage and to the collection of contributions, and are the responsibility of the Minister of Human Resources and Social Development and the Quebec Pension Board, respectively, for the part that relates to benefits.

Until the 2016 announcement to enhance the CPP, the CPP and QPP were broadly similar in the benefits and qualifying conditions, although the contribution rate on the QPP was higher at 5.25% for both employers and employees. This chapter describes the main provisions of the CPP/QPP in force as of January 2016, and notes any significant differences between the two programs.

Contributions

Contributions to the CPP/QPP are paid on earnings between the YBE and the YMPE. Both the employer and the employee contribute equally at 50% of the total contribution rate. Self-employed persons contribute both the "employee" and "employer" portion.

The YMPE is linked to the average Canadian wage and is adjusted annually. Beginning in 1975, the amount of the YBE for an employee or a self-employed person changed from 12% of the YMPE to 10% of the YMPE, rounded down to the next $100. Since 1996, the YBE has been $3,500 (it was frozen at this level in 1998). Although the YBE has been frozen since 1998, the amount that a person who is collecting a CPP disability pension can earn without reducing his or her benefits continues to increase each year ($5,400 in 2016).

Historically, CPP and QPP contribution rates were aligned until 2012. Until 1986, the total contribution rate was 3.6%. However, as shown in the following table, this rate was progressively increased commencing in 1987. At that time, a new schedule of contribution rates was introduced when it became evident in the respective CPP and QPP Statutory Actuarial Reports that the 3.6% rate was inadequate to meet the long-term benefit obligations of the plans. For the same reasons, a revised higher rate schedule was introduced in 1992. In January 1998, new CPP/QPP contribution rates were implemented. These new rates were introduced in order to ensure that the plan remained adequately financed and sustainable in the long run, without placing too much financial burden on future generations. The rate increases were based on a six-year schedule that provided for annual increases in the combined employer-employee contribution rate from 6.0% in 1997 to 9.9% in 2003. It has remained at 9.9% since then for CPP. For QPP, contributions levels were again increased, this time beginning in 2012.

The 2016 CPP expansion announcment includes a new tier of contributions that will apply for earnings between the YMPE and a new maximum limit that is 14% higher than the current limit. This increase will be phased in over two-year period from 2024 to 2025. The contribution rate for this new tier of contributions will be approximately 4% of earnings for both employers and employees, and these contributions will be tax-deductible, as opposed to being eligible for tax credits.

					Maximum contributions by	
Year	YBE	YMPE	Maximum contributory earnings	Contribution rate	Each of Employer and Employee	Self-Employed Person
	(1)	(2)	(3) = (2) - (1)	(4)	50% X (3) X (4)	(3) X (4)
1967	600	5,000	$ 4,400	3.6%	79.20	158.40
1972	600	5,500	4,900	3.6%	88.20	176.40
1977	900	9,300	8,400	3.6%	151.20	302.40
1982	1,600	16,500	14,900	3.6%	268.20	536.40
1986	2,500	25,800	23,300	3.6%	419.40	838.80
1987	2,500	25,900	23,400	3.8%	444.60	889.20
1988	2,600	26,500	23,900	4.0%	478.00	956.00
1989	2,700	27,700	25,000	4.2%	525.00	1,050.00
1990	2,800	28,900	26,100	4.4%	574.20	1,148.40
1991	3,000	30,500	27,500	4.6%	632.50	1,265.00
1992	3,200	32,200	29,000	4.8%	696.00	1,392.00
1993	3,300	33,400	30,100	5.0%	752.50	1,505.00
1994	3,400	34,400	31,000	5.2%	806.00	1,612.00
1995	3,400	34,900	31,500	5.4%	850.50	1,701.00
1996	3,500	35,400	31,900	5.6%	893.20	1,786.40
1997	3,500	35,800	32,300	6.0%	969.00	1,938.00
1998	3,500	36,900	33,400	6.4%	1,068.80	2,137.60
1999	3,500	37,400	33,900	7.0%	1,186.50	2,373.00
2000	3,500	37,600	34,100	7.8%	1,329.90	2,659.80
2001	3,500	38,300	34,800	8.6%	1,496.40	2,992.80
2002	3,500	39,100	35,600	9.4%	1,673.20	3,346.40
2003	3,500	39,900	36,400	9.9%	1,801.80	3,603.60
2004	3,500	40,500	37,000	9.9%	1,831.50	3,663.00

CPP/QPP CONTRIBUTION HISTORY FOR SELECT YEARS UP TO 2011

CPP/QPP CONTRIBUTION HISTORY FOR SELECT YEARS UP TO 2011						
Year	YBE	YMPE	Maximum contributory earnings	Contribution rate	Maximum contributions by	
					Each of Employer and Employee	Self-Employed Person
	(1)	(2)	(3) = (2) - (1)	(4)	50% X (3) X (4)	(3) X (4)
2005	3,500	41,100	37,600	9.9%	1,861.20	3,722.40
2006	3,500	42,100	38,600	9.9%	1,910.70	3,821.40
2007	3,500	43,700	40,200	9.9%	1,989.90	3,979.80
2008	3,500	44,900	41,400	9.9%	2,049.30	4,098.60
2009	3,500	46,300	42,800	9.9%	2,118.60	4,237.20
2010	3,500	47,200	43,700	9.9%	2,163.15	4,326.30
2011	3,500	48,300	44,800	9.9%	2,217.60	4,435.20

CPP CONTRIBUTION HISTORY FROM 2012 to 2016						
Year	YBE	YMPE	Maximum contributory earnings	Contribution rate	Maximum contributions by	
					Each of Employer and Employee	Self-Employed Person
	(1)	(2)	(3) = (2) - (1)	(4)	50% X (3) X (4)	(3) X (4)
2012	$3,500	$50,100	$46,600	9.9%	$2,306.70	$4,613.40
2013	3,500	51,100	47,600	9.9%	2,356.20	4,712.40
2014	3,500	52,500	49,000	9.9%	2,425.50	4,851.00
2015	3,500	53,600	50,100	9.9%	2,479.95	4,959.90
2016	3,500	54,900	51,400	9.9%	2,544.30	5,088.60

The recent CPP expansion announcement states that CPP contributions are expected to increase by a total of 2% (phased-in from 2019 to 2023), shared by employers and employees at 1% each (to a total contribution rate of approximately 11.9%). This rate of 11.9% would apply on the current YMPE level (i.e. prior to the YMPE increase from 2024 to 2025).

In order to improve the funding of the QPP and to achieve intergenerational equity, Quebec implemented contribution rate increases in its March 2011 Budget. These contribution rates are shown in the table below. The contribution rate for 2012 increased to 10.05% and is scheduled to increase by 0.15% per year until it reaches 10.8% in 2017. Thereafter, the contribution rate will be adjusted automatically each year to align it with the QPP's steady-state rate.

QPP CONTRIBUTION HISTORY FROM 2012 to 2016						
					Maximum contributions by	
Year	YBE	YMPE	Maximum contributory earnings	Contri - bution rate	Each of Employer and Employee	Self- Employed Person
	(1)	(2)	(3) = (2) - (1)	(4)	50% X (3) X (4)	(3) X (4)
2012	$3,500	$50,100	$46,600	10.05%	$2,341.65	$4,683.30
2013	3,500	51,100	47,600	10.20%	2,427.60	4,855.20
2014	3,500	52,500	49,000	10.35%	2,535.75	5,071.50
2015	3,500	53,600	50,100	10.50%	2,630.25	5,260.50
2016	3,500	54,900	51,400	10.65%	2,737.05	5,474.10

Contributions for the CPP/QPP are required from persons who earn in excess of $3,500 annually from attainment of age 18 to the date of death, commencement of retirement pension, or attainment of age 70, whichever comes first.

The contributory period is the above period, less any month for which a disability pension was payable to a contributor, or when there are no earnings or earnings have fallen below $3,500 annually or any month for which a family allowance was payable to a contributor for a child less than seven years of age.

Contributions by self-employed persons for a year are paid directly to the Canada Revenue Agency (CRA) or Revenue Quebec, as the case may be, by April 30 of the following year, when submitting income tax returns. Employee contributions are deducted from pay and remitted by the employer monthly, together with employer contributions, to the CRA or Revenue Quebec.

Contributions are charged month by month on all earned income in excess of the YBE until the maximum for the year has been paid. If an employee works for more than one employer in any year, deductions must nevertheless be made by each such employer without regard to the other(s). The employee may apply for a refund of any overpayments through their income tax return, although the employer may generally not obtain such a refund.

Qualifying Conditions

Retirement Pension

The normal commencement age for a CPP/QPP retirement pension is age 65. A CPP retirement pension may become payable to a person who has made at least one valid contribution to the CPP and who has reached the age of 60. A QPP retirement pension may become payable to a person who has made valid contributions for at least one year to the QPP and who has reached the age of 60. Prior to 2012, before a CPP pension could commence for a person under age 65, that person must have earned less than the allowable maximum pension payment ($1,092.50 in 2016) in the month before the pension began and in the month in which it began. Once a person started receiving a CPP pension, he or she could work as much as desired without affecting the pension amount. However, there could be no further contributions to the CPP on earnings received while the CPP pension was being paid.

Beginning in 2012, a contributor who has reached the age of 60 can now commence the CPP pension while continuing to work. The employee (and employer) must continue making contributions until the employee retires or until age 65, whichever is earlier. An employee who continues to work past 65 has the option to continue making contributions until retirement up to age 70. The employer must also contribute in these circumstances.

Contributions made to the CPP while the employee is working and drawing a CPP pension serve to increase the CPP pension. The increase in the CPP pension for each year that contributions are made is 2.5% of the maximum CPP pension payable, adjusted to reflect the contributor's actual earnings (if less than the YMPE) and age. This adjustment is known as the Post-Retirement Benefit (PRB), and the increases to the employee's CPP pension will be made on January 1 following each year CPP contributions are made.

For example, suppose an employee who turned 65 on January 1, 2015 decided to continue working for at least another year and also decided to start the CPP pension and continue making CPP contributions. The employee earned $60,000 in 2015. Effective January 1, 2016 the increase in the employee's CPP benefit would be $355.28 per year, calculated as follows:

The maximum CPP pension in 2016 is $13,110 per year.

> The employee is age 66, and would receive an increase of 8.4% on the additional retirement benefit earned in 2015.

$13,110 x 1.084 x 2.5% = $355.28

Under the QPP and prior to 2014, a person under the age of 65 had to have either ceased working or have entered into a progressive retirement agreement with his or her employer that reduces the applicant's income by at least 20% in order to begin receiving a pension. Effective January 1, 2014, this requirement was removed. An individual is now able to start the QPP pension early while continuing to work, however they must continue to make regular contributions to the QPP while working. These contributions serve to increase the QPP pension by an amount referred to as the retirement pension supplement. The increase in the QPP pension for each year that contributions are made is 0.5% of the earnings on which the employee contributed in the previous year. The adjustment to the employee's QPP pension will be made on January 1 following each year QPP contributions are made.

For example, suppose an employee who commenced his or her QPP pension on January 1, 2015 decided to continue working for the rest of the year. The employee earned $60,000 in 2015, and therefore contributed $2,630.25 (one half of 10.50% of $50,100, the maximum contributory earnings, as shown in the QPP contributions chart earlier in this chapter). Effective January 1, 2016 the increase in the employee's CPP benefit would be $250.50 per year, calculated as follows:

The employee contributed based on earnings of $50,100

$50,100 x 0.5% = $250.50

Early and Postponed Retirement Adjustments

Bill C-51 changed the adjustment factors to be applied to CPP benefits on early or postponed retirement. Prior to 2012, if a contributor commenced the CPP retirement pension before age 65, the amount of pension was calculated as though the person were age 65, but was reduced by 0.5% for each month between the month in which the pension commenced and the month in which the contributor attained age 65. Beginning in 2012, this reduction will increase gradually over a period of four years to 0.6% for any early retirement pensions commencing in 2016 or later.

Commencement of retirement pensions may also be deferred to any age between age 65 and 70. For retirements occurring prior to 2011, the pension was increased by 0.5% for each month between the attainment of age 65 and the month of retirement. For postponed retirements in 2011 and later years, the rate of increase was raised gradually to a rate of 0.7% per month for retirements in 2013 or later.

Now that these early and late retirement adjustments have been fully phased in, pensions commencing at age 60 will be 36% lower, and at age 70 will be 42% higher, than the amount calculated on the regular formula for persons at age 65.

In a move to encourage experienced workers to remain in the labour force, Quebec also introduced changes to the adjustment factors for early and postponed retirement in the QPP. The changes are similar to those implemented for the CPP. The ultimate adjustment factors and the year in which they are reached are the same; however, the phasing in of these ultimate adjustment factors was different. The other main difference is that, under the QPP, the reduction factors for individuals retiring early will depend on the level of their QPP pension.

The following table shows the monthly adjustment rate for early or postponed retirements, depending on the year of retirement, under both the CPP and QPP.

Schedule of New Adjustment Factors				
Year of Retirement	Monthly Early Retirement Reduction Factors		Monthly Postponed Retirement Increase Factors	
	CPP	QPP*	CPP	QPP
2011	0.50%	0.50%	0.57%	0.50%
2012	0.52%	0.50%	0.64%	0.50%
2013	0.54%	0.50%	0.70%	0.70%
2014	0.56%	0.53%	0.70%	0.70%
2015	0.58%	0.56%	0.70%	0.70%
2016	0.60%	0.60%	0.70%	0.70%

*Applicable to maximum pension

Under the QPP, an individual receiving a lower pension who wishes to retire early will receive a lower early retirement reduction (0.5%) than someone who is entitled to the maximum QPP pension (0.6%) in 2016 or later. The table below illustrates how the early retirement reduction would be applied.

QPP Pension as % of Maximum	Monthly Reduction Factor for Early Retirements in 2016 and After
25%	0.525%
50%	0.550%
75%	0.575%
100%	0.600%

Retroactive Retirement Pension

For the CPP and QPP, if an employee retires after his or her 65th birthday, he or she may receive up to 12 months of retroactive payments, but no earlier than the month following his or her 65th birthday.

Disability Benefits

CPP/QPP disability benefits comprise a pension to the disabled contributor and a pension to dependent children who meet certain conditions. These pensions are payable to a contributor who has a severe and permanent disability and the contributor is unable to engage in any substantially gainful occupation with earnings in excess of $15,489 per year in 2016.

If an individual under age 65 became disabled after December 31, 1997, he or she must have contributed to the CPP in four of the last six years on earnings that are at least 10% of the YMPE to be entitled to these disability pensions under the CPP. Bill C-36, which was passed on May 3, 2007, reduced the CPP contribution requirement to three of the last six years. Under the QPP, an individual who is less than age 60 must have contributed during:

1) At least two of the last three years in his or her contributory period; or

2) At least five of the last 10 years in his or her contributory period; or

3) At least half of the years in his or her contributory period, with a minimum of two years.

Additionally, under the QPP, an individual aged 60 to 64 (inclusive) can be deemed to be disabled if he or she can no longer regularly pursue the gainful occupation that he or she left because of disability. Effective January 1, 2013, an individual in this age range (60 to 64, inclusive) must have contributed to the QPP for four of the last six years in his or her contributory period to be eligible for a disability pension.

Effective January 1, 2013 the QPP introduced an "additional amount for disability" which can be paid to individuals currently collecting QPP if they meet the following criteria:

- They meet the criteria of being disabled;
- They have been receiving their QPP pension for at least 6 months;
- They can no longer cancel their application for a retirement pension in order to receive a disability pension instead; and
- They contributed to the QPP for at least four of the last six years in their contributory period, which ends in the month that they are deemed to be disabled.

Under the CPP/QPP, the disability pension of the disabled contributor is payable as long as the employee is alive and continues to be disabled, or until age 65, when it is replaced by the retirement pension. The retirement pension is calculated based on the YMPE at the time of disablement, indexed to age 65. When payment of this disability pension is approved, the pension is payable monthly, beginning with the fourth month following the month in which the contributor became disabled.

Survivor Benefits

Under the CPP/QPP, survivor benefits are paid to a surviving spouse or common-law partner, dependent children, and a deceased contributor's estate. There are three different types of benefits: the survivor's pension, the dependent children's benefit, and death benefits.

Survivor's Pension

Under the CPP, a survivor – defined as a person who was married to or who was the common-law partner of the contributor at the time of the contributor's death — aged 35 or older at the time of the contributor's death, or a survivor regardless of age if the survivor has dependent children or is disabled at the time of the contributor's death, is entitled to receive a CPP survivor's pension.

A surviving spouse (a person who was married to the contributor, was in a civil union with the contributor, or was living with the contributor in a de facto union on the day of the death of the contributor) under the QPP, is entitled to a surviving spouse's pension, regardless of age, but the amount of the pension is different for surviving spouses according to the spouse's age, whether or not they have children and whether or not they are disabled.

CPP/QPP survivor benefits are payable if contributions were made for not less than one-third of the total number of calendar years within the contributory period (but not less than three years), or for at least 10 years.

Orphan's Benefit

According to the CPP/QPP, an orphan's benefit is to be paid to each dependent child of a deceased contributor who has made contributions for at least the minimum qualifying period. The deceased contributor must have made contributions for the same minimum qualifying period as for a survivor's pension discussed above.

Death Benefits

A lump-sum death benefit is also payable upon the death of a contributor, under the same eligibility provisions as for the survivor pension.

For contributors who died after December 31, 1997, the CPP death benefit is a lump-sum payment that amounts to six times the amount of the deceased contributor's monthly retirement pension, to a maximum of $2,500. Under the QPP, the death benefit is a lump-sum payment of $2,500.

Determination and Payment of Benefits

Retirement Pension

The CPP/QPP retirement pension is based on the contributor's past earnings. This involves the calculation of the average earnings up to the YMPE of each year in the period from January 1, 1966 or from age 18, whichever is later, to the date of the claim. The earnings of a contributor are therefore taken into account over the entire contributory period, excluding any "drop-out" months determined as described below.

To compensate for periods of unemployment, low earnings and sickness and disability, the plan allows certain periods to be dropped out or ignored in computing the average earnings. These include:

- Periods while receiving CPP disability benefits;

- Periods while caring for children under the age of seven (CPP/QPP);
- Up to 15% of the contributor's months of lowest earnings prior to age 65, provided that at least 120 months are left in the contributory period (CPP/QPP);
- Months included in a period of indemnity (QPP); and
- Periods after age 65 while contributing to CPP.

Effective in 2012 and for CPP only, the percentage of low earnings increased to 16%, allowing up to 7.5 years of the contributor's lowest earnings to be dropped from the calculation. In 2014, the percentage increased to 17%, allowing up to 8 years of the contributor's lowest earnings to be dropped from the calculation. For QPP, the percentage of low earnings to be dropped from the calculation has remained at 15%.

A contributor may also substitute a month of earnings after age 65. The months to be dropped out will be those in which the earnings were the smallest, in order to maximize the average earnings and, therefore, the pension.

The CPP/QPP allow for increases in the general level of wages by providing for an adjustment in each year's covered earnings in the computation of average earnings. Before calculating average earnings, the actual contributory earnings in each year are adjusted by the ratio of the average YMPE for the five years ending with the year in which the pension commences to the YMPE for the year in question.

The amount of a retirement pension payable to a contributor aged 65 and over is a basic monthly amount equal to 25% of his or her average monthly pensionable earnings, adjusted to reflect the average of the final five-year maximum pensionable earnings. With the June 2016 CPP expansion announcement, this ratio has been set to increase for the CPP, phased-in over a five year period from 2019 to 2023 from 25% to 33%. As noted above, the YMPE has also been announced to increase by 14%, phased-in over a two-year period from 2024 to 2025.

The first step in calculating the adjusted average pensionable earnings is to calculate the average of the YMPE for the year of retirement and the four preceding years. For example, for retirements in 2016, the average YMPE is calculated over 2012, 2013, 2014, 2015, and 2016, giving $52,440. Then, for each month in the contributory period (excluding any "drop-out" months), the adjusted pensionable earnings are calculated by multiplying the actual pensionable earnings for the month by the ratio of the average YMPE for the retirement year to the YMPE for the year in which the earnings were paid.

For example, suppose a person who is retiring in 2016 had pensionable earnings of $2,000 in each month of 1988 (i.e., total 1988 pensionable earnings of $24,000, which is less than the 1988 YMPE of $26,500). Each $2,000 of monthly earnings would be adjusted by multiplying by the ratio of the average YMPE for 2012 to 2016 to the YMPE for 1988 (i.e., by $52,440/$26,500) to give adjusted monthly earnings of $3,957.74 (i.e., total adjusted earnings for 1988 of $47,492.88).

If the annual 1988 earnings had been at or above the YMPE for 1988 of $26,500, then the 1988 pensionable earnings would have been $26,500, and the total of the monthly adjusted pensionable earnings for 1988 would have equalled the average YMPE for 2016 of $52,440.

The adjustment calculation described above is done for every month in the non-drop-out contributory period. The adjustment increases the earnings for most months, but for months in the two or three years just prior to retirement the adjustment decreases the earnings because the YMPE for those years is greater than the average YMPE.

The final steps of the calculation are to total the adjusted monthly pensionable earnings for the whole non-drop-out contributory period and then divide the total by the number of months in the non-drop-out period to give the average adjusted monthly pensionable earnings. The monthly CPP/QPP pension (before any reduction for retirement prior to age 65) is currently 25% of the average monthly adjusted pensionable earnings as of 2016. Phased-in from 2019 to 2023, the calculation will change from 25% of the average monthly adjusted pensionable earnings to 33%.

For an individual who has earned at or above the YMPE in all years included in the non-drop-out contributory period, the average of the monthly adjusted pensionable earnings in the whole non-drop-out contributory period will be equal to 1/12 of the average YMPE for the year of retirement (i.e., $52,440/12, which equals $4,370 for 2016). Such a person would be entitled to the maximum possible CPP pension (i.e., 25% of $4,370, which equals $1,092.50 for 2016).

The Pension Index is used as a mechanism for determining the increases in the amount of benefits payable from one year to the next. The Pension Index is tied to the CPI, unless the CPI decreases, in which case the Pension Index will remain the same.

Disability Benefits

As noted above, disability benefits consist of a pension for the disabled contributor and an additional pension for any eligible dependent children.

A disabled contributor is entitled to receive a pension that is equal to a flat-rate pension plus an earnings-related component equal to 75% of the contributor's retirement pension. The maximum disability pension in 2016 is $471.40 under the QPP) plus 75% of $1,092.50, which amounts to $1,290.81 a month ($1,290.78 under the QPP).

Pensions for dependent children of disabled contributors are payable at the same amounts as for dependent children of a deceased contributor (see below).

Survivor Pension

The survivor benefits payable by the CPP/QPP consist of a pension payable to an eligible spouse or common-law partner, plus a pension to dependent children.

Pension to Eligible Spouse/Survivor

While the survivor is under age 65, the pension is equal to the sum of a flat-rate pension plus an earnings-related component of 37.5% of the contributor's retirement pension. Where the survivor is between the age of 35 and 45 (not disabled and without dependent children) he or she receives reduced benefits. If the survivor is under the age of 35 (not disabled and without dependent children), he or she will not receive any benefits.

The CPP benefits for a survivor under age 65 are shown in the table below:

Age/Status of Survivor At Date of Contributor's Death	Description of Benefit	Maximum Benefit
a. 45 to 64, or b. under 45 and has a disability or a dependent child	Flat rate ($183.93 per month in 2016) plus 37.5% of contributor's pension	$593.62 per month in 2016
c. 35 to 44 and does not have a disability or a dependent child	Same as for (a) minus 1/120 for each month the survivor is under 45 at the time of the contributor's death	

Age/Status of Survivor At Date of Contributor's Death	Description of Benefit	Maximum Benefit
d. under 35 and does not have a disability or a dependent child	No benefit until the survivor reaches age 65 or is diagnosed with a disability	

Under the QPP, there are three different flat-rate pensions depending on the surviving spouse's age, disability status, and whether or not there are dependent children, as shown in the table below.

Age/Status of Surviving Spouse at Contributor's Date of Death	Flat-Rate Pension in 2016 (per month)	Maximum Pension in 2016 (per month)
45 to 64	$471.40	$881.09
Disabled (any age)	$471.40	$881.09
Non-disabled under age 45 with dependent child	$437.70	$847.39
Non-disabled under age 45 without dependent child	$120.73	$530.42

Thus, unlike the CPP, the QPP pays a survivor's pension to a non-disabled eligible spouse without dependent children who is under age 35.

An individual may receive both a survivor's pension and a retirement pension as a contributor in his or her own right. Under the CPP, for a survivor who has reached 65 years of age, the amount of the combined pension will be the retirement pension, plus the lesser of: (1) 60% of the deceased's retirement pension minus the lesser of 40% of that amount and 40% of the survivor's retirement pension before an actuarial adjustment; and (2) the ceiling of the maximum retirement pension in the year of entitlement to the second benefit.

If the survivor is between the ages of 60 and 65, the amount of the combined pension will be the adjusted retirement pension, plus the survivor flat-rate benefit, plus the lesser of: (1) 37.5% of the deceased's retirement pension minus the lesser of 40% of that amount, or 40% of the survivor's retirement pension before actuarial adjustments; and (2) the maximum survivor's retirement pension in the year of entitlement to the second benefit plus the survivor flat rate.

Combined pensions are permitted under the QPP as well. When a surviving spouse is under the age of 65 and becomes entitled to both a retirement pension and a surviving spouse's pension, the monthly amount of the surviving spouse's pension is equal to the sum of:

- The flat-rate benefit for a surviving spouse (a maximum of $471.40 in 2016); and
- An amount equal to the lesser of:
  - i.   37.5% of the amount of the deceased contributor's retirement pension, and
  - ii. the difference between the maximum monthly retirement pension for the year and the amount of the surviving spouse's retirement pension.

Where a surviving spouse becomes entitled to both a retirement pension and a surviving spouse's pension after reaching 65 years of age, the monthly amount of the surviving spouse's pension is equal to the lesser of:

- The difference between the maximum retirement benefit and the surviving spouse's retirement pension established; and
- The greater of:
  - i.   37.5% of the amount of the contributor's retirement pension, and
  - ii. 60% of the amount of the contributor's retirement pension minus 40% of the amount of the surviving spouse's retirement pension.

Pension to Dependent Children

A survivor's pension is payable to each dependent child of the deceased contributor. Under both the CPP and QPP, this pension is a flat-rate pension, and it stops when the child attains age 18. Prior to 2012, the amount of the flat-rate pension under the QPP was only about a third of that payable under the CPP. Effective January 1, 2012, Quebec legislation tripled this amount. In 2016, the dependent child's pension is $237.69 per month under both the CPP and QPP. There are some differences between the dependent child's pension under the CPP and QPP:

- Under the CPP only, the pension is also payable while the child is between the ages of 18 and 25 and is attending school full-time; and

- Under the CPP only, an orphan is eligible for double benefits if both deceased parents were contributors.

Lump-Sum Death Benefits

A lump-sum death benefit is payable in addition to the survivor pensions described above. Under the CPP, the amount of this lump-sum benefit is six times the actual or calculated contributor's retirement pension, to a maximum of $2,500. Under the QPP, the death benefit is a lump-sum payment of $2,500 in respect of a contributor who dies after December 31, 1997.

According to the CPP, if there is a will, the executor of the estate must apply for the death benefit within 60 days of the date of death. If there is no will, or the executor did not apply within the 60-day period, payment will be made (1) to the person who paid for the funeral expenses; (2) to the surviving spouse or common-law partner of the deceased; or (3) to the next-of-kin of the deceased, in that order.

According to the QPP, the death benefit will be paid to the person or charity who paid the funeral expenses. An application must be made within 60 days of the contributor's death. If an application is not made within 60 days, it will be payable to the first of the following applicants: (1) the person or charity who paid the funeral expenses; (2) the heirs of the contributor; (3) the surviving spouse of the contributor (if no surviving heirs); (4) the descendants of the contributor (if no surviving heirs or surviving spouse); or (5) the ascendants of the contributor (if no surviving spouse or descendants).

Benefit Amounts

The following table gives a history of the maximum monthly retirement, survivor and disability pensions, and lump-sum death benefits under the CPP/QPP at the time of commencement.

CPP/QPP MAXIMUM BENEFIT HISTORY FOR SELECTED YEARS								
Year of Commencement (1)	Retirement Pension	Disability Pension		Survivor's Pension				Lump Sum Death Benefit
				Spouse		Children		
	CPP/QPP	CPP	QPP	CPP (2)	QPP (2)	CPP	QPP	CPP/QPP
1967	10.42	N/A (3)	N/A(3)	N/A (4)	N/A (4)	N/A (4)	N/A (4)	N/A(4)
1972	67.50	111.98	111.98	69.79	69.79	27.60	27.60	550.00
1977	173.61	175.05	245.17	109.94	180.06	44.84	29.00	930.00
1982	307.65	301.42	411.92	186.05	296.55	70.68	29.00	1,650.00
1987	521.52	634.09	634.09	290.36	506.39	94.79	29.00	2,590.00
1992	636.11	783.89	783.89	359.68	631.06	154.70	29.00	3,220.00
1999	751.67	903.55	903.52	414.46	681.47	171.33	54.40	2,500.00
2002	788.75	956.05	956.02	437.99	695.37	183.77	58.35	2,500.00
2004	814.17	992.80	992.77	454.42	704.90	192.68	61.18	2,500.00
2005	828.75	1,010.23	1,010.20	462.42	710.37	195.96	62.22	2,500.00
2006	844.58	1,031.05	1,031.02	471.85	716.31	200.47	63.65	2,500.00
2007	863.75	1,053.77	1,053.74	482.30	729.84	204.68	64.99	2,500.00
2008	884.58	1,077.52	1,077.49	493.28	745.77	208.77	66.29	2,500.00
2009	908.75	1,105.99	1,105.96	506.38	765.18	213.99	67.95	2,500.00
2010	934.17	1,126.76	1,126.73	516.57	776.41	214.85	68.22	2,500.00
2011	960.00	1,153.37	1,153.34	529.09	793.34	218.50	69.38	2,500.00
2012	986.67	1,185.50	1,185.47	543.82	815.47	224.62	224.62	2,500.00
2013	1,012.50	1,212.90	1,212.87	556.64	833.18	228.66	228.66	2,500.00
2014	1,038.33	1,236.35	1,236.32	567.91	846.94	230.72	230.72	2,500.00

CPP/QPP MAXIMUM BENEFIT HISTORY FOR SELECTED YEARS								
Year of Commence-ment (1)	Retire-ment Pension	Disability Pension		Survivor's Pension				Lump Sum Death Benefit
	CPP/QPP	CPP	QPP	Spouse		Children		CPP/QPP
				CPP (2)	QPP (2)	CPP	QPP	
2015	1,065.00	1,264.59	1,264.56	581.13	865.19	234.87	234.87	2,500.00
2016	1,092.50	1,290.81	1,290.78	593.62	881.09	237.69	237.69	2,500.00

(1) amounts are those payable in January of year; pension is indexed starting on the January 1 following its year of commencement
(2) payable to a spouse aged 45 or more but under 65
(3) first paid in 1970
(4) first paid in 1968

General Provisions

Indexing of Benefits

Indexation of benefits before retirement is based on a wage index through the indexation of the YMPE, whereas after retirement the indexation is based on the CPI.

The YMPE, which governs the earnings on which contributions are made and benefits are calculated under the CPP/QPP, has historically been adjusted annually to reflect changes in the Industrial Aggregate Wage Index of weekly wages and salaries in Canada published by Statistics Canada. The YMPE is the previous year's YMPE, multiplied by the ratio of the average wage index during the 12 months ending June 30 of the previous year to the similar average one year earlier (the resulting amount is rounded to the next lower multiple of $100). Commencing in 2024 and phased-in over a two-year period until 2025, a new tier of contributions will apply for earnings between the YMPE and a new maximum limit that is 14% higher than the current limit.

Pensions in pay are adjusted each January 1 by the ratio of the average of the Consumer Price Indices for the 12 months ending with October of the preceding year to the similar average one year earlier. However, under the CPP/QPP, pensions in payment cannot be decreased, even if the CPI decreases.

Income Tax

CPP/QPP benefits are taxable income to the beneficiary. Contributions by employers are fully tax deductible, while employees receive a tax credit. For 2001 and subsequent taxation years, the tax credit is 16% of contributions for all employees. Prior to the 2001 taxation year, self-employed individuals were allowed a credit in respect of all their premiums payable under the CPP (which included both the employer and employee portions of the premiums). Beginning in 2001, a self-employed person can deduct one-half of his or her CPP premiums payable on his or her self-employed earnings, which effectively means that the employer portion of the premiums is deductible from income, while the employee portion is allowed the credit.

Credit Splitting

When a marriage or common-law relationship ends, the CPP credits built up by a couple while they lived together can be divided equally between them. These credits can be split even if one spouse or common-law partner did not pay into the CPP.

Assignment

A retirement pension in payment may be divided between the two spouses or common-law partners in proportion to the period of cohabitation, provided that both spouses or common-law partners are at least age 60 and have ceased contributing to the CPP/QPP. On death, divorce, separation (after 12 months), or request of both spouses or common-law partners, the assignment will come to an end and the amount of the pension will revert to the same amount as if there had been no pension sharing. The assignment will also come to an end if one of the spouses or common-law partners had never paid into the CPP/QPP but begins contributing.

Reciprocal Agreements with Other Countries

The federal government and the Quebec Government have reciprocal social security agreements with various countries to help people qualify for benefits from either country (i.e., eligible service under the foreign plan may be taken into account to quality for the CPP/QPP benefits). As of 2016, the federal government has entered into 57 agreements and the Quebec Government has entered into 33 such agreements.

Integration with CPP/QPP Benefits

Other private or public arrangements may reduce benefits to take into account the benefits payable from the CPP/QPP. For example, the GIS will be reduced by $1 for each $2 of retirement pension payable under CPP/QPP. Some Workers' Compensation programs take the CPP/QPP disability pension into account.

Many private pension plans may also integrate their employee contribution and benefit level with the CPP/QPP. Integration may be direct (i.e., 2% of final average earnings minus the CPP/QPP benefit) or indirect (i.e., step-rate pension of 1.25% of final average earnings up to the YMPE and 2% above). The second method is by far the most popular integration method if there is CPP/QPP integration.

Similarly, contributions may be integrated directly (i.e., 5% minus CPP/QPP contributions) or indirectly (4.5% up to the YMPE and 6% above).

If the benefits or contributions are in addition to the CPP/QPP benefits or contributions, they are referred to as stacked benefits.

Funding and Future Contributions

The sustainability of the CPP/QPP has been of considerable concern for both the federal government and the Quebec Government. The CPP/QPP were established as pay-as-you-go arrangements, and reserve funds were established to cover two to three years of benefit payout to smooth fluctuations. The 15th Actuarial Report on the CPP (1993) disclosed the unfunded liability of that plan alone at $570 billion. The pay-as-you-go nature of these plans meant that substantial increases in contributions would be required in the future to sustain current benefit levels. The increased contribution needs were due to the maturation of the plans (full retirement benefits have been payable since 1977, when contributions were made for only a portion of employment years), higher than expected disability payments, an aging population, and slower than expected economic growth since these plans were first implemented.

In 1997, the federal and provincial governments agreed to changes to the CPP to ensure its future sustainability. These changes came into effect in 1998. As a result, the increases to the total employee plus employer annual CPP contribution rates were accelerated and reached 9.9% of employee contributory earnings in 2003. The total CPP contribution rate has remained at 9.9% since then and there are no more increases currently scheduled.

The changes also included a new investment policy. One of the most significant aspects of this new policy was the creation of the CPP Investment Board. The objectives of the Board, as set out in section 5 of the *Canada Pension Plan Investment Board Act* are:

- To manage funds in the best interests of the contributors and beneficiaries under the CPP; and
- To invest its assets with a view to achieving a maximum rate of return, without undue risk of loss, having regard to the factors that may affect the funding of the CPP and the ability of the CPP to meet its financial obligations.

The CPP Investment Board is a Crown corporation that acts at arm's length from the government, and the intent is that this independent board will both diversify and enhance the performance of the CPP assets. As a result, a proportion of the CPP funds are now permitted to be invested beyond government bonds and into other investment vehicles.

In June 1996, the Quebec Government released a working paper, "A Reform of the Quebec Plan", in which it made several proposals to ensure the financial security of the QPP. One of the issues reviewed was the potential contribution rate increases and their effect on the economy and public finances. On December 17, 1997, Bill 149, *An Act to reform the QPP and to amend various legislative provisions*, received Royal Assent and provided for several significant amendments to the QPP, most of which were to take effect January 1, 1998. As with the CPP, the total employee plus employer annual QPP contributions rose to 9.9% of employee contributory earnings by 2003. The QPP funds are invested by the Caisse de depot et placement du Quebec in a combination of government bonds and private-sector assets.

On June 6, 2002, new legislation was introduced to consolidate the investment management of all CPP assets into the CPP Investment Board, over a three-year phase-in period. As of March 31, 2002, the Board had investment assets of approximately $14 billion, while the assets being transferred had an approximate value of $40 billion. The Chief Actuary of Canada estimated at the time that these changes were expected to increase returns on CPP assets by approximately $75 billion over the following 50 years.

The CPP/QPP employ the concept of the "steady-state" contribution rate in measuring the long-term financial sustainability of the plans and in assessing whether contribution rates need to increase to ensure sustainability and inter-generational fairness. The steady-state contribution rate is the minimum contribution rate that is required to maintain a level ratio of assets to annual expenditures over the long term.

In addition, the CPP introduced the principle of fully funding any changes to the CPP that increase or add new benefits. Under this principle, any such changes must be fully funded over a defined period of time consistent with common actuarial practice. (Common actuarial practice suggests this period to be about 15 to 20 years.)

The results summarized in the report on the December 31, 2009 valuation of the CPP concluded that current legislated contribution rates were sufficient to maintain the financial health of the CPP.

The results summarized in the report on the December 31, 2009 valuation of the QPP resulted in the need for change in contribution levels. As of December 31, 2009, the QPP assets were $29.6 billion, about three times expenditures in the following year. With the 9.9% legislated contribution rate, expenditures will begin to exceed contribution income as early as 2013.

In 2011, Quebec acted on the findings of the December 31, 2009 valuation report and introduced phased-in contribution rate increases in its March 2011 Budget. In 2012, the contribution rate increased to 10.05%, and it is scheduled to increase each year by 0.15% until it reaches 10.8% in 2017. Thereafter, it will automatically be adjusted to keep it in line with the QPP's steady-state rate.

December 31, 2012 Actuarial Report on the CPP

The Twenty-Sixth Actuarial Report on the CPP, as of December 31, 2012, concluded that the current 9.9% legislated contribution rate is more than sufficient to pay for future expenditures over the period 2013 to 2022 and to accumulate assets projected to grow to $300 billion by 2020. A key measure of the financial stability of the CPP is the ratio of assets to the following year's expenditures. The valuation projected that this ratio will grow from 4.7 in 2013 to 5.4 by 2025 and 5.9 by 2075.

This legislated contribution rate of 9.9% was applied to the first three years after the valuation year (from 2013 to 2015).

The minimum contribution rate required to financially sustain the CPP is 9.84% of contributory earnings for the year 2016 and thereafter. This minimum contribution rate has decreased since the December 31, 2009 report, which disclosed a minimum rate of 9.86% for years 2013 to 2022 and 9.85% thereafter. Compared to the legislated contribution rate of 9.90%, the minimum contribution rate of 9.84% was projected to grow the ratio of assets to the following year's expenses from 4.7 in 2013 to 5.3 by 2025 and to remain at 5.3 50 years later in 2075.

The number of CPP contributors is expected to grow from 13.5 million in 2013 to 14.5 million by 2020. Under the legislated 9.9% contribution rate, annual contributions are expected to increase from $42 billion in 2013 to $56 billion in 2020.

The number of retirement beneficiaries is expected to increase from 4.6 million in 2013 to 10.2 million in 2050.

Plan experience of the CPP was more financially favourable than expected from 2010 to 2012 (especially regarding migration, benefits and investment returns). This experience was partially offset by higher projected life expectancies at age 65 and lower assumed real wage increases at Dec. 31, 2012. The overall net result was a small decrease in the minimum contribution rate.

With the 9.9% legislated contribution rate, the assets are projected to grow over the decade following the valuation date, with contribution revenue projected to exceed expenditures over that period. After that period, assets are still projected to grow however at a slower pace, with the ratio of assets to the following year's expenditures expected to grow to 6.0 by 2050. The report concluded that despite the expected increase in benefits to be paid to an aging population, the CPP is expected to be able to meet its obligations and remain financially sustainable over the long term.

The next valuation of the CPP which will be completed as at December 31, 2015 will reveal the impact that the June 2016 CPP expansion announcement will have on the financial status and future outlook of the Plan.

December 31, 2012 Actuarial Report on the QPP

The results summarized in the report on the December 31, 2012 valuation of the QPP concluded that the contribution rate of 10.8% as of 2017 would not be altered at least until the next valuation as at December 31, 2015.

The report projected that contributions would be greater than cash outflows until 2018, after which a portion of the investment income would need to cover the shortfall between contributions and cash outflows. The ratio of the reserve at the end of one year to the cash outflows for the following year was estimated as 3.4 in 2013, and projected to reach a maximum of 3.6 in 2020 and decrease thereafter.

The report recognized that the maximum contribution rate of 10.8% that will come into effect in 2017 may not be sufficient to ensure a long-term stable ratio between the reserve and cash outflows for the following year, and that this contribution rate may need to be changed as early as in 2018.

Chapter 3

EMPLOYER PENSION PLANS — TERMS AND CONDITIONS

Executive Summary[1]

This chapter outlines the principal terms and conditions that must be included in a pension plan document, together with the choices and considerations involved in designing a plan. The considerations will vary, depending on whether the pension plan is a defined benefit or a capital accumulation plan, whether the plan is single employer or multi-employer, and whether the employer is in the private sector or public sector. Certain plan provisions will be driven by the minimum standards in the provincial and federal pension standards legislation, which are discussed in more detail in Chapter 9. Other provisions are required by the registration rules of the *Income Tax Act* (ITA), described in Chapter 8. This chapter will briefly examine pension plan design and focus on the most common types of provisions that are included in a registered pension plan (RPP).

The principal provisions for pension plans relate to:

- Eligibility;
- Pension formula;
- Pensionable service;
- Employee contributions (for contributory plans);
- Retirement age;
- Normal and optional forms of pension;
- Death benefits before retirement;
- Termination benefits;
- Disability benefits; and
- Inflation protection.

---

[1] For more information on the terms and conditions that must be included in a pension plan, please consult the multi-jurisdictional charts in the *Canadian Employment Benefits & Pension Guide*. Morneau Shepell, *Canadian Employment Benefits & Pension Guide*, loose-leaf (Toronto: LexisNexis Canada, 2003). The table of contents for these charts appears at the back of this Handbook.

If established, a pension plan constitutes a legal promise and the pension plan text (also known as a pension plan document) quantifies what the promises are, when they will be paid, who will pay for them, and other obligations of the employer and employees. The plan text informs employees and their representatives, the government authorities that register the pension plan, and the employer and its representatives what those promises are at any given time in the future.

A plan text is a written and signed legal document that describes the terms and conditions that apply, including a detailed description of all relevant rules and regulations that relate to the rights and obligations of both the employees and employer under the plan.

Eligibility Requirements

The eligibility requirements of a pension plan determine the date on which an employee may (or must) become a member of the employer's plan. Once an employee becomes a member, pension credits begin to accumulate. In a pension plan that requires the members to make contributions, the date on which the employee becomes a member also determines the date from which the member's contributions commence.

Most pension standards legislation requires that employees be eligible for membership no later than on the completion of two years of employment, regardless of their age, if they belong to the class of employees for whom the plan was established. Some employers make membership in the pension plan compulsory or mandatory. Compulsory membership ensures that all employees receive some pension benefit in respect of their period of employment with the plan sponsor.

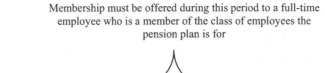

Membership must be offered during this period to a full-time
employee who is a member of the class of employees the
pension plan is for

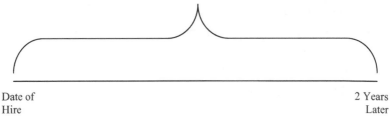

Date of   2 Years
Hire   Later

Eligibility conditions based on age were at one time common, but are now contrary to human rights legislation. Different eligibility conditions for females and males, while also once common, are now prohibited for the same reason.

In most jurisdictions, part-time employees who are in the same class as eligible full-time employees, and who have earned at least 35% of the Year's Maximum Pensionable Earnings (YMPE), as defined under the *Canada Pension Plan*, for two consecutive years must be allowed to join the pension plan. Alternatively, the employer may set up a separate plan for part-time employees if it provides reasonably equivalent benefits.[2]

Once an employer has decided to establish a pension plan, the eligibility rules are often set to balance administrative complexity with employee enrolment objectives. For example, eligibility may be set after the probationary period for a new employee to avoid the need to enroll and settle pension benefits for terminated employees with very short periods of employment, particularly in jurisdictions that require immediate vesting of benefits.

Pension Formula

The pension formula defines how pension benefits will accumulate during years of plan participation to deliver either the targeted retirement income in the case of a defined benefit plan or the accumulation of assets from which a retirement income can be derived in the case of a defined contribution plan. The employer will determine what level of income replacement to target when designing the defined benefit plan. In the case of a defined contribution plan it is the level of contributions to be made for the objective of accumulating assets for retirement that is the primary design decision. Often, but not always, the level of retirement benefit that can reasonably be expected to be achieved in a defined contribution plan under various economic scenarios is modeled and considered in the setting of contribution rules.

The decision on the amount of retirement benefit is perhaps the most difficult one. It is obviously related to cost considerations, benefit adequacy, and competitiveness of the program. The most common approach used by plan sponsors in determining adequacy of a pension is to consider the ratio of total retirement income to salary prior to retirement, called the replacement ratio. Various studies have set a target replacement ratio of 60% to 80% over a full career of participation, or more simply set 70% as a good starting point to preserve employees' standard of living at retirement. However, few employers would design a plan to provide a full replacement ratio, because government pension benefits provide a portion of the necessary income and employees are

---

[2]   Details of the pension standards legislation on eligibility can be found in Chapter 9.

generally expected to save for their own retirement outside of the employer sponsored programs

In addition to a basic salary, the definition of earnings used in the pension plan may include commission income, overtime, or bonuses. For defined benefit plans, to smooth out the volatility of salary prior to retirement, pension plans will commonly use an average of earnings prior to retirement, over a number of years in the determination of the retirement benefit.

The nature of the pension formula or promise varies with the objectives of the plan sponsor and can be one of several types or a combination of the types.

Defined Benefit Plans

As described in Chapter 1, a defined benefit plan specifies the formula to determine benefit entitlements. The specific formula will vary depending on the type of defined benefit plan.

Final Average Earnings Plans

In a final average earnings plan, a typical pension formula is 1.5% of average earnings for the last five or best five years prior to retirement, multiplied by years of service. For example, Jan Jones is an employee of "X" Co., where she has been employed for the last 35 years. Her plan has a pension formula, which is 1.5% of her average earnings for her last five years (being $70,000 in this case) prior to retirement. Jan's annual pension would be $36,750 (1.5% X 70,000 X 35).

If the plan is contributory (that is, if plan members are required to make contributions), the benefit credit is generally higher than for non contributory plans.

Often the benefit formula is integrated with Canada Pension Plan and Quebec Pension Plan (CPP/QPP) benefits to deliver a pension of about 70% of final average earnings at retirement for a long-service employee, inclusive of the government benefits. Historically the CPP/QPP benefit aimed to provide 25% of average earnings covered by the CPP/QPP; that is, earnings up to the YMPE. For a working career of 35 years, that was equivalent to a pension of about 0.7% of the YMPE for each year of employment. As such, many private pension plans are designed to provide a step of 0.7%, for example, by a formula under which the pension accrued per year of service is 1.3% of earnings up to the YMPE, and 2% of earnings in excess of the YMPE.

Goal of Step-Rate Pension Formula:

Pension provided by CPP	
Pension provided by employer on income up to YMPE	Pension provided by employer on income above YMPE

As noted in Chapter 2, in June 2016 the Candian Federal and Provincial Finance Ministers agreed to expand the CPP, aiming to provide 33% of average earnings covered by the CPP. CPP premiums are set to increase to 5.95% for both employee and employer and are being phased in over a 5 year period starting in 2019. In addition, the level of earnings covered by the CPP is set to increase by 14% from $54,900 in 2016 to approximately $62,600 as measured in today's dollars by the year 2025 (or $82,500 by 2025). This increase in the earnings covered under CPP is expected to be phased in over 2 years starting in 2024, and premium rates on this second tier will be set at 4% and be tax deductible.

The Quebec Government also began consultation on expansion of the QPP in the summer of 2016.

It remains to be seen if and how pension plan sponsors will vary their contribution structures to take into account the expanded CPP and higher YMPE. However, we expect that many sponsors of both DB and DC programs as well as other retirement arrangements will begin to consider whether any amendments to their pension plans are necessary to accommodate and take into account these changes.

The examples in this chapter are based on the CPP/QPP structure as of the time of publication.

Example of Step-Rate Integration with CPP/QPP

Jan Jones has pensionable earnings of $70,000 and she is entitled to the maximum CPP retirement pension payable in 2016, which equals $13,110. Jan has worked for 35 years and retires at age 65. Assume that under her employer's pension plan, the pension formula is 2%. With no integration the following result would occur:

Pension plan

$70,000 X 2% X 35 .... $ 49,000

Canada Pension Plan.. $ 13,110

Total.......... .... $ 62,110

As a result, Jan would actually receive approximately 89% of her pre-retirement income, which is more than the intended 70% of her final average earnings.

Now assume that Jan's employer's pension plan calls for a step-rate integration. The formula is 1.3% of earnings up to the YMPE and 2% of earnings in excess of the YMPE (the YMPE in 2016 is $54,900).

1.3% X $54,900 X 35 .... $24,979.50

2% X $15,100 X 35 .... $10,570

Canada Pension Plan $13,110

Total $48,659.50

As a result of the integrated model, Jan will receive approximately 70% of her pre-retirement earnings.

Typically, in a final average earnings plan with step-rate integration, the average YMPE would be used in the formula, where the YMPE is averaged over the same years that the earnings were averaged.

Another type of integration method is the direct offset method, in which a portion of the employee's CPP/QPP benefit is deducted directly from his or her pension benefit payable under the employer's pension formula.

While the amount of the Old Age Security (OAS) benefit may be taken into account in establishing the income replacement objectives of a private pension plan, it is generally prohibited in most provinces to make an explicit reduction for the OAS in the pension formula.

Career Average Earnings Plan

In a pure career average earnings pension plan, a typical formula is a pension equal to 1.5% (or an integrated formula that credits 2%) of the employee's earnings in each year. This approach is equivalent to averaging the employee's earnings over his or her career, and multiplying this average by the employee's years of service and the formula rate. Such plans are usually updated from time to time to reflect increases in wages and salaries. If the updates are made regularly, the pension benefit approximates that of a final average earnings plan. Career average earnings plans that are not updated are not common; their design is not tax-effective, because a 2% career average earnings plan produces the same reduction in Registered Retirement Savings Plan (RRSP) contribution room as a 2% final average earnings plan, but would produce a lower pension benefit.

Another variation in a career average earnings plan is to apply a final earnings minimum to the basic career average earnings plan. For example, the basic benefit may be 2% of career earnings, which will be supplemented, if necessary, up to a minimum level of 1.25% of the final five years' average earnings for each year of service.

Flat Benefit Plan

The pension formula in a flat benefit plan is normally expressed as a dollar amount for each year of service. Most flat benefit plans result from labour negotiations, in which case the benefit level is settled upon by the parties to the agreement. These plans are generally easier to explain to plan members, and relatively easy to administer, compared to final average or career average earnings plans.

Typical settlements in larger plans provide basic pensions of $30 to $70 per month for each year of service, paid for by the company. Different benefit levels may apply for employees in different wage classes and for past and future service.

Bridge Benefits

Defined benefit plans may include a supplemental pension in the form of a bridge benefit payable from retirement until the age at which government pensions can be received. The bridge benefit can take the form of a dollar amount per year of service, or it can be determined by reference to the CPP/QPP and/or OAS benefits. The purpose behind a bridge is to provide an approximately level retirement income to the individual without a sudden increase in income when government pensions commence.

Goal of Bridge Benefits:

Bridge paid from retirement to age 65	Pension provided by CPP

Lifetime pension provided by employer on early retirement

Shared Risk/Target Benefit Plans

A Target Benefit Plan or Shared Risk plan is similar to a Defined Benefit Plan, in that a formula is defined which calculates the level of pension payable to a member upon retirement, based on their earnings and years of service Contributions required to provide this benefit are fixed (or are variable within a pre-defined narrow range). If the contributions, and the investment returns on those contributions are not deemed to be sufficient to provide the target benefit to the plan members, benefits may be reduced to a more affordable level or contributions required may be adjusted.

Shared Risk / Target Benefit Plans are currently permitted in New Brunswick, Alberta and British Columbia, and there are strict restrictions on the types of employers who can offer this type of plan.

Capital Accumulation Plans

Under a capital accumulation plan (CAP) [which includes defined contribution pension plans (often referred to as money purchase pension plans), group savings plans (RRSPs, DPSPs, TFSAs), or profit sharing pension plans], there is no pension formula that defines the pension benefit on retirement. Instead, the plan defines the level of contributions to be made by the employer and the employee.

A typical CAP in Canada would have employer and employee contributions of anywhere from 1% to 6% of earnings, for a total contribution of anywhere from 2% to 12% of earnings. There are many variations available for structuring the contributions. Matching programs permit employees to elect a level of contribution that they will make to the plan that the employer will "match" (e.g., up to 5% with a 100% match). Others could require a certain minimum contribution from either or both the employee and employee (e.g., minimum of 2% or 3% from each) with the remaining contributions available to be elected by the employee with possibly an employer match to be offered. Still others are designed to deliver a set level of employer contribution without requiring employees to contribute (e.g., employer contributions of 5%). In any case the employer may structure the formula differently for different defined classes of employees or structure the formula to deliver different benefit levels based on years of service or "points" which are generally based on age+years of service. Similar to how defined benefit plans are often designed to provide a benefit that is integrated with the delivery of CPP/QPP benefits in retirement, many CAP sponsors also consider the integration of CPP/QPP required contributions into their CAP contribution formulas and in light of the recent changes that have been announced to the CPP program, more CAP sponsors may begin to consider whether integrated formulas would be desirable.

How a plan formula is ultimately structured is highly dependent on the guiding principles, objectives and constraints of the employer including whether or not they are designing the plan to deliver a certain level of retirement benefit adequacy within a reasonable probability, the desired level of competitiveness for their programs, how they view employer/employee sharing of responsibility for retirement savings, and cost constraints, to name a few. Contributions to CAPs are allocated to individual member accounts. In the past it was typical for CAPs to invest all contributions in a common fund, and the income from the investments would be allocated to the individual member accounts in proportion to their amount invested. Advances in technology and administrative software now permit CAPs to offer a variety of investment choices to plan members, enabling them to transfer their assets from one investment to another on a daily basis, or to divide their assets amongst a number of investment funds.

The pension, when the employee retires, is whatever can be purchased or provided by the contributions and the investment income (net of expenses) that was earned on the contributions. Thus, the employee does not know the exact benefit that will be received until retirement.

In some jurisdictions, defined contribution pension plans are permitted, but not required, to allow a retired member's funds to remain in the plan with the retired member withdrawing amounts as if the defined contribution plan were a Life Income Fund (LIF). This form of self-annuitizing of a CAP allows the member to take advantage of the lower administration and investment costs negotiated by the employer.

Uniformity in the Plan

An employer may cover one or all classes of employees in a plan. In the latter case, one may find different pension formulas for different classes of employees (i.e., a 2% benefit for executives and 1.5% for other employees). Legislation does permit different benefit levels or qualifying conditions that depend on the employee's position in the company or salary level. However, there must be no discrimination by age, sex, or marital status, and all employees in the same class must receive the same benefit.

Past Service Benefits

When a new pension plan is implemented by an employer who has been in business for many years, there are usually some long-service employees who are fairly close to retirement. These employees will receive inadequate pensions unless they receive pension credit for their employment before the effective date of the pension plan. Very few employees are able to make any significant contribution themselves towards these past service pensions.

Ideally, the past service pension formula would be the same as for future service. This way, the employee would be in the same position as he or she would if the pension plan had been in effect during the entire period of prior service. In practice, in order to reduce the employer's cost and in recognition of the fact that the employee made no contributions in respect of past service, the past service pension formula is often lower than the formula for future service.

For example, if the formula for future service is 2% of final average earnings, the employee might receive a pension equal to 1% for each year of past service that is credited.

Today, there are also tax implications for the employee when new benefits are provided for past service, because the employee must have enough RRSP contribution room to receive the benefits.

This is explained in Chapter 8 under "Past Service Pension Adjustments".

Note that past service benefits cannot be established on a defined contribution basis, only on a defined benefit basis.

Pensionable Service

The plan must define the period of service for which the employee will earn pension benefits, typically defined as "credited" or "pensionable service". Certain periods of absence are required by law to be included as pensionable service (i.e., maternity or parental leave).

The *Income Tax Act Regulations* limit the periods of service that can be recognized for pension purposes under a defined benefit plan.[3]

Employee Contributions

Pension plans may be either contributory (that is, the employees are required to contribute and the employer pays the balance of the cost) or non-contributory (that is, the employer pays the full cost). Traditionally, most union-negotiated pension plans have been non-contributory. Although it is estimated   approximately half of private-sector pension plans require members to make contributions to their plan, nearly all plans in the public sector are contributory.

---

[3]   The related rules are explained in Chapter 8.

Advantage to Employer of a:	
Contributory Plan	**Non-Contributory Plan**
> Costs employer less or employer may provide higher benefit for same cost. > Employees are more interested in plan because they pay for part of it.	> Simpler and less costly to administer. > All eligible employees covered by plan. > Employer may have more autonomy in investment and benefit provision decision making (because there are no employee assets).

Required Employee Contributions

Contributory pension plans are more common in Canada than in the United States because pension plan contributions are tax deductible in Canada, unlike the United States.

The level of contribution is governed by factors such as the level of benefits provided and the employer's willingness and/or ability to pay. Employee contributions in defined benefit pension plans tend to fall in the range of 5% to 8% of earnings. The large public-sector pension plans, including those for federal and provincial public servants and teachers, mostly require a basic employee contribution in the range of 7% to 9% of earnings.

Where the defined benefit pension plan benefits are integrated with CPP/QPP benefits, employees' contributions are nearly always reduced to integrate them with the contributions required for the CPP/QPP. This preserves the equity between the benefits received and the contributions paid. Integration has typically taken the form of step-rate contributions (i.e., 3.5% on earnings up to the CPP/QPP YMPE limit and 5% on earnings above the YMPE limit). Alternatively, there may be a direct reduction to contributions to the company plan by the amount of the CPP/QPP contributions. Many such plans, however, have changed their contribution formula because this approach results in erosion of employee contributions to the pension plan as the CPP/QPP YMPE level increases.

50% Rule

In contributory defined benefit plan designs, the cost sharing objectives may have been determined based on the entire membership group. While this goal may have been met in aggregate, it was not always the case for each individual plan member.

To remedy this effect, pension standards legislation introduced in the late 1980s and early 1990s requires that the employer fund at least 50% of the value of the benefits that are paid to each individual plan member with respect to their membership after the date the legislation came into effect. This is commonly known as the 50% rule. The 50% rule does not apply to CAPs.

In cases where the 50% rule applies, the plan member's contributions with interest are compared to the value of the pension benefits being provided, and the excess, if any, above 50% of the value of the pension benefits is either refunded to the plan member or used to provide additional benefits.

Additional Voluntary Contributions (AVCs) by Employees

Many contributory pension plans historically allowed employees to make extra "voluntary" contributions to increase the amounts of the pensions they would otherwise receive from the plans. However, employees may prefer to use their personal RRSPs to make additional tax-deductible contributions, because they are more flexible than the pension plan in allowing for in-service withdrawals and use towards permitted withdrawals under the Home Buyer's Plan and Lifelong Learning Program. As a result, voluntary contribution clauses in some defined benefit pension plans have been eliminated as not enough members make voluntary contributions to justify the additional administrative cost to the plan sponsor. For a defined contribution pension plan, the additional administrative cost of allowing voluntary contributions is minimal and such clauses may be more popular in a defined contribution vehicle, as they encourage the accumulation of assets for retirement in a single program for ease of employee retirement planning.

Optional contributions are created in some defined benefit plans to enhance the level of benefit. Flexible pension plans, which are emerging in response to tax limits on pension benefits, allow plan members to make tax-deductible contributions towards ancillary benefits (i.e., indexing) without triggering a pension adjustment that reduces RRSP contribution room.[4]

---

[4]   More details on flexible pension plans are found in Chapter 1.

Retirement Age

A pension plan needs to specify the normal retirement age, the earliest retirement age, and the conditions that apply when a pension commences early or is postponed.

Normal Retirement

Normal retirement age is the age specified in the pension plan text at which the employee has the right to retire on a full, unreduced pension. Nevertheless, accrued pensions payable on an unreduced basis are sometimes available before normal retirement age.

Normal retirement age is usually age 65, which is the commencement age for unreduced benefits from the CPP/QPP. Pension standards legislation in several jurisdictions prohibits a pension plan from having a normal retirement date later than the attainment of age 65 or 66.

Early Retirement

Many employees retire before age 65, and some plans provide unreduced pensions for early retirement at ages younger than 65. The ITA permits pensions to be paid on an unreduced basis as long as one of the following conditions is met:

- The member is aged 60 or above;
- The member's number of years of age plus service totals 80 "points"; or
- After 30 years' service, regardless of age (30 and out).

If the employee is employed in a public safety occupation (i.e., paramedic, commercial airline pilot, air traffic controller, corrections officer, police officer, or firefighter), the age 60 requirement above is reduced to age 55, the 80-point requirement is reduced to 75 points, and the 30-year requirement is reduced to 25 years. In the early 1980s, when many companies were forced to reduce their staff, early retirement was encouraged by a variety of special early retirement incentives both within and outside the pension plan.

The trend to earlier retirement ages is anomalous, in view of the great advances in health and life expectancy that have been experienced over the past decades. Further, the population is aging as a result of the 1950-1965 baby boom, followed by a period of low birth rates. This means that the ratio of those aged 60 and over to those between the ages of 20 and 60 is rapidly increasing and suggests that retirement ages should not be reduced. Retirement well before age 65 is popular with many employees, particularly those with defined benefit pensions that offer access to unreduced early pensions, some of whom then find other paid work, and receive both pension income and earned income.

However, a recent trend amongst employees, particularly those who are members of CAPs, is to work beyond age 65. This trend has arisen as a result of lower contribution levels, accumulation of insufficient assets, and reductions in the level of pension that can be purchased from CAPs, resulting in employees working longer in order to afford the retirement they had planned.

A pension plan will ordinarily allow the employee to retire at his or her own wish, up to 10 years before the normal retirement age. Pension standards legislation in most jurisdictions gives an employee the right to retire at any time within 10 years of normal retirement age. The early retirement pension may be the actuarial equivalent (that is, of equal value on an actuarial basis) of the pension the employee has earned up to the date of early retirement, payable at normal retirement age.

Actuarial equivalents can result in quite severe reductions to the accrued pension. For example, depending on the actuarial assumptions used, the reduction on an actuarial basis may be about 30% for someone who chose to start their pension at age 60 rather than age 65. A plan member who is considering early retirement must choose between taking a reduced pension immediately, or deferring commencement until normal retirement, at which point the full pension is payable.

Consider the following example for a member of a 2% final average earnings plan that compares the reduced pension at age 60 to the pension the individual would have received if he or she had remained employed to age 65.

	Retirement Age	
	60	65
Final average monthly salary	$3,000	$3,800
Years of service	20	25
Monthly pension before reduction	$1,200	$1,900
Monthly pension after reduction	$ 840	$1,900

A member who works the additional five years to normal retirement has a significantly greater pension than the early retiree for a number of reasons: five years of additional service, the higher final average salary, and the absence of any early retirement reduction factor.

A plan may reduce the pension by less than the full actuarial adjustment. Frequently the early retirement reduction factors are formula-based, such as a reduction of 3% or 6% for each year of early retirement. In the example above, with a 3% reduction, the pension at 60 would be $1,020 (85% of $1,200) per month, instead of $840. The rationale for the lesser formula reduction is that the full actuarial discount is simply too severe. Use of a lesser reduction factor means that the pension plan is in fact subsidizing a portion of the cost to retire early. Some employers are prepared to accept this increase in the cost of the plan as it encourages the orderly retirement of employees.

As noted earlier in this chapter, a plan may provide bridge benefits on early retirement. Depending on early retirement frequency, subsidies to early retirement reductions and bridge benefits can significantly increase plan costs.

For employees retiring from defined contribution pension plans, the process is simpler. As early as age 55 but no later than the year in which turning age 71, the employee can choose to use the accumulated assets in their defined contribution account to purchase either an immediate or a deferred annuity (no later than age 71) from an insurance company or can transfer their locked in account balances to either a "locked in retirement account" or LIRA (also known as a locked-in RRSP) which will hold the assets until the individual is ready (or required) to begin their withdrawals, or to a "Life Income Fund" (LIF) or "Locked In Retirement Income Fund" ("LRIF"), depending on the province of jurisdiction from which withdrawals may begin immediately, subject to legislated minimum and maximum percentages and spousal consent.

Phased Retirement

Phased retirement generally refers to the gradual reduction of work by older employees transitioning into full retirement. Some older Canadian employees continue to work as a result of inadequate income following retirement. In addition, many employees consider the abrupt movement from full employment to full retirement to be stressful, often with too much time on their hands too soon. A properly designed phased-retirement program can assist older employees with the transition to full retirement, both financially and psychologically. Current trends in Canadian demographics and predictions of impending labour shortages also provide incentives for employers to begin considering the implementation of a phased-retirement program.

A phased-retirement program includes any program that provides employees with assistance or incentive in the transition from employment to retirement. It will almost always involve a gradual reduction of work time during a specified period immediately prior to some formal retirement date.

Because the concept is intended to gradually reduce the employee's work time, the employer must carefully structure a formal agreement to minimize the potential for any misunderstanding that might lead to litigation. Moreover, the phased-retirement program should not be imposed by the employer, but provided as an option to the employee.

Effective in 2008, the ITA permits the accrual of defined benefit pension credits while receiving a lifetime pension from the same registered pension plan during a period of phased retirement. However, the ITA and supporting regulations impose conditions and restrictions on the benefit accrual limits, contribution limits, and the permissiveness and timing of distributions for a phased retirement program. Most jurisdictions have formally implemented provisions to regulate phased retirement.[5]

Postponed Retirement

Some pension plans allow the pension payments to commence at normal retirement age even though the employee continues to work and draw salary or wages. However, the employee cannot continue to accrue further pension credits in this event. This practice has been criticized as conflicting with the basic purpose of a pension plan, which is to provide an income when earnings cease. The practice has been defended on the ground that pensions are essentially deferred pay, and that the payment of an employee's pension should not be suspended as the result of postponed retirement.

Another design for postponed retirement allows pension credits to continue to accumulate after the normal retirement date (with the employee continuing to pay the required contributions, if any), so that when postponed retirement occurs, a larger pension may commence. Alternatively, the pension, on postponed retirement, may be the actuarial equivalent of the pension that would have been paid at normal retirement age. In any event, the ITA requires that the pension commences no later than the end of the year in which the member attains age 71.

In Quebec, plans must actuarially adjust benefits to reflect the post-postponement period. Members are allowed to receive payment of all or part of their normal pension during the postponement period. This amount

---

[5]   See Chapter 3 and 9 for further information on phased retirement.

cannot exceed the sum necessary to offset any permanent reduction in remuneration during the postponement period. However, a member may receive all or part of his or her pension, regardless of the limit, under an agreement with his or her employer, if the pension plan document permits. The amount of pension not paid out during the postponement period must be adjusted at the end of the postponement period. An adjustment is made to ensure that the pension payable at the end of the postponement period is actuarially equivalent to the pension at the member's normal retirement date had that pension not been postponed.

Normal and Optional Forms of Pension

Normal Form of Pension

Every pension plan must define the normal form of pension that will determine what benefits, if any, an employee's beneficiary or estate will receive when the employee dies after retirement. In some plans, the normal form of pension will be different for members who do not have a spouse and those who do. (See discussion below on pre-retirement death benefits regarding the definition of spouse.)

Pensions are always payable for the lifetime of the retired employee. The plan may provide a minimum guarantee that if death occurs within a certain number of years, the pension will continue for the balance of the period. If the period is five years, this type of pension is known as a "life annuity guaranteed five years". In a contributory plan, there may be a guarantee that if death occurs before the pensioner has received payments equal to his or her contributions, with interest, up to the retirement date, the balance will be paid in a lump sum to the estate or beneficiary. This is known as a "refunding life annuity" or "modified cash refund annuity".

Another approach provides that the pension continue after the member's death to the surviving spouse for the surviving spouse's lifetime. This form of pension is a joint and survivor annuity. The spouse's pension is usually 50% or 60% of the amount paid to the retired member and is more common today as a result of pension standards legislation. More specifically, if the normal form of pension is not joint and survivor, the pension standards legislation in all jurisdictions requires that the pension elected must be a joint and survivor annuity continuing to a spouse, unless a waiver is signed by the spouse. The annuity payable to the spouse must not be less than 60% of the pension payable before the member's death. Typically, the joint and survivor pension is payable in a reduced amount to reflect the more expensive nature of this form of pension. As a result of legislation requiring joint and survivor pensions, some plans have changed their normal form for members with a spouse to a joint and survivor pension, so that these members do not have to bear full cost. This is discussed in more detail in the following section.

The ITA allows the normal form of the pension to be as generous as a joint and survivor annuity, which provides a survivor pension not in excess of $66^2/_3$% of the member's pension, combined with a guaranteed period of five years. If a survivor annuity is not provided, the maximum guarantee period is 15 years.

Optional Forms of Pension

Pension plans customarily allow the employee to elect a pension different from the normal form before pension payments commence. Therefore, an employee can choose the form that best suits his or her needs at retirement, subject, of course, to the rules in pension standards legislation and the ITA. The amount of pension paid under the optional form is usually the actuarial equivalent of the normal pension, so that the election does not result in either a gain or loss for the pension fund.

The following forms of pension are normally offered by a pension plan:

- Pension with a guarantee period;
- Joint and survivor;
- Integrated/level income; and
- Small pension commutation.

These options are further described below.

Pension with a Guarantee Period

Some pension plans allow the retiring member to elect a pension payable for his or her lifetime, and for a minimum guarantee period if the pensioner dies within this period. Common guarantee periods are 5, 10, or 15 years. The ITA restricts the maximum guarantee period to 15 years. A pension with no guarantee period is known as a "life only annuity".

Joint and Survivor Option

After the member's death, a percentage of the member's pension will continue to the member's joint annuitant for that person's lifetime. Common percentages are 50%, 60%, 66¾%, 75%, or 100%. The pension may reduce only on the death of the member or, in some provinces, on the first death of the member and spouse.

Integrated/Level Income Option

This option (sometimes called the "level income" or "notched" option) allows an employee who retires prior to age 65, at which time OAS and CPP/QPP benefits are normally payable, to take a higher pension from the employer's plan up to age 65 and a lower pension thereafter, so as to produce a roughly level total income from both sources. The calculation may reflect the fact that CPP/QPP payments are available prior to age 65 on a reduced basis. However, once the integrated pension has been calculated, the payments cannot be changed to allow for a change in the commencement date or the actual amount of CPP/QPP payments.

Some of the optional forms of pension discussed above can be combined. For example, a joint and survivor annuity can be paid with a guarantee of at least five years.

Small Pension Commutation

The commutation of a small pension is an option provided by plans but is not actually a pension. Each jurisdiction has a provision allowing the value of a small pension to be paid in cash. In general, a "small" pension is one in which the annual pension due is less than 4-10% of the YMPE, or, depending upon the jurisdiction and the member's age, if the commuted value is less than 10-40% of YMPE. Each jurisdiction must be reviewed as the conditions for commutation vary from province to province. Pension standards legislation in some jurisdictions permits 25% of the value of an employee's pension benefit, earned before the legislation was revised, to be taken in cash if employment terminates before retirement, even if the termination occurs very shortly before normal retirement age.

In some jurisdictions, pension plans may also permit the transfer on retirement of the commuted value of an employee's pension to another locked-in arrangement (see "Termination Benefits" below). However, the employee is still required to ultimately receive those benefits in some form of lifetime annuity or stream of income payments.

Death Benefits Before Retirement

Every pension plan must define what benefits, if any, an employee's spouse, beneficiary, or estate will receive if the employee dies before retirement. These benefits are referred to as pre-retirement death benefits.

The definition of spouse, the rules on pension credit split upon a marriage breakdown, and the treatment upon remarriage vary considerably by jurisdiction.[6] The registered pension plan should include a definition of "spouse", and that definition is subject to minimum provincial standards. All of the provinces have amended their pension benefits standards legislation to include same-sex spouses, under either the definition of "spouse" or "common-law partner".

The pension standards legislation in all jurisdictions requires pension plans to provide pre-retirement death benefits. Prior to legislated minimum standards in this area, death benefits were minimal. In a non-contributory pension plan, there was often no benefit payable on death before retirement. If the pension plan was contributory, the death benefit payable to the deceased employee's beneficiary or estate was generally a return of employee contributions with interest. Group life insurance plans were thought to meet the needs of most employees.

Some pension plans did provide, prior to pension reform, death benefits from the pension plan in the form of spouses' and children's pensions. A plan of this type might have provided a deceased employee's spouse with one-half of the pension that had been earned for service up to the date of death, perhaps with a minimum amount. However, these spouses' pensions were somewhat restrictive. For example, the pension typically ceased if the spouse remarried, or the spouse's pension was paid only if the employee had been married for at least one year prior to death. The definition of spouse was usually limited to widows, and did not include widowers.

Changing social attitudes and the frequency of common-law relationships prompted reform of pension plans in the area of pre-retirement death benefits. Pension standards legislation, as amended in the 1980s and 1990s (giving rise to the pre-reform period and the post-reform period), now requires the payment of specific benefits to the surviving spouse if a plan member dies before retirement. The definition of spouse has continued to evolve (as discussed above).

Provincial legislation usually requires a minimum pre-reform benefit equal to a return of the member's own pre-reform contributions, if any, with interest. Beyond this, there is usually no specific requirement to provide a pre-reform, pre-retirement death benefit.

Depending on the jurisdiction, the minimum post-reform, pre-retirement death benefit that is payable to a spouse is the commuted value of the post-reform benefit that would have been payable to the plan member if he or she had terminated service at the date of death. The

---

[6]   Details on these legislative requirements are found in Chapter 9.

spouse does have the right to waive entitlement to this death benefit in some jurisdictions.

A beneficiary who is not the member's spouse may not be entitled to the same benefits as the spouse. Some jurisdictions provide a commuted value to the plan member's spouse, but a beneficiary who is not the member's spouse is only entitled to contributions with interest. In other jurisdictions, a beneficiary who is not the spouse is only entitled to contributions with interest if the contributions have not vested.

Plan sponsors may consider exceeding minimum legislated requirements for pre-retirement death benefits by applying post-reform rules on all service. The distinction between pre-reform and post-reform provisions is then removed, making the communication and administration of the plan easier.

Termination Benefits

Every pension plan must define the benefits and rights of the employee upon termination of employment other than by death or retirement. The employee is always entitled to his or her own contributions. An employee who is vested is entitled to his or her accumulated pension commencing at normal retirement age, or to an actuarially reduced pension at an earlier age. If a pension is locked-in, both the employee and employer contributions must be used to provide a pension at retirement, and cannot be withdrawn in cash (unless specific conditions are met which permit the pension to be withdrawn as cash, for example the small benefit provisions discussed earlier).

Vesting, Locking-In, and Portability

"Vesting" means the right of an employee who terminates employment to the portion of the pension benefit provided by employer contributions, as a result of achieving a certain age and/or length of service or plan membership. It is taken for granted that terminating employees have a right to their own contributions with credited interest.

"Locked-in" means that the employee cannot withdraw any contributions or portion of the benefit in cash. The benefit can only be received in the form of retirement income.

"Portability" means that the commuted value of a terminating employee's pension may be transferred on a locked-in basis to another RPP, or to a prescribed retirement arrangement.

Pension standards legislation has established minimum standards of vesting, locking-in, and portability. These standards vary across jurisdictions.[7] Where existing pension standards legislation was amended in the 1980s and 1990s, different standards may apply for pre-amendment date service. Locking-in of contributions typically occurs at the same time as vesting.

National employers, therefore, have had to decide whether to adopt the minimum vesting rules of each jurisdiction for employees in those jurisdictions, or a common vesting rule that meets the requirements of all jurisdictions. All employers have also had to decide whether the new vesting standard should be made retroactive to all service, or whether different treatment should be given to pensions accrued before and after the effective dates of the pension standards legislation.[8]

Pension standards legislation currently gives a terminating employee the right to transfer the commuted value of the vested pension to another retirement savings arrangement prescribed in the legislation. The institution receiving the transferred amount must agree to administer it on a locked-in basis as prescribed by legislation.

Interest on Employee Contributions

Employees who leave an employer before satisfying the vesting requirement are entitled to a refund of their own contributions accumulated at a prescribed minimum rate of interest, usually the investment return earned on the pension fund or the average of five-year personal term deposit rates. The rate to be credited on additional voluntary contributions is normally the same as for required contributions or the actual rate of return earned on the pension fund. Most pension standards legislation prescribes both the minimum rate of interest and the manner in which interest shall be credited.[9]

Reciprocal Transfer Agreements

The vesting requirements may be satisfied if a group of related employers (such as a group of Crown corporations) allows the transfer of an appropriate sum of money from the pension fund of one employer directly to the pension fund of another, on behalf of an employee who leaves the first employer and who finds employment with the second. This procedure

---

[7]   These standards are detailed in Chapter 9.
[8]   This issue of uniformity is discussed in Chapter 1.
[9]   See Chapter 9 for details.

is actually portability in a literal sense; the paying and receiving pension plans need not be identical to accommodate these transfers.

Reciprocal transfer agreements between pension plans in the public sector are common. Because public-sector plans are generally similar in design, the amount to be transferred is often determined by a simple but arbitrary formula, such as twice the employee's contributions with interest. The employee is then credited with a number of years of service in the second employer's plan.

Today, more plans are using an actuarial-based formula. The commuted value of the employee's pension, as calculated by the actuary of the first plan, is transferred. The actuary of the second plan then calculates the amount of pension or the period of credited service that may reasonably be granted to the employee in respect of the transferred funds. The details of the calculation method are contained in the reciprocal transfer agreement or in the plans.

Under general portability, arrangements may be made to transfer pension reserves or refunds of contributions to any other pension fund willing to receive them without a specific reciprocal transfer agreement. The transferred funds would normally be deemed to be additional voluntary contributions made by the employee, rather than funds that credit the employee with past service.

Multi-Employer Pension Plans

In multi-employer pension plans, an employee may work for several employers in the industry for short periods of time and will continue to be a member of the industry-wide plan. Pension credits earned with various employers will accumulate as if the employee had worked for only one employer. These plans contain vesting and locking-in rules similar to those in single employer plans, except that the rules are usually based on participation in the plan or employment in the industry, rather than service with one employer.[10]

Disability Benefits

A pension plan should specify what provisions are to apply to an employee who becomes disabled, and should contain a clear definition of disability for purposes of the plan.

---

[10]   Multi-employer pension plans are discussed in more detail in Chapter 11. Financing issues specific to multi-employer plans are found in Chapter 25.

A majority of employees are covered by their employers under some form of short- or long-term disability plan. These plans provide for regular payments to the employee to replace a portion of the employee's wages or salary while the employee remains disabled.[11] If such a plan is in place and delivers adequate benefits, there will be no need for the pension plan to provide disability pensions. However, as the payments from nearly all long-term disability plans stop at age 65, it is necessary to provide an appropriate pension after age 65. Hence, a pension plan member who is receiving disability income usually continues to accrue pension credits so that the pension at age 65 will be based on service as an active employee plus deemed service while disabled. Under the ITA Regulations, an employee must satisfy prescribed definitions of disability to continue to accrue benefits under the pension plan. In contributory pension plans, it is usual to waive any required employee contributions during the period of disability.

If the employees are not covered or are not eligible for insured long-term disability benefits, the pension plan can be designed to provide an immediate unreduced pension. The pension is usually equal to the full pension accrued to the disability date with no adjustment for early commencement. Sometimes the pension is equal to the full estimated pension the employee would have earned had he or she remained at work until normal retirement. The ITA imposes limits on the qualifying conditions and the additional projected pension benefits that can be provided.[12]

Inflation Protection

Before Retirement

In the 1970s and 1980s, when the rate of inflation was high, considerable attention was given to ways of maintaining the purchasing power of pensions. Final average earnings plans generally provide inflation protection up to the point of retirement, although there may be some shortfall, since the last five-year-average salary can fall well below the salary at retirement date in periods of high inflation.

By contrast, career average earnings and flat benefit pension plans do not compensate for inflation that occurs prior to the employee's retirement age, unless they are updated from time to time.

---

[11]   See Chapter 21.
[12]   These are described in Chapter 8.

With much earlier vesting and locking-in, a large number of vested deferred pensions will be created and these will lose their purchasing power unless they are updated during the period up to commencement date. A possible solution is the transfer of the commuted value to a locked-in RRSP/locked-in retirement account, where favourable investment earnings could compensate for inflation, as in a defined contribution pension plan.

In the province of Quebec, the legislation was modified, effective January 1, 2001, to provide for an additional benefit representing partial inflation protection between the date the employee ceases active membership in the plan until the date that is 10 years prior to the normal retirement date. Just 5 years later on January 1, 2016 this requirement was removed.[13]

CAPs automatically make some adjustment for inflation prior to retirement, provided that the investment return of the pension fund rises with the rate of inflation.

After Retirement

Protecting against inflation prior to retirement is only part of the issue. Post-retirement adjustments are also necessary if the purchasing power of pensions is to be maintained. Historically, the industry tended to believe that the income needs of pensioners decline as they get older, and thus their purchasing power does not have to be fully protected against increases in the cost of living. This view is understandably unpopular with some employees and pensioners and some studies have found that pensioners' spending needs do not decline significantly over time. Post-retirement inflation protection can take several forms.

Indexation

The obvious way to protect the pensioner from loss in time of inflation is to index pensions according to a wage or price index. Pensions that increase 1% for every 1% increase in the Consumer Prices Index (CPI) maintain their purchasing power to the extent that the CPI is a good measure of the prices of goods and services that pensioners buy. Pensions that are increased in line with increases in the average industrial wage typicall provide better inflation protection — they also give pensioners a share in the growing productivity, by keeping their pensions in line with pay rates of active workers.

---

[13]   Additional detail on this requirement is provided in Chapter 9.

A pension that is adequate at retirement and thereafter is adjusted for cost-of-living increases is ideal for the retired employee. However, private-sector employers usually regard it as too costly and risky to promise fully indexed pensions. Generally, automatic indexing after retirement is prevalent only among public-sector pension plans. Where automatic indexing is provided, a plan will often contain provisions that limit the increase, either by limiting increases to a percentage of inflation, or by providing increases equal to inflation but capped at a certain percentage.

Mandatory Inflation Protection

To date, no pension standards legislation requires that pensions and deferred pensions be adjusted to provide inflation-related increases. Although the Ontario pension standards legislation provides for mandated increases in accordance with a prescribed method, as of 2016 the province has not prescribed an indexation formula and, therefore, inflation protection is not required.

Ad Hoc Adjustments

Ad hoc adjustments have been used by nearly all large employers in the private sector in recent years to compensate for post-retirement cost of living increases. Union groups often bargain for ad hoc pension adjustments on behalf of their retired members.

The amount of the *ad hoc* increase varies from plan to plan. It may be a percentage increase in all pensions that have been paid for a number of years or a percentage for each year since the last increase (or retirement if sooner). Other approaches include a flat addition of, for example, $50 a month, the introduction of a minimum pension, or a combination of these approaches.

Ad hoc adjustments are made on a one-time only basis, with no promise of any future increases. A company may adopt a policy of regular review and upgrading, but without a firm commitment to future increases.

Ad hoc adjustments are popular with employers because the related costs are completely under the employer's control. Employers are reluctant to provide automatic indexation due to uncertain costs, but are often willing to make substantial ad hoc adjustments, as long as they are not committed to repeat the practice on a regular basis.

A second advantage of *ad hoc* increases is that all the circumstances — inflation, the company's financial position, and changes in social security — may be taken into account. A company that has a good year or that has a surplus in the pension fund may tend to give larger increases and to give them more frequently. A company in a poor financial situation will tend to defer and to minimize the increase. Members who retired under a recently improved plan may be treated differently than those who retired before the improvements came into effect.

Limitations Under the ITA

The ITA permits defined benefit pensions to be adjusted for inflation both before and after retirement, subject to certain limits.[14]

---

[14]   These rules are described in Chapter 8.

Chapter 4

GOVERNANCE OF RETIREMENT, SAVINGS, AND OTHER BENEFIT PLANS

Executive Summary[1]

The term "governance" is now a standard part of the pension lexicon, but its meaning in the present-day context is not always clear, and it is often overlooked as it relates to benefits other than pensions. In the broadest sense, every action that is taken by an organization (or a committee or agent acting on behalf of an organization) related to the operation of its pension or benefits plans falls under the rubric of "governance". When regulators or consultants talk about pension governance though, they are usually referring to something more specific, that is, the formal framework that defines how the tasks and duties involved in the operation, management, and oversight of a pension plan will be carried out in order to meet the fiduciary and other obligations of the plan.

Effective governance establishes a documented framework that defines roles and responsibilities for:

- *Administration and communication* — including establishing programs, addressing regulatory compliance, and establishing the processes, systems, and technologies required to administer contributions and benefits;

- *Financial management* — including determining whether to secure benefit obligations, how and in what amounts to accumulate funds and how to measure and recognize pension costs in the plan sponsor's financial statements; and

- Investment management of fund assets.

---

[1] For more information on plan administration and governance, please consult the multi-jurisdictional charts in the *Canadian Employment Benefits & Pension Guide*. Morneau Shepell, *Canadian Employment Benefits & Pension Guide*, loose-leaf (Toronto: LexisNexis Canada, 2003). The table of contents for these charts appears at the back of this Handbook.

The nature of the plan sponsor's governance role depends on plan type — whether it is registered or non-registered and whether it is defined benefit (DB) or defined contribution (DC).

This chapter will commence with a brief overview of the roles and responsibilities of those involved with the establishment and administration of a registered pension plan, including the concepts of fiduciary duty and prudence. We will then provide an historical perspective on the development of pension governance in Canada, describe two sets of guidelines released in 2004 that marked a turning point in the attention paid to governance in this country, and outline a number of significant developments in governance since the issuance of these guidelines

This chapter also recommends that a similar framework that follows the pension governance model be considered for other employer-sponsored benefit plans as well. As support for this proposition, some governance issues that have arisen with regards to employer benefits programs are described.

The process of documenting a more rigorous approach to governance can be a daunting task, and it does call for a significant commitment. Therefore, this chapter also provides some suggestions as to how an organization might commence working on governance issues with respect to their retirement arrangements. If a long-term approach centering on continuous improvement is adopted it can be appreciably less painful, and more effective, as there will continue to be developments in pension governance in Canada and around the world.

Overview

A pension plan is established by the plan sponsor. "Plan sponsor" is not defined in the legislation, but is usually:

- an employer or group of employers in a related industry;
- a union or professional association;
- a government; or
- more than one of the above.

Typically, an employer offers a pension plan to its employees, or a group of its employees. Membership in a pension plan is so closely associated with the employment relationship that "employee" and "member" are frequently used interchangeably, as are "employer" and "sponsor".

Once established, the focus shifts to the operation of the plan. The operation of the plan requires meeting certain responsibilities, such as:

- defining the roles and responsibilities of all parties involved in the operation of the plan;
- ensuring that the persons delegated with those responsibilities have the education and skills required to perform their duties;
- selecting service providers;
- completing the regulatory requirements;
- maintaining complete plan documentation;
- communicating with employees; and
- funding the benefits, monitoring the plan fund performance, and managing the fund assets.[2]

Together, these responsibilities constitute pension plan governance and are necessary for sound management of the plan.

Roles and Responsibilities

The following lists a number of entities who are commonly involved in the administration of a pension plan:

- plan administrator;
- pension committee;
- board of directors, if the employer is a private-sector corporation;
- plan fund trustees;
- actuaries and auditors;
- regulators;
- external service providers; and
- bargaining agent.

Plan Administrator

Pension standards legislation defines who can be the administrator, and generally includes:

- the employer;

---

[2]   Chapter 6 addresses financial management of plans and Chapter 7 covers pension fund investment management.

- a pension committee comprising one or more representatives of the employer, or any person required to make contributions under the plan, and possibly, members of the plan;
- a pension committee comprising representatives of members of the plan (in some cases, may include former or retired members);
- the insurance company guaranteeing the benefits provided under the plan;
- in the case of a multi-employer plan, a board of trustees; or
- a board, agency, or commission appointed or established by an Act of the Legislature.

Outside of Quebec and Manitoba, the plan administrator is usually, but not always, the corporation acting through its board of directors or board of pension trustees. In this chapter, the term "plan administrator" will generally be used to cover all situations, rather than plan sponsor, employer, union, trustees, or committee. Furthermore, the plan sponsor is sometimes referred to as the plan (upper case) "Administrator." This is different from the (lower case) "plan administrator" role that is taken on by some service providers.

The plan administrator is subject to the "prudent person rule" in a number of jurisdictions. The Ontario *Pension Benefits Act* states that "[t]he administrator of a pension plan shall exercise the care, diligence and skill in the administration and investment of the pension fund that a person of ordinary prudence would exercise in dealing with the property of another person". The prudent person rule is difficult to define precisely, and therefore could be difficult to enforce with certainty, but demands that the administrator act fairly and honestly, without conflict of interest, and with consideration for the best interests of the plan members, beneficiaries, and the plan. Given these expectations, plan administrators of registered pension plans are considered to stand in a fidicuary capacity in relation to plan members and other benficiaires. While only the new pension legislation in Alberta and British Columbia expressly identify plan administrators as fiduciaries, this is how the relationship is viewed in all jurisdictions across Canada, regardless of whether the pension plan is a DB, DC or hybrid arrangement. The concepts of fiduciary responsibility and prudence are discussed in detail later in this chapter.

Pension legislation implicitly recognizes that there are many tasks involved in the administration and management of a plan and fund and that it would be impossible for the plan administrator to carry out all tasks or acitivites on its own. While pension legislation permits the plan administrator to delegate many activities related to plan administration and the investment of the fund to employees and external service providers, ultimate fiduciary responsibility remains with the plan administrator and cannot be delegated away. This means that, regardless of who performs duties related to collecting and investing contributions, safeguarding assets accumulated in the plan, making benefit payments, paying plan expenses, maintaining accounts and records, and communicating with employees, ultimately, the plan administrator retains its fiduciary responsibility to the plan members and other beneficiaries. Those who are delegated duties may also owe a fiduciary duty depending on the activity they are performing, especially if they are viewed as an agent of the plan administrator. Accordingly, this necessitates the supervision and ongoing monitoring of all delegated tasks, in one form or another.

When a single employer sponsors a pension plan, it must be careful to recognize that there will be times when decision-making by its board of directors will be done in its role as the plan sponsor, and other times decisions will be made in its role as the plan administrator; as a plan sponsor, the employer does not owe a fiduciary duty to plan members and other beneficiaires and may act in the best interest of the company. The inherent conflict that exists in this context has been characterized in common law Canadian jurisdictions as the "two hats" doctrine or theory. This doctrine, as indicated in the section *Pension Governance Milestones in Canada* has evolved over time and further buttressed the need for good pension plan governance.

Pension Committees

Québec legislation requires that a pension committee be appointed to administer the plan. The committee must have at least three members, of whom two must be members of the plan appointed in accordance with the terms of the plan, and one must be independent of both the employer and the plan members. This pension committee is responsible for all aspects of the plan administration.

In Manitoba, as of May 31, 2011, most single-employer plans registered in Manitoba, except those with fewer than 50 members, must establish a pension committee to act as plan administrator.

Under the federal, British Columbia, Newfoundland and Labrador, and Saskatchewan pension standards legislation, if the majority of members in the plan (with a minimum number of 50 members in the plan) request a pension advisory committee, the employer must establish one.

In Nova Scotia and Ontario, if the administrator is a pension committee and that committee includes at least one member appointed by plan members, there is no right to form an advisory committee. If the administrator is not a pension committee, the members and former members may establish an advisory committee by majority vote. Ontario has recently revised its legislation to strengthen the rules around the establishment of an advisory committee and to make it easier for the plan members to require a committee to be established. The legislation in each jurisdiction must be reviewed to determine not only if there is a right to form an advisory committee and what requirements are necessary to establish one, but also to determine the powers of such a committee.

The purposes of pension advisory committees are outlined in the applicable pension standards legislation, and could include such duties as:

- promoting awareness and understanding of the pension plan;
- making recommendations for improvements in the pension plan;
- reviewing/monitoring the administrative aspects of the pension plan; and
- attending to any other matters as requested by the employer.

Board of Directors

Within private-sector corporations, the board of directors generally has final responsibility and accountability for matters pertaining to the plan. Often a subcommittee of the board is formed to have direct dealings on pension matters — this pension committee would normally be composed not only of board members, but would also include senior management representatives from human resources and finance. At times, there may even be two such subcommittees involved — one responsible for overseeing the investment area, while the second one deals with pension policy and benefit matters. The structure will depend on the size of the company and of the pension fund. A number of external parties may be involved in the administration of a pension plan.

Trustee of the Plan Fund

The trustee is responsible for holding and ensuring the safekeeping of the assets of the plan for the benefit of plan members. The trustee must be someone other than the employer.

Actuaries and Auditors

In the case of a DB plan, there must be an actuary who prepares the actuarial valuations and advises the administrator on the financial position of the plan. Auditors are also involved as generally, audited statements of the fund holdings must be prepared.

Regulators

The regulators are also important players in the administration of a pension plan. They are responsible for interpreting pension legislation and ensuring that the interests of plan members are safeguarded.

External Service Providers

In lieu of hiring one or more investment managers as employees of the plan sponsor, the administrator may appoint one or more investment management firms to be responsible for the selection of the investments of the plan. There are strict rules under pension legislation regarding the types of investments that can be held by a pension plan fund. In addition, investment managers must follow the statement of investment policies and procedures (also sometimes referred to as the "statement of investment policies and goals") adopted under the plan. Like the administrator, the investment manager is subject to the prudent person rule.[3]

Other external service providers that may be retained by the plan administrator include an independent communication expert, fund custodian, plan recordkeeper, and lawyer or law firm. It is always important to understand whether the external service provider is retained in the capacity of an agent or advisor of the administrator. While agents of a plan administrator are generally held to a fiduciary standard in performing the specific duties for which they have been retained, advisors are not.

Bargaining Agent

A bargaining agent can be a member of a pension committee or board of trustees, which is the administrator of the pension plan. This often occurs, but not always, in unionized environments.

---

[3]   These issues are examined further in Chapter 7.

Fiduciary Responsibility and Prudence

Fiduciary Responsibility

As noted above, in all jurisdictions in Canada, a plan administrator is viewed as a fiduciary in the responsibilities it owes to the plan, its members, and other beneficiaries. The Guideline No.4: Pension Plan Governance Consultation Draft-Guideline, released by CAPSA in March 2016, defines fiduciary relationship to be "one of trust between two or more parties where one (or more) person(s) (the fiduciary[ies]) has an obligation to act in the best interests of the other party". The Draft-Guideline goes on to provide that fiduciary obligations are owed when legislation imposes such duties or when:

- a plan administrator and/or any delegates can exercise discretionary power to affect the interests of members or beneficiaries;
- a plan administrator and/or any delegates can unilaterally exercise that power so as to affect the interests of the members or beneficiaries; and
- the members and/or beneficiaries are in a position of vulnerability at the hands of the plan administrator and/or any delegate.

In the pension plan context, therefore, fiduciary responsibilities include:

- treating members and beneficiaries impartially;
- acting with the care, skill, and diligence of a prudent person;
- interpreting the plan terms fairly, impartially, and in good faith;
- managing conflicts of interest; and
- within the scope of such duties and its authority, ensuring that members and beneficiaries receive promised benefits.

Fiduciary responsibilities cannot be delegated by the fiduciary. Duties may be delegated, but the responsibility for proper and complete fulfillment of those duties remains with the original identified holder of the fiduciary duty.

Prudence

While fiduciary responsibility refers to the impartial consideration of outcomes, prudence refers to the decision-making process that leads to those outcomes. Prudence demands caution, attentiveness, and care. The intent is to make the right decisions for the specific situation and the specific group of people. Just because a decision is prudent for one situation and one group of people, does not mean that it is prudent for another situation or group of people.

When considering decisions made around pension plan administration, prudence dictates that if an administrator does not have the expertise to advise in certain situations, that administrator should obtain qualified professional advice. Due to the evolving nature of the requirements of plan administration throughout the lifetime of the plan, there is no single set of administrative standards that can be universally adopted by administrators of all types and sizes of pension plans.

Generally, any breach of the duties set out in the pension legislation is an offence under the legislation, is subject to prosecution by the regulatory authority, and, on a finding of guilt, may result in significant fines. To the extent that a plan administrator or its agents and advisers are under a fiduciary obligation in respect of the plan, civil remedies including an accounting and payment to the beneficiaries and/or the fund for breaches of that fiduciary duty may be awarded at common law.

Introduction to Governance

At the risk of oversimplifying, a governance structure is not so much about *doing* as about *planning what to do, how to do it and who should do it*. While the "doing" is the end goal, good governance is more likely to happen if the stakeholders document the "what", the "how", and the "who".

Looked at another way, governance can be split into two parts:

Level 1 — Determine who does what	This is essentially the "who". It includes a delineation of roles and the type and frequency of communication between the various parties involved in governance. When a board of directors commissions a governance study, for example, they often mean a review of who does what.
Level 2 — Ensure the pension or benefit plan operation runs smoothly	This is the "what" and the "how". This includes the quality of the administration being done, processes to ensure consistency from one period to the next, consistency between administration, legal documents and employee communication, setting investment and funding policy where applicable, risk management, etc.

While this is a little simplistic, it may be helpful. Later, this chapter will discuss how the Canadian pension regulatory authorities have defined good governance in terms of 11 principles.

The Emergence of Pension Governance in Canada

Canada has long maintained a three-pillar approach to funding the retirement of its citizens. One pillar consists of government-sponsored arrangements, primarily the Canada and Quebec Pension Plans (CPP/QPP) and Old Age Security (OAS). Personal savings through individual Registered Retirement Savings Plans (RRSPs) and other investments represents another pillar. The third pillar is a voluntary system of employer-sponsored pension and savings plans, including group RRSPs and Deferred Profit Sharing Plans (DPSPs). It is around this pillar that the attention to governance matters has revolved in recent years.

The governance hype is a relatively recent phenomenon. Some of the history of the development of this concept in Canada is set out below, focusing on the more significant milestones.

Pension Governance Milestones in Canada

Date	Development	Impact
June 1993 (Court of Appeal — October 1995)	*R. v. Blair (Enfield Case)*[4] — Pension Committee sued for failing to supervise investment manager.	Better understanding of the duties owed by the "administrator" under the PBA and the limitations on delegation of duty.
December 1994	Release of Dey report: "Where were the Directors?" — Commissioned by the Toronto Stock Exchange to address corporate governance issues.	Provided pension industry with some guidance in developing governance for pension plans.
August 1995	*Imperial Oil Limited Retirement Plan* (1988) *and the Pension Plan for Former Employees of McColl-Frontenac Inc.* — case before the Pension Commission of Ontario (PCO) on whether the employer was in breach of its fiduciary duties for amending its plan to (prospectively) eliminate an early retirement benefit.	The PCO provided the first articulation of the "two hats" doctrine which states that an employer plays two distinct roles *vis-à-vis* a pension plan and that the employer is not an "administrator", subject to fiduciary duties, for all purposes (*e.g.*, when it amends its plan or carries out its other employer duties).

---

4   *R. v. Blair*, (1995) CarswellOnt 1135.

Date	Development	Impact
May 1996	*Froese v. Montreal Trust Co. of Canada*[5] — Montreal Trust responsible for improper payments from the pension fund.	Expanded the concept of fiduciary duty to include the trust company, despite attempt to limit liability, based on an overarching obligation to protect beneficiaries' interests.
February 1997 to May 1998	PIAC — Effective Pension Plan Governance; ACPM — Governance of Pension Plans; OSFI — Guidelines for Governance of Federally Regulated Pension Plans.	Formal guidance on appropriate standards for governing pension plans in Canada begins to be generated by Canadian associations and regulators.
November 1997	Re *Unisys Savings Plan Litigation* (U.S. case)[6] — Investigating the liability of company regarding investment options available to members.	Held that liability for poor investment performance does not attach to sponsor where sponsor has exercised appropriate due diligence.
November 1998	Report of the Standing Senate Committee on Banking, Trade and Commerce "The Governance Practices of Institutional Investors".	Provided useful forum to examine questions respecting the accountability of institutional funds and the extent of their economic influence.
December 1999	Release of ACPM/PIAC/OSFI joint recommendation on Pension Plan Governance and Self-Assessment.	Pension industry finally has widely accepted, clear written guidelines to work with to develop governance practices.
April/May 2001, respectively	Release of draft Joint Forum Proposed Regulatory Principles for CAPs, and CAPSA Pension Governance Guideline and Implementation Tool.	Pension industry given opportunity to participate in development of governance principles for Canadian pension and specified capital accumulation plans.
Late 2001	Collapse of Enron, then WorldCom, then Global Crossing.	Leads to increased regulation of auditing and accounting in the U.S. under the *Sarbanes-Oxley Act*, with spillover

---

[5]   *Froese v. Montreal Trust Co. of Canada*, [1995] B.C.J. No. 423 (S.C.).
[6]   *Re Unisys Savings Plan Litigation*, 74 F.3d 420, 445 (3d Cir. 1996).

Date	Development	Impact
		effects in Canada
May 2004	Release of Guidelines for Capital Accumulation Plans.	Guidance on the proper management of a Capital Accumulation Plan.
October 2004	Release of CAPSA Pension Plan Governance Guidelines and Self Assessment Questionnaire.	Guidance on the proper governance of a pension plan.
March 2004 to March 2008	Régie des rentes du Québec (as Retraite Québec was previously known) released collection of publications called "Administering a pension plan well".	Offers guidelines aimed at helping pension committees that act as the plan "administrator" to perform their role in a competent and prudent manner
December 2006	Quebec Bill 30 legislatively requires plan administrators to adopt a written set of internal by-laws addressing governance related topics.	This was the first Canadian jurisdiction to legislate the requirement to adopt a broad written document related to governing a pension plan beyond the statement of investment policies and procedures or goals.
June 2008	CFA Institute Centre for Financial Market Integrity, "Code of Conduct for Members of a Pension Scheme Governing Body".	Recommended to public companies, government agencies, unions and pension administrators as best practice for members of pension governing bodies.
December 2009	R. v. Christophe,[7] charges brought by FSCO against the Board of Trustees and Investment Committee of CCWIPP for breach of standard of care and non-compliance with pension legislation.	In obiter, the court commented that proper record-keeping and a detailed governance system are essential to fiduciary oversight and personal liability for trustees or fiduciaries may arise if this duty is breached. In addition, in order to make prudent decisions, fiduciaries lacking specialized knowledge have a duty to seek expert advice or

---

[7]   R. v. Christophe Lewis, [2011] O.J. No. 5927, 2011 ONSC 7631 (Ont. S.C.J.).

Date	Development	Impact
		assistance to help them fulfill their role.
June/July 2009	Organization for Economic Co-operation and Development released the OECD Guidelines for Pension Fund Governance.	Not of significant impact in Canada. Although the Canadian Government is a member of the OECD, these Guidelines did not go as far as the guidance already released by various organizations within Canada.
June 2010	FSCO policy on the Management and Retention of Pension Plan Records by the Administrator.	Provides detailed guidance respecting the issues around record retention in relation to pension plans and provides a sample format for documenting retention practices.
March 2011	CAPSA Guideline on Fund Holder Arrangements.	Highlights good governance practices related to fund holder arrangements for pension plans and pension funds.
May 2011	Manitoba regulations require pension committees to establish rules of procedure and governance.	This is the second jurisdiction in Canada, and the first common law jurisdiction, to legislate written rules of pension governance.
April 2011	FSCO policy on Administrator's Management of Inquiries and Complaints from Plan Beneficiaries.	Clarifies the responsibilities of the plan administrator in responding to inquiries and complaints from various plan beneficiaries and other person(s) who have an entitlement under the plan. The policy also provides the administrator with specific guidance on how to effectively manage inquiries and complaints from plan beneficiaries.
November 2011	CAPSA Pension Plan Prudent Investment Practices Guideline.	Provides guidance to plan administrators on how to demonstrate the application of

Date	Development	Impact
		prudence to the investment of pension plan assets. Clearly identifies this as the role of the plan administrator.
November 2011	CAPSA Pension Plan Funding Policy Guideline.	Provides guidance on the development and adoption of funding policies. Clearly identifies this as the role of the plan sponsor.
May 2012	British Columbia Bill 38 receives Royal Assent.	Requires the plan administrator to establish a governance policy. Details to be released in the regulations.
December 2012	Alberta Bill 10 receives Royal Assent.	Requires the plan administrator to establish a governance policy. Details to be released in the regulations.
February 2013	*Sun Indalex Finance, LLC v. United Steelworkers.*[8]	The Supreme Court of Canada addressed and further refined the "two hats" doctrine by examining the obligation of the employer, in the context of a corporate insolvency, to be aware of its legal requirements as plan administrator when making corporate decisions and ensuring that it deals with any conflicts which may flow from its statutory obligations.
March 2014	CAPSA DC Pension Plans Guideline.	Supplements the CAP Guideline in relation to DC plans by, amongst other things, outlining and clarifying the rights and responsibilities of various stakeholders, providing guidance regarding tools and information to provide to

---

[8]   *Sun Indalex Finance, LLC v. United Steelworkers*, [2013] S.C.J. No. 6, [2013] 1 S.C.R. 271 (S.C.C.).

Date	Development	Impact
		members in both the accumulation and decummulation phases.
July 2014	Alberta approves regulations to Bill 10.	Provides the details of what is required to be included in a governance policy as well as other policies such as the SIPP, participation agreements and funding policies.
November 2014	Ontario approves new amendments to General Regulation 909.	Effective January 1, 2016, all SIPPs for Ontario pension plans must include information about whether environmental, social and governance (ESG) factors are incorporated into the SIPP and, if so, how the ESG factors are addressed in the plan's investment strategy.
May 2015	British Columbia approves regulations to Bill 38.	Provides the details of what is required to be included in a governance policy as well as other policies such as the SIPP, participation agreements and funding policies.
November 2015	Québec adopts *An Act to amend the Supplemental Pension Plans Act* (Bill 57).	Effective January 1, 2016, funding and annuity purchase policies are required; details to be prescribed in regulation. In addition, as of January 1, 2016, plan administrators are required to include, in internal by-laws, measures to be taken to quantify and manage plan risks.

Until the middle of the 1990s, only the largest of pension plans devoted much time to formal governance reviews. Other employers saw it as an abstract, nebulous concept. The lack of specific regulatory guidelines on pension governance at that time did not help matters. As a result, most organizations did not deal directly with governance issues, either because they felt their agents were handling them or that doing so would not materially affect overall results. To an extent, the one exception was Quebec-based plans where the requirement to have a pension committee put the focus on governance earlier than in other jurisdictions.

As explained later in this chapter, 2004 marked a watershed year in pension plan governance with the introduction of best-practice guidelines for both registered and non-registered arrangements. Since then, there has been a steady and constant initiative on the part of regulators, individually and collectively, as well as governments to clearly define what pension governance means, what it entails, and what is required. As a consequence, pension plans of all sizes have started devoting more time to formal plan governance.

Governance Developments in our Civil Law Jurisdiction

Retraite Québec has a number of documents and training programs for members of pension committees. For example, a new member of a pension committee can attend a training program held by Retraite Québec which will help members acquire better knowledge about pension plans and the responsibilities of a pension committee member.[9] In 2004, the Régie des rentes du Québec, as Retraite Québec was then known, commenced publication of a collection called "Administering a pension plan well"; this collection applies to pension plans in the private, municipal, and university sectors. The first instalment, issued in March 2004, was entitled "Sound administration: what you should know". The Preface of the collection noted that: "This collection offers guidelines aimed at helping pension committees to perform their role in a competent and prudent manner. You will find ways for improving the administration of pension plans in the private, municipal and university sectors, protecting the members of pension committees and increasing members' and beneficiaries' trust."

The remaining instalments were published as follows:

- Instalment 2: "The role and responsibility of a pension committee" (last updated June 2011)
- Instalment 3: "How a pension plan operates" (last updated March 2008)
- Instalment 4: "Key players in plan administration" (last updated March 2007)

---

9   Information on this training course can be located on Retraite Quebec's website at http://www.retraitequebec.gouv.qc.ca.

- Instalment 5: "Information for Members and Beneficiaries" (last updated March 2009)
- Instalment 6: "Pension Plan and Pension Plan Administration Documents" (last updated December 2012).

Instalments 2 and 3 were revised in part to reflect the new plan governance requirements imposed by Québec Bill 30, in December 2006. The requirements imposed by Bill 30 are described in further detail later on in this chapter. In addition to requiring pension committees to develop internal policies and controls (effective December 13, 2007), this Bill also imposed new responsibilities on administrative service providers (effective December 13, 2006) and permitted pension committee members to be indemnified in respect of any lawsuits resulting from their activities on the pension committee (effective June 14, 2006).

Legislative Guidance on Pension Governance

Although Canadian pension standards legislation mandates a specific standard of care for pension plan administrators, many Canadian jurisdictions offer little else, from a legislative perspective, to guide plan administrators in managing their governance responsibilities.

Québec was the first province to legislatively require that the plan administrator adopt a written set of internal bylaws addressing governance-related topics. This became a requirement in December 2007. For most pension plans registered in Quebec, the "internal bylaws" must address:

- duties of the committee members;
- ethical rules governing the committee members;
- rules mandating the designation of committee officers;
- procedure and frequency of meetings;
- professional development of committee members;
- risk management, including, as of January 1, 2016, measures to quantify and manage risks;
- internal controls;
- keeping of books and registers;
- service provider selection and supervision; and
- service standards on communicating with plan members.

Manitoba also included a governance-related requirement in the regulations to its pension standards legislation, effective May 31, 2011. In that province, the regulations require pension committees to establish rules of procedure and governance. The prescribed minimum requirements are not as fulsome as the requirements specified in Quebec, and must be reviewed at least once every three years.

In 2012, both British Columbia and Alberta passed Acts to replace their existing pension legislation. The new pension legislation specifically requires the administrators of all pension plans registered in these jurisdictions to establish governance policies and to ensure that plans are administered in accordance with these policies. In July 2014, Alberta approved regulations to the new pension legislation which prescribed the minimum requirements of the governance policy; British Columbia followed suit with almost identical regulations in May 2015. Generally speaking, the governance policies for plans registered in these provinces must do the following:

- set out the structures and processes for overseeing, managing and administering the plan;
- explain what those structures and processes are intended to achieve;
- identify all participants who have authority to make decisions in respect of those structures and processes, and describe the roles, responsibilities and accountability of those participants;
- set performance measures and establish a process for monitoring, against those performance measures, the performance of each of the participants identified;
- establish procedures to ensure that the administrator and, as necessary, any other participant in those structures and processes have access to relevant, timely and accurate information;
- establish a code of conduct for the administrator and a procedure to disclose and address conflicts of interest of the administrator;
- establish an ongoing process to identify the education requirements and skills necessary for the administrator to perform his or her duties in relation to the plan;
- identify the material risks that apply to the plan and establish internal controls to manage those risks; and
- establish a process for the resolution of disputes involving members or other persons who are entitled to benefits under the plan.

Coupled with the requirement to establish a governance policy for each plan is the requirement, on a triennial basis, for the plan administrator to assess the administration of the plan, and prepare a written report that includes the:

- plan's compliance with the respective legislation and its regulations;
- plan's governance;

- funding of the plan;
- investment of the pension fund;
- performance of the trustees', if any; and
- performance of the administrative staff and any agents of the administrator.

Industry Guidelines Supplement Legislation

Long before the pension standards legislation began expanding on governance requirements and largely due to the dramatic corporate failures involving Enron, WorldCom, and others, many boards started taking steps to tighten up their corporate governance practices in general and pension governance in particular. At the same time, the pension funding crisis commencing in 2001 exposed how the health of an organization's DB pension plans can affect the health of the corporation itself, not just the retirement security of the members. This realization spurred organizations to devote more attention to pension matters.

It is at least partly serendipitous that the Canadian pension regulators and industry associations were working in the background to develop better governance standards for pension and capital accumulation plans at the very time the need for them was starting to become apparent.

To assist plan administrators with understanding what their governance responsibilities might entail, CAPSA, an association made up of representatives of the various pension regulators across Canada, developed several guidelines related to the governance of pension and other retirement savings plans. Two of these guidelines are as follows:

- Working in a "Joint Forum" with the Canadian securities and insurance regulators, CAPSA released the *Guidelines for Capital Accumulation Plans* (the CAP Guidelines) in May 2004; and
- CAPSA released the *Pension Plan Governance Guidelines* and Self-Assessment Questionnaire (the CAPSA Governance Guidelines), in October 2004; in 2014, the CAPSA Pension Plan Governance Committee in conjunction with an Industry Working Group undertook a review of the guideline and a revised draft was released for public consultation in March 2016. At the time of writing this chapter, the revised CAPSA Governance Guideline had not yet been released in final form.

The similarity in name between "CAPSA" and "CAP" is purely coincidental and a source of some confusion. As the chart shows, each has a somewhat different sphere of influence.

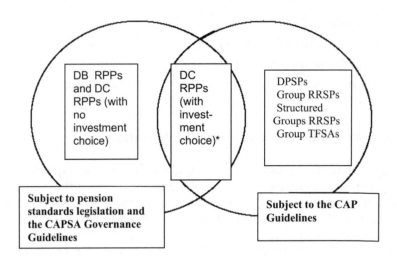

Also includes the DC component of hybrid or flex DB plans.

The CAP Guidelines are not just about governance, but they do contain a number of good governance principles. Plan administrators who want to achieve compliance with the CAP Guidelines might be best advised to do so in conjunction with working through the CAPSA Governance Guidelines to avoid duplication of effort.

CAPSA versus CAP Guidelines

	CAPSA	CAP
Formal Name	CAPSA Pension Plan Governance Guidelines and Self-Assessment Questionnaire	Guidelines for Capital Accumulation Plans
Developed By	Canadian Association of Pension Supervisory Authorities (pension regulators across Canada)	Joint Forum of Financial Market Regulators = CAPSA plus securities and insurance regulators across Canada
Final Form Release Date	October 25, 2004 (revised guideline released in draft form for public consultation in March 2016)	May 28, 2004

	CAPSA	**CAP**
Target Audience	Plan administrators of DB and DC registered pension plans	Plan administrators of DC plans, which offer member investment choice, sponsors of DPSPs, group RRSPs, structured group RRSPs, Tax-Free Savings Accounts, hybrid plans and flexible DB plans offering member investment choice
Compliance Date	None	December 31, 2005

CAPSA Pension Plan Governance Guidelines

The CAPSA Governance Guidelines consist of 11 principles.[10] The following are things the CAPSA Governance Guidelines recommend the plan administrator do or cause to be done:

1. Understand its **fiduciary and other responsibilities to plan members, beneficiaries and other stakeholders**.

2. **Establish governance objectives**.

3. **Document roles and responsibilities** for all participants in the governance process.

4. **Establish and monitor performance measures** for key decision makers.

5. **Apply the knowledge and skills** needed to meet governance responsibilities.

6. Have **access to relevant, timely, and accurate information**.

7. Establish an internal control framework to **manage the pension plan's risks**.

8. Establish mechanisms to **oversee and ensure compliance** with legislative requirements and administrative policies.

9. Provide for the communication of the governance process to plan members to **facilitate transparency and accountability**.

---

[10] Copies of the CAPSA Governance Guidelines are available on the CAPSA website at http://www.capsa-acor.org.

10. Establish a code of conduct and policy to **address conflicts of interest**.

11. Conduct **regular reviews** of its plan governance.

Included with the CAPSA Governance Guidelines is a Self-Assessment Questionnaire that allows plan administrators to track their progress toward achieving and maintaining compliance. The Questionnaire is intended to be reviewed annually by the "plan administrator" and does not have to be filed with the pension regulator. There are 21 questions on the Questionnaire, roughly two questions for each of the 11 principles. Its purpose is to help the plan administrator determine which principles it has instituted and what steps are still required to improve the governance of the plan.

By deliberate design, the CAPSA Governance Guidelines do not prescribe how a plan administrator is supposed to respond to each principle. Plan administrators are expected to develop processes that are appropriate to their plan and their company. In 2005, CAPSA released a number of frequently asked questions (FAQs) and responses related to the principles. The FAQs describe possible methods for dealing with various governance issues. As mentioned above, the CAPSA Governance Guidelines were reviewed in 2014 and a revised draft was issued for public consultation in March 2016. The proposed revisions to the guideline maintain the 11 principles. The Self-Assessment Questionnaire has been changed to add additional questions (there are now 27 questions rather than the initial 21), and the FAQ document has been significantly expanded and revised. The CAPSA Governance Guidelines (including the Self-Assessment Questionnaire and the FAQ document) have been principally revised to emphasize that governance and administrative practices need to be documented, and to make it easier for plan administrators to review their compliance with the governance principles. Some of the more notable revisions include the following:

- Expanded discussion of fiduciary duties;
- Guidance for creating a governance framework;
- Guidance for documenting roles and responsibilities, including a sample tool;
- Clarifying the duty to monitor plan administration;
- Guidance on how to develop an appropriate level of knowledge and skills for participants in administration (such as pension committee members);
- Examples of risks faced by pension plans;
- Guidance on methods and substance of communications with members; and

- Guidance with respect to conducting a governance review.

Initially, the CAPSA Governance Guidelines were reflective of best practices on governance. However, with many Canadian organizations adopting formal governance structures for their plans based on the CAPSA Governance Guidelines, and with several Canadian legislators building the requirement to adopt a formal governance structure into their pension standards legislation, the Guidelines are quickly gaining minimum standards status.

Specific Regulatory Guidelines

As noted above, OSFI and Retraite Québec both issued governance related guidelines before and around the same time as CAPSA, respectively. In recent years, other jurisdictions have also supplemented the guidelines released by CAPSA by issuing their own policies, interpretative guidelines and the like. While these policies do not have the force of law, and plan administrators cannot be compelled to follow them, they are a good indicator of what pension regulators expect from administrators of plans registered in their respective jurisdictions.

The regulator in Alberta, for example, has issued an interpretive guideline that addresses the statutory requirements for a plan administrator to establish a governance policy and specifically directs plan administrators to the CAPSA Guidelines.[11] FSCO has released policies on record retention and management, administrator roles and responsibilities, management of plan member inquiries and complaints, and fees and expenses payable from the pension fund. The regulator in Saskatchewan has published a specific guide to assist plan administrators and their service providers in the management of DC pension plans registered in that jurisdiction. Not only does the guide make it clear that the regulator expects plan administrators to establish a governance policy and procedure manual that covers a number of items, but it goes on to say that should an examination of a plan's administration practices be performed, the regulator will review the administrator's governance practices, policies and procedures.[12]

---

[11] The interpretive guideline can be found at http://www.finance.alberta.ca/publications/pensions/interpretive-guidelines/IG-12-Governance-Investment-Funding-Policies.pdf.

[12] The guide can be found at http://www.fcaa.gov.sk.ca.

Regulatory Risk Based Frameworks

Over the last few years, governance has become a key consideration for many pension regulators across the country, particularly as they concentrate more time and resources on dealing with plans that are considered at risk of failing. FICOM, FSCO and OSFI have all implemented risk based approaches to overseeing pension plans that generally consist of three related processes: risk monitoring, risk assessment, and risk response.

As indicated in the following chart, pension plan governance is, either directly or indirectly, a key consideration under these risk based regulatory frameworks:

	OSFI	**FSCO**	**FICOM**
When	Since early 2011	Since 2011	Since 2014
Relevance of Governance Risk	Not identified as a separate risk, but built into significant activities that are monitored, including administration and communication to members	Part of risk universe categorization Associated with lack of or poor governance practices	Identified as a fundamental risk Associated with poor oversight, poor internal controls and ineffective plan management
Factors to Consider	Documents policies and procedures for the operation of the plan Contract for all work done by third parties and performance monitoring Degree of controls and oversight mechanisms	Existence of code of conduct/policies and procedures Use of qualified outsourced providers and oversight by the plan administrator Existence of oversight/ monitoring/ supervision policies and evidence that polices are followed (through internal controls) Information, performance measures and risk management processes	Existence of oversight, monitoring and supervision policies and evidence (through internal controls) that policies are followed Use of qualified service providers and oversight by the plan administrators Management reporting, performance measures and risks management processes Degree of compliance with regulatory filing requirements Extent of member communication

Also Pertinent to Benefit and Other Plans

Note that the CAPSA Governance Guidelines are intended for the governance of DB and DC registered pension plans. While not directly applicable, the Guidelines can also be usefully applied to the governance of a company's DPSP or group RRSP and also to an organization's employee benefits programs. The principles are flexible and provide ideas on best practice related to governance generally.

Possible Governance Issues in Benefit Plans

There are organizations that are taking advantage of the good guidance provided by the CAPSA principles to improve the structure of and processes relating to their benefits programs. Considering the increasing importance group benefits play and the increasing cost to organizations of providing these benefits both before and after retirement, employers are looking at governance principles to assist with the risk management of these programs. Largely due to the lack of comparable minimum standards legislation and accounting practices as they relate to active employees, many employee benefit plans are not maintained with the same level of scrutiny as compared to pension plans. However, outdated benefit policies and employee communication material coupled with a lack of strict administrative processes and accurate financial management have left many employers exposed to potential financial risk. For example, consider the employer who allows the benefit plan administrator to exercise judgment in policy setting within the benefit plan. In the event an exception is made in a health plan which allows one employee coverage for a particular medical expense, that employer may have subjected themselves to a precedent requiring that all employees receive the same coverage, or may face a complaint of discrimination, each having significant cost implications for an employer. For many other reasons, including privacy and access to information, employers should identify who in their organization has access to information, how decisions are made and should ensure these individuals understand this potential fiduciary responsibility.

We have seen certain practices being adopted in relation to the *Sarbanes-Oxley Act* in the U.S. starting to make their way into Canada, and impacting primarily on the benefit plans of Canadian subsidiaries of American companies. The practices being adopted in these organizations are sure to flow through to a broader subsection of the industry as governance continues to be a hot button on boards of directors' agendas.

Even in the absence of specific case law or legislative authority, it may be reasonable to conclude that employers have a fiduciary-like duty towards their employees in relation to health and non-retirement benefit arrangements: once such programs are established an employer may need to consider what is in the best interest of members and other beneficiaries when making certain decisions, independent of financial considerations. Furthermore, a recent Ontario Court of Appeal decision suggests that the "two-hat" doctrine may apply in the health and non-benefit plan context to assess the role of an employer *vis-à-vis* its employees, particularly where there is an allegation of conflict of interest and breach of fiduciary duty.[13]

In light of the foregoing, governance is as important and necessary for health and benefit plans as it is for retirement arrangements. More specifically, governance in this area should, at the very least, focus on processes and procedures for the proper administration of such arrangements, consistent and clear documentation, proper financial management, clear and effective communication, and timely and accurate legislative compliance.

Understanding the roles of those external to the organization should also be considered. For example, the insurance carrier is assumed to bear the responsibility for accuracy of claims payments; however, without sufficient review and audit of information an employer may be accused of leaving too much responsibility in the hands of a third party.

Some plans contain sensitive information as it relates to an employee's personal health status or cause of disability and need to be treated with care. Clear policies that address the rights and entitlements of those not actively at work should also be considered. Having a well-documented and openly communicated policy on benefits for retired or terminated employees could avoid class action lawsuits or liabilities associated with severance packages that may not be available through standard insurance provisions.

Furthermore, as with pensions, employees need accurate and clear information in order to make informed decisions with respect to their benefit coverage. Employers leave themselves exposed to possible complaints from employees who may have made decisions impacting their retirement, for example, on erroneous assumptions about their plan provisions. Governance principles should also address compliance with key legislative requirements (*e.g.*, human rights, employment standards, privacy, and income tax) as well as oversee the ongoing financial

---

[13]   *Garcia v. Labourers' International Union of North America, Local 1059*, [2015] O.J. No. 1694, 2015 ONCA 230 (Ont. C.A.).

management of the plans, particularly if employee contributions are allocated to the plan. Consider the impact of a surplus or deficit emerging within a self-insured plan and the need to ensure transparency in rate-setting if rates are differentiated between classes of employees within any organization.

If each CAPSA principle is carefully reviewed for its applicability to the benefit plans, this can go a long way in addressing the above concerns and improving the company's overall risk management.

Capital Accumulation Plan Guidelines

DB and DC pension plans share similar governance issues but with at least one significant difference: in DC plans, it is clearly the members who bear the investment risk and who are usually given investment options. This factor can increase the potential liability faced by a DC plan administrator and also create additional responsibilities.

The Joint Forum of Financial Market Regulators (Joint Forum), with significant industry input, developed the CAP Guidelines over a three-year period.

The objectives of the CAP Guidelines were to:

- Outline and clarify the responsibilities of CAP sponsors, service providers, and CAP members;
- Ensure that CAP members have the information and assistance they need to make investment decisions in a CAP; and
- Ensure that there is a similar regulatory result for all CAP products and services, regardless of the regulatory regime that applies to them.

The Guidelines apply to all tax-assisted plans that have member-directed investments. This includes most DC pension plans, DPSPs, group RRSPs, EPSPs, TFSAs, structured group RRSPs, hybrid plans, and flexible DB plans. They do not apply to CAPs where the member has no investment choice. As mentioned earlier, these Guidelines are in addition to, not a replacement for, the CAPSA Governance Guidelines.

In a CAP, the plan administrator determines which investment options will be offered to plan members, the rules for inter-fund transfers and the default option if a member does not make an investment election. The member, however, bears the investment risk. This places the onus on the plan administrator to choose the right array of fund options and to provide the members with the information necessary to make good choices.

The CAP Guidelines provide recommendations respecting the selection of investment options and the oversight of these options, but they also address many other topics, such as: fee disclosure, member communications generally, record retention, and service provider selection and monitoring.

What the CAP Guidelines Cover
> Introduction and Setting up a CAP
> Investment Information and Decision-Making Tools for CAP Members
> Introducing the Plan to CAP Members
> Ongoing Communication to Members
> Maintaining a CAP
> Termination (of the CAP and/or a Member's Participation in the CAP)

Focus on Communications

Given that plan members have to make choices and assume investment (and survival or longevity) risk, member communication is even more important than it is in a DB plan. The plan administrator is responsible for providing investment information to help members better understand their investment choices. The emerging question is, "How far should the plan administrator go?"

At present, most plan administrators provide investment information to members, either directly or through their record-keepers or investment managers. Some of this will be general information on investment basics and some will be specific data on the characteristics and past performance of each of the investment options. They may also make certain tools available, such as self-assessment questionnaires that members may use to determine their risk tolerance and make their investment choices. The dissemination of all of this information has one thing in common: in the vast majority of cases, it is provided to members and the members can decide whether or not to use it. The problem is that a good proportion (in many cases, more than half) of the membership will not make use of the information and will not be qualified to make investment decisions.

A second level of action by the plan administrator would involve *monitoring* what members do. For example, if a plan administrator gets monthly reports and notices that a member is invested solely in a money market fund for a prolonged period, it may be prudent to ensure the member understands what a money market fund is (up to a third of them may not know) and how it's typically used. While this type of monitoring can be beneficial to the members, it means the plan administrator has to "raise the bar" to monitor member behavior.

One level higher yet is to engage in *testing* the understanding of CAP participants. Morneau Shepell (MS) surveys of CAP participants suggest that a large percentage of participants do not understand investment basics and are not fully qualified to choose from an extended list of investment options. Most plan administrators agree with this assessment. Testing would address this, at least in theory. Employees would need to pass an investment test before being given unfettered access to all of the investment options. Those who do not pass the test could either be given a restricted set of options, such as life cycle funds, or be required to sign a waiver agreeing to accept full responsibility before being permitted access to the full range of funds. While the concept has its merits, and its supporters, the fact is that few, if any, Canadian plan administrators currently do testing, nor was it contemplated in the CAP Guidelines.

At the highest level, plan administrators could actually arrange for an outside expert (which may be the CAP record-keeper or a firm with financial planners) to give participants investment *advice* rather than just guidance. Until recently, advice-giving was regarded as too risky but that view seems to be changing. It is gaining popularity in the U.S. and more Canadian plan administrators are now starting to believe that giving advice reduces their potential CAP liability rather than increases it. Time will tell if this trend takes hold.

Whether it is advice, monitoring, or self-assessment questionnaires, it is important to remember that employees may have personal savings outside the employer-sponsored CAP. An individual's investment policy should take all personal assets into account, not just those in the CAP. For instance, a member might have reason to invest 100% of his or her CAP assets in a fixed income fund if he or she holds only equities outside of the CAP. It is not the plan administrator's job to monitor a member's entire investment portfolio, but it is prudent to ensure that people who appear to be candidates for additional help are offered it.

While not a part of the CAP Guidelines, information given to members should take into account their different educational backgrounds and investment literacy. One idea is to offer descriptions of all concepts on three levels: "basic", "intermediate", and "advanced". A one-size-fits-all method of information dissemination can leave some members with significant gaps in understanding. Nevertheless, the CAP Guidelines do allow for one-size-fits-all education, provided it is aimed at the "median".

Suggested Documentation

Any organization that sponsors a CAP should review and incorporate the CAP Guidelines when designing a governance structure. Some of the documents that a company may wish to consider creating in response to the CAP Guidelines are set out below:

- Notice of member responsibilities;
- Document/record retention policy;
- Certificate of compliance for service providers;
- Policy on selection and supervision of service providers;
- Policy on selection and retention of investment options; and
- Policy on responding to member/employee questions.

While communications, such as participant statements and plan booklets, have been required by pension legislation for many years, the formal concept of notifying members of their responsibilities is new. The CAP Guidelines specifically recognize that members have responsibilities when they participate in a DC retirement plan. This is a significant first as far as the pension regulators are concerned. How can members be held responsible, however, if they have not been formally advised of the responsibilities they owe? Therefore, it is recommended that the plan administrator notify the members of their responsibilities.

Support can also be found in the CAP Guidelines for developing specific policies and generating or requiring the other documents noted above. Depending on an organization's particular circumstances, of course, some of this documentation may already be in place. As noted above, FSCO, in 2010 and 2011, released policies that encourage the adoption by plan sponsors of a record retention policy and a policy on the management of inquiries and complaints from plan members.[14] These policies are recommended by FSCO not only for CAPs but for all Ontario registered pension plans. Plan administrators in other jurisdictions may also want to consider the material in these policies, as two of the principles under the CAPSA Governance Guidelines, risk management

---

[14] These policies can be found online at: http://www.fsco.gov.on.ca/en/pensions/policies/active/Documents/A300-200.pdf and http://www.fsco.gov.on.ca/en/pensions/policies/active/Documents/A300-450.pdf respectively.

(Principle 7) and transparency (Principle 10), support the adoption of policies in these two areas.

As best practices develop and governance of CAPs improves across the board, there will undoubtedly be additional actions a company can take, and more detailed policies it can put in place, to respond to the spirit of the CAP Guidelines.

Review of the CAP Guidelines

At the time the CAP Guidelines were released, the Joint Forum committed to review the guidelines after a period of time to assess to what extent the Guidelines have been successful in achieving their original objectives and to determine whether any changes to the Guidelines are required.

In January 2008, two voluntary and anonymous surveys were distributed to the pension industry, one in relation to CAP sponsors and another one canvassing service providers, to gauge their experiences with the CAP Guidelines since they were introduced in 2004. Based on the responses to the surveys at that time, the Joint Forum decided that no changes to the CAP Guidelines were required. Another review of the CAP Guidelines was undertaken in 2012, but no changes resulted from that review.

In January, 2010, the Joint Forum did issue an FAQ to address two questions: whether a TFSA was to be considered a CAP, and whether all provisions of the CAP Guidelines were applicable to CAP arrangements that offer members access to the full universe of investment options, including investment funds, as well as the assistance of an advisor.[15] As noted above, TFSAs are considered CAPs. With respect to the second question, the Joint Forum advised that while the CAP Guidelines would still apply to such plans, some provisions would not be applicable, and therefore, would not need to be followed.

Why Comply?

It is important to note that compliance with both the CAPSA and CAP Guidelines is voluntary. Subject to the earlier discussion of the legislative requirements to adopt governance bylaws or policies, there is no legislative requirement, yet, to comply with these two sets of Guidelines.

---

[15]   The Q&A can be found at http://jointforum.ca/en/init/cap_accumulation/CAP%20QA%20Final%20English.pdf.

The rationale to take action, therefore, depends not on any legally binding obligation, but on a calculated effort to manage the risks related to administering a pension plan and a real desire to improve plan performance, increase efficiencies, and help participants (in the case of CAPs). Plan administrators now have a much clearer picture of what they can and should do with respect to the governance of their programs. Should a plan administrator ever be subject to litigation, it is important to remember that the reasonableness of the administrator's actions will depend in good part on the documented policies and processes that are in place and compliance with those policies and processes, which in turn should largely reflect the CAPSA and CAP Guidelines.

Getting Started

If this has not already been done, plan administrators should analyze the gaps between what they are currently doing and what is recommended by the CAPSA Governance Guidelines (and CAP Guidelines, too, if applicable). The most difficult hurdle to getting started may be determining who initiates activity. This may be easiest in Quebec or Manitoba where the pension committee is the plan administrator.

The board may be responsible, but board members may not realize the extent of that responsibility, be aware of the existence of the CAPSA Governance Guidelines (the CAP Guidelines seem to have received broader recognition), or know what they need to do to get started. In our experience, a corporation's senior management may be positioned to get the ball rolling.

Organizational Charts

A reasonable starting point is for the plan administrator to take inventory of the current governance structure, which might involve preparing an organizational chart documenting who is responsible for each aspect of the operation of a plan. When done for the first time, this can be an eye-opener since there will be tasks for which no one is formally responsible (or aware they are responsible) and others where two individuals might claim responsibility. Once the chart is complete, responsibilities can be realigned as appropriate. Then, job descriptions can be developed setting out the pension-related responsibilities for each person.

What does an organizational chart look like? In the example below, the work is delegated down from the board of directors/trustees, and the delegates do the front-line work. As already noted the board of directors/trustees is ultimately the entity responsible for the governance of the plan and must perform an oversight function. As we describe the roles and responsibilities below, recall that in the provinces of Quebec and Manitoba, as we have mentioned earlier, a pension committee acts as the "Board".

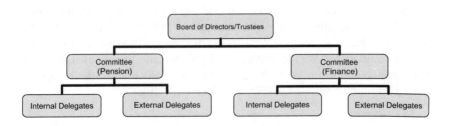

Possible Pension Committee Duties	Possible Finance Committee Duties
Plan design recommendations	Selecting and monitoring of investment managers
Administration of the plan	Selecting and monitoring of plan investments
Maintenance of plan documents	Approving valuations (selecting assumptions)
Regulatory compliance	Accounting disclosure
Member communication	Funding/contributions

Other models are possible, such as one in which a single committee oversees both pension and finance responsibilities. What is appropriate for a given organization depends on the size of an organization as well as the skill sets and interest levels of the various parties.

To evaluate the information it receives from the various delegates, monitor performance and make informed decisions, the members of the board must have a shared knowledge about their role. A governance program could therefore set forth:

- The minimum knowledge a member must have;
- The period of time in which the member must acquire or upgrade that knowledge;
- The different programs or sources of training available and considered appropriate; and
- A training budget and rules related to that.

Strategic Versus Tactical, the Role of the Board

The role of the board in governing a pension plan should be viewed as a strategic one. Many governance specialists recommend that the board (in Quebec and Manitoba, the pension committee) spend its limited and valuable time developing policy, rather than drilling down to implementation issues. This is not always what occurs.

Whether the plan is DB or DC, the board can get distracted by operational matters, especially investment specifics. It is tempting for boards to focus on short-term investment strategies or even the stock picks of the fund's investment managers. Even though investment returns have a significant impact on pension expense (and hence on the bottom line of a corporate balance sheet), getting the long-term investment policy right is much more important than security selection. A focus on detailed investment activity draws attention away from other areas of governance with which a board should be dealing.

For organizations that do not have a formal governance structure, or have one that has not been reviewed to take the CAPSA Governance Guidelines into account, the most important role the board can take is to initiate action to improve its governance structure.

Monitoring Governance and Responding to Developments

The implementation of a governance structure based on the CAPSA Governance Guidelines and CAP Guidelines is a good starting point, but it is not the end of the road. It is necessary to monitor the overall process on a regular basis to ensure ongoing compliance and to keep informed and respond to new developments as they occur. Principles 8 and 11 of the CAPSA Governance Guidelines (oversight and compliance, and governance review) provide the foundation for monitoring and reviewing the governance process on a regular basis. There are other publications in Canada that provide additional guidance respecting good governance practices.[16]

---

[16]   For example, refer to "20 Questions Directors Should Ask About Their Role in Pension Governance," and the sequel "A Call to Action for Boards: Governance of Employer-Sponsored Pension Plans," published in 2003 and 2005 respectively by The Canadian Institute of Chartered Accountants, Author Gordon M. Hall.

The CFA Institute

As noted above, it is necessary to keep abreast of developments in governance best practices. For example, in June 2008, the CFA Institute Centre for Financial Market Integrity (the CFA Institute) released their "Code of Conduct for Members of a Pension Scheme Governing Body".[17] This Code was developed in concert with a multinational coalition that sought public comment from all major global financial markets and stakeholders. The CFA Institute has recommended the Code to public companies, government agencies, unions, and pension scheme administrators as best practice for members of pension governing bodies when complying with their duties to the scheme. Although adoption of the Code is voluntary, the CFA Institute has suggested that adopting it will establish an ethical framework for pension plan governing board members, and evidence a commitment to the best interests of pension participants and beneficiaries.

Ten principles are outlined in the Code, and they are said to apply equally, (a) to a governing body member's responsibilities for overseeing the administration of benefits as well as the investment decision-making process, and (b) regardless of the type or nature of a pension scheme. It would appear, however, that the Code does have a considerable bias towards investment-related issues, and a DB rather than a DC environment.

Principal 10 of the CAPSA Governance Guidelines advocates the adoption of a code of conduct for the plan administrator and its delegates. The Code proposed by the CFA Institute may provide plan administrators who have not already developed a code of conduct with considerable assistance in responding to this CAPSA governance principle.

Recent CAPSA Guidelines

CAPSA has also remained engaged with governance issues. In 2011 it released three new Guidelines that touch on governance topics: Guideline No. 5 — *Guideline on Fund Holder Arrangements*; Guideline No. 6 — *Pension Plan Prudent Investment Practices Guideline and the Self-Assessment Questionnaire on Prudent Investment Practices*; and Guideline No. 7— *Pension Plan Funding Policy Guideline*. Furthermore,

---

[17]   The Code can be found online at http://www.cfainstitute.org/learning/products/publications/ccb/Pages/ccb.v2008.n3.1.aspx.

in 2014, CAPSA released Guideline No. 8 — *Defined Contribution Pension Plans Guideline.*

The *Guideline on Fund Holder Arrangements* expands on the CAPSA Governance Guidelines by highlighting the governance principles related to fund holder arrangements (*i.e.*, trusts and insurance contracts). It identifies the permitted types of arrangements and discusses the roles and responsibilities of the key players in these arrangements (the administrator, fund holder, and custodian) and the responsibilities of other important figures, like the employer, plan sponsor, any third-party service providers, and the regulators. Finally, it provides stakeholders with information on what the pension standards regulator will look for when reviewing existing fund holder arrangements.

The CAPSA Guidelines on prudent investment practices and funding policies were developed and released together. It is useful to review them at the same time and it should be noted that the requirement to develop an investment policy is stated to be a responsibility of the plan administrator, while the requirement to develop a funding policy is a responsibility of the plan sponsor. It is specifically stated that "the plan sponsor is not held to a fiduciary standard of care" in the course of its activities related to establishing a funding policy. The Guidelines are not legislation, however, and their provisions should be considered in this light.

Prudent Investment Practices

The *Pension Plan Prudent Investment Practices Guideline* is intended to help plan sponsors demonstrate the application of prudence to the investment of plan assets. The Guideline provides a very good description of the differing roles of the plan sponsor and plan administrator, and the necessity for communication between the entities, if they are different. It also describes situations where the roles may overlap.

The Guideline explains that the establishment of a Statement of Investment Policies and Procedures or Goals (both referred to hereinafter as SIPP) is a statutory requirement, and CAPSA encourages plan administrators to consider the circumstances of their particular plan and the specific requirements of the legislation in their jurisdiction as they apply the Guideline. Although the SIPP could be used by itself as the plan's "investment policy document", a plan administrator may decide to have a broader investment policy. An investment policy guides investment decision-making and sets out how the administrator is to comply with investment principles.

The self-assessment questionnaire that was released as a companion document to the Guideline is meant to help administrators review their practices, and assist them in satisfying the prudent person rule and identifying strengths and weaknesses.

Funding Policy

The *Pension Plan Funding Policy Guideline* provides guidance on the development of funding policies for DB pension plans. It describes how a funding policy documents the objectives of the plan sponsor with respect to the funding of the pension promise, and can serve as the foundation for plan member benefit security and investment decision making. The focus of the funding policy is more on the plan liability side rather than the plan investment or asset side.

The Guideline sets out some of the many factors that may be relevant to the pension plan or the plan sponsor in the development of the funding policy (for example, the affordability of contributions or the demographic characteristics of the plan's beneficiaries).

A number of advantages in the development of a funding policy are proposed and CAPSA sets out what it believes is best practice for issues that should be considered in establishing a policy. Consideration of the following elements for inclusion in the policy is recommended:

- Plan overview;
- Funding objectives;
- Key risks faced by the plan;
- Funding volatility factors and management of risk;
- Funding target ranges;
- Cost sharing mechanisms;
- Utilization of funding excess;
- Actuarial methods, assumptions, and reporting;
- Frequency of valuations;
- Monitoring; and
- Communication policy.

The Guideline recognizes that all of the above issues will not apply equally to all plans, and that there are special considerations that must be taken into account when developing a policy for a multi-employer pension plan.

It should be noted that the new pension legislation in both British Columbia and Alberta requires the adoption of funding policies for all DB pension plans. The regulators in both jurisdictions recommend plan administrators refer to the Guideline when drafting their funding policies.

Defined Contribution Pension Plans Guideline

The Defined Contribution Pension Plans Guideline builds on the guidelines and documents related to DC plans (and other types of CAPs) previously released by CAPSA, including the CAP Guidelines, by clarifying the rights and responsibilities of plan administrators, employers, plan sponsors, service providers, fund holders and members; and what constitutes an adverse amendment (*e.g.*, reduction of employer contributions, changes in expense allocation, changes in possible member retirement age, and lengthening vesting requirements in jurisdictions where vesting is not immediate). A key consideration for DC plans is the information and tools that should be provided to members during the accumulation phase and as they approach the payout phase at retirement. The Defined Contribution Pension Plans Guideline provides considerable guidance for both phases. With respect to the accumulation phase, the guideline provides direction on, and examples of, the types of information that should be provided to members in regards to investment choices, contributions, and projected account balances "as well as an estimate or example of the benefit that may result from the accumulated values". With respect to the payout phase, the guideline contains an explicit expectation that plan administrators will provide members with information regarding all of the regulated retirement's products (*e.g.*, locked-in retirement account, locked-in retirement income fund, life income fund, life annuity contract, etc.) and their unlocking options and thereby allowed them to make informed decisions regarding their retirement benefits.

Conducting a Governance Audit or Review

Continued focus and improvement is necessary where pension governance is involved. If an organization has already responded to the CAPSA and CAP Guidelines, this does not mean that it has achieved good governance and will be protected from risk. A regular review mechanism, like an audit, needs to be established so that the material put in place remains relevant to the organization.

What is a Governance Audit?

A governance audit is a review of the structure and procedures surrounding one or more aspects of the administration and investment of the pension plan, and includes a review of the documentation relating to the above. This can involve looking at:

- The role of the administrator versus the plan sponsor;
- Policy development and implementation;
- Delegation and monitoring of duties and responsibilities;
- Plan documentation and compliance;
- Operating procedures and practices;
- Investment management;
- Service provider services; and
- Other aspects of the administration of the pension plan.

What is the Purpose of a Governance Audit?

There is no one single perfect governance system. What is appropriate for one organization may not be appropriate for another. Although the exact nature of a governance audit may vary from plan to plan and from organization to organization, at their very core, governance audits serve one or more of the following purposes:

- *Legal and regulatory compliance* — While not a legal requirement in most Canadian jurisdictions except for Alberta and British Columbia, one of the main reasons to engage in a governance audit is to ensure that the terms of the pension plan, as well as how the plan is administered, are in compliance with applicable legislation and regulatory regimes and best practices guidelines.

- *Improving and optimizing pension plan administration* — Regular governance audits of pension plans and their administration can also assist in improving and optimizing the administration process. A governance audit by an independent third party can identify legal compliance or administration problems so that appropriate remedies can be instituted before problems become difficult to manage and the ability of an administrator to carry out its fiduciary duties becomes compromised. In addition, a governance audit forces the plan administrator to examine or re-examine plan administrator issues that are raised during the course of the audit and that may otherwise not be brought to the attention of the administrator. Lastly, the use of an independent third party not only allows for an objective assessment of how the plan is being administered, but also enables comparisons to be made to industry benchmarks and best practices, and facilitates the identification of measures that may improve and optimize the efficiency and efficacy of the administration.

- *Pre-emptive identification, assessment and management of risk* — Regular governance audits of a pension plan also allow for the pre-emptive identification, assessment, and management of various plan specific risks, such as investment irregularities or non-compliance issues, communication (or more precisely miscommunication or misrepresentation) problems, funding deficiencies, etc. Ultimately, a failure to detect these and other issues early enough and thereby implement corrective measures may leave the fund, sponsor/administrator, officers and directors, or other persons involved in the administration of the plan susceptible to legal claims. A pre-emptive approach to risk may afford the plan administrator the best defence to claims that it breached its fiduciary duties towards plan beneficiaries either under the governing pension legislation or common law.

What Should a Governance Audit Cover?

A governance audit can focus on various areas. It is important to identify the scope and the depth of an audit before starting. The more common types of audits include:

- *High-level overview audit* — where the focus is on policy-making, its implementation, and the structure of the governance system.
- *Administration audit* — where day-to-day administration is examined in detail for processes, accuracy, completeness, consistency, efficiency, compliance, and risks.
- *Financial audit* — where financial issues are reviewed and risks are assessed. This looks at the investment process, including manager selection and review, as well as other financial issues, such as contributions, corporate reporting, and the plan's financial position.
- *Compliance audit* — where the focus is on ensuring that the plan documentation and processes and procedures are compliant with, and facilitate compliance with, legislative and regulatory requirements.
- *Benchmarking audit* — where the focus is on comparing aspects of the governance of the organization with an appropriate peer group.

Who Should Perform a Governance Audit?

In certain circumstances, self-assessments may be sufficient, but there are some obvious advantages to having an independent experienced third party, such as an accountant, actuary, consultant, or lawyer conduct the governance audit. The third party will provide a fresh perspective on the plan documentation, administrative structures, and operational procedures and processes, unaffected by internal culture or politics. While many internal people are knowledgeable about good governance, it can often be with limited experience of alternative structures and processes. As a result, the current system may get great marks for completeness, but it may be inefficient or ineffective for the organization.

In addition, having a governance audit supervised or managed by legal counsel, either in-house or external, should also be considered. Legal counsel, particularly counsel with pension law experience, can assist in identifying compliance issues as well as determining an appropriate strategy for dealing with these issues. Moreover, the participation of legal counsel, if not in the actual audit, at least in the requesting of the audit and the receiving of the audit report, has the best likelihood of affording the organization the protection of solicitor-client privilege. Solicitor-client privilege will be particularly useful if there is a chance of a lawsuit.

What Can be Done When Problems are Uncovered?

Some common types of problems uncovered by a governance audit include:

- Lack of understanding regarding the differing roles of plan administrator and plan sponsor;
- Ineffective focus of the board on detailed investment issues to the detriment of policy development;
- Lack of documentation of the governance structure and processes;
- Lack of appropriate delegation and oversight mechanisms;
- Service provider contracting issues (*i.e.*, lack of a contract, out-of-date contact, or non-competitive terms);
- Benefit processing issues (*e.g.*, inconsistent or incorrect interpretation of plan terms, records management and retention, *etc.*);
- Poor or improper documentation of plan administration practices and procedures;

- Plan terms or administration practices that are inconsistent with the terms of an applicable collective agreement;
- Ineligible expenses being paid from the plan;
- Issues with member communications (*i.e.*, out-of-date or inaccurate communications, or missing deadlines);
- Other member-related issues (*i.e.*, eligibility, monitoring investment behaviour, or providing investment advice versus information);
- Funding issues (especially with multi-employer plans or when a plan sponsor is facing financial difficulties);
- Investment issues (*e.g.*, the setting of benchmarks, performance measurement, manager selection and supervision, out-of-date investment policies, etc.); and
- Conflict of interest issues.

A written report is an essential product of an audit, even if it is often only issued in draft form. It serves to document the base from which the organization is starting, as well as the fact that the organization has recognized its obligation (whether fiduciary or not) to recognize and strive to achieve good governance. Once a report has been prepared, the next step should be a full understanding and evaluation of the recommendations in terms of importance and cost. They can be prioritized and an orderly process established for implementation. It is not always necessary to implement all recommendations. However, where recommendations are not implemented, it is wise to document the consideration of the recommendation and the reason why the organization has decided not to respond to it (*i.e.*, the recommendation may involve a high cost with minimal benefit).

Frequency of an Audit

Many plan administrators wait until a problem has occurred before commencing a governance audit. By then it may be too late. A governance audit could be very valuable if conducted on a regular (even if infrequent) basis or on a dynamic basis when there is suspicion that all is not as it should or could be. This will probably be about every five to 10 years. Another time to consider an audit is following a significant change in organizational structure or personnel. If the recommendations of an audit report have largely been implemented, the benefits should be evident long into the future.

If an organization is doing all of this with respect to its pension and savings plans there still may be work to be done, as suggested earlier in this chapter, on the governance of its benefits program.

Pension Governance in Jurisdictions Other than Canada

A number of other jurisdictions have experienced developments in corporate and/or pension governance as well. In the U.S. one can look to the *Sarbanes-Oxley Act of 2002*, the *Pension Protection Act of 2006* (which covers a multitude of topics, but includes some governance-related measures, for example, permitting the provision of investment advice under certain conditions), and the *Dodd-Frank Wall Street Reform and Consumer Protection Act of 2010*, which focused on financial regulatory reform and was passed as a response to the 2008-2012 global recession. In the U.K., the primary review of governance-related issues occurred in 2001 with *Institutional Investment in the U.K.: A Review* (better known as the *Myners Report*), which was followed up, in December 2004, with *Myners principles for institutional investment decision-making: review of progress*. A further review was opened in March 2008 and resulted in *Updating the Myners principles: a response to consultation* in October 2008. In response to the consultation, the U.K. Government established an independent Investment Governance Group under the chairmanship of the Pensions Regulator.

In January 2006, the Organisation for Economic Co-operation and Development (OECD), of which Canada is a member country, approved the *OECD Guidelines on Pension Fund Asset Management* and followed them up with the *OECD Guidelines for Pension Fund Governance* in June 2009. In addition, in June 2012, the OECD Working Party on Private Pensions endorsed the OECD *Roadmap for the Good Design of Defined Contribution Pension Plans* which contains 10 recommendations based on good design and public policy. The OECD Guidelines and Roadmap are not legally binding and are intended to be guides for countries to determine their own requirements and to set minimum international standards. These documents demonstrate that pension governance is not specifically a Canadian issue, but rather one that is being considered by a host of countries. The World Economic Forum[18] has called for an international set of pension governance principles, but that may take some time to develop. As Canada is clearly a leader in the area of pension governance, there may be a role for it to play in assisting other countries with their governance development efforts.

---

[18] Described on its website as being "the foremost global community of business, political, intellectual and other leaders of society committed to improving the state of the world". Refer to http://www.weforum.org.

Chapter 5

DESIGN, REGISTRATION, AND ADMINISTRATION OF PENSION PLANS

Executive Summary[1]

This chapter focuses on the requirements of administering a pension plan, including the major considerations in designing, establishing, and maintaining a registered pension plan (RPP), and details the impact of pension and tax legislation on the administration of a registered plan. A description of the various entities involved in establishing and administering a pension plan, and their roles and responsibilities, including fiduciary duties where applicable, can be found in the chapter on Governance of Retirement, Savings, and Other Benefit Plans.

The success of any retirement savings arrangement will depend on many things, such as:

- Good plan design to meet employee retirement needs;
- Plan sponsor goals and commitment;
- Efficiency of operation;
- Effective communication to the employees;
- Appropriate plan governance; and
- Plan member goals and satisfaction.

These factors are important to ensure that the promised benefits are delivered appropriately and that employees understand their retirement savings benefits and are satisfied with them. These principles apply to both registered and non-registered arrangements, but administration of RPPs is complicated by considerable regulatory requirements and governance guidelines.

This chapter also provides an in-depth review of the selection of service providers, the registration process, and the operation of the plan.

---

[1] For more information on plan administration and governance, please consult the multi-jurisdictional charts in the *Canadian Employment Benefits & Pension Guide*. Morneau Shepell, *Canadian Employment Benefits & Pension Guide*, loose-leaf (Toronto: LexisNexis Canada, 2003). The table of contents for these charts appears at the back of this Handbook.

Reporting requirements are reviewed, as are the main considerations for plan members.[2]

Overview

The nature of the pension promise is defined by the design of the plan. Once the plan is operational, the design should be revisited periodically, and some adjustments may be made to reflect the changing realities, for example:

- Changes in the profile of the workforce;
- Industry competitiveness and trends;
- Changes in legislation;
- Financial considerations;
- New benefit trends and technologies;
- Changes in government programs; and
- The impact of collective bargaining agreements.

Pension legislation has assigned statutory obligations to certain players involved in plan administration. Litigation on pension matters has become quite common in Canada, although not as prolific as in the United States. Litigation issues have included surplus ownership, the employer's right to contribution holidays, conversion from DB to DC plans, communications and promises made to employees, benefit division on marriage breakdown, death benefit entitlement, and deemed trust issues on employer insolvency. The need for closer oversight of investment management has attracted considerable attention in recent years, and has led to litigation. Pension litigation is often brought in the form of a class action suit by members, former members and retirees who work together to bring legal action against a plan sponsor and administrator.

Well-publicized interpretations of pension legislation and high-profile litigation have contributed to raising the public's awareness of pension plan issues, and to redefining the roles of the various parties in the pension arena. A number of them are considered to have fiduciary obligations. Penalties have been applied in cases where there has been a breach of fiduciary obligations.[3] Fiduciary duties are described more fully in Chapter 4, Governance of Retirement, Savings, and Other Benefit Plans.

---

[2]   See Chapter 29 for a detailed discussion of communication; see Chapter 4 for a detailed discussion of governance.

[3]   Chapter 10 provides detailed discussions of key pension decisions.

RPPs are subject to more than one piece of legislation, with pension standards legislation playing a central role in affecting plan administration. Pension legislation in Canada is not harmonized among the jurisdictions with enacted pension legislation, although the Association of Canadian Pension Management and others in the industry have encouraged increased harmonization for years. What the different pension standards laws have in common is that they describe:

- Minimum standards for plan benefits and administrative requirements;
- Minimum funding standards;
- Minimum disclosure requirements;
- Plan wind-up requirements;
- Reporting requirements;
- Roles and responsibilities for the supervisory body and for the employer; and
- Remedial actions.

The requirements are very detailed and need to be satisfied for each jurisdiction affecting the pension plan.

As of 2016, most jurisdictions in Canada have pension standards legislation. Nunavut, Northwest Territories, Yukon Territory, and Prince Edward Island do not have enacted pension legislation. Nunavut and the Territories are governed by federal pension legislation. Prince Edward Island introduced a new *Pension Benefits Act* (Bill 41) on May 17, 2012, but Bill 41 failed to pass.

The federal *Income Tax Act* (ITA) also has jurisdiction over RPPs.[4] The ITA defines acceptable benefits and the applicable limits for RPPs. It also defines maximum contribution levels that can be made to a plan and deducted by the employer and by the employee. The ITA also has significant reporting requirements.

While pension standards legislation generally defines the minimum standards and requirements that must be provided by a pension plan, the ITA defines the maximum benefits that are available.[5]

Other areas that can have significant impact on the administration of pension plans and of members' benefits include legislation in both the provincial and federal jurisdictions, covering:

---

[4]   The ITA also governs some types of non-registered pension plans, such as Retirement Compensation Arrangements (RCAs), which are discussed in Chapter 13.

[5]   Chapters 8 and 9 examine the ITA requirements and pension standards legislation in more detail.

- Human rights legislation;
- Employment standards legislation;
- Estates and succession law;
- Family law (both property division and support);
- Bankruptcy and insolvency law; and
- Trust law.

Plan Design

A pension plan operates with significant constraints. The design of the pension plan must balance these constraints with the goals and desires of the plan sponsor and members.

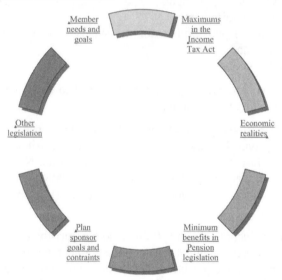

There are many questions an employer should ask before deciding on the design of the pension plan or amendments to an existing pension plan. The first step for the employer is to decide what type of plan to offer on a go-forward basis. Will it be a defined benefit plan, a defined contribution plan, a hybrid plan or a target benefit plan, where permitted by legislation?

Each type of plan has its own advantages and disadvantages and is more suitable for some employee groups than others.[6]

---

[6]   Chapter 1 discusses the different types of plans that a sponsor can offer.

As employees have different needs, the average characteristics of the employee group that will be covered should be considered in plan design, such as:

- Type of work — are employees office workers, or do they perform physically demanding work? Are employees unionized and what does the collective bargaining agent want?
- Length of service and average age — do employees spend their full careers with the employer or do they make frequent career moves?

The type of plan may depend on the goals of the sponsoring employer. The employer may want to:

- Attract employees in a competitive marketplace;
- Retain employees and, where necessary, provide incentives for early retirement;
- Reward long service employees; or
- Defer compensation for executives and other highly paid employees.

One of the most important considerations is cost. Establishing a pension plan is a significant undertaking, and once established, can demand significant resources to maintain:

- Will the plan provide modest or substantial benefits?
- Will the employees be required to contribute as a condition of membership?
- How much of the cost of the plan is the employer willing to assume?
- How much investment risk is acceptable for the employer and the employees?

Other cost-related provisions to consider in defined benefit plan design include:

- What survivor and death benefits will be offered?
- What reductions will be made for early retirement from the plan?
- Will the employer provide full pensions at an earlier age to individuals if they meet certain criteria?
- Will the pensions be indexed?

All of these considerations, and other plan details, must be clearly documented within the terms of the official plan text. Once completed, the official text must be filed with the Canada Revenue Agency (CRA) and the jurisdiction affecting the plan.

When setting up a plan, the plan sponsor should also factor in the expected plan operation expenses such as actuarial and administrative charges, custodial and fund management fees.

Establishing a Plan

As a rule, an application for registration of a retirement plan must be made with the regulatory authorities by the plan sponsor, or on behalf of the plan sponsor within 60 days after the establishment of the plan. The descriptive documents that must be filed in support of an application for registration depend on the jurisdiction, but typically include:

- A prescribed application form;
- A certified copy of the plan document;
- A certified copy of the funding arrangement (*i.e.*, the trust agreement or insurance contract);
- A certified copy of a board of directors' resolution adopting the plan;
- A certified copy of a collective agreement (if any);
- A certified copy of any reciprocal transfer agreement related to the plan (if any);
- A copy of the plan booklet provided to members;
- Any other documents by virtue of which the plan is established, such as a declaration of trust;
- An initial actuarial report (for defined benefit pension plans only); and
- A statement of investment policies and procedures.

For RPPs, a registration fee must be paid to the appropriate jurisdiction of registration.

In order to receive a tax deduction for employee and employer contributions, the following documents must be submitted to the CRA for registration:

- A completed CRA application form (Form T510);
- A certified copy of the pension plan text;
- An initial actuarial valuation report (for defined benefit pension plans only);
- A certified copy of the funding arrangement (typically a trust agreement or insurance contract); and
- A certified copy of any other relevant documentation, such as a declaration of trust.

The CRA also imposes registration and filing obligations on non-registered pension arrangements. One example is a Deferred Profit

Sharing Plan (DPSP), which is an arrangement whereby the employer contributes a portion of the annual profits from its business or a related-business, to a trustee. The trustee, in turn, holds and invests the contributions for the benefit of employees. These plans offer tax deferral benefits that are similar to RPPs. To obtain these tax advantages, the plan must be registered and the following documents must be submitted to the CRA for registration:

- Form T2214, with which the trustee and the employer apply for registration of the plan as a DPSP;
- A certified copy of the resolution of the directors authorizing the application to be made, if the employer is a corporation; and
- A certified copy of the trust agreement and plan text (these can be combined in one document) constituting the terms of the DPSP. These documents must be compliant with ITA rules concerning DPSPs.

Selection of Service Providers

Plan sponsors often require the help of one or more of the following service providers to set up and maintain their retirement plans:

- Actuaries, consultants, and legal counsel;
- Custodian (*i.e.*, trustee or insurance company)
- Investment managers;
- Administration service providers; and
- Communication specialists.

The role of each of these service providers is discussed below.

Actuaries, Consultants, and Legal Counsel

If the plan sponsor is establishing a defined benefit plan, an actuary is required to complete the initial valuation report and cost certificate. Actuaries also provide information regarding the financial impact of plan improvements; if the cost of the plan improvement affects the funding of the plan, actuaries are required to complete an actuarial cost certificate. Actuaries, pension consultants, and legal counsel can also assist plan sponsors with:

- Drafting the plan document;
- Making board resolutions;
- Reviewing trust agreements or insurance contracts;
- Preparing or reviewing communication material for employees;
- Selecting other suppliers; and
- Preparing regulatory submissions.

Plan sponsors may elect to do some or all of the above tasks themselves, depending on their own internal resources. The actuary or consultant may be hired based on a prior relationship, a recommendation, or through a formal selection process where proposals are solicited from a number of firms, interviews are conducted, and a selection is made.

Custodian (Trustee or Insurance Company)

Custodial services, also known as fund holder services, are offered by most of the major trust and life insurance companies. The fund holder is the actual holder of the plan assets and is responsible for those assets. Fund holders are entitled to rely on instructions given by the administrator. They are also responsible for providing an accounting to the administrator showing the income and outflow of the funds and assets, as well as maintaining the integrity of the pension fund. Selection criteria for custodians include reporting capabilities, service, compatibility with the investment manager selected, financial strength, experience, and fees.

Trust agreements and insurance contracts are the two fundamental models for delivering pension plans in Canada. The distinction focuses on the vehicle for holding the assets, but it has many implications.

The trust-based model, which is very common for DB plans as well as larger DC plans, is often synonomous with an unbundled approach where the plan administrator selects specialized independent vendors for custodial services and cash management, administration services (i.e., recordkeeping) and investment management. There are a number of key advantages to this model:

- Plan administrators have access to a very broad range of independent providers, including almost unlimited range of investment managers, providing the ability to construct the solution that suits them best;plan administrators have a direct relationship, and are able to negotiate directly with each vendor;
- Plan administrators with both DB plans and CAP arrangements are able to benefit from integrated administration as well as lower custody and investment management fees based on the combined scale of their plans;
- Plan sponsors avoid the need to "seg-wrap" their investment products – a process by which investments are converted into insurance products for distribution by insurance companies. Seg-wrapping adds cost and inefficiencies, which typically results in underperformance of the segregated fund versus the original investment product;

- Separation of roles minimizes potential conflicts of interest and promotes disclosure and transparency.

In an insurance-based model, the insurance company generally offers a pre-packaged or "bundled" solution that includes custodial services and cash management, administration services (recordkeeping) and investment management. The insurer model is common for small and mid-sized defined contribution plans, but is rare for defined benefit plans. Key advantages to this model include:

- Convenience of a one-stop shop for plan sponsors;
- Vendor management and contracting is simplified with a single provider;
- Access to multiple investment managers on the insurer platform, based on the aggregate assets of the plan, which benefits smaller plans who do not have the scale to negotiate directly with investment managers. We note, however, that in recent years, insurance platforms have heavily emphasized proprietary, rather than third-party, investment products.

It should also be noted that the plan administrator may have problems trying to "unbundle" the services if there is an issue with asset performance or the insurance company's service at a later date. This can cause disruption when the administrator needs to change service providers.

Investment Manager

Investment managers are often hired directly by plan sponsors to manage the plan assets. There are a number of options the plan sponsor should consider when hiring an investment manager.[7]

- The plan sponsor may use pooled funds, which tend to have lower fees if the plan assets are not sizable; however, using pooled funds reduces investment flexibility for the plan sponsor and means that the investment manager is bound by the pooled fund's investment policy statement.
- If the plan sponsor elects to have its assets managed directly by an investment manager, the fees may be higher (depending on the amount of assets in the plan) but the sponsor has more influence in the investment mix of the plan assets.
- All jurisdictions require that a pension plan have a Statement of Investment Policies and Procedures (SIPP) as part of ensuring that

---

[7]   Chapter 7 discusses these issues in detail.

the plan is administered with the goals of good governance. An investment manager that directly manages plan assets will be expected to comply with the SIPP in managing the pension fund. The SIPP details the investment goals and procedures for the pension fund, such as:

- o Performance objectives and benchmarks;
- o Risk tolerance;
- o Diversification and target asset allocation of equities, such as stocks and shares, debt instruments, such as bonds and mortgages, foreign investments, and cash (defined benefit plan);
- o Number and type of investment options and default fund (defined contribution plan);
- o Rules for monitoring investment performance, including minimum frequency for investment performance review by the board of directors or pension committee;
- o Selection, monitoring and changes in investment managers or funds; and
- o Methods of valuation of assets, voting rights, and rules for determination of materiality of transactions.

When choosing an investment manager, the plan administrator may want to consider:

- The investment manager's style, objectives, and risk tolerance, and how these will match with the SIPP;
- Whether or not the manager has a proven track record, *i.e.*, is there a well-established stable organization with solid pension investment experience;
- Key personnel;
- Fees.

Monitoring the performance of the investment funds should be an ongoing process, as poor performance will have a detrimental effect on the health of the plan fund. In a defined benefit plan, poor investment performance will ultimately lead to an increased cost to the employer; and in a defined contribution plan, poor investment performance can result in increased costs to the member or an inadequate pension for the member.

Administration Service Providers

A plan sponsor may decide to outsource the administration of the plan or administer the arrangements internally. Issues that plan sponsors often consider when outsourcing administration are reporting capabilities, service, experience, and costs.

If the plan sponsor wants to outsource the administration duties for a defined contribution plan, the duties may be performed by the custodian of the plan or an independent recordkeeper.

A plan sponsor who chooses to administer a defined benefit plan internally will need specialized pension administration software for this purpose. If the sponsor decides to outsource the defined benefit plan administration, there are a number of firms capable of performing the administration. The plan sponsor may have the administration done by the consulting firm that performs the actuarial valuations, or may decide to ask a number of firms to bid on the work. Considerations for the selection of a service provider, and more information on the various functions involved in recordkeeping are provided in a later section of this chapter.

Communication Specialists

Plan sponsors often retain communication specialists to prepare communication materials for plan members. Given the specialized nature of pension benefits, the expertise necessary to adequately communicate pension benefits can be found in employee benefits consulting firms.[8]

Plan Jurisdiction

A pension plan is registered in the jurisdiction in which the plurality of its members report to work. For example, if a plan has 100 members in Ontario, 125 members in Manitoba, and 150 members in Alberta, the plan will be registered in Alberta, because the plurality of the members report to work in Alberta. Should the plurality of membership shift between jurisdictions, the plan registration will change jurisdictions.

The exception to the plurality rule is plans covering employees in industries subject to federal regulation, such as airlines, telecommunications, shipping, railroads, and banking; these plans are registered with the federal regulators.

All of the jurisdictions with pension legislation are parties to a memorandum of reciprocal agreement, which confirms that the applicable regulator will ensure that all plan members have equal protection. In the example above, the Alberta regulator, the Superintendent of Pensions, as well as ensuring that the benefits of Alberta members are administered according to Alberta legislation, assumes responsibility for ensuring that the benefits of the Manitoba members of the plan are administered in

---

[8]   The range of services varies widely and is discussed in more detail in Chapter 29.

accordance with the Manitoba legislation, and that the benefits of the Ontario members of the plan are administered in accordance with Ontario legislation.[9] Since July 1, 2016, British Columbia, Nova Scotia, Ontario, Quebec and Saskatchewan are party to a new Multi-Jurisdictional Pension Plans Agreement that replaces the memorandum of reciprocal agreement and formalizes the rules for changing jurisdiction of plan registration.

Table of Regulators

Jurisdiction	Applicable Law	Regulator
Alberta	*Employment Pension Plans Act*	Treasury Board and Finance (Superintendent of Pensions)
British Columbia	*Pension Benefits Standards Act*	Financial Institutions Commission (Superintendent of Pensions)
Manitoba	*The Pension Benefits Act*	Manitoba Pension Commission (Superintendent of Pensions)
New Brunswick	*Pension Benefits Act*	Financial and Consumer Services Commission (Superintendent of Pensions)
Newfoundland and Labrador	*Pension Benefits Act, 1997*	Service NL, Pension Benefits Standards Division (Superintendent of Pensions)
Nova Scotia	*Pension Benefits Act*	Finance and Treasury Board (Superintendent of Pensions)
Ontario	*Pension Benefits Act*	Financial Services Commission of Ontario (Superintendent of Financial Services)
Quebec	*Supplemental Pension Plans Act*	Retraite Québec — Direction des régimes de retraite

---

[9]   See Chapter 9 for more information on plan jurisdiction.

Jurisdiction	Applicable Law	Regulator
Saskatchewan	*The Pension Benefits Act, 1992*	Financial and Consumer Affairs Authority (Superintendent of Pensions)
Federal, Yukon, Northwest Territories and Nunavut	*Pension Benefits Standards Act, 1985*	Office of the Superintendent of Financial Institutions

The Registration Process

Registered Pension Plans

The following chart illustrates the process of a successful registration from start to finish.

Plan Sponsor decides to establish a retirement plan
(or is required through collective bargaining)

↓

Plan Sponsor selects service providers to assist in
design/registration/implementation of new plan

↓

Plan Text, Board Resolution and Trust Agreements, and any other
applicable documents, are drafted and finalized

↓

Application filed including appropriate documents and
filing fees with regulatory authorities and CRA

↓

Pension plan is approved by CRA
and the appropriate jurisdiction

Plan documentation (text and related records) should, along with other matters, specify:

- Classes of employees eligible to participate
- Eligibility conditions required to join the plan;
- Amount and form of pension benefits to be provided, including any ancillary benefits;
- Method of determining contributions of the employer, and of the employees, if any;
- Timing and form of benefit payments;
- Rights of participants upon termination of employment and retirement;
- Power to amend the plan;
- Investment of plan assets;
- Right to, and use of, excess assets in an ongoing plan and surplus assets on plan termination; and
- Ability to deduct fees and expenses from the fund.

Operation of the Plan

Differences by Type of Arrangement

Registered pension plans must be registered under pension standards legislation and under the federal ITA in order to qualify as a tax-sheltered arrangement. The actual operation of these RPPs is dictated by the various requirements of the regulatory authorities.

Other pension arrangements are not subject to pension standards legislation, although the federal ITA still imposes some requirements. Thus, the operation of these plans is simpler, being driven more by the principles of prudence and good management.

The balance of this section will deal with the operation of registered pension plans.

Recordkeeping — Issues and Alternatives

Defined Benefit Plans

In every RPP, there is detailed administration work that must be done. This includes keeping records of individual members, sending each member an annual statement, processing retirements, deaths and terminations, answering questions, and filing returns with federal and provincial governments.

Detailed records must be set up and maintained for each plan member, which includes active members, disabled members, inactive members, pensioners, and survivors of deceased members. These records contain important member data, such as:

- Dates of birth, hire, plan entry, and retirement;
- Social Insurance Number and employee ID used by the employer;
- Contributions, service, and earnings history;
- Special dates, such as periods of leave and disability, and whether or not pension credit was earned for the period;
- Marital status, spouse, and beneficiary information, including information on any partition of benefits resulting from a marriage breakdown.

The data must be stored with integrity to ensure that plan members receive the correct benefit entitlements. The records also serve as the source of information for actuarial valuations and various periodic reports required by regulatory authorities, for producing annual member statements, and for calculating Pension Adjustments, Pension Adjustments Reversals, and Past Service Pension Adjustments. This data is also necessary for the calculation of pension assets in the case of marriage breakdown proceedings. Marriage breakdown proceedings normally give rise to increased recordkeeping requirements in order to administer pension benefits in accordance with court orders and separation agreements.

These recordkeeping functions may be performed in-house or delegated to outside advisers such as the custodian (*i.e.*, a trust or an insurance company), an actuarial consulting company, or a company specializing in third-party pension administration.

Pension legislation has made pension plan administration extremely complex, and an important decision is determining who will manage the day-to-day administration of the plan. This decision should be revisited periodically. It may be appropriate for a plan sponsor to perform the administration of the plan internally for some time and, subsequently, to retain the services of an outside supplier. Conversely, the employer may initially contract out administration until sufficient expertise is available internally to repatriate this function.

Employers wishing to exercise more control over the management and day-to-day administration of their program(s) may prefer to opt for a software service model, such as a Software as a Service (SaaS) or installed option. The SaaS solution is a subscription-based model allowing the employer remote access to the selected SaaS provider's recordkeeping system. The SaaS provider is responsible for keeping data secure and all system maintenance (including hardware and software).

In the installed option, the selected system is installed on the employer's own servers. The plan sponsor is responsible for managing the technical environment, including operating and managing the hardware and upgrades.

Some major factors to be considered when making these decisions are:

- *Number of plans and complexity* — are the calculations straightforward or are they complex?
- *Plan membership and annual turnover* — how many calculations are performed each year?
- *Corporate philosophy* — how much control does the employer want to maintain over the administration of the plan versus outsourcing?
- *Availability and depth of knowledge of existing staff* — will existing staff understand the increasing regulatory requirements of pension administration or will specialists need to be hired?
- *Key person dependency* — what happens in the event of illness or vacation?
- *Internal structure of the company* — will the administration be handled centrally or locally?
- *Internal resources of the company* — will the purchase of computer equipment, specialized software, or the addition of new staff be necessary?
- *Likelihood of future plan restructuring* — will any decisions resulting in significant cost be obsolete in the future as a result of future restructuring?
- *Available budget* — how much money will be set aside to administer the plan?

Member Rights and Responsibilities

Although plan sponsors, pension committees, and employers bear significant responsibilities in the administration of a pension plan, members also have obligations that they must fulfill, including:

- Completing the plan enrolment and any required forms;
- Completing the appropriate forms when there is a change in designated beneficiary;
- Informing the plan administrator of address changes and contact information;
- Informing the plan administrator of significant events that could result in a third-party claim on the benefit, such as a marriage breakdown, which will affect the members' benefits;

- Advising the administrator of inaccurate information to be updated; and
- Providing appropriate documentation to expedite benefit payments at termination or retirement.

Plan members have rights, which plan sponsors must ensure are met. These rights include:

- Access to plan description documentation, such as plan booklets and plan summaries (commonly made available online in addition to hard copy, although rules concerning electronic communications must be considered);
- An annual pension statement, describing the benefits accrued in the plan;
- Opportunity to review plan documentation at the sponsor's address;
- Notification of plan amendments, and explanations of the amendment; and
- Timely statements of benefits earned and the options available upon termination, retirement, or death.

Defined Contribution Plans

While the alternatives discussed above can be applied to all types of RPPs, they are directed primarily at the administration of defined benefit plans.

An employer administering a defined contribution plan may not have the same registration and reporting procedures. The plan may offer investment alternatives for the members to select. If this is the case, the employer needs to ensure that members can obtain information about the options and their pension investments on an ongoing basis. The administration of defined contribution plans, as a result of increased flexibility in member investment choice, has become highly sophisticated. The trend in the services offered by outside advisers is shifting from pure recordkeeping to leading-edge services such as:

- Providing online access to member pension records;
- Linking the member's pension information with their group benefits;
- Access to pension and savings mobile apps designed to run on mobile devices such as smartphones and tablet computers;
- Access to online videos and tutorials designed to educate plan members about their program(s) and saving for retirement;
- Providing interactive voice response services and/or online access to frequently asked questions;
- Providing online access to plan documentation;

- Tools designed to assist plan members with converting pension savings to retirement income (decumulation);
- Providing investor profile questionnaires and cross-validation to ensure plan members' asset mix is appropriate to their investment style;
- Providing targeted and customized real-time messaging advising plan members whether they are on track to meet their retirement goals; and
- Adopting e-signatures to reduce the administrative effort associated with obtaining physical signatures.

The ability to provide these services, and more, will continue to require a significant commitment and investment in technology and innovation.

Benefit Determination and Delivery

A member's benefit entitlement must be calculated and provided to the member within time limits set by the regulatory authorities, according to the relevant provisions of the pension plan and the applicable legislation.

Benefits are calculated on a member's termination of employment, retirement or death and, in some jurisdictions, on marriage breakdown. Benefits are also calculated in the event of termination or partial termination of the pension plan. It is the responsibility of the administrator to provide the member with a written statement outlining the options available to the plan member and to ensure that payment is made in accordance with the elected options.

In certain circumstances, such as in the case of calculating transfer values in the event of termination of employment or death, the requirements set out by the Canadian Institute of Actuaries (CIA) must be adhered to as well.[10] The general principles of the standard of practice are to ensure that the transfer value reflects current financial market conditions, is calculated independently from the plan's financial position, and reflects the full benefit which the plan member is entitled to under the terms of the plan.

---

[10]   Canadian Institute of Actuaries, Standard of Practice for Determining Pension Commuted Values, online: http://www.actuaries.ca.

Financial Reporting

Investment/custodial reporting and reconciliation must be done at least annually; however, they are often done more frequently. Audited financial statements prepared in accordance with generally accepted accounting principles must be filed annually with regulators for registered pension plans, although pension plans below certain asset thresholds and defined contribution pension plans are sometimes exempt.[11] Where pension plnas are exempt, certified financial statements, as opposed to audited financial statements, may be filed.

Regulatory Reporting

Once a plan is registered with the regulatory authorities, reports must be filed periodically. The timing and nature of reports required by provincial standards legislation vary by jurisdiction. The following reports are examples of reporting requirements common to all jurisdictions.

Annual Information Return

An Annual Information Return (AIR) must be filed annually by the administrator of the pension plan in the jurisdiction in which the pension plan is registered. Each jurisdiction has its own prescribed return that must be filed within a specified time frame. A fee, based on membership in the reporting year, must accompany the return. If the information return is filed late and no extension has been obtained, there may be late filing fees.

The AIR generally requires the following information:

- Plan membership, by province and sex;
- A reconciliation of the annual plan membership that includes the number of new members, retirements, terminations, and deaths;
- Total employee required contributions;
- Total employee voluntary contributions;
- Total employer current service contributions;
- Credits or surplus used to reduce employer current service contributions;
- Employer payments to liquidate unfunded liabilities;
- Employer payments to liquidate experience deficiencies; and

---

[11]   See CPA Canada Handbook-Accounting.

- Information relating to the value of fund assets.[12]

As part of ongoing initiatives by the CRA and CAPSA to reduce the administrative requirements on pension plan administrators, a single return has been developed to accommodate the joint filing of the AIR, which meets both the ITA requirements and the requirements under pension standards legislation. All provinces, with the exception of Quebec, have harmonized their AIR forms with the CRA. For Quebec RPPs, separate CRA and provincial AIRs must be filed within six months following the end of the fiscal year of the plan.

A number of jurisdictions provide for electronic filing of the AIR, namely Alberta, British Columbia, Ontario and the federal jurisdiction. Some of these jurisdictions provide for online filing of other information, such as financial statements, investment information summaries, and actuarial valuation reports.

Amendment Filing Requirements

All pension plan amendments must be filed within time limits prescribed by pension legislation. Notice of amendments of a non-technical nature must generally be provided to plan members, and those that adversely affect member benefit or increase member contributions may require advance notice and/or filing with regulators when the amendment is filed.

Generally, when an amendment to a plan affects the cost of benefits, creates unfunded liabilities, or otherwise affects the solvency of the plan, an actuarial report or a cost certificate must be filed in support of the amendment. The prescribed time limits within which the supporting actuarial reports and cost certificates must be filed vary by jurisdiction.

Canada Revenue Agency Requirements

Once registered status is conferred by the CRA, registration is ongoing. Certain filings are required; for example, a copy of each amendment to the plan must be filed. The CRA does not acknowledge or confirm the acceptance of amendments; however, the plan administrator will be notified of any changes the CRA may require in order for a plan amendment to comply with the ITA.

---

[12]   See Chapter 9 for more information on specific jurisdictional requirements regarding benefit determination, delivery, and financial and regulatory reporting.

T3P

If the pension plan is funded through a trust (or a corporate pension society), the trustee (or society) is required to file a pension plan income tax return, the T3P, annually with the CRA. The T3P must be filed within 90 days following the end of the taxation year of the trust (or society). All receipts and disbursements of the pension fund during the taxation year must be reported on the T3P. A statement of assets of the fund at year-end with a reconciliation to the previous year-end must be attached to the T3P.

Pension Adjustments and Pension Adjustment Reversals

Pension Adjustments (PAs) were introduced with the 1990 taxation year. A PA is reported annually for each member of the pension plan who has earned a benefit during the year. The PA is intended to represent the value of the pension benefit earned by the member during the year, and it will affect the member's available Registered Retirement Savings Plan (RRSP) contribution room for the subsequent year.

The defined benefit PA calculation formula is specified by the ITA and does not take into account provisions of individual pension plans. As a result, in some cases the PA can overstate the value of the pension benefit that the member will eventually receive. This is particularly true in the event of termination prior to the member being eligible to retire.

The PA formula for defined benefit provisions is:

(Benefit earned in the year " $\times$ " 9) less the PA offset.

The PA offset was $1,000 from 1990 to 1996, and has been $600 from 1997 to date.

For defined contribution plans, the PA is the sum of contributions made on behalf of the member, by both the member and the employer, plus any additional contributions made, such as redistribution of forfeitures made by terminating members.

If the pension plan is a hybrid plan, combining both defined benefit and defined contribution provisions, the PA is the sum of the two calculations above.

The annual PA for each plan member must be reported on the member's T4 slip, which must be distributed to the member and filed with CRA by the last day of February of the following year. Once the plan member's income tax return is filed, the CRA will then reduce the member's available RRSP room by the PA amount, and will include the maximum deductible RRSP contribution room available to the member on the notice of assessment forwarded to the member by CRA.

A member's RRSP contribution room is calculated as:

- 18% of earnings in the previous year, to a cap of $25,370 for 2016 ($26,010 for 2017, to be indexed thereafter);
- Less the PA reported for the previous year;
- Less any Past Service Pension Adjustments (PSPAs) filed for the member;
- Plus any Pension Adjustment Reversal (PAR) filed for the member in the current year;
- Plus any unused RRSP room carried forward from previous taxation years.

The PAR is used to restore RRSP contribution room that has been previously foregone as a result of the PA reporting during the years of the member's participation in the plan.

Upon termination from a defined benefit plan, if the lump sum benefit received by the plan member is less than the sum of the historical PA amounts reported on the T4 slips and any PSPAs, the difference is reported as the PAR. PARs are only calculated and filed when 100% of the benefit is paid out to the member in full and final settlement. If the member has service in the pension plan prior to 1990, only the value of the benefit earned from 1990 forward is used in the PAR calculation. A PAR restores lost RRSP room immediately and is effective with the current taxation year. A member receiving a PAR will receive a revised notice of assessment from the CRA.

A PAR is calculated for a defined contribution member as the sum of contributions made minus the sum of contributions withdrawn, as valued at the dates of contribution. PARs for defined contribution pension plans do not take into account changes in investment value.

PARs are reported on a T10 form and a copy of the form is forwarded to both the plan member and the CRA. The administrator must file the T10 form no later than 60 days after the end of the calendar quarter in which the member termination occurs. The one exception is for the last quarter of the year, when the PAR must be filed within 30 days of the end of the year. If the PAR is filed late, there may be late filing fees.

It is not required to file a PAR if the value is less than $50, unless the member specifically requests it. In practice, many administrators file all PARs over $0.

Past Service Pension Adjustment

PSPAs are calculated and reported to the CRA when plan members' benefits are improved retroactively, either through a plan change affecting all members or a group of members, or an individual member's purchase of past service benefits in the plan. The PSPA is the sum of the PAs that would have been reported during the affected period, had the improved benefit been in place at that time, less the PAs that were actually reported for the member.

If a PSPA requiring certification is less than $50, it does not have to be reported to CRA. A PSPA that is exempt from certification does not have to be reported to the CRA if it is less than $250. However, it must be tracked by the plan administrator, as this rule is cumulative, and any subsequent situation requiring a PSPA calculation must take into account any previous unreported PSPAs under $50/$250.[13]

Table of Maximum Benefits under the *Income Tax Act*

Year	Maximum benefit accrual	Maximum Defined Benefit PA	Maximum Defined Contribution PA	Maximum RRSP Contributions for the year
1990	1,277.78	10,500	11,500	N/A
1991	1,388.89	11,500	12,500	11,500
1992	1,388.89	11,500	12,500	12,500
1993	1,500.00	12,500	13,500	13,500
1994	1,611.11	13,500	14,500	14,500
1995	1,722.22	14,500	15,500	15,500
1996	1,722.22	14,500	13,500	13,500
1997	1,722.22	14,900	13,500	13,500
1998	1,722.22	14,900	13,500	13,500
1999	1,722.22	14,900	13,500	13,500
2000	1,722.22	14,900	13,500	13,500
2001	1,722.22	14,900	13,500	13,500
2002	1,722.22	14,900	13,500	13,500
2003	1,722.22	14,900	15,500	13,500
2004	1,833.33	15,900	16,500	14,500
2005	2,000.00	17,400	18,000	15,500
2006	2,111.11	18,400	19,000	18,000

---

[13]   Additional discussion of PAs, PARs, and PSPAs can be found in Chapter 8.

Year	Maximum benefit accrual	Maximum Defined Benefit PA	Maximum Defined Contribution PA	Maximum RRSP Contributions for the year
2007	2,222.22	19,400	20,000	19,000
2008	2,333.33	20,400	21,000	20,000
2009	2,444.44	21,400	22,000	21,000
2010	2,494.44	21,850	22,450	22,000
2011	2,522.22	22,370	22,970	22,450
2012	2,646.67	23,220	23,820	22,970
2013	2,696.67	23,670	24,270	23,820
2014	2,770.00	24,330	24,930	24,270
2015	2,818.89	24,770	25,370	24,930
2016	2,890.00	25,410	26,010	25,370
2017	1/9 the money purchase limit	Indexed	Indexed	26,010

Annual Statements

As mentioned earlier in this chapter (Recordkeeping — Issues and Alternatives), plan members are entitled to periodically receive a pension statement. Even though these statements are usually refered to as annual statements, the Newfoundland and Labrador legislation requires that they be issued at least once every three years.

The general rule is that statements must be issued to all active members, but certain juridictions also require that statements be provided to non-active members (i.e., former members, retired members), spouses and other beneficiaries. Issuing statements to non-active members, spouses and beneficiaries has been a long time requirement in Quebec. With the new enactments recently introduced in Alberta and British Columbia, persons receiving a pension (i.e., retired members and surviving spouses) are entitled to receive a statement. The Ontario and federal legislations also provide for statements to both retired members and members entitled to a deferred pension. By July 1, 2017, these members should have received their first statement.

Ontario statements to non-active members, spouses and beneficiaries are required every two years. Nova Scotia legislation also includes a provision for statements to both deferred and retired members, but this requirement will only come into force when enabling regulations are adopted.

Annual statement requirements vary by legislation and according to member classes.

Typically, active member statements will include the following:

- Name of the plan and registration number;
- Contact information;
- Member's name and date of birth;
- Date of hire;
- Date of plan entry;
- Name of beneficiary;
- Name of spouse;
- Period covered by the statement;
- Vesting date;
- Normal retirement date;
- Early retirement date;
- Right to examine documents;
- Information about amendments during the past year; and
- Information about the SIPP (Ontario only).

For a DC plan:

- Account balance at beginning and end of plan year;
- Amounts contributed by employer and employee (if applicable) in the plan year;
- Cumulative amounts contributed by employer and employee; and
- Amount of pension benefits provided by amounts transferred into plan (under certain circumstances).

For a DB plan:

- Credited service to date, amount of pension to date, and any integration with public pension benefits;
- Solvency or transfer ratio;
- If plan is not fully solvent, statement that plan assets are not sufficient to cover liabilities on a plan termination basis, and confirmation that special payments are being made;
- Employee contributions and AVCs (separately) for the year and accumulated employee contributions and AVCs (separately) plus interest;
- Rate of interest applied to the different types of contributions;
- Earliest retirement date with an unreduced pension;
- Information related to optional ancillary contributions and benefits;
- Transfer Value of benefits;

- Information on the financial position of the plan; and
- Surplus rights.

Statements issued to federally regulated members must be addressed to both the member and his or her spouse.

It is important to note that the coming into force of the 2016 Agreement Respecting Multi-Jurisdictional Pensions Plans on July 1, 2016, affects the production of annual statements. For any financial year ending on or after July 1, 2016, statements issued to British Columbia, Saskatchewan, Ontario, Quebec, or Nova Scotia members will have to satisfy the requirements and deadlines applicable in the province in which the plan is registered, not the jurisdiction where the member is located.

For example, if an Ontario registered plan has members in Ontario, British Columbia and Saskatchewan, active and non active members in these three jurisdictions will receive statements based on Ontario requirements. On the other hand, for a Nova Scotia registered plan that also has Quebec members, only active members will be entitled to statements; it will no longer be required to issue statements to Quebec non-active members, spouses and beneficiaries as Nova Scotia legislation does not provide for these yet.

Statements on Termination, Retirement, Death and Marriage/Spousal Relationship Breakdown

When a member of a pension plan terminates membership, retires, or dies, the administrator must provide the member or his or her survivor(s) with a written statement of the member's benefits payable under the plan within a prescribed period.

The termination, retirement, or death statement updates the member's data for the period between the date of the most recent annual statement issued and the date of event. The statement must also present the addressee's available options for the payment of benefits along with explanations of these options. The statement will also include the deadline to select an option and the consequences of not meeting the deadline, such as any default option that will be imposed on the recipient.

Statements also have to be provided with respect to pension division upon marital breakdown. Depending on the pension division rules applicable in the jurisdiction, the statement will include either a standard calculation of pension value as prescribed by legislation, or the necessary data for an independent actuary to perform an evaluation of the benefits or data and benefit options. Some jurisdictions prescribe fees that may be imposed by the plan administrator in return for producing a statement valuing the member's benefits or processing the marriage breakdown. The prescribed fee may not cover the full cost of servicing the marriage breakdown to the plan or the employer, however.

Enrollment Form

In order to properly administer a pension plan, the administrator must collect and validate numerous elements of data. As an employee is onboarded, they are set up in the employer's system with personal data such as their employee number, tombstone data (including date of birth), date of employment, and date of membership. Information about the member's spouse, if any, and beneficiary designation(s) are typically collected via the administrator's online enrollment tool.

Administrative Procedures upon Retirement

When a member retires in a defined benefit plan, the administrator must confirm his or her marital status, given the rights to a survivor pension granted to the spouse by legislation. A *Declaration of Marital Status* form is typically used.

If the member has a spouse and the spouse wishes to waive his or her right to the mandatory survivor pension, a spousal waiver form will have to filed with the administrator. This form is either a prescribed form prepared and made available by the regulator or a form with a prescribed minimal content.

The member will be asked to provide banking information for the purpose of direct deposit. Income tax forms will be required for tax withholding from the pension consistent with the member's tax situation.

Proof of age will also be required from the member, and if the elected form of pension provides for a survivor pension payable to the spouse, a proof of age of the spouse.

Administrative Procedures upon Termination of Membership

Upon termination of active membership of a plan member, it is very likely that a transfer form such as CRA's T2151 (Direct Transfer of Single Amount under Subsection 147(19) or Section 147.3) or an administrator-made replacement form will be used to record the details of the transaction and confirm that any locked-in funds will be administered in accordance with legislation.

Federal and New Brunswick legislation requires the use of a prescribed form to confirm that locked-in funds will be administered in accordance with the legislation. In other jurisdictions, the confirmation requirement will be satisfied by a written document signed by a representative from the financial institution receiving the transferred money.

If the terminating member has a spouse, some jurisdictions will also require a spousal waiver to allow certain fund transfers, generally when funds are directed to life income funds. Where such waiver is required, the administrator will want to confirm the marital status of the member and a *Declaration of Marital Status* form will then be used.

Proof of age will also be required from the member and certain plans will also need proof of age for the spouse, if applicable.

Administrative Procedure upon Pre-Retirement Death

If a member dies prior to retirement, the administrator must confirm the member's marital status given that the spouse has priority rights to the death benefit, even over a named beneficiary, pursuant to legislation. A *Declaration of Marital Status* form will then be used.

If permitted by legislation, and the spouse wishes to waive his or her right to the death benefit, a spousal waiver form will have to be filed with the administrator prior to the member's death. This form is either a prescribed form issued by the regulator or a form drafted by the administrator. All provincial pension legislation, except for Newfoundland and Labrador, provides for the spousal waiver. Under the federal legislation, a plan may permit the spouse to make written surrender of his or her right to the pre-retirement death benefit in favour of dependant beneficiary as defined in the *Income Tax Act*.

Transfer forms may be required if the spouse is transferring the benefit to an RRSP or locked-in account. Some provinces require a pre-retirement death benefit payable to a spouse to be paid on a locked-in basis or paid in the form of a pension. A pre-retirement death benefit payable to a non-spousal beneficiary is paid as a cash lump sum.

Once again, proof of the age of the member will be required and if the benefit is payable to spouse, depending on the form of the benefit, a proof of the age of the spouse will be needed.

Administrative Procedures on Marriage/Spousal Relationship Breakdown

The administration of pension division on a marriage or spousal relationship breakdown is typically prescribed by legislation, but also depends on the terms of the court order or separation agreement (which may be termed a domestic contract, matrimonial property agreement, or some other term specified by legislation). The administrator is required to review the forms and supporting documents submitted by the parties and determine how and whether they can be administered as requested. If the terms of the documents are ambiguous or contravene legislation, the administrator may require clarification by the parties or even the revision of the court order or separation agreement.

Property division situations can be contentious and family lawyers may not fully understand the restrictions on property division set out by pension legislation. It is important that administrators understand the law and clearly communicate their concerns to the parties in an even-handed manner.

Use of Prescribed Forms

For their own protection, pension administrators should be using the prescribed forms that are set out by pension legislation or issued by the pension regulator (if any). Typically, the action will only be valid if the prescribed form is used.[14] If prescribed forms are not available, care should be taken that forms accurately reflect the current legislation, are not misleading, and do not create any potential liability for the administrator or service providers. A legal review of the forms is essential.

Electronic Communications

There has been increasing interest by plan administrators and members in the use of electronic communications and electronic signatures. However, regulatory guidelines and legislative requirements of the applicable jurisdiction must be considered. Typically, these require the member's or recipient's consent to electronic communications, along with a certain number of disclosures by the administrator.

CAPSA Guideline No. 2, published in 2002, sets out regulatory expectations for member's consent to receive communications in an electronic format, including communications that must be provided in written format pursuant to legislation. The Guideline addresses matters such as obtaining the member's consent, the required disclosures to go along with the member's consent, and subsequent communications, and the process for revoking consent. The Guideline also provides that paper copies of the communication must be made available to the member and that the information provided electronically must be capable of being

---

[14]   *Smith v. Casco Inc.*, [2011] O.J. No. 1817, 2011 ONCA 306 (Ont. C.A.).

retained. The Guideline also addresses requirements for electronic signatures.

Rules respecting electronic commnications have been written into the legislation of several jurisdictions, including Nova Scotia, Ontario, and the federal jurisdiction. Typically, these rules reflect some of the contents of CAPSA Guideline No. 2, although the federal rules are the most specific and detailed.

Chapter 6

FINANCIAL MANAGEMENT OF PENSION PLANS

Executive Summary[1]

Extensive media coverage of the financial health of Canadian pension plans and pension-related labour conflicts over the last few years has resulted in the public becoming much more aware of pension plans costs and finances. For some large organizations, the pension plan represents a significant cost and risk, and has resulted in significant analysis from the investment community.

It is important to note that there are many measurements to assess the "financial position" of a pension plan: going concern, solvency, wind-up, and accounting. Each of these measurements would normally result in a different stated financial position. In addition, the annual "cost" of a pension plan is often expressed using different bases: the going concern current service cost, which is the cost of benefits accruing in the current year determined on a going concern basis; the solvency or wind-up incremental annual cost, which is the estimated change in solvency or hypothetical wind-up liabilities over the current year; the required employer contributions to the plan, which would normally be the employer portion of the going concern current service cost and any special required contributions to fund past service deficiencies; and an accounting pension cost, as determined under the accounting standards on an accrual basis.

All these bases to measure the financial position and cost can result in many different outcomes. Investors and management will often focus on the figures presented in the financial statements, which are on an accounting basis. At the same time, management needs to understand their current cash contribution requirements, which are based on the going

---

[1] For more information on actuarial valuations and the calculation of solvency assets and liabilities, please consult the multi-jurisdictional charts in the *Canadian Employment Benefits & Pension Guide*. Morneau Shepell, *Canadian Employment Benefits & Pension Guide*, loose-leaf (Toronto: LexisNexis Canada, 2003). The table of contents for these charts appears at the back of this Handbook.

concern and solvency valuations. At times, management will also need to understand the financial impact of terminating the plan, which is provided by the wind-up financial position.

The financial management of a pension plan depends in part on which financial measurements are important to an organization balanced against how the organization wishes to manage their available cash.

This chapter will review the financial management of pension plans and its implications on a sponsoring company. Included for discussions are various standards used to determine the funding of the plan, including solvency funding versus going concern funding. Finally, a section on accounting for pension costs and obligations in the financial statements is presented.

Funding Policy Considerations

Funding policy deals with the allocation of assets towards the fulfillment of the pension promise. Sooner or later, assets must be transferred from the employer to the employee to provide the pension. At one extreme, the assets are transferred only as the benefits are paid to the retired employee or his or her survivors. This approach is referred to as "pay-as-you-go". At the other extreme, assets could be transferred immediately, so that the employee takes on the entire responsibility for ensuring that the assets are ultimately used for their intended purpose. Neither of these approaches involves "advance funding" or "funding" in the way that term is usually used.

In typical usage of the term, "advance funding" or "funding" of pension benefits involves the creation of a fund held by an outside third party, such as a trust company, a group of individual trustees or an insurance company. This fund receives the employer's contributions (and the employees' contributions, if any), earns investment income, and pays out the benefits promised by the plan as they arise.

Reasons for Funding

With the exception of supplemental arrangements for executives, private-sector pension plans have generally been funded over the last several decades. There are two significant reasons why this has occurred:

- The *Income Tax Act* (ITA) provides significant tax advantages for advance funding. In order to benefit from these advantages the pension plan has to be registered with Canada Revenue Agency;

- Pension standards legislation in the provincial and federal jurisdictions require advance funding to increase benefit security. It has been shown that these legislative funding requirements alone were insufficient in ensuring plan members would get 100% of their benefits upon plan wind up with an insolvent employer.

Even in the case of plans where these two reasons do not exist, there are nevertheless good reasons to fund a pension plan:

- The accumulated pension fund provides security that the employees will receive the promised benefits, regardless of the employer's fortunes in the future. In the absence of an adequate fund or other security, the employees' pension benefits may just be one of a long list of unsecured debts of the employer.

- Funding provides the employer with an orderly method of managing cash resources, and avoids the situation where contribution requirements rise out of control as the plan matures. It can also help insulate the employer from being hit with a double whammy of high pension payments during a period of economic distress. There is little comfort to employees in an unfunded pension plan when honouring financial commitments helps bring about the collapse of the employer — resulting in both lost jobs and lost pensions.

- Generally accepted accounting principles require the allocation of pension costs over the years that employees perform their services, regardless of when the benefits are ultimately paid. In the absence of advance funding, the recognition of accounting costs will ultimately lead to a large pension liability in the employer's financial statements. In some cases, this could impair the employer's ability to raise additional financing. When the pension promise is funded, the funding contributions offset this build-up of liability.

- Advance funding at an appropriate level can reduce or eliminate transfers of cost between generations of employees, shareholders, taxpayers, or other stakeholders.

Reasons for Not Funding

Where funding is not required by legislation, there may be other reasons not to fund a pension program in advance. In the private sector, the most commonly advanced reason for not funding is that the employer is able to achieve a higher after-tax rate of return by retaining assets within the business than would be possible in an invested fund. In that situation, funding the pension plan would increase its ultimate cost.

In the public sector, other reasons have been advanced for not funding the pension program. In particular, it has been argued that the perpetual nature of governments, combined with their vast ability to tax and borrow, eliminates any concerns regarding benefit security and cash management. It has been further argued that investment by government of large amounts of money in private capital markets is neither socially desirable nor necessarily financially advantageous, given the opportunity for politically motivated interference in the investment process.

How Much to Fund — Going Concern Versus Wind-Up

The assets needed for a plan to be "fully funded" can be considered from more than one perspective. A plan can be said to be fully funded on a "wind-up basis" if the existing assets are sufficient to provide for all benefits that have been accumulated for service to date, determined as if the pension plan were to be discontinued or wound up immediately. On a "going concern basis", the plan is assumed to remain in place indefinitely, and will be considered fully funded if the existing assets plus the service cost contributions in the future (which will depend upon the funding method used) and assumed investment income will be sufficient to enable all benefits, in respect of future service as well as past service, to be paid as they fall due.

It is quite possible for a pension plan to be fully funded on one of these bases (wind-up or going concern) and have a significant unfunded liability on the other basis. For example, a plan that bases benefits on end-of-career earnings might be able to meet all of its obligations if it were discontinued today, but not have sufficient assets to provide benefits that are based on significantly higher earnings levels expected in the future — at least not without significant increases in future rates of contribution. Conversely, some plans may call for special benefits to be provided in the event of plan discontinuance that would not normally arise in the normal operation of the plan. In these situations, a plan could be fully funded on a going concern basis, but underfunded on a wind-up basis.

How Much to Fund — Risk and Conservatism

Any approach to funding a pension plan involves making assumptions about future events — assumptions that will most likely turn out not to have been entirely accurate. In some cases, the future will turn out to be more favourable than assumed, and in other cases less favourable. In the past, actuaries included a degree of conservatism in selecting going concern actuarial assumptions for pension funding. That is, they made funding recommendations such that the likelihood of overfunding was greater than the risk of underfunding. Effective December 31, 2010, the Canadian Institute of Actuaries no longer required or permitted the use of margins for conservatism except as required by law or the terms of engagement with the plan's sponsor. The majority of regulators and plan sponsors still request that a margin of conservatism be included in the going concern assumptions.

In some ways, it seems almost obvious that overfunding a pension program is a more favourable outcome for everyone than is underfunding. After all, if the plan is overfunded, the benefits are more secure and the employer can enjoy reduced future costs. On the other hand, if the plan is underfunded, the benefits are less secure, and the employer's future contributions will need to increase.

However, things are not always so simple. In some cases, overfunding may mean that past generations of employees have received lesser benefits than they might have otherwise enjoyed. In other cases, there may be great pressure from employees for benefit improvements when a plan is overfunded. If a plan has become overfunded partly as a result of favourable investment returns and if these surplus funds are used up to improve benefits, when the financial markets experience their next downturn, these funds will not be available to offset investment losses, the plan could become underfunded and the plan sponsor may have to fund the deficit. Finally, the ongoing debate over surplus ownership, the *Monsanto* decision, which requires that employers deal with surplus distribution in the event of partial wind-up, and the limit on the amount of surplus that can be recognized under the accounting standards, have caused some employers to view an underfunded plan as the preferred approach.

Regardless of one's perspective on what is favourable or unfavourable, there is often a cost associated with adopting a conservative funding stance (for example, foregone use of cash and investment returns to the company). The need to manage the costs and risks associated with a particular funding approach has led to increasing use of a variety of tools, such as pension forecasting, pension modelling, scenario testing, and asset and liability matching.

Funding Methods

According to the Canadian Institute of Actuaries, the objectives in advance-funding a pension plan may include:

- Security of benefits;
- Orderly and rational allocation of contributions among time periods; and/or
- Intergenerational equity.

Any particular "orderly and rational allocation of contributions among time periods" is a funding method. Many funding methods have been developed, modified, redeveloped, and used over the years. The terminology used to describe and classify these various funding methods has also undergone significant modification over the years.

Cost Allocation Methods

Cost allocation methods are those that start by determining the total "cost" of the projected benefits to be provided (for both past and future service), and then allocating that cost directly to time periods. Typically, the allocation attempts to make the cost allocated to each future year equal in some sense — in dollar terms perhaps, or as a percentage of pay. This equal cost allocation may be done on an individual-by-individual basis, or only in respect of the plan as a whole. The allocation of cost to past time periods may be carried out on the same basis as for future periods, or on some entirely different basis.

Funding methods that fall into this family of methods go by names such as "entry age normal", "attained age normal", "aggregate", and "individual level premium". This family of methods has also been called "projected benefit methods" or "level premium methods".

One essential characteristic of this family of methods is that the cost of the plan for the current group of members, expressed in whatever measure is appropriate to the particular method, is designed to remain stable over the future working lifetime of the current group of members — provided, of course, that the various assumptions made in the calculations turn out to accurately reflect future events. As members come and go, however, and as actual experience unfolds, the actual contribution requirements may go up or down over time.

Benefit Allocation Methods

Benefit allocation methods allocate the projected benefits that are to be provided to specific time periods. The cost associated with a particular time period is then directly determined from the benefit allocated to that period. Benefits may be allocated based upon the way they accrue under the plan provisions, using only historical earnings and service, or they may be projected to retirement (or earlier death or termination) and allocated in proportion to service, salary, or some other relevant quantity.

Funding methods that fall into this family go by names such as "unit credit", "traditional unit credit", "accrued benefit", "projected unit credit", and "projected benefit method prorated on services". The benefit allocation family of methods has also been called "accrued benefit methods" or "single premium methods".

One characteristic of the benefit allocation method is that when it is applied to a closed group of plan members, the cost associated with future years tends to increase steadily, and sometimes quite steeply. This increase is mostly due to the ever-shortening period of time over which the compounding of interest can occur. It can also be magnified by the benefit allocation methodology, and by the decreased likelihood of termination as employees near retirement. As more and more private sector defined benefit pension plans are closed to new entrants, it is becoming more common to see significant increases in costs expressed as a percentage of covered payroll in these plans. For those defined benefit pension plans that are not closed to new entrants, new members are joining continually. As long as the average age of the plan membership is kept reasonably stable by new members joining at younger ages, the contribution rates required can also remain reasonably stable.

All things being equal, benefit allocation methods tend to result in lower levels of funding prior to retirement than do the corresponding cost allocation methods. At retirement, if all assumptions are met, the level of funding should be the same under both methods.

Forecast Methods

Unlike the previous two families of funding methods, which assess the funding adequacy of a pension plan at a single point in time based only on the current membership population, forecast methods are designed to assess funding levels over a lengthy period into the future, and typically involve consideration of new entrants. Using forecast methods, one could develop a funding regime that satisfies a broad range of criteria. For example, one might require that the plan be fully funded on a wind-up basis at each year end for the next 30 years, be fully funded on a going concern basis using one of the other methods at the end of that 30-year period, and ensure that benefit payments during the next 30 years can be met from contributions and investment income, without requiring a sale of assets — all while keeping the variation in the employer's contribution rate within some reasonably tight boundary.

Prior to December 31, 2010, the Canadian Institute of Actuaries' *Standards of Practice — Practice-Specific Standards for Pension Plans (2010)* indicated that if a plan is a registered pension plan (RPP) under the ITA, the forecast method should not be used in valuing the plan's liability for funding purposes. Effective December 31, 2010, the Canadian Institute of Actuaries' *Standards of Practice* indicates that forecast methods are an acceptable actuarial cost method for RPPs.

Forecast methods can provide valuable insight into how the funding of the pension plan under one of the more traditional methods is likely to proceed. This can assist the plan sponsor in developing funding policy, or in managing the funding decisions that must be made from valuation to valuation.

Traditionally, these methods have been applied only in the context of large pension plans, due to the cost associated with complex computerized pension models. However, with today's technology, similar techniques can now provide very valuable planning information at more reasonable cost even for small plans.

Terminal Funding

Under terminal funding, the employer contributes the present value of the benefits promised to each employee as that employee retires or terminates. There are no funds set aside in respect of employees who are still rendering service to the employer. Obviously, the employer's cost will vary widely from year to year, because the retirement pattern is usually irregular — particularly so in a plan with a small membership.

This form of funding was first recognized by the ITA in 1952, and was used in the context of pensions promised under collective bargaining agreements. Under many of those agreements, employees retiring during the term of the agreement were entitled to receive a pension for life, but those retiring after the agreement expired were not legally entitled to anything.

Terminal funding is not acceptable under pension standards legislation, but it often arises in the context of supplementary plans not subject to that legislation. In this context, the lack of benefit security while actively employed may be justifiable or even desirable, if the covered employees are senior executives whose own actions are responsible for the financial viability of the employer, or if the benefit is only payable if the senior exectuvie remains in the company up to retirement. However, in light of the ongoing inclusion of employees below the executive level in supplemental pension plans, questions of the appropriateness of terminal funding are often raised.

A variation on the concept of terminal funding is the use of letters of credit to secure supplemental pension promises to executives. In this case, it is the termination of the employer that triggers the funding, rather than the retirement of the employee. As long as the employer is financially viable, and makes the pension payments as they fall due, no funding is in place. As soon as that situation changes, the trustee that holds the letter has the responsibility to call on the letter of credit to fund the balance of the benefits owing to the employee.[2]

Pay-As-You-Go

Pay-as-you-go is not really a funding method at all, because there is no fund accumulated. The employer or plan sponsor simply pays the pension benefits out of current revenue as they fall due — or in the context of a national social security program, the current generation of employees/taxpayers pays for the benefits provided to the current generation of retirees. The advantages and disadvantages of this approach are precisely the reverse of the advantages and disadvantages of funding already discussed.

The pay-as-you-go method is prohibited under the provincial and federal pension standards legislation. However, it is a common method of providing supplemental executive benefits.

Old Age Security (OAS) and the Guaranteed Income Supplement (GIS) are operated on a pay-as-you-go basis. In contrast, the Canada and Quebec Pension Plans (CPP/QPP) operate on partial funding. Based on the December 31, 2012 valuation report for the CPP, the existing level of funding on a closed group approach is 17.4%.

Actuarial Assumptions and Methods

In order to assess the funding level of the plan or the pension cost and obligations for accounting purposes, it is necessary to make assumptions about a wide variety of possible future events and possible future characteristics of the plan and its members. Here are examples of matters about which assumptions are required:

- *Economic* — the discount rate or rate of return on investments, the rate of wage and salary increases, and the rate of increases in external indexes, such as the Consumer Price Index, the industrial aggregate wage index, the Year's Maximum Pension Earnings

---

[2]   More information on letters of credit is found in Chapter 13.

(YMPE) under the CPP/QPP, the maximum pension limit under the ITA, and the number of hours worked by employees, affecting benefits;

- *Social* — family composition, the likelihood of a spousal relationship at termination, death, or retirement, and the likely age differences between spouses;

- *Benefit entitlement and benefit continuance* — the incidence of early, normal, and deferred retirement, the incidence of disability and disability recovery, the incidence of death both before and after retirement or disability, and the incidence of termination of employment; the propensity of members to elect from among the various optional forms of benefit delivery; and future benefit adjustments; and

- *Other* — the level of administrative, investment and other expenses, taxes, and changes in levels of benefits and contributions under social security programs, etc.

The classification of assumptions into these groups is neither unique nor uniformly applied, because many of the assumptions are interrelated, and some contain aspects of more than one group.

Relationships Between Assumptions

Many assumptions are interrelated, particularly the economic assumptions. It is therefore not sufficient to consider each assumption in isolation. The assumptions must also be considered in relation to each other. For example, investment returns are commonly considered to comprise three components: an inflation component, a basic "risk-free" real rate of return, and a risk premium that reflects the market's demand for additional return to compensate for the acceptance of risk, in whatever form that may be. Similarly, increases in wages and salaries are commonly considered to comprise a number of components: an inflation component, a component reflecting increases in productivity generally, and components reflecting individual increases due to merit, seniority, and promotion. Normally, the inflationary component of these two assumptions, as well as of other assumptions that may be affected by inflation, should be the same.

The effect of a component that is common to several assumptions can be offsetting. For example, assuming a higher level of inflation will typically mean a higher discount rate (reducing pension costs), a higher rate of wage and salary increases (typically increasing pension costs), and a higher rate of post-retirement benefit increases, if applicable (also increasing pension costs).

Often the effect of differing assumptions and the way in which assumptions interrelate depends on the specifics of the plan provisions and the plan membership. For example, the expected future rate of increase in wages and salaries has a very considerable effect on the valuation of a final pay pension plan, but would generally have no effect on the valuation of a typical flat benefit pension plan. In addition, the rate of increase in general wages and salaries can affect the relative impact of the plan's integration with CPP/QPP and also the relative impact of the maximum benefit limits imposed under the ITA.

The assumptions selected by the actuary should be appropriate in the aggregate and independently reasonable unless the selection of assumptions that are not independently reasonable can be justified. The Canadian Institute of Actuaries' Standards of Practice — General Standards (effective January 1, 2012) define an appropriate assumption as the best estimate assumption, modified to incorporate margins for adverse deviations required by law or the terms of the engagement. The margin in each assumption, if required, should reflect the uncertainty of that assumption and of any related data.

Asset Valuation Methods

In the context of an ongoing funded pension plan, the assets are accumulated in the fund in order to pay the benefits as they become due. As the liabilities of the plan represent the value of these benefits, it would generally not be appropriate to measure the liabilities of the pension plan using a discount rate that is significantly higher than the rate of investment return that can reasonably be expected to be achieved in the long term by the assets held in the pension fund.

It is not obvious why or how the value placed on the assets might be affected by the pension plan's liabilities. Surely what you could realize by selling the assets is not related to the pension liabilities. Although the market value of assets, if such a value exists, is not dependent upon the pension liabilities, the market value may not always be the most appropriate value to use in the context of a going concern valuation, particularly if the assets are not expected to be sold. Market value is, after all, just a point-in-time value that is highly sensitive to changes in short-term outlooks.

For a going-concern valuation, it may be appropriate to use an asset valuation method that moderates or smooths out short-term market fluctuations in order to reduce the volatility of contributions.

As another example, a pension plan may hold a portfolio of assets — bonds perhaps — that produce cash inflows that are roughly matched to the expected cash outflows needed to pay a certain class of benefits. In that case, it may be most appropriate for those assets to be valued using a discount rate assumption comparable to that used to value the related liabilities. Why should the values be significantly different if the cash flows match?

The Standards of Practice of the Canadian Institute of Actuaries – Pension Plans (Part 3000) and the guidance notes issued by the Canadian Institute of Actuaries provide direction with respect to an actuary's advice regarding the "funded status" or "funding" of a pension plan.[3]

Funding Policy

Pension plans of all types invest assets in financial markets where the future performance cannot be predicted with accuracy. On the benefit side, defined benefit, multi-employer, and other forms of target benefit plans provide benefits whose costs also cannot be predicted accurately owing to the many unpredictable factors involved.

Given this, many pension plans have developed funding policies that plan for actions to be taken in response to future outcomes, whatever they may be. The New Brunswick Shared Risk Pension Plan Regulations require the establishment of an explicit funding policy with certain prescribed priority actions. So does Chapter 29 of the pension legislation in Quebec and section 55 of the Alberta pension regulation

Generally, the purpose of a funding policy is to support the plan reaching its goals by documenting level and timing of funding that the plan sponsor is willing to commit to, the strategies that may be employed as corrective actions to address over and underfunding situations based on defined requirements under the plan's founding documents, and to efficiently and effectively meet the pension plan's primary objectives. A common approach is to make indexing conditional on certain funding criteria.

Generally, a funding policy will cover the following items:

- Purpose of pension plan and funding policy;
- Benefit objectives;
- Stability of contributions;
- Risk management;

---

[3]   These standards can be viewed at the Canadian Institute of Actuaries website at http://www.cia-ica.ca.

- Actions contemplated when in an underfunded position;
- Actions contemplated when in an overfunded position;
- Margin in actuarial assumptions;
- Annual review.

The funding policy itself could be developed as a result of sophisticated modeling or as general guidance on actions acceptable to the plan sponsor or plan partners and considerations of risk tolerance limits.

Accounting for Pension Costs and Obligations

Background

In early 1986, the Canadian Institute of Chartered Accountants (CICA) who became in 2015 the Chartered Professional Accountants (CPA) Canada issued a revised accounting standard on accounting for pension costs and obligations: *CICA Handbook, Section 3460.* The revision dealt with the accounting for, and disclosure of, pension costs and obligations, and how they are to be reflected in corporate financial statements. In the United States, the equivalent requirements of the Financial Accounting Standards Board (FASB) were issued in 1985 and are now known as Accounting Standards Codification (ASC) 715.

The Section 3460 standards came into existence because it was thought that financial reporting of pension costs and obligations was inadequate. In fact, prior to that time most companies did not even disclose the existence of pension plans in their financial statements.

Rationale

The main objectives of accounting for pension costs are:

- To allocate the cost of the pension plan to the years in which employee services are provided;
- To facilitate comparability in financial statements between periods and between entities; and
- To provide disclosure of the value of plan assets and liabilities.

Prior to the Section 3460 standards, actual contributions required for funding purposes would be the *de facto* pension expense, which was not considered an appropriate basis for accounting for defined benefit pension plans. In years when the sponsor took a contribution holiday, pension expense would be nil; in other years, it would be the sum of contributions for current service cost and past service amortizations. The potential for large variations in pension costs from year to year and between companies, and thus on reported income, was considerable.

In 1994, the Accounting Standards Board (AcSB) established a task force to develop reporting standards that would be harmonized with the U.S. standards and also, wherever possible, would be in line with international standards. In 1999, the AcSB issued *CICA Handbook, Section 3461*, "Employee Future Benefits" (Section 3461). Section 3461 dealt with accounting for both pension plans and other post-employment benefit plans (post-retirement health plans, retirement awards, etc.).

Section 3461 was effective for fiscal years beginning on or after January 1, 2000, and superseded Section 3460. Changes were made in 2004 related to disclosure. These applied to fiscal years ending on or after June 30, 2004.

Canadian accounting standards underwent significant changes in 2010 and 2011, with the requirement that publicly accountable entities report in accordance with International Accounting Standard 19 — Employee Benefits (IAS 19), while non-public entities could continue to report under an amended version of Section 3461 for Private Enterprises, which was further replaced by Section 3462 in 2013 (Section 3463 for not-for-profit organizations). The remainder of this chapter provides a brief overview of some of the more important issues to be dealt with in accounting for pension costs and obligations.

In order to simplify presentation, only IAS 19 (as revised in 2011 and became effective January 1, 2013) will be covered in this section, as this is the pension accounting standard followed by the majority of Canadian publicly accountable entities.[4] Some parts of the following commentary are reproduced from the text of the revised IAS 19.

Objectives

As stated in IAS 19, the objective of accounting for the cost of future employee benefits "is to recognize a liability when an employee has provided service in exchange for employee benefits to be paid in the future, and an expense when the entity consumes the economic benefit arising from service provided by an employee in exchange for employee

---

[4]   For more detailed information, please visit the CPA Canada website at http://www.cpacanada.ca, as well as its standards boards' website at http://www.frascanada.ca.

benefits". Benefit plans are regarded as a component of an employee's compensation arrangement. Certain benefit plans require an entity to provide benefits to an employee in future periods for service currently performed by the employee.

Application

IAS 19 accounting standards apply to all employee benefit plans, including pension plans of publicly accountable enterprises, other than those in the public sector. Private enterprises and not-for-profit organizations can choose to report under IAS 19 or under Sections 3462 and 3463 of the CPA Canada Hanbook, respectively. For public sector financial reporting, Section PS3250 of the *CPA Public Sector Accounting Handbook* applies for pension benefits.

Defined Contribution Plans

A defined contribution plan is a benefit plan under which an entity pays a fixed contribution into a separate fund, and for which the entity has no legal or constructive obligation to pay further contributions if the fund has insufficient assets to pay for all employee benefits in respect of service to date. For a defined contribution plan, the expense is equal to the entity's contributions.

Defined Benefit Plans

A defined benefit plan is any plan other than a defined contribution plan. The determination of expense for a defined benefit plan is much more complex.

Terminology

The following are some of the terms used in IAS 19, which will be useful in understanding the accounting concepts discussed below.

- *Actuarial Assumptions* — These are the best estimates of the variables that will determine the ultimate cost of providing post-employment benefits (*i.e.*, discount rate, retirement age, mortality, rates of employee turnover, disability claim rates, rate of salary increases, *etc.*).

- *Actuarial Valuation* — This is an assessment of the financial status of a benefit plan. It includes the valuation of plan assets, if any, and the present value of the defined benefit obligation.

- *Present Value* — This is the discounted value of an amount or series of amounts payable or receivable at various times, determined as of a given date by the application of a particular set of actuarial assumptions.

- *Present Value of a Defined Benefit Obligation* — This is the present value, without deducting any plan assets, of expected future payments required to settle the obligation resulting from employee service in the current and prior periods. It is also known as "defined benefit obligation".

- *Fair Value of Plan Assets* — This is comprised of assets held by a long-term benefit fund and qualifying insurance policies. When no market price is available, the fair value of plan assets is estimated, for example, by discounting expected future cash flows using a discount rate that reflects both the risk associated with the plan assets and the maturity of those assets. Plan assets exclude unpaid contributions due from the entity to the fund, as well as any non-transferable financial instruments issued by the entity and held by the fund. Plan assets are reduced by any liabilities of the fund that do not relate to employee benefits, for example, trade and other payables and liabilities resulting from derivative financial instruments.

- *Net Defined Benefit Liability (Asset)* — This is the deficit or surplus (equal to the difference between the present value of the defined benefit obligation and the fair value of plan assets, if any), adjusted for any effect of limiting a net defined benefit asset to the asset ceiling. This net defined benefit liability (asset) is recognized in the entity's balance sheet.

- *Current Service Cost* — This is the increase in the present value of the defined benefit obligation resulting from employee service in the current period, reduced to reflect employee contributions during the period.

- *Past Service Cost* — This is the change in the present value of the defined benefit obligation for employee service in prior periods, resulting from a plan amendment (the introduction or withdrawal of, or changes to, a defined benefit plan) or a curtailment (a significant reduction by the entity in the number of employees covered by a plan, such as the closing of a plant, the discontinuance of an operation, or termination or suspension of a plan).

- *Settlement* — This is a transaction that eliminates all further legal or constructive obligations for part or all of the benefits provided under a defined benefit plan, other than a payment of benefits to, or on behalf of, employees that is set out in the terms of the plan and included in the actuarial assumptions. In practice, a settlement generally occurs when a significant number of employees are terminated, and annuity purchases or lump-sum payments are offered to employees in exchange for their rights to receive benefits.

- *Actuarial Gains and Losses* — These are changes in the present value of the defined benefit obligation resulting from experience adjustments (the effects of differences between the previous actuarial assumptions and what has actually occurred) and the effects of changes in actuarial assumptions.

- *Asset Ceiling* — This is the present value of any economic benefits available in the form of refunds from the plan or reductions in future contributions to the plan.

Actuarial Assumptions

The first step in accounting for defined benefit plans is to determine the actuarial assumptions. IAS 19 requires that the actuarial assumptions used for accounting purposes, represent management's best estimate based on market expectations for each of the assumptions and that they shall be unbiased and mutually compatible. Actuarial assumptions are unbiased if they are neither imprudent nor excessively conservative. Accounting assumptions differ from funding assumptions because the latter are usually made with the objective of benefit security and may include a provision for adverse deviations. In general, the assumptions for accounting purposes will differ from those used for funding purposes. This is confirmed by surveys that have consistently shown assumptions used for accounting purposes are less conservative than those used for funding purposes.

Plan sponsors will usually adopt and document a methodology for setting and reviewing the actuarial assumptions that will provide auditors with the confirmations that they require. Management must also keep the assumptions internally consistent, except for the discount rate for which specific guidance is provided. For example, the rate of inflation underlying an assumption about future increases of payable pensions should be the same as the rate of inflation underlying the assumption regarding future salary levels.

Discount Rate

Under IAS 19 the rate used to discount post-employment obligations (funded and unfunded) shall be determined by reference to market yields at the end of the reporting period on high quality corporate bonds. Although IAS 19 does not set out what "high quality corporate bonds" are, AA (or higher) corporate bonds are generally presumed to meet this qualification.

Furthermore, IAS 19 also states that market yields on government bond rates at the end of the reporting period should be used if there is no deep market for these high-quality corporate bonds. The Canadian corporate bond market is a deep market at low durations but there are very few long duration bonds. In 2011, the Canadian Institute of Actuaries published an Educational Note, "Accounting Discount Rate Assumption for Pension and Post-Employment Benefit Plans", which offered guidance to pension actuaries on the determination of discount rates to use for accounting purposes. The Educational Note described a methodology to extrapolate the long end of the high-quality corporate yield curve using yield information from high-quality corporate and provincial bonds.

IAS 19 states that the discount rate should reflect the estimated timing of benefit payments.

The traditional approach was to achieve this by determining a single-weighted average discount rate that reflects the timing and amount of the defined benefit obligation's expected benefit payments and use this discount rate for the determination of the current service and interest cost.

A refinement of the traditional approach is to determine a separate single-weighted average discount rate based on the expected benefit payments associated with the current service cost and use this rate to determine the current service cost.

A further refinement is to use the expected benefit payments and the individual spot rates to determine the interest cost. Under IAS 19, the corresponding average discount rate would have to be used to determine other cost components like interest income on plan assets and interest on the effect of the asset limit.

After the Securities and Exchange Commission indicated (in September 2015) that it was open to the application of alternative methods for determining the current service and interest cost under ASC-715, accounting for employee benefits, the major auditing firms are now open to using alternative approaches for accounting for pension and post-retirement benefits plans under both International Accounting Standards and US GAAP.

Actuarial Valuation Method

To determine the present value of the defined benefit obligation, the related current service cost, and past service cost (where applicable), the projected unit credit method (sometimes known as the accrued benefit method pro-rated on service) must be used.

Attributing Benefit to Periods of Service

Under IAS 19, an entity normally attributes benefit to periods of service based on the plan's benefit formula. If an employee's service in later years will lead to a materially higher level of benefit than in earlier years, an entity is required to attribute benefits on a straight-line basis.

Components of Defined Benefit Cost for the Period

For a defined benefit plan, the cost for a period under IAS 19 consists of three components:

- *Service cost (recognized in the profit or loss of the entity)* — This is comprised of three elements:
  - Current service cost (see terminology section);
  - Past service cost (see terminology section); and
  - Any gain or loss on settlement. This is the difference between the present value of the defined benefit obligation being settled (as determined on the date of the settlement) and the settlement price, including any plan assets transferred and any payments made directly by the entity in connection with the settlement.
- *Net interest on the defined benefit liability (asset) (recognized in the profit or loss of the entity)* — This is calculated by applying the discount rate discussed above to the net defined benefit liability (asset), both determined at the start of the reporting period, taking into account any changes in the net defined benefit liability (asset) during the period as a result of contribution and benefit payments. This can also be viewed as comprising:
  - Interest income on plan assets, which is calculated by applying the discount rate to the fair value of plan assets, determined at the start of the reporting period, taking into account any changes in the plan assets held during the period as a result of contribution and benefit payments;
  - Interest cost on the defined benefit obligation, which is calculated by applying the discount rate to the defined benefit

obligation, determined at the start of the reporting period, taking into account any changes in the defined benefit obligation during the period as a result of service cost and benefit payments; and

o   Interest on the effect of the asset ceiling, which is calculated by applying the discount rate to the effect of the asset ceiling, determined at the start of the reporting period.

- *Remeasurements of the net defined benefit liability (asset) (recognized in other comprehensive income)* — This is comprised of three elements:

o   Actuarial gains and losses (see terminology section);

o   The actual return on plan assets, excluding amounts included in net interest on the net defined benefit liability (asset), as described above. In determining the return on plan assets, the entity must deduct the costs of managing the plan assets, but not the other administration costs; and

o   Any change in the effect of the asset ceiling, excluding amounts included in net interest on the net defined benefit liability (asset), as described above.

- While the above components are recognized as other comprehensive income, they are not to be reclassified to the profit and loss statement in a subsequent period. The entity may transfer these amounts within equity.

Limit on a Defined Benefit Asset

IAS 19 limits the measurement of a net defined benefit asset to the lower of the accounting surplus in the defined benefit plan and the asset ceiling. The asset ceiling is the present value of any economic benefits available in the form of refunds from the plan or reductions in future employer contributions to the plan. The entity must determine the maximum amount that is available from refunds, reductions in future employer contributions, or a combination of both (although this combination should not be based on assumptions that are mutually exclusive).

A refund is available to the entity only if the entity has an unconditional right to it. This could occur during the life of the plan, irrespective of whether the liabilities are settled, or at the plan's wind-up. If the amount of the refund is determined as the full amount or a proportion of the surplus, rather than a fixed amount, no adjustment shall be made for the loss in value of money over time.

Questions have arisen about when refunds or reductions in future contributions should be regarded as available, particularly when a minimum funding requirement exists. In Canada, minimum funding requirements exist to improve the security of pension benefit promises made to members of an RPP. Such requirements normally stipulate a minimum amount or level of contributions that must be made to a plan over a given period. Therefore, a minimum funding requirement may limit the ability of the entity to reduce future contributions.

The International Financial Reporting interpretation Committee provided an interpretation on the matter (IFRIC 14), as set out below.

If there is no minimum funding requirement for contributions relating to future service, the economic benefit available as a reduction in future contributions is the future service cost to the entity for each period over the shorter of the expected life of the plan and the expected life of the entity. The future service cost to the entity excludes amounts that will be borne by employees. The future service costs shall be determined using the same assumptions as those applicable for the defined benefit obligation at the end of the reporting period. Thus, no change in benefits and a stable workforce shall be assumed, unless the employer is demonstrably committed to reducing its workforce, in which case the assumption would account for this reduction.

If there is a minimum funding requirement for contributions relating to future service, the economic benefit available as a reduction in future contributions is the sum of:

(a) Any amount that reduces future minimum funding requirement contributions for future service because the entity made a prepayment (*i.e.*, paid the amount before being required to do so); and

(b) The estimated future service cost in each period (as defined in the previous paragraph), less the estimated minimum funding requirement contributions that would be required for future service in those periods if there were no prepayment as described in (a). If the future minimum funding requirement contributions for future service exceed the future IAS 19 service cost in any given period, that excess reduces the amount of the economic benefit available as a reduction in future contributions (without being less than zero).

If an entity has an obligation under a minimum funding requirement to pay contributions to cover an existing shortfall on the minimum funding basis in respect of services already received, the entity shall determine whether the contributions payable will be available as a refund or reduction in future contributions after they are paid into the plan. To the extent that the contributions payable will not be available after they are paid into the plan, the entity shall recognize a liability when the obligation arises. The liability shall reduce the defined benefit asset or increase the defined benefit liability.

Termination Benefits

Benefits may be provided to employees by entities upon termination, and such benefits may take various forms such as lump-sum payments, periodic future payments, enhancements of post-employment benefits, or a combination thereof. Termination benefits result from either an entity's decision to terminate the employment or an employee's decision to accept an entity's offer of benefits in exchange for termination of employment. The liability and expense should be recognized when the entity can no longer withdraw the offer, or when the entity recognizes costs for a restructuring and involves the payment of termination benefits, whichever happens first.

Disclosures

While the disclosure requirements for defined contribution plans are very straightforward and simple, the requirements for defined benefit plans are significant and very detailed. The required disclosures enable users of financial statements to understand the entity's obligation to provide employee future benefits, and the costs, risks, and uncertainties associated with those obligations, for the purposes of making resource allocation decisions and assessing management stewardship.

Chapter 7

PENSION FUND INVESTMENT MANAGEMENT

Executive Summary[1]

This chapter begins with a review of the fundamental document of the investment program, the Statement of Investment Policies and Procedures. It then examines three core elements of an investment program: risk management, conflicts of interest, and investment manager selection, monitoring, and termination. A review of topical issues follows. These sections explore the benefits and challenges of alternative investments, liability-driven investments, outcome investing, the separation of alpha from beta, and responsible investing. The chapter also provides commentary on the investment principles in defined contribution plans. As well, the transfer of knowledge from Canada to other jurisdictions is examined. The chapter concludes with a summary of Canadian investment rules and regulations.

The Statement of Investment Policies and Procedures

The Statement of Investment Policies and Procedures ("SIPP") is the principle governing document for the investment process. It states the investment objectives. It discloses what the plan will invest in, how it will select, or terminate, an investment manager, how it will measure performance, and what risks are acceptable. It defines governance and accountability. It provides disclosure and continuity for stakeholders. All Canadian defined benefit pension plans are required by law to have a written SIPP. Member-directed pension plans, federally registered pension plans and certain provincially registered plans do not require a SIPP. Beginning in 2016, all Ontario-registered pension plans are required to file an initial SIPP, and any amendments thereto, with the Financial Services Commission of Ontario ("FSCO").

---

[1] For more information on Statements of Investment Policies and Procedures and permitted investments for pension plans, please consult the multi-jurisdictional charts in the *Canadian Employment Benefits & Pension Guide*. Morneau Shepell, *Canadian Employment Benefits & Pension Guide*, loose-leaf (Toronto: LexisNexis Canada, 2003). The table of contents for these charts appears at the back of this Handbook.

SIPP Content

Section 7.1(1) of the federal *Pension Benefits Standards Regulations, 1985* ("PBSR"), which is incorporated by reference into regulations governing pension plans registered in Ontario and in most other provinces, states the SIPP must disclose the following:

- Categories of investments and loans, including derivatives, options and futures.
- Diversification of the investment portfolio.
- Asset mix and rate of return expectations.
- Liquidity of investments.
- Lending of cash and securities.
- Retention or delegation of voting rights acquired through plan investments.
- The method of, and basis for, the valuation of investments not regularly traded at a marketplace.
- Related party transactions and the criteria to be used to establish whether a transaction is nominal or immaterial to the plan.

Section 7.1(1) and 7.1(2) of the PBSR also state that the plan administrator must have regard to the plan's liabilities and funded status in setting investment policy; determine what factors affect the funding and solvency of the plan; and describe the relationship of those factors to the investment policies and procedures. Aside from statutory disclosure, the Office of the Superintendent of Financial Institutions ("OSFI") has issued the guidelines on the content of a SIPP.[2] While the guidelines are not directly referenced in any specific law, the guidelines are consistent with the statutory requirement of an administrator of a pension plan to maintain a high standard of care for the members of the pension plan. Consequently, while the guidelines specifically address federally-registered pension plans, the guidelines are also the standard of good practice for provincially-registered plans. In accordance with the guidelines, the SIPP should:

- Identify responsibilities and accountabilities — the requirement covers the board, prominent sub-committees, such as the investment committee or pension committee, management, staff, and key external service providers, such as custodians, record keepers, investment managers and consultants.

---

[2] Office of the Superintendent of Financial Institutions Canada, *Memorandum: PPPD Investment Policy Guideline*, 2000.

- Set out the process for approving and implementing decisions.
- Enunciate relevant investment risks, how they are measured and how they are managed.
- Determine the frequency and format of reporting and performance measures.
- Identify policies and procedures to protect the plan assets from conflicts of interest.
- Address borrowing and pledging.

Administrator-directed defined contribution pension plans are expected to follow the required and recommended disclosures discussed above; however, the requirements for member-directed defined contribution plans have been amended recently to better conform to the unique characteristics of these types of plans.

In April 2015, the content requirements set out in section 7.1 of the PBSR were amended so they no longer apply to the investment of member-directed defined contribution pension plans; instead, the administrator is required to provide annually to members of such a plan a written statement that:

- Includes a description of each investment option available that indicates:
  o its investment objective;
  o the types of investments and the degree of risk associated with it;
  o its 10 largest asset holdings based on market value, each expressed as a percentage of total assets;
  o its performance history;
  o that its past performance is not necessarily an indication of future performance;
  o the benchmark that best reflects its composition;
  o the fees, levies, and other charges that reduce return;
  o its target asset allocation.
- Includes a description of how the member's funds are currently invested.
- Indicates any timing requirements that apply to the making of an investment choice.

For Ontario-registered pension plans that are member-directed defined contribution plans, or include a member-directed defined contribution provision, the expectation is that the SIPP will be prepared in accordance with the administrator's required standard of care and that the administrator "will give due consideration" to include the following information in the SIPP:[3]

- General investment philosophy.
- Permitted asset classes from which investment funds can be selected.
- The default investment option for member accounts where no selection is made.
- Monitoring service providers.
- Selecting, monitoring and terminating investment managers and funds.
- Plan expenses and investment fees related to the defined contribution plan or provision.
- Related party transactions.
- Information guidelines for plan members on investment options.

The administrator may set out the above information in a separate document and incorporate it by reference into the SIPP, or may simply include relevant excerpts in the SIPP. Additional details are provided in the section on defined contribution plans.

Administrators should note two additional content requirements that are applicable to all types defined benefit plans and defined contribution plans, whether administrator-directed or member-directed. First, the terms and provisions of the SIPP must be consistent with Schedule III of the PBSR. Second, in Ontario, effective January 1, 2016, a SIPP must disclose its policy regarding environmental, social and environmental ("ESG") factors. These points are discussed in greater detail in subsequent sections.

Review, Approval and Filing

According to the PBSR, an administrator must review and confirm, or amend, the SIPP with respect to the assets of a defined benefit or administrator-directed defined contribution plan or provision, at least once each plan year. However, the PBSR does not require an annual review and confirmation of SIPPs for member-directed defined contribution plans. The review frequency is subject to the demands of prudence. Further, there are no requirements to file a SIPP.

---

[3]   Financial Services Commission of Ontario, Statement of Investment Policies and Procedures (SIPPs) for Member-Directed Defined Contribution Pension Plans, IGN-003, 2015.

Ontario regulation imposes additional rules on the review, approval, and filing process. In addition to the requirements of the PBSR, Ontario-registered plans must:

- Ensure that the plan assets are invested in accordance with the SIPP at all times; as a result, amendments to a SIPP must be made before any change in investment policy is implemented.
- File with FSCO an initial SIPP and any amendments thereto within the prescribed time frame.
- Make the SIPP available to prescribed parties.
- Include prescribed content about the SIPP in annual or biennial statements to members or former members, respectively.

Risk Management

- In the section on the SIPP, it was stated the pension plan should identify key risks and its risk management program. Risks may be classified as asset-based risks, liability-based risks or asset-liability risks. An example of a liability-based risk is longevity risk, whereby members may live longer than actuarial projections. One investment tool used to manage longevity risk is the longevity swap, whereby the pension plan swaps its schedule of fixed pension payment, based on its estimate of longevity, with an insurer who, for a premium, will make additional payments to the member should they live longer than the plan's estimate.
- An example of an asset-liability risk is solvency risk, whereby assets are insufficient to satisfy liabilities upon a wind up of the plan. To assess solvency risk, an asset-liability study may be appropriate. Examples of asset-based risks are: active management risk, alternative asset risk, asset concentration risk, compliance risk, counterparty risk, country risk, currency risk, derivatives risk, index tracking risk, inflation risk, interest rate risk, investment style risk, leverage risk, liquidity risk, market risk, operational and settlement risks, and securities lending risk.
- Once the risks are identified, the fiduciaries may document their assessment of the severity of the risk to their pension plan, establish measurement tools, and articulate strategies to mitigate those risks. The process is illustrated below.

Risk	Description	Impact	Sample Measurements	Sample Strategies to Mitigate
Market	Risk that equity returns are below expectations	High	CBOE Volatility Index or "VIX" Standard deviation Value at risk or "VaR"	Diversify equity allocation by traditional means (geography, market capitalization and sectors, etc.) Diversify equity characteristics that produce desired outcomes (growth, yield, low volatility) Apply derivatives to lower market risk Lower the allocation to equity
Interest Rates	Risk that the value of obligations increases faster than the value of the assets due to interest rate changes	High	Duration Convexity Yield curve stress tests	Improve the match between the interest rate sensitivity of assets with obligations (duration match, cash flow match, hybrid match) Neutralize through a full immunization strategy
Inflation	Risk that inflation and costs are higher than anticipated	Moderate	Consumer Price Index Real return bonds Break-even inflation	Invest in assets sensitive to inflation
Currency	Risk of foreign currency denominated assets will depreciate against the base local currency	Low	Dollar exposure Hedged, benchmark Correlations of foreign currency exposures	Review relevant factors for hedging, which include, asset size, base currency, investment horizon, asset class, fees, etc.
Active Management	Active management detracts from instead of adding value above stated benchmarks	Low	Value-add Tracking error Information ratio Batting average	Differentiate the probability of success of active management by asset class and determine if the specific market has suitable characteristic for index tracking

Conflicts of Interest

The CFA Institute states the first guiding principle for pension plan fiduciaries is to "act in good faith and in the best interest of the scheme participants and beneficiaries".[4] Canada's Chief Justice McLaughlin has written that "the essence of a fiduciary relationship is that one party exercises power on behalf of another and pledges himself or herself to act in the best interest of the other".[5] In this section, we examine how conflicts of interest undermine the members' best interests in the context of investment issues. The scope of the discussion is necessarily broad since the affected parties are numerous, the specific situations varied, and the goal is to manage not only conflicts of interest, but also the appearance of conflicts of interest.

Affected Parties

Conflicts of interest apply to the legal pension plan administrator, often the sponsoring company or organization, through its governing board. In Ontario, the *Pension Benefits Act* prohibits an administrator from knowingly permitting its interests to conflict with its duties. If an administrator delegates responsibility for a specific task to an agent, that agent assumes a fiduciary role, and is subject to the same standard of care regarding conflicts of interest. Agents may be, among others, pension committees, investment committees, finance committees, human resource committees, employees, investment managers, actuaries, third-party administrators, or custodians. The wide scope of affected parties means a wide scope of potential situations that may trigger conflicts of interest.

Conflict Situations

The following list provides examples of situations that pose conflicts or potential conflicts of interest in the investment function:

- Acceptance of any gift, service, favor, entertainment, or any other thing of value from anyone currently engaged by or seeking business from the pension plan if it could reasonably be expected to influence a decision or be considered a reward.

---

[4] CFA Institute, Code of Conduct for Members of a Pension Scheme Governing Body, 2008.

[5] Mitch Frazer, "Minimizing the Risks of Personal Liability in Pension Plan Governance by Meeting Fiduciary Duties", Canadian Institute's 12th Annual Advanced Forum on Pension Law, Litigation and Governance, Toronto, January 25-26, 2011.

- Participation in an investment manager search or investment provider search while employed by the investment manager or investment provider.

- Ownership of an investment fund that is managed by an individual who is a plan fiduciary.

- Captive execution, whereby an investment manager conducts all securities trading through a single, often affiliated, broker-dealer, rather than seeking the best available execution for the pension plan's securities trading.

- "Soft dollar" arrangements, whereby a pension plan pays a higher trading commission in return for services other than trade execution, such as research.

- Revenue sharing arrangements, in which a mutual fund charges a pension plan for mutual fund expenses and allocates a portion of its expense ratio to pay a third-party administrator. If the third party administrator provides a bundle of services to the sponsor and its pension plan, the administrator must direct the reimbursement exclusively to the pension plan.

- The party responsible for the valuation of the pension assets and for the investment of the pension assets is one and the same party.

Managing Conflicts

To manage conflicts of interest, the pension plan may establish a written policy on conflicts of interest. The Canadian Association of Pension Supervisory Authorities ("CAPSA") recommends the following:

The plan administrator should provide for the establishment of a code of conduct and a policy to address conflicts of interest. The plan administrator should establish a code of conduct for both the plan administrator and its delegates. The code of conduct should set out required behaviour, establish a control procedure for conflicts of interest, and provide for due process and a dispute resolution mechanism. The plan administrator should always behave in a manner that reflects its fiduciary and other obligations.

To ensure the code of conduct is effective, and that it also applies to delegates, the plan administrator should set up a review process. The conflict of interest policy should set out an appropriate procedure to disclose and address conflicts of interest. The policy should address both actual conflicts and the appearance of conflicts.[6]

Practical applications of the CAPSA guidelines may include:

- The provision of training on conflicts of interest.
- For new fiduciaries to the pension plan, an initial conflicts certification, that includes a declaration of all potential conflicts, and an annual certification thereafter.
- Acceptable limits on the acceptance of gifts in a variety of contexts and documentation of any gifts received.
- The manner (written or verbal to the chair, secretary or other party) and the timing (immediate, within five days, etc.) of disclosure of real or perceived conflicts of interests as they occur.
- A conflicts registry that records conflicts of interest disclosure, including the acceptance of any gifts.
- Required action in the event of a conflict of interest, such as abstention from a vote or exclusion from any deliberations.
- Receipt of disclosure of:
  o the conflicts of interest policy of the plan's investment service providers;
  o the affiliations of the pension plan's investment manager with other investment firms, broker-dealers, mutual funds;
  o the trading allocation policy of the plan's investment managers;
  o revenue sharing.
- Separation of the office of the chair of the committee that oversees investments from the chair of board of trustees or board of directors or from the chair of any delegated committee that oversees pensions.
- Inclusion by reference to the conflicts of interest policy in the plan's SIPP.

Two Hats

In the event an organization fulfills two roles, or wears "two hats", by serving as both the pension plan sponsor and the pension plan administrator, the organization may find it is in a conflict position in

---

[6] Canadian Association of Pension Supervisory Authorities, Guideline No. 4 Pension Plan Governance Guidelines and Self-Assessment Questionnaire, 2004, p. 9.

which a decision may favour the sponsor to the detriment of the pension plan or vice-versa. In these situations, the organization should consider carefully which "hat" it is wearing and, if it is wearing its pension plan hat, it must act in the best interests of the pension plan.

Manager Selection, Monitoring, and Termination

Manager Selection

Once an investment policy has been established by the board, management must implement the policy. Because very few Canadian funds have a large internal investment staff, external manager selection is a key implementation issue.

The first step in manager selection is to consider the following issues relating to manager structure:

- Number of managers.
- Type (specialty or balanced).
- Style (growth, core, or value).
- Primary approach (fundamental or quantitative).
- Active management or passive index investment.

The factors affecting the issues relating to manager structure include:

- Cost.
- Resources required to supply oversight.
- Diversification.
- Volatility relative to a benchmark.
- Varying expertise within one manager in different asset classes.
- Ability to add value by switching among asset classes.
- Market efficiency of different asset classes.

Once the manager structure has been settled, the search for an individual manager begins with a determination of the essential attributes of the desired manager. These attributes may include the following:

- Expertise in a specific asset class.
- An established, stable investment team.
- A minimum level of assets under management.

No significant issues involving the overall organization;

- Low portfolio turnover.
- Above median performance over the past five years.

- Below median performance volatility over the past five years.
- Reasonable fees.

These attributes are used to screen a large universe of managers into a long list of candidates.

The long list of candidates is then subjected to detailed quantitative and qualitative examination, which analyzes organizational stability, personnel turnover, investment philosophy, investment process, performance results, volatility results, and the return correlation with other incumbent managers. The outcome is a short list of candidates from which finalist candidates are interviewed and the successful manager is selected.

Superior past performance is not predictive of superior future performance. Consequently, it is imprudent to select a manager based principally on superior past performance. Further, the fiduciary responsibility of the administrator is not to guarantee a certain performance result. The fiduciary responsibility of the administrator is to ensure that the manager search is soundly based on the application of a systematic and informed decision-making process.

Manager Monitoring

It is the fiduciary responsibility of the plan administrator to regularly monitor and evaluate investment performance. Individual portfolios and individual managers within the fund are measured against portfolio specific benchmarks. These individual portfolios, for example, a Canadian equity portfolio, will often be similar across funds. As a result, peer comparisons are also useful to assess manager performance.

The assessment of groups of managers is less straightforward, because total fund return corresponds closely to the fund's policy asset mix. To the extent that the policy asset mix of a fund reflects the unique characteristics of the fund, total fund return is not directly comparable across different funds. However, total fund return is also measured against an overall policy benchmark specified in the SIPP. The difference between the fund's total return and its policy benchmark return is the fund's value-added return.

Some SIPP's specify that, for the purpose of strengthening pension fund governance, independent third parties are responsible for monitoring, evaluating, and reporting to the board or investment committee on the investment program's performance relative to policy and benchmarks.

In respect of promoting comparability in the measurement of manager performance, the CFA Institute provides guidelines in its Global Investment Performance Standards (GIPS). GIPS specifies the use of total return, time-weighted rates of return that adjust for external cash flows (except for private equity, which uses an internal rate of return calculation), geometric linking of sub-period returns, the inclusion of cash and cash equivalents, and the deduction of trading expenses.[7]

Manager monitoring involves the measurement of risk as well as return. Risk-adjusted return measures for equity managers include the following: tracking error, information ratio, Sharpe Ratio, Treynor Ratio, Sortino Ratio, standard deviation, value at risk, upside and downside capture and batting average.

Manager Termination

Manager underperformance is typically handled through a process that defines a progression of steps that are undertaken if underperformance persists. The following describes a four-step plan of action:

- A manager who fails to achieve a predetermined performance level for a predefined period is placed "on watch".
- If the manager fails to achieve an acceptable performance level after a defined period, a series of reviews are triggered as follows: a review of the portfolio's mandate, a review of the appropriateness of the benchmark, a review of the manager's compatibility with the fund's objectives, and an attribution review of where the manager is adding or subtracting value.
- A complete reassessment of the manager's structure, decision-making, and personnel.
- Termination of the manager and the search for a replacement manager.

Alternative Investments

Types of Alternatives

Alternative investments comprise private equity, hedge funds, commodities, and infrastructure. Private equity provides capital to enterprises not quoted on a stock market. The two main types of private equity are venture capital and buyout. Venture capital can be used to develop new products and technologies. Buyout capital facilitates the buyout of a privately owned business or the buy-in of a business by

---

[7]   CFA Institute, Global Investment Performance Standards Handbook, 2012.

experienced managers. Methods of investment include limited partnerships, co-investment, and direct investment.

Hedge Fund Research, Inc., a specialist in hedge fund indices, tracks 7,000 hedge funds and funds of hedge funds. It categorizes its database into four principal hedge fund strategies: equity hedge funds, event driven funds, macro funds, and relative value funds. Equity hedge funds hold long and short positions in equities and equity derivatives. For example, 130/30 hedge funds are equity funds in which the manager short sells 30% of the portfolio and uses the proceeds to maintain a long position of 130%. Market neutral funds are equity funds in which 100% of the underlying market exposure is removed.

Event driven funds maintain equity and debt positions in companies involved in significant corporate transactions such as mergers, restructurings, or takeovers. Macro funds search for return in equity, fixed income, currency, and commodity markets based on movements in major underlying economic variables. Relative value funds seek to exploit price discrepancies between related securities such as the price difference between an equity issue and its related convertible debt.

With respect to commodities, funds hold a wide range of these types of alternative investment: energy, agricultural, industrial metals, and precious metals. Securities used include commodity index futures, over-the-counter derivatives, commodity futures, and commodity-linked bonds. The final category of alternative investments is infrastructure. The $9 billion infrastructure portfolio of the Ontario Teachers' Pension Plan, held at the end of 2011, illustrates the range of possible infrastructure investments: gas and water distribution networks, toll roads, pipelines, airports, power generation facilities, and port facilities.

The Benefits of Alternative Investments

Proponents of alternative investments cite three main benefits: higher return, better matching, and greater diversification. Alternative markets may offer a premium return because they are less efficient and less liquid. Hedge funds argue further that the prospect of additional gain is driven by an opportunity set that is larger than that of the traditional portfolio manager. Hedge funds can short sell and capitalize on poor performing equities, and hold leveraged long positions with the proceeds of short sales.

Advocates of alternatives also highlight the ability of infrastructure assets and private equity to match the long-term character of liabilities. Matching is also achieved through the ability to hedge inflationary increases in the benefit promise with assets that rise with inflation such as commodities and many infrastructure assets. Finally, it is held that there is a reduction of overall portfolio risk because alternative assets have a low correlation with stocks and bonds.

Potential Pitfalls and Challenges of Alternative Investments

Valuation and performance measurement are challenges for alternative assets. The determination of fair value in infrastructure and private equity will involve subjective judgments. Furthermore, there are no standard benchmarks for many alternative investments. The implication is that two funds with identical investments in the same private equity venture will likely report radically different value-added returns if they use different benchmarks.

Another concern is the use of leverage in many alternative investments. The multibillion dollar losses at Barings and Société Générale, and the bankruptcies of Orange County, Long Term Capital Management, and Amaranth Advisors are reminders of the dangers of leverage.

Emerging strategy risk should also be acknowledged. Alternative assets have short histories and lack robust data. These short histories should temper confidence regarding studies showing weak correlations between alternative assets and traditional assets.

Alternatives also tend to be high cost assets. A hedge fund manager will often charge a base fee and a fee for performance. Such fees are often several times the investment management fee for a stock or bond portfolio. High cost is compounded when, to diversify risk, a pension fund may own private equity or hedge funds in a fund of fund arrangement. This arrangement introduces a manager of manager tier of fees. Investing in alternative assets also tends to be labour intensive dealing with non-standard transactions, which involve higher costs.

There may also be less control over alternative investments. For example, the standard separation of duties between a discretionary investment manager and a custodian, where the manager who makes the investment decisions does not have direct access to the assets, and the custodian who safeguards the assets does not make the investment decisions, is not always in place for alternative investments.

Finally, funds should be aware of the regulation to which alternative asset portfolio managers are subject. In Canada, portfolio managers or advisers to hedge funds are registered. In the U.S., most hedge fund advisers are exempt from regulation.

Liability-Driven Investing

Risk management often focuses on asset return risk: the variation in returns of individual investment managers either on an absolute basis or around a benchmark or the variation in total returns for the whole asset portfolio. However, the greater risk is the risk that a plan fails to meet its funding objectives due to an imbalance between the values of assets and liabilities. If assets are growing but liabilities are growing faster, the mismatch between assets and liabilities trumps any concern over asset return volatility. The thesis of liability-driven investing is that if the investment policy is to help meet the pension liabilities, a superior result is achieved when liabilities are included in the investment process.

The first step in liability-driven investing is to model plan liabilities. Essentially, all investments and all plan liabilities can be expressed as a stream of future expected cash flows. After the cash flows have been estimated, there are numerous ways to match assets and liabilities. One straightforward method is to try to match the annual cash flows over time. A second method is to match the average cash flows over specified period ranges (such as one to five years, six to 10 years, 11 to 15 years, and so on).

A third model represents the "low risk" match for plan liabilities as a portfolio of nominal and real return bonds. This model measures how liabilities change in value according to changes in nominal interest rates and real rates. Changes in its value would correspond roughly to changes in the value of the benefit promise due to fluctuations in inflation and nominal interest rates. The liability model allows an examination of the match or mismatch between assets and liabilities.

If it is observed that the duration of the liability portfolio is much longer than the duration of the asset portfolio, the latter duration can be extended by adding long-term bonds, by substituting long-term bonds for short-term bonds, or through interest rate swaps. Alternatively, if the liability portfolio contains a high proportion of real return bonds (reflecting inflation-indexed benefits), the policy asset mix could raise its inflation sensitivity by allocating funds to inflation-linked assets.

Limitations of Liability-Driven Investing

The limitation of liability-driven investing is the impact on asset returns. Perfect matching between assets and liabilities, called "immunization", means asset growth equals exactly liability growth. The mismatch risk is zero. However, higher expected long-term return is sacrificed to achieve a closer match with the liabilities. In the event that the plan's liabilities exceeded assets before immunization, the assets will never "catch up" to the liabilities under immunization. Furthermore, under immunization, where asset growth equals exactly liability growth, asset returns can never contribute to higher benefits or lower contributions. The limited availability of certain types of securities, such as Canadian real return bonds, also constrains liability-driven investing.

Outcome Investing

Given the limitations of a strict liability-driven approach, a strategy that combines return-seeking assets with liability-hedging assets likely has more application to most pension funds. For example, the typical 60%/40% allocation between equities and fixed income could be replaced with a 60% allocation to return-seeking assets and a 40% allocation to liability hedging assets. The liability hedging can be accomplished by the methods described above.

The determination of return-seeking assets needs to be carefully considered. The temptation is to select highly aggressive return-seeking assets to compensate for the significant portion of the pension fund that has been allocated to hedging. On the contrary, the return-seeking assets should stress long-term value added with protection against risk of loss and excessive volatility.

One strategy that combines return-seeking and liability-hedging assets focuses on diversifying return-seeking assets by objective or outcome. The outcome–based portfolio may include absolute return assets, yield-generating assets, and low volatility assets, uncorrelated or lowly correlated with the rest of the funds assets. The focus represents a departure from the traditional basis for equity asset allocation, which is based on geography (Canadian, U.S., and international equities) and style (growth, core, and value).

Further, the allocation between return-seeking assets and liability-seeking assets should not be static; rather, it should be dynamic. To illustrate, as risk in the pension plan decreases, as evidenced by an increase in the funding ratio (the ratio of assets to liabilities), the pension fund should lower its risk profile, reducing the allocation to return-seeking assets and increasing the allocation to liability-hedging assets.

The Separation of Alpha and Beta

Alpha as Skill or Chance

Beta is the return of the portfolio that is attributable to the exposure to the broad market. Alpha is the return in excess of that which is attributable to the broad market. The central question is whether alpha is the product of an investment manager's superior knowledge, analysis, and skill, or simply the product of random chance.

There are two opposing views. Supporters of the efficient market hypothesis argue that security prices reflect all available public information. Manager skill cannot generate additional returns. Over the short term alpha is the product of random chance, and over the long term will net to zero. Also, to the extent that the broad market return represents the return of all market participants, in aggregate, alpha must sum to zero.

On the other hand, behaviouralists contend that markets are populated by participants who act irrationally. These irrational investors render markets inefficient. They create the opportunities for skillful managers to capture alpha. On a global basis, large pension funds allocate roughly 70% of their total assets to active management in search of alpha. These funds appear to believe that they can beat the market.

In practice, the arguments in favour of passive index investing are:

- Low percentage management fees relative to active management.
- No active management risk.
- Low portfolio transaction costs.
- Returns close to benchmark returns.

The arguments against passive investing are:

- High dollar minimums make index investing impractical for small-sized pension funds.
- No opportunity to lower risk relative to the benchmark.
- Returns that are typically less than the benchmark by the amount of the index management fees.

The Alpha-Only Portfolio and Beta-Only Portfolio

Financial engineering is able to separate alpha from beta. In a Canadian equity portfolio, a manager can create a derivative position so that any rise or fall in the portfolio due to the general market is offset exactly by a fall or rise in the derivative position. The manager is left with an alpha-only "market neutral" portfolio. The fund meanwhile can gain market exposure through passive indexation or enhanced indexation to satisfy the requirements of its policy asset mix.

Proponents of the separation of alpha and beta cite potential benefits in performance, risk, and cost. A fund may want to hire a manager who is judged to be very skilled but who invests in a market deemed to be too risky. If the fund separates alpha from beta it is possible to hire the manager but avoid exposure to the undesirable market. Risk management is facilitated because the return correlation of an individual alpha portfolio can be measured against all other alpha portfolios and all beta portfolios. The fund can then strive to lower overall asset risk or seek higher returns per unit risk. In addition, the separation of alpha from beta provides a clear delineation for governance purposes.

However, the separation of alpha and beta is based upon the belief that alpha will be positive. If positive alpha is not achieved, this approach could lead to higher agency costs and therefore lower after-fee returns.

Some plans in Canada and Europe have adopted the alpha/beta separation on a plan-wide basis. Investment teams are constructed as beta teams or alpha teams. Other plans are contemplating the same plan-wide approach.

Responsible Investing

Background

Established in 1989, Canada's Responsible Investment Association ("RIA") (formerly the Social Investment Organization) describes responsible investment as "the integration of environmental, social and governance… factors into the selection and management of investments…".

Examples of Environmental, Social and Governance Issues

The CFA Institute provides the following list of key environmental, social and governance ("ESG") issues, with the caveat that the list is not exhaustive.[8]

Environmental	Social	Governance
• Carbon emissions, greenhouse gas emissions • Climate change • Ecosystem change • Facilities citing environmental risks • Hazardous waste disposal / clean up • Pollution • Renewable energy	• Animal welfare • Child labour • Discrimination • Diversity (employee / Board) • Facilities citing social risks • Genetically modified organisms • Living wage disputes • Predatory lending	• Cumulative voting • Dual-class share structure • Executive compensation • Majority voting • Poison pills • Say on pay • Separation of chairperson / CEO position

---

[8]　CFA Institute, Social, Environmental and Social Issues in Investing, 2015.

Environmental	Social	Governance
• Resource depletion • Toxic chemical use	• Political contributions • Political risk of involvement in troubled markets, countries • Sexual harassment • Slave labour	• Shareholder rights • Staggered Boards • Takeover defenses

Global Trend to Responsible Investment

The RIA estimates there was more than $600 billion managed under responsible investment guidelines in Canada in 2013, compared with $50 billion in 2000.[9] The Principles of Responsible Investment Association ("PRI"), an independent organization supported by the United Nations, reports that the trend to responsible investment is a global phenomenon. There are nearly 1,500 signatories, including 79 Canadian signatories, to its key principles. The signatories are from over 50 countries and represent US$60 trillion in assets.

Common Responsible Investment Strategies

Positive and Negative Screens

Screening is the application of social or environmental value judgments to the investment process. Negative screens exclude companies that engage in activities that the screener judges to be negative such as tobacco production, child labour, weapons manufacturing, or pornography dissemination. Companies that operate in countries known for human rights violations may also be excluded. Positive screens include companies that engage in socially positive activities such as progressive employee relations policies, strong community involvement, or a commitment to a healthy and sustainable environment.

Community Investment

The objective of community investment is to improve the economic and social development of local communities. Community investments help to create local jobs, develop local enterprises and expertise, and provide valuable services to low income or disadvantaged groups. Entrepreneurs,

---

[9]   Responsible Investment Association, 2015 Canadian Responsible Investment Trends Report, 2015.

co-operatives, and not-for-profit groups are often the recipients of community investments.

Shareholder Advocacy

Shareholder advocacy involves the attempt by a shareholder to influence corporate behaviour through corporate communication, shareholder proposals, proxy voting, and divestment.

Integration of ESG Factors into Security Analysis

Unlike positive or negative screening, to create a suitable universe for further analysis, the integrated approach is more nuanced, embedding ESG factors into the analysis process for individual securities. The use of ESG factors is one component part of the overall security analysis process so that, on their own, ESG factors do not necessarily determine the inclusion or exclusion of a security from a portfolio.

Proponents of and Opponents to ESG

The Canadian Pension Plan Investment Board believes that "organizations that manage environmental, social and governance (ESG) factors effectively are more likely to endure, and create sustainable value over the long term, than those that do not".[10] The belief is more aspirational then empirical since research indicates that there is no statistically significant performance difference between responsible investment mutual funds and conventional mutual funds, or between responsible investment indices and traditional indices.

Some pension plans reject ESG factors on the basis that any constraint, no matter how well intentioned, contravenes the plan's fiduciary obligation to achieve the best long-term return for the plan's participants and their beneficiaries.

Further, while ESG factors may be conceptually appealing and easy to understand, there are practical difficulties which arise, as ESG issues can be subjective and complex. For example, a pension plan may decide to avoid equity securities involving alcohol, tobacco, or gambling. How then does the pension plan treat the debt securities of governments that earn tax revenue from alcohol, tobacco and gambling?

---

[10]   Canadian Pension Plan Investment Board, *2014 Report on Sustainable Investing*, 2014, p. 2.

Regulatory Ramifications of ESG

Effective January 1, 2016, FSCO requires that pension plans registered in Ontario disclose in the pension plan's SIPP whether or not ESG factors are incorporated into the plan's investment policies and procedures. If ESG factors are incorporated into the plan's investment policies and procedures, FSCO requires a description of how these factors are incorporated.[11] The disclosure requirement is the first of its kind in Canada, although similar provisions exist in the U.K., France, Germany, Sweden and Belgium.[12] FSCO highlights the fact that the issue of ESG factors is one of disclosure not advocacy. It requires pension plans to disclose their policies on ESG factors, not necessarily to adopt ESG factors. Given the recent effective date of the regulation, we expect pension plans and their investment managers will be developing and updating their policies and procedures on ESG factors, so it will be important to monitor the evolving response to this requirement.

Defined Contribution Plans

Difference from Defined Benefit Plans

Defined contribution plans differ from defined benefit plans in respect of goals and risk, and these differences have ramifications for the investment programs of each type of plan. The goal of a defined benefit plan is to provide a defined or set retirement benefit to its members, the terms of which are established in the pension plan's constating documents. On the other hand, the goal of a defined contribution plan is to accumulate assets for the member during his or her years of work service that may be used to contribute to the member's income during the member's retirement years.

The key difference between the plans is the party who bears the investment risk. Given the employer's guarantee to the member, the investment risk of a defined benefit plan is borne by the employer. Defined contribution plans provide no comparable guarantee, so the investment risk is borne entirely by the member.[13]

---

[11]   Financial Services Commission of Ontario, Environmental, Social and Governance (ESG) Factors, IGN-004, 2016.

[12]   Rick Baert, "Ontario Requiring All DB Funds To Disclose ESG Data", Pension and Investments, January 9, 2015.

[13]   Exceptions to this general rule may be found in hybrid plans. A hybrid plan combines the elements of defined benefit and defined contribution plans; for example, a hybrid plan may provide the member with a benefit that is the greater of a defined benefit provision and a benefit achievable through the plan's defined contribution provision.

Basic Types of Defined Contribution Plans

There are two basic types of defined contribution plans that vary according to the party that directs the investment decisions: administrator-directed plans and member-directed plans. In an administrator-directed plan, the administrator establishes the investment policy, including the policy asset mix, and determines the number of investment managers to retain and selects the investment managers based on considered criteria. In this regard, the administrator-directed plan is similar to the defined benefit plan. In a member-directed plan, the member decides on how to invest the member's contributions and those of his or her employer.

Bundled and Unbundled Structures

A defined contribution plan may be established on an unbundled or bundled basis. In the unbundled case, the administrator selects, by asset class, the individual investment managers from a universe of available managers; selects a custodian to safe keep the assets; and selects a record keeper to maintain individual member records.

In the bundled case, the administrator selects a third-party administrator that combines the custodial, record keeping, and investment functions into a single service package. In the bundled case, the administrator chooses investment options that are offered by the third-party administrator on an investment platform comprising investment funds eligible for defined contribution plans. The third-party administrator is usually an insurance company that can offer the administrator similar services for other retirement assets such as registered and non-registered retirement savings plans.

Standard of Care

It is important to note that the delegation of functions, whether to individual investment managers, record keeper, and custodian, or to a bundled service provider, does not remove the administrator's ultimate responsibility for these functions. The administrator has a duty to provide a standard of care appropriate to a fiduciary and, in the particular case of these delegations, has a duty to reasonably monitor the investment managers, record keeper, custodian, and third-party administrator.

Earlier, it was stated for Ontario-registered pension plans that are member-directed defined contribution plans, or include a member-directed defined contribution provision, the expectation is that the SIPP will be prepared in accordance with the administrator's required standard of care and that the administrator "will give due consideration" to certain key elements of an investment program. In other words, whether or not there is disclosure in the SIPP, the administrator should consider certain core investment elements in establishing its investment program for the purpose of good governance. Below we provide added detail.

- The investment philosophy:
  - o This refers to the plan's investment principles, beliefs and assumptions and the investment strategies and vehicles that are appropriate to the investment philosophy. Here the administrator can express its views on active versus passive management, the advantages and disadvantages of different fund vehicles, the virtues of diversification and liquidity, and the relationship between risk and return.
- Permitted asset classes from which investment funds can be selected:
  - o The administrator may itemize the permitted asset classes and, more importantly, describe the essential characteristics, including the risks, associated with the asset categories.
- The default investment option for member accounts where no selection is made and an explanation as to why the default option is appropriate to the plan members:
  - o The default may consider member demographics and the interest rate environment. The default is a key decision made by the administrator because research shows members tend to leave their contributions in the default option for long periods. Therefore, the value of a member's account will vary dramatically depending on the default option chosen by the administrator. Over the long term, in a low interest rate environment, the value of contributions to a default money market fund will differ widely from the value of contributions to a default target date fund.
- Monitoring service providers:
  - o This refers to the frequency and type of reporting required of service providers such as the record keeper, the third-party administrator, and custodian.
  - o If a service provider fails to meet established criteria, CAPSA suggests a consideration of the following factors when deciding on a course of actions:[14]

---

[14] Canadian Association of Pension Supervisory Authorities, *Guideline No. 3 Guidelines for Capital Accumulation Plans*, 2004, p. 14.

- the length of time the criteria has not been met;
- any complaints from members;
- the effect of remedial action on members;
- the availability of alternative service.

- Selecting, monitoring and terminating investment managers and funds:
  - In the selection of investment options, CAPSA recommends a consideration of the number to be offered and the diversity and demographics of the members, and, for each option, the associated fees, the ability to review, the diversification, the liquidity and the risk; and in the selection of specific investment funds, CAPSA recommends a consideration of the fund's objectives, strategies, risks, manager, performance and fee.[15]
  - In monitoring, CAPSA recommends a review be conducted at least annually.[16]
  - In termination, the considerations are those described above for a service provider.

- Plan expenses and investment fees related to the defined contribution plan:
  - This determination and disclosure may include which expenses that will be paid by the employer and which will be paid by the members; guidelines for monitoring expenses and an explanation on how fees may vary by asset class, structure (single manager versus manager of managers) or fundamental approach (active versus passive).

- Related party transactions:
  - Refer to the section on rules and regulations for recent changes to permitted and prohibited related party transactions.

- Information guidelines for plan members on investment options:
  - Here the focus is on assisting members to make informed investment choices. At a high level, the administrator should determine the types of information to provide to members.

---

[15] Canadian Association of Pension Supervisory Authorities, p. 8.
[16] Canadian Association of Pension Supervisory Authorities, p. 14.

Member Communication

Nobel Laureate Daniel Kahneman, reflecting on the onus placed on members to make investment choices, says: "Research indicates that decision biases, a lack of understanding of financial markets and too much personal discretion are likely to turn average workers into bad managers of their retirement accounts."[17]

Although the average worker may not be equipped to be a fund manager, the administrator is in a position to support informed decision-making by its members.

FSCO recommends reference to CAPSA Guidelines No. 3 and 8 and section 7.3 of the PBSR on investment option information to plan members. Section 7.3 of the PBSR was referred to earlier. CAPSA Guideline No. 3 outlines the responsibility of members to make investment decisions and their rights to information on investment option characteristics such as objective, returns, type of investments held, significant changes in investment policy, fees, and how additional information can be accessed. Guideline No. 8 suggests member communications should be tailored to member life cycle, meaning communications will vary if the member is new, if the member is accumulating assets, or if the member is approaching retirement.

The Transfer of Knowledge from Canada to Other Jurisdictions

The Canadian pension fund industry is fortunate to have institutions that are well established, practices that are sophisticated, and participants who are knowledgeable. In fact, large Canadian pension funds operate some of the most advanced investment and risk management programs in the world. This high level of development allows for a significant transfer of knowledge to other jurisdictions. The opportunity for this knowledge transfer from Canada to Bermuda and the Caribbean region is illustrated below.

In the Caribbean, the general tendency is to emphasize quantitative rules as opposed to the prudent person rule. These quantitative rules often establish not only maximum exposures but also minimum exposures for currency, for asset classes, such as real estate, for foreign assets, and for specific investments, such as local government bonds. The practice in

---

[17]   Daniel Kahneman, Terrance Odean, and Brad Barber, "Private Pensions: An Irrational Choice." *Global Agenda, a publication of the World Economic Forum,* 2005.

Canada demonstrates that an increased reliance on the prudent person rule can mean an enhanced investment opportunity set and an increased risk management capability. The principles underlying the prudent person rule are discussed in the next section.

Another underlying issue in the region is the subordination of the interests of the pension plan members to government policy in matters of debt management or local economic development. The practical impact is that a pension fund may suffer illiquidity, asset concentration, opportunity cost, and, with a high allocation to local government securities, an undiversified exposure to volatile, local interest rates. The appropriate response to these policies is to reassert fundamental investment principles — diversification, asset quality, and asset liquidity — and to re-establish the interest of the pension plan members as the prime responsibility of the pension plan.

Costs always matter, but the management of investment costs in the region requires particular attention for two reasons. First, thousands of U.S., Canadian, and European investment products (pooled funds or mutual funds) are restricted to eligible domestic subscribers. Second, the small size of a typical pension fund in the region will often fail to meet the minimum size required for segregated asset management. The reduced supply of available funds and the small asset size frequently mean high investment management cost. In Canada, cost-effectiveness drives industry pension plans, association pension plans, and multi-employer pension plans. A similar motive recently changed pension legislation to allow large pension funds to manage for small pension funds.

One unique feature in certain countries in the region, including Bermuda, the Cayman Islands, and the Bahamas, is that a large part of the work force comprises expatriates. To attract these workers, employers provide competitive compensation packages that often include pension benefits. The difficulty is that the investment time horizon of these expatriate members, which is limited to the term of a work permit, is markedly shorter than that of local members. Expatriate workers highlight a larger issue, which is the need for a pension plan to offer not one investment option but multiple investment options. These different options serve the different segments of the pension plan membership. In Canada, this need is commonly satisfied through life cycle funds, risk profile funds, and target date funds.

Rules and Regulations: Prudent Person Principles, Quantitative Rules, and Other Rules

Prudent Person Principles

The administrator, as well as the custodian, the trustee, the asset managers, and the investment advisor, all have a fiduciary responsibility to members of the plan. Under pension legislation, the standard of care that fiduciaries must exercise is broadly defined as "the care, diligence and skill . . . that a person of ordinary prudence would exercise in dealing with the property of another person". However, to the extent that these professionals have, or ought to have, additional knowledge or skills, the professionals are also expected to apply this additional expertise.

The prudent person rule has been expressly adopted in the federal legislation as well as in the pension fund laws of all provinces except Saskatchewan and Newfoundland and Labrador. However, a fiduciary relationship exists in all provinces whether or not the pension legislation explicitly states that it applies.

Pension plans are also subject to the prudent portfolio rule, which relates to the overall reasonable level of risk the plan should undertake as a whole and the appropriate level of diversification of the entire pension fund. Risk is evaluated on a total portfolio level, rather than on a security-by-security basis. While the pension legislation still contains some quantitative rules, compliance with the quantitative rules alone does not ensure that the fund is being prudently managed.

Quantitative Rules

Pension plan investments are subject to compliance with investment regulations under the federal PBSR or provincial pension standards legislation. Many of the provinces have adopted the federal rules. All plans are also subject to federal *Income Tax Act* rules.

Federal investment rules limit pension funds to owning no more than 30% of a company's shares eligible to elect a board of directors.

Federal investment rules also limit investments or loans in excess of 10% of the value of the plan's assets in a single entity. The 10% limit is based on the market value of the assets at the time of purchase and aggregates the combined value of debt and equity. In a member-directed defined contribution plan, the 10% rule applies at the member account level, although there are exemptions for qualifying investment funds and segregated funds.

Other Rules

Federal investment rules have refined and amended related party transactions. They now distinguish between investment and non-investment transactions. Non-investment transactions conducted for the operation or administration of the pension plan are permitted if the terms and conditions are not less favourable than market terms and conditions.

The administrator of a plan may invest in a related party (often the company stock of the employer) subject to certain conditions. The most relevant condition is that the investment is made through an investment fund or segregated fund that is available to investors other than the administrator or its affiliates. This new provision is effective July 1 2016. Plans have until July 1, 2021 to remedy non-compliant related party investments.

Finally, federal investment regulations continue to permit a related party transaction if the value of the transaction is nominal where the administrator has defined what is nominal.

Chapter 8

REGISTRATION OF PENSION PLANS UNDER THE INCOME TAX ACT AND TAXATION OF RETIREMENT SAVINGS

Executive Summary

This chapter will review the restrictions on registered pension plans (RPPs) imposed by the federal *Income Tax Act* (ITA). Because a registered pension plan receives significant tax advantages in the form of tax-deferral, the purpose behind the benefit restrictions is to reduce the tax loss by indirectly limiting the funding of pension plans. Included in the review is the pension adjustment system, consisting of Pension Adjustments, Past Service Pension Adjustments, and Pension Adjustment Reversals, and its connection to the Registered Retirement Savings Plan system. Finally, the ability to transfer funds between the registered pension plan system and the Registered Retirement Savings Plan system will be discussed.

History of Registration of Pension Plans

To obtain preferred tax treatment, a pension plan must be accepted for registration by the Canada Revenue Agency (CRA). Once registration has been granted, it continues until the plan is terminated by the pension plan sponsor and all assets are distributed from the plan, or plan registration is revoked by the CRA. The registration rules are intended to limit the type and extent of benefits that may be paid from an RPP, thereby limiting tax assistance and deferrals.

Contributions to an RPP are deductible up to certain limits, and benefits are fully taxable to employees when paid. Income and capital gains earned by investing the assets of an RPP are not taxable.

From 1972 to 1990, the registration rules for pension plans were not formally included in the ITA, but were described in an Information Circular, the last edition being Information Circular 72-13R8. The Information Circulars outline the CRA's views and administrative policies but do not constitute laws. It was the practice of pension plan sponsors to conform to the rules set out in the Information Circular, but as time passed, the government decided that the preferred way to regulate pension plans was to give the rules the force of law by including them in the ITA and *Income Tax Act Regulations.*

On June 27, 1990, the Government of Canada passed Bill C-52, *An Act to Amend the Income Tax Act and Related Acts.* This legislation significantly changed the system for granting tax assistance for retirement savings, introduced many new plan registration rules, and incorporated into law some of the old plan registration rules.

The government's stated objectives in implementing the new regime were:

- To establish a tax framework to encourage increased private retirement savings;
- To eliminate inequities that resulted in some taxpayers being unable to benefit from as much tax assistance as others, depending on the type of their pension and retirement savings plans;
- To enhance the flexibility in the timing of retirement savings; and
- To introduce a system under which dollar limits on contributions and benefits are adjusted for inflation and therefore do not decline in real value.

In this chapter, the main provisions of the legislation, the rules for registration of pension plans, and the rules regarding taxation of RPPs are outlined.

It is important to note that the applicable pension standards legislation and the provsions of the applicable pension plan set out the member's benefit accruals. The federal *Income Tax Act* imposises maximums to ensure the stated objectives outlined above are met.

Retirement Savings Limits

The legislation is based on the principle that the availability of tax assistance should be the same for all individuals with the same incomes, whether they save for retirement through participation in a defined contribution pension plan, a defined benefit pension plan, a Registered RetirementSavings Plan (RRSP), a Deferred Profit Sharing Plan (DPSP), or through a combination of these plans.

The system of retirement saving limits became effective for the 1991 tax year. The following is an outline of the provisions that apply these savings limits to contributors to RRSPs and members of RPPs and DPSPs.

Comprehensive Savings Limit

There is a comprehensive retirement savings limit, regardless of whether contributions are made by the individual or an employer, equal to 18% of the taxpayer's compensation, subject to a dollar maximum. Tax preferences are not given to retirement savings contributions above these limits.

Pension Adjustments

The system requires that accruals under pension plans in each year be converted to approximate lump-sum values. The approximate lump-sum value, known as a Pension Adjustment (PA), is then compared to the individual's savings limit (referred to in the paragraph above) in order to determine whether the plan member has reached his or her annual comprehensive savings limit. To calculate in each year the permitted RRSP contribution for an individual who is a member of an RPP or a DPSP, the individual's accrued retirement savings limit for the year is reduced by the individual's previous year's PA. Taxpayers who do not contribute the maximum allowed for a year to their RRSPs have the right to carry forward indefinitely the unused RRSP contribution room for use in subsequent years.

Employers operating RPPs or DPSPs are required to report the PAs of plan members to CRA on a T-4 slip by the end of February each year. These reports are used by CRA to calculate the RRSP contribution room for a plan member for the following year.

PAs were first calculated and reported for 1990, affecting 1991 RRSP limits.

In a defined contribution pension plan, the PA is calculated as the sum of employer and employee contributions in the year, plus any forfeited amounts (from unvested terminated members) reallocated to the employee's defined contribution account. In a DPSP, which has no employee contributions, the PA is equal to the employer contributions on behalf of the employee.

In a defined benefit pension plan, the PA is calculated as nine times the approximate amount of annual pension accrued in the year, minus $600. This formula applies regardless of the design of the defined benefit plan, and whether or not the employee is vested. The factor of nine was chosen by the federal Department of Finance as an appropriate average factor to produce the approximate value or cost of a dollar of lifetime pension income under the most generous defined benefit pension plan permitted under the registration rules. The factor, while appropriate for estimating the value of pension benefits under generous plans for employees who participate over their full careers in those plans, is unfortunately applied to estimate the value of accruals under all defined benefit pension plans, even the less-generous plans, and is applied to employees of all ages. The factor of nine overstates the value of pension accruals in most private-sector defined benefit plans, particularly for younger employees who most likely will not remain in the same pension plan for their full careers. It thus overstates the amount by which the RRSP of those taxpayers should be reduced by a PA.

The PA is calculated with regard to the individual's "pensionable earnings" in earnings-based defined benefit plans, without projection for future pay increases. Hence, the PA formula does not distinguish between career earnings and final earnings plans, the assumption being that a career earnings plan will probably be updated so as to give much the same result as a final earnings plan.

Past Service Pension Adjustments

If an employer amends an RPP to increase pensions already earned, a Past Service Pension Adjustment (PSPA) is calculated for each affected member. The PSPA is the difference between the sum of PAs actually reported for the earned pensions, and the sum of the PAs that would have been reported for that period had pensions been earned at the upgraded level. A PSPA reduces the amount that the affected member may contribute to an RRSP, and are applied against unused RRSP contribution room. A PSPA is generally created if the benefit formula in a defined benefit pension plan is increased, or if past service benefits are added for years after 1989. However, a PSPA does not arise if ancillary benefits are improved, such as early retirement subsidies or increased death benefits. PSPAs are not created by upgrading or improving pensions for service before 1990 (although other restrictions apply to upgrades of pre-1990 service).

There are two types of PSPAs that plan administrators would report to the CRA:

1. PSPAs requiring certification from the CRA:

   Past service upgrades that are applicable to one employee or a small number of employees fall under the first category and require certification.

2. PSPAs that are exempt from certification:

   When the past service upgrades affect most of the employees who are members of the plan (and if relatively few of those employees are highly paid), the PSPA must be reported but does not need to be certified.

With respect to certification, the administrator must calculate the PSPA for the employees and then report that amount to the CRA using Form T1004. If the PSPA (net of qualifying transfers from other registered savings vehicles) does not exceed the sum of $8,000 plus the member's unused RRSP contribution room, then certification will be granted. As a result, an increased past service benefit can be paid to the member and the benefit can be funded by additional contributions. A PSPA can cause negative RRSP contribution room (but not more than negative $8,000 if it was a "certified" PSPA), which reduces the taxpayer's RRSP contribution limit in future years.

If a certifiable PSPA for a member exceeds the above amounts (i.e., if the PSPA is more than $8,000 greater than the available contribution room), the member may create PSPA room by withdrawing funds from his or her RRSP. In that case, the member or the plan administrator must file a Form T1006 with the CRA to demonstrate that the "qualifying withdrawal" was completed. The member will be taxed on any such withdrawals.

Past service upgrades granted in respect of service after 1990 may be paid and funded without certification by the Minister if all of the following conditions are met:

- There are at least 10 active members accruing benefits under the provisions being upgraded;
- No more than 25% of the members receiving the upgrade are "specified individuals" (i.e., those who are expected to earn more than 2.5 times of the Year's Maximum Pensionable Earnings (YMPE) in the year of improvement);
- Substantially all active plan members will receive upgraded past service benefits; and
- Disproportionate benefits are not payable to high earners, or to active versus inactive members.

If certification of a PSPA is not required, the plan administrator reports the amount to CRA using a Form T215. PSPAs that are exempt from certification can produce a negative balance of unused RRSP contribution room for the taxpayer. Unlike the certified PSPA (where negative RRSP must not be more than negative $8,000), the exempt PSPA has no limit on its impact on negative RRSP room.

Pension Adjustment Reversal

The Pension Adjustment Reversal (PAR) was introduced in 1997 to correct the problem of RRSP inequities. It helps where a terminated employee's benefit (either as a lump-sum payment or transfer to RRSP or Registered Retirement Income Fund (RRIF)) is less than the cumulative PAs and PSPAs reported for the employee for the plan. The PAR restores RRSP contribution room that was previously lost as a result of PAs and PSPAs. The PAR, which is reported to the CRA by the plan administrator, will permit the employee to make additional contributions to an RRSP. The intent behind the PAR is to recognize the fact that PAs are often overstated for members of defined benefit pension plans (as a result of the factor of nine calculation), as well as for employees who terminate employment from a defined contribution pension plan or a DPSP before becoming fully vested.

Contribution Limits to Registered Plans

The current contribution limits are:

- For RRSPs, 18% of compensation in the previous calendar year, subject to the following dollar limits; and
- For defined contribution RPPs, 18% of compensation in the year, subject to the following dollar limits:

Year	DC RPPs	RRSPs
2016	$ 26,010	$ 25,370
2017	Indexed	$ 26,010
2018		indexed

The dollar limit increases each year according to increases in the average wage as defined in the *Income Tax Act*.

The DPSP contribution limit continues to be set at half of the contribution limit for money purchase pension plans in each year.

Registration Rules and Contribution Limits for Pension Plans

The policy of the federal government to examine pension plans arose during and shortly after World War II. At that time, Canada had a wage freeze and an excess profit tax, but no restrictions on employee benefits. As a result, corporations were tempted to pay large and perhaps unnecessary sums to pension plans, the actual cost to the shareholders being next to nothing.

Over the years, the government policy became concerned that pension plans should be *bona fide* retirement savings vehicles. Government policy would be opposed to considering pensions only as a device to avoid tax on savings. Therefore, it would be concerned that the tax-deductible contributions should not exceed amounts that it considered reasonable in the circumstances. The allowable contributions are described later in this chapter.

Before it will grant registration under the ITA, the CRA requires a pension plan sponsor to also apply for registration under the provincial or federal pension standards legislation (where there is such legislation applicable to members of the plan). A pension plan sponsor may apply for registration retroactively, but the effective date must be in the same calendar year in which the application for registration is submitted.

Regulations to the ITA to prescribe registration rules for pension plans were introduced in December 1989, and apply to all benefits provided under pension plans submitted to the CRA for registration on or after March 28, 1988, as well as to benefits accruing for service after 1991 under defined benefit pension plans submitted for registration prior to March 28, 1988. However, the guidelines outlined in Information Circular 72-13R8 continue to be applied to benefits accrued for service prior to January 1, 1992, under defined benefit pension plans submitted for registration prior to March 28, 1988. For all defined contribution pension plans, the new rules became law on June 27, 1990, but some rules are retroactive to January 1, 1989.

The regulations apply to three categories, as follows:

1.   All pension plans;
2.   Defined contribution pension plan provisions; and
3.   Defined benefit pension plan provisions.

Some of the more important registration rules are described below, but the descriptions are not comprehensive descriptions of all the registration rules. When trying to determine if a particular provision would be permitted, reference should also be made to Chapter 9, which deals with pension standards legislation for all of the jurisdictions.

CRA Supervision

Upon application for registration, the CRA will typically issue a provisional registration number in order to allow for the plan to be administered while a full review is undertaken. The CRA will fully review the terms of the pension plan for compliance with the registration rules, and may require amendments to the pension plan documents before the plan may be permanently registered.

Failure to adhere to the registration rules at any time after initial registration causes the plan's registered status to become revocable. If the plan's registration is revoked, the arrangement will then be classified as a retirement compensation arrangement from the date it ceases to comply with the rules, and becomes subject to non-preferential tax treatment.

On July 18, 2015, the CRA issued Newsletter No. 15-1: "Comprehensive Risk-Based Cyclical Review of Registered Pension Plans".[1] Since April 1, 2015, CRA has commenced the comprehensive review of all pension plan documents at least once every six years based on a risk-based regulatory model.

Under the CRA's new approach, unless the CRA identifies a high-risk issue for a plan, any amendment submitted after a pension plan's last comprehensive review will be reviewed only when the plan's next review date comes up. At that time, a CRA analyst will review the plan documentation and some aspects of plan administration for compliance with the Act. Any areas of non-compliance will be brought to the attention of the plan administrator. After all of the issues have been resolved and the terms of the plan comply with the Act, the analyst will send a letter to confirm compliance.

Once an amendment is submitted, as long as it is reasonable to assume the CRA will accept the amendment, the amendment must be administered as if it were part of the plan. If, at the time of a later review, the CRA refuses the amendment, a plan administrator will be prohibited from administering the plan in accordance with that amendment.

A cyclical risk-based review differs from a pension plan audit. An audit ensures that a plan is administered in line with the revenue rules and the plan terms. A plan may be chosen for an audit for various reasons, including random and risk-based selection. Audits may also result from a referral or cross-reference from another audit or another area. A plan may also be chosen for an audit if significant non-compliance was found in a prior audit.

---

[1]   http://www.cra-arc.gc.ca/tx/rgstrd/nwslttrs/15-1-eng.html.

Rules and Limits Applicable to All Pension Plans

Primary Purpose to Provide Pension Benefits

The primary purpose of an RPP is to provide employees with pension payments after retirement.

The pensions must be payable for the employee's lifetime in equal periodic amounts, except where they are adjusted for inflation or reduced after the death of the member or his or her spouse. Additional reasons for varying the amount of pension benefit are included in the ITA Regulations.

Pension Commencement Date

Employees may not participate in RPPs after the end of the year in which they reach age 71, and must start to receive pensions by that date.

Non-Assignability of Rights Under a Pension Plan

All RPPs must include a specific clause prohibiting plan members from assigning or transferring to another, or pledging as security for a debt, their rights under the pension plan. Similarly, plan members cannot surrender or voluntarily forfeit their pension rights. Creditors cannot charge, or apply to seize a member's rights under an RPP in order to satisfy debts owed by the plan member. However, these provisions do not prevent the assignment of benefits pursuant to a court order or settlement agreement upon the breakdown of a marriage or conjugal relationship. They also do not prohibit the surrender of benefits to avoid the revocation of a plan's registration, nor do they prohibit the distribution of benefits by a deceased plan member's legal representative.

Investments

RPPs must comply with all minimum standards investment regulations of the jurisdictions of registration. As well, the ITA registration rules prohibit RPP assets from being invested in shares or debt instruments of any plan member, any employer who participates in the plan, and generally, any individual connected or related to a plan member or participating employer. The prohibition, however, does not extend to shares or debt obligations of a participating employer where the shares of the corporate employer are listed on a prescribed stock exchange inside or outside of Canada.

An RPP may not borrow funds, except:

- Where the term of the loan does not exceed 90 days and none of the RPP's assets are used as security for the loan (except where borrowing is necessary for current payment of benefits); or
- Where the borrowed money is used to acquire real property, as long as no RPP asset other than the real property acquired is used as security for the loan.

Prior to February 2005, the ITA limited investments of registered pension fund assets in foreign property to 30% of the pension fund, measured by the original cost of the assets in the fund. Where foreign content in the fund exceeded 30%, a penalty tax was assessed.

Since the 2005 federal Budget, the foreign content limit is no longer applicable to investments held under pension plans (and RRSPs).

Administration

RPPs must be administered pursuant to the provisions of the plan text as registered with the CRA. Failure to administer in accordance with the registered plan text will place the RPP's registration in a revocable status.

The provisions of an RPP must include the designation of a specific administrator who is responsible for the overall operation and administration of the RPP, and for filing information returns about the RPP to the CRA. The administrator may be a participating employer, a Canadian resident, or a group of persons, the majority of whom reside in Canada. Non-Canadian administrators are permitted only with the written permission of the Minister.

Contributions

An RPP must require the employer to contribute. If employees are required or permitted to contribute, the documents must contain specific information on the amount and nature of contributions. A plan can be designed that neither requires nor permits employee contributions.

Contributions must be made in accordance with the terms of the plan as registered and are subject to the relevant PA limits.

Spouse

The "spouse" of an RPP member is entitled to special privileges under the ITA and under the pension standards legislation. The ITA generally defines a spouse as a person who is married to the taxpayer, or the common-law partner (whether opposite sex or same sex). For tax purposes the non-married spouses would have to cohabit in a conjugal relationship for at least one year. Note that pension standards legislation generally have different cohabitation requirements for recognizing a person as the member's "spouse".

Foreign Service

In certain circumstances, employment outside of Canada can be included as eligible service. The CRA published a comprehensive Newsletter, No. 93-2, "Foreign Service Newsletter", which was updated by No. 00-1, "Foreign Service Newsletter Update".[2]

The CRA permits foreign service to be accrued under a defined benefit provision for up to five years during service with a foreign employer who is affiliated with the Canadian employer. Until 2001, this limit was three years.

Defined contribution pension plan contributions can also be made during foreign service, provided that CRA consent is obtained.

In order to accrue service while employed abroad, the individual must have previously been employed by the employer in Canada. The five year limit can be renewed if the employee returns to and works in Canada for an additional 12 months.

Rules and Limits Applicable to Defined Contribution Pension Plan Provisions

Contributions

Employer contributions must be made in respect of particular employees, and must be allocated to the employees with respect to whom they are made. Unallocated contributions cannot be made.

Employer contributions cannot be made at a time when there is surplus in a defined contribution plan that has not been allocated to employees' accounts, or while there are unallocated pre-1990 forfeited amounts.

---

[2]   http://www.cra-arc.gc.ca/tx/rgstrd/nwslttrs/00-1-eng.html.

In order to remain registered, the CRA requires an annual employer contribution of at least 1% of the active members' pensionable earnings, on a collective basis.

Amounts (of employee contributions) forfeited after 1989 by plan members who terminate employment before vesting, and earnings thereon must be reallocated to plan members, used to pay administrative expenses of the plan, used to satisfy the employer's contribution obligations, or refunded to the employer before the end of the year following the year of forfeiture. A refund ordinarily requires advance approval by the appropriate pension regulator in the jurisdiction where the plan is registered.

All contributions and forfeitures allocated to an employee's credit must be included in the PA of the employee for the year in which they are made or, if the contributions are made before the end of February and relate to the previous calendar year, for the previous calendar year.

Lifetime Pensions

Pensions must be provided by the purchase of annuities from a person licensed or otherwise authorized under the laws of Canada or a province to sell life annuities (generally life insurance companies). Alternatively, though not common, a plan may permit a member to elect RRIF-style payments directly from the member's defined contribution account, without purchasing an annuity.

Generally, pensions must be payable in equal periodic amounts for the member's lifetime. However, the defined contribution pension plan regulations permit the payment of certain other benefits that are not payable for the duration of the member's life, or that cause the pension to be payable in unequal amounts, in addition to ordinary lifetime pension benefits. For example, pension benefits may be increased as a result of increases in the cost of living, as measured by the Consumer Price Index (CPI), or increased at a rate specified in the pension plan terms, where the rate cannot exceed 4% *per annum*. Temporary bridge benefits may be provided to a member retiring before normal pensionable age, ending no later than the end of the month following the month in which the member reaches age 65, to bridge the time until Old Age Security (OAS) and Canada or Quebec Pension Plan (CPP/QPP) benefits start at age 65. These ancillary benefits, payable in addition to the lifetime retirement pension, must be provided by the balance in the member's account. Defined contribution benefits are limited by the contributions and earnings in each member's account. If ancillary benefits are elected by a member at retirement, the amount of lifetime pension payments is reduced compared to that possible had the ancillary benefits not been elected.

Pre-Retirement Death Benefits

In the event that the member dies before starting to receive the pension, the defined contribution plan must provide a pension to the surviving spouse.

The pension can be paid in any form — other than joint and survivor — that would have been allowed to be paid to the member. For example, it could be in the form of a pension guaranteed for up to 15 years. Pension payments to the surviving spouse must begin no later than the end of the year when the spouse reaches 71; if the spouse has already reached 71 years of age at the time of the member's death, the survivor pension must begin within one year of the member's death.

The defined contribution plan may also permit a lump-sum payment to be made to the spouse or to a beneficiary. It cannot exceed the amount in the member's account. The spouse, but not a non-spouse beneficiary, can transfer the lump-sum benefit to his or her RRSP.

Post-Retirement Death Benefits

A retiring plan member may elect to receive a form of lifetime pension that provides a death benefit to his or her beneficiary. The pension can be guaranteed for up to 15 years from the date the pension commences; if the plan member should die before 15 years of pension payments, the designated beneficiary will receive the remainder of the 15 years of payments. Under this form of guarantee, the retiree may select any individual to receive any benefits that may be payable after the retiree's death. If the plan member has a spouse, he or she may elect a form of joint and survivor life annuity, whereby the pension is payable for the retiree's life, and after the retiree's death, the pension will continue in the same or in a lower amount to a surviving spouse.

Minimum pension standards legislation restricts the payment options on the death of a member by requiring payment of death benefits to the member's surviving spouse; however, the jurisdictions permit the spouse to waive his or her entitlement to the survivor pension.

In the case where the retirement benefits have been guaranteed, rather than receiving continuing payments, the surviving spouse or beneficiary may elect to receive the commuted value of the remaining payments in a lump sum. If a lump sum is payable, only the spouse of the member is permitted to transfer the amount to his or her own RRSP.

Rules and Limits Applicable to Defined Benefit Pension Plan Provisions

Eligible Service

Defined benefit pension plan formulas are calculated with reference to the duration of membership in the plan, which in turn reflects part or all of the employee's employment with a participating employer as defined in the plan text. Pensions must be earned relatively evenly over a number of years of service; the registration rules prohibit granting large pensions for only a few years of service. As well, the registration rules permit pension accrual for "eligible service" only.

Eligible service is employment in Canada with an employer who participates in the pension plan, or with a predecessor employer whose business has been acquired by the participating employer. Periods of absence from active employment due to disability qualify as eligible service, regardless of the duration of the disability. Periods of unpaid leave of absence from employment for reasons other than disability qualify as eligible service, subject to an overall lifetime limit on such unpaid leaves of five years, plus up to three additional years for parental leaves.

Service with a former employer can count as eligible service in the current employer's pension plan if the service was included in pensionable service under the former employer's pension plan and the plan member does not retain rights to benefits from that former employer's pension plan.

Maximum Benefit Accrual Rate

The annual benefit accrual rate cannot, in general, exceed 2% of such remuneration or the defined benefit limit. This rate increases to 2.33% for public safety occupations where the pension is integrated with CPP or QPP.

Post-Retirement Cost of Living Increases

After retirement, pensions can be indexed to reflect increases in the cost of living. The most common indexing formulas are based on increases in the CPI, or a fixed rate *per annum* (not to exceed 4% *per annum*) from the date the pension commences to be paid. Also permitted is a less-common "excess earnings approach". In that case, the rate of pension indexation depends on the amount by which investment returns exceed a pre-determined target.

A longer-term CPI restriction also applies. At any time after pension commencement, the overall pension cannot exceed the maximum pension at pension commencement, adjusted for CPI.

Early Retirement Lifetime Pension

An employee may retire and receive a lifetime pension commencing prior to normal retirement age. In this circumstance, the registration rules permit the plan to provide either a benefit that is reduced for earlier commencement, or, in certain circumstances, the accrued pension without reduction, subject to restrictions. To receive the accrued pension without reduction, before normal retirement age, the employee must have satisfied one of the following criteria:

- Attainment of age 60 at pension commencement date;
- 30 years of service; or
- Age plus years of service totalling 80 or more.

For employees in public safety occupations (firefighters, police officers, paramedics, commercial pilots, corrections officers, and air traffic controllers) the criteria are:

- Attainment of age 55 at pension commencement date;
- 25 years of service; or
- Age plus years of service totalling 75 or more.

If a reduced early retirement pension is provided, the reduction must at least equal 0.25% for each month by which the pension commencement date precedes the earliest date at which an unreduced pension could have been paid. This is quite a generous standard, as many pension plans provide a much greater reduction on early retirement.

Postponed Retirement Lifetime Pension

A defined benefit pension must commence to be paid prior to the end of the year in which the individual attains age 71. The administrator may apply an actuarial increase to compensate for the fact that a pension commences after age 65, but it is not required to do so.

Bridge Benefits

An RPP may pay "bridge benefits" any time during the period after pension commencement until the member attains age 65. This allows an income supplement to be paid until the member can collect OAS benefits and the full unreduced CPP/QPP retirement pension.

The maximum amount of periodic bridge benefit payments from a defined benefit RPP is the sum of the CPP/QPP and OAS benefits the member would be able to receive if he or she were age 65 at the date the bridge benefit commences. However, if the plan member has not attained age 60, or has not completed at least 10 years of pensionable service, the maximum bridge benefit is reduced by 0.25% for each month by which the bridge benefit commencement date precedes age 60. If the member has less than 10 years of service, the maximum bridging benefit is also reduced on a prorated basis.

The limit above describes the maximum bridging benefit that a defined benefit plan can provide without affecting the member's lifetime pension. Bridging benefits in excess of that amount are, however, permitted where the excess portion is provided in place of a part of the member's lifetime retirement benefit. The member's lifetime benefit reduction will be calculated on an actuarially equivalent basis. The total annualized amount of bridging benefit cannot exceed 40% of the YMPE for the year in which the bridging benefit begins. However, pension standards legislation may impose restrictions on the extent to which a lifetime pension may be reduced to provide a level income benefit option.

Disability Benefits

If an employee is unable to perform the duties of employment as a result of a physical or mental impairment, a defined benefit pension plan may permit the employee to continue accruing pension benefits for the period of disability. The plan may require the disabled employee to continue making the ordinary contributions to the pension plan, or may waive contributions for the period of disability.

An employee who is unable, by reason of physical or mental impairment, to engage in any employment for which he or she is reasonably suited by education or training or experience, and who can reasonably be expected to remain disabled until death, is "totally and permanently disabled" for the purpose of the registration rules, and may continue to receive pension accruals or may receive an immediate lifetime disability pension. The pension plan may provide the full accrued pension to the totally and permanently disabled employee, unreduced by reason of its early commencement. The normal rules regarding when an unreduced early retirement pension may commence do not apply to a member who is totally and permanently disabled.

The maximum annual lifetime retirement benefit that may be paid to an individual who is totally and permanently disabled is equal to the greater of

- The accrued benefits at the time of the disability retirement, without reduction for early retirement; and
- The lesser of:
  - The projected pension that would otherwise have been earned by the employee under the pension plan had he survived and remained employed to age 65, assuming no increase in pay, and
  - The YMPE for the year in which disability pension payments start.

The determination of whether an employee is disabled or totally and permanently disabled must be made by the plan administrator, based upon the written report of a medical doctor.

Pre-Retirement Death Benefits

When an employee dies before pension commencement, the plan can provide that a designated beneficiary or spouse receive, in a single lump-sum payment, the value of part or all of the employee's accrued pension. Alternatively, a lump-sum payment equal to twice the member's own required contributions to the plan plus interest, may be paid.

Lump-sum payments may be tax-sheltered through transfer to an RRSP or a RRIF, or to another plan only if the recipient is the deceased member's spouse or former spouse.

In lieu of paying a single lump-sum payment to a beneficiary or surviving spouse, the plan may provide a surviving spouse or dependant with an immediate pension equal to up to $66^2/_3\%$ of the pension accrued to the plan member. The survivor's pension may be paid to the spouse for life. A survivor pension payable to eligible dependants may only be paid for the period during which they remain dependent. A dependant can include a parent, grandparent, brother, sister, child, or grandchild who was dependent on the member for support at the time of the member's death. The survivor's pension must end once a person no longer qualifies as a dependant. If the survivor's pension is payable to more than one person, the level of survivor's pension can be increased to up to 100% of the pension accrued to the employee at date of death. No more than two-thirds of the accrued pension may be paid to any one particular beneficiary. If the survivor pension is payable to a spouse or former spouse, it can be paid to the spouse in a form that is guaranteed for up to 15 years.

Post-Retirement Death Benefits

In the case of a member's death following the commencement of pension benefits, a pension plan may provide post-retirement survivor benefits to the spouse and dependants of the deceased member. An employee's pension may be guaranteed for up to 15 years after the date on which the pension commences, if paid in the form of an annuity payable for a single life. Any remaining guaranteed payments after the member's death may continue to be paid to the beneficiary, or may be commuted and paid in a lump sum. A life only pension need not be actuarially reduced on account of the guarantee period, although the plan may apply the reduction if provided under the plan terms.

The survivor's pension payable to the spouse generally cannot exceed $66^2/_3\%$ of the pension previously payable to the employee, with a maximum guarantee of five years. However, if an actuarial reduction is applied to the employee's lifetime pension, the surviving spouse may receive up to 100% of the pension previously payable to the employee or may receive a longer guarantee period (up to 15 years).

Survivor benefits to an eligible spouse may continue for the spouse's remaining lifetime, whereas survivor benefits to a dependant may only continue for the eligible survivor period of the dependant. This period ends at the end of the year in which the dependant reaches age 18, or, if later, the time at which the dependant ceases to be a full-time student. However, if the dependant is infirm, the payments may continue for as long as the infirmity continues.

Total monthly payments to the spouse and any beneficiary after the survivor pension has begun may not exceed the total monthly benefits that would be payable to the member if the member were alive. A plan may also provide a guarantee that total payments in respect of a member will not be less than the member's contributions to the plan with accumulated interest.

The form of pension is determined at the date of pension commencement, but may change on a go-forward basis at a later date (for example, due to marriage breakdown), subject to the plan terms and applicable pension legislation.

Benefits on Termination of Employment

On termination of employment before retirement, a pension plan may provide a deferred pension, or one of the following alternate payments:

- A refund of member contributions with interest;
- A refund equal to twice member contributions with interest, if certain conditions are met; or
- A lump-sum payment equal to the value of the pension accrued to the member at date of termination of employment.

Termination benefits are also subject to pension standards legislation.

Commutation of Pension

Under the ITA Regulations, a plan member may commute all or any portion of his or her pension either before or after the pension has started. However, the right to commute a pension in pay is also governed by pension standards legislation and is usually prohibited.

Plan Participation After Retirement

Subject to special phased retirement provisions under the ITA, an employee cannot continue to accrue further defined benefit pension benefits with the same employer for a period of employment after the employee has started receiving pension payments. However, if the pensioner subsequently is re-employed by his or her previous employer, and wishes to recommence participation in the defined benefit RPP, the member may elect to suspend payment of the pension. In that case, he or she would be permitted to recommence participation in the plan and earn further pension credits. This restriction does not apply to accrual of benefits under a defined contribution provision with the same employer. It also does not apply to accrual of benefits under a defined benefit provision of an unrelated employer. As a result, after a member commences receiving a defined benefit retirement pension, he or she could begin to accrue benefits under a defined contribution provision, or a defined benefit provision sponsored by an unrelated employer.

Some provincial jurisdictions have enacted phased retirement provisions in their pension standards legislation that do not contravene the traditional ITA provisions.[3]

---

[3]   See Chapter 3 for more information on phased retirement.

Since 2008, the ITA Regulations have allowed pension plans to offer phased retirement arrangements. A member could start receiving a "partial" pension while continuing to be employed and accruing additional pension. The member must have reached the earliest unreduced retirement age under the plan (which may not be earlier than age 55) or age 60. The pension plan may permit the member to receive up to 60% of accrued benefits. If the plan provides bridge benefits, the plan could permit the member to start receiving up to 100% of accrued bridge benefits.

Maximum Pension Rules

A defined benefit pension plan is limited in the amount of pension it may provide. At the time of pension commencement, the lifetime pension paid to an employee cannot exceed the lesser of:

- The defined benefit limit multiplied by the employee's years of pensionable service; and
- 2% of the employee's highest average indexed compensation, multiplied by the employee's years of pensionable service.

The defined benefit limit is equal to $\frac{1}{9}$ of the defined contribution RPP contribution limit for the year. The limit is $2,890 for 2016.

The "highest average indexed compensation" is equal to the average of the best three non-overlapping, 12-month periods of the employee's highest compensation. The three periods are not required to be consecutive. The indexed compensation for a given month is the compensation actually paid in that month, updated to the year of pension commencement to reflect post-1986 increases in the average industrial wage.

There is a different limit with respect to the pension granted after 1989 for years of past service before 1990 in which the employee did not participate in any RPP or DPSP. The benefits payable in respect of those years of past service cannot exceed two-thirds of the defined benefit limit for each year of pre-1990 pensionable service, in recognition of the fact that the employee enjoyed a higher level of RRSP contribution room in those years than individuals who were RPP participants.

The maximum pension outlined above would be reduced by 0.25% for each month by which pension commencement precedes the earliest of the following dates:

- The date on which the member would attain age 60;
- The date on which the member would have had 30 years of service; or

- The date on which the member's age plus years of service would have equaled 80.

For employees in public service occupations, the maximum pension is reduced if pension commencement occurs before the earliest of:

- The date on which the member would attain age 55;
- The date on which the member would have had 25 years of service; or
- The date on which the member's age plus years of service would have equaled 75.

Where a defined benefit pension plan provides bridge benefits to persons whose pension commenced before age 65, the combined annual lifetime pension and bridge benefit payable is limited to:

- The defined benefit limit for the year of pension commencement multiplied by the employee's pensionable service;

plus

- 25% of the average YMPE (in the last three calendar years including the pension commencement year), multiplied by the ratio (not exceeding 1.0) of years of pensionable service divided by 35, indexed from the year of commencement to the particular year in line with increases in the CPI.

This limit on combined lifetime retirement benefits and bridging benefits only applies to lifetime retirement benefits and bridging benefits for post-1991 pensionable service.

These maximum limits severely restrict the bridging benefits discussed previously that may be paid to highly compensated members whose lifetime retirement benefits are close to or at the maximum permitted, as well as lower-income members with relatively short periods of service.

Downsizing Programs

An employer who initiates a downsizing program in order to reduce the size of its workforce may apply to the Minister of National Revenue for approval of the downsizing program. If the Minister approves the downsizing program, the employer will be able to offer enriched pension benefits to downsized employees.

The Minister has administratively set criteria for approval of downsizing and early retirement programs. The criteria require that the workforce must be reduced by the greater of 50 employees or 10% of employees in a locality. As well, no more than 35% of the target employees can be in the top earnings quartile for the locality.

If the program is approved, the employer may grant downsized employees, aged 55 or older, extra pensionable service to their normal retirement date, subject to a maximum of seven additional years. As well, early retirement reductions can be waived under a downsizing program if downsizing benefits are paid on or after the earliest of:

- Attainment of age 55;
- Attainment of 25 years of service; or
- Age plus years of service, equal to 75.

Any additional benefits provided under an approved downsizing program are not subject to the ordinary maximum pension rule, as they are subject to their own rule.

Designated Plans

A defined benefit pension plan is a "designated plan" if it is not maintained pursuant to a collective agreement and if the PAs of specified members exceed 50% of all PAs earned under the plan in that year. Specified members are:

- Individuals who earn over 21/2 times the YMPE;
- Individuals who own 10% or more of the issued shares of any class of shares of the employer or a related corporation; and
- Individuals who do not otherwise deal at arm's length with the employer.

Contributions to a designated plan cannot exceed the amount specified according to the designated plan rules, which apply an artificial cap on employer contributions and plan funding levels.

The Minister may exempt a plan with at least 10 active members from designated plan status if the plan operates as a traditional defined benefit plan. A traditional plan is a plan in which:

- The benefit formula does not vary from member to member;
- Members are not involved in the decision-making process regarding the amount of contribution made in respect of the member;
- Members do not have control over the investment of any of the assets; and
- Surplus is not tracked individually for each member.

Individual Pension Plans

The 2011 federal Budget proposed new tax measures that would apply to "individual pension plans" (IPPs). For this purpose, an IPP is a defined benefit RPP with three or fewer members, if at least one member is "related" for tax purposes to an employer that participates under the pension plan; or that is a designated plan, if it is reasonable to conclude that the rights of one or more members under the plan exist primarily to avoid this new definition. As is the case for designated plans, the Minister of National Revenue has the power to waive IPP status in appropriate circumstances. The Budget proposed that, commencing in 2012, annual minimum amounts would be required to be withdrawn each year after the member attains 71 years of age. The amounts would be equal to the greater of the regular annual pension payment and a new minimum amount calculated as if the member's share of IPP assets were held in an RRIF.

The Ontario and Quebec pension regulators objected to this stance, and in 2013 the CRA clarified that it would not require such withdrawals if the regulator publicly objects to such withdrawals. However, such withdrawals may be required if the plan permits such withdrawals from surplus on an ongoing basis.

Employer Contributions to Defined Benefit Plans

Contributions made by an employer to a defined benefit plan are deductible, if based on the recommendation of an actuary certifying that the contributions are required to ensure the assets of the plan are sufficient to fund the benefit promises made under the plan. A contribution must be made in respect of an actuarial report with a valuation date less than four years old, and the actuary's recommendations must be approved by the CRA. An employer contribution is deductible if made in the current year or in the first 120 days of the subsequent year (in respect of benefits earned in prior years).

Where the funding status of the plan is in a surplus position, there are restrictions placed on further employer contributions. For plans in actuarial surplus, a certain portion of the surplus in a defined benefit plan may be disregarded in determining whether an employer may make eligible contributions. The amount that may be excluded is equal to 25% of the actuarial liabilities under the plan. This threshold was increased in 2010 from the previous rule, which was effectively 10% of the actuarial liabilities under the plan, allowing more surplus to be accumulated under the plan.

If excess surplus exists, it must be used to reduce employer and employee contributions in respect of current service, used for benefit improvements, or paid out of the plan.

Employee Contributions

Contributions made by an employee to a defined benefit pension plan or to a defined benefit provision of a pension plan for current service are fully deductible in determining taxable income if made in the calendar year or in the first 120 days of the subsequent year (in respect of contributions for the prior year). The contribution must be made in accordance with the terms of the plan. Each employee's current service contributions to a defined benefit plan for each calendar year must not exceed the lesser of:

- 9% of the employee's compensation for the year; and
- $1,000 plus 70% of the employee's PA for the year.

For a plan that provides a termination or pre-retirement death benefit of twice employee contributions, the figure "70%" is reduced to "50%".

The CRA may waive the contribution limits if member contributions are determined in a way that is acceptable to the Minister. It must also be reasonable to expect that, on a long-term basis, the total regular current service contributions made under the provision by all members will not fund more than half of the related benefits. The CRA will also verify that member contributions over the above limit do not result in larger benefits for most of the members because of the minimum employer contribution rule. Details on obtaining the CRA waiver are found in Actuarial Bulletin No. 3.[4]

If an employee makes a contribution to purchase past service pension benefits for years of employment after 1989, that contribution is deductible against the employee's income in the taxation year of the contribution.

If an employee wishes to make contributions to purchase pension benefits in respect of pre-1990 employment with the employer, the deductibility of such contributions depends on whether or not the employee was or was not a contributor to any RPP in respect of those particular years. Where the past service contribution is made with respect to years of service before 1990 in which the employee was not a contributor to any RPP, the total deductible contribution is limited to

---

[4]   http://www.cra-arc.gc.ca/tx/rgstrd/blltn/ctrlblltn03-eng.html.

$3,500 times the number of years of purchased past service. The deduction for such a past service contribution can be taken at the rate of $3,500 per year in the current and future taxation years.

Where the past service contribution was made in respect of years of service prior to 1990 during which the employee contributed to an RPP, the amount paid to purchase pension benefits for such years of past service can be deducted at a rate of $3,500 per year in the current and future taxation years. This deduction is further reduced by all other current and past service contribution deductions claimed by the employee in the year, so that if the employee makes current or past service required or voluntary contributions in the year totalling $3,500, this deduction is completely eliminated.

Transfer of Assets Between Pension Plans and Registered Retirement Savings Arrangements

Upon separation from employment, especially upon termination of employment, pension benefits are often payable as a commuted value lump sum. To avoid immediate taxation in the employee's hands of the lump-sum payment, the ITA permits transfers of the lump-sum amount, on a tax-deferred basis, between registered retirement savings arrangements. The following types of transfers are recognized:

- A transfer from a money purchase provision of an RPP to a money purchase provision of another RPP, or to an RRSP or RRIF;
- A transfer from a money purchase provision of an RPP to a defined benefit provision of an RPP;
- A transfer between defined benefit provisions of RPPs; and
- A transfer from a defined benefit provision of an RPP to a defined contribution provision in another RPP, or to an RRSP or RRIF.

A transfer from a defined benefit plan to an RRSP, RRIF or a defined contribution plan is subject to specified limits in the regulations. With few exceptions, the amount eligible for tax-free transfer is equal to the amount of post-age-65 lifetime retirement benefit that is foregone or surrendered, multiplied by a maximum transfer value factor corresponding to the member's age at the time of transfer.

It is important to note that the maximum transfer limit does not apply for other types of transfers from a defined benefit pension plan, such as a transfer to a spouse or former spouse in respect of death benefits or a division of pension on spousal relationship breakdown. The maximum transfer rules only apply to transfers from defined benefit pension plans and are not applicable to transfers from defined contribution pension plans or other types of plans.

Annuity Purchase

A pension benefit may also be used to purchase an annuity. In the case of a defined contribution plan, the annuity is the pension benefit payable under the plan and the purchase may be made directly from the pension plan. The annuity must be for the member's lifetime and must meet the requirements of revenue rules and pension standards legislation.

In the case of a defined benefit plan, an annuity must replicate the benefit payable from the pension plan in order to be a qualifying annuity. A qualifying annuity is exempt from the maximum transfer limits. The CRA has acknowledged that the pension benefit may not be completely replicable by an annuity.

Alternatively, the commuted value of a defined benefit pension may be transferred to an RRSP, RRIF or defined contribution pension plan, and subsequently used to purchase an annuity. However, the first transfer will be subject to maximum transfer limits.

The use of a pension by the member to purchase an annuity should not be confused with situations where a pension plan administrator purchases an annuity to purchase an annuity to pay or fund the pension benefits under a defined benefit plan. Such annuity purchase may be termed a buy-out or buy-in annuity.

Chapter 9

PENSION STANDARDS LEGISLATION[1]

Executive Summary

Control of the terms and operations of the pension plan is the primary focus of pension standards legislation. Under pension standards legislation the operation of a pension plan is governed by a comprehensive set of rules, and a regulator has the duty and the remedial authority to enforce compliance with those rules. Pensions are provincially regulated and standards legislation exists for all provinces, except one, and for those employees who work within the province unless the work is within the legislative authority of the federal government (in which case federal pension legislation applies). The scope of pension legislation is similar in each jurisdiction, but the details differ substantially among the various jurisdictions. Some of the key minimum standards set by legislation are eligibility for membership, vesting and locking-in, retirement age, pre- and post-retirement death benefits, and pension credit splitting on marriage breakdown. This chapter reviews these and other minimum standards and sets out jurisdictional differences. The chapter also analyzes the impact of pension standards legislation on the financial operations of the plan, including discussions of such topics as solvency liabilities, contribution holidays and surplus, as well as the legislation's impact on plan investments.

History of Pension Standards Legislation

Pension plans are regulated from two perspectives — the control of the terms and operations of the plan, and maximum limits on the tax deferral available. Improving benefit security through control of the terms and operations is the primary focus of pension standards legislation. The federal government controls the tax shelter provided for pension plans through the *Income Tax Act* (ITA).

---

[1] For more information on pension standards legislation, please consult the Morneau Shepell Summary of Pension Legislation in Canada charts in the Canadian Employment Benefits & Pension Guide. Morneau Shepell, Canadian Employment Benefits & Pension Guide, loose-leaf (Toronto: LexisNexis Canada, 2003).

The Development of Pension Standards Legislation

The initiation of pension standards legislation was spurred by the phenomenal growth of private pension plans in the 1950s and 1960s, and the concern that employees were losing all of their pension rights when they terminated employment before retirement. A long delay in the vesting of pension rights was the main problem. Vesting is the unconditional right to retain a pension entitlement (or the value thereof). When vesting was available, employees were able to and often did forfeit their pension rights in order to receive refunds of their contributions. Because of delayed vesting, many employees who had been in several employer-sponsored pension plans received little or nothing from these pension plans upon retirement. A major thrust of pension standards legislation was to preserve pensions on termination of employment prior to retirement so that many workers would benefit, the pressure for public plans would be reduced and the mobility of skilled labour would be improved.

In addition, within organized labour, the theory that pensions are deferred pay has prevailed over the idea that they are provided in recognition of long service. The concept of pensions as deferred pay calls for early, if not immediate, vesting.

Another reason for action by the provinces in the 1960s was to fill the void left by the breakdown and withdrawal of the federal rules on pension plans. Under Canada's constitution, most pension plans are under provincial, not federal, jurisdiction. Until 1958, the federal authorities in Ottawa were in the unhappy position of trying to do indirectly through the ITA what they were not allowed to do directly. Pressures built up and the federal statement of Principles and Rules Respecting Pension Plans was withdrawn. After a gap of several years the old statement was replaced first by Information Circular 71-4 and then by successive versions of Information Circular 72-13.

In light of these developments, provincial governments stepped in to regulate the terms and operations of employer-sponsored pension plans. Over the 30-year period between 1965 and 1995, pension standards statutes were enacted by most provincial governments, and by the federal government for federally regulated employees. Discussions and negotiations led to a large measure of agreement among the authorities having pension legislation and the resulting original statutes and regulations were uniform in their main essentials. Over time, many jurisdictions have amended their pension standards legislation to extend the regulation of pension plans. Many of the original statutes have been substantially revised to improve the minimum benefit standards. The effective date of these comprehensive changes to the standards is commonly referred to as the reform date. The effective dates (as opposed to the date the legislation was actually enacted) of the first pension standards legislation, and reform dates, are as follows:

Jurisdiction	Effective Date	Reform Date	Date of Replacement Pension Legislation
Alberta	January 1, 1967	January 1, 1987	September 1, 2014
British Columbia	January 1, 1993	July 15, 1999	September 30, 2015
Manitoba	July 1, 1976	January 1, 1985	May 31, 2010
New Brunswick	December 31, 1991	—	—
Newfoundland and Labrador	January 1, 1985	January 1, 1997	—
Nova Scotia	January 1, 1977	January 1, 1988	June 1, 2015
Ontario	January 1, 1965	January 1, 1988	—
Quebec	January 1, 1966	January 1, 1990	—
Saskatchewan	January 1, 1969	January 1, 1993	—
Federal	October 1, 1967	January 1, 1987	—

Prince Edward Island passed a *Pension Benefits Act* in 1990, but it has never been proclaimed in force. The province introduced Bill 41, a new *Pension Benefits Act*, on May 17, 2012 which was never passed into force. As a result, there are no references to Prince Edward Island legislation in this chapter.

Some provinces have since completely replaced their pension benefits legislation, namely Alberta, British Columbia, Manitoba and Nova Scotia. The effective dates of this replacement legislation are set out in the table above. Note that the Alberta and British Columbia pension legislation is closely harmonized, following the 2008 recommendations of the Alberta/British Columbia Joint Expert Panel on Pension Standards.

Quebec made some major changes effective January 1, 2001, and subsequently in the 2014-2016 period. In particular, Quebec Bill 57 came into force on January 1, 2016, making significant changes to pension funding regimes in Quebec, among other things.

Pension standards regulation now governs such matters as eligibility for membership, vesting, portability of pensions, death benefits, and disclosure of information. Each jurisdiction has enacted its own pension standards legislation to meet the needs of that particular jurisdiction. Today, Canadian pension standards legislation varies considerably from jurisdiction to jurisdiction. These differences have made pension plan administration complicated for pension plans that have members located in various jurisdictions across Canada.

The federal government has also reformed the provisions of the ITA relating to pension plans. Amendments to the ITA concerning assistance for retirement saving became law on June 27, 1990. These amendments replaced, for the most part, the rules under the old Information Circular 72-13. The focus of the rules since 1990 has been on limiting the amount of funds that can be tax-sheltered by a registered pension plan (RPP).

Registration Requirements and Applicable Laws

Pension standards legislation provides two things:

- A comprehensive set of rules governing the operation of pension plans; and
- A regulator that has the duty and the remedial authority to enforce compliance with those rules.

No employer is required to set up or maintain a pension plan for its employees although all employees must contribute to the Canada or Quebec Pension Plans (CPP/QPP) and the employer must contribute on their behalf. If a pension plan is established by an employer with employees in a jurisdiction that has pension standards legislation, the plan must be registered and must comply with that legislation. Registration under both the federal ITA and the pension standards legislation is essential for an RPP for tax status and compliance. Alternatives to RPPs, such as Deferred Profit Sharing Plans (DPSPs), Supplemental Employee or Executive Retirement Plans (SERPs), group Registered Retirement Savings Plans (group RRSPs), Retirement Compensation Arrangements

(RCAs) and Pooled Registered Pension Plans (PRPPs) are subject to the ITA, but are exempted from pension standards legislation in most cases.[2]

Pension standards legislation exists for all provinces except Prince Edward Island, and applies to employees who work in the province unless the work comes within the application of the federal *Pension Benefits Standards Act, 1985* (PBSA). The PBSA applies to employees in any province who are employed in any work, undertaking, or business that is within the legislative authority of the federal government. This includes businesses in shipping, railways, telephones, broadcasting, and banking, as well as employees in the territories.[3]

Quebec and the federal government have not signed the Memorandum of Reciprocal Agreement (discussed in the following section). Accordingly, a plan with both Quebec and federal members would have to be registered both federally and in Quebec. If the number of federal members exceeds the number of members in other jurisdictions, then the plan is registered federally and in no province other than Quebec, but the federal regulator will have to administer in line with provincial law. If the number of federal members is less than the number of members in other jurisdictions, then the plan is registered provincially and the provincial regulator will be required to regulate federal members in line with federal law.

Pension legislation states that a person is deemed to be employed in the province in which the establishment of the employer where he or she reports to work is situated. If there is no such establishment, the person is deemed to be employed in the province from which his or her remuneration is paid.

Each government has included in its legislation a provision to allow pension plans to be registered in, and supervised by, the jurisdiction in which the plurality of active members are employed. Thus, the functions, authorities, and duties provided to the appointed regulator under each piece of pension standards legislation can be delegated to another regulator. However, the standards of one jurisdiction are not necessarily substituted for another. A plan operating in more than one jurisdiction must comply with the funding standards of the jurisdiction of registration but is still required to apply the particular benefit standards rules of each jurisdiction for the employees in that jurisdiction. The regulator of the jurisdiction in which the pension plan is registered is expected to enforce all applicable benefit standards, including those of other jurisdictions where the plan has members in more than one jurisdiction.

---

2   See Chapters 13 and 14 for detailed discussion of these topics.
3   *Pension Benefits Standards Act, 1985*, R.S.C. 1985, c. 32 (2nd Supp.), s. 4(4).

On October 21, 2008, the Canadian Association of Pension Supervisory Authorities (CAPSA) released a proposed *Agreement Respecting Multi-Jurisdictional Pension Plans* for public consultation. The Agreement would replace the existing Memorandum of Reciprocal Agreement originally signed in 1968. Consultations were held and a revised draft was released on June 30, 2009. A Commentary Guide was released in November 2009.

The Agreement was finalized on May 20, 2011. Ontario and Quebec adopted the Agreement effective July 1, 2011. Other provinces did not sign the Agreement at the time. Effective July 1, 2016, British Columbia, Nova Scotia, Ontario, Quebec, and Saskatchewan signed a *new interim Agreement Respecting Multi-Jurisdictional Pension Plans* that is extremely similar to the 2011 version, but adjusts the rules for determining priority claims on assets in wind-ups and other situations for provinces such as Quebec that abolish solvency funding of defined benefit provisions. A fully revised Agreement is intended to be adopted by 2018.

The Agreement sets out provisions that are subject to the jurisdiction where the plan is registered (the major jurisdiction), including matters such as plan registration, administrators' duties, plan records, funding (with the exception that certain benefits such as post-retirement indexing that are required to be funded under a minor authority's rules must still be funded), investments, and provision of information to members. Member rights are mostly reserved to the province of employment, with the exception that annual statements are subject to the rules of the major jurisdiction.

The Agreement also provides a mechanism for transferring jurisdiction from one province to another. Essentially, the plan will be registered in the province with the plurality of active members. A change in province of registration will occur: after three fiscal years in which a plurality is reported elsewhere, if the number of active members is less than 75% of the number in another province in any year, or if there are zero active members in the province of registration and there are active members in any other jurisdiction. The transfer takes place five days prior to the end of the following fiscal year after the conditions for a transfer are recognized.

Finally, the Agreement provides rules for the enforcement of rules by the major authority, transition provisions, and for asset allocation between jurisdictions on the wind-up of a multi-jurisdictional plan.[4]

---

[4]   See also Chapter 15 for a discussion of the CAPSA Agreement Respecting Multi-Jurisdictional Pension Plans.

Regulatory Cooperation Toward Uniformity

As early as 1968, most supervisory authorities entered into a Memorandum of Reciprocal Agreement to facilitate administration and streamline regulation of plans having members in more than one jurisdiction. This Agreement was the impetus for the legislative provisions permitting plans to be registered in and supervised by the jurisdiction where the plurality of active members are employed. There is no such agreement between the Quebec government and the federal government. Under the Agreement, administrative and procedural matters are to be determined according to the legislation of the province of registration. Matters pertaining to a member's rights are to be determined according to the legislation in a member's jurisdiction (province of employment or federal jurisdiction). On July 26, 2000, the Ontario Divisional Court ruled in *Régie des rentes du Quebec v. Pension Commission of Ontario*[5] (the "Leco" case) that the Agreement does not allow the regulator in the province of plan registration to ignore the legislation of the province where a minority of members resided in the case of a surplus sharing application.

The Canadian Association of Pension Supervisory Authorities was established in 1974. CAPSA is an association of senior government officials who are responsible for the administration of pension standards legislation. Originally, one of CAPSA's prime objectives was to work towards uniformity in the regulatory legislation. However, the political difficulties involved in this process have become evident, and each jurisdiction continues to support whichever policies are felt to be most appropriate for that jurisdiction. CAPSA's mandate is now to facilitate an efficient and effective pension regulatory system in Canada.

In 1993, CAPSA issued the first draft of a *Multilateral Agreement Among Canadian Jurisdictions Respecting Pension Plan Regulation and Supervision*. By 1994, the draft Agreement had been revised, and in September 1994, the members of CAPSA agreed to submit the proposed Agreement to their respective governments with the intention of obtaining the necessary legislation for its implementation.

The concept of the Agreement was to permit a pension plan to be governed entirely by the pension legislation of the jurisdiction in which the plan is registered (with some exceptions). Thus, if a plan were registered in Saskatchewan, for example, then only Saskatchewan pension

---

[5] *Régie des rentes du Quebec v. Pension Commission of Ontario*, [2000] O.J. No. 2845, 189 D.L.R. (4th) 304 (Ont. Div. Ct.).

legislation would apply, even if some plan members worked in Alberta or Quebec.

The Agreement was problematic in that it would have obliged governments to permit the laws of another jurisdiction to apply to their residents. It was never adopted by provincial governments.

On January 19, 2004, CAPSA released for consultation a document entitled "Proposed Regulatory Principles for a Model Pension Law". According to CAPSA at the time, the proposed principles sought to balance the protection of pension plan members' rights with the need to simplify the administrative requirements for multi-jurisdictional pension plans in Canada.

CAPSA proposed a two-step solution to harmonizing Canadian pension legislation. In the short term, the reciprocal agreement would be revised to clearly establish the legislation applicable to various matters regarding pension plans with members who fall under more than one jurisdiction. In order to have effect, the agreement revised by CAPSA must be signed by the respective governments.

In the long term, CAPSA will encourage the Canadian governments to amend their pension legislation in order to adopt key regulatory principles.

From January 19, 2004 until June 30, 2004, CAPSA consulted pension stakeholders across Canada regarding the proposed principles. A separate and parallel consultation was conducted in Quebec during this period by the Regie des rentes du Quebec, as Retraite Quebec was then known.

CAPSA published Proposed Funding Principles for a Model Pension Law in June 2005.

On October 31, 2008, CAPSA released the final "Report on CAPSA's Work on Regulatory Principles for a Model Pension Law". The Report noted CAPSA's decision in 2006 to cease work on principles viewed as contentious, since it would be difficult to achieve stakeholder consensus in light of strong disagreements. However, about 70% of the principles were considered non-contentious. The majority of these principles related to plan administration and minimum standards for entitlements to benefits on termination, death, or retirement.

Contentious issues included the proposed model for plan administrators, pension splitting on marriage breakdown, proposed funding rules, surplus distribution, and reporting by advisors. The report was shared with governments so they can consider the principles in making future legislative changes.

Although no move towards uniform pension legislation seems likely, a degree of harmonization appears to be emerging as pension regulators and government officials share information and agree on best practices in pension regulation. For example, following Manitoba pension reform in 2010, Manitoba legislation tracks legislation in the rest of Canada more closely. The Nova Scotia *Pension Benefits Act* tracks Ontario legislation quite closely, with the exception of some policy differences. The proposed *Pension Benefits Act* of Prince Edward Island found in former Bill 41 tracked Nova Scotia (and consequently Ontario) legislation quite closely. In addition, the Alberta/British Columbia Joint Expert Panel on Pension Standards issued a report in 2008 recommending harmonization of pension legislation between the two provinces. As a result, Alberta and British Columbia adopted nearly identical pension benefits standards legislation in 2014 and 2015.

Minimum Standards

The scope of pension standards legislation in each jurisdiction in Canada is similar. However, the details differ substantially among the various jurisdictions. For example, all pension standards legislation prescribes a minimum period of time after which benefits must become vested, yet even jurisdictions that have undergone pension reform do not all impose the same vesting rules. Some of the key minimum standards are described below. While not exhaustive, the summary describes the prevalent trend and some notable differences.

Eligibility for Membership

An employer is not required to provide a pension plan for its employees. However, when a pension plan does exist, pension standards legislation generally requires that every full-time employee who belongs to the class of employees for whom the plan was established must be allowed to join the plan after two years of employment. It is permissible in some provinces to require employees to join a plan.

In most jurisdictions, part-time employees who are in the same class as eligible full-time employees and who have earned at least 35% of the Year's Maximum Pensionable Earnings (YMPE), as defined under the CPP, for two consecutive years must be allowed to join the pension plan. Alternatively, the employer may set up a separate plan for part-timers if it provides reasonably equivalent benefits. Ontario, Saskatchewan, and Nova Scotia also extend participation to part-time employees who have completed at least 700 hours of employment in each of two consecutive calendar years.

Manitoba compels all eligible full-time employees to join a pension plan, if one exists, after two years of employment, except for certain groups that are exempted under the legislation. Part-time employees must join after two years of employment and after satisfying the requirements set out in the plan, which include some combination of the 700 hours and 35% of the YMPE rule over two consecutive calendar years.

Quebec employees covered by a pension plan must be allowed to join if they have either earned at least 35% of the YMPE or worked 700 hours of employment in the preceding calendar year.

Outside of Manitoba, an employer has the right to make plan membership optional or mandatory for its employees. In addition, Alberta and British Columbia legislation permits "auto-enrollment", in which employees are automatically enrolled if they do not opt out within a specified time limit.

Vesting and Locking-In

"Vesting" means the right of a plan member who terminates employment to receive a benefit in excess of their own contributions with interest, if any, from the pension plan. "Locking-in" is the requirement that the vested entitlement must provide retirement income. The criteria for vesting are the completion of a specified period of employment or plan membership. These are also the criteria for the locking-in of a member's pension. Age requirements for vesting and locking-in have been abolished in all jurisdictions. However, service earned prior to legislative changes abolishing age requirements is governed by the previous rules, because the changes were not retroactive. In all provinces other than New Brunswick, Newfoundland and Labradord and Saskatchewan, all benefits are immediately vested.

The following table lists the vesting and locking-in minimum requirements in the respective jurisdictions with respect to post-reform benefits.

Jurisdiction	Minimum Vesting Requirements	Minimum Locking-in Requirements
Federal	Immediate	2 years of membership
Alberta	Immediate	Immediate
British Columbia	Immediate	Immediate
Manitoba	Immediate	Immediate
New Brunswick	a) 5 years of continuous service; or b) 2 years of plan membership beginning on or after January 1, 2001.	Same as vesting rule
Newfoundland and Labrador	2 years of plan membership	Same as vesting
Nova Scotia	Immediate	Immediate
Ontario	Immediate	Immediate
Quebec	Immediate	Immediate
Saskatchewan	2 years of continuous service	Same as vesting

Exceptions to Locking-In (Unlocking)

There are exceptions to the locking-in rule that permit a plan to pay a cash sum in lieu of all or part of the pension entitlement.

Employees whose employment terminates before meeting the vesting requirement of a contributory pension plan are entitled to a refund of their own contributions with interest. Excess amounts under cost sharing (50% rule), which is discussed later in this chapter, are unlocked in most jurisdictions, with the exception of Quebec and the federal jurisdiction. Additional voluntary contributions are unlocked in all jurisdictions.

Pre-reform pensions may be unlocked as follows:

- 100% of pension earned before January 1, 1967 (Alberta), July 1, 1976 (Manitoba), January 1, 1977 (Nova Scotia), and January 1, 1993 (British Columbia);
- 50% of pension earned before January 1, 1993 (Saskatchewan);
- 25% of the value of pension earned before January 1, 1985 (Manitoba), January 1, 1987 (Ontario) and January 1, 1988 (Nova Scotia).

All provinces provide a small benefit unlocking rule for pension plans. Generally, a pension plan may provide for unlocking if the annual pension at the normal retirement date is less than 4% of the YMPE (not applicable in Alberta, British Columbia, Quebec, and the federal jurisdiction) or the commuted value is less than 20% of the YMPE in Alberta, British Columbia, Manitoba, Nova Scotia, Ontario, Quebec, Saskatchewan, or the federal jurisdiction (10% in Newfoundland and Labrador).[6] The applicable YMPE is from the year of termination in most provinces, but the current YMPE can be used in Alberta, British Columbia and Saskatchewan. Notwithstanding the above, New Brunswick provides for unlocking if the age-adjusted commuted value is less than 40% of the YMPE in the year of termination. Unlocking is a mandatory provision for plans in Alberta, British Columbia, Manitoba, and Quebec, and is optional elsewhere.

All provinces also provide for small benefit unlocking from locked-in accounts, but the rules vary by province.

New Brunswick permits plans to require a compulsory transfer to a locked-in account if the commuted value of the pension is less than 10% of the YMPE. Alberta and British Columbia also permit a plan to require forced portability for all defined contribution plan members who join a plan after August 10, 2006. Ontario, Quebec, Saskatchewan, and the federal regulator permit a plan to require lump-sum cash payments, which may be transferred to an unlocked Registered Retirement Savings Plan (RRSP), pursuant to the regular small benefit unlocking rule discussed above. Manitoba requires plans to make a lump-sum cash payment or transfer to an unlocked RRSP all benefits that fall below the small benefit unlocking threshold.

---

[6]   Note that certain provinces provide that the figure "must not exceed" rather than be less than a certain figure, but we ignore that distinction here.

Some jurisdictions have created further exceptions to the locking-in requirements for pension plan members or locked-in account holders. In nearly all cases, if there is a spouse, spousal consent is a precondition to unlocking pension funds.

It is optional for a plan to offer commutation of pension benefits to non-residents of Canada in Manitoba and Saskatchewan, and mandatory for plans in Alberta, British Columbia, New Brunswick, Quebec, and under the federal jurisdiction. It is optional for locked-in accounts to offer commutation of pension benefits to non-residents of Canada in Manitoba, and mandatory for locked-in accounts in Alberta, Bristish Columbia, New Brunswick, Ontario, Quebec, Saskatchewan, and the federal jurisdiction. Generally speaking, non-residency is established via a letter from the CRA stating that the person is non-resident for income tax purposes.

Exceptions to locking-in can apply for the entire value of the pension where the terminating employee's life expectancy is shortened. This is a mandatory requirement for pension plans in Alberta, British Columbia, Ontario, and Nova Scotia , and is optional in all other jurisdictions. It is a mandatory requirement for locked-in accounts in Alberta, Bristish Columbia, Manitoba, New Brunswick, Nova Scotia, Ontario, and Quebec (LIRA only), and optional elsewhere. The definition of shortened life expectancy is set out in the applicable legislation, but typically requires a physician's letter and a life expectancy of less than two years.

In Alberta, Bristish Columbia, Nova Scotia, Ontario, and the federal jurisdiction, an individual may also be able to access funds in locked-in vehicles in situations involving financial hardship. However, financial hardship unlocking from a pension plan is not allowed. The locked-in account holder must apply to the locked-in account administrator for permission to unlock the funds, and the account holder must meet specific qualifying circumstances set out in the legislation. Qualifying circumstances include such things as the need to pay first and last month's rent, to avoid eviction for unpaid mortgage payments, to pay for medical treatment, to renovate property to accommodate for illness or disability, and low income below a specified threshold. Information on how to apply for financial hardship unlocking is available directly from the regulatory authority in a jurisdiction.

A number of jurisdictions now permit former members who meet certain age requirements to make a one-time election to unlock part of their pension funds in, or on transfer to, certain locked-in accounts. Saskatchewan is the most permissive, allowing full withdrawal after age 55. Alberta permits a one-time option to unlock up to 50% upon transfer from a plan or LIRA to a Life Income Fund (LIF) or LIF-style account within a DC pension plan for a member who has reached age 50. New Brunswick permits a one-time unlocking of up to 25% from a defined benefit plan, where the plan permits, and up to the lesser of 25% or three times the maximum withdrawal permitted for that fiscal year from a LIF. Ontario permits a one-time transfer of up to 50% from a LIF within 60 days of transfer to the LIF. The federal jurisdiction permits one-time unlocking of up to 50% of the value of a locked-in account for a person age 55 or older who transfers funds to a Restricted LIF. Manitoba permits a one-time only transfer option of up to 50% of the balance in a LIF or Retirement Income Fund (RIF) to a creditor-protected Registered Retirement Income Fund (RRIF).

Portability

Portability refers to the ability of a plan member to transfer the commuted value of his or her deferred vested pension to another retirement savings arrangement on termination of employment before retirement age. In all jurisdictions it is permissible, but not mandatory, for a pension plan to provide portability rights to plan members who have attained early or normal retirement age for a defined benefit plan. Some jurisdictions require a plan to provide portability rights to defined contribution plan members who have reached early but not normal retirement age. Alberta, British Columbia, Manitoba, New Brunswick, and Quebec give portability rights to a defined contribution plan member upon termination of employment at any age. In practice, plan sponsors typically allow portability out of a defined contribution plan at any age, since in most cases the only alternative for a defined contribution account is the purchase of an annuity.

In Ontario, the wording of the *Pension Benefits Act* is such that a member who has reached normal retirement date is considered a "retired member". As a result, the Financial Services Commission of Ontario has taken the position that a DB member who has reached normal retirement age under the plan is not permitted to transfer his or her benefit out to the plan. Nova Scotia has similar wording in its legislation, but the Nova Scotia regulator has not yet taken a position on the matter.

In Quebec, pursuant to Bill 57, as of January 1, 2016, the commuted value may be paid out of a defined benefit pension fund only in proportion to the degree of solvency of the plan (up to 100%) unless:

- the member or beneficiary does not have the option of maintaining his benefits in the pension plan; or
- the plan is amended to provide for the full payment of the value of members' and beneficiaries' benefits in a proportion that is greater than the degree of solvency of the plan.

Quebec is the first province in Canada to apply such rules to all defined benefit pension plans, although many multi-employer pension plans, negotiated cost plans, or target benefit plans apply such measures in other provinces.

The locked-in retirement savings arrangements to which a member who is entitled to a deferred pension can transfer the value of benefits are as follows:

- Another registered pension plan (RPP), if that other plan permits;
- A locked-in Registered Retirement Savings Plan (locked-in RRSP), which is offered only in the federal jurisdiction;
- A Locked-In Retirement Account (LIRA), which is the equivalent of a locked-in RRSP and is offered in all other jurisdictions;
- A Life Income Fund (LIF);
- A Locked-In Retirement Income Fund (LRIF), which is now only offered in Newfoundland and Labrador;
- A Registered Retirement Income Fund (RRIF);
- A LIF-style account within a defined contribution pension plan; and
- An insurance company for purchase of an immediate or deferred life annuity.

In 2002, Saskatchewan introduced the creditor-protected RRIF as a portability option giving employees access to their formerly locked-in pension money. The creditor-protected RRIF remains locked-in until age 55, and replaces LIFs and LRIFs in Saskatchewan.

The following table summarizes the transfer options that must be provided in each jurisdiction.

Jurisdiction	Transfer Vehicles
Federal	RPP, locked-in RRSP, LIF, Restricted LIF (after age 55 and after 50% unlocking option is taken), life annuity, or, if the plan permits, a LIF-style account within the plan
Alberta	RPP, LIRA, or, if the plan permits, LIF (after age 50), life annuity, or a LIF-style account within the plan
British Columbia	RPP, LIRA, or, if the plan permits, LIF (after age 50), life annuity, or a LIF-style account within the plan

Jurisdiction	Transfer Vehicles
Manitoba	RPP, LIRA, LIF, life annuity, or, if the plan permits, a LIF-style account within the plan
New Brunswick	RPP, LIRA, LIF, or life annuity
Newfoundland and Labrador	RPP, LIRA, LIF, LRIF, or life annuity
Nova Scotia	RPP, LIRA, LIF, life annuity, or, if the plan permits, a LIF-style account within the plan
Ontario	RPP, LIRA, LIF, or life annuity
Quebec	RPP, LIRA, LIF, locked-in account of a VRSP, life annuity, or, if the plan permits, a LIF-style account within the plan
Saskatchewan	RPP, LIRA, life annuity, creditor-protected RRIF, or, if the plan permits, a LIF-style account within the plan

In a number of jurisdictions, the consent of a member's spouse (if any) is required for a transfer to a LIF or a LIF-style account within a pension plan, but not to other portability options. This is due to the possibility that the LIF will be depleted before the death of the member, leaving the spouse without a survivor pension. Beginning on July 1, 2016, the federal jurisdiction has required the consent of the spouse for a transfer from a pension plan to a locked-in RRSP, LIF or Restricted LIF after the member has reached the early retirement age under the plan.

LIF-Style Accounts within Defined Contribution Pension Plans

The pension benefit provided under a defined contribution pension plan is comprised of a life annuity purchased from an insurance company using the member's account. In reality, most former defined contribution members transfer their benefits to a LIRA or locked-in RRSP, and then to a LIF from which they make annual withdrawals.

The *Income Tax Act* and the legislation in various jurisdictions have been amended to permit a defined contribution pension plan to make LIF-style payments directly from the member's account within the pension plan. This allows members to keep their accounts within the plan through retirement. The pension legislation in Alberta, British Columbia, Manitoba, Nova Scotia, Quebec, Saskatchewan, and the federal jurisdiction permits such LIF-style accounts within a defined contribution pension plan. Ontario has released draft regulations to permit such accounts.

Normal, Early, Postponed, and Phased Retirement

All jurisdictions require that a pension plan contain rules concerning the earliest age or "normal retirement date", at which a pension is paid without reduction, or the normal retirement age for the plan. The normal retirement date remains relevant, despite the fact that mandatory retirement has been effectively abolished in most Canadian jurisdictions. The concept of a normal retirement date is more meaningful for defined benefit plans, since reduction for early commencement can apply before that date.

In Ontario, New Brunswick, and Nova Scotia, the normal retirement date cannot be later than one year after age 65 is attained. In Manitoba, this age cannot be later than the first of the month following the month in which unreduced retirement benefits are payable under the CPP. In Quebec, this age cannot be later than the first of the month following the month in which age 65 is attained, and in Newfoundland and Labrador, it cannot be later than the date the member attains 65. Other jurisdictions such as Alberta, British Columbia, Saskatchewan, and the federal jurisdiction leave the normal retirement date to the discretion of the employer, although 65 is typical.

Legislation in Alberta, British Columbia, Manitoba, New Brunswick, Nova Scotia, Ontario, Quebec and Saskatchewan requires that a plan member whose employment or plan membership ceases within the 10 years before the normal retirement date is entitled to receive an immediate pension. The federal legislation has a similar rule that states that early pension entitlement occurs within 10 years of "pensionable age", which is the earliest date on which a pension can be received without reduction and without employer consent. Newfoundland and Labrador prescribe that the entitlement occurs at age 55. All jurisdictions require that if a pension is reduced for early commencement, the reduced pension must be at least actuarially equivalent in value to the pension deferred to normal retirement date.

A phased retirement agreement in line with the standards of the ITA is permitted in Alberta, British Columbia, Manitoba, New Brunswick, Nova Scotia, Quebec, Saskatchewan, and the federal jurisdiction. [7] Legislation permitting phased retirement has been passed in Ontario, but

---

[7]   More information on phased retirement is contained in Chapter 3.

not yet proclaimed into force. These rules allow a member to receive a partial pension under a pension plan to compensate for a reduction in work hours. Alberta and Quebec also provide another type of lump-sum withdrawal in relation to phased retirement.

Pension standards legislation sets minimum standards for the treatment of plan members who remain employed beyond the normal retirement date. Generally, a member can delay receipt of pension and continue to earn benefits, subject to any plan rules concerning maximum service or benefit amounts or, as an alternative, commence receiving the pension at normal retirement age even though employment continues. The pension does not have to be actuarially adjusted to account for the postponed pension commencement in most jurisdictions, although the plan administrator may elect to do so. In Manitoba, the pension payable cannot be less than the pension that would have been payable at normal retirement age actuarially increased for the postponement.

In Quebec, members may postpone their normal pension if employment continues with the same employer they were employed with at normal retirement date. During the postponement period, members may require payment of all or part of the normal pension, but only to the extent necessary to offset any permanent reduction in remuneration. The amount of the postponed pension not paid is adjusted at the end of the postponement. However, if an agreement is made between the member and the employer, a member may receive all or part of his pension, regardless of the limit (unless otherwise stated in the pension plan). If contributions are paid during the postponement period, the resulting additional amount of pension must be of an equal or greater value than that of the benefits that could be purchased, at the end of the postponement period, with the member's contribution paid during such a period, including accrued interest. An adjustment will be made to ensure that the pension payable at the end of the postponement is actuarially equivalent to the pension had the pension not been postponed

Death Benefits Before Pension Commencement

Every pension plan must define what benefits, if any, a vested plan member's spouse (as defined by the pension standards legislation), beneficiary, or estate will receive if the member dies before pension commencement. These benefits are generally referred to as pre-retirement death benefits.

Pension legislation requires a pension plan to provide pre-retirement death benefits if a vested plan member dies before pension commencement, either before or after termination of employment. The specifics of the requirements vary considerably. In most jurisdictions

100% or 60% of the commuted value of the vested pension earned by the member must be paid to the spouse, or if there is no spouse, to another beneficiary or the member's estate. Some jurisdictions require only a refund of contributions if there is no spouse. Most jurisdictions have provisions whereby a spouse may waive entitlement to a pre-retirement death benefit. An eligible spouse is entitled, depending on the jurisdiction, to choose an immediate or deferred pension, to transfer the death benefit to a locked-in account, to transfer the death benefit to an unlocked RRSP, or to take the death benefit in a lump-sum cash payment. These measures are consistent with the idea that survivors should be protected, and that vested pensions should not be forfeited.

The following table sets out details of the pre-retirement death benefit requirements in the respective jurisdictions.

Jurisdiction	Pre-Retirement Death Benefit Requirement
Federal	100% of the commuted value of the pension
Alberta	100% of the commuted value of the pension
British Columbia	100% of the commuted value of the pension
Manitoba	100% of the commuted value of the pension
New Brunswick	100% of the commuted value of the vested pension
Newfoundland and Labrador	100% of the commuted value of the vested post-1996 pension
Nova Scotia	100% of the commuted value of the post-1987 vested pension. Pre-1988 contributions with interest.
Ontario	100% of the commuted value of post-1986 vested pension. Pre-1987 contributions with interest.
Quebec	(a) If, prior to member's normal retirement date, a lump-sum benefit equal to or greater than the commuted value of post-1989 vested pension; and (b) if, after normal retirement date, the spouse is entitled to a pension equal to at least the greater of (a) above and a 60% joint and survivor pension.

Jurisdiction	Pre-Retirement Death Benefit Requirement
Saskatchewan	If member was eligible to retire, a 60% joint and survivor pension for post-1993 service and a pension equal to the value of pre-1994 contributions with interest; if member was not eligible to retire, a pension equal to 100% of the commuted value of the pension.

Death Benefits After Pension Commencement

Every pension plan must specify the form of pension that it will be. This determines what benefits, if any, the pensioner's spouse, beneficiary, or estate will receive when the pensioner dies after pension commencement.

Pension standards legislation does not prescribe forms of pension except:

- To require that the pension must be payable to the pensioner for his or her lifetime; and
- To provide a retiree's eligible spouse (if any) with the right to a survivor pension.

In all jurisdictions, for a member who has an eligible spouse (as defined by pension standards legislation) at the time of pension commencement, the form of pension that must be paid is a joint and survivor pension unless a waiver is signed by the spouse. In all the jurisdictions that require a joint and survivor pension, the pension payable to the spouse after the member's death cannot be less than 60% of the pension that the member was receiving. An eligible spouse is typically a spouse that is not living separate and apart from the member, although in some cases a married but separated spouse is also eligible for a survivor pension.

Cost Sharing (50% Rule)

Cost sharing is a minimum standard applicable to contributory defined benefit pension plans. It requires the employer to pay for a minimum percentage, namely 50%, of a member's pension entitlement. This cost-sharing requirement is commonly referred to as the "50% rule". All jurisdictions require contributory defined benefit pension plans to provide employer cost sharing. In most jurisdictions, cost sharing was introduced when pension standards legislation was reformed in the 1980s and 1990s.

The 50% rule is applied at the time of an employee's death or termination of service. At that time, if the value of the employee's required contributions made after the prescribed date with credited interest is greater than 50% of the commuted value of his or her vested pension earned over the same period, the excess amount of member contributions must be refunded or used to provide additional benefits. In some jurisdictions, the 50% cost-sharing rule applies to the member's vested pension, while in other jurisdictions, it applies to the member's vested contributory pension.

There are a couple of exceptions to the 50% rule. In New Brunswick, the 50% minimum limit applies unless the plan specifies a different percentage. Plans subject to the federal PBSA do not have to apply the 50% rule if the pension plan provides for the annual indexation of deferred pensions (to payment date) at a rate that is at least 75% of the increase in the Consumer Price Index (CPI), less 1%, or an equivalent rate acceptable to the federal authorities.

The following table summarizes the options that must be given to a plan member with respect to excess contributions under the 50% rule:

Jurisdiction	Effective Date	Required Options
Federal	January 1, 1987	• increase pension • plan may instead require choice of locked-in transfer to RPP, locked-in RRSP, LIF, or transfer to insurance company to purchase annuity
Alberta	January 1, 1987	• lump-sum refund • transfer to RPP • transfer to RRSP or RRIF • transfer to insurance company to purchase annuity • plan may offer increased pension
British Columbia	January 1, 1993	• lump-sum refund • transfer to RPP • transfer to RRSP or RRIF • transfer to insurance company to purchase annuity • plan may offer increased pension
Manitoba	January 1, 1985	• lump-sum refund • transfer to RRSP or RRIF • plan may offer increased pension

Jurisdiction	Effective Date	Required Options
New Brunswick	December 31, 1991	• lump-sum refund • transfer to RRSP or RRIF
Newfoundland and Labrador	January 1, 1997	• lump-sum refund • transfer to RPP • transfer to retirement savings arrangement • transfer to insurance company to purchase annuity • plan may offer increased pension
Nova Scotia	January 1, 1988	• lump-sum refund • transfer to RRSP or RRIF
Ontario	January 1, 1987	• lump-sum refund
Quebec	January 1, 1990	• increase pension • transfer on locked-in basis as permitted by plan
Saskatchewan	January 1, 1969	• lump-sum refund • transfer to RPP • transfer to RRSP • transfer to insurance company to purchase annuity • plan may offer increased pension

Under the ITA, excess contributions may be transferred to another retirement arrangement on a tax-deferred basis only if the member also elects to transfer the commuted value of pension out of the pension plan. The sum of the commuted value and the excess contributions is subject to the maximum transfer limit under the ITA.

Inflation Protection

Subject to the paragraph set out below respecting Quebec, it is not necessary for any pension plan to provide inflation protection in order to comply with pension standards legislation. However, a federally regulated pension plan must provide either employer cost sharing, or inflation protection for pensions at the rate of 75% of increases in the CPI minus 1%.

In Ontario, the pension standards legislation contains provisions that appear to mandate inflation protection. However, the legislation stipulates that the inflation protection be provided according to a prescribed formula. Ontario has not prescribed the formula for such indexation and so the requirement is treated as having no force or effect.

In Quebec, the requirement for partial indexation if the member ceases active membership or dies 10 years or more before the normal retirement age (usually age 55) was introduced on January 1, 2001, and repealed as of January 1, 2016, as part of Bill 57. The indexation period only applies to years of service accumulated on or after January 1, 2001 and before the plan is amended to remove partial indexing (if applicable). Indexing only applies to the period between the date the membership ended and the date that is 10 years before the plan's normal retirement age (usually age 55). Bill 57 provided that an amendment to a pension plan to remove partial indexation on service prior to 2016 is permitted, despite the reduction in accrued benefits, if made prior to 2017.

Deadline for Employer Contributions

An employer is required to make its contributions within deadlines specified by legislation, or by the plan text or other plan documents if earlier. Pension legislation also requires the employer to notify the pension fund holder in advance of the contribution schedule, and requires the pension fund holder (and possibly the administrator) to notify the provincial regulator if contributions are not made by a specified deadline.

The employer contribution deadlines are as follows.

Defined Benefit Plan (Normal Cost):

Jurisdiction	Remittance Deadline
Alberta, Bristish Columbia, Manitoba, Nova Scotia, Ontario, Saskatchewan, and Federal	Within 30 days after the end of the month for which contributions are payable.
Newfoundland and Labrador,	Within 30 days after the end of the quarter for which contributions are payable
Quebec	Last day of the month for which contributions are payable.

Defined Benefit Plan (Normal Cost):

Jurisdiction	Remittance Deadline
New Brunswick	Within 30 days after the last day of the month in which the normal cost is incurred, if benefits would decrease or member contributions would increase as a result of later payment. Otherwise, for a plan with a solvency ratio of less than 100%, within 90 days after the last day of the month in which the normal cost is incurred, or for a plan with a solvency ratio of 100% or greater, within 120 days after the last day of the pension plan year in which the normal cost is incurred.

Defined Contribution Plan:

Jurisdiction	Remittance Deadline
Alberta, British Columbia, Manitoba, Newfoundland and Labrador, and Saskatchewan	Within 30 days after the end of the month to which contributions relate, unless contributions relate to profits, in which case 90 days after the end of the fiscal year.
Quebec	Last day of the month following the month of receipt.
New Brunswick, Nova Scotia, Ontario, and Federal	Within 30 days after the end of the month to which contributions relate.

Protection of Employee Contributions

Required and voluntary employee contributions to a pension plan that are received by an employer from the member or deducted directly from the employee's pay are deemed to be held in trust until deposited to the pension fund.

Each jurisdiction requires the employer to remit employee contributions to the pension fund within certain times.

The following table summarizes the timetable for the receipt of member contributions and remittance to the pension fund for each jurisdiction.

Jurisdiction	Remittance Deadline
Alberta, British Columbia, Manitoba, Newfoundland and Labrador, Nova Scotia, Ontario, and Saskatchewan	Within 30 days after the end of the month of receipt or deduction.
Quebec	Last day of the month following the month of receipt or deduction
Federal	30 days from the end of the period in which contributions were deducted
New Brunswick	15 days from the end of the month of receipt or deduction

Minimum Interest Rate Credited to Employee Contributions

Prior to regulatory controls, employers were able to determine the interest rate (if any) to be credited to employee contributions. All jurisdictions now require that a prescribed minimum rate of interest be credited to employee-required and voluntary contributions.

Generally, the annual rate of interest to be credited to employee contributions made to a defined contribution pension plan is the investment rate of return earned by the pension fund, less administration expenses if the plan so provides.

For employee-required contributions made to a defined benefit pension plan, most jurisdictions permit the pension plan to provide a rate based on five-year personal fixed-term chartered bank deposit rates (CANSIM series B14045, also known as series V122515) averaged over a period not exceeding 12 months, or the rate of return earned by the pension fund less administration expenses. Saskatchewan permits the CANSIM rate to be rounded down to the next 0.1%.

Defined benefit plans in the federal jurisdiction, and in New Brunswick, and Newfoundland and Labrador may apply either of the two rates (above) to employee voluntary contributions. Alberta, British Columbia, Manitoba, Nova Scotia, Ontario and Saskatchewan require that the pension fund rate of return (less administration expenses) be credited to employee voluntary contributions. Quebec requires that the pension fund rate of return (less administration expenses) be credited to both employee-required contributions and employee voluntary contributions.

Legislation in many of the jurisdictions requires interest to be credited to employee contributions from the first of the month following the month contributions are required to be deposited into the pension fund. Interest must be credited to a member's date of termination of service. Where contributions are refunded to a member, most jurisdictions require that interest be credited to the month of payment.

Pension Credit Splitting on Marriage Breakdown

In *Clarke v. Clarke*, the Supreme Court of Canada stated that pension benefits are matrimonial assets and subject to division, unless the legislation specifically states otherwise. As such, all provinces treat pension benefits as family property.

Several jurisdictions, such as British Columbia, Manitoba, and Saskatchewan, provide for division of family property for common-law spouses, while the majority only provide for division of family property for married spouses who have experienced a separation or divorce. As a result, most separations of common-law spouses do not result in a division of pension.

Regulations concerning the calculation of pension credits available for division vary considerably in each jurisdiction. Furthermore, the federal jurisdiction adopts pension division rules based on the member's province of residence, with certain modifications.

In addition, the different jurisdictions have different options regarding when the non-member spouse will receive his or her portion of the benefit. At times, there will be an immediate payment, while at other times the benefit will not be paid until a triggering event occurs, such as termination or retirement.

All of the jurisdictions permit separating spouses to offset the value of pension benefits against other matrimonial assets, as opposed to dividing the actual pension benefits. Manitoba requires specific procedures where a spouse intends to opt out of otherwise mandatory pension splitting.

The following table summarizes some of the main characteristics of pension splitting rules as they apply to spouses and the jurisdictions in which they apply. The following are general guidelines. Each jurisdiction must be reviewed for specific exceptions.

Jurisdiction	Earliest Date that Pension is Payable to Spouse of Non-Retired Member
Nova Scotia (defined benefit)	Payment can be made at the earlier of termination or pension commencement.
Alberta, British Columbia, Manitoba, New Brunswick, Newfoundland and Labrador, Nova Scotia (defined contribution only), Ontario, Quebec, Saskatchewan, and Federal	Payment to member's spouse can be made immediately after domestic agreement or court order.
Jurisdiction	**Maximum Amount Payable to Member's Spouse**
Alberta, Manitoba (domestic contract), New Brunswick (domestic contract), Newfoundland and Labrador, Nova Scotia, Ontario, Quebec (domestic contract)	50% of amount earned during marriage/relationship
Saskatchewan	50% of value of entire pension
British Columbia, Manitoba (court order), New Brunswick (court order), Quebec (court order), and Federal	100% of entire pension

Evolution of Marriage-Like Relationships and Same-Sex Marriage

One area of the law that has evolved is the extension of rights and obligations to persons who are living with same-sex partners, both under marriage and common-law status.

Beginning in the late 1990s, courts began to rule that various spousal benefits should be payable to same-sex spouses on the same terms as opposite-sex spouses. (For example, see the 1999 Supreme Court of Canada ruling in *M. v. H.*).[8] As a result, a number of jurisdictions provided spousal rights under pension legislation to same-sex couples on the same terms as opposite-sex couples who cohabited for a set period (*i.e.*, common-law couples).

---

[8]   *M. v. H.*, [1999] S.C.J. No. 23, [1999] 2 S.C.R. 3 (S.C.C.).

From about 2003 to 2005, courts in a number of provinces ruled that the opposite-sex definition of marriage violates the Charter of Rights and Freedoms. As a result, same-sex marriage was considered legal in provinces where the courts so ruled.

The federal Parliament passed Bill C-38, the *Civil Marriage Act*, in 2005. It became law upon Royal Assent on July 20, 2005. As a result, same-sex marriage is now legally recognized across Canada.

While the federal government has authority over the definition of marriage, the provinces regulate spousal status under pension benefits standards legislation. Each jurisdiction, including the federal jurisdiction, specifies which spousal relationships are recognized for the purposes of pension plan entitlements. The definition of spouse is important in determining entitlements to pre-retirement death benefits as well as survivor pensions after retirement. In addition, the unlocking of pension benefits is typically subject to the spouse's consent, where applicable.

Certain jurisdictions define a "spouse" to include both married and common-law couples, whereas others have separate definitions of "spouse" and "common-law partner". Ontario originally had a separate definition of "same-sex partner", but the term was abolished by Bill 171 in 2005. Alberta uses the term "pension partner" for both opposite-sex and same-sex couples. New Brunswick adopted an amended definition of "spouse" and "common-law" partner in order to recognize same-sex spouses in 2011.

With regard to benefit determination, spousal status *at the relevant time* is the determining factor. For example, survivor pensions and pre-retirement death benefits are not payable to a spouse who is not living separate and apart from the member at the relevant time. Other provinces require a minimum separation period or include all separated, but married spouses. In some cases, the term "living separate and apart" is present in the actual definition of spouse, whereas in others it is found elsewhere in the legislation.

Pension benefit standards legislation varies in a number of other ways across jurisdictions, including the period of cohabitation required for recognition of a common-law relationship, the entitlements of married but separated spouses and the period of separation, if any, required for the termination of spousal status. The ITA recognizes common-law spousal status after one year of cohabitation, but many provinces impose longer cohabitation requirements.

The registration of common-law unions has been instituted in Nova Scotia and Manitoba. In Nova Scotia, couples can file domestic-partner declarations with the province to create legally-recognized "domestic partnerships". As a result, domestic partners are entitled to enjoy all of the same rights as married spouses under pension benefits legislation. The same applies in Manitoba to couples who register a common-law relationship under the *Vital Statistics Act*.

In Quebec, a "marriage-like" state has been created — the civil union — because common-law partnerships are generally not recognized under the *Civil Code of Québec* (although they are recognized for death benefit purposes in pension legislation). The civil union was introduced in Quebec before same-sex marriage was legally recognized by the federal government. The civil union continues to exist under the *Civil Code of Québec*. It is defined as "a commitment by two persons eighteen years of age or over who express their free and enlightened consent to live together and to uphold the rights and obligations that derive from that status". Individuals in a civil union must be unmarried and cannot be parties to another civil union, nor may the parties be siblings, ascendants, or descendants. The union must be formally solemnized by an officiant who is legally authorized to solemnize marriages in Quebec.

The following table sets out the definitions of spouse and common-law partner as provided in the various minimum pension standards legislation.

Jurisdiction	Definition of Spouse/Common-Law Partner
Federal	A "spouse" of an individual is defined as a person who is married to the individual and includes a void marriage. A "common-law partner" is a person who is cohabiting with another individual in a conjugal relationship, having so cohabited for a period of at least one year.
Alberta	A "pension partner" is (a) a person who, at the relevant date, was married to the member and had not been living separate and apart from the member for a continuous period longer than three (3) years; or if clause (a) does not apply, a person who has been living with the member in a marriage-like relationship, for a continuous period of at least three (3) years preceding the relevant date; or of some permanence, if there is a child of the relationship by birth or adoption.
British Columbia	A "spouse" means (a) a person who at the relevant date was married to the member, and not living separate and apart from the member for a continuous period longer than two years; or (b) a person who lived with the member in a marriage-like relationship for a period of at least two years immediately preceding the relevant date.

Jurisdiction	Definition of Spouse/Common-Law Partner
Manitoba	A "spouse" of an individual is a person who is married to the individual. Spouse loses entitlement if living separate and apart. A "common-law partner" of a member or former member means a person who, not being married to the member or former member, cohabited with him or her in a conjugal relationship (a) for a period of at least three years, if either of them is married; or (b) for a period of at least one year, if neither of them is married. It also includes a person with whom the member has registered a common-law relationship under the *Vital Statistics Act*.
New Brunswick	A "spouse" means either of two persons who (a) are married to each other; (b) are married to each other by a marriage that is voidable and has not been voided by a declaration of nullity; or (c) have gone through a form of marriage in good faith that is void and have cohabited within the preceding year. A "common-law partner" means either of two persons who are not married to each other and who have cohabited in a conjugal relationship for a continuous period of at least two years.
Newfoundland and Labrador	A "spouse" means (except in relation to the splitting of credits upon marital breakdown, in which case "spouse" must meet the definition set out in the *Family Law Act*) a person who (a) is married to the member or former member; (b) is married to the member or the former member by a marriage that is voidable and has not been voided by a declaration of nullity; (c) has gone through a form of marriage in good faith that is void and is cohabiting or has cohabited with the member or former member within the preceding year. Spouse loses entitlement if there is a cohabiting partner. A "cohabiting partner", (a) in relation to a member or former member who has a spouse, means a person who is not the spouse of the member or former member and who has cohabited continuously with the member or former member in a conjugal relationship for not less than three years; or (b) in relation to a member or former member who does not have a spouse, means a person who has cohabited continuously with the member or former member in a conjugal relationship for not less than one year; and is cohabiting or has

Jurisdiction	Definition of Spouse/Common-Law Partner
	cohabited with the member or former member within the preceding year.
Nova Scotia	A "spouse" means either of two persons who (a) are married to each other; (b) are married to each other by a marriage that is voidable and has not been annulled by a declaration of nullity; (c) have gone through a form of marriage with each other, in good faith, that is void and are cohabiting or, if they have ceased to cohabit, have cohabited within the twelve-month period immediately preceding the date of entitlement; (d) are domestic partners within the meaning of the *Vital Statistics Act*; or (e) not being married to each other, cohabited in a conjugal relationship with each other: (i) for a period of at least three years, if either of them is married, or (ii) for a period of at least one year, if neither of them is married. Spouse loses rights if living separate and apart with no prospect of resumption of cohabitation, and spouse has signed waiver or is not entitled to benefits due to separation agreement or court order.
Ontario	A "spouse" means two persons who (a) are married to each other; or (b) are not married to each other and are living together in a conjugal relationship, (i) continuously for a period of not less than three years, or (ii) in a relationship of some permanence, if they are the natural or adoptive parents of a child, both as defined in the *Family Law Act*. Spouse loses rights if living separate and apart.
Quebec	A "spouse" of a member is a person who (a) is married to or in a civil union with the member; or (b) has been living in a conjugal relationship with the member who is not married or is not in a civil union for a period of not less than three years or for a period of not less than one year if (i) they have at least one child, (ii) they have adopted jointly at least one child, or (iii) one of them has adopted at least one child who is the child of the other. Spouses loses entitlement if legally separated from bed and board.

Jurisdiction	Definition of Spouse/Common-Law Partner
Saskatchewan	A "spouse" means (a) a person who is married to a member or former member; or (b) if a member or former member is not married, a person with whom the member or former member is cohabiting as a spouse at the relevant time and who has been cohabiting continuously with the member or former member as his or her spouse for at least one year prior to the relevant time.

Gender Discrimination

Legislation in all jurisdictions other than Newfoundland and Labrador and Quebec prohibits the use of different eligibility rules for plan membership, different employee contribution rates and different pension benefits based on the gender of an employee. Quebec mandates the use of a sex-distinct mortality table for benefit calculations. In most jurisdictions that impose these unisex standards, the requirements apply to pension benefits earned after the effective date of pension reform.

Financial Issues

Pension standards legislation focuses on the funding and financial operations of pension plans, as well as on benefit standards. While Chapter 6 deals with the financial management of pension plans, the focus of the following section of this chapter is to provide an overview of the impact of pension standards legislation on the financial operations of a pension plan. The concepts discussed here, such as solvency liabilities, are in many jurisdictions defined with considerable precision and there is significant variation from jurisdiction to jurisdiction.

Funding Requirements — Defined Benefit Plans

Ongoing and Solvency

When an employer establishes a defined benefit pension plan, it assumes an obligation to fund the plan in accordance with applicable pension standards legislation. That legislation requires that a pension plan must be pre-funded or be in the process of becoming fully pre-funded. The reason for the pre-funding requirement is to provide security for the benefits the employer has promised to the members and that have accrued to their credit. In contrast, the thrust of the ITA provisions governing an employer's contributions to a pension plan is to ensure that there is adequate actuarial justification for the contributions, with a view to ensuring that the employer does not overfund.

Pension standards legislation requires that a plan be valued at least every three years (one year in some cases where the plan is underfunded). An actuarial valuation involves the comparison of the value of the assets in the plan fund to the value of the benefits the plan is expected to pay. Valuations to determine funding requirements are required on two very different bases — an ongoing basis, and a solvency basis. An ongoing valuation focuses on the ability of the plan to meet its obligations, assuming that it continues to operate. For example, in a final average earnings plan, the valuation on an ongoing basis views the plan as if members will continue to accrue benefits and receive pay increases, in accordance with the plan terms and assumptions used in the valuation respectively. The ongoing valuation attempts to show whether the funding of the plan is on course, just as a personal review of income and expenses would show if an individual is on course to meet his or her financial targets.

Most defined benefit plans are required to also fund their benefits on a solvency basis, although exceptions are made for some multi-employer pension plans, jointly sponsored pension plans, and public sector pension plans. A solvency valuation focuses on the ability of the plan to meet its obligations if it is terminated as at the review date. At first glance, it may seem more likely that a plan will be fully funded on a solvency basis simply because members cease to accrue benefits. However, the plan terms or pension standards legislation may result in the plan having additional liabilities on termination that it does not have if it continues on an ongoing basis. The solvency of a plan is determined as the aggregate of the market value of the plan assets and the present value of future special payments, over the liabilities of the plan where the liabilities are determined on a plan termination basis, including additional benefits that may become payable as a result of plan termination. If liabilities exceed assets, the plan has a solvency deficiency, and if assets exceed liabilities, the plan has a solvency excess.

In Quebec, Bill 57 has amended, since January 1, 2016, the funding rules for private sector defined benefit plans by eliminating the solvency-basis funding requirement. However, it has added a stabilization provision that must be funded on a going-concern basis.

The 2016 Ontario Budget announced a review of the solvency funding framework for Ontario-registered defined benefit plans, which may involve the modification or abolition of solvency funding rules.

Contributions

There are two basic types of payments that must be made by an employer to a pension plan: current service cost (sometimes referred to as normal cost) and special payments. The current service cost is the employer's obligation to contribute to the plan in respect of benefits expected to accrue to members in each year of the valuation period. Special payments are required if actuarial liabilities exceed the value of pension fund assets. "Special payments" is a catch-all term encompassing payments that must be made to fund the plan as a result of certain triggering events, such as an amendment that increases accrued benefits, a change in actuarial methods or assumptions, or plan experience (*e.g.*, investment returns or mortality rate) that is less or more favourable than anticipated. Generally, when special payments are required, the employer is not required to fully fund the amount of the special payments immediately. Instead, the special payments may be amortized over a period of five to 15 years, as set out in the applicable pension standards legislation. Payments made to fund a solvency deficiency are included in the special payments. As of January 1, 2016, Quebec requires the accumulation of a "stabilization provision" in defined benefit plans.

Contribution Holidays

When the assets of a plan exceed its liabilities, the plan is said to have surplus assets. In the jurisdicitons of Alberta and British Columbia, the term actuarial excess is used to distinguish surplus assets in an ongoing plan from surplus assets on plan termination. It is normal actuarial practice to take the surplus into account when determining whether or not an employer must make contributions in order to properly fund a plan.

A "contribution holiday" occurs when the sponsoring employer decides not to make new contributions to the pension plan, because an actuary has determined that the plan is more than fully funded, having assets in excess of its liabilities. All pension standards legislation now permits the employer to take a contribution holiday, if the plan permits, for as long as the actuary determines that the plan will remain fully funded without further contributions. In Alberta and British Colmbia, the up to 20% of the plan's actuarial excess may be used to reduce or eliminate employer contributions. However, Alberta, British Columbia, Manitoba, Nova Scotia, and the federal jurisdiction now require that a contribution holiday may only be taken in respect of surplus exceeding 5% of liabilities (going concern or solvency, depending on the jurisdiction). Newfoundland and Labrador permits a contribution holiday only in respect of surplus exceeding 10% of solvency liabilities. Saskatchewan requires Superintendent consent to contribution holidays. Alberta, British Columbia, Nova Scotia and Saskatchewan require disclosure of contribution holidays to members.

In Quebec, new rules restricting contribution holidays were added in 2001 to the legislation. These rules were abolished and replaced as of January 1, 2016.

In Quebec, the rules regarding the use of a plan's actuarial surplus (while the plan is ongoing and in the event of plan termination) were significantly altered by Bill 57 which became effective January 1, 2016.

Subject to applicable requirements, when the plan reaches a funding ratio of at least 105%, plus the stabilisation provision, and funding on a solvency basis is at least 105%, the excess surplus that may be used is prescribed, depending on which amount is the lesser.

All provisions concerning the use of surplus assets (while the plan is ongoing and in the event of plan termination) must be grouped in an easily identifiable section of the plan. There is a mechanism for member consultation to amend the plan to include such provisions. If 30% or more of the members and beneficiaries oppose the proposed amendment, it is deemed rejected and cannot be made.

The provisions regarding the principle of equitable use of surplus assets have been eliminated.

The new rules also introduced a legislative framework for a "banker's clause" provision, which can be used for the payment of employer and member contributions when the plan shows an actuarial surplus and, in certain circumstances, can be used for benefit improvements or refunded to the employer. The banker's clause assets must be monitored separately and includes investment returns.

Under the ITA, contributions are not permitted if surplus exceeds set limits (set out later in this chapter). An employer may not make contributions exceeding these limits regardless of plan terms or provincial legislation.

Funding Relief for Defined Benefit Plans

Defined benefit pension plans hit a "perfect storm" of funding difficulties in the first few years after 2000, due to poor stock market returns and historically low discount rates. Matters became even worse in 2008 and 2009, due to the global financial crisis. This made it more expensive for employers to fund their solvency deficiencies. As a result, numerous employers pressed legislators and regulators for relief from legislated solvency funding requirements.

As a result, most jurisdictions introduced defined benefit solvency funding relief measures, for limited periods of time, during the past few years. In many cases, additional notice to members was required and restrictions on benefit improvements were imposed during the relief period. The main types of funding relief were a moratorium on funding the deficit identified as resulting from the financial crisis, consolidating prior deficits into a single five-year funding period, and extending the solvency funding period from five to 10 years. Solvency funding measures applicable to defined benefit pension plans are listed in the following table.

Jurisdiction	Temporary Solvency Funding Relief Measure
Federal	Funding relief was available in respect of a new solvency deficiency identified in an actuarial valuation report with an effective date between November 1, 2008, and October 31, 2009. In the first year of the 10-year period, all plan sponsors were able to fund the solvency deficiency on a reduced basis. There were three options available after the first year: • Option 1: Extend the solvency funding payment period by an additional year; • Option 2: Extend the solvency funding payment period to 10 years with member and retiree support; or • Option 3: Extend the solvency funding payment period to 10 years with letters of credit.
Alberta	Single employer pension plan administrators could apply for a three-year moratorium from making special solvency payments before the end of 2009. Alternatively, single employer pension administrators could extend the solvency funding amortization period from 5 to 10 years for newly arising solvency deficits. The application could be made for a valuation report with a valuation date between September 1, 2008 and December 31, 2009. An additional period of funding relief was offered in 2012. Two options were available: (a) consolidation of previous solvency deficiencies, and (b) extension of the amortization period from 5 to 10 years.

Jurisdiction	Temporary Solvency Funding Relief Measure
British Columbia	Pension Bulletin PEN-2009-01, issued in January 2009, set out an application process and some specific factors the Superintendent will consider in an application for an extension of the solvency funding period. The Superintendent will not approve a solvency funding extension beyond 15 years. Pension Bulletin PEN-11-002, issued in August 2011, provided further guidance to plan administrators on making an application for a solvency extension request.
Manitoba	In 2008, Manitoba provided for a consolidation of past solvency deficiencies and extension of the amortization period to 10 years for solvency deficiencies reported in the first actuarial valuation filed between December 30, 2008 and January 2, 2011. In 2011, Manitoba adopted a regulation providing for a consolidation of past solvency deficiencies and temporary extension of the amortization period to 10 years for solvency deficiencies reported in the first actuarial valuation filed between December 30, 2011 and January 2, 2014.
New Brunswick	The plan administrator was permitted to consolidate all existing solvency schedules and amortize the solvency shortfall over a 10-year period for a valuation report with a review date between April 1, 2010 and January 1, 2012. Notice was required to be provided to all members and other plan beneficiaries. During the extended period, annual actuarial reports are not required. Any benefit improvements during the extended amortization period must be fully funded.
Newfoundland and Labrador	With respect to a valuation report dated between January 1, 2010 to January 1, 2013, a plan could elect one of the following funding methods: • Consolidating previous solvency deficiencies into a new, single five-year period, • Extending the solvency funding period from 5 to 10 years, provided that no more than 1/3 of active or inactive plan members and beneficiaries object, or • Extending the solvency funding period from 5 to 10 years, making up the difference with a letter of credit. Similar options applied to an actuarial report with a valuation date between January 1, 2007 and January 1, 2009.

Jurisdiction	Temporary Solvency Funding Relief Measure
Nova Scotia	A plan sponsor could elect a 10-year amortization period in the first actuarial report with a valuation date between December 30, 2008 and January 2, 2011, provided that fewer than 1/3 of the members, former members, and beneficiaries under the plan object. Benefit improvements were prohibited during the first 5 years if they would create additional liabilities, unless funded by the employer. A plan sponsor could also elect a 15-year amortization period in the first actuarial report with a valuation date between January 3, 2011 and January 2, 2014, provided that fewer than 1/3 of the members, former members, and beneficiaries under the plan objected. Benefit improvements were prohibited during the first 10 years if they would create additional liabilities, unless funded by the employer.
Ontario	An administrator could elect up to three options in respect of a valuation report with an effective date between September 30, 2008 and September 30, 2011: • Option 1: delay the start of the new special payment schedule for up to one year after the filing of the actuarial valuation report; • Option 2: Consolidate previously established solvency deficiencies into a new 5-year payment schedule; and • Option 3: Extend the solvency payment amortization period to 10 years, provided that no more than 1/3 of active or inactive plan members and beneficiaries object. Option 1 was made permanent for all defined benefit plans in 2012 and Options 2 and 3 were extended as Options 4 and 5. In 2016, regulations were adopted extending those two options as Options 6 and 7 for private sector single employer plans only.

Jurisdiction	Temporary Solvency Funding Relief Measure
Quebec	Solvency funding relief was provided to private sector pension plans for a two-year period starting December 31, 2013. The employer or board of trustees was permitted to elect one or more of the following measures for the first actuarial valuation of the plan dated after December 30, 2013: (1) smoothing of assets over a period of up to 5 years; (2) elimination of amortization payments related to any actuarial deficiency on a solvency basis determined on the date of a previous actuarial valuation; and (3) extension of the solvency amortization period to up to 10 years. Previous solvency relief measures were in place from December 31, 2008 to December 31, 2013.
Saskatchewan	Administrators could elect a three-year moratorium from funding a new solvency deficiency in a valuation with an effective date between December 31, 2008 and January 1, 2011.

A number of jurisdictions also passed special funding relief provisions with respect to certain pension plans. These could apply to an employer emerging from corporate restructuring (for example, Air Canada, Algoma Steel, General Motors, and Stelco) or to other employers in either the public or private sector considered worthy of relief.

Alberta, British Columbia, Nova Scotia, Newfoundland and Labrador and Ontario have also passed temporary solvency funding relief measures for certain multi-employer pension plans. Special funding provisions also apply in respect of some or all public sector pension plans in many provinces. Ontario exempts jointly sponsored pension plans (large unionized public sector plans) from solvency funding requirements altogether and has provided temporary solvency funding relief in an attempt to restructure pension plans in the broader public sector, in particular, universities and health care.

Letters of Credit

Alberta, British Columbia, Manitoba, Ontario, Quebec, Nova Scotia, and the federal jurisdiction have taken measures to permit employers to use an irrevocable letter of credit to fund an employer's solvency contributions on a permanent basis. This type of funding arrangement is typically limited to 15% of the plan's solvency liabilities, although there is no such limit in Alberta, British Columbia, and Manitoba. The letter of credit must be issued by a financial institution and must be renewed annually. If the employer does not provide evidence of renewal at the end of the year, then the employer must replace the amount of the letter of credit in the pension fund or the letter of credit will be called from the financial institution.

Insufficient Assets — Defined Benefit Plans

The prospect of a plan winding up with insufficient assets to meet its liabilities is dealt with in pension standards legislation in a number of ways. Typically, the legislation requires the employer to continue to fully fund the plan upon termination. (Saskatchewan and the federal jurisdiction only require funding of the liabilities accrued to the date the plan was terminated.)

Where that is not possible, there are provisions for the orderly reduction of benefits. Some jurisdictions provide for pro rata reductions for all members, whereas others allow plan provisions to distinguish between different classes, such as retirees, those eligible to retire, and younger employees.

Ontario is unique in Canada, as it maintains a fund, the Pension Benefits Guarantee Fund (PBGF), that guarantees a minimum level of pension benefits in the event an employer is insolvent and the pension plan is underfunded. The PBGF guarantees specified benefits in respect of service in Ontario in a pension plan registered under Ontario legislation where the plan is wound up in whole or in part, and the Superintendent of Financial Services is of the opinion that the funding requirements prescribed by the legislation cannot be satisfied. In theory, PBGF benefits are to be reimbursed by the employer who continues to have an obligation to fund the benefits. In practice, payments are made from the PBGF where the employer is bankrupt or insolvent. The PBGF has no application to a plan that has been established for less than five years, benefits that have been granted within the preceding five years, multi-employer and jointly sponsored pension plans, benefits under a defined benefit plan where the employer's contributions are set by collective agreement, and designated pension plans.

Payments under the PBGF are specified in the regulations under the Ontario legislation. Generally, for qualifying individuals, these payments are 100% of the benefits guaranteed by the PBGF, plus a proportion of other benefits included in calculating the Ontario wind-up liability. The PBGF fully guarantees the first $1,000 per month of pension payable. Certain benefits such as consent benefits, special allowances, escalated adjustments, prospective benefit increases, potential early retirement window benefit values, and plant closure and permanent lay-off benefits are excluded from coverage.

In theory, the PBGF is intended to be self-financing via contributions from sponsors of defined benefit plans. However, on several occasions since its inception, the PBGF has faced claims that exceeded the total amount in the fund. The provincial government provided financial assistance to the fund in the form of loans or grants.

In order to limit its financial losses, the Ontario government increased PBGF assessments of plan sponsors effective January 1, 2012. A sponsor of a defined benefit pension plan with Ontario members must pay an assessment rate each year equal to:

- A minimum assessment of $250, or
- The higher of:
    - $300 multiplied by the number of Ontario plan members, or
    - $5 for each Ontario plan member plus 0.5% of any portion of the PBGF assessment base that is less than 10% of the PBGF liabilities, 1% of any portion of the PBGF assessment base that is 10% or more but less than 20% of the PBGF liabilities, and 1.5% of any portion of the PBGF assessment base that is 20% or more of the PBGF liabilities.

The PBGF assessment base for a plan is defined as the amount by which the PBGF liabilities exceed the solvency assets multiplied by the ratio of PBGF liabilities to solvency liabilities. Essentially, it measures the funded level of benefits covered by the PBGF. The PBGF liabilities are the liabilities of the plan that are covered by the PBGF. The formula ensures that less well-funded plans pay higher assessments corresponding to their higher risk levels.[9]

Investment Rules

For the sponsor of a defined benefit pension plan, investments are obviously an important consideration, as they determine in large part the employer's required contributions to the plan. If a greater proportion of the benefits can be funded via investment returns, then the employer will not be required to contribute as much.

Pension standards regulators and the tax authorities also have an interest in pension fund investment. Pension standards legislation is concerned with ensuring that a plan is sufficiently funded to meet its obligations, both on an ongoing basis and in the event the plan is terminated. It follows that pension standards legislation is concerned with

---

[9]   See Chapter 15 for additional discussion of the PBGF.

ensuring that pension funds are invested appropriately, as determined under the applicable statute. The CRA, through the ITA, is also interested in the appropriateness of pension fund investments. As contributions to a pension fund are tax deductible, the tax authorities do not want pension funds losing large amounts of capital or investing in speculative investments. The CRA is also concerned with preventing employers from using pension fund investments to subsidize the employer's business or shelter income by investing in related companies.

Income Tax Act

The ITA prohibits investment in shares (unless they are shares listed on a prescribed stock exchange) or other obligations of an employer who participates in the plan, and anyone who participates in the plan or is connected or does not deal at arm's length with the plan sponsor.

Since 2005, the former restriction on investments in foreign property to 30% of the book value of the pension fund has been abolished. In the event a pension plan exceeded this limit, the excess was subject to a penalty tax of 1% per month.

Pension Standards Legislation

In evaluating a given investment, pension standards legislation follows the prudent portfolio approach. A given investment is analyzed from the perspective of how it affects the risk and return of the portfolio taken as a whole. This differs from the traditional "legal for life" approach, in which the risk and return characteristics of the particular investment are analyzed in isolation from the rest of the portfolio. The legal for life approach was followed under the federal PBSA prior to July 1, 1993. There has been a distinct move away from legal for life investment in Canada and other countries (most notably England and the United States).

Most jurisdictions have adopted the prudent portfolio approach in some form, some more specific than others. Prior to recent reforms, the Quebec *Supplemental Pension Plans Act* specified that a pension fund could not invest more than a maximum of 10% of the book value of the plan assets in any one property or individual. This 10% rule was eliminated and replaced by a new "diversified" rule, and thus Quebec has taken the furthest step forward towards true "prudent portfolio" investment. Section 171.1 of the *Supplemental Pension Plans Act* now states "unless it is reasonable in the circumstances to act otherwise, the pension committee must endeavour to constitute a diversified portfolio so as to minimize the risk of major losses."

The other aspect of prudence is the prudent person. In most Canadian jurisdictions, the plan administrator and its agents are required to exercise the care, diligence, and skill in the investment of the pension fund that a person of ordinary prudence would exercise in dealing with the property of another person. In addition, the relevant persons must exercise all relevant knowledge that they possess or ought to possess by reason of their business. This requirement is explicit in the federal jurisdiction, Alberta, British Columbia, Manitoba, Ontario, Quebec, New Brunswick, and Nova Scotia. A plan administrator breaching this provision would be guilty of an offence under pension legislation and potentially liable for damages.

A slightly different approach is taken in, Newfoundland and Labrador, and Saskatchewan. The legislation of Newfoundland and Labrador and Saskatchewan states that the administrator holds the pension fund in trust for the members. In addition, the legislation of Alberta, British Columbia, and Saskatchewan states that the administrator owes a fiduciary duty to the members. A fiduciary duty requires that a person in a position of trust meet a standard of care, act in good faith, avoid conflicts of interest, and act even-handedly and in the best interests of plan members.

Because prudence requires that the portfolio as a whole be analyzed, it is necessary to have a Statement of Investment Policies and Procedures (SIPP) governing the permitted investments and procedures for investing the pension fund. All jurisdictions require that a written SIPP be adopted by the plan administrator, with the exception that a SIPP is not required for a defined contribution plan where investments are directed by members in Alberta, British Columbia, Saskatchewan, and the federal jurisdiction. Many jurisdictions also require annual review of the SIPP by the plan administrator. A SIPP must be filed with the provincial regulator in New Brunswick and, starting on January 1, 2016, in Ontario. The required contents of this statement are discussed in Chapter 7.

Since January 1, 2016, Quebec also requires that the SIPP be established by giving particular consideration to the funding policy for the plan.

Most jurisdictions (with the exception of New Brunswick and Quebec) have adopted similar investment rules to those set out in Schedule III of regulations to the federal *Pension Benefits Standards Act, 1985*. These rules include the following restrictions on investments:

- No more than 10% of the market value (book value for Nova Scotia) of the plan's assets may be held directly or indirectly in a single person or corporation or a single corporation or group of associated associations. The 10% limit does not apply to real estate, resource, and investment corporations.

- A plan may hold no more than 30% of the voting shares of any one corporation.

Some large public sector plans have argued that Schedule III is unnecessarily restrictive for them, particularly in respect to the restrictions on control of a corporation. Accordingly, in 2010 the federal government abolished previous restrictions that limited a plan's investments in any piece of real property to 5% of book value, investments in Canadian resource property to 15% of book value, and overall investments in real property and Canadian resource property to 25%. Restrictions on voting control and the 10% concentration limits were retained but, in 2016, the federal government commenced a review of the 30% rule.

Special Situations

Successor Employers

Most pension standards legislation addresses the pension rights of employees who are affected by the sale of their employer's business. The legislation preserves entitlement to the benefits accrued to the date of sale or merger.

Where a business or part of a business is sold, the affected employees either lose their jobs or become employed by the purchaser of the business. In many jurisdictions, the pension legislation provides that where the purchasing employer does not provide a pension plan for the transferred employees to join, the vendor's pension plan is deemed to be terminated or partially terminated, and the plan termination rules will govern. However, where the purchaser does have a pension plan that is provided to some or all of the transferring employees (a successor plan), the legislation provides different rules.

Generally, where a vendor who contributes to a pension plan sells, assigns or otherwise disposes of all or a portion of its business or business assets, a member of the pension plan who continues employment with the purchaser continues to be entitled to those benefits accrued under the vendor's plan prior to the effective date of the sale. Alternatively, the purchaser and vendor can agree that the purchaser will assume liability for the pension benefits earned prior to the sale in the vendor's plan. In that case assets from the vendor's plan are transferred to the successor plan.

Where the purchaser provides a successor plan, the employment of employees who continue with the purchaser is deemed by most pension standards legislation not to be terminated. The major exception to this standard is Quebec, where no successor plan rules exist and the employee's membership in the vendor's plan is simply terminated with the usual transfer options. Therefore, regardless of whether or not the purchaser assumes liability for the pension benefits accrued under the vendor's plan, the "service" of an employee will include service with both the vendor and purchaser in both the vendor's and purchaser's pension plans when determining:

- The vesting of benefits;
- Eligibility for ancillary benefits that depend on length of service or plan membership;
- The locking-in of benefits; and
- Eligibility for membership in the purchaser's pension plan.

The successor pension plan is not required by pension legislation to recognize past service with the vendor for the purposes of benefit accruals. The purchaser's plan simply commences the accrual of pension benefits by the transferred employees from the date of sale forward, as it would for any new employee. In order to ensure that service with the purchaser is taken into account for vesting and other purposes in the vendor's plan, the benefits in the vendor's plan are typically not paid out until eventual termination of employment with the purchaser.

The consent of the regulatory authority in the jurisdiction in which the vendor's plan is registered is required before any assets are transferred from the vendor's plan to the successor plan. Typically something like the Ontario standard of review will apply, so that consent will not be granted unless the benefits of affected members are protected.

Under the ITA, the transfer of assets to cover liabilities that may be assumed by a purchaser is governed by the rules set out in section 147.3.

Merger

The merger of two or more pension plans is a subject that is sparsely addressed, if at all, in pension legislation. The Quebec legislation, however, does contain rules specific to plan mergers that grant the regulatory authority the power to approve a merger on conditions it may prescribe. In addition, the legislation requires that either the merging plans have provisions dealing with the treatment of surplus on plan termination that are of identical effect, or the terms of the absorbing plan are more advantageous for the members and beneficiaries. Alternatively, if the provisions do not have identical effects and the terms of the absorbing plan are not more advantageous, the plan merger can still be approved if, after receiving the prescribed notice, fewer than 30% of the affected members object to the merger. Among the other jurisdictions, the regulatory control over the merger process is derived from the regulator's general authority to consent to or deny approval for the transfer of assets from one plan to another.

In Ontario, the regulator imposed a moratorium on certain types of mergers in the wake of the 2004 Court of Appeal decision in *Aegon Canada Inc. v. ING Canada Inc.*[10] However, the courts have taken a more lenient approach to approving plan mergers in subsequent decisions such as *Baxter v. National Steel Car*[11] from the Ontario Divisional Court in late 2004. Therefore, the Ontario regulator released a checklist for plan mergers and defined benefit asset transfers whereby it can determine what trust issues potentially apply.[12]

The Ontario legislation governing asset transfers were reformed effective January 1, 2014, allowing for more defined benefit mergers and asset transfers. The key concern under the old Ontario rules had been whether trust rules limit the use of surplus arising under a defined benefit plan to fund another defined benefit plan. Likewise, members transferred from a defined benefit plan in surplus to a plan in deficit would be concerned about losing their entitlement to surplus. The reformed Ontario rules impose certain funding requirements on a plan merger or asset transfer and require a portion of surplus to be included in the transfer. The new rules have reduced the need for a costly legal review of the plan's trust history and significantly sped up the approval process.

Generally speaking, the regulators' requirements for approval are that valuations be prepared to report on the financial status of the merging plans, and that benefits earned prior to the merger are preserved or otherwise protected.

Under the ITA, an asset transfer due to the merger of pension plans is governed by the transfer rules contained in section 147.3. Advance approval is not required. However, a new valuation report for the continuing plan will be necessary.

Termination of a Pension Plan

The terms "terminate" and "wind-up" are often used interchangeably. However, their technical meaning is distinct. The termination of a pension plan results in members ceasing to accrue further pension benefits. The

---

[10]   *Aegon Canada Inc. v. ING Canada Inc*, [2003] O.J. No. 4755, 38 C.C.P.B. 1 (Ont. C.A.).

[11]   Baxter v. Ontario (Superintendent of Financial Services), [2004] O.J. No. 4909 (Ont. S.J.C.).

[12]   See Chapter 10 for further discussion of merger and asset transfer case law.

wind-up process involves the disposition of the pension fund assets, including the settlement of pension benefits for the members, former members, and other persons, such as beneficiaries, who have entitlements under the plan.[13]

The termination and winding-up of a pension plan is a complex process subject to a myriad of legislative requirements. The wind-up of a defined benefit pension plan involving the ownership and distribution of any surplus assets can be an especially complex and lengthy process.

A pension plan is not considered to be fully wound up until the employer, plan sponsor or superintendent-appointed administrator has satisfied all of the legislative requirements, received approval from the applicable regulatory authority, and arranged for the disposition of all of the pension fund assets, including the settlement of pension benefits to plan members.

In many cases, the termination of a pension plan is the result of a voluntary decision made by the employer or plan sponsor to discontinue the plan. The decision is often the result of a business event, such as a sale, merger, or corporate reorganization, where a number of employees cease to be employed, although an employer can terminate a plan where members' employment continues. Pension plans and funding agreements generally include provisions that provide the employer with the authority to voluntarily terminate the pension plan, in whole or in part, at any time. Pension plans established through a collective bargaining agreement will be subject to the legal obligations applicable under those circumstances.

The pension regulators in each of the jurisdictions have a discretionary power to declare or order the full or partial termination of a pension plan if certain circumstances exist. The main grounds for a regulatory authority to order a full or partial termination of a pension plan include the discontinuance of all or part of an employer's business operations, bankruptcy of the employer, the discontinuance or suspension of employer contributions, failure to satisfy prescribed solvency tests, or non-compliance with applicable pension standards legislation. If there is no pension plan administrator, or the administrator fails to act on an order to fully or partially terminate a pension plan, most jurisdictions permit the regulatory authority to appoint an administrator or trustee to manage the plan termination and wind-up.

When a partial or full plan termination occurs, affected plan members gain certain special rights by virtue of the pension standards legislation.

---

[13] Chapter 15 contains further discussion about the distinction between "termination" and "wind-up" and explores the wind-up process.

Most jurisdictions generally require that members be fully vested in their pension benefits accrued to the termination date, regardless of the vesting provisions provided under the pension plan. The majority of jurisdictions also explicitly provide for transfer rights with respect of the commuted value of their pension upon termination of the pension plan.

A pension plan can be partially terminated in most provinces. There is a recent trend towards abolishing or limiting partial wind-ups, as in most cases a partial termination would simply provide for immediate vesting and grow-in rights (explained below). In provinces that have provided for immediate vesting and do not provide grow-in rights, there is no advantage to members in a partial plan termination.

In Quebec, as a result of changes to the legislation granting full and immediate vesting of members' rights, partial terminations of pension plans were eliminated, effective as of January 1, 2001. Partial plan terminations have been abolished in Ontario (effective July 1, 2012), Alberta (effective September 1, 2014), and British Columbia (effective September 30, 2015). Federal legislation has abolished employer-sponsored partial terminations, although the regulator can still order a partial termination.

The partial termination of a pension plan involves the settlement of pension benefits for a specific group of plan members. Partial pension plan terminations are normally the result of the sale or discontinuance of a part of the employers business operations or a significant reduction in plan membership resulting from employee terminations and lay-offs. All jurisdictions (except Quebec) require that plan members who are affected by the partial termination of a pension plan be given the same rights that they would have under a full termination of the plan. New Brunswick indicates that surplus may be distributed to plan members unless the plan provides for payment of surplus to the employer.

On July 29, 2004, the Supreme Court of Canada released its judgment in *Monsanto Canada Inc. v. Ontario (Superintendent of Financial Services)*,[14] interpreting the Ontario legislative provisions respecting partial termination. The result was a requirement to distribute a proportional share of the actuarial surplus when a defined benefit plan is partially wound up. A later federal Court of Appeal case, *Cousins v. Canada (Attorney General)*,[15] found that the requirement for surplus distribution does not apply to federally regulated pension plans.

---

[14]   *Monsanto Canada Inc. v. Ontario (Superintendent of Financial Services)*, [2004] S.C.J. No. 51, 2004 SCC 54, [2004] 3 S.C.R. 152 (S.C.C.).

[15]   *Cousins v. Canada (Attorney General)*, [2007] F.C.J. No. 635, 2007 FC 469 (F.C.).

The legislation in some jurisdictions includes provisions relating to early retirement in the context of a plan termination. Legislation in Nova Scotia and Ontario also requires that certain members be given "grow-in" rights. Eligible members are those whose age plus years of employment equal 55 or more. They are entitled to receive the following:

- An immediate pension in accordance with the terms of the pension plan, if eligible under the plan;
- A pension in accordance with the terms of the plan to begin at the earlier of:
  - The plan's normal retirement date, or
  - The date the member would have been entitled to an actua-rially unreduced pension if the plan had not wound up and if membership had continued; and
- An actuarially reduced pension in the amount payable under the plan and commencing on the date the member would have been entitled to a reduced pension, if the member's membership had continued to that date.

These "grow-in" rights are significant for pension plans that provide generous early retirement benefits, such as an unreduced pension at a specified age prior to normal retirement age. Eligible members also grow into bridge benefits, if they have at least 10 years of employment or plan membership at the date of the plan termination.

The Nova Scotia government considered eliminating grow-in benefits in 2004, but ultimately amended the regulations under the Nova Scotia *Pension Benefits Act* to remove the requirement to fund grow-in benefits under a solvency valuation. Grow-in provisions continue to apply on full or partial pension plan wind-up, but their priority on pay-out would be second to the basic pension that all employees would receive. Moreover, grow-in benefits would only be paid out if there were sufficient assets in the fund at the time of wind-up of a plan to provide for those benefits. In 2007, however, the Nova Scotia government passed Bill 4 to force full plan funding on wind-up for solvent employers, including grow-in benefits. Because grow-in benefits are not included in solvency valuations, this imposes a significant additional burden on employers in a wind-up situation.

Effective as of January 1, 2003, multi-employer pension plans are exempt from the "grow-in" requirements under the Nova Scotia legislation.

Ontario amended its legislation, effective July 1, 2012, to provide for grow-in benefits upon any involuntary termination. Previously, grow-in benefits were only provided on partial or full plan termination. This expansion of grow-in benefits is seen as a trade-off for the abolition of partial plan terminations. Generally speaking, grow-in benefits have to be provided upon any termination of employment by the employer, except if the employment is terminated as a result of wilful misconduct, disobedience, or wilful neglect of duty by the member that is not trivial and has not been condoned by the employer. Given that these grow-in benefits are a part of solvency funding requirements, this is a significant new burden for employers who provide early retirement subsidies in their defined benefit pension plans.

At the same time, Ontario amended its legislation to permit multi-employer pension plans and jointly sponsored pension plans to opt out of the requirement to provide grow-in benefits. This option expired for pre-existing multi-employer pension plans and jointly sponsored pension plans as of July 1, 2013. New multi-employer pension plans and jointly sponsored pension plans have one year from the date of registration to opt out of grow-in.

It should also be noted that the Federal regulator, OSFI, interprets the provisions of the *Pension Benefits Standards Act, 1985* to require a form of grow-in as well. OSFI's view is that, if a former member has met all requirements other than an age requirement to receive a pension benefit at the "pensionable age" (the earliest unreduced retirement date), the former member is assumed to grow-in to any age requirement under the plan.

Pension standards legislation in all jurisdictions contains specific provisions setting out the wind-up procedures that must be followed by the plan administrator. The following is a brief summary of the major requirements in effect in most jurisdictions:

- A written notice of the proposal to terminate the pension plan must be provided to all affected plan members and the pension authority. Other interested parties, such as a trade union that represents affected members and any advisory committee are also entitled to notice. The timing of transmission of the notice is also generally stipulated by regulation or by the regulator's policies.

- The written notice must include information concerning the name and registration number of the pension plan, the proposed termination date, notification that each member will be provided with an individual statement that sets out his or her pension entitlements and settlement options, and where a plan provides contributory benefits, notice of the member's right to make contributions in respect of the period of notice of termination of employment.

- As soon as notice has been given, the payment of benefits to affected members is prohibited until the regulatory authority has approved the plan wind-up report. All jurisdictions permit pensions already in payment to continue, and also permit refunds of member contributions to be made, as exceptions to this asset freeze.

- The wind-up report must be filed with the regulatory authority within a certain time frame following the termination date of the pension plan. The report must be prepared by an actuary and must include information on the benefits to be provided to members, former members, and other persons who have pension entitlements, the assets and liabilities of the plan, and the methods of allocating and distributing the pension plan assets.

- Members must be provided with a written statement that sets out information concerning their pension benefit entitlements and settlement options.

Subject to the following, where a pension plan is terminated, Canadian jurisdictions require the employer to contribute to the fund the amount owing but not yet paid, or the amount required to fund the plan on a solvency basis. The only exception is Saskatchewan.

Ontario is the only jurisdiction that operates a Pension Benefits Guarantee Fund, which is designed to provide benefits to members until the employer has funded the benefit. A more detailed description of the Ontario PBGF is found under the heading "Financial Issues" in this chapter. Most pension standards legislation also contains specific rules governing the reduction of benefits on a plan termination, where there are insufficient assets to secure all benefits and no prospect of full funding.

Surplus on Plan Termination

Pension standards legislation defines surplus, with minor differences, essentially as the excess of the value of plan assets over the liabilities of the plan. Additional discussion of surplus is found under the heading "Financial Issues" in this chapter.

Where a defined benefit pension plan is fully terminated, there may be surplus assets in the pension fund. When a plan is fully terminated, surplus represents the value of any excess pension fund assets, i.e., assets not needed to pay or settle all benefits. For partial plan terminations, pension standards legislation requires that the surplus attributable to the part of the plan being terminated be identified in the wind-up valuation report.

The full termination of a pension plan that is in a surplus position will require the assessment of surplus rights in order for the assets to be fully distributed. It is always possible for the employer to pay surplus to members, either as benefit improvements (subject to maximums imposed by the ITA) or as cash payments, provided that the plan contains provisions that specify how this will be done (or is amended to so provide). If the employer wishes to withdraw the surplus, the consent of the regulatory authority is required. Generally this consent cannot be given unless the employer is entitled to withdraw the surplus according to the plan terms. Although the legislation typically states this requirement, in most cases the regulatory authority does not have the ability to make a binding determination of entitlement. An employer may have to obtain a court ruling on the entitlement in order to proceed. Many jurisdictions impose further requirements, such as notice to all members of the proposed withdrawal. In New Brunswick, notice need only be given to the trade union and each member of the advisory committee.

The legislation of some jurisdictions permits the employer and plan members to agree on the terms of the withdrawal of surplus, in lieu of the employer requirement to show entitlement to the surplus (whether through the plan terms or by court order). Ontario and Nova Scotia legislation allows (a) the employer, (b) two-thirds of the plan members (with the collective bargaining unit consenting on behalf of its members), and (c) such number of former members and other persons entitled to plan benefits as the Superintendent requires, to agree to the withdrawal. Ontario and Nova Scotia also provide for surplus distribution based on a court order establishing employer entitlement to surplus or, in the absence of agreement between the employer and members, binding arbitration interpreting the plan provisions.

The legislation in Alberta and British Columbia permits defined benefit and target benefit plans to apply to the Superintendent to use surplus on plan termination. In both of these jurisdictions, defined benefit plans may establish solvency reserve accounts which are separate from the main plan fund, in which surplus assets may accumulate. Where the plan text of a defined benefit plan provides for the withdrawal of surplus on plan termination, or if the application is to withdraw surplus from the plan's solvency reserve account, member consent is not required. However, if the plan text does not provide for the withdrawal, at least 2/3 of all active members and 2/3 of all deferred and retired members must consent to the employers's proposal to withdraw the surplus from the main fund of the plan. Surplus may not be withdrawn from a target benefit plan, however it may be used to improve benefits for members. In all situations, withdrawal of surplus from the main plan fund or the solvency reserve account requires the written consent of the Superintendent.

In Quebec, since January 1, 2016, any surplus assets of a terminated pension plan are first allocated to the employer and to the members up to the amount of the contributions recorded, respectively, under the "banker's clause" provision. Any remaining surplus assets must be allocated in accordance with the conditions and procedure set out in the pension plan. The portion allocated to the members and beneficiaries is apportioned among them proportionately to the value of their accrued benefits or according to another method set out in the plan documents.

A surplus withdrawal by an employer on partial plan termination is governed by the rules for surplus withdrawal from an ongoing plan.

Surplus in an Ongoing Pension Plan

The rules for surplus withdrawal from an ongoing plan are generally more prohibitive than those rules that apply on full plan termination. This is consistent with the purpose of the legislation (to ensure the continued financial health of a pension plan) and with the fact that surplus exists only notionally in a plan that has continuing liabilities. In Quebec, an employer may not withdraw surplus from an ongoing plan.

The legislation in Alberta and Bristish Columbia makes a distinction between surplus and actuarial excess. Actuarial excess is defined as the amount by which the value of plan assets exceeds the value of plan liabilities in an ongoing pension plan. Target benefit plan provisions may use actuarial excess to improve benefits in prescribed circumstances, however, it may not be withdrawn. If the plan text does not provide for withdrawal of actuarial excess, at least 2/3 of all active members and 2/3 of all deferred and retired members must consent to the withdrawal. Where the plan has established a solvency reserve account, member consent to withdraw actuarial excess is not required. However, similar to the conditions for withdrawal of surplus, the written consent of the Superintendent is required to withdraw actuarial exess.

Most pension standards legislation requires a plan text to contain provisions that specify how surplus is to be dealt with in the plan while it is a going concern, and on plan termination. Some legislation further provides that if the plan is silent, the plan will be deemed to provide that the employer is not entitled to withdraw surplus from the plan.

For purposes of the plan as a going concern, strict controls are imposed on any withdrawal of surplus by the employer. Regulatory approval of the withdrawal is required, and, in most cases, that approval cannot be granted unless the employer has the required consent of the plan members or has established an entitlement to withdraw the surplus. An employer who wishes to withdraw surplus from an ongoing plan faces significant procedural requirements, such as an extensive notification and disclosure process for all plan members. Pension standards legislation typically restricts the amount of surplus that can be withdrawn, in order to ensure that a sufficient amount remains in the plan to preserve the fully funded status of the plan.

Pension standards legislation does not impose any restrictions on the amount of surplus that may accumulate in a pension plan. This is consistent with the underlying purposes of pension standards legislation to ensure that a pension plan is adequately funded. However, investment income earned by a pension fund is not taxed. As a means of controlling tax revenue foregone arising as a result of not taxing the investment income, the ITA prohibits the accumulation of surplus beyond a specified level. ITA standards were revised in 2010 so that an employer cannot contribute to a pension plan if the plan has surplus greater than 25% of the plan's actuarial liabilities, which is higher than the previous limit of the greater of 10% of the plan's actuarial liabilities and two times the estimated current service contributions that would be required to be made by the employer and employees for the 12 months following the effective date of the actuarial valuation on which the actuary's recommendation for contributions is based. The previous limit was blamed for limiting the amount of surplus a pension plan could accumulate and reducing the security of defined benefit pension plans, resulting in the termination of a number of underfunded pension plans during the financial crisis in 2008 and 2009.

Although the pension standards regulators would undoubtedly prefer that the ITA not impose a cap on the surplus in a plan, pension standards legislation does not require or authorize funding in excess of contributions permitted by the ITA.

Chapter 10

CASE LAW AFFECTING PENSION PLANS

Executive Summary[1]

This chapter deals primarily with significant Canadian court decisions resolving pension disputes over the past few decades and also notes those disputes still before the courts that are likely to have an impact on pension plans once a final decision has been reached.

While pension standards legislation, discussed in Chapter 9, attempts to cover many of the legal requirements for pension plans, the courts and other adjudicative bodies are often left to fill in the gaps not addressed by legislation and to lend guidance in interpreting unclear or apparently conflicting legislative provisions. Some of the major pension issues arising in these decisions include surplus entitlement, marriage breakdown and spousal entitlement, pension plan mergers and asset transfers, mandatory retirement, bankrupt or insolvent plan sponsors, and payment of plan expenses. We explore these common topics in this chapter.

Case Law

Given the potential financial significance of pension issues for employers, plan members, retirees, and other pension plan beneficiaries, it is inevitable that the courts and other adjudicative bodies are asked to resolve questions of legal entitlement. In addition, heightened awareness of plan governance has brought new issues of plan administration before these bodies, while increased use of class proceedings to forward pension claims has been noted across Canadian jurisdictions.

In all jurisdictions that have pension standards legislation in force, a regulatory authority is charged with interpreting the statute and

---

[1] For more information on topics that have frequently been the subject of litigation in Canada, such as surplus, contribution holidays, and pension splitting on marriage breakdown, please consult the multi-jurisdictional charts in the *Canadian Employment Benefits & Pension Guide*. Morneau Shepell, *Canadian Employment Benefits & Pension Guide*, loose-leaf (Toronto: LexisNexis Canada, 2003). The table of contents for these charts appears at the back of this Handbook.

regulations and for making decisions that affect employers and plan members, among others. An appeal of such decisions to a court is normally available, or in some jurisdictions, to a regulatory tribunal, such as Ontario's Financial Services Tribunal. The following discussion is an overview of a number of the major decisions made by Canadian courts and other adjudicative bodies on pension matters.[2]

Surplus

Although there are ordinarily legislative provisions that deal with matters of pension plan surplus, no legislation specifically overrides explicit plan provisions allowing a sponsoring employer to take a contribution holiday or to recapture surplus on plan termination or in an ongoing plan. Consequently, courts have seen considerable activity on the subject of whether plan provisions prohibit or permit contribution holidays, or provide surplus rights to the employer or to plan members. However, the frequency of these court actions has decreased in the last decade, as a result of the economic climate, as fewer pension plans have featured a surplus.

Contribution Holidays

Canada's common law jurisdictions differed regarding contribution holidays until the Supreme Court of Canada decision in *Schmidt v. Air Products*.[3] In this case, which is considered a "foundational" decision, the Supreme Court held that contribution holidays are permitted if provided for explicitly or implicitly by plan provisions, and that the right to take contribution holidays is not dependent on who is entitled to the surplus in the event of plan termination. The Supreme Court clearly stated that a contribution holiday is not a derogation of members' rights to surplus on plan termination, where that right exists. This decision also suggests that, in the absence of a restrictive amending clause or contractual obligations of the employer prohibiting the amendment, an amendment that changes the nature of the employer's contribution obligation from a fixed obligation to one that can fluctuate depending on the funded status of the plan, is valid.

Prior to the Supreme Court providing a definitive answer on this issue in *Air Products*, the courts were arriving at different results, not only

---

[2]   Full citations for cases discussed in this chapter can be found in the Case Table.
[3]   *Schmidt v. Air Products Canada Ltd.*, [1994] S.C.J. No. 48, [1994] 2 S.C.R. 611 (S.C.C.).

because of the particularities of the plan provisions being considered, but also from disagreement about what principles of law should be applied. Some courts considered the use of surplus for a contribution holiday to be the same as a withdrawal of surplus by the employer, while others took the approach that was eventually confirmed by the Supreme Court.

In the wake of *Air Products*, the results in each case can differ depending on the court's interpretation of the particular contribution provisions of the pension plan. In *Hockin v. Bank of British Columbia*,[4] the British Columbia Court of Appeal accepted the *Air Products* holdings, but decided the employer was not entitled to take contribution holidays because the plan text did not permit it. The Court of Appeal also found that the provisions of the federal *Pension Benefits Standards Act* prior to 1987 did not permit it (all pension standards legislation now permits contribution holidays if the plan provisions permit). In *Maurer v. McMaster University*,[5] the Ontario Court of Appeal also followed the reasoning set out in *Air Products*, and held that plan language stating that the employer's contribution obligation is determined by the actuary, based on the sufficiency of the fund, permits the employer to take contribution holidays if the fund is in surplus.

In *Kerry (Canada) Inc. v. Ontario (Superintendent of Financial Services)*,[6] the Ontario Court of Appeal was faced with the issue of whether contribution holidays were permitted in a plan that did not contain a formula for determining the employer's required contributions or make reference to actuarial calculations. The Court of Appeal concluded that contribution holidays were implicitly permitted in such cases, because the only way the employer's contributions could reasonably be determined was through actuarial calculations.

On appeal, the Supreme Court of Canada affirmed the employer's right to take contribution holidays, noting that the wording of plan amendments in 1965 supported the conclusion that the employer's contributions were determined by actuarial calculations. The Supreme Court agreed that, from its inception, the plan permitted the employer to take contribution holidays. The majority of the Supreme Court held that because no statute or regulation prohibited having both defined benefit and defined contribution components in a single plan or prohibiting a contribution holiday in respect of either component, whether or not an employer could take a contribution holiday depended on the governing

---

[4]   *Hockin v. Bank of British Columbia*, [1995] B.C.J. No. 1219 (B.C.C.A.).
[5]   *Maurer v. McMaster University*, [1995] O.J. No. 1538 (Ont. C.A.).
[6]   *Kerry (Canada) Inc. v. Ontario (Superintendent of Financial Services)*, [2009] S.C.J. No. 39, 2009 SCC 39 (S.C.C.).

plan documents. The majority of the Supreme Court found that the defined benefit portion and the defined contribution portion were part of a single plan, and that, provided the plan was retroactively amended to make members of the defined contribution portion beneficiaries of the defined benefit trust fund, the terms of the plan permitted the contribution holiday.

Despite the decision in *Air Products,* the Quebec courts determined the contribution holiday issue quite differently under civil law, until the decision of the Quebec Court of Appeal in *Association provinciale des retraités d'Hydro-Québec v. Hydro-Québec,*[7] which followed the approach of common law jurisdictions in permitting the use of surplus in an ongoing plan to fund contribution holidays. In the *Hydro-Québec* case, a group of retirees filed a class action, challenging the employer's ability to amend the plan to use surplus to improve benefits of active employees and to grant employer and employee contribution holidays. The retirees claimed that they should have been consulted on the amendment and demanded compensation for their share of the surplus in the form of improved pension benefits. The retirees relied on the Quebec Court of Appeal decision in *Châteauneuf v. TSCO of Canada Ltd. (Singer),*[8] which had previously been the leading case in Quebec respecting an employer's right to take contribution holidays, for the principle that their contingent right to surplus entitled them to benefit enhancements equivalent to those provided to active employees. At the trial level, the Superior Court dismissed the retirees' claim. The Court of Appeal upheld the Superior Court's decision, ruling that the retirees were not entitled to any compensation arising from the employer's use of surplus to fund contribution holidays. The Court of Appeal found that such use did not infringe on any contingent rights to surplus the retirees may have on plan termination. The Court of Appeal based its decision on the Civil Code of Québec provisions governing trusts, on the Quebec *Supplemental Pension Plans Act* (QSPPA), and on the principles set out in *Air Products.*

The QSPPA was modified as a result of this decision to introduce an equity principle when using surplus to fund plan amendments and a consultation process of active and non-active members. These surplus rules were revised again effective January 1, 2016. [See Chapter 9 for more details.]

---

[7]   *Association provinciale des retraités d'Hydro-Québec v. Hydro-Québec,* [2005] J.Q. no 1644, 2005 QCCA 304 (Que. C.A.).

[8]   *Châteauneuf v. TSCO of Canada Ltd. (Singer),* [1995] J.Q. no 86 (Que. C.A.).

Surplus and Cross-Subsidization

Over the last two decades, there has been a general movement away from defined benefit plans toward defined contribution plans. Defined contribution plans are seen as more simple to administer and to fund, and they do not have the large funding fluctuations that are sometimes associated with their defined benefit counterparts. Some employers have maintained their defined benefit plans, while adding a defined contribution component and, typically, new employees are allowed to participate only under the defined contribution part of the plan.

Stemming from such arrangements is the issue of cross-subsidization, that is, whether surplus generated in the defined benefit portion of the plan can be used for funding obligations in the defined contribution part of the same plan. The *Kerry* decision, referenced above, dealt with this very issue.

In *Kerry*, the employer amended its defined benefit plan to introduce a defined contribution component and attempted to use the surplus the plan had generated over the years to fund the ongoing employer contributions under the new defined contribution component. The Ontario Financial Services Tribunal (Ontario FST) ruled that the provisions in the plan that permitted cross-subsidization were inconsistent with the terms of the trust agreement, but that the issue could be resolved by amending the trust agreement to make the defined contribution members beneficiaries under the trust. The Ontario Divisional Court disagreed, finding that the plan was, in effect, two separate plans (a defined benefit plan and a defined contribution plan), and that the employer could not use surplus funds from one plan to fund the other. On appeal, the Ontario Court of Appeal restored the Ontario FST's decision and agreed that the cross-subsidization should be allowed. As noted above, the Court of Appeal ruled that it was one plan with two separate components, and that the employer was not prohibited from using surplus for the benefit of defined contribution members, so long as they were made beneficiaries under the trust.

As it did on the issue of the employer's right to take contribution holidays, the Supreme Court of Canada largely adopted the reasoning of the Court of Appeal and found that no statute or legislation prohibited having both defined benefit and defined contribution components in a single plan. The majority of the Supreme Court affirmed that the defined benefit and defined contribution portions were part of a single plan, and that no legislation prevented a retroactive amendment to make defined contribution members beneficiaries of the defined benefit trust fund. Defined benefit members had no rights to actuarial surplus in an ongoing plan and a retroactive amendment such as the one proposed by the employer did not take away any vested property rights of defined benefit members.

Entitlement to Surplus on Plan Termination

In addition to entitlement to surplus in an ongoing plan, there has also been uncertainty concerning the issue of surplus entitlement on plan termination. The uncertainty existed because pension plans had not received much judicial attention until significant surpluses arose in the 1980s, and because many pension plans established in the preceding decades were silent or ambiguous with respect to the disposition of surplus on plan termination. Employers had an expectation, even where the documentation was silent, that they were entitled to surplus in accordance with the principle that the plan fund had been established only to ensure that the promised benefits would be paid.

Faced with silent or ambiguous plan documentation, the courts disagreed about whether a pension plan should be treated as a contract or as a trust, even where the plan's funding documents clearly fell into one or the other category. Even within trust law or contract law, various principles could be applied. Neither body of law by itself adequately addressed the fact that a pension plan consists of a bundle of rights typically created unilaterally by an employer, concerning an ever-changing group of beneficiaries, and applying over a long period of time, and neither could bridge the gap between the employer's expectations of entitlement versus the apparent effect of the plan documentation. Complicating the matter was the fact that in many cases, the plan members had developed their own expectations, which were often inconsistent with the plan documents or the employer's understanding of its rights. The result was considerable variance in surplus entitlement determinations, depending on the particular facts in each case and on the legal analysis preferred by the court.

The Supreme Court of Canada's *Air Products* decision, referenced above, settled much of the uncertainty for common law jurisdictions, particularly with respect to the application of trust principles to pension plans whose funds are established pursuant to a trust. The Supreme Court confirmed the principle that the settlor of a trust cannot revoke the trust unless the power to do so is expressly reserved in the original terms of the trust, and clarified that a general power of amendment is not sufficient to give the employer the power to revoke the trust. Consequently, if a pension trust fund is established that has the effect of giving the beneficiaries an interest in surplus funds, the employer cannot later unilaterally amend the trust to take that interest away, unless the plan clearly allows such an amendment to be made. One of the two pension plans in question was subject to a trust and did not contain language allowing the employer to revoke the trust.

The *Air Products* decision also establishes that if a pension plan is not subject to a trust, then surplus entitlement can be determined in accordance with principles of contract. The Supreme Court dealt with a plan that was subject to a contract. That plan contemplated from its inception that surplus on termination could revert to the employer and also included wording that no amendment could divert part of the pension fund to purposes other than for the exclusive benefit of the members. The Supreme Court was of the view that this language applied only to the benefits defined in the plan. This, combined with the surplus reversion provision, resulted in the employer owning the surplus in that part of the plan. In matters of contract, considerable uncertainty still exists because a myriad of considerations will apply, including the terms of the plan documentation as they are amended from time to time and relevant communications between the employer and the plan members.

The importance of the *Air Products* decision in establishing the framework for analyzing surplus entitlement can be seen in the 2011 Ontario Court of Appeal decision in *Sutherland v. Hudson's Bay Co.*[9] In this case, the members of Simpsons trusteed defined benefit pension plan, which was established in 1971 and funded pursuant to a trust agreement incorporated into the plan, challenged amendments made by the successor employer Hudson's Bay Company. The plan prohibited Simpsons and its successors from reducing accrued benefits or returning any amounts to Simpsons prior to the payment of all pension and other benefits, and the trust agreement restricted the fund's use to members' exclusive benefit and prohibited any amendments resulting in any other use of trust monies. The challenged amendments provided for adding defined contribution components for employees of two Hudson's Bay Company subsidiaries, and using surplus in the plan's fund to satisfy the company's obligations in respect of these plans.

The employees lost their challenge at trial, with the trial court concluding that Hudson's Bay Company could use the defined benefit surplus to pay its contributions under the defined contribution component. However, the court also found that plan assets were impressed with a trust in favour of plan members, that Hudson's Bay Company was not a beneficiary of the trust, and on plan termination, the plan members were entitled to any surplus assets in the trust fund. On appeal by the Hudson's Bay Company, the Ontario Court of Appeal relied on the reasoning set out in *Air Products* in deciding the question of surplus. Following that

---

[9]   *Sutherland v. Hudson's Bay Co.*, [2011] O.J. No. 4208, 2011 ONCA 606 (Ont. C.A.).

analysis, and on the basis of its review of plan documentation, the Court of Appeal upheld the trial court's conclusion regarding members' entitlement to surplus assets on plan termination. The Supreme Court of Canada denied leave to appeal the Court of Appeal's decision.

The law in Quebec regarding surplus entitlement on plan termination has developed quite differently compared to the common law jurisdictions. In *Syndicat national des salariés des outils Simonds c. Eljer Manufacturing Canada Inc.*,[10] the pension plan was analyzed as a contract by the Quebec Court of Appeal. The plan provided that surplus on wind-up would be paid to members and that the employer could amend the plan, provided the amendment did not adversely affect the inherent or acquired rights of the members. The Court of Appeal held that surplus entitlement was an "inherent right", and therefore the plan could not be amended to provide surplus reversion to the employer. In *Châteauneuf c. TSCO of Canada Ltd.*, previously mentioned under "Contribution Holidays" above, the pension plan was characterized as a "stipulation pour autrui" by the Quebec Court of Appeal. The effect of such a characterization is that surplus rights cannot be altered without the consent of the members. The Court of Appeal held invalid an amendment providing surplus reversion to the employer, since the employer did not obtain member consent.

Surplus on Partial Plan Wind-Ups

Another surplus issue that has entered the court system is the issue of distribution of surplus on partial wind-up of a defined benefit plan.

A pension plan can be partially terminated, also known as a partial wind-up, a process which involves the settlement of the pension benefits of a specific group of plan members. Partial wind-ups are normally the result of the sale or discontinuance of a part of the employer's business operations or a significant reduction in plan membership resulting from employee terminations and lay-offs.

Partial wind-ups have been phased out in some jurisdictions but continue to be permitted in Newfoundland, New Brunswick, Manitoba, Nova Scotia, and Saskatchewan. With certain exceptions, jurisdictions that permit partial terminations provide that the same rights be given to affected members as would have been given under a full plan wind-up. Under federal pension legislation, employers are not permitted to declare partial plan terminations, however, the Superintendent may declare part of a pension plan terminated. Further, the federal PBSA does not

---

[10]   *Syndicat national des salariés des outils Simonds c. Eljer Manufacturing Canada Inc.*, [1995] J.Q. no 189 (Que. C.A.).

automatically trigger the wind-up of a pension fund, including a distribution of surplus, when a pension plan is terminated, either in whole or in part.

The issue of surplus on partial wind-up was decided by the Supreme Court of Canada in its 2004 landmark decision in *Monsanto Canada Inc. v. Ontario (Superintendent of Financial Services)*.[11] The issue first arose when the Ontario Superintendent refused to accept a partial wind-up report submitted by Monsanto. Although there were other reasons for refusal, the most significant was that Monsanto failed to provide for distribution of surplus to terminated members. This refusal was in contrast to the Superintendent's prior practice of approving partial wind-ups in the same circumstances. Monsanto then appealed to the Ontario FST. The majority of the Ontario FST agreed with Monsanto that then current subsection 70(6) of the Ontario *Pension Benefits Act* (Ontario PBA), entitling those affected by partial wind-up to rights and benefits "not less than" their rights and benefits on full wind-up, did not oblige Monsanto to distribute the surplus upon partial wind-up. Additionally, the majority stated that Monsanto had a legitimate expectation that its report would not be refused. The Ontario FST's decision was appealed to the Ontario Divisional Court, which set aside the Ontario FST's order and directed the Superintendent to carry out the proposal to refuse the partial wind-up report submitted by Monsanto.

The Ontario Court of Appeal upheld the Divisional Court's decision and dismissed Monsanto's appeal. The Court of Appeal applied the standard of reasonableness to the Ontario FST's decision and found that interpreting subsection 70(6) of the Ontario PBA as excluding surplus distribution was unreasonable. The Court of Appeal also explicitly rejected one of the Ontario FST's other findings, namely that the decision in *Air Products* compelled the conclusion that no surplus could arise on partial wind-up.

In the final stage of litigation, the Supreme Court of Canada dismissed Monsanto's appeal from the decision of the Court of Appeal. The Supreme Court gave less deference to the Ontario FST's decision than the Court of Appeal, reviewing the decision on the basis of whether the decision was correct, as opposed to whether it was reasonable. In applying that standard, the Supreme Court concluded that the Ontario FST's interpretation of subsection 70(6) was incorrect. The Court found that the ordinary sense of subsection 70(6), together with other provisions of the Ontario PBA regarding distribution of surplus, in the context of the

---

[11]   *Monsanto Canada Inc. v. Ontario (Superintendent of Financial Services)*, [2004] S.C.J. No. 51, 2004 SCC 54 (S.C.C.).

legislation's overall public policy objective, led to the conclusion that subsection 70(6) required the distribution of surplus on the effective date of the partial wind-up. This decision prompted the Ontario regulator to issue revised policies with respect to approval of partial wind-ups and to post other guidance for plan sponsors and plan members on its website. The Ontario legislation has since, as of July 1, 2012, eliminated partial wind-ups.

More recently, in *McGee v. London Life Insurance Co.*,[12] the employer established a defined benefit pension plan in 1916 pursuant to a corporate by-law. In 1973, the by-law was revised to provide the employer with the right to surplus upon plan termination. The employer, as was common practice for Canadian life insurance companies, did not enter into a trust agreement and segregate the plan assets until later, in 1993. The trust agreement provided that the employer retained the right to terminate or amend the trust agreement or plan, and also that the trust fund would be distributed in accordance with the employer's instructions. In 1996, a partial wind-up of the plan occurred, and the employer took the position that plan members had no entitlement to surplus. At trial, following *Air Products*, the Ontario Superior Court examined the plan documentation since inception, and determined that the by-laws did not create a trust over the plan assets, nor did the employer intend to create a trust, as benefits were paid out of the employer's general assets. Finding that there was no trust as of 1973, the employer had the authority to amend the plan to incorporate its entitlement to surplus assets.

A decision from the Federal Court of Appeal clarifies that the decision in *Monsanto* does not directly apply to federally-regulated pension plans. The decision, *Cousins v. Canada (Attorney General)*,[13] involved a federally-regulated defined benefit plan. The employer, a marine company, effected successive downsizings over a period of years and filed partial wind-up reports in 1997 and 1998 with the Office of the Superintendent of Financial Institutions (OSFI). The reports did not provide for distribution of surplus on partial wind-up, and the federal Superintendent approved the reports. After *Monsanto*, when the employer was preparing another partial wind-up report in connection with a subsequent downsizing, members challenged the approval of prior reports as well as the current report on the grounds that the reports were required to provide for distribution of surplus. The Court of Appeal ruled that the differences between the wording in the then current Ontario PBA and the federal PBSA were material and justified distinguishing the case at bar from *Monsanto*. Consequently, the Court of Appeal held that *Monsanto* is

---

12   *McGee v. London Life Insurance Co.*, [2011] O.J. No. 4206, 2011 ONSC 2897 (Ont. S.C.J.).

13   *Cousins v. Canada (Attorney General)*, [2008] F.C.J. No. 1011, 2008 FCA 226 (F.C.A.).

not a binding authority for the proposition that members of a federally-regulated pension plan are entitled to a distribution of surplus on partial termination under the federal PBSA.

Pension Plan Governance

Governance has played an increasingly important role for pension plan administrators in recent years.[14] There is an increasing understanding of the importance of good governance policies and procedures. Formal governance policies are now mandated by the legislation in some jurisdictions (*i.e.*, Alberta and British Columbia), while the regulators in other jurisdictions recommend that a comprehensive governance manual be developed. In the courts and other adjudicative bodies, governance issues may arise regarding accountability for administrator and trustee decisions in the area of investments, as well as other areas such as proper recordkeeping and other related administrative practices.

For example, *R. v. Blair* (also referred to as the *Enfield* case),[15] is an Ontario case dealing with the responsibilities of plan administrators for the governance of the decision-makers dealing with pension fund investments. At the trial division level, the members of the pension committee appointed by the plan sponsor to administer the plan were convicted for having failed to properly supervise the internal investment manager of the pension fund. The manager invested a large proportion of the fund assets in securities of the plan sponsor, in violation of the limits prescribed under the Ontario PBA. The trial judge found that, though the plan text named the individual corporate plan sponsor as administrator, the committee was the *de facto* administrator of the plan and, therefore, personal liability attached to its members for not ensuring that appropriate systems for plan and fund administration were in place and operating adequately. The judge further stated that a plan administrator cannot delegate, to an external trustee, the responsibility of monitoring the daily activities of the investment manager with respect to complying with regulatory restrictions on pension investments.

On appeal, the Ontario Court of Justice exonerated the members of the pension committee, holding that the Ontario PBA permits the appointment of only one administrator, and that it would be impossible to have a "legal administrator" and a separate "*de facto* administrator" with each having liability as "administrator" under the Ontario PBA. The

---

[14] See Chapter 4, Governance of Retirement, Savings and Other Benefit Plans for further information.

[15] *R. v. Blair*, 1995 CarswellOnt 1135.

corporate plan sponsor named in the pension plan was the administrator, and the committee was simply the agent of the administrator to which some functions had been delegated. Based on the facts of the case, the court concluded that the investment manager was not an agent of the committee, but an agent of the plan sponsor. Therefore, the committee members did not have the responsibility for assessing the investment manager's qualifications and activities. The court also stated clearly that it was appropriate for an agent to sub-delegate the investment monitoring function to a professional pension fund trustee. The court implied that there might in fact have been a breach of duty by the plan sponsor, as administrator, in the supervision of the investment manager. However, charges were not laid against the corporation.

In *R. v. Christophe*,[16] the Crown brought criminal charges against the board of trustees as a whole and individually, and against the investment committee of the Canadian Commercial Workers Industry Pension Plan Trust Fund, based on imprudent administration, investments that violated the 10% investment rule, and failure to properly supervise as required under the Ontario PBA. The fund had a diverse investment portfolio in the range of $1 billion. Ten-and-a-half per cent of the fund was invested in a complex investment mechanism under which the plan advanced money to investment corporations owned by the plan, some of which were linked to Caribbean hotel properties, which caused losses to the plan. The trustees were found not guilty of the imprudent investment charge because the Crown failed to produce expert evidence as to what constituted the prudent investment standard. However, the investment committee was found guilty of exceeding the 10% rule, and the board as a whole was found guilty of failure to supervise. In the result, the trustees were fined a total of $202,500, which included a penalty of $18,000 and a $4,500 victim surcharge imposed on each trustee.

Good governance also relates to proper record retention. The decision in *Hunte v. Ontario (Superintendent of Financial Services)*,[17] illustrates how important it is for an employer to retain records in relation to member pension entitlements, especially where issues can arise decades into the future. In this case, an employee worked for the employer from 1970 to 1975, left employment for a few weeks, and was rehired and worked again with the employer until 1982. Decades later, the employee asserted that he was a member of the employer's defined benefit pension plan from 1970 to 1975, that he made both required and additional voluntary contributions during this period, and did not receive a refund of these contributions

---

[16]   *R. v. Christophe*, [2009] O.J. No. 5296, 2009 ONCJ 586 (Ont. C.J.).

[17]   *Hunte v. Ontario (Superintendent of Financial Services)*, [2014] O.J. No. 935, 2014 ONSC 1270 (Ont. S.C.J.).

when he left in 1975. He also asserted that when he returned in 1975, the employer agreed that he would be treated as a plan member continuously from 1970. As a result, the employee claimed that he was entitled to a deferred pension based on approximately 12 years of service. The employee, however, had no documents to support his claims.

The employer had sparse documentary records relating to the employee's employment and pension history, but was able to produce evidence (such as CRA tax summaries and corporate memorandums) that showed that the employee no longer had any entitlements under the plan. The Ontario FST agreed with the employer, and found that the employee's entitlements had been paid out of the plan when he terminated his employment in 1982, and he was therefore not entitled to a deferred pension. The Ontario FST did note that there were defects in the employer's record-keeping system, but that these defects were not of sufficient gravity to raise fiduciary concerns. This decision was upheld by the Ontario Superior Court of Justice.

Good governance also deals with ensuring that proper administrative procedures are followed in accordance with applicable pension legislation and regulatory policy. In *Smith v. Casco Inc.*,[18] a plan member elected to retire early. The member elected to receive a life-only pension, rather than a default joint and survivor pension. To give effect to this election, the member's spouse signed a spousal waiver form that had been prepared by the employer, and not the prescribed form produced by the Ontario pension regulator. The spouse "glanced at" the form before signing it. When the member died, and his spouse only received the balance of the payments owing for the remainder of his guarantee period, the spouse challenged the validity of the form. The Ontario Court of Appeal closely compared the employer's form with the prescribed form, and found that the differences affected the substance of the form (for example, the caution given to spouses to obtain independent legal advice was not in bold type), and that the form was therefore invalid. As a result, the spouse was entitled to survivor benefits for her life under the default joint and survivor pension.

Pension Plan Conversions

In recent years, a number of cases (particularly class actions) have related to pension plan conversions, where the plan sponsor converts a defined benefit plan to a defined contribution plan, or where the employer introduces a defined contribution component to an existing defined benefit

---

[18]   *Smith v. Casco Inc.*, [2011] O.J. No. 1817, 2011 ONCA 306 (Ont. C.A.).

plan. Many of these cases proceed on the basis of negligent misrepresentation and breach of fiduciary duty, with claims largely related to losses caused by alleged misinformation provided from the plan sponsor/employer about the defined contribution option.[19] For example, in *Beaulieu v. Compagnie Abitibi-Consolidated du Canada*,[20] the Quebec Superior Court concluded that the employer breached its duty to inform plan members when introducing a new defined contribution plan for non-unionized employees. Employees were offered the choice to remain in the defined benefit plan or to participate in the new defined contribution plan. During information sessions, the plan members were informed by human resources that the defined benefit plan would not be improved in the future and that it would eventually disappear. Based on this information, plan members elected to join the defined contribution plan. The defined benefit plan, however, was later improved in the context of a harmonization of pension plans following the employer's business acquisitions. According to the court, the employer knew that its verbal representations could cause prejudice, and was ordered to pay $4.4 million in damages.

In *NCR Canada Ltd. v. International Brotherhood of Electrical Workers, Local 213*,[21] employees used a different legal argument, namely estoppel, to successfully prevent their employer's attempt to require them to participate in a defined contribution plan rather than a defined benefit plan. In this case, the employer amended its defined benefit plan in 2001 to introduce a defined contribution component. Pursuant to the amendment, employees who became members of the plan prior to January 1, 2002 could elect to remain in the defined benefit component or move to the defined contribution component. Nineteen unionized members elected to stay in the defined benefit component.

In 2012, the employer again amended the plan to provide that all defined benefit members would commence participation in the defined contribution component. The union filed a grievance on behalf of the 19 members, arguing that the employer was "estopped" (or prevented) from amending the plan in this manner because of representations made to the members in 2001 when they elected to stay in the defined benefit part. These representations told the employees that, if they elected to remain in

---

[19]   See, for example, *McLaughlin v. Falconbridge Ltd.*, [1999] O.J. No. 2403 (Ont. S.C.J.), *Dawson v. Tolko Industries Ltd.*, [2010] B.C.J. No. 479, 2010 BCSC 346 (B.C.S.C.); and *Weldon v. Teck Metals Ltd.*, [2013] B.C.J. No. 1696, 2013 BCCA 358 (B.C.C.A.).

[20]   *Beaulieu v. Compagnie Abitibi-Consolidated du Canada*, [2008] J.Q. no 7075, 2008 QCCS 3386 (Que. S.C.).

[21]   *NCR Canada Ltd. v. International Brotherhood of Electrical Workers, Local 213*, [2015] B.C.J. No. 170, 2015 BCCA 44 (B.C.C.A.).

the defined benefit part, this election would continue in effect throughout their employment. At arbitration, the arbitrator agreed, finding that the employer was estopped from amending the plan, mainly based on the representations the employer made to employees during the conversion. Further, although the communications also stated that the employer had the right to amend the plan, the arbitrator did not allow the employer to rely on this clause to later force the remaining defined benefit members to switch to the defined contribution component in light of the other statements. In the result, the employer was precluded from forcing these members to participate in the defined contribution component.

Marriage Breakdown/Spousal Entitlement

The division of pension benefits upon relationship breakdown is another complex area of pension law. Adding to the complexity is the fact that this area is regulated by provincial family law and matrimonial property legislation, as well as by pension legislation. Further, as with many pension matters, the rules pertaining to pension splitting are not consistent across jurisdictions. As described in Chapter 9, some legislation states that the splitting of pension benefits can occur either as of the date of marital breakdown or as of the date of the member's termination or retirement. Further, rules regarding when the non-member spouse is entitled to receive his or her share of the pension benefits also vary — payment may be made immediately, or only on the occurrence of a specified event, such as the member's retirement or termination, or at any of these times. In recent years, as described in Chapter 9, pension jurisdictions have attempted to harmonize these different rules.

As a result of this lack of legislative clarity, it is often left to the courts to provide some form of guidance. One such issue that required clarification was "double-dipping", also referred to as "double recovery". Double-dipping occurs if, on marriage breakdown and before retirement, the parties divided the value of the pension accrued during the marriage period and subsequently, after the member's retirement, the spouse obtains spousal support based on the member's pension income. The Supreme Court of Canada's decision in *Boston v. Boston*[22] established the basic jurisprudential framework for challenging the issue. In *Boston*, the parties had consented to a judgment dividing their assets. As part of the equalization process, the husband retained the value of his pension, the wife retained other assets, and the husband agreed to pay spousal support in the amount of $3,200 monthly, indexed to the cost of living. At the time

---

[22]   *Boston v. Boston*, [2001] S.C.J. No. 45, 2001 SCC 43 (S.C.C.).

of judgment, the husband was earning $115,476, while the wife had no employment income.

Subsequently, the husband retired and began receiving pension income of $8,000 per month, of which $5,300 was derived from pension assets retained on equalization, and $2,300 was derived from pension assets acquired after equalization, and the balance was a Canada Pension Plan (CPP) benefit. His net assets totaled $7,000, while the wife's assets had grown to more than $493,000. The husband brought a successful application to reduce the amount of spousal support. He claimed that his retirement on a reduced income and the "systematic depletion" of his pension amounted to a material change in circumstances sufficient to vary the spousal support order. The reduced amount of spousal support, for $950 per month on the motion to vary, was changed by the Ontario Court of Appeal to $2,000 per month. The husband appealed to the Supreme Court, which allowed the appeal and restored the $950 per month award. The Supreme Court concluded that it is *generally* unfair to permit double-dipping with respect to pensions.

If post-retirement spousal support is paid out of income from pension assets that were not subject to equalization, then the double-dipping issue does not arise. In *Boston*, the motions judge rightfully concluded that the quantum of support should be based on the portion of the husband's pension that was acquired after the equalization date. The wife did not suffer economic hardship from the avoidance of double recovery.

Despite the Supreme Court's ruling against double recovery in *Boston*, the Supreme Court also clearly stated that double recovery cannot always be avoided. Court decisions following *Boston* begin with the premise that the prohibition against double recovery is not absolute,[23] identifying certain situations in which a pension that has been equalized can also be used later to provide support when the pension is in pay. Double recovery may be permitted where:

- the member has the financial means to pay support;
- the non-member spouse has made a reasonable effort to use the equalized assets in an income-producing way, and yet despite this, economic hardship continues; and
- spousal support orders are based on need as opposed to compensation.

---

[23]   See, for example, *Kopp v. Kopp*, [2012] M.J. No. 2, 2012 MBQB 2 (Man. Q.B.), *Swales v. Swales*, [2010] A.J. No. 1105, 2010 ABCA 292 (Alt. C.A.), *Scott v. Scott*, [2009] O.J. No. 5279 (Ont. S.C.J.), and *Murphy v. Murphy*, [2015] B.C.J. No. 496, 2015 BCSC 408 (B.C.S.C.).

Prior to the *Boston* decision, the Supreme Court of Canada considered another contentious issue in *Best v. Best*:[24] the determination of the appropriate pension valuation method upon marital breakdown. Pension valuation involves determining the present value of an income stream that will be received in the future, based upon certain presumed factors and assumptions. This amount will then be divided between the spouses. In the *Best* decision, the parties had a relatively short marriage of 12 years and during their relationship, the husband worked as a school principal, and continued to work as such at the time of trial. His pension plan was a defined benefit plan, which provided that the benefit was equal to 2% of the average of the husband's five highest annual salaries, multiplied by the total number of years of service prior to retirement.

In the calculation of the parties' net family property, a dispute arose over the value to be assigned to the pension at the date of marriage. The husband favoured the *pro rata* method, while the wife favoured the value-added method. The *pro rata* method calculates the pension benefit accrued during the marriage by first calculating the present value of the pension benefit accrued on the date of separation. Second, the pension's value on the date of marriage is determined by multiplying the first value by the ratio of the number of years of pensionable service prior to the marriage, divided by the total pensionable service up to the date of separation. The amount attributable to the period of marriage is the difference between the value on the date of marriage and the value on the date of separation. The value-added approach is calculated by subtracting the pension's value at the date of marriage from the value of the pension at the date of separation. Each successive year of pensionable service is of increasingly greater value, if the value-added method is used. It apportions more value to the later years of pension holding than to earlier years.

In the *Best* matter, the amount attributable to the period of the marriage was smaller under the *pro rata* method. The trial court valued the pension using the "termination value-added" method, therefore ruling in favour of the wife. The Ontario Court of Appeal upheld the trial decision and the husband subsequently appealed to the Supreme Court. Speaking for the majority, Justice Major concluded that, absent special circumstances, a *pro rata* method of pension valuation best achieves the purpose of the *Family Law Act* (Ontario), that is, the equitable division of assets between spouses. This was particularly clear under the facts of the case, where the value-added method apportioned 88% of the value of the appellant's 32 years of pensionable service to the 12-year marriage, whereas the *pro rata* method, treating all pensionable service years

---

[24]   *Best v. Best*, [1999] S.C.J. No. 40, [1999] 2 S.C.R. 868 (S.C.C.).

equally and the pension increasing in value at a constant rate over time, apportioned 37% of the pension's value to the period of marriage.

The Supreme Court also noted that the *pro rata* method will not always be preferable. However, as a general rule, the *pro rata* method will be favoured due to the nature of a defined benefit plan. Justice Major commented that legislative changes were required to provide guidance on pension valuation. In fact, some jurisdictions in Canada do endorse some form of *pro rata* approach to pension valuation. The lack of direction in other jurisdictions requires parties to select an agreed-upon valuation method, although the results can vary significantly, depending upon the valuation method selected.

Another problematic pension-splitting issue that required judicial resolution is the valuation date applicable to a split in the absence of clear legislative prescription fixing the valuation date. In *Stairs v. Ontario Teachers' Pension Plan Board*,[25] the Ontario Court of Appeal resolved nine years of litigation on this issue. When the parties separated, they agreed that Ms. Stairs was entitled to an interest in the pension plan death benefits (calculated on an "if and when" basis), regardless of whether the member had another spouse at the time. However, on the pre-retirement death of the member, the administrators paid the entire benefit to the new spouse as per the terms of the plan. The Ontario FST dismissed Stairs's complaint. That decision was overturned by the Divisional Court, and the Divisional Court's ruling was upheld by the Court of Appeal, thus granting Stairs's entitlement to an appropriate portion of the death benefit.

The Court of Appeal found that the terms of the separation agreement took precedence over the plan terms. The Court of Appeal also resolved the issue of determining the proper date for calculating the value of the death benefit assigned to Stairs in order to apply the 50% limit. The Court of Appeal ruled that nothing in the Ontario PBA or what was then in section 56 of the Regulations under the Ontario PBA spoke directly to the issue of valuation date for purposes of calculating the pension split. In the absence of statutory prescription, the Court of Appeal gave effect to the date agreed to in the separation agreement, which was the date the benefit became payable, *i.e.*, the date of the member's death.[26]

---

[25]   *Stairs v. Ontario Teachers' Pension Plan Board*, [2004] O.J. No. 331 (Ont. C.A.).

[26]   Seemingly in response to the *Stairs* decision, the Ontario PBA was revised to adopt the definition of "valuation date" as defined in the *Family Law Act* (Ontario). In theory, this definition would avoid the application of *Stairs* and the use of post-breakdown vaulation dates. Ontario's new pension splitting rules retain the same definition of "valuation date".

Interest payable on payments to spouses can also become an issue in marriage breakdown proceedings. In the Ontario decision, *Heringer v. Heringer*,[27] the parties agreed that the husband would pay the wife a global settlement payment of $137,000 by way of transfer of the husband's pension to the wife. Upon receipt of the wife's application for transfer, the plan administrator initially advised the wife that the payment would include interest. In addition, the Ontario regulator forms used by the wife and the plan administrator indicated that interest would be added to the beginning of the month in which the transfer was made. However, when the transfer was made, the administrator did not add interest, as the settlement documents did not address interest. The wife sought interest to be added to the amount, but this was dismissed by the Ontario Superior Court of Justice. Based on its review of the Ontario PBA and the *Family Law Act* (Ontario), there was no legislative basis for a payment expressed as a specific amount (as opposed to an amount expressed as a percentage) to be modified on account of interest. Rather, if the court order or domestic contract does not provide for interest to a specified amount, the plan administrator has no discretion to add interest.

Finally, pension-splitting issues often arise in the context of successive or simultaneous spouses. Pension jurisdictions vary as to cohabitation requirements establishing who is the eligible spouse entitled to a share of the pension or the pre- or post-retirement death benefit. A significant Ontario decision on this issue is *Carrigan v. Quinn*.[28] Prior to this case, the widespread understanding was that the Ontario PBA made a pre-retirement death benefit payable to a common-law spouse, even if the deceased member was separated from, but still married to, an earlier spouse. However, in this case, this common understanding was reversed. Mr. Carrigan married Mrs. Carrigan and had two daughters. Mr. and Mrs. Carrigan separated in 1996, but never divorced or formalized their separation by a separation agreement or court order. Mr. Carrigan participated in a workplace registered pension plan and in 2002, designated Mrs. Carrigan and their daughters as his beneficiaries under the plan. Mr. Carrigan began living with Ms. Quinn in 2000, and they continued to do so until Mr. Carrigan's death prior to retirement in 2008.

In determining who was entitled to the pre-retirement death benefit, the majority of the Ontario Court of Appeal found that both Mrs. Carrigan and Ms. Quinn met the definition of "spouse" set out in section 1 of the Ontario PBA, and confirmed that subsection 48(1) of the Ontario PBA gives a member's spouse priority to pre-retirement death benefits. The majority then held that because Mrs. Carrigan (the married spouse) was

---

27   *Heringer v. Heringer*, [2014] O.J. No. 6340, 2014 ONSC 7291 (Ont. S.C.J.).
28   *Carrigan v. Quinn*, [2012] O.J. No. 5114, 2012 ONCA 736 (Ont. C.A.).

living separate and apart from Mr. Carrigan at the date of his death, subsection 48(3) of the PBA was invoked. Once invoked, subsection 48(3) caused subsection 48(1) to become inapplicable. Based on this analysis, neither Ms. Quinn nor Mrs. Carrigan was entitled to the death benefit. The majority then awarded the benefit to Mrs. Carrigan and her daughters as the designated beneficiaries under subsection 48(6). The Supreme Court of Canada denied leave to appeal this decision.[29]

In another case dealing with successive spouses, *Vladescu v. CTV Globe Media Inc.*,[30] a member of a federally-registered defined benefit plan executed a separation agreement, which purported to authorize the plan administrator to pay all "survivor benefits" to the former spouse, and that the former spouse was "solely entitled" to "survivor benefits". The agreement also required the member to make all possible efforts to enter into an agreement with any future spouse that would release the subsequent spouse's rights to his pension. The member remarried, and died prior to retirement. When paying the death benefit, the plan administrator treated the separation agreement as containing an irrevocable beneficiary designation in favour of the former spouse, and since a beneficiary cannot receive death benefits in preference to an eligible surviving spouse under the federal PBSA, the subsequent spouse was entitled to the benefit. The Ontario Superior Court of Justice came to the same conclusion, finding that the federal PBSA permitted the member to assign his pre-retirement death benefit, but that assignment must feature "clear and unambiguous" language. In this case, the separation agreement was found to be an irrevocable beneficiary designation in favour of the former wife, rather than an "assignment".

On appeal, the Ontario Court of Appeal similarly found that clear language is needed to allow plan administrators to fulfill their duty to pay benefits to the correct recipients. In this case, the language merely described the member's pension benefit and acknowledged the former spouse's legal rights to those benefits at the time the separation agreement was executed. In the result, the former spouse was not entitled to the pre-retirement death benefit.

---

[29] The Ontario PBA was amended effective July 24, 2014, to reverse the impact of *Carrigan*, clarifying that the common-law spouse is entitled to a pre-retirement death benefit or joint and survivor pension benefit in a "dual spouse" situation. Note that the new Ontario PBA provisions provide a discharge to plan administrators who made the payment to a common-law spouse prior to July 24, 2014, in the case of a post-retirement death benefit. They also provide a discharge for a payment made prior to October 31, 2012 (the date of the *Carrigan* decision) in the case of a pre-retirement death benefit.

[30] *Vladescu v. CTV Globe Media Inc.*, [2013] O.J. No. 3024, 2013 ONCA 448 (Ont. C.A.).

In *Linder v. Regina (City)*,[31] the Saskatchewan Court of Queen's Bench was required to determine whether the definition of "spouse" in the Saskatchewan *Pension Benefits Act* (Saskatchewan PBA), giving priority to pre-retirement death proceeds to a legally married spouse over a cohabiting spouse, violated the Canadian *Charter of Rights and Freedoms* (Charter). In this case, the common-law spouse and the member had lived together for 25 years at the date of the member's death, but the pension administrator refused to pay the pre-retirement death benefit to the common-law spouse on the grounds that the member's legally married wife was still alive. The Court ruled that the definition of "spouse" in the Saskatchewan PBA constituted discrimination on the basis of marital status, contrary to section 15 of the Charter. The court directed a trial on the issue of whether the spousal definition was saved under section 1 of the Charter, which permits discriminatory legislation if it can be shown to be just and reasonable in a democratic society.

There was no trial of the issue in the *Linder* case. Years later, in *Holmes v. Boreen*,[32] the Saskatchewan Court of Queen's Bench agreed that the *Linder* decision was binding in a similar circumstance, but was not prepared to rule on the constitutionality and Charter implications of the Saskatchewan PBA. Therefore, it is still not clear if a Charter challenge to the definition of spouse under the Saskatchewan PBA (or other jurisdictions that give priority to married spouses over common-law spouses) would be successful.

Pension Plan Mergers and Asset Transfers

Another area with significant court rulings is that of plan mergers and asset transfers, typically occurring in the case of corporate transactions and reorganizations.

In *Aegon Canada Inc. v. ING Canada Inc.*,[33] the Ontario court ruled on the issue of validity of a plan merger, effected in 1989, when one of the merged plans was a defined benefit plan in a surplus position subject to a 1969 trust agreement. The merger of plans resulted from the share purchase of the company sponsoring the defined benefit plan. The purchaser represented in the share purchase agreement that its plan, which it intended to be merged with the vendor's plan, was fully funded on an ongoing and solvency basis (later, actuarial reports disclosed an unfunded deficit).

---

[31]   *Linder v. Regina (City)*, [2006] S.J. No. 75, 2006 SKQB 68 (Sask. Q.B.).
[32]   *Holmes v. Boreen*, [2015] S.J. No. 572, 2015 SKQB 333 (Sask. Q.B.).
[33]   *Aegon Canada Inc. v. ING Canada Inc.*, 2004 CarswellOnt 2994.

In compliance with Ontario PBA, the employer applied to the Superintendent and received approval for an "asset transfer" or merger of the plan funds. The employer undertook to keep the assets of each plan separate and did so, but at the same time, used the assets of the plan in surplus to determine funding requirements and future service costs of the "combined" plan. As a result, the employer took contribution holidays. In essence, the surplus assets of one of the merged plans were used to make up for the deficit in the other merged plan.

Aegon sued ING, disputing the terms of the share purchase agreement. The pension issue was central to the resolution of the dispute, and the court was required to rule on the validity of the plan merger and the subsequent contribution holidays. At the trial level, the Ontario Superior Court ruled that the first plan remained impressed with a trust after the merger, and its assets could not be used for the benefit of persons who were not beneficiaries of that trust. Because the transferred assets could not be used to satisfy plan liabilities, they could not be taken into account when determining contribution holidays.

In 2003, the Ontario Court of Appeal upheld the lower court decision, agreeing that the terms of the 1969 trust agreement precluded use of the assets for any purpose other than for the exclusive benefit of the trust beneficiaries. The Court of Appeal also found that the *Air Products* analysis of surplus did not apply, noting that just because the beneficiaries of the surplus plan had no present entitlement to the surplus, this did not justify the use of the surplus for a purpose contrary to the terms of the trust. The Supreme Court of Canada refused to hear an appeal from the decision. Following the *Aegon* decision, the Ontario regulator released a policy statement about asset transfer approvals where one or more of the plans are subject to a trust. In effect, the policy created a moratorium on plan transfers unless the transfer qualified as one of the exceptions outlined in the policy. However, with recent amendments to the Ontario PBA prescribing detailed rules for asset transfers effective January 1, 2014, the effect of *Aegon* on asset transfers will likely be ameliorated.

In *Buschau v. Rogers Communications Inc.*,[34] the employer merged several plans, and the original plan was a trusteed defined benefit plan, closed to new members and in a surplus position at the time it was merged in 1992. As beneficiaries of the trust, members of the original plan were successful at trial in obtaining an order to terminate the plan and gain access to its surplus. They invoked an established common law rule, known as the Rule in *Saunders v. Vautier*, permitting the termination of a trust and distribution of its proceeds upon consent of all the beneficiaries.

---

[34]   *Buschau v. Rogers Communications Inc.*, [2006] S.C.J. No. 28, 2006 SCC 28 (S.C.C.).

The Court of Appeal reversed the decision to terminate the plan. Although the Court of Appeal found that the original trust continued to exist despite plan merger, it determined that consent of all plan beneficiaries had not been obtained, as some of the designated beneficiaries of members had not been located and some members had not designated specific beneficiaries, leaving their estates to benefit. Nevertheless, the Court of Appeal granted a three-month extension to give members time to revoke designations of unlocatable beneficiaries and to replace them with beneficiaries who would give consent. Those conditions were satisfied, and the Court of Appeal ruled that the trust was terminated.

On further appeal, the Supreme Court of Canada concluded that the rule in *Saunders v. Vautier* would rarely, if ever, apply to a pension plan. The Supreme Court recognized that a pension trust is not a standalone instrument and cannot be terminated without taking into account the plan for which it was created and the specific legislation governing the plan. Accordingly, the plan could not be terminated unless the provisions of the applicable legislation were followed (in this case, the federal PBSA). The Supreme Court made it clear that not all general trust law principles are applicable to pension plans, particularly where there are legislative provisions in place that have the effect of displacing such principles.

In *Burke v. Hudson's Bay Co.*,[35] the Ontario Court of Appeal determined that a transfer of surplus assets was not required on the sale of a business where the plan members did not have entitlement to surplus on a pension plan wind-up. The Hudson's Bay Company provided a defined benefit pension plan for its employees. The plan was in surplus position at the time when the Hudson's Bay Company sold one of its divisions, resulting in the employees of that division becoming employees of the purchaser. The purchaser established a pension plan (a successor plan) for the transferred employees. The question arose as to whether some share of the surplus from the Hudson's Bay Company's plan ought to be transferred to the successor plan on behalf of the transferred employees.

The trial court judge held that a transfer of assets without surplus from the Hudson's Bay Company's plan amounted to a breach of trust. However, the Ontario Court of Appeal overturned the trial court's decision. The Court of Appeal concluded that based on the terms of the Hudson's Bay Company's plan and trust documents, plan members had no entitlement to surplus, even if the plan were wound-up. The original plan document only promised members a right to the defined benefits calculated in accordance with the plan's benefit formulas and implicitly provided that any surplus would be returned to the employer. (A later plan amendment giving the Hudson's Bay Company express rights to

---

[35]   *Burke v. Hudson's Bay Co.,* [2010] S.C.J. No. 34, 2010 SCC 34 (S.C.C.).

termination surplus was therefore found to be valid.) Accordingly, the Hudson's Bay Company was not required to transfer any surplus amounts to the successor plan on behalf of the members who were transferred out of the Hudson's Bay Company's plan.

On appeal by the members, the Supreme Court of Canada affirmed that given the plan documentation at issue, there was no obligation to transfer surplus assets on the sale of business. The original plan documentation clearly limited the employees' interest in the trust fund to their defined benefits only, and later "exclusive benefit" language in the trust agreement was found to have limited application in light of the original plan wording.

Section 80 of the Ontario PBA, which relates to successor plans in a sale of business situation, has also come into play in other decisions relating to asset transfers. In *Ontario Pension Board v. Ratansi*,[36] certain Ontario public servants employed with Ontario's Ministry of Revenue participated in the Public Service Pension Plan (PSPP). Due to a subsequent reorganization, they transferred employment to the Canada Revenue Agency (CRA) and became members of the federal public service pension plan. The employees sought confirmation that those who qualified for early unreduced pensions under the PSPP could begin receiving their pensions as soon as they transferred employment. The PSPP administrator found that such pensions could not commence as long as employment continued with the CRA, based on subsection 80(3) of the Ontario PBA, which deems employment to continue for purposes of the act where there is a sale of business. The Ontario FST narrowly interpreted subsection 80(3) to mean that employment was deemed to continue for the purposes of the act alone. In this case, the plan text did not prohibit the commencement of a pension despite continued employment with the CRA. On appeal, the Ontario Superior Court of Justice,[37] reversed the Ontario FST decision, and found that subsection 80(3) deemed the employees' employment to be continuous for purposes of the entire Ontario PBA. Further, in the event of any inconsistency between the Ontario PBA and the plan text, the former prevails.

In a related decision, *Provost v. Superintendent of Financial Services*,[38] the Ontario FST had another opportunity to address subsection 80(3), but in the context of a "successor to a successor" sale of business transaction. In this case, the member was employed by Alcan and

---

[36]   *Ontario Pension Board v. Ratansi*, 2012 CarswellOnt 7355.

[37]   *Ontario Pension Board v. Ratansi*, [2013] O.J. No. 911, 2013 ONSC 1092 (Ont. S.C.J.).

[38]   *Provost v. Superintendent of Financial Services*, 2012 CarswellOnt 7106.

participated in its pension plan, but due to two separate transactions, his employment was transferred first to Eaglebrook and then to Kemira. In connection with the first sale transaction, the Alcan plan was partially wound up. The member chose to maintain his deferred benefits in the Alcan plan. A few years later, upon attaining age of 55 and after his employment had been transferred to Kemira, the member applied to have his pension paid out of the Alcan plan, but was refused on the basis that he was working with a successor employer within the meaning of section 80. Following the outcome in *Ratansi*, the Ontario FST concluded that the deemed continuation of employment provision in section 80 could apply in successor to successor situations for certain Ontario PBA purposes. However, in order for the provisions to apply, there had to be a "clear continuity" of the business, a fact that could not be assumed. In this case, the Ontario FST made no finding in regards to successorship since the parties had proceeded on the assumption that Alcan's business had passed to Kemira. It was not clear, however, that the business purchased by Kemira was in fact Alcan's business. The Ontario FST warned that the absence of relevant information presented would have made it difficult to make a finding of successorship.

Class Actions

Pension plans are offered to "classes" of employees. As a result, a contentious pension plan issue (such as a plan amendment) may affect an entire group of individuals. As a result, class actions have become a prevalent litigation mode for members who wish to challenge the actions of trustees and administrators in regard to pension issues.

Each jurisdiction has specific legislation setting out requirements that must be satisfied in order for the action to be certified as a class action. Among other things, the court must conclude that a class action is the preferable route for resolving the issues. In unionized settings, a much-litigated issue arose around whether a unionized member group could proceed with a class action or whether it had to use the arbitration procedure available under its collective agreement. The Supreme Court of Canada delivered a fairly clear answer to that question in *Bisaillon v. Concordia University*.[39] In that case, the members challenged the validity of amendments to the University's pension plan. The applicable collective agreements relating to certain University employees referred to the plan, some in more detail than others. The remaining plan members were non-unionized University employees.

---

[39]   *Bisaillon v. Concordia University*, [2006] S.C.J. No. 19, 2006 SCC 19 (S.C.C.).

Eight of the unions supported the application to be certified as a class action. One union opposed the application and was successful in having it dismissed. On appeal, however, the dismissal was overturned, and Bisaillon was authorized to proceed with the class action. The Quebec Court of Appeal found that the plan was independent of the collective agreement and that arbitral jurisdiction could not resolve all claims of all employee groups, making class action the proper way to resolve the dispute. The Supreme Court, however, in a split decision, reversed the Court of Appeal and held that the essential matter of the dispute, concerning how the plan should be administered, arose out of the plan and therefore was within the exclusive jurisdiction of the grievance arbitrator. As long as the collective agreement expressed a relationship to the plan, either directly or indirectly, the plan was a term or condition of employment and within the exclusive jurisdiction of the arbitrator under the regime of labour law.

This reasoning was followed by the British Columbia Court of Appeal in *Ruddell v. B.C. Rail Ltd.*[40] Pursuant to the requirements of the then current British Columbia *Pension Benefits Standards Act,* the B.C. Rail plan contained an arbitration clause for the settlement of all disputes. When the retirees challenged a plan amendment that provided for contribution holidays, they sought to use a class action to make that challenge. The trial court certified the class action, but the Court of Appeal overturned that decision, ruling that a binding arbitration clause must be given effect. It also noted that an arbitration decision had a potentially broad application to all persons who could be affected by the decision and therefore was not inferior to class action as a route to secure speedy and inexpensive justice.

In an ongoing and largely contested class action relating to the use of surplus, *Lacroix v. Canada Mortgage and Housing Corp.,*[41] former members of a federally-regulated pension plan commenced parallel class actions seeking to add as common issues whether the court can order the partial termination of the plan or order damages calculated on the basis of surplus arising from partial termination. The members are terminated employees who elected to transfer the commuted value from the plan and who, following subsequent benefit enhancements by the employer, were not entitled to the enhancements. The enhancements were funded from plan surpluses arising after the employees' terminations. The company also used surplus for its own purposes. The members argued that the company contravened the conflict of interest provisions of subsection

---

[40]   *Ruddell v. B.C. Rail Ltd.,* [2007] B.C.J. No. 918, 2007 BCCA 269 (B.C.C.A.).
[41]   *Lacroix v. Canada Mortgage and Housing Corp.,* [2012] O.J. No. 1674, 2012 ONCA 243 (Ont. C.A.).

8(10) of the federal PBSA and that subsection 8(11), which permitted a court to order any terms on contravention of subsection 8(10), gave the court jurisdiction to order partial termination of the plan. The Ontario Court of Appeal found that the federal PBSA gave plan termination authority to the Superintendent, and the Court of Appeal had no jurisdiction to compel wind-up. As it could not compel wind-up, neither could it order damages premised on wind-up, these common issues could not be certified.

This case, however, is continuing through the courts. In 2013, the plaintiffs in the *Lacroix* action sought to add additional common issues relating to the alleged breach by the plan trustees of the conflict of interest provisions of the federal PBSA when it failed to advise class members that they had or may have had beneficial interest in pension fund surplus prior to those class members electing to take their commuted value and leaving plan, when it took the position that it owned the surplus to the exclusion of plan members, and when it implemented its surplus sharing decisions without including class members as beneficiaries. In 2015, the Ontario Superior Court certified the additional common issues in both actions. The certification of these additional issues was upheld on appeal in 2016.[42]

Class action proceedings are also used to have pension plan amendments declared null. In *Samoisette v. IBM Canada ltée*,[43] the Quebec Court of Appeal authorized a class action in which the plan members contested the elimination of the bridge benefit provided under the plan. The Quebec Superior Court rendered a decision in 2016 in this case.[44] In 1994, IBM introduced a defined contribution (DC) pension plan. As an incentive for employees in the defined benefit (DB) plan to elect the new DC plan, IBM offered to increase by 40% the contributions accrued by each member. Such additional contribution was intended to compensate for certain differences between the DB plan and the DC plan, including the bridge benefit available to members who retired before age 65. The choice between the DB plan and DC plan was irrevocable. In January 2006, IBM amended the plan to eliminate the bridge benefit for members who become eligible to retire after December 31, 2007.

The explanations and documents provided to assist employees to choose between the DB plan and the DC plan in 1994 contained no information or warning to the effect that the bridge benefit could be modified or abolished. Nor did the software tool made available at the

---

[42] *Lacroix v. Canada Mortgage and Housing Corp.*, [2016] O.J. No. 2131, 2016 ONSC 2641 (Ont. S.C.J.).

[43] *Samoisette v. IBM Canada ltée*, [2012] J.Q. no 4711, 2012 QCCA 946 (Que. C.A.).

[44] *Samoisette v. IBM Canada ltée*, [2016] J.Q. no 6461, 2016 QCCS 2675 (Que. S.C.).

time or the annual updates subsequently provided to employees make any mention to the effect that the bridge benefit could be modified or abolished. It was only after the changes were announced in 2006 that IBM added a provision to benefits statements which stated the right to modify the plan. The explanations provided in 1994, including the assurance to receive the bridge benefit, had the effect of modifying the existing employment contract. The evidence showed that employees relied on the documents to make a decision to remain in the DB plan and were comforted by the thought that they would receive a specific amount at the time of retirement.

The Superior Court held that the amendment provision was abusive as it gave IBM the right to modify an essential condition of the employment contract. The Superior Court also concluded that the amendment provision was abusive as the employees relied on representations made by IBM in 1994 to exercise an election with respect to their pension plan and that the bridge benefit was presented as being an integral part of the compensation that could be expected by employees upon retirement. IBM could not withdraw it in January 2006.

The Superior Court ordered the collective recovery of the bridge benefit and that IBM pay to members of the group an amount of $23,519,000 with interest and additional indemnity provided under the Civil Code of Quebec. IBM was also ordered to pay to each of the members of the group the amount of their individual claim with respect to the bridge benefit, adjusted as at October 1, 2015, with interest and additional indemnity provided under the Civil Code of Quebec.

Another recourse for authorization of a class action with respect to plan amendments was rejected by the Quebec Superior Court in *Association des retraités de l'École polytechnique v. Corporation de l'École polytechnique*.[45] In this case, the association of retirees sought a declaration of nullity of certain plan amendments with respect to indexing of retirees' pension. The *ad hoc* indexing provisions were amended to provide for automatic indexing where certain conditions were satisfied. The lower court declined to authorize the class action on the grounds that there was no appearance of serious right, no fault of the employer was demonstrated even *prima facie*, and that the recourse was prescribed. In this case, the association of retirees was informed throughout the process and had acknowledged the conditions applicable to pension indexing under the plan. The plan amendments were presented to plan members at a referendum and it was found that the employer could not be held liable

45   Association des retraités de l'École polytechnique v. Corporation de l'École polytechnique, [2011] J.Q. no 6600, 2011 QCCS 2784 (Que. S.C.).

if the pension committee omitted to provide all relevant information. This decision was affirmed at the Quebec Court of Appeal.[46]

An emerging issue in pension-related class action proceedings is whether the common issues are indeed common to all plan members. In *Sommerville v. Catalyst Paper Corp.*,[47] the employer made a number of changes to non-unionized employees' benefits, including ceasing accruals under its defined benefit plan and transferring all members to its defined contribution plan. Employer contributions to the defined contribution plan were also reduced. A class action was commenced, and the British Columbia Supreme Court certified the action. However, there were a number of common issues that the court would not certify on the basis that the issue required an individual assessment particular to each class member, including any question relating to whether the employees' contracts of employment required the employer to provide notice of the change in benefits.

Mandatory Retirement/Discrimination Based on Age

To date, most provinces have passed legislation to abolish mandatory retirement, subject to certain exceptions. Some of those exceptions involve pension plans, and the Supreme Court of Canada decision in *New Brunswick (Human Rights Commission) v. Potash Corp. of Saskatchewan Inc.*[48] sheds some light on how those exceptions are to be applied.

The *Potash* case involved a miner who was forced to retire from Saskatchewan Potash when he reached age 65 because of the mandatory retirement policy in the company's pension plan. The employee complained to the New Brunswick Human Rights Commission alleging age discrimination. The New Brunswick *Human Rights Act*, like all other federal and provincial human rights legislation in Canada, prohibits age discrimination. However, the statute contained an exception that allows mandatory retirement under a *bona fide* pension plan or group insurance plan. The Commission took the matter to a Board of Inquiry, which used a three-part test to determine whether the pension plan mandatory retirement policy was *bona fide*: the policy was established for a purpose rationally connected to the job; the policy was adopted in good faith; and the policy was reasonably necessary because accommodating an

---

[46]   *Association des retraités de l'École polytechnique v. Corporation de l'École polytechnique*, [2013] J.Q. no 398, 2013 QCCA 130 (Que. C.A.).

[47]   *Sommerville v. Catalyst Paper Corp.*, [2011] B.C.J. No. 464, 2011 BCSC 331 (B.C.S.C.).

[48]   *New Brunswick (Human Rights Commission) v. Potash Corp. of Saskatchewan Inc.*, [2008] S.C.J. No. 46, 2008 SCC 45 (S.C.C.).

individual member over age 65 imposed undue hardship on the employer or the plan administrator.

The Board's decision was overturned on review, and the reviewing judge used a two-part test requiring the employer to establish both the *bona fides* and the reasonableness of the mandatory retirement policy. The New Brunswick Court of Appeal disagreed that either test was appropriate in an employment context. It found that the clear intent of the New Brunswick legislature was that employers would not have to defend mandatory retirement policies in pension plans. On final appeal, the Supreme Court of Canada clarified that such a mandatory retirement policy was acceptable if the pension plan was subjectively and objectively *bona fide*. As such, it must be a legitimate plan, adopted in good faith and not for the purpose of defeating protected rights. In other words, as long as the plan was not a "sham", then it would be considered *bona fide* and allow the employer to enforce a mandatory retirement provision. This decision may be applicable to other jurisdictions where human rights legislation contains exceptions to age discrimination similar to New Brunswick's exception for *bona fide* pension plans.

The *Potash* decision was raised in the Nova Scotia context in *Foster v. Nova Scotia (Human Rights Commission).*[49] Effective July 2009, the Nova Scotia legislature amended the Nova Scotia *Human Rights Act* to remove the exemption from the age discrimination for mandatory retirement, but retained the exemption from the age discrimination for a *bona fide* pension plan. Prior to July 2009, the employer had a mandatory retirement policy in place along with a defined benefit plan that included a mandatory retirement provision. A defined contribution plan did not include an express mandatory retirement provision, but members were subject to the employer's mandatory retirement policy. With the statutory changes in 2009, the employer amended the defined contribution to provide for mandatory retirement at the age of 65.

One affected employee brought a complaint before the Nova Scotia Human Rights Board of Inquiry alleging discrimination on the basis of age. Applying *Potash*, the Board concluded that the defined contribution plan maintained its *bona fide* status and protection under the statute. On appeal, the Nova Scotia Court of Appeal upheld the Board's decision that the pension plan was a well-funded, registered pension plan with a significant number of members and was not a sham. Further, the plan amendment was made in good faith and for the valid policy reason to treat all employees equally.

---

[49]   *Foster v. Nova Scotia (Human Rights Board of Inquiry)*, [2015] N.S.J. No. 258, 2015 NSCA 66 (N.S.C.A.).

In *Welk v. Université McGill/McGill University*,[50] at issue was not mandatory retirement, but rather whether contributions could be related to a member's age. In this case, the University's pension plan provisions were amended to increase the age at which a member must begin to receive a pension to age 71, in line with the changes to the *Income Tax Act*. Despite this change, the plan provision with respect to the age until which the employer and members may contribute to the plan was not changed and remained fixed at age 69. Plan members alleged that the University was depriving them of a benefit by reason of their age, which is a form of discrimination based on age that is contrary to the Quebec *Charter of Human Rights and Freedoms* (Quebec Charter). The Quebec Superior Court concluded that the QSPPA did not require that a plan allow payment of contributions after a member had attained age 65. As this distinction was authorized by law, there was no discrimination under the Quebec Charter, which is worded differently than the Charter. This decision was upheld by the Quebec Court of Appeal.[51]

Bankrupt or Insolvent Plan Sponsors

A growing and complicated area within pensions is the interaction between pension law and bankruptcy and insolvency law. Unfortunately, when an employer encounters financial troubles, the employer's pension plan often suffers as well. While pension funds are held in trust for plan members and do not form part of the company's assets, issues often arise regarding required plan contributions that the employer cannot remit in times of financial hardship, or where the plan is fully or partially wound up (either before or after entering the insolvency or bankruptcy proceedings) and a deficit remains. In such situations, plan members are often pitted against the company's creditors, and the courts are left with the difficult task of reconciling pension standards legislation with bankruptcy and insolvency legislation.

The Supreme Court of Canada's 2013 decision in *Sun Indalex Finance LLC*[52] was transformative in this area. In this case, Indalex filed for creditor protection under the *Companies' Creditors Arrangement Act* (CCAA) in 2009. The Ontario Superior Court of Justice authorized Indalex to borrow funds pursuant to a debtor-in-possession (DIP) credit

---

50   *Welk v. Université McGill/McGill University*, [2009] J.Q. no 5424, 2009 QCCS 2430 (Que. S.C.).

51   *Welk v. Université McGill/McGill University*, [2011] J.Q. no 2861, 2011 QCCA 578 (Que. C.A.).

52   *Sun Indalex Finance, LLC v. United Steelworkers*, [2013] S.C.J. No. 6, 2013 SCC 6 (S.C.C.).

agreement among Indalex, Indalex's U.S. parent company and a syndicate of lenders (DIP Lenders). The court order also gave the DIP Lenders a super-priority over all other creditors.

Indalex was the sponsor and administrator of two defined benefit plan pension plans: a plan for salaried employees that had been wound up prior to the CCAA filing (Salaried Plan); and a plan for executive employees that was still ongoing (Executive Plan). Both plans were underfunded and had wind-up deficiencies.

In July 2009, Indalex sought court approval of the sale of its assets and the distribution of the sale proceeds to the DIP Lenders. The purchaser assumed no responsibility for the defined benefit plans and the proposed distribution of the sale proceeds would result in no funds to cover the plans' wind-up deficiencies. Employee groups objected to the proposed distribution of sale proceeds and asserted a deemed trust claim over the sale proceeds to cover the plans' deficiencies. The court approved the sale of Indalex's assets, with the sale proceeds going to the monitor. The monitor was ordered to retain a reserve fund, representing the approximate value of the plans' deficiencies. At issue was whether the reserve fund was payable to the DIP Lenders or to the pension plans.

In 2011, the Ontario Court of Appeal ordered the monitor to pay into each of the plans an amount sufficient to satisfy the wind-up deficiencies, in priority over the DIP Lenders. With respect to the Salaried Plan, the Court of Appeal expanded the scope of the deemed trust provision set out at subsection 57(4) of the Ontario PBA to include the entire wind-up deficiency under that plan. With respect to the Executive Plan, the Court of Appeal refused to find that a deemed trust under the Ontario PBA existed, since that plan was not wound up at the time Indalex entered into CCAA protection. However, the Court of Appeal held that Indalex breached its fiduciary obligations as the plan administrator in the CCAA proceedings and further held that the remedy for the breach was to impose a constructive trust over a portion of the reserve fund, with the result that the pension deficiency in the Executive Plan was also found to rank ahead of the DIP Lenders' super-priority.

On appeal, the Supreme Court of Canada issued a split decision. The Supreme Court unanimously found that the super-priority granted to the DIP Lenders in the federal CCAA proceedings prevailed over any deemed trust under the Ontario PBA on the basis of the legal doctrine that grants paramountcy to federal laws where they conflict with provincial laws. The Supreme Court also unanimously found that Indalex breached its fiduciary duty in failing to appropriately address its conflict of interest that it encountered when it sought the super-priority for the DIP Lenders. According to the majority, Indalex should have given the plans' beneficiaries proper notice of the DIP financing motion. However, the majority of the Supreme Court rejected and overturned the use of a constructive trust as an appropriate remedy for the breach.

Importantly, the Supreme Court upheld the Court of Appeal's expanded interpretation of the deemed trust provisions of the Ontario PBA, and found that the deemed trust applies to the entire wind-up deficiency of a plan upon its wind-up. The Supreme Court also confirmed that the deemed trust in subsection 57(4) of the Ontario PBA did not apply to the estimated wind-up liability of the ongoing Executive Plan, as the section is not invoked until actual plan wind-up.

Since the Supreme Court's decision in *Indalex*, courts in other jurisdictions have grappled with its application in the context of their own pension standards legislation. In Quebec, in *White Birch Paper Holding Company, Re*,[53] Justice Mongeon rendered a decision declaring that section 49 of the QSPPA did not create a real or deemed trust that would render unpaid special payments to a pension plan payable in priority over other secured claims and that the reasoning of the Ontario Court of Appeal in *Indalex* (later confirmed by the Supreme Court of Canada) did not apply under Quebec law.

Later, in 2014, Justice Mongeon rendered another decision in an unrelated matter, *Timminco ltée, Re*,[54] in which he revisited his conclusions made in the 2012 *White Birch* decision and held that, as between two creditors subject to Quebec law and in the absence of super-priorities affecting the assets, unpaid special payments were subject to a deemed trust under section 49 of the QSPPA and are also unassignable and unseizable under section 264 of the QSPPA. *Timminco* thus allowed the pension plan to recover special payments that the employer had failed to pay despite a secured creditor having a prior secured claim over the employer's assets. Justice Mongeon distinguished *White Birch* on factual grounds, on the basis that the secured creditor in *Timminco* was not the DIP lender, as in *White Birch*, so the secured creditor did not have the benefit of super-priority under the CCAA.

Justice Mongeon released a further decision in 2014 in *White Birch Paper Holding Co., Re*.[55] In this case, a purchaser of the debtors' assets was concerned about the possible effect of the *Timminco* judgment on the continuation of the *White Birch* CCAA proceedings, as it may reopen the debate as to whether the debtors had the obligation to pay into the pension

---

[53]   *White Birch Paper Holding Co., Re*, [2012] J.Q. no 3643, 2012 QCCS 1679 (Que. S.C.).

[54]   *Timminco ltée, Re*, [2014] J.Q. no 402, 2014 QCCS 174 (Que. S.C.).

[55]   *White Birch Paper Holding Co., Re*, [2014] J.Q. no 10777, 2014 QCCS 4709 (Que. S.C.).

plans the special payments unpaid since 2010. Justice Mongeon found that the *White Birch* decision was final and not appealed.

The Quebec courts had another chance to consider the application of *Indalex* in *Aveos Fleet Performance Inc.*,[56] but under the federal PBSA. In this case, the insolvent employer was located in Québec and the plans were not wound up before the insolvency proceedings began. As a result of a solvency deficit, the employer continued to make special payments to the plan until March 2012. In the CCAA initial order, the court suspended special payments to the plan, but allowed the employer to make normal cost contributions. In May 2012, OSFI wound up the plans. Upon wind-up, the employer owed both the special payments owing on the date of the initial order, along with the special payments owed for the period between the initial order and the end of the year. OSFI claimed that the deemed trust created by the federal PBSA obliged the employer to pay to the plan, in priority to the employer's secured creditors, the unpaid special payments.

The court disagreed and held that the amounts owed to the employer's secured creditors ranked in priority to the special payments owed under the plan. In this case, when the deemed trust arose, the employer's assets were already encumbered by fixed charges in favour of the secured creditors that were created in 2010 and 2011. In contrast, the deemed trust in respect of the plan arose either upon the employer's liquidation (which would not have been before the CCAA filing) or, at the earliest, when a special payment became due following the plan's actuarial actual report filed in June 2011. In other words, the secured creditors' security interest was created before any deemed trust in respect of the plan could have existed. Since the assets were already charged, any deemed trust under the federal PBSA would be subordinate to the interests of the secured creditors.

In the Ontario context, in *Grant Forest Products Inc. v. The Toronto-Dominion Bank*,[57] the employer and other related companies sought creditor protection under the CCAA. Under the CCAA initial order, the employer was entitled, but not required, to pay outstanding and future pension contributions to its two defined benefit pension plans. In February 2012, the Ontario Superintendent ordered the plans wound up. The wind-up order gave rise to significant wind-up payment obligations for the employer. The employer made contributions until June 2012, when it

---

[56]   *Indalex* in *Aveos Fleet Performance Inc.*, [2013] J.Q. no 15967, 2013 QCCS 5762 (Que. S.C.).

[57]   *Grant Forest Products Inc. v. The Toronto-Dominion Bank*, [2015] O.J. No. 1366, 2015 ONCA 192 (Ont. C.A.).

sought an order declaring that it not be required to make further contributions pending the Supreme Court's decision in *Indalex*. Following release of the *Indalex* decision, the CCAA judge stated that the wind-up deemed trust will prevail in an insolvency where the wind-up occurs before insolvency, but not when the wind-up occurs after the initial order is granted, as it did in this case. On appeal, the Ontario Court of Appeal upheld the lower court's decision, distinguishing the facts of *Indalex* on the basis that the pension plan giving rise to the Ontario PBA deemed trust in *Indalex* had been wound up prior to the CCAA initial order. In this case, the plans were only wound up after the CCAA initial order was made.

Most recently, in *Bloom Lake, G.P.L. (Arrangement of)*,[58] on initiating CCAA proceedings, the petitioners requested that the Québec Superior Court approve an interim financing arrangement as part of the CCAA initial order, which would give the interim lender a super-priority charge over all charges against the petitioners. The petitioners had two underfunded defined benefit plans. As part of the interim financing arrangement, the petitioners would be required to suspend special payments in relation to these plans. The court granted the initial order approving the interim financing, but provided for a comeback hearing to determine whether the interim lender could be granted a super-priority charge over the statutory deemed trusts created by the federal PBSA and Newfoundland and Labrador PBA (N&L PBA).

Ultimately, the court confirmed that Parliament's intent was for federal pension claims to be protected only to the limited extent set out in the CCAA and the *Bankruptcy and Insolvency Act*, notwithstanding the broader scope of protections in the federal PBSA. On this basis, the deemed trust provisions in the federal PBSA did not prevent the court from granting a super-priority charge to the interim lender. With respect to the N&L PBA, the lower court held that the deemed trust provisions were in conflict with the CCAA. Based on *Indalex* and the doctrine of federal paramountcy, the lower court held the interim lender could be given priority over the N&L PBA deemed trust. This decision was upheld at the Quebec Court of Appeal.

---

[58]   *Bloom Lake, G.P.L. (Arrangement of)*, [2015] Q.J. No. 7736, 2015 QCCA 1351 (Que. C.A.).

Payment of Pension Plan Expenses

Another useful topic covered by *Kerry (Canada) Inc. v. DCA Employees Pension Committee,*[59] referenced at the beginning of this chapter, was determining when employers are permitted to pay plan expenses out of the pension fund. Pension standards legislation typically does not authorize the payment of plan expenses from the fund (although some pension standards legislation provides that reasonable administrative expenses may be permitted based on the pension plan text). Instead, such determinations are left to the wording of the particular pension plan text or trust agreement.

In *Kerry*, the original plan text contained no provisions dealing with the payment of plan expenses, and a disagreement arose as to whether the employer was entitled to be reimbursed for expenses it incurred in operating and administering the plan. The Ontario Court of Appeal held that "silence does not create an obligation on the Company to pay" and concluded that, in accordance with general trust practice and principles, it was appropriate for the fund to bear the plan expenses. The Court of Appeal did, however, disallow the claim for the payment of expenses relating to advice on the addition of a defined contribution component to the plan, since that advice was for the employer's own benefit and not for the benefit of plan members. Accordingly, the employer was solely responsible for those expenses.

On appeal, the Supreme Court of Canada affirmed the Court of Appeal's decision on payment of plan expenses, holding that while the plan stated it was being provided for the "exclusive benefit" of the members, this did not preclude paying administrative expenses associated with maintaining the plan from the plan fund. The Supreme Court noted that the plan was a benefit to the employees, and that payment of plan expenses was necessary to "ensure the Plan's continued integrity and existence". The Supreme Court concluded that it was "to the exclusive benefit of the employees that expenses for the continued existence of the Plan were paid out of the Fund".

Soon after the *Kerry* decision, in *Burke v. Hudson's Bay Co.,*[60] the Supreme Court of Canada again concluded that the employer had no obligation to pay plan expenses when the plan text was silent on the matter, and that the employer made a valid subsequent amendment to the plan explicitly authorizing expense payments from the fund. Following its

---

[59]   *Kerry (Canada) Inc. v. Ontario (Superintendent of Financial Services)*, [2009] S.C.J. No. 39, 2009 SCC 39 (S.C.C.).

[60]   *Burke v. Hudson's Bay Co.*, [2010] S.C.J. No. 34, 2010 SCC 34 (S.C.C.).

analysis in *Kerry,* the Supreme Court reiterated that in the absence of any statutory or common law obligations for an employer to pay administrative expenses, any obligation would be determined by the plan text and trust documents. Silence in the original trust and plan documents, and subsequent trust agreements allowing plan administrator expenses to be paid from the fund, and confirming what was already implicitly provided for in the original trust agreement, supported the employer's authority to pay expenses from the fund.

While *Kerry* helped clarify the issue of payment of plan expenses, the Supreme Court's analysis underscored that each particular case will turn on a careful examination of the relevant historical plan and trust documentation (along with pension standards legislation, where applicable).

Funding of Deficits under a Multi-Employer Pension Plan

The issue of funding a deficit upon participating employer withdrawal from a multi-employer pension plan (MEPP) was extensively considered in Quebec. In *Multi-Marques Distribution Inc. v. Régie des rentes du Québec*, a MEPP registered in Quebec was funded by participating employers only, and provided that employers' contributions to the plan were limited to the contributions as provided for in the applicable collective agreement. In 1996-1997, the MEPP, which had both defined benefit and defined contribution components, was partially terminated as a result of the closure of certain company divisions. The MEPP had a deficit of approximately $5 million at that time because of the cost related to the past service credited to the employees of the divisions in question.

In the first decision in this case (*Multi-Marques 1*),[61] the Quebec Court of Appeal decided in 2008 that the plan's provisions were not incompatible with the provisions of the QSPPA, as members' benefits are at first determined according to the pension plan provisions and not the QSPPA. In this case, the plan members were only entitled to the benefits that were funded by the employer at the time of the MEPP termination. The Court of Appeal ordered that the file be returned to the Régie des rentes du Québec (the Régie) in order for the Régie to render decisions in the partial wind-up process in accordance with the decision of the Quebec Court of Appeal in *Multi-Marques 1*.

As a result of *Multi-Marques 1*, the QSPPA was amended in June 2008 by Bill 68 in order to "counteract" the effects of that decision. In the

---

[61]   *Multi-Marques Distribution Inc. v. Régie des rentes du Québec*, [2008] J.Q. no 2587, 2008 QCCA 597 (Que. C.A.).

meantime, the Régie formed a review committee to apply the *Multi-Marques 1* decision. The review committee confirmed the Régie's decisions as it was of the opinion that Bill 68, which was a declaratory statute, established the scope of the QSPPA provisions that was always intended.

An appeal of the decision was heard by the Quebec Court of Appeal in 2011 (*Multi-Marques 2*).[62] The Court of Appeal provided useful explanations with respect to the scope of a declaratory statute, which is retroactive. The Court of Appeal concluded that the Régie was bound by the *Multi-Marques 1* decision rendered in 2008 regardless of the declaratory statute subsequently adopted. The Court of Appeal also confirmed that a declaratory statute cannot affect a judgment that is *res judicata*, unless the declaratory statute expressly provides that it applies to such judgments. Otherwise, the parties must comply with the judgment. The Régie was ordered to modify its decisions in accordance with the conclusions in *Multi-Marques 1* and the fact that the plan provisions were compatible with the QSPPA.

The *Multi-Marques* legal saga finally came to an end with the 2013 Supreme Court of Canada decision in *Kelly (Trustee of) c. Québec (Régie des rentes)*.[63] The Supreme Court found that the Régie was correct in applying the provisions of the declaratory legislation and in refusing to allow members' benefits related to past service to be reduced. According to the Supreme Court, the legislature's objective in Bill 68 was to overrule the Court of Appeal's decision in order to protect members and beneficiaries. Also, declaratory provisions are an exception to the general rule that legislation is prospective, as they have an immediate effect on pending cases. In this case, since the Court of Appeal returned the file to the Régie in 2008, the case was still pending. In the result, the withdrawing employers from the MEPP were required to remedy any solvency deficit based on the QSPPA requirements.

In another recent Quebec decision relating to employer withdrawal from a MEPP, *Kelly c. Québec (Régie des rentes)*,[64] two participating employers ceased contributing to a MEPP on behalf of certain of their employees in 2003 and 2002 as a result of those employees being represented by a different union. The Tribunal administratif du Québec (TAQ) was required to decide whether the employers had withdrawn from the plan. According to the TAQ, by no longer making contributions to the

---

[62]   *Multi-Marques Distribution Inc. v. Régie des rentes du Québec*, [2011] J.Q. no 10713, 2011 QCCA 1518 (Que. C.A.).

[63]   *Kelly (Trustee of) c. Québec (Régie des rentes)*, [2013] S.C.J. No. 46, 2013 SCC 46 (S.C.C.).

[64]   *Kelly c. Québec (Régie des rentes)*, 2014 LNQCTAQ 7, 2014 QCTAQ 01130.

MEPP, the employers effectively withdrew from the MEPP under section 198 of the QSPPA. However, these withdrawals were not yet in force, because under section 198, a withdrawal of employer is conditional upon a modification of the pension plan, which must be filed with the Régie. In other words, the withdrawal only takes effect on the date the plan modification is registered with the Régie.

In a similar case, *Louben Sportswear inc. c. Caisse de retraite des industries de la mode (U.I.O.V.D.)*,[65] an employer ceased making contributions to a MEPP in 2010, as it no longer had active employees. However, no application for the registration of a plan amendment was ever filed with the Régie in order to effect the withdrawal. The Régie terminated the MEPP in 2012. Upon termination, there was a deficit to be paid by the participating employers, of which $940,480 was claimed from the employer. The employer contested this payment, alleging that it had not had any employees covered by the Plan since 2010, and that the calculation of its debt should be made as at the date it withdrew, not as at the MEPP's termination date. The Quebec Superior Court held that the mere fact that the employer ceased to contribute to the MEPP in 2010 did not in and of itself constitute a withdrawal, but that withdrawal is conditional upon an amendment to the plan that must be authorized by the Régie. In addition, the QSPPA provides that no plan amendment can take place after the termination of the pension plan. In the present case, any amendment to the MEPP would necessarily take place after the termination date in 2012, which is not permitted by the QSPPA. As a result, the MEPP could no longer be modified after 2012, so as to confirm the employer's withdrawal, and so the employer's action was doomed to fail. This decision was affirmed at the Quebec Court of Appeal.

Outside of Quebec, in *Northern Employee Benefits Services v. Rae-Edzo Community Services Authority*,[66] the MEPP at issue was not subject to any pension standards legislation. A participating employer notified the MEPP administrator that a number of its employees would be terminating their plan membership. At the same time the employer stopped making contributions. The administrator terminated the employer's participation in the plan and claimed a payment representing the employer's share of the plan's solvency deficiency, pursuant to its internal policy. The NorthWest Territories Supreme Court reviewed the administrator's by-laws as well as the policy, to determine if the administrator had the authority to impose a solvency deficiency payment on the employer. The

---

[65] *Louben Sportswear inc. c. Caisse de retraite des industries de la mode (U.I.O.V.D.)*, [2015] J.Q. no 117, 2015 QCCA 42 (Que. C.A.).

[66] *Northern Employee Benefits Services v. Rae-Edzo Community Services Authority*, [2012] N.W.T.J. No. 67, 2012 NWTSC 61 (N.W.T.S.C.).

court found that the by-laws provision that required any outstanding balance to be refunded or paid by the member and its participating employees on termination did not include solvency payments. Further, the court noted that the policy had been amended in 2002 to require an employer to make solvency deficiency payments; however, the amendment was never distributed nor explained to participating employers. As a result, the employer was not responsible for its share of the solvency deficiency.

Plan Amendments Reducing Benefits

A significant issue that has come to the forefront of pension cases in recent years is the ability to amend a plan to reduce pension and other ancillary benefits. At issue in these cases is whether a benefit is "accrued" or "vested", and therefore cannot be reduced in respect of past service under applicable pension legislation or in the plan text.

Plan sponsors often question their right to reduce accrued benefits under pension plans. In *Synertech Moulded Products, Division of Old Castle Building v. Tribunal administratif du Québec*,[67] the Quebec Superior Court considered the issue of amendments that reduce pension benefits retroactively. The court ruled that the Régie could not arbitrarily refuse to register plan amendments to which the affected members had given their consent. According to the court, the Régie could not act arbitrarily, unreasonably, or unfairly when exercising a discretionary power, such as the power to authorize or not an amendment reducing benefits.

In this case, the Régie refused to register pension plan amendments reducing the pension formula for all service under two individual defined benefit pension plans for two key employees of Synertech. The Régie considered that the amendments significantly reduced the benefits retroactively. The Superior Court analyzed section 20 of the QSPPA, which allows amendments that retroactively reduce benefits for all service if the affected members give their consent and the Régie has authorized the amendment. In this case, the two affected members had given their written consent to the reducing amendment.

The Superior Court pointed out that in the absence of criteria in the legislation, the Régie's decisions must be based on the provisions as set out in the QSPPA. It should be noted that the Régie's non-official internal position was not to authorize retroactive amendments that reduced the

---

[67] *Synertech Moulded Products, Division of Old Castle Building v. Tribunal administratif du Québec*, [2011] J.Q. no 12370, 2011 QCCS 4770 (Que. S.C.).

value of members' benefits by more than 5%. Plan sponsors who wish to introduce amendments reducing benefits should consult the applicable legislation to determine the specific applicable requirements.

The decision in *Halliburton Group Canada Inc. v. Alberta*,[68] considered this issue in the context of the Alberta *Employment Pension Plans Act* (EPPA). The defined benefit plan at issue originally provided a benefit based on a member's five best consecutive years of salary in the 10 years preceding the member's normal retirement date. The employer later amended the plan to "freeze" all accrued defined benefit entitlements as of January 1, 2002, and to require all members to participate in a defined contribution component for future service. The employer later amended the plan to provide that members' salary for purposes of the closed defined benefit component would be the annualized average of members' salary in the 36 months preceding the date members joined the defined contribution component.

The Alberta Superintendent rejected these amendments, taking the position that, by freezing salary for purposes of the defined benefit component at a date earlier than immediately before the member's retirement, the amendments constituted a retroactive reduction of "accrued" benefits contrary to the EPPA. More specifically, section 81 of the EPPA provides that a plan amendment cannot reduce accrued benefits. The plan text also prohibited retroactive reductions of "vested" benefits. On appeal, the Alberta Court of Appeal upheld the Superintendent's decision, agreeing that defined benefit members had a vested entitlement to have their pension for pre-2002 service calculated based on the previous definition of salary prior to their retirement dates, and not frozen as at the date of conversion.

A similar fact scenario subsequently arose in the Ontario context in *ROMCA v. Superintendent of Financial Services*,[69] but the Ontario FST came to a different conclusion based on the wording of the Ontario PBA and the plan text at issue. In this case, the employer maintained a defined benefit plan for both salaried and hourly employees, with benefits calculated based on the best 36 consecutive months of earnings prior to retirement. The employer amended the plan's benefit formula to provide that earnings would be based on the greater of: (i) the best 36 consecutive months of earnings for employment prior to January 1, 2010; and (ii) the best 60 consecutive months of employment prior to retirement.

---

[68]   *Halliburton Group Canada Inc. v. Alberta (Minister of Finance)*, [2010] A.J. No. 1001, 2010 ABCA 254 (Alta. C.A.).

[69]   *ROMCA v. Superintendent of Financial Services*, 2013 ONFST 9.

The Ontario regulator subsequently registered the amendment. However, one of the unions representing hourly employees complained to the Ontario Superintendent, challenging the amendment as void under paragraph 14(1)(a) of the Ontario PBA, which prohibits reductions to "accrued" pension benefits. The Superintendent rejected the union's position, finding that the amendment preserved the highest average salary accrued under the plan prior to the amendment's effective date and that future earnings are contingent events that do not form part of the benefit that accrued as at the effective date of an amendment. On appeal, the Ontario FST similarly found that paragraph 14(1)(a) of the Ontario PBA only prohibits the reduction of the "amount" of a pension benefit accrued based on employment before the amendment's effective date, calculated as of the date of the amendment and based on service and earnings up to that date. The Ontario FST distinguished *Haliburton* based on differences in the wording of the Ontario PBA and the EPPA and on the specific language of the plan text in question.

The issue of changes to "accrued" or "vested" benefits was again considered by the Ontario FST in *General Motors of Canada Limited v. Ontario (Superintendent of Financial Services)*.[70] The defined benefit plan at issue provided contractual indexing of benefits. Initially, the plan's termination section described a deferred pension in accordance with various provisions, including the indexing provision "as applicable". However, the termination section was amended in 2003, retroactive to 1995 (being the establishment of the defined benefit component), to remove the reference to the indexing provision. From the time the defined benefit provision was added in 1995, the employer applied contractual indexing only to members who retired from active employment. The employer later amended the plan to freeze the accrual of defined benefit entitlements. This amendment also confirmed that contractual indexing applied only to active employees who had already become retirement-eligible on June 30, 2011.

As a result of the employees' challenge, the Ontario Superintendent declared the employer's amendment void on the grounds that it reduced an accrued pension benefit, being the contractual indexing, contrary to subsection 14(1) of the Ontario PBA. The Ontario FST upheld the Superintendent's decision, holding that all members were entitled to contractual indexing based on the plan's language, not only those who retired or terminated after reaching retirement age. The Ontario FST also held that the employer's past administrative practices were not relevant.

---

[70]   *General Motors of Canada Limited v. Ontario (Superintendent of Financial Services)*, 2014 ONFST 11.

Importantly, the Ontario FST held that contractual indexing could not be removed for past service because it is a "pension benefit" for the purpose of the Ontario PBA. The Ontario PBA provides a higher protection to pension benefits as opposed to "ancillary benefits", in that the statute voids any amendment that purports to reduce a pension benefit accrued for service prior to the amendment's effective date, but in contrast, ancillary benefits "vest" on the date a member has met all eligibility requirements necessary to exercise the right to receive the benefit. The Ontario FST held that the only ancillary benefits that can be provided to Ontario members are those listed in subsection 40(1) of the Ontario PBA. Since indexing is not a listed ancillary benefit in that section, it must be a "pension benefit" and accordingly, it cannot be reduced or eliminated once accrued.

Chapter 11

Multi-Employer Pension Plans

Executive Summary[1]

Multi-employer pension plans (MEPPs) are typically defined as plans to which two or more, usually unrelated, employers in the same industry contribute. Although MEPPs are generally subject to the same statutory minimum standards that apply to single-employer pension plans, the pension legislation in each Canadian jurisdiction as well as the *Income Tax Act* (ITA) contain specific conditions and exemptions that recognize the uniqueness of such arrangements. This chapter starts off with an examination of the concept of MEPPs, their history in Canada, and their main characteristics. The second part of this chapter addresses the various statutory provisions applicable to MEPPs from the perspective of pension legislation and the ITA. The chapter concludes by examining the issue of governance in the context of MEPPs.

Introduction

Although the majority of pension plans in Canada are single employer plans, which are addressed in Chapter 9, a significant number of Canadian workers, in both the public and private sectors, are members of pension plans that are sponsored or established by two or more, usually unrelated, employers. Such plans are known as multi-employer pension plans or MEPPs.

According to Statistics Canada, as of December 31, 2014, there were 400 MEPPs in Canada covering approximately 1,006,900 workers.[2] While Ontario regulates more MEPPs than any other Canadian jurisdiction, a

---

[1]   For more information on multi-employer plans, please consult the multi-jurisdictional charts in the *Canadian Employment Benefits & Pension Guide*. Morneau Shepell, *Canadian Employment Benefits & Pension Guide*, loose-leaf (Toronto: LexisNexis Canada, 2003). The table of contents for these charts appears at the back of this Handbook.

[2]   *CANSIM Table 280-0013 (Registered pension plans (RPPs), members and market value of assets, by number of employers sponsoring the plan, sector, type of plan and contributory status)*, Statistics Canada.

significant number of MEPPs are also regulated under the federal jurisdiction, British Columbia, Alberta, Quebec, and New Brunswick.[3]

This chapter outlines the various characteristics that make MEPPs different from single employer pension plans (SEPPs) and considers their treatment under both pension and income tax legislation. Where appropriate, consideration will also be given to negotiated cost defined benefit plans, which operate similarly in certain respects even though they may not technically all be MEPPs. Recent changes to pension legislation, especially in New Brunswick and British Columbia, have led to several MEPPs in these jurisdictions converting to shared risk or target benefit plans and much of the information in this chapter still applies to these plans.

Although this chapter emphasizes the requirements under the Ontario *Pension Benefits Act*, statutory requirements under other Canadian jurisdictions are also considered, particularly where these requirements are different from those in Ontario.

General Definition of a Multi-Employer Pension Plan

Although pension legislation in each Canadian jurisdiction provides its own definition of a MEPP, a multi-employer pension plan may be generally defined as a plan to which two or more, usually unrelated, employers in the same industry contribute. Employees who may work for several employers within the industry for relatively short periods of time are members of such plans, with the result that an individual employee's pension benefit entitlement is based on the aggregate of pension credits earned while employed with various employers, as if the employee had worked for only one employer. These plans contain vesting and locking-in rules similar to those in SEPPs, except that the rules are usually based on participation in the plan or employment in the industry, rather than service with one employer.

History of Multi-Employer Pension Plans

Historically, workers employed in industries such as construction, entertainment, clothing, food and service, trucking, graphic communication, and hotels were excluded from employer-sponsored pension plans. Unique to these industries was the fact that most individuals did not stay

---

3   E. Shilton, *Current Issues Concerning Multi-Employer Pension Plans in Ontario*, Research Report, The Ontario Expert Commission on Pensions (31 October 2007).

with any one employer long enough to qualify for benefits that the employer may have offered and if they were fortunate enough to qualify, worker mobility increased the costs of administration in dealing with frequent short-term payouts and transfers. These barriers, coupled with the demand for occupational pension plans at the time, led to the establishment of MEPPs within the private sector. The first MEPP in Canada appeared in the 1940s as a consequence of an agreement between the Amalgamated Clothing Workers of America and the Associated Clothing Manufacturers of Toronto.

More recently, governments and quasi-public sector agencies have adopted the concept of MEPPs in order to provide pension benefits to public sector unions and, at the same time, control the inherent risks and costs associated with SEPPs.

Broadly speaking, there are three types of MEPPs:[4]

1. *Classic MEPPs*: are traditional MEPPs that have been established by trade unions (or otherwise through the collective bargaining process) in industries such as construction. Classic MEPPs tend to be defined benefit plans in which the pension benefit is based on a formula that gives the employee a fixed dollar amount per month for every year of employee service or for every hour worked. Employer contributions are typically fixed by a collective agreement for the duration of the agreement.

2. *Public Sector MEPPs*: are MEPPs that are established by governments, agencies, boards, commissions, municipalities, universities, schools, and hospitals, as well as certain social services and other organizations that are funded through government transfers. Many of these MEPPs are established by statute and include the Ontario Teachers' Pension Plan, the Ontario Municipal Employees Retirement System, the British Columbia Public Service Pension Plan, and the Manitoba Civil Service Superannuation Fund. These MEPPs tend to be career average or final average earnings plans, much like single employer defined benefit plans. A number of the Ontario Public Sector MEPPs are classified as Jointly Sponsored Pension Plans (JSPP) today.

3. *Co-operative MEPPs*: are MEPPs that are established to achieve administrative efficiencies and economies of scale. Co-operative MEPPs are different from Classic MEPPs in that there is an absence of an underlining collective agreement; employer participation is usually bargained on a unit-by-unit basis. In the

---

[4]   *Ibid.*, at x-xi.

private sector, they may arise as a result of industry affiliations or associations. In the not-for-profit sector, they may arise out of church or education affiliations.

The remainder of this chapter will focus on Classic MEPPs.

Characteristics of a Multi-Employer Pension Plan

There are a number of characteristics that distinguish a MEPP from a SEPP including:

- *Board of Trustees*: MEPPs are generally administered by boards of trustees. While some MEPPs are administered by the relevant union only, most boards are comprised of equal representation from the union and participating employers. The union component of the board generally consists of elected members or union officials, often including the president and business manager. The employer component is typically appointed by the employer bargaining association and is often made up of representatives of senior management of the plan's largest employers.

- *Employer contributions are fixed*: Typically, only employers are required to contribute to MEPPs (although many Public Sector and Co-operative MEPPs do require employee contributions), and the amount is fixed by the most recent collective bargaining agreement between the participating employer and union. The implication is that a board of trustees normally has no power to increase contributions. Please note that different union locals may negotiate different contribution rates, or a local may have different contracts and contribution rates with different employers. Also note that, in industries where work levels can be heavily dependent on seasonal work or economic cycles, contribution levels can vary quite a bit.

- *Funding rules*: In some provinces, SEPP funding rules apply equally to MEPPs in determining the minimum amount of required contributions that result from the current service cost and any special payments for deficit funding. Given the fixed contribution nature of MEPPs, the actuary must demonstrate to the pension regulator that the scheduled contributions are sufficient to cover the minimum amount of required contributions. If the current level of contributions is sufficient, then the MEPP can continue as is and may even consider making a benefit improvement. However, if contributions are insufficient to cover the minimum costs, then the board of trustees must submit an action plan to reduce benefits in some fashion (this could include accrued benefits and pensions in pay) and/or to increase contributions (subject to negotiations for most MEPPs). This differs significantly from SEPP funding in that an increased SEPP deficit typically results in increased employer contributions. Unless given the express power to do so, the board of trustees does not have the power to unilaterally increase contributions. It is important to note that some jurisdictions currently offer temporary solvency funding exemptions to MEPPs in recognition of the much lower risk of plan insolvency as compared to SEPPs. Some jurisdictions also exempt MEPPs from solvency funding entirely if certain other funding criteria are met (e.g., target benefit plans in British Columbia). Actuaries have generally developed more conservative funding methods for MEPPs in hopes of avoiding pension reductions due to poor market conditions and periods of employment slowdowns.

- *Target benefits*: The trustees apply a prescribed formula outlined in the plan terms to convert negotiated contributions into a defined benefit pension at retirement. If the negotiated contributions are insufficient to cover the minimum required amount of contributions based on the applicable funding rules (see section above), then pension legislation in most jurisdictions permits the board of trustees of a MEPP to reduce benefits for future service and past service. As a result, the pension amount for members of a MEPP is dependent on the financial position of the plan and may be reduced or increased from year to year or valuation to valuation. This is the fundamental difference between SEPPs and MEPPs — SEPPs offer a fixed pension amount whereas MEPPs can only offer a targeted pension amount. Benefit reductions and benefit improvements are common within MEPPs.

- *Membership and worker mobility*: The eligibility rules for MEPPs are the same as SEPPs except that a member of a MEPP can work for more than one participating employer during a single year or period to qualify for membership. This feature of a MEPP addresses worker mobility within a specific industry or group of employers that participate in the same MEPP. Membership can also be drawn from more than one local of a particular union. Service is often based on hours of work or hours of contributions. In addition, the definition of an hour of work may include hours, periods of disability, temporary layoff, service for the union, and certain unpaid time off for which the employer is contracted to contribute. Many MEPPs operate on an hour banking system to compensate for periods of low employment. A full year may be defined as a number of hours less than normally considered full time (2,080 hours in a year). Hours in excess of this number can be banked and used to increase the credit up to a full year when the member would otherwise only have credit for a partial year.

- *Benefit formulas*: Benefit formulas in MEPPs do not vary greatly from SEPPs and indeed a cross section of MEPPs will reflect the same types of benefit formulas that a cross section of SEPPs will have, including: final or average salary plans, flat dollar benefit plans, and defined contribution plans. However, different benefit levels may apply to different locals and groups of members. Given the mobility of workers and sporadic employment characteristics of MEPPs, the method for crediting service and benefit accruals tends to be more liberal for MEPPs as compared to the month of work equals a month of service rule for SEPPs.

- *Ownership of funds and surplus*: There is a minimum requirement in most pension standards legislation that any registered SEPP must deal with the matter of surplus ownership, both when the plan is ongoing and on plan termination. In the absence of such a provision, no surplus withdrawals can be made. Funds in a MEPP do not belong to any one employer or even to all employers or the union; rather, they generally belong to the members. Complications of ownership of surplus that arise in defined benefit SEPPs are eliminated in MEPPs. Trust agreements must also specify conditions governing the funds when the plan is wound up or terminated. All remaining funds must be used for the benefit of existing members and former members.

- *Pooling & shared administration costs*: MEPPs offer many smaller employers and their employees access to a pension plan supported by professional advisors and a more sophisticated investment structure at a much lower price than if they were to establish a SEPP because the administration costs and professional advisor fees are shared across all participating employers. Furthermore, the pooling of assets means that individual returns and longevity risks associated with defined contribution pension plans are minimized and members generally can expect to receive a larger retirement income for their contribution dollars than if they had been participating in a defined contribution SEPP.

The Collective Agreement and Trust Agreement

Most private sector MEPPs are established pursuant to a formal written trust agreement, with a collective agreement often stipulating the defined contribution.

The trust agreement usually contains a declaration of the purposes of the trust and authorizes the trustees to receive contributions and hold assets in order to fulfill those purposes. The trust agreement also contemplates the creation of a whole set of subsidiary documents that are necessary to carry out trust purposes. Principal among these is the plan text, which the trustees are empowered to establish in order to govern the distribution of benefits from the pension fund. Additionally, a trust agreement may recognize other types of documents or agreements that oblige an employer to make contributions to the plan. Most importantly, the trust agreement is the source of the trustees' authority to operate the pension fund, and in that regard it spells out the scope of their powers and duties.

After the initial power to establish the pension plan, one of the most important powers conferred on trustees is the power to amend that plan consistent with its purposes. This includes the power to effect plan improvements by increasing benefits or making benefit reductions, when necessary. Sometimes the settlors of the trust, namely, the union and employers, reserve to themselves the power of amendment and the power to negotiate benefit changes.

A trust agreement may authorize the trustees to delegate administrative powers and responsibility for decision making to subcommittees of the trustees, to their agents, or other individuals. Typically, MEPP trustees will retain a number of professional advisers to assist them in determining minor policy and investment issues. Additionally, the trust agreement will commonly address the following matters:

- The removal, resignation, or replacement of trustees;
- Requirements respecting frequency of meetings, quorum, audits, etc.;
- Procedures for breaking trustee deadlocks.

Other important documents are the employer participation agreement and reciprocal agreements. Participation agreements between trustees and the employer are essential in those cases where there is no collective agreement requiring participation in a MEPP and are helpful even where there is a collective agreement in giving trustees a direct contractual relationship with participating employers. Reciprocal agreements provide for continuity of service even when a plan member works in another jurisdiction either within the same trade or otherwise (e.g., there are reciprocal agreements between a large number of different trades in the construction industry).

Legislative Requirements Applicable to Multi-Employer Pension Plans

Definition of a MEPP

The terms MEPP and specified multi-employer pension plan (SMEPP) are specifically defined in the ITA. This enables legislation to include specific rules and regulations relating to special characteristics of MEPPs. In a MEPP or SMEPP, 100% of the members cannot be employed by related employers, i.e., employers that do not deal at arm's length with each other.

Pension plans where there are no employers that are required to contribute pursuant to a collective bargaining agreement cannot qualify as a SMEPP. All SMEPPs are MEPPs but not all MEPPs are SMEPPs.

Theoretically, a MEPP could be established other than as a result of collective bargaining or pursuant to statute, but in practice few are. There are some groups of employers, e.g., members of a trade association or a board of trade, that do establish defined contribution plans on a multi-employer basis to reduce administrative costs. This pension plan would therefore be called a MEPP, even though contributions are not required pursuant to a collective bargaining agreement, but it would not qualify as a SMEPP.

Once established, a MEPP exists and may continue to exist beyond the duration of any collective agreement. For example, a MEPP continues to exist to provide for the payment of benefits, even if any collective agreement ceases to exist and contributions to the plan cease.

Under the Ontario *Pension Benefits Act*, a pension plan is a MEPP if it is established and maintained for employees of two or more employers who contribute, or on whose behalf contributions are made, to a pension fund by reason of agreement, statute, or municipal by-law to provide a pension benefit that is determined by service with one or more of the employers. However, a pension plan is not a MEPP if *all* of the employers are affiliates within the meaning of the *Business Corporations Act*. The Regulations under the Ontario *Pension Benefits Act* also provide for a unique type of MEPP called a Specified Ontario Multi-Employer Pension Plan (SOMEPP). Provided that certain eligibility criteria are satisfied, a MEPP may be declared a SOMEPP by the regulator on or after September 1, 2007, and before September 1, 2017. SOMEPPs are temporarily not required to make solvency special payments.

Federal pension legislation, as well as the pension legislation in British Columbia, Alberta, Manitoba, Saskatchewan, Quebec, New Brunswick,

Nova Scotia, Newfoundland and Labrador, and Prince Edward Island (in place but never proclaimed), all contain similar definitions with some minor variations.

Using a variation on Ontario's theme, under the Federal *Pension Benefit Standards Act*, a pension plan is not a MEPP if 95% or more of the employers are affiliated.

Amendments to the British Columbia *Pension Benefits Standards Act* in 2015 and the Alberta *Employment Pension Plans Act* in 2014 harmonized many of the legislative provisions under both provinces, including the definition of MEPPs. Legislation under both provinces outlines two subsets of MEPPs. "Collectively bargained MEPPs" are defined as plans that are established through a collective agreement and broadly represent "Classic MEPPs". "Non-collectively bargained MEPPs" are defined as plans that are established other than through a collective agreement and broadly represent "Co-operative MEPPs". Legislative provisions which apply to the two subsets are notably different. Note that the regulator has the power to make the decision to designate a plan as a SEPP or MEPP.

Manitoba is different from these other jurisdictions in that while MEPPs are not actually defined under the province's pension legislation, they are covered by the term multi-unit pension plans. The Manitoba regulator is permitted to designate a plan as a multi-unit pension plan where the trustees have declared their intention to be regulated as such in writing and the plan complies with the provisions of the pension legislation and regulations. MUPPs must have a board of trustees and representation of plan members on the board must be at least equal to the representation of management. In Manitoba, employees of a plan that is about to be designated a MUPP have the right to opt out.

New Brunswick's *Pension Benefit Regulations* define a MEPP as a pension plan established and maintained for employees of two or more employers who contribute or on whose behalf contributions are made to a pension fund by reason of agreement, but does not include a pension plan where all the employers are affiliates within the meaning of the *Business Corporations Act*.

Nova Scotia's *Pension Benefit Regulations* provide for a MEPP that is designated as a SMEPP under the ITA. The definition of a SMEPP under the ITA is addressed later on in this chapter.

Under the Quebec *Supplemental Pension Plans Act* definition of a MEPP, a MEPP is a plan in which the members are the employees of two or more employers. However, parent companies and their subsidiaries who, under the terms of the plan, agree that the plan should not be considered a MEPP, are permitted to opt out.

Saskatchewan's *Pension Benefits Act* defines a SMEPP as a plan that is administered for employees of two or more employers and is specified by the superintendent as such.

Multi-Employer Pension Plan Administration

The collective agreement typically calls for the establishment of a trusteed pension plan (an arrangement where contributions are paid to a trustee who acts as custodian of the pension fund and, in some cases, is responsible for investing funds and paying pension benefits in accordance with the terms of the trust agreement). MEPPs are typically administered by a board of trustees — most often comprised of employers or management representatives and union officials. Some boards or trustees are comprised of union officials only. The board of trustees is responsible for the overall administration of the multi-employer trust and plan in accordance with the trust agreement and related subsidiary documents (like the plan text) until such time as all obligations of the trust and the plan have been fully met (i.e., termination of the trust). This responsibility continues until the last surviving pensioner has received his or her benefits or until the promised benefits have been purchased from an insurance company or the plan is wound up by regulators.[5] While some administrative functions can be contracted to an administration service provider, the ultimate responsibility for all the trust fund operations remains with the trustees.

The following chart summarizes administration requirements by jurisdiction.[6]

Jurisdiction	Type	Administrator	Representation
Federal	MEPP established by collective agreement	board of trustees	• no requirement
	MEPP established by other means	pension committee	• members — at least one, if majority requests • pensioners — at

---

[5]   This topic is discussed in Chapter 15.

[6]   Unless indicated otherwise, for the purpose of this chart, the term MEPP includes all variations of MEPPs such as specified multi-employer pension plans and the Specified Ontario Multi-Employer Pension Plan as applicable.

Jurisdiction	Type	Administrator	Representation
			least one, if plan has at least 50 pensioners and majority requests
Alberta and British Columbia	collectively bargained MEPP	board of trustees	• members — not less than number representing employers
	non-collectively bargained MEPP	participating employer or board of trustees	• no requirement
Manitoba	MUPP	board of trustees	• members — not less than number representing employers, and at least one representing non-active members
Newfoundland and Labrador	MEPP established by collective agreement	board of trustees	• members — at least one-half
	MEPP established by other means	pension committee	• no requirements
New Brunswick, Nova Scotia, Ontario and Prince Edward Island (to be proclaimed)	MEPP established by collective agreement or trust agreement	board of trustees	• members — at least one-half • employees — no requirement, but permitted • pensioners — no requirement, but permitted
Quebec	all MEPPs	pension committee	• members — active, inactive • pensioners
Saskatchewan	all SMEPPs	board of trustees	• members — at least one-half

While the existence of a board of trustees is crucial to a MEPP, pension legislation is typically silent or defers to the trust agreements on how trustees are to be chosen and whether member representatives will be selected by the trade union where one exists. While some jurisdictions, like Ontario, require that trustees be Canadian citizens or landed immigrants, this is generally the extent of the consideration afforded to them under the relevant statutes. Consequently, in order to avoid confusion and unnecessary litigation, it is imperative that the trust agreement or other plan document set out specifically how trustees are to be appointed and by whom.

Trustees as Fiduciaries

Like the administrators of SEPPs, trustees of MEPPs have a fiduciary duty to the members of those plans. The trustees' fiduciary responsibilities are:

- To act solely for the benefit of the trust and not for their own self-interest;
- To exercise their duties with integrity and due standard of care;
- To make every effort to educate themselves and seek expert opinion where necessary;
- To act impartially between beneficiaries; and
- To attend trustee meetings.

These duties extend to agents that the trustees may engage for purposes of carrying out the administration.

Unlike most SEPPs, however, in a MEPP there is usually a separation in the legal identity between the administrator and the plan sponsors, and the former's obligations are normally spelled out in the trust agreement, pension plan text, or other legal document between the parties.

In addition to the duties specified in the plan document, the administrator/trustees must comply with their statutory duties. One such statutory duty is to avoid conflicts of interest. The prohibition against any conflict between personal interest and duty is codified in most pension legislation. Under the Regulations to the Ontario *Pension Benefits Act*, there are limited exemptions to the conflict of interest prohibition, particularly where a plan is jointly governed. For a MEPP, cost-sharing transactions are not considered to be a conflict of interest where pursuant to the pension plan document the administrator of a MEPP enters into a transaction with one or more of the plan sponsors to purchase or lease office space for legal, accounting, or other services or purchase materials and equipment necessary for the administration and operation of the plan, provided that the compensation paid is reasonable in the circumstances.

There are a number of methods used by trusteed MEPPs to perform the administrative function. Because of the complexity of MEPPs as compared to SEPPs, the majority of trusteed MEPPs use a contract administration service provider to perform many of the day-to-day activities.

- Self-administration — Self-administration can take several forms, including salaried self-administration, client-owned self-administration, and cooperative self-administration. Most larger plans happen to be self-administered.

  o *Salaried self-administration.* Administration is performed by staff that is directly employed by the trust, working under the direction of the trustees. This type of administration is sometimes used by benefit trusts that are located outside the major business centres and want more tailored and personal service than the contract administrators are accustomed to providing. It is also used by larger trust funds that have the resources to administer in-house. Sometimes the administration is carried out through a wholly owned subsidiary corporation.

  o *Client-owned self-administration.* Administration is performed by a corporation that is owned by one or more of the benefit trusts it serves. Generally, a number of boards of trustees come together, regionally or nationally, to create a larger block of administration work that is judged to be big enough to support a full service and technically advanced administration firm. The trustees may or may not come from the same industry. Their benefit trusts may or may not be merged. The commonality of interest is, simply, better and less expensive service than they perceive to be available on the open market.

  o *Cooperative self-administration.* Administration is performed by a nonprofit organization that serves several unrelated trusts. The trusts share the operating expenses for the service and dictate the operating policy. This type of administration originated from the same objectives as those for the salaried self-administration approach, but it was first introduced in western Canada where the concept of a cooperative is well founded.

- Contract administration — Administration is performed by a person, organization, or firm that is usually unrelated, through ownership or other control, to the trust, the trustees, the participating employers, or the sponsoring union(s). This was the first kind of benefit trust administration to develop in Canada (imported from the United States) and still remains the predominant kind of benefit trust administration across the country.

MEPP trustees (or their administration service provider) are generally responsible for several functions that the administrator of non-trusteed single employer plans is generally not responsible for. These functions include:

- Maintaining a database on all participating employers and their employees;
- Maintaining trustees' documents, including related collective agreements, trust agreement, and employer participation agreements and collection control program;
- Maintaining plan documents, including any reciprocal agreements with other trust funds/plans;
- Preparing minutes of trustees' meetings;
- Creating and modifying rules relating to the administration of the trust/plan;
- Receiving and verifying for deposit all negotiated contributions to the trust fund pursuant to employer participation and related collective agreements and the timeliness thereof;
- Receiving and verifying for deposit all contributions to the trust fund received pursuant to reciprocal agreements and the timeliness thereof;
- Recording of required contributions (from the collective, employer participation, and reciprocal agreements) and, where applicable, updating members' credits;
- Receiving, verifying, and recording additional voluntary contributions (e.g., top-up contributions) and updating members' credits earned toward a pension;
- Pursuing and collecting delinquent contributions, including establishing procedures for these activities;
- Calculating and redirecting monies to other trust funds/plans in accordance with reciprocal agreements; and
- Receiving and verifying acceptability of claims for benefits, as provided by the plan.

Adverse Plan Amendments

An amendment is adverse if it would take away a right or obligation of a member, former member or any other individual entitled to payment from a pension plan. Pension legislation typically requires notification of such amendments to members, and in certain provinces, notification is required in advance of the amendment being registered. In New Brunswick, Nova Scotia, Ontario, Prince Edward Island, and Quebec, this requirement may be dispensed with by the appropriate regulator in certain circumstances, including where the amendment pertains to a MEPP established by a collective agreement.

The rationale for this exemption is that because, in theory, plan members are represented on the board of trustees by member representatives, they would be advised of the "adverse amendment" before the amendment was actually approved. Consequently, a formal notice to the participants of a MEPP would be unnecessary.

Right to Reduce Benefits

As a general rule, pension legislation in all jurisdictions expressly prohibits the retroactive reduction of accrued benefits. However, subject to plan terms, pension legislation in certain jurisdictions permits the board of trustees of a MEPP established pursuant to a collective agreement or a trust agreement to reduce accrued benefits. (This exception also applies to negotiated cost defined benefit pension plans.)

It should be emphasized that a MEPP amendment that purports to reduce accrued benefits is only valid if the plan documents that establish the MEPP permit such an amendment either expressly or by virtue of being silent. If the plan documents prohibit a benefit reduction, the regulatory authority is unlikely to permit such an amendment.

The following chart summarizes the permissibility of accrued benefit reductions under a MEPP by jurisdiction.

Jurisdiction	Permissibility of Accrued Benefit Reduction in an Ongoing MEPP
Federal	If the MEPP is a negotiated contribution plan, an amendment to reduce benefits may be made. The regulator has discretion to permit reduction for any plan.

Jurisdiction	Permissibility of Accrued Benefit Reduction in an Ongoing MEPP
Alberta and British Columbia	If the MEPP is a negotiated cost plan, the trustees may, with the written consent of the superintendent, amend the plan text document to reduce benefits if the circumstances of the plan require reduced benefits. If the MEPP contains a target benefit provision, benefits may be reduced without regulatory approval.
Manitoba	The trustees of a MUPP can amend the plan to reduce benefits to meet solvency funding requirements, and the amendment must be approved by the regulator.
New Brunswick	If the MEPP is a shared risk plan, benefits can be reduced in accordance with the funding policy.
Nova Scotia, Newfoundland and Labrador and Prince Edward Island (to be proclaimed)	Permissible for a MEPP under a collective agreement or a negotiated cost defined benefit plan.
Ontario	Permissible provided the MEPP is established pursuant to a collective or trust agreement.
Quebec	Not permissible.
Saskatchewan	Plan must provide for reduction for purposes of meeting prescribed solvency tests in an ongoing plan and subject to regulatory approval.

Funding

MEPPs typically rely on fixed contributions, and legislation is evolving to provide appropriate funding rules and exemptions from the general funding requirements that exist in most jurisdictions for SEPPs. The funding requirements unique to MEPPs are examined below.

Employer Contributions

Under a MEPP, employer contributions are fixed by the collective agreement or trust agreement and must be remitted to the plan administrator, typically, 30 days after the end of the month in which they become due or as specified by the collective agreement, whichever is earlier. The contributions are used to meet the cost of the current service benefits and to fund any deficit in the plan. The contribution rate must be sufficient to cover the expected cost of benefits and an orderly funding of any deficit. Contributions greater than that amount are permitted.

Aside from investment income, contributions are the main source of income to a MEPP trust fund. Contributions to a MEPP are usually made by employers at the rate or amount set by the collective agreement. It is important to note that the contributions are made to the trust fund, not the union. This means that it is the responsibility of trustees to see that the trust receives the correct amounts at the correct time. This is one of the functions usually delegated to the administration service provider, but it still remains the ultimate responsibility of the trustees. Collection of all monies due and owing to the trust is one of the most basic duties of the trustees.

It can be an extremely difficult task, given the large number of contributing employers and the fact that most contributions are the subject of reports submitted by employers without the ability to verify all the information. Nevertheless, a serious delinquency problem can impair the ability of any trust fund to deliver its benefits, deprive plan members of proper benefits, and unfairly punish employers that report accurately and pay on a timely basis. It is important that the handling of delinquencies be given special priority by trustees.

Administrator's Responsibilities

The MEPP administrator/board of trustees is responsible for collecting employer remittances. Having a copy of the collective agreement or other document that sets out employer contributions assists the administrator in knowing the amount of individual employer contributions it is required to enforce.

Pension legislation generally requires that the administrator, at the beginning of each fiscal year, provide to the custodian trustee of the pension fund a summary of contributions required to be made in respect of the pension plan. This requirement is not necessary under a MEPP because the plan administrator stands at arm's length to the plan sponsor and therefore is well suited to ensure that each employer under the MEPP makes their required contributions.

Often, the administrator may retain an intermediary to assist in the collection of contributions, and most pension legislation permits the administrator to require persons involved in receiving contributions to the pension fund or who administer or invest the pension fund to be bonded.

Solvency Requirements

(a)   Ontario

Given the negotiated fixed contribution element of MEPPs, the rules for preparing actuarial valuations are different from those that apply to SEPPs. For example, under the Regulations to the Ontario pension legislation, a MEPP's actuary is only required to perform such tests as would show the sufficiency of the contributions, as required by the collective agreement or agreements, to provide the benefits set out in the plan. These tests include consideration of adequate funding of current service costs as well as any deficit but are not to take into account any possible reduction of benefits provided under plan terms or legislation. Where the contributions are not sufficient, the actuary must propose options available to the administrator so the contributions will be sufficient to provide those benefits.

Employers contributing to a MEPP are not required to remit special payments. Any contribution required to fund a deficit under the plan is part of the required contributions referred to above. In addition, once the actuary has advised the administrator of an insufficiency and proposed options, it is the duty of the administrator to adopt and inform the regulator of the course of action that will be taken. Reduction of accrued benefits is one option that the board of trustees may adopt. However, the *Pension Benefits Act* does not mandate a reduction of accrued benefits.

Another key aspect of the valuation requirements in Ontario is that the duty imposed on the actuary to determine the sufficiency of contributions is done so without any reference to going-concern or solvency funding. Many within the pension industry had argued that the solvency funding and the corresponding five-year amortization requirements under the legislation should not, and did not, apply to MEPPs because the existence of two or more unrelated employers greatly reduced the likelihood of a plan wind-up. However, in July 2000, the Superintendent of Financial Services issued a letter clarifying that solvency funding did apply to MEPPs and that this had been the regulator's position consistently over time. Any doubts regarding the requirement to fund a MEPP on a solvency basis were laid to rest in August 2007, with Regulation 489/07 to the *Pension Benefits Act*, which made it clear that the sufficiency of the required contributions under MEPPs is to be determined on the basis of a going-concern and a solvency valuation.

In addition, Regulation 489/07 introduced temporary solvency funding relief for eligible MEPPs that choose to become a SOMEPP. This relief was extended to cover actuarial valuations prior to September 1, 2017. A SOMEPP is given special lower funding rules for a temporary period.

(b)   Other Jurisdictions

Similar solvency funding obligations and amortization requirements, particularly in relation to required contributions, are found across most other jurisdictions. Certain jurisdictions have also implemented temporary and permament solvency relief.

For example, in Alberta MEPPs are permitted, subject to certain conditions, to temporarily suspend solvency payments, subject to the regulator's approval. British Columbia provided similar relief measures, but MEPPs can no longer apply for these measures and must convert to a target benefit plan to avoid solvency funding obligations. Shared risk plans in New Brunswick and all Quebec pension plans, including MEPPs, are also exempt from solvency funding, however, certain other funding criteria must be met.

Termination of Membership

Under a MEPP, members may frequently terminate employment without terminating participation in the plan. Termination of membership for MEPPs is typically triggered when a member works less than a specified number of hours with all participating employers during a certain length of time.

As well, members may change employment and be covered by a different MEPP but their pension contributions are sent back to the original plan under the terms of a reciprocal agreement. As a result the portability provision applicable to a SEPP might cause a premature transfer of benefits out of the plan. Certain jurisdictions have made attempts to accommodate these unique factors.

The following chart summarizes, by jurisdiction, when membership in a MEPP is considered terminated and therefore portability rights triggered. The below table omits circumstances where the member dies, elects to retire when eligible, or when the MEPP is terminated.

Jurisdiction	Termination of Membership in a MEPP
Federal and Quebec	General SEPP member termination provisions apply to MEPP members.
Alberta and British Columbia	A member in a MEPP is considered to terminate membership in the plan when the total period of employment is less than 350 hours during a period of two consecutive fiscal years of the plan unless the plan provides otherwise.
Manitoba	Earliest of when: both the member's period of continuous employment and the member's membership in the union in that employment end; no contributions to the plan have been made by or on behalf of the member for a period of two years; or the member ceases to be eligible for active membership under the terms of the plan.
New Brunswick	Member entitled to be deemed to have terminated membership if no contributions are paid or are required to be paid to the pension fund by or on behalf of the member for 24 consecutive months or as provided for under the plan, whichever is less. This provision does not apply if there is a reciprocal transfer agreement respecting two MEPPs.
Newfoundland and Labrador	The member is entitled to cease membership in the plan when no contributions have been made in respect of that member by a participating employer for a period of 24 months, or a shorter period as provided under the plan, and the member is not in receipt of an immediate pension benefit.

Jurisdiction	Termination of Membership in a MEPP
Nova Scotia	A member of a MEPP is entitled to terminate membership in the pension plan if no contributions are paid or are required to be paid to the pension fund by or on behalf of the member for 24 consecutive months or for such shorter period of time as is specified in the pension plan. This provision does not apply if there is a reciprocal transfer agreement respecting two plans. A member is deemed not to have terminated employment until the member terminates membership in the plan. Where a trade union which represents a member of a MEPP ceases to represent that member and the member joins a different pension plan, the member is entitled to terminate membership under the first MEPP.
Ontario	Member entitled to terminate membership if no contributions are paid or are required to be paid to the pension fund by or on behalf of the member for 24 consecutive months or as provided for under the plan, whichever is less. This provision does not apply if there is a reciprocal transfer agreement respecting two MEPPs. Entitlement to a deferred pension under the MEPP is not determined until a member who terminates employment with a participating employer also terminates membership in the MEPP. In the absence of a reciprocal transfer agreement, where a trade union which represents a member of a MEPP ceases to represent that member and the member joins a different pension plan, the member is entitled to terminate membership under the first MEPP.
Prince Edward Island (to be proclaimed)	Member entitled to terminate membership if no contributions are paid or are required to be paid to the pension fund by or on behalf of the member for 24 consecutive months or as provided for under the plan, whichever is less.

Jurisdiction	Termination of Membership in a MEPP
Saskatchewan	A member in a MEPP is considered to terminate membership in the plan when: the total period of employment is less than 350 hours during a period of two consecutive fiscal years of the plan unless the plan provides otherwise; or has ceased membership in a class of employees that is required to contribute to the plan.

Termination of a Multi-Employer Pension Plan

The general rules regarding the termination of pension plans, particularly in the context of SEPPs, are discussed in Chapter 8. Given the definition of a MEPP and the fact that the participating employers under such an arrangement are usually unrelated, the entry or exit of any one particular employer should not in theory have an impact on the plan. Consequently, it is rare for a MEPP to wind-up, in whole or in part, where an employer withdraws from participating in the plan. This is the case in New Brunswick, Nova Scotia, and Prince Edward Island where the legislation provides that a MEPP will not be wound up by reason only of the withdrawal of a participating employer. In these jurisdictions, however, the regulator does have the authority to require the wind-up of a MEPP if in their opinion the circumstances warrant it.

Despite the foregoing, under certain jurisdictions the general wind-up rules apply to MEPPs, thereby exposing the plan to issues such as surplus distribution and grow-in rights (Ontario and Nova Scotia), as well as increased costs of administration. For example, under the Ontario *Pension Benefits Act*, the regulator has the authority to order a wind-up of a MEPP where (i) there is a significant reduction in the number of members, or (ii) there is cessation of contributions under the plan or a significant reduction in such contributions.

Under the federal *Pension Benefits Standards Act*, the terms "termination" and "wind-up" are defined separately to mean "cessation of crediting of benefits to plan members generally" and "distribution of the assets of a plan that has been terminated" respectively. Once a plan is terminated, the regulator has broad discretion to order a distribution of assets. As in Ontario, there are no special provisions or exemptions for MEPPs.

Like the federal legislation, the British Columbia *Pension Benefits Standards Act* and the Alberta *Employment Pension Plans Act* distinguish between plan termination and wind-up. However, the legislation does recognize the unique features of MEPPs by providing that the cessation or termination of contributions on the part of a participating MEPP employer does not result in a partial termination of the plan. Furthermore, while the requirements to wind-up a pension plan after termination apply to both MEPPs and SEPPs, sponsoring employers of MEPPs or negotiated cost defined benefit plans who remain solvent after a wind-up are not required to cover the wind-up costs.

In the case of Quebec, the Retraite Québec may terminate a MEPP only where all participating employers cease to make contributions. Similarly, a plan may be terminated voluntarily only where all of the employers acting jointly give notice of termination.

Under the Saskatchewan *Pension Benefits Act*, the term "termination" is synonymous with wind-up. The legislation provides that the failure of an employer to make contributions to a MEPP does not terminate the plan unless the plan provides that it does.

Pension legislation in Manitoba and Newfoundland and Labrador appear to be silent on the issue of MEPP termination.

Taxation and Multi-Employer Pension Plans

Generally speaking, MEPPs must comply with the registration rules applicable to SEPPs under the ITA.[7] There are, however, a number of exemptions and conditions unique to MEPPs. These are addressed below.

Multi-Employer Pension Plans and Specified Multi-Employer Pension Plans under the Income Tax Act

A registered plan is considered a MEPP if, at the beginning of the year, it is reasonable to expect that at all times during the year, no more than 95% of the active plan members will be employed by a single participating employer or by a group of related participating employers.

In addition, a SMEPP is a particular type of MEPP that is administered by a board of trustees or similar body that is not controlled by participating employers. In order to qualify as a SMEPP, the plan must fall into one of three categories. Under the first category, a plan qualifies as a SMEPP if it satisfies a number of conditions including, but not limited to:

---

[7]   These rules are discussed in Chapter 8.

- all or substantially all of the participating employers in the plan are not exempt from tax under Part I of the ITA (persons exempt from tax include labour organizations, municipalities, Crown corporations, and registered charities);

- employer contributions are fixed by a collective bargaining or similar agreement and not dependent on the financial experience of the plan; and

- the contributions that are to be made by each employer in the year are determined, in whole or in part, by reference to the number of hours worked by individual employees of the employer or some other measure that is specific to each employee.

Under the second category, the Minister of National Revenue may designate a plan to be a SMEPP. Lastly, under the third category, a plan that was a SMEPP in the preceding year will continue as a SMEPP in a subsequent year even though one of the conditions in the first category is no longer satisfied.

In addition, for a plan to remain a SMEPP, the total contributions to be made each year must reasonably be expected not to exceed 18% of the total compensation of plan members.

Calculating Pension Credits and Pension Adjustments

Generally, pension credits and Pension Adjustments (PA) for a defined benefit MEPP are determined in the same manner as a defined benefit provision of a SEPP. However, where a member worked for two or more employers in the year, worked part-time or less than a full year, or ended employment in the year, the ITA allows the employer to prorate the pension credit and PA formula for both the benefit earned and the $600 offset by the portion of the year worked with each employer. Each employer calculates the pension credit and PA as if the member had not worked for any other employer. The amount earned by the member is annualized, and the fraction of the year actually worked by the member is used to calculate the benefit earned.

Pension credits under a defined contribution MEPP are calculated in the same way as a SEPP. In certain circumstances, PAs for a defined contribution MEPP are prorated as described above.

If a MEPP qualifies as a SMEPP, it is allowed to report PAs using the rules that apply to defined contribution pension plans. As a result, a member's PA is equal to the total contributions made in the year by the employer and the member. This rule recognizes two characteristics of many SMEPPs whereby many members work for a number of different employers during the year and the benefit earned can change by action of the trustees. Both of these characteristics would make it extremely difficult for employers to determine PAs under the defined benefit formula.

Past Service Pension Adjustments and Pension Adjustment Reversals

For purposes of Past Service Pension Adjustments (PSPAs) and Pension Adjustment Reversals (PARs), SMEPPs are treated differently from all other pension plans. Under a SMEPP, a PSPA only arises where a member makes a contribution in respect of a post-1989 past service benefit. The PSPA will equal the member's past service contribution made in a particular year and will include any contributions the member made that are conditional on certification of the PSPA. The PSPA must be certified by the Canada Revenue Agency before the related benefit can be paid to the member. A PAR will not be determined when a member terminates membership in a SMEPP; pension credits are deemed to be zero. This special treatment of SMEPPs is consistent with the special rule for calculating PAs.

Generally, PSPAs and PARs under MEPPs are determined in the same manner as a SEPP.

Additional Considerations

There are a number of other considerations unique to MEPPs and SMEPPs that merit mention.

- Under a SEPP a member is precluded from accruing benefits under an employer's pension plan after pension payments have commenced from either that plan or another plan sponsored by the employer. The same restriction does not apply to a member of a MEPP. If a member receives a pension from his or her employer's SEPP, they can still continue to accrue benefits under a MEPP to which their employer is contributing on their behalf.
- MEPPs sponsored by a non-taxable organization that has been exempted from application of the maximum pension rules in Information Circular 72-13R8 are exempted from the maximum limit on the pension payable in respect of pre-1992 service.
- The maximum pension rule does not apply to SMEPPs.[8]

---

[8]   See Chapter 8.

- The five and three year leave of absence provisions do not apply to SMEPPs.
- Employee contributions to a SMEPP are not subject to the maximum limits.[9]
- The restriction on contributions when there is an excess surplus do not apply to SMEPPs.
- Under a SEPP, if post-retirement indexing exceeds increases in the Consumer Price Index, a PA must be reported. This does not apply to SMEPPs and indexing may be given in any amount without generating a PA or PSPA.

Multi-Employer Pension Plan Governance

Pension governance continues to be in the spotlight, and pension regulators are increasingly turning their attention towards the operation and management of pension plans.

While there has been progress in some jurisdictions in terms of legislative guidance[10] on pension governance, best practice follows the guidelines recommended by various organizations, including the Canadian Association of Pension Supervisory Authorities (CAPSA). The CAPSA Guidelines are as relevant to MEPPs as they are to SEPPs; however, the existence of a board of trustees for purposes of administering the plan, and the absence of any meaningful statutory guidance on the powers and duties of trustees, have necessitated the need for MEPP-specific guidelines.

The Office of the Superintendent of Financial Institutions (OSFI) in May 1998 published guidelines for governance of federally regulated pension plans, including in Appendix V the special governance issues that arise when a board of trustees is the administrator.[11] A synopsis of the best practices detailed in Appendix V is outlined below.

- *Composition and Orientation of the Board*: boards of trustees should pay special attention to educating the board members and planning for an orderly succession. In addition, various groups with an interest in the plan should be represented or mechanisms to obtain their views should be instituted.

---

[9] See Chapter 8.

[10] See Chapter 4 for a discussion of the current legislative guidance on pension plan governance.

[11] The guidelines can be found online at: http://www.osfi-bsif.gc.ca/Eng/pp-rr/ ppa-rra/gvn/Pages/govengl3_let.aspx.

- *Investments*: the trustees should take special care to ensure that they are managing the funds to achieve the plan objectives and in a manner that is consistent with the plan's investment policies and their own fiduciary responsibilities.

- *Obtaining Independent Objective Advice*: the adversarial nature of collective bargaining connected to the operation of the plan must not hinder trustees from acting on independent and objective advice.

- *Benefit Increases:* in order to preserve equity among generations of members, trustees should ensure that each generation pays for the benefits it receives, and not rely on contributions of the members who follow.

- *Compensation of Trustees*: the board of trustees should establish a policy for compensating its members for their time and earnings lost while they work as trustees. Expense reimbursement should be based on actual out-of-pocket expenses.

- *Collection of Data and Contributions*: trustees should consider refusing participation to a group of employees if their collective agreement does not provide the plan with adequate authority to collect contributions and data. They should establish a delinquency control program, including procedures for the collection of unremitted contributions.

In addition, CAPSA published a "frequently asked questions" (FAQ) to provide pension plan administrators with general guidance, additional clarification and examples related to CAPSA Guideline No. 4, Pension Plan Governance Guidelines and Self-Assessment Questionnaire. Key among the questions and responses was a section on MEPPs established by trade unions, wherein the various participants were identified and guidelines on their roles and responsibilities were described. A summary of the roles and responsibilities is provided below:

- Pension Plan Board of Trustees:

- Role: Plan administrator

   o Ensure that members of the board of trustees receive training and ongoing education to assist them in carrying out their governance responsibilities.

   o Hire staff and service providers to carry out aspects of the administration of the plan.

   o Review performance of plan staff and service providers against established standards.

   o Monitor the funding of the plan.

- o Take action where employers are delinquent in making required contributions to ensure contributions are made.
- o Establish the investment policy for the investment of plan assets.
- o Monitor the investment of the assets of the plan.
- • Plan Manager:
- • Role: Day-to-day responsibilities for the administration of the pension plan
  - o Perform day-to-day functions related to the administration of the plan.
  - o Make required filings with regulatory authorities.
  - o Monitor required contributions paid by employers and where employers are delinquent in making required contributions, bring them to the attention of the board of trustees for action.
  - o Pay members' benefits accurately and in a timely manner.
  - o Respond to members' inquiries.
- • Agents/Service Providers:
- • Role: Provide services or advice required in the administration of the plan (pension legislation may limit the parties who can provide certain services or advice)
  - o Invest the assets of the plan in accordance with the investment policy established by the board of trustees and in compliance with legal requirements.
  - o Periodically perform actuarial valuations of the plan and report the results to the board of trustees.
  - o Calculate benefit entitlements of members and other beneficiaries.
  - o Prepare and provide required statements to members.

As the preceding discussion indicates, the OSFI and CAPSA guidelines are only "guidelines" and do not have the force of law. Moreover, the OSFI guidelines only apply to federally regulated pension plans. Nonetheless, trustees would be ill-advised to ignore these guidelines.[12]

Note that, in certain jurisdictions, the increasing focus on governance is becoming quite apparent. For example, recent changes in legislation in Alberta and British Columbia now require pension plans to have formal

---

[12]   See Chapter 4 for additional discussion of CAPSA guidelines.

governance documents drafted. The legislation also broadly outlines the requirements of these documents, which closely mirror the CAPSA Guidelines. Effectively speaking, what was once considered best practice is, in these provinces, now a legislated requirement. See Chapter 4 for a closer examination of pension plan governance.

Chapter 12

PUBLIC SECTOR PENSION PLANS

Executive Summary

Public sector pension plans had played and will continue to play a significant role in the overall Canadian pension coverage and capital landscape. With the change in the economic and demographic landscapes, governments at all levels are evaluating the continued long term sustainability of their pension plans. The focus of this chapter is to look across Canada the evolving trends of public sector pension plans. It concludes with a review of a high level risk management framework that is evolving in the public sector pension plans (which is equally applicable to the private sector pension plans) and a discussion of the significant contributions that large Canadian public sector pension plans have made both locally and abroad and the reputation they have earned on the world stage of pension and capital market.

The Public Sector Pension Landscape

Public sector pension plans play a significant role in the overall Canadian pension landscape. These are not government-sponsored programs such as the Canada and Quebec Pension Plans (CPP/QPP). Instead, public sector pension plans are pension plans sponsored by employers (or co-sponsored by employee representative groups) in the broader public sector (such as the municipal, provincial and federal governments and entities, crown corporations, government boards, commissions and agencies, and public educational and health institutions) for their employees.

According to the latest available information from Statistics Canada, there are approximately just over 6 million Canadians who are members of a registered pension plan. This represents a pension coverage rate of just under 40% amongst working Canadians. However, dissecting the landscape by public versus private sector unveils the dominance of public sector pension plans — they account for over 50% of the total active membership and 70% (or approximately $1.1 trillion) of the $1.6 trillion in total market value of assets of all registered pension plans.

	Pension Coverage as a % of Number of Employees	Total Invested Assets in Market Value ($ Trillions)	Annual Contributions ($ Billions)	Annual Benefits ($ Billions)
Public Sector	86%	$1.1	$36.5	$36.5
Private Sector	24%	$0.5	$18.5	$24.6
Total	**38%**	**$1.6**	**$55.0**	**$61.1**
Public Sector Share	**n/a**	**70%**	**66%**	**60%**

Canada's public sector pension plans are among the best in the world — they are generally large, efficient and well-managed. Historically, public sector pension plans in Canada are predominantly of a traditional defined benefit design with cost-of-living protection coverage (less than 5% of the membership belongs to a pure defined contribution plan). The exception to this norm is Saskatchewan which moved much of that province's public sector from defined benefit plans to defined contribution plans in 1977. By contrast, less than 50% of the members in the private sector are covered by a pure defined benefit plan.

Most public sector pension plans in Canada are funded and regulated (just like their private sector counterparts and unlike their US counterparts) although there remains some that are run under a book reserve system (for example, the defined benefit pension plans for federal government workers are funded for service earned after 2000 but benefits earned before then are book reserved).

Pension benefit is a key component of the total compensation of public servants. They are generally viewed as generous and their generosity was historically rationalized as a compensation for the generally lower cash rewards that public servants receive compared to their private sector counterparts.

Public sector defined benefit plans are no different from their counterparts in the private sector in that benefits are guaranteed (with a few exceptions, such as New Brunswick's Shared Risk Pension Plan) and in the face of a funding shortfall, a plan sponsor is left to shoulder the impact of any corrective measures which come in the form of either an increase in contributions or reduction in benefits, subject to applicable legislation. The difference, however, lies in the source of funding. For the private sector pension plans, funding is confined to plan sponsors and plan participants. For the public sector pension plans, funding comes from the government coffers which, in turn, are derived from taxation. Tax payer dollars pay the government's share of pension contributions; they also pay the employees' salaries and thus their share of contributions. Tax payers at large also shoulder the costs for any corrective measures, to the extent that they come in the form of contribution increases, and these taxpayers might not be the beneficiary of these pension plans. There is always this fiscal tie to the tax payers whether the government is the sole sponsor or co-sponsor of the public sector pension plans in question.

Drivers of Change

Historically, there have not been any significant reforms with respect to the public sector pension plans with the exception of Saskatchewan in 1977. Pensions were (and should still be) viewed as having long life and there was also the perception that governments perhaps have unlimited ability to raise funds through its taxing power to meet any pension funding requirements. The changing tide perhaps began in the early 2000s. Most public sector pension plans had enjoyed an era of high interest rates and double digit investment returns in the late 1990s due to strong equity markets — these led to "runaway" surpluses in many of the public sector pension plans. As a result, many benefit improvements were made and contribution holidays were taken. On the heels of these was the first market downturn of the decade in 2001 and 2002. This was shortly followed by the second market downturn of the decade, the 2008 financial crisis, which derailed any funding improvement progress that was in play. During the diminishing surplus of the 2000s, benefits were generally not reduced. Instead, since 2000, most provinces have seen repeated increases in the contribution rates to their public sector pension plans — some more significant (*e.g.*, British Columbia, Alberta, Manitoba, Ontario, Nova Scotia, Newfoundland & Labrador) while others are more modest (*e.g.*, New Brunswick and Prince Edward Island). In addition, special payments were also made to address funding deficits in some cases.

New Norm and Public Perception

Following the financial crisis at the turn of the decade is the realization of the new operating norm of pension plans. These include:

- Expected prolonged periods of a low interest environment and volatile market makes it increasingly difficult to generate high consistent investment returns; and

- Continued maturity of plans both in terms of longer life expectancy and the mass retirement of baby boomers. The latter causes a general rise in the ratios of retirees to active members in the plans which, in turn, reduce the plans' risk bearing capacity going-forward.

These new operating norms caused many plans to set more realistic assumptions about the future, driving costs for members and employers (and ultimately, tax payers) even higher.

The continued divergence of pension coverage between the public and private sector (fueling pension envy between the have's and the have-not's) resulted in the general view, perceived or real, that public sector pension plans are overly generous and expensive.

Heightened contributions, the lack of timeliness of pension reform in the public sector pension plans, and the realization of the above new norm brings to question the sustainability of these plans.

Reform Trends and Development

In response to the debate about the rising costs of public sector pension plans and sustainability issues, governments in many Canadian jurisdictions have, since the beginning of this decade, begun to review their public sector pension plans, and in some cases make changes to them. Some common reform themes emerging include:

- 50-50 cost and risk sharing between employers and contributing members;
- Conditional indexing used as a sustainability lever; and
- Less generous early retirement benefits.

In addition, some jurisdictions have established a two-tier plan structure, with new employees entitled to less generous benefits (in particular, early retirement benefits). Generally, accrued benefits are protected, with the noted exception of New Brunswick's SRPP. Some jurisdictions, but not too many, have also reduced the benefit accrual rate — for example, from a 2% formula to a 1.5% formula; changes to the provision of how earnings are averaged have been adopted by some.

Below are commentaries of the general public sector pension reform themes in various Canadian jurisdictions (some reforms are specific to certain plans in the jurisdiction in question and details differ among specific plans):

Federal

In 2012, the Federal Government introduced a two-tier *Public Service Pension Plan* — new members after 2012 will contribute less for less generous early retirement benefits. Key reform themes are:

- Cost sharing

  Contribution rates for all active and future members were increased effective January 2013 with the objective of reaching a balanced cost-sharing ratio for employer/employee contribution of 50/50 by 2017.

  It is important to note that the 50/50 cost-sharing is confined to current service costs only. The government remains responsible for the funding of any deficits.

- Early retirement benefits

  New members after 2012 will need five more years (compared to those before 2013) to be entitled to unreduced pension (at age 65 or age 60 with 30 years of service).

The defined benefit pension plans for federal government workers are funded for service earned after 2000 but benefits earned before then are book reserved. Investments of all four federal pension plans — the Public Service, the Canadian Forces, the Royal Canadian Mounted Police and the Reserve Force, are managed by the Public Sector Pension Investment Board (PSP Investments) which was incorporated as a Crown Corporation under the *Public Sector Pension Investment Board Act* in 1999. Today, PSP Investments is one of Canada's 10 largest pension investment managers, with $112 billion of assets under management at March 31, 2015.

British Columbia

There have not been any notable reform discussions. Provisions for conditional cost of living protection based on affordability have generally been in place since the early 1980s. Two of the public sector plans have recently implemented a cap on the annual indexing adjustment — the B.C. College Pension Plan (starting with 2011) and the B.C. Municipal Pension Plan (starting with 2016).

Most of British Columbia's public sector pension plans are administered by the B.C. Pension Corporation which was incorporated in 2000 under the *Public Sector Pension Plans Act* as a Crown corporation, governed by a board of directors made up of plan member and plan employer representatives from each of the College, Municipal, Public Service and Teachers' pension plan boards. The B.C. Pension Corporation is responsible for administering the four afore-mentioned statutory pension plans, as well as other plans such as the Members of the Legislative Assembly Pension Plan for MLAs in B.C.'s provincial government and the Workers' Compensation Board Superannuation Plan. Investment of many of these pension funds are also pooled and managed collectively by the British Columbia Investment Management Corporation (bcIMC) which was created in 2000. As at March 31, 2015, bcIMC had over $100 billion of pension assets under management, making it one of Canada's 10 largest pension fund managers.

Alberta

The previous Progressive Conservative Alberta Government withdrew its public sector reform bill (Bill 9) that would have imposed the following changes to some or all of Alberta's four public sector pension plans after 2015 (the Local Authorities Pension Plan, the Public Service Pension Plan, the Management Employees Pension Plan and the Special Forces Pension Plan):

- a contribution cap;
- replace guaranteed indexing with targeted indexing;
- provide less generous early retirement benefits; and
- transition into a joint sponsorship governance model.

In face of significant union opposition, the previous government announced in September 2014 that it will not be reintroducing the Bill. To date, the new NDP government has not indicated its public pension reform agenda, if any.

Many of Alberta's public sector pension plans are administered by the Alberta Pensions Services Corporation (APS) which was incorporated in 1995 under Alberta's *Business Corporations Act* with the Government of Alberta as the sole Shareholder. APS is responsible for administering seven statutory pension plans under the direction of four pension boards and the Government of Alberta, as well as two supplementary retirement plans. Investment of many of these pension funds are also pooled and managed collectively by the Alberta Investment Management Corporation (AIMCO) which was created in 2008. At the end of 2015, AIMCO had about $90 billion under management and more than half of which are public pension plan assets, making it one of Canada's 10 largest pension fund managers.

Saskatchewan

Saskatchewan public sector pension plans are mostly defined contribution plans. However, legacy defined benefit pension plans such as the *Municipal Employees Pension Plan* and the *Healthcare Employees' Pension Plan* remain. Some of latest movements with these legacy plans include:

- In July 2014, the *Municipal Employees Pension Plan* undertook a consultation with its membership with the view to engage them and discuss the standing of the plan and how to ensure the Plan's long term sustainability. The results of the consultations were to provide a proactive measure on how and when changes will be implemented to support sustainability of the Plan; to date, no actions have been announced.

- Following a threat by the Saskatchewan Government in 2014 to deregister the *Regina Civic Employees' Superannuation and Benefit Plan* for non-compliance and lack of progress on reaching agreement to address the Plan's unfunded liability, the Plan submitted proposed sustainability measures (which the government accepted in March 2015) for benefits earned after 2015, as follows:
  - Rule of 85 for retirement eligibility (changed from Rule of 80);
  - Pension calculated on best consecutive five years of service (changed from best three);
  - Overtime compensation to be excluded in pensionable earnings; and
  - Cost of living adjustments will be conditional on the Plan's financial health and on the rate of return earned on the fund.

- The *Regina Police Pension Plan* moved to a target benefit plan model on July 1, 2014. Employer took over deficit for service to July 1, 2014; deficit liability is shared after that date. Benefits were reshaped significantly based on affordability.

It is also interesting to note that the Saskatchewan teachers switched its pension from defined benefits to defined contributions in 1979 as a result of a collective bargaining process. However, this was later switched back to a defined benefit arrangement in 1991 and the *Saskatchewan Teachers' Retirement Plan* (STRP) was established with the Saskatchewan Teachers' Federation being the sole sponsor of the Plan. Despite being a member-sponsored plan, STRP also made some changes effective July 1,

2015 to address its sustainability challenge to include changing its benefit formula from final average earnings based to career average earnings based, from guaranteed indexing to conditional indexing and less generous early retirement and survivor benefits going forward.

Manitoba

There have not been any notable reform discussions.

Ontario

Most of Ontario's largest public sector pension plans are jointly-sponsored (with the exception of the Ontario *Public Services Pension Plan*, managed by the Ontario Pension Board). In these plans, decisions on benefits and contributions are shared between employer sponsors and representatives of plan members. As well, plan members make contributions to pay for the benefits they are earning and are responsible for sharing in the cost of funding any deficits. In most cases, plan members pay for half the cost of their benefits, with the employer matching plan members' contributions. These Ontario's pension funds are recognized as some of the best-managed funds in the world — five of Canada's 10 largest pension funds are from the Ontario public sector, representing almost $400 billion in assets.

Despite the above, many Ontario public-sector employees, particularly in the university and electricity sectors, are members of single-employer pension plans. Under these plans, the employer is solely responsible for funding shortfalls. Employers typically contribute more than plan members — in some cases, two or three times more. The Ontario Government believes that single-employer public-sector plan members should share the ongoing cost of their pension benefits equally with the employer as with jointly-sponsored pension plans.

In May 2011, the government provided temporary solvency funding relief to public-sector single-employer pension plans. In exchange for this relief, these plans were expected to negotiate plan changes that would improve sustainability and affordability over the long term. Unless these plans can demonstrate progress toward this objective, additional solvency funding relief would be denied. As of March 2016, 25 plans have been granted relief (19 of them in the university sector) — most have already negotiated plan changes, including increased employee contributions and reduced future benefits.

The Ontario Government announced, in its 2012 Budget, that it would consider additional tools to make public-sector pensions more affordable for taxpayers and sustainable for pension plan members. Some of the key items include:

- **Jointly-Sponsored Public Sector Pension Plans** — Given that most of the largest Ontario public-sector pension plans are jointly-sponsored and given that they account for almost 80 per cent of the Province's direct pension expense, the government proposed to focus on ensuring that measures used to improve plan funding do not add to employer and taxpayer expense, beyond what has already been agreed to. The government also wished to ensure that all jointly-sponsored plans move to 50/50 funding between employers and employees.

  Following consultations, the government reached agreement in 2012 with the Hospital of Ontario Pension Plan, the OPSEU Pension Plan and the Colleges of Applied Arts and Technology (CAAT) Pension Plan, and in 2013 with the Ontario Teachers' Pension Plan to freeze contribution rates until December 31, 2017, except in exceptional circumstances. If in the meantime, a plan experiences a new funding shortfall, the plan would be required to reduce future benefits, up to a limit, before further increasing employer contributions. Any benefit reductions necessary to address a new deficit during this period would apply to future benefits only, not those that have already been accrued. Current retirees would not be affected.

- **Single-Employer Public-Sector Pension Plans** — The government announced its support of efforts to convert single-employer defined benefit public-sector pension plans to jointly-sponsored pension plans with equal cost-sharing. The government believes that by adopting the features of a jointly-sponsored pension plan, these plans will have greater transparency, be better governed, have a more predictable cost and be more likely to provide sustainable benefits in the long term.

  In 2014, the government amended the *Pension Benefits Act* to create a framework that would facilitate single-employer pension plans in the broader public sector mergers with existing jointly-sponsored pension plans or conversions to new jointly-sponsored pension plans. The legislative framework for these transactions was proclaimed into force effective November 1, 2015 with accompanying regulations. Effective January 1, 2016, the *Royal Ontario Museum (ROM) Pension Plan* joined the CAAT Pension Plan — the first transaction effected under the framework.

  At this time, the Ontario university sector (which has about 25 different single-employer pension plans with total assets of about $15 billion) is considering the viability of consolidating the various plans into a sector-based University Pension Plan or the merit of joining another existing jointly-sponsored pension plan.

The government also recognizes that the availability of an exemption from solvency funding rules for new jointly-sponsored pension plans is an important factor for stakeholders exploring conversions. Employers and plan members joining an existing jointly-sponsored pension plan that is already exempt from solvency funding requirements would receive the same treatment. In April 2015, the government released for consultation proposed criteria to be used in determining whether new multi-employer jointly-sponsored pension plans or a jointly-sponsored pension plan created out of the amalgamation of existing single employer pension plans receive a solvency exemption. While there has been interest from the broader public sector employers about whether a solvency exemption would be available should the single employer pension plans they sponsor simply convert to new single-employer jointly-sponsored pension plans, these will not be considered at the time.

- **More Efficient, Effective Pension Asset Management** — The government believes in maximizing the effectiveness of asset management. A pooled asset management framework would allow smaller public-sector pension plans to benefit from the lower investment management costs, improved access to alternative investments and enhanced risk management that larger pension funds typically enjoy. Under this framework, management of assets could be transferred to a new entity or to an existing large public-sector fund.

In 2012, the government appointed Bill Morneau as Pension Investment Advisor to consult with interested parties and develop recommendations for consideration. Mr. Morneau estimated that, if fully implemented, savings of $75 million to $100 million annually could be realized. In 2013, the government established a technical working group to advise on the design, governance and transition issues associated with the implementation of a new pooled asset management entity for Ontario's broader public-sector funds, including other non-pension public funds.

On July 1, 2016, the government established the Investment Management Corporation of Ontario (IMCO) which would operate at arm's length from government as a member-based non-profit corporation and is set to be up and running by spring of 2017. The Ontario Pension Board — which administers provincial government employees' pensions as well as those of workers at government agencies, boards, and commissions — and the Workplace Safety and Insurance Board are founding members, with combined investment assets of about $50 billion. Participation will be voluntary, through a managed process, for other broader public sector organizations with investment funds that are interested in accessing the services of IMCO.

Quebec

In the wake of the D'Amours Report (*"Innovating for a Sustainable Retirement System"*) — the result of the work undertaken by the Expert Committee on the Future of the Québec Retirement System in 2013 at the request of the Québec Government, the Québec Government sprang into action with public sector pension reforms, specifically with respect to the municipal and university sectors:

- **Municipal Sector** — On December 4, 2014, the Québec Government passed Bill 3 to introduce a significant change to the structure of defined benefit pension plans in the Québec municipal sector. Effective January 1, 2014, any pension plan in this sector will include two components — one for service credited prior to January 1, 2014 (past service component) and one for service credited after December 31, 2013 (current service component).

  With respect to the current service component, Bill 3 required, among many other provisions, a limit of the current service cost, 50/50 current cost-sharing, risk-sharing as well as the elimination of automatic indexing provision. Employers and employees are allowed to negotiate a range of how much they will contribute toward the past deficit — 45-50% for employees and 50-55% for employers. If no agreement is reached, the default of 50/50 contribution applies.

  With respect to the past service component, indexing is allowed to be suspended as of January 1, 2017.

  Bill 3 set out a one-year term for a negotiated settlement starting at the latest on February 1, 2015; however, for plans that are in better financial shape and where a collective agreement was in force at December 31, 2016, the Bill allowed the deferred of negotiations to start no later than January 1, 2016.

  It should be noted that consolidation of municipal plans was not part of the Québec Government reform platform and there are numerous small municipal plans in Québec.

- **University Sector** — On June 8, 2016, the Québec government passed Bill 75 under which all university-sector defined benefit plans must be restructured by December 31, 2017 in accordance with the provisions of the Act, based on a complete actuarial valuation as at December 31, 2015, to be submitted no later than June 30, 2016.

Bill 75 is very similar to Bill 3 in many aspects with the following noted exceptions:

- o   Bill 75 does not apply to any pension plans in the university sector that is a defined contribution or hybrid plan;
- o   The current service and past service components are split as at December 31, 2015;
- o   With respect to the current service component, the parties may, if they wish, keep the automatic indexing provision; and
- o   The parties must reach an agreement within 9 months of undertaking their negotiations, which must start no later than June 30, 2016.

Many of Québec's public sector pension plan assets are pooled and managed collectively by Caisse de dépôt et placement du Québec (CDPQ) which was established in 1965. Over $200 billion of the $250 billion managed by CDPQ as at the end of 2015 are pension fund assets, including the over $50 billion of QPP assets, making it one of Canada's 10 largest pension fund managers.

New Brunswick

In its bid to find sustainable pension solutions, the New Brunswick Government introduced its SRPP model in 2012. The following is a high level summary of the key features of an SRPP:

- •   A more modest base benefit promise, based on career average earnings with no guaranteed indexing provision;
- •   Conservatively funded at a level where future surpluses are expected to be adequate to pay for both pre-retirement and post-retirement indexing;
- •   Contributions are constrained within a relatively narrow range from the initially agreed level and the benefit distributions may vary depending on the plan's financial performance;
- •   Accrued benefits can be reduced; however, contribution rates, benefit levels and investment strategies are subject to a stringent risk management process to ensure a high probability that base benefits will be secure;
- •   Rules around surplus distribution are also pre-determined, thus ensuring member participation in positive plan experience and avoiding the debate of surplus ownership;
- •   No solvency funding is required; and
- •   Joint governance.

In December 2013, the New Brunswick Government passed legislation converting its *Public Service Superannuation Plan* into a SRPP — the *Public Service Shared Risk Plan*. As a result, retirees lost their guaranteed cost of living increases; instead, these increases became conditional and discretionary and Pension Coalition NB alleges that New Brunswick has breached their rights under the Canadian Charter of Rights and Freedoms.

Many other New Brunswick public sector pension plans have also since converted into an SRPP model.

In 2016, two plans (the *Public Service Shared Risk Plan* and the *New Brunswick Teachers' Pension Plan)* announced the creation of the Vestcor Corporation, or organization independent from the government, which will provide pension administration and investment services for their combined membership as well as to a number of other public sector client plans. The new organization aims to fully launch on October 1, 2016, and will include two companies — the existing fund manager, the New Brunswick Investment Management Corporation (NBIMC) which manages $13 billion of pension assets and other public capital will become Vestcor Investment Management Corporation, and the existing administration, the Pensions and Employee Benefits Division (PEBD) of the Department of Human Resources which administers 11 pension plans and benefit programs for 55,000 actives and 30,000 retired provincial government workers, will become Vestcor Pension Services Corporation. Both NBIMC and PEBD are currently under the control and direction of government. Transferring the oversight of these organizations, ultimately, to representatives of the two plans' boards of trustees provide better alignment with the needs and requirements of the plans and meet industry best practices. In addition, it is also believed that the independent organization will be in a better position to capitalize on future opportunities, both investment and pension administration, to continue to gain scale efficiency and advantage.

Although there were some discussions about merging the many small municipal plans to gain efficiency, to date, this has not materialized.

Nova Scotia

Reform to Nova Scotia's public sector pension platform began in 2010 with its largest pension plan, the *Public Service Superannuation Plan*. Essentially, a two-tier plan was introduced with new hires on or after April 6, 2010, entitled to less generous benefits:

- New employees of the Province of Nova Scotia on or after April 6, 2010 will not be eligible to retire per the Rule of 80 (entitlement to unreduced pension if age is at least 50 and age plus service equals at least 80). These new employees will be eligible to retire per the new Rule of 85 (entitlement to unreduced pension if age is at least 55 and age and service equals at least 85); and

- New employees who started work on or after April 6, 2010 will be eligible for a reduced level of survivor benefits.

In addition, effective April 6, 2010, indexing will be tied to the health of the plan. As a result, indexing was set at 1.25% per year, for the 5-year cycle starting January 1, 2011 to December 31, 2015 — the changes apply to all pensioners, including those already receiving a pension. This approach is similar to New Brunswick as there is no protection of accrued benefits. In addition, amendment to the *Public Service Superannuation Act* was also passed to implement a five-year funding review cycle commencing in 2015. Under this approach, indexing will not be permitted unless the *Public Service Superannuation Plan* is fully funded and the extent of indexing will also dependent on the amount of surplus. For the January 1, 2016 to December 31, 2020 cycle, indexing was set at 0.85% per year with the next review in 2020.

As part of the reform, a joint governance framework was also rolled out in 2013 for the *Public Service Superannuation Plan* to be similar to the *Nova Scotia Teachers' Pension Plan* which adopted such model in 2006. In addition, the previous Nova Scotia Pension Agency was devolved and the Nova Scotia Pension Services Corporation was established as a separate entity from government. The new pension corporation continues to administer the pension benefits and investment assets of the *Nova Scotia Teachers' Pension Plan,* the *Public Service Superannuation Plan* and a few other public sector plans but the oversight was shifted from the minister of finance to a joint ownership structure involving the trustees of the plans that the agency serves (the new Pension Services Corporation is jointly owned by the Teachers' Pension Plan Trustee Inc. and the Public Service Superannuation Plan Trustee Inc.).

In 2015, Nova Scotia also introduced legislation that allows university pension plans to be transferred to the *Public Service Superannuation Plan.* This allows the smaller public sector pension plans to gain scale advantage from both pension administration and investment perspectives. As a result, members of the Acadia University pension plan and the school's board of governors agreed to transfer its 700 members to the *Public Service Superannuation Plan* effective July 1, 2015. On July 1, 2016, pension plans from the Université Sainte-Anne and the University of King's College were also transferred into the *Public Service Superannuation Plan.*

Prince Edward Island

In 2013, the government of Prince Edward Island announced a number of significant changes that will impact the two large public sector pension plans that cover the province's civil servants (as well as health sector workers) — the *Civil Service Superannuation Fund*, and teachers — the *Teachers' Superannuation Fund*. Some of the key changes are:

- Moving from a "best three years" formula to an "indexed career average earnings" formula, effective January 1, 2014. While indexing for 2014 to 2016 were preset, indexing thereafter would be based on increases in average industrial wages but contingent on the plans' being fully funded;
- Beginning in 2017, cost of living adjustments to retirees will no longer be guaranteed (previously, indexing is guaranteed at full CPI for civil servants and at 60% of CPI for teachers) but will be granted based on funded status of the plans. Once awarded, cost of living adjustment increases will be protected and not subject to future reductions;
- Effective 2019, the retirement age for an unreduced pension will be raised from 60 to 62 and changing the service requirement from 30 to 32 years, after attaining age 55 (for service from 2019); and
- Additional member and employer contributions would also be required if funding level drops below a specified percentage.

Unlike New Brunswick and Nova Scotia, the PEI approach is to continue to protect the dollar amount of pension payable (including indexing received to date). While future increases may be lower as a result of these changes, the dollar amount of members' benefits is protected under the reform.

In addition, the government has also expressed interest in looking at new governance structure in the future.

Newfoundland and Labrador

In 2014, the Government of Newfoundland and Labrador announced an agreement with the major unions to reform its *Public Service Pension Plan*. The government will make additional contributions over 30 years to address the existing unfunded liability. In return, unions have agreed to plan changes effective January 1, 2015 (with transition provisions), including the following:

- Increases in matching member and employer contributions;

- Future service benefits will be calculated using the best six year average earnings, instead of five;

- Entitlement to unreduced early retirement will be changed to age 60 with a minimum of 10 years of service (instead of the previous age 60 and 5 years of service) or age 58 with a minimum 30 years of service (instead of the previous age 55 and 30 years of service); and

- Indexing on future service is suspended but current retirees will not be affected.

The *Public Service Pension Plan* also will be transitioned to a jointly trusteed structure with equal sharing of future surpluses and deficits between the members and government. In addition, an independent corporation will oversee the administration of the plan. Legislation that will set out the framework for the corporation will be introduced.

Evolving Risk Sharing Trends

Better risk sharing is the main reform theme among public sector pension plans across Canada. Some of the evolving best practice risks sharing mandates include:

- Intergenerational equity — Not spending on current generations of members (actives and pensioners) at the expense of future generations.

- Equity between membership groups — To the extent possible, treat different member groups (active and retired members) equally when comes to risk or gain sharing, realizing that absolute equity can never be achieved given the risk-pooling nature of a defined benefit arrangement.

- Benefit security — A core or base suite of benefits will either be guaranteed or protected with a high degree of certainty. Other benefits beyond these core or base benefits (*e.g.*, indexing) are subject to reduction. Adjustments to plan contributions cannot be the only lever for addressing plan deficits.

- Stability of plan contributions — Generally a higher but more stable and predictable contribution requirements from both employers and members (although not necessarily equally shared), with caps and built in reserving and buffering provisions during good times for the rainy days.

To execute against these risk-sharing mandates, many plans are now formalizing and operationalizing their risk management procedures with greater transparency. These include annual valuations and projection of plan's funded status, regular asset/liability studies and scenario stress-testings.

The New Brunswick Shared Risk Pension Plan model provided explicit and prescribed metrics with respect to many of the above risk-sharing mandates and risk-management procedures. However, the same outcome can also be achieved with other plan model — what is needed is a plan that requires both sides (employers and members) to understand their plans and look at what would happen if benefits become unaffordable. A jointly-sponsored pension plan model, which many public sector pension plans across the country had adopted, provides a viable platform for these discussions to unfold. Joint decisions allow better understanding and alignment of the collective priorities and no parties can abdicate their responsibility. To best capitalize on this joint sponsorship platform, an iterative process that captures the following attributes is required:

- Education — Spending sufficient time upfront to understand stakeholders' priorities, base lines and pain points and to get educated about the range of possible outcomes that could affect a pension and its payouts, including demographics, prolonged market volatility and low interest rates.

- Filling the toolbox — Understand what levers and tools are available — these tools can be in the form of adjustments to contribution rates, benefit provisions, investment strategies, risk transfer strategies and reserving and statutory filing policies. It is also important to establish boundaries around each tool — e.g., contributions will not go above a certain threshold.

- Evolve and adapt — Develop a built-in response mechanism as internal and external environment changes by triggering the appropriate tools in the toolbox at the appropriate time — this adaption goes both ways — risk sharing as well as gain sharing.

The end result is an integrated blue print for the plan, comprising of the plan's benefits policy, investment policy and funding policy. This integrated blue print allows the plan sponsors to know exactly what to do under various circumstances — when and how much each party in question is paying or receiving. This blue print can be principle-based or can be prescriptive depending on the comfort level and the dynamics of the plan sponsors (although care should be given not to make the parameters too prescriptive as it is not possible to predict all possible outcomes ahead of time). This blue print has to be kept alive via regular reviews and validations.

While both the New Brunswick Shared Risk Pension Plan model and the more generic jointly-sponsored pension plan model (specifically

Ontario's JSPPs) could achieve the same results, it is important to note two key differences between the two models:

- The New Brunswick Shared Risk Pension Plan model allows the reduction in accrued benefits while the plan is on-going (it remains to be seen whether similar models that might be introduced in other jurisdictions allow the reduction in accrued benefits); however, reduction in accrued benefits is only allowed under an Ontario jointly-sponsored pension plan on wind-up (if there is not sufficient assets).

- Although the initial conversions of the New Brunswick plans into Shared Risk Pension Plans were carried out in collaboration between the government and the affected unions, the legislation does not actually require consent or input from plan members and retirees as a condition for conversion. By contrast, consent is required under the Ontario framework that facilitates single-employer pension plans in the broader public sector mergers with existing jointly-sponsored pension plans or conversions to new jointly-sponsored pension plans.

The Maple Revolutionaries

Another evolving trend among the Canadian public sector pension plans is consolidation for scale and capacity. To understand this trend, a discussion of how the largest Canadian public sector pension plans are managed and their economic impact and reach is warranted. The distinct Canadian approach to public pension fund management was labeled "Maple Revolutionaries" by The Economist in 2012 and is a Canadian success story on the world stage.

The 10 largest public pension funds (including the Canada Pension Plan Investment Board) have a total of over $1 trillion in assets under their management. Eight of them are among the top 100 pension funds globally and three of them in the top 20. According to the latest Boston Consulting Group report in 2015:

- During the 10 year period from 2003 to 2014, the funds' assets were tripled, fueled by approximately $600 billion in net investment returns (which represented 80% of the source of growth).

- The funds collectively invested over $600 billion across various asset classes in Canada and are the investors behind many Canadian landmark assets and flagship companies.

- They are a stable source of employment — collectively, they directly employed approximately 11,000 professionals across

Canada and office unique global experience to many investment professionals.

These plans are now viewed as a new brand of financial institution that not only contribute to the retirement security of many Canadians but also to the Canadian and global economy at large.

Broadly speaking, three inter-linked attributes contribute to the overall success of many of these Canadian plans:

- **Scale** — The larger size of these Canadian plans permits broader investment diversification. In addition to investing in public markets, these plans also invest in private equity, private debt, intellectual property, infrastructure and real estate. Many of these alternative asset classes are capital intensive and would be off-limits to the smaller plans. Size also permits a more global orientation to investing versus the typical home country bias evident in smaller plans.

- **Internal Capacity** — Most of the large public sector Canadian plans have sizable, professional internal teams performing pension administration functions as well as conducting direct investing programs across the public and private markets. Scale is a precondition to building effective internal capabilities. Building internal capacity allows better plan management/sponsors/ members alignment. It allows the development of professional and cost efficient pension-delivery organizations, more control over investments (specifically the timing of turnover of many of the illiquid alternative asset classes) and could also result in lower cost structure — for example, many external managers of private assets have a two and twenty fee structure (*i.e.*, a charge equal to a flat 2% of asset value as a management fee plus an additional 20% of any profits earned); it is believed that internal execution would cost less.

- **Investment Horizon** –Another common attribute of the Canadian public pension funds is their long investment horizon. All these plans are defined benefit schemes with associated long duration liabilities and predictable cash flows. This enables and encourages these plans to adopt a long-term investment mindset, allowing them to allocate assets to the less liquid, higher return private assets such as private equities, real estates and infrastructures. These asset classes generally have lower correlation with other public assets and hence will reduce the funds' exposure to market volatility. According to the Boston Consulting Group report, the top 10 Canadian public pension funds have almost 1/3 of their assets invested in alternative classes (compared to less than 10% for most other pension funds and less than 5% for retail investors). Such allocation is substantially higher than many of their counterparts globally. According to a 2015 survey done by the Organization for Economic Cooperation Development (OECD), allocations to alternatives increased among the large pension funds around the globe (and the trend is even stronger among public pension reserve funds, such as the CPP and their global counterparts); but the average allocation was only 15.3% of total assets in 2014.

In addition to the above, well-developed governance structure is also a strong contributor to their success. Although the structures are not uniform across the board, most plans have independent professional fiduciary and oversight boards. These large Canadian public sector pension plans also influence, encourage and help shape good corporate governance practices in Canada's capital markets.

Potential lower cost structure, coupled with broader investment diversifications, could, in turn, lead to outperformance. Based on a study by Alexander Dyck and Lukasz Pomorski from the University of Toronto, it was found that larger plans outperform smaller ones by half a percent annually on average, and that difference is much larger for high performing large funds such as those in Canada. Compounding that difference over many years makes an enormous impact upon accumulated fund assets.

These large Canadian public sector funds, with their long investment horizons, can act as counter forces to the increasing short-term orientation of most market participants; this is especially valuable in times of market stress. In addition, they represent important sources of long-term capital for the much needed infrastructure investments which are critical to economies and societies globally. They are patient investors which make them the ideal owners of these assets since they have the incentive to reinvest in them to maintain their cash flow generative capabilities to match pension payments over the long haul.

The successes of these large public sector plans have been used as an aspiration benchmark for many of the smaller public sector plans across the country and have fuelled many of the consolidation discussions, the introduction of associated enabling legislation and regulatory framework, and actual consolidation implementations. The ultimate driving force is the establishment of cost-efficient, independent and integrated pension service delivery organizations (encompassing both investment and pension administration centres of excellence).

Chapter 13

SUPPLEMENTARY PENSION ARRANGEMENTS

Executive Summary[1]

When an employer provides a registered pension plan (RPP) to employees, the level of benefits that can be provided from that plan is limited by the registration rules of the Income Tax Act (ITA). A supplementary arrangement is needed if the pension income that the employer wishes to provide is in excess of that limit.

Supplementary pension arrangements are commonly known as Supplemental Executive Retirement Plans or Supplementary Employee Retirement Plans (SERPs), or Supplementary Retirement Plans. They are also called top-up or top hat plans. SERPs may take a variety of designs and may be formal or informal, funded or unfunded. The continuing increase in the ITA limits, as well as the movement to defined contribution plans, is starting to reduce the need for defined benefit SERPs.

This chapter looks at the emergence of supplementary arrangements, the design of these plans, funding issues and approaches, and documentation.

Emergence of Supplementary Arrangements

ITA Limit for Registered Pension Plans

Supplementary arrangements emerged following the inclusion in the ITA of a limit on the retirement income payable from an RPP. In 1976, the annual pension limit was $1,715 per year of pensionable service, to a maximum of 35 years, for a maximum annual pension of $60,025 after 35

---

[1] For more information on supplementary employee retirement plans, please consult the multi-jurisdictional charts in the *Canadian Employment Benefits & Pension Guide*. Morneau Shepell, *Canadian Employment Benefits & Pension Guide*, loose-leaf (Toronto: LexisNexis Canada, 2003). The table of contents for these charts appears at the back of this Handbook.

years of service. This limit affected employees earning more than $85,750 in a plan providing an accrual rate of 2%, and an income replacement of up to 70% could be achieved. In 1976, the affected earnings level was approximately six times the average industrial wage, and therefore supplementary arrangements were needed only for executives. This limit remained unchanged from 1976 to 1990. By 1990, earnings of $85,750 were approximately 2 1/2 times the average wage, and the limit had begun to affect employees below the executive level.

As part of the tax reform of 1990, the annual pension limit was set at $1,722.22 per year of pensionable service, and was originally scheduled to be indexed to the average wage beginning in 1995. In addition, the 35-year limit on pensionable service was eliminated for service after 1989 (1991 for plans in place on March 27, 1988). The indexing was intended to stop the erosion of the limit, but the federal government repeatedly postponed such indexation. The limit remained at $1,722.22 through 2003, until it was finally increased to $1,833.33 for 2004 retirements. In 2016, the limit is $2,890.00, and it will increase at the same rate as the average industrial wages. In 2016, for plans providing a 2% accrual rate, employees earning over $144,500 would be affected by the limit. This is expected to be slightly more than 2½ times the average wage and is comparable to the situation that prevailed in 1990.

The provision of supplementary pension arrangements was once only a concern for executive employees. The trend since the late 1980s has been for more employers to put supplementary arrangements in place, and to expand the membership of existing arrangements to include all employees affected by the maximum.

Competitive Compensation

Supplementary arrangements are not only used for topping up the benefits that would otherwise be paid from a registered plan if not for the maximum; they also contribute to attracting and retaining executive employees. A supplementary arrangement, being unencumbered by registration requirements, is a flexible tool that can provide more or less generous pensions on bases that differ from those normally used in an RPP. Hence, for executives hired at mid-career for whom the registered plan can provide only a relatively small benefit, the supplementary arrangement can be designed to compensate for short service. For example, a supplementary arrangement could provide pension income based on an accrual rate of 4% of earnings or two years of service being credited for each year of "natural" service, or simply promise an income replacement of 70% of final pay.

Where the market for talented executives is competitive, a supplementary arrangement can be an important element of the total compensation package.

Prevalence of Supplementary Arrangements

The size of the company and the nature of the industry have been major determinants in the prevalence of supplementary arrangements. For example, all of Canada's large banks offer supplementary arrangements to their executives. Banks are typical of stable, long-term-oriented enterprises that develop talent over many years and want to retain it.

Even with the ongoing growth in the maximum pension limits, supplementary arrangements continue to be offered to employees below executive ranks, in smaller companies, and in new industries.

Canadian Securities Administration (CSA) Disclosure

The Ontario Securities Commission requires publicly traded companies to disclose the compensation of named executive officers (NEOs). The NEOs include the CEO, the CFO, and the three other most highly paid executives whose total compensation each exceeds $150,000. Until 2007, this disclosure included estimated annual pension benefits payable, but did not require that values be reported.

In 2005, the CSA provided additional guidelines on disclosure related to executive retirement packages for companies that chose to report on the value of pension benefits granted to NEOs. Many large Canadian publicly traded companies followed these guidelines.

On February 22, 2008, the CSA released a proposal for a completely revised Form 51-102F6 Statement of Executive Compensation.

The 2008 proposal was adopted by all jurisdictions effective for the first fiscal year ending on or after December 31, 2008.

The CSA's revised Form 51-102F6 significantly changed executive compensation disclosure requirements. A "pension value" is required to be disclosed in the summary compensation table. This value includes the "compensatory value" of benefits provided to each NEO under all registered and non-registered defined benefit and defined contribution plans.

Benefits provided under defined benefit and defined contribution plans are to be disclosed in separate retirement plan benefit tables. Details to be disclosed for defined benefit plans are:

- Years of credited service;
- Annual benefits payable at year-end and at age 65;
- Accrued obligation at the start of the year;
- Compensatory change in the accrued obligation in the year;
- Non-compensatory change in the accrued obligation in the year; and
- Accrued obligation at the end of the year.

The assumptions that are used for financial statement reporting purposes are, in general, to be used in the calculation of the accrued obligation, including future earnings projections, termination and retirement rates. To the extent that different assumptions are used, they should be disclosed along with their impact on the disclosed values, if material. For defined contribution plans, accumulated values at the start and end of the year are to be reported, as well as the compensatory and non-compensatory changes in value that occurred during the year.

In 2011, the CSA amended Form 51-102F6 with several updates, including the requirement to disclose the benefits paid or earned for the year, not the intended amounts. This means that the pensionable earnings used for disclosure on the form may differ (e.g, be more current and coordinate with the the proxy statement disclosures) than those used in determining the obligation in the financial statements.

Design Issues

When designing supplementary arrangements, there are a number of concerns and questions that must be addressed in order to deliver supplementary benefits that will meet the objectives of the employer in an efficient manner. These are discussed in the following pages.

Eligibility

The first question to be addressed is who should be eligible to participate in the supplementary arrangement.

Most commonly, supplementary arrangements are designed to meet the needs of highly compensated employees whose registered pensions are limited by the registration rules of the ITA. Supplementary arrangements can be grouped into two categories in relation to the eligibility criteria:

"Top-Up" Plans

In top-up plans, enrolment is automatic as soon as any employee's registered plan entitlement is restricted by the maximum. It is the most straightforward kind of supplementary arrangement.

Selected Enrolment Arrangements

The criteria to determine who participates in selected enrolment plans vary widely. Plan enrolment may be:

- For the CEO only;

- Automatic for selected officers;

- At the board's discretion for selected officers;

- For all employees above a certain position; or

- For all employees above a certain salary.

Benefit Formula

The majority of supplementary arrangements are of the defined benefit type. However, where the base plan is a defined contribution plan, the supplementary arrangement is more often also a defined contribution plan with real or notional contributions.

Top-up plans generally provide for benefits in excess of those payable from the RPP to produce a total benefit from both sources that would equal the benefit that would have been available from the RPP if the ITA maximum had not existed.

In selected enrolment arrangements, provisions may be very similar to those of the RPP covering the named executives, but in many instances, they are structured to meet special criteria for employees in senior positions. For example:

- To provide an attractive retirement income for executives hired in mid-career or to make up for pension credits forfeited as a result of leaving prior employment; and

- To help retain key executives as they approach retirement age.

These special provisions may include:

- An accrual rate higher than 2%;

- Additional service credits; or

- Pensions as a flat percentage of final average earnings (i.e., 60%), irrespective of service or after a specified number of years of service (such as 15 or 20 years).

Covered earnings are usually tightly related to the corresponding RPP provision, especially for top-up plans. Earnings used under the supplementary arrangement may either include or exclude cash bonuses. Should bonuses be included in earnings, there is a trend away from the use of actual bonuses (or some fraction of them), toward the use of target bonuses (or a fraction of them), usually as a cost containment measure, as well as increasing certainty for all.

Some plans have a maximum on covered earnings or on credited service. A fairly common provision for selected enrolment arrangements using a benefit rate in excess of 2% is to specify a maximum benefit as a percentage of covered earnings (i.e., 60%).

Covered service is generally the same as for the registered pension plan. However, some plans may only recognize service since the inception of the supplementary plan, or may recognize service with a previous employer.

Ancillary Benefits

One consideration when designing a supplementary arrangement is to ensure that the combination of benefits provided by the RPP and the supplementary arrangement achieves the desired objective at an acceptable cost. For example, one way to control costs and increase tax effectiveness is to maximize the ancillary benefits under the RPP and provide reduced ancillary benefits under the supplementary arrangement.

The rules and benefits for early retirement are often based on the same conditions as in the RPP. However, in many cases, generous supplementary arrangement provisions are accompanied by stringent vesting or early retirement provisions in order to retain executives. For example, it is not uncommon to provide no benefits under the supplementary arrangement if the employee terminates employment before becoming eligible to retire. In some circumstances, early retirement subsidies are subject to retirement with company consent. Also, it is not unusual to see variation in benefits according to whether termination of employment is voluntary or involuntary.

Indexing is another example where benefits under the supplementary arrangements and the RPP may be coordinated. Many supplementary arrangements provide for the same indexation pattern as the RPP (discretionary or automatic). However, to optimize tax effectiveness and benefit security, some supplementary arrangements provide that the total benefit is not indexed, or only partially indexed, but that the registered plan portion is fully indexed so that the supplementary arrangement portion of the total obligation reduces over time.

In the case of death prior to retirement, most plans provide for a spousal pension or for the payment of the commuted value. Some plans have a service condition and others provide that the benefit is only payable if death occurs after an age condition, such as age 55. Finally, some plans provide for no benefit at all. In the case of death after retirement, plans typically provide a joint and survivor pension or a life pension with a guaranteed period as the normal form of payment.

One of the key considerations when designing a SERP is to ensure that it will not be treated as a Salary Deferral Arrangement (SDA) by the Canada Revenue Agency (CRA). In 2007, the CRA surprised many observers by taking what appeared to be a new stance that a SERP that goes beyond ignoring the tax limits applicable to an underlying RPP would be treated as an SDA, leading to undesirable tax treatment for executives and making SERPs much less appealing. After several months of uncertainty surrounding this matter, the CRA re-confirmed its long-standing policy to the effect that reasonable pension arrangements would not automatically be considered an SDA. This is a relief for a lot of employers and their executives. Nevertheless, employers should remain prudent; employers who intend to set up a SERP should keep in mind that it is always possible to request an advance income tax ruling to confirm whether the proposed SERP arrangement would be viewed as reasonable by the CRA.

Contributions

Almost all supplementary arrangements are non-contributory. For those plans that are contributory, most supplementary arrangements use the same contribution formulas as those contained in the underlying RPP.

In order for employee contributions to a SERP to be tax-deductible, they need to be mandatory and the plan must require employer contributions to at least equal employee contributions. Otherwise, non-deductible contributions can still be made to the plan and the payment of benefits at retirement will not be taxed until the total amount of employee contributions has been paid out.

Other Provisions

There are other provisions that may appear in some supplementary arrangements. These include non-compete provisions where the provision of benefits is conditional on the executive not engaging in certain activities considered to compete with his or her former employer. These non-compete clauses must be carefully crafted in order to be legally binding. There may also be a provision to cover the continuity of benefits or enhancement of benefits under the supplementary plan in the event of a change in control or ownership of the organization.

Retiring Allowances

A supplementary arrangement may be designed to utilize the tax advantages available under the ITA with respect to retiring allowances. However, the tax advantage related to retiring allowances is much less relevant today.

Under the ITA, a retiring allowance is an amount received upon or after retirement from an office or employment, in recognition of long service or in respect of loss of office or employment. A retiring allowance is usually paid as a single sum, but it can also be paid out in a limited series of installments. Retiring allowances are often paid in addition to the RPP benefits to encourage an employee to retire. In the absence of a pension plan, they are also used to reward long-service employees.

Although a retiring allowance must be included as taxable income in the year received, tax may be deferred if the retiring allowance is transferred to an RPP or to a Registered Retirement Savings Plan (RRSP), subject to certain limits. The amount that can be transferred to an RPP or RRSP is limited to:

- $2,000 times the number of years before 1996 during which the employee was employed by the employer or a related employer; plus

- An additional $1,500 for each of these years of service, prior to 1989, in respect of which employer contributions to an RPP or a Deferred Profit Sharing Plan had not vested in the employee.

The above limits are in addition to any available RRSP room the individual may have. The tax relief available in respect of service prior to 1996 is becoming less relevant as time goes by. Retiring allowances are used mostly as severance payments to long-service terminated employees, or as "sweeteners" to induce long-service employees to accept an early retirement offer. It also makes sense to take advantage of the tax relief, such as it is, upon planned retirement. Supplemental arrangements may be used to provide retiring allowance payments.

Funding

The tax relief that makes funding RPPs attractive is not available when assets are set aside to fund the benefits promised under a supplementary arrangement. Therefore, historically, few supplementary arrangements were funded. Today, anecdotally, around half of all DB SERPs are funded. Where supplementary arrangements are not funded, the pension benefits are paid as they fall due out of the company's current revenues (pay-as-you-go basis).

There are as many reasons to fund supplementary pensions as there are not to fund them. Certainly, the lack of funding can be a source of concern to employees who expect to receive supplementary pensions. There is a risk that the fortunes of the employer will deteriorate, rendering the employer unable to pay.

On the other hand, some companies feel that funding executive pensions is inappropriate; "if the ship goes down, those on the bridge are expected to go with it". Depending on the reasons why the supplementary arrangement was put in place, a corporation might consider the supplementary pension to be part of incentives for active employees rather than as a provision for the employee's retirement security in the future. Despite this rationale, it is nevertheless difficult to dismiss the concern of the retired employee to have a secure income that does not depend on the future success of the company.

Funding is only one way to provide security. In certain companies, the prospect of corporate failure during the remaining lifetime of its retiring employees is not a concern, and pay-as-you-go arrangements are felt to be secure. In other situations and for many reasons, security is an issue, and can be achieved in whole or in part, depending on the means.

When a SERP is funded through a Retirement Compensation Arrangement (RCA), contributions and investment gains attract a 50% refundable tax (see the section "Funded Retirement Compensation Arrangements" below for more details on refundable taxes). Funding for SERPs has been influenced by the evolution of the accounting treatment for these plans. Prior to 2000, accounting discount rates used for valuing funded SERPs were typically set at half of the discount rates used for valuing an unfunded plan. Consequently, funded SERPs impacted a company's income statement and balance sheet much more than would an unfunded SERP. This impediment to funding was removed when new accounting rules were introduced on January 1, 2000, which required that the same (unadjusted) discount rates be applied whether or not a SERP was funded. Under changes to international accounting standards, funded SERPs are assumed to earn a return equal to the discount rate regardless of how the funds are invested. SERP surveys conducted by Morneau

Shepell have shown that the proportion of funded SERPs has increased since 2000. Recent data extracted from proxy circulars of large publicly-traded corporations suggest that nearly 50% of SERPs are secured.

Methods for Securing Benefits

Security against default of payment may be obtained, or at least enhanced, in various ways. A brief description of possible approaches follows. It should be noted that the most common are the funded RCA followed by an RCA that holds a letter of credit.

Funded Retirement Compensation Arrangements

Under the ITA, where assets are transferred by an employer to another person (typically a trustee), or are held in trust by the employer to secure supplementary pension benefits, the arrangement is treated as an RCA. The contributions to an RCA and the investment income earned by RCA assets attract a 50% refundable tax.

It should be noted that there are specific arrangements that are excepted from the definition of an RCA, and these excluded arrangements include RPPs, SDAs, and plans that are dealt with under other provisions of the ITA, such as a Deferred Profit Sharing Plan, an Employee Profit Sharing Plan, an RRSP, a Tax-Free Savings Account, an employee trust, certain health, disability, and unemployment benefit plans, and certain foreign-service plans for non-residents. There is also an exception for plans established for the purpose of deferring the salary of a professional athlete. Life insurance premiums and insurance policies are also excluded. However, there are instances where a life insurance policy can be deemed to be an RCA. Additionally, certain "prescribed plans or arrangements" under the *Income Tax Act Regulations* will not be considered an RCA.

Employer contributions to an RCA are deductible under the ITA. Employee contributions made to an RCA are deductible provided they are mandatory and are matched by the employer. Non-deductible employee contributions may also be made. Distributions from the RCA fund are taxable income in the hands of the employee on receipt, except for the non-deductible employee contributions, which are accorded more favourable tax treatment. However, 50% of the contributions and the realized investment earnings of the fund must be remitted to the CRA as a refundable tax. This 50% tax is refunded, without interest, at the rate of 50% of all disbursements made by the fund. The net effect is that only half the monies contributed to an RCA generate investment returns.

The main advantage of funding through an RCA is that it provides security to the participating employees, because the assets in the RCA will be separate from company assets and protected from the employer's creditors.

The cost related to funding through an RCA is greater than for an RPP, because it does not benefit from the same favourable tax treatment.

Letter of Credit

After the funded RCA, the most common mechanism to provide security for a supplementary pension arrangement is a letter of credit. Although the letter of credit is not an immediate source of funding itself, it can provide a form of security in circumstances such as bankruptcy and change of control.

A letter of credit is an irrevocable promise by a financial institution, usually a bank, to pay a specified amount if certain conditions unfold (such as the failure to pay a pension). The letter of credit strategy defers the actual funding of the non-registered benefit until such time as the company does not meet its obligation to pay the benefit or to provide a replacement letter of credit. At that time, upon request of the appointed trustees, the lending institution advances the face amount of the letter of credit, subject to the 50% RCA tax remittance requirements, to fund the benefit, and thereby becomes a creditor of the employer. As the contribution is made by the lending institution, the employer does not receive a tax deduction credit for the face amount of the letter of credit.

The premium paid to the bank for the letter of credit in the amount needed to secure the unfunded accrued pension promise is analogous to an insurance premium for coverage that will facilitate payment of these benefits. It is a recurring expenditure. Normally, the term of a letter of credit is one year. For purposes of securing a long-term obligation such as pension income, successive letters of credit are put in place, each of which will become payable for the benefit of the RCA trust if the company fails to provide the next letter of credit.

Letter of credit rate-setting is dependent upon the issuing institution's assessment of the employer's credit-worthiness, and will be influenced by a number of factors, including risk assessment, usage of overall credit by the employer, terms of the promissory note from the employer to the institution in the event that the letter of credit is called, terms of the letter of credit, and the nature of the banking relationship. The annual charge for a letter of credit is typically in the range of 1/2% to 1-1/2% of the face amount.

Generally, the employer will establish an RCA and will contribute twice the fee charged by the financial institution issuing the letter of credit and 1/2 of the contributions will be paid to the Receiver General. This contribution will be done on an annual basis as letters of credit are put in place. The RCA will use the contributions to purchase the letter of credit from the financial institution. Seeing as there is no property held in the RCA, other than the letter of credit, there are no earnings inside the RCA subject to the refundable 50% tax.

The benefits would be paid out to the employee on a pay-as-you-go basis, and the letter of credit would only be called upon where the employer failed to make the payments or some other specified event occurred that would trigger the letter of credit.

Life Insurance Policies

As a result of special deeming rules under the ITA, when an employer acquires an interest in a life insurance policy with the intent of using that policy to fund retirement benefits, the RCA rules will apply. These special deeming rules can be summarized as follows:[2]

- The employer who purchased the policy is deemed to be the custodian of an RCA;

- The policy is deemed to be the property of the RCA;

- Twice the amount of any premium paid in respect of the policy is deemed to be a contribution to an RCA and will be subject to the 50% refundable tax;

- A repayment of a policy loan is also considered to be a contribution to an RCA; and

- Any payments received pursuant to the policy, including policy loans, will be treated as distributions from an RCA and will trigger the 50% refund.

Accordingly, the person who holds the interest in the policy will be liable to pay refundable tax equal to the amount of any policy premiums and repayments of policy loans.

Because the proceeds of the insurance policy are the unencumbered property of the company, the executive may have no security should the company encounter financial difficulties or a take-over bid.

---

[2]   These rules also apply to annuities.

An exempt life insurance policy held by an RCA trust to fund retirement benefits can provide advantageous tax treatment. The income earned under an exempt life insurance policy is not subject to the 50% RCA refundable tax. Thus, this can be a more cost-effective way to fund supplementary pension benefits than other securities such as Guaranteed Investment Certificates and bonds. However, such potential cost effectiveness must be measured against the additional cost of insurance, the need for additional life insurance coverage, the long period of time required before the alleged cost effectiveness materializes, and the security provided by the issuer. Further to the latter point, the failure of American International Group during the financial crisis in 2008 and 2009 serves as a reminder that no financial institution can claim to be fully secure.

When held outside an RCA trust, payments from the life insurance policy would cause the refundable tax to be paid out to the employer, who is the custodian. Refunds from the RCA to the employer will be included in the employer's income. As for the employee, there will be no tax consequences until the employee actually receives the benefit, at which time he or she will be taxed. Additionally, any death benefits paid out to beneficiaries are considered taxable.

However, the above situation must be distinguished from the situation whereby the RCA trust purchases a life insurance policy (or annuity contract) on the life of the employee to fund retirement benefits. In such a situation, the employer would have funded the RCA previously and paid the refundable tax at that point. Therefore, the insurance premiums paid by the custodian of the RCA would not have been subject to the 50% refundable tax. As mentioned above, if the insurance policy is an exempt policy, any income earned will not be subject to the 50% refundable tax on income earned in an RCA trust. The death benefits paid out of an insurance policy to the RCA are exempt; however, any such proceeds paid out to the employee or a beneficiary will be taxable income to either the employee or the beneficiary.

Secular Trusts

A secular trust is an arrangement whereby the employer pays to the employee additional salary on the condition that the employee will in turn establish a trust to hold the additional amounts. The employee is the beneficiary of the trust. To ensure that the funds are used to provide retirement income, the employee agrees that the trust will contain terms that constrain the timing and amount of income the employee can withdraw from the trust. The capital used to establish the secular trust is taxable income to the employee. As a result, a gross-up may be required to offset the personal taxes paid. The employee pays tax on the income of the trust; thus, such trusts do not defer tax. The employer can normally obtain a deduction for the additional salary paid. A secular trust can be tax-effective if the top marginal tax rate is less than the 50% rate applicable to RCAs. Under the current tax regime, capital gains and dividends enjoy an effective tax rate below the 50% RCA tax rate. This may be seen as an advantage for using a secular trust instead of an RCA.

Terminal Funding

Under this approach, the employer pays the present value of the employee's pension in a lump sum or in installments over a short period of time, at the time the employee retires. Terminal funding has the disadvantage that the employer's outlay may be substantial in certain circumstances. It will also vary widely from year to year, because the retirement pattern is usually irregular. This may not be an issue when such a case outlay is small relative to the size of the organization.

Paying a lump sum at retirement rather than periodic payments may be an acceptable compromise in many cases from a security perspective for the employee, but the lump-sum amount is fully taxable to the employee in the year of receipt. From the employee's perspective, the lump-sum value of the supplementary arrangements entitlement should be calculated using the employee's expected after-tax rate of return.

However, many employers believe that where a lump-sum option exists, any additional tax liability should be the responsibility of the executive, and they would require the lump sum to be determined using the employee's or employer's pre-tax expected rate of return. Plan documents need to be clear on the basis to be used when lump-sum payments are available. Often, the same basis used under the RPP to determine pension commuted values is used under the SERP.

Where it is the intention to provide the employee with a given amount of after-tax income each year, assumptions as to the employee's future marginal tax rate have to be made and a prescribed annuity contract can be purchased from a life insurance company to provide the desired level of income. The employer would provide a special lump sum to the employee, who would then use the after-tax proceeds to purchase the annuity.

Cost of Funding

As noted in Chapter 5, determination of the cost of unfunded supplementary arrangements and, in particular, the choice of an appropriate discount rate assumption, involves a multi-faceted set of considerations. The additional cost of advance funding of the supplementary arrangement involves quantifying the return forfeited, if any, as a result of investing capital in a segregated trust versus investing in the business entity.

Whether or not the supplementary arrangement is funded, employers are required to account for its costs and to disclose its related obligations in their financial statements.[3]

Documentation

The documentation of the supplementary pension promise is important and should not be neglected. The wording of the plan text or individual agreements is very important to the security of the promise, and is also crucial at the employee termination or retirement date, especially in the context of a difficult separation. If the documentation of a supplementary arrangement is restricted to a board of directors' resolution or to a letter signifying intent, the lack of details concerning benefit delivery or the contractual underpinnings of the commitment can cause significant problems years after the supplementary arrangement is established.

A more formal policy can be in the form of a contract between the employee and the company, or a plan text accompanied with a designation letter to the employee.

Plan sponsors should be aware that the documentation will also have an impact on the ease (or lack of it) of plan administration and communication to the members of the plan.

---

[3]   Chapter 6 discusses these financial management issues related to supplementary arrangements.

Chapter 14

OTHER RETIREMENT INCOME, SAVINGS, AND DEFERRED COMPENSATION ARRANGEMENTS

Executive Summary

Over the last few decades, retirement income arrangements other than pension plans, as well as other savings programs that can generate additional retirement income, have gained in importance. The group Registered Retirement Savings Plan (RRSPs), various types of profit sharing and other savings plans, and deferred compensation arrangements are the major alternatives to pension plans. These vehicles are generally grouped under the label "Capital Accumulation Plans" (CAP). Added to the CAP spectrum in 2009 was the next tax-assisted savings vehicle, the Tax-Free Savings Account (TFSA). Of these vehicles, group RRSPs have been the most popular thus far. This chapter provides a detailed discussion of the history, main features, and taxation and investment requirements of RRSPs, profit sharing plans and other retirement and savings arrangements. There is also a chart comparing significant aspects of RRSPs and TFSAs. In addition, the chapter delivers thorough explanations of different types of deferred compensation arrangements, profit sharing plans and stock purchase plans, as well as their tax considerations.

Introduction

Over the last few decades, the pension legal environment in Canada has grown in complexity – there has been important reform of pension standards legislation as well as of the *Income Tax Act* (ITA), including the establishment of a new tax-assisted savings program. Further, the cost of defined benefit pension plans have increased due to lower interest rates and increased life expectancies. As a result, some employers, especially smaller ones, have chosen to terminate their defined benefit pension plans in favour of CAPs, including defined contribution Registered Pension Plans (RPPs), group RRSPs, and Deferred Profit Sharing Plans (DPSPs). Also, many employers have viewed a CAP arrangement as a vehicle to help them control future costs and support a new element of corporate culture – the shift of responsibility to employees. In 2009, the TFSA was added to the CAP spectrum. In 2012, the federal government introduced the Pooled Registered Pension Plan (PRPP) to provide employees and self-employed individuals who do not have access to a work-place retirement arrangement, the opportunity to save for retirement and benefit from lower fees compared to an individual RRSP.

Registered Retirement Savings Plans

The legislation creating RRSPs was enacted in 1957 and was designed to encourage individuals to save for their retirement on a tax-sheltered basis. Assets under RRSPs have grown rapidly, particularly since the 1991 changes to the ITA that increased contribution limits, and now constitute a significant proportion of total Canadian retirement savings.

These plans are of particular value to the self-employed, who do not have access to employer-sponsored retirement arrangements to accumulate retirement savings on a tax-preferred basis. RRSPs may also be used by employees, whether or not they are members of pension or profit sharing plans.

An RRSP is a contract between an individual and an authorized insurer, trustee, or corporation (an issuer). Contributions made by a taxpayer are deductible for taxation purposes, within the contribution limits described in Chapter 8. Taxpayers may also elect to contribute to their spouses' RRSPs within the prescribed limits, however, certain restrictions apply on withdrawals of money from a spousal RRSP. The investment earnings on the assets of RRSPs are tax-sheltered, however, withdrawals from the plans are taxable unless they are "excluded withdrawals" pursuant to the Home Buyers Plan or the Lifelong Learning Plan.[1]

Initially, the funds from an RRSP had to be used to purchase a life annuity from an insurance company. Such annuities may be based upon the life of the taxpayer alone, or on the lifetime of the taxpayer and the taxpayer's spouse. This type of annuity may have a guaranteed term, but the guaranteed term must not exceed 90 minus the age of the annuitant, or when

---

[1]   The Home Buyers Plan allows individuals to withdraw up to $25,000 from RRSPs tax-free to purchase *or build* a first home *or a home for a related person with a disability*. They are allowed a period of up to 15 years to repay the withdrawn funds. Under the Lifelong Learning Plan (LLP), an individual is allowed to withdraw funds from his or her RRSP on a tax-free basis for the purpose of financing full-time studies of the individual or the individual's spouse or common-law partner. The aggregate withdrawal is limited to $20,000 with a maximum yearly withdrawal of $10,000. The amounts withdrawn under the LLP must be repaid to the RRSP over a period not exceeding 10 years, beginning with the earlier of the second year after the last year that the student was enrolled in full-time studies and the fifth year after the first year in which an LLP withdrawal was made.

the annuitant's spouse is younger and the annuitant elects, 90 minus the age of the annuitant's spouse. Previous amendments to the ITA have allowed two retirement income options in addition to the life annuity:

- An annuity certain (a fixed-term annuity) for the term of years equal to 90 minus the age of the annuitant when the annuity commences, or if the annuitant so elects, 90 minus the age of the annuitant's spouse where the spouse is younger than the annuitant; and

- The Registered Retirement Income Fund (RRIF) was introduced in order to allow the individual more control over the investment of the fund after the RRSP matures and more flexibility in the timing of withdrawals from the fund.

Therefore, there are three tax-effective options: a life annuity, a fixed-term annuity, or an RRIF.

The RRSP may be matured or annuitized at any time, except that the annuitant payments must commence or the funds must be transferred to an RRIF prior to the end of the year in which the taxpayer's 71st birthday is reached.

The ITA and pension standards legislation generally allow the value of the pension benefits from the RPP of a terminating member to be transferred into an RRSP. In most cases, the pension benefits are locked-in, meaning the transfer must be made, depending upon the applicable pension standards legislation, to either a locked-in RRSP, a Locked-In Retirement Account (LIRA), a Life Income Fund (LIF), or a Locked-In Retirement Income Fund (LRIF). Pension benefits may be exempt from the locked-in rules if the amount is less than various limits outlined under applicable pension standards legislation.

Locked-in RRSPs are similar to regular RRSPs. However, they differ from regular RRSPs in that a locked-in RRSP, as the name implies, is locked in until retirement age and the money must be used to provide retirement income. Subsequent to the advent of the locked-in RRSP, the LIRA was introduced and is essentially identical to a locked-in RRSP. A LIF or LRIF is very similar to a RRIF, except that maximum and minimum annual withdrawals are prescribed by the applicable pension standards and tax legislation. Some jurisdictions distinguish between LIFs and LRIFs, with the principal difference being that under a LIF a life annuity must be purchased with the balance of the fund at an age not exceeding 90. In jurisdictions that do not distinguish between LIFs and LRIFs, the life annuity requirement does not apply.

In recent years, a number of pension jurisdictions have relaxed locked-in rules to allow portions of locked-in accounts to be unlocked. In some instances there are special rules for unlocking in the event of financial hardship, shortened life expectancy, or non-resident status. In other instances, the unlocking of a significant portion is permitted if certain other criteria are met, as follows:

- Alberta amended the Employment Pension Plans Regulation, effective November 1, 2006, to permit unlocking of up to 50% of an amount that would otherwise be transferred to a LIF (or a LIF-style account in a DC plan) from a LIRA or pension plan provided the individual has attained age 50. LIFs and LRIFs were also consolidated into a single LIF structure with this amendment.

- The federal government amended the Pension Benefits Standards Regulations, effective May 8, 2008, to permit unlocking of up to 50% of an amount transferred to a Restricted LIF (RLIF) from a Locked-in RRSP, LIF or pension plan, within 60 days of such transfer.

- Manitoba amended the Pension Benefits Regulation, effective May 31, 2010, to permit a member to transfer (on a one-time basis and if the plan permits) up to 50% of his or her pension to an RRIF. This amendment is subsequent to the May 25, 2005 amendment that permits a one-time transfer of up to 50% of the funds in a LIF or LRIF to an RRIF. Please note the unlocking of benefits under the amendments, whether from a pension plan, LIF, or LRIF, may only be done once in a lifetime.

- New Brunswick amended the *Pension Benefits Act*, effective December 1, 2003, to permit a member, upon termination of employment, to transfer up to 25% of the member's pension benefits to an RRIF, if the plan so permits. Further, the Regulation under the *Pension Benefits Act* permits a one-time transfer from a LIF to an RRIF of up to the lesser of 25% of the account balance at the start of the year or three times the maximum LIF withdrawal amount for the year.

- Ontario amended the Regulations to the *Pension Benefits Act*, effective January 1, 2010, to permit a one-time unlocking of up to 50% of an amount transferred to a "New LIF" from an LIRA or pension plan, within 60 days of such transfer.

- Saskatchewan introduced the Prescribed Registered Retirement Income Fund (PRIF) as a new portability option in 2002, giving employees over age 55 (or the plan's early retirement age, if younger) access to their formerly locked-in pension money. This new option replaced LIFs and LRIFs in Saskatchewan.

Group Registered Retirement Savings Plans

Group RRSPs have been very popular in recent years as an alternative to pension plans. This popularity follows a general trend away from defined benefit arrangements toward more defined contribution arrangements. Some employers have chosen a group RRSP as opposed to a defined contribution pension plan, a primary reason being that RRSPs are not subject to pension standards legislation. More particularly, there is:

- No plan text to be registered with a governmental supervisory authority;
- No locking-in requirements;
- More flexibility to vary employer contributions among plan members;
- More flexibility in establishing eligibility conditions;
- No restriction on beneficiary designations;
- No mandatory joint and survivor pension to be paid to a spouse;
- No requirement to report Pension Adjustments (PAs);
- No pension committee required (as required for Quebec RPPs and Manitoba RPPs with at least 50 members);
- No plan members annual meeting required (as required for Quebec RPPs); and
- Opportunity for the employee to arrange income splitting through spousal RRSPs.

On the other hand, there are some employer costs in operating a group RRSP as compared to a defined contribution pension plan, because employer contributions to RRSPs are considered salary to the employee. Under the ITA, only individuals can contribute to their RRSP accounts and group RRSPs are merely a collection of individual RRSPs. Thus employer contributions are deemed to be paid to the employee who, in turn, contributes the amount to their RRSP. As a result, employer contributions, in effect, immediately vest in the employee. As well, there are often additional costs associated with employer contributions in the form of contributions to government plans:

- Canada/Quebec Pension Plan (employer and employees);
- Employment Insurance (employer and employees);
- Provincial health care plans in some jurisdictions (employer); and
- Workers' Compensation (employer).

However, it also important to note, that if the employee's remuneration is greater than the maximum assessable earnings for payroll taxes, an increase in the employee's compensation as a result of employer contributions to a group RRSP will not create an increase in the amount of payroll taxes.

Group RRSPs also provide some advantages to the employees as opposed to individual RRSPs, even if the employer does not contribute. Advantages include:

- Saving for retirement through payroll deductions is very convenient, and the tax deductibility of the contribution reduces the amount of withholding taxes;
- Employees can benefit from the greater purchasing power of a group, through:
- Reduced administration and fund management costs, which may be paid or partially paid by the employer, and
- Access to a wide variety of investment funds (GICs, short-term deposit funds, equity funds, fixed-income funds, balanced funds, foreign equity funds, target date or lifecycle funds, etc.).

Some of the very features in a group RRSP that offer employees flexibility make it difficult for employers to use this arrangement as a human resources management tool. As previously noted, notional "employer contributions" to the group RRSP are, in effect, immediately vested to the employee. There is no way to ensure that the funds will eventually be used for retirement purposes rather than for any other personal purpose, or even prevent employees from making withdrawals from their group RRSP while they are still employed by the employer. It may be possible when such a plan is established to include non-withdrawal clauses, however care should be taken in the implementation of such clauses. Otherwise, there is no legal basis on which to prevent withdrawals. To discourage contribution withdrawals, some employers suspend matching contributions for a period of one to five years in the event withdrawals are made during employment.

Plans featuring notional "employer contributions" and non-withdrawal clauses are often referred to as "Structured Group RRSPs". These types of plans may carry some regulatory risks. In the late 1990s there were some instances where pension regulators declared group RRSPs with withdrawal restrictions to be pension plans subject to pension standards legislation, and that as such they were non-compliant. Any document describing a plan featuring employer contributions and withdrawal restrictions should be carefully reviewed to ensure that it does not meet the definition of a "pension plan" under pension standards legislation.

Group RRSPs are often used on a stand-alone basis, but they are also found as a supplement to a non-contributory defined benefit or defined contribution pension plan or to DPSP. A DPSP is used in these cases to receive employer contributions, as they are not considered to be salary subject to payroll taxes. Other conditions governing DPSPs are described later in this chapter.

Fiduciary Responsibility for Group Registered Retirement Savings Plans

Even though a group RRSP is not subject to pension standards legislation, the employer establishing it may face some fiduciary or fiduciary-like responsibility. It is usually the employer who selects the administrator and fund manager(s) who will act within the parameters set by the employer.

In such circumstances, the employer has a responsibility to make the selection with prudence and diligence. After the initial selection, the employer also has a responsibility to monitor and evaluate the fund manager's performance on an ongoing basis. These functions are crucial under a group RRSP, because the benefits to the participants are directly related to the performance of the fund manager and the investment selections.[2]

Group RRSPs are also subject to the CAP Guidelines.[3]

Registered Retirement Savings Plan Investments

RRSPs may be invested in a wide variety of securities, including Canadian and foreign common stocks, fixed-income securities, and mortgages chosen by the annuitant, provided that they are qualified investments for RRSPs under the ITA. Prior to 2005, there were limits on the amount of foreign securities that could be held in RRSPs. Since the 2005 federal Budget, the foreign content limit no longer applies to investments held under RRSPs.

Generally, RRSPs are invested in a combination of fixed income and equity investments. In making the investment decision, the individual will consider the type and amount of his or her other savings and investments, the economic outlook, individual tolerance for investment risk, and the time remaining until retirement. Individuals may also choose to invest RRSPs in a deferred annuity contract with an insurance company, in the pooled funds of a trust company, or in a mutual fund. Pooled funds and mutual funds have gained in popularity, giving a choice of investment in equities, bonds, mortgages, or a combination thereof. Target date funds, also known as life cycle funds, are another popular choice that automatically adjusts the individual's asset mix as they approach retirement. Alternatively, a self-administered RRSP can be established under an agreement with a corporate trustee or other authorized corporation, which permits the annuitant to select the individual securities.

---

[2]   Chapter 7 discusses these issues in further detail.
[3]   More information on the CAP Guidelines is found in Chapter 29.

Taxation of Registered Retirement Savings Plans

Assets

The list of permitted investments for RRSPs is defined under the ITA and includes investments in cash, guaranteed income certficiates, government and corporate bonds, mutual funds, and securities listed on a designated exchange ("qualified investments"). Although RRSPs are generally considered tax-free until withdrawal, taxes become payable if the assets are invested in "non-qualified" investments or non-arm's-length securities or transactions.

Contributions

Contributions to an RRSP are tax deductible within set limits. Prior to 1991, self-employed persons and individuals who were not members of an RPP or DPSP were permitted a higher maximum contribution than those who participated in such a plan. Today, the deductibility of RRSP contributions is governed by a retirement savings system based on the principle that tax assistance should be the same for all individuals with the same income, regardless of the arrangement in which they participate.

Post-1990 calculation of an individual's RRSP contribution limit

Contribution Limit = A + B + C - D

A = Taxpayer's unused contribution room at the end of the preceding taxation year

B = (lesser of 18% of taxpayer's "earned income" for preceding year and "RRSP dollar limit") minus PA for preceding year

C = Taxpayer's PAR for the year

D = Taxpayer's net PSPA for the year.[4]

What constitutes "earned income" is set out in the ITA and includes such things as employment income, business income, royalties, rental income, alimony or maintenance payments, payments received under a supplementary unemployment benefit plan, and research grants.

- A taxpayer's "RRSP dollar limit" is defined in the ITA as:
- For 2012, $22,970;
- For 2013, $23,820;

---

[4]   See Chapter 8 for definitions of PA, PAR, and PSPA.

- For 2014, $24,270;
- For 2015, $24,930;
- For 2016, $25,370; and
- For 2017, $26,010.

The RRSP dollar limit will be increased based on the growth in the average industrial wage in 2018 and later.

If an individual borrows money to finance an RRSP contribution, the interest payable on the loan taken is not tax deductible.

Investment Income

Investment income earned in an RRSP is not taxable until paid out, at which time the entire amount of any withdrawal is taxable as ordinary income unless it is an "excluded withdrawal" pursuant to the Home Buyers Plan or the Lifelong Learning Plan. Lump sums payable from a spousal plan are added to the contributor's income if the withdrawal is made within three years of a contribution; otherwise they are taxed as income of the spouse. Assets may be transferred from one RRSP to another, or to an RRIF or RPP, without attracting tax at the time of transfer. Similarly, there is no tax on lump-sum transfers to an RRSP from an RPP or DPSP. Retiring allowances may be transferred to an RRSP, tax-free, subject to specified maximum amounts described in Chapter 13.

Registered Retirement Income Funds

This alternative to annuity purchase as a form of settlement under an RRSP was introduced in 1978. An annuitant may elect to have the RRSP assets transferred into a RRIF before the RRSP reaches maturity; however, RRSP funds that are locked-in by virtue of pension legislation are not eligible for transfer to a RRIF unless they meet one of the unlocking rules discussed above.

Similar to RRSPs, the entire amount of any withdrawal is taxable as ordinary income. The annuitant may elect to receive any amount up to the total balance in the fund, but must make a minimum annual withdrawal. The minimum annual withdrawal follows a table of factors varying according to the attained age prescribed in the ITA.

Under normal conditions, if only the minimum payments are made, the payments will initially be less than the investment return, although they will rise from year to year. Hence, the amount of the RRIF assets can be expected to rise for several years and then start to decrease; consequently, the fund can provide a substantial estate if death occurs before age 90.

An RRIF tends to appeal to those who have maintained an individually managed RRSP until retirement. It enables such taxpayers to continue to control their investments during retirement.

A taxpayer must transfer his or her RRSP into a RRIF or retirement annuity (or some combination of both) by the end of the year he or she attains 71 years of age. A taxpayer does not have to withdraw any amount in the year the RRIF is established. However, commencing in the following year, a minimum amount must be withdrawn. The minimum amount is computed by multiplying the fair market value of the property held in connection with the fund at the beginning of the year by a prescribed factor based on the taxpayer's age at the beginning of the year. The taxpayer can make a one-time election, at the time the RRIF is established, to have the prescribed factor based on his or her spouse or common-law partner's age. In 2015, the factors were reduced in order to reflect decreased investment returns on RRIFs. The prescribed factors for 2015 and subsequent years are listed in the following table:

Age	Minimum Withdrawal %
71	5.28
72	5.40
73	5.53
74	5.67
75	5.82
76	5.98
77	6.17
78	6.36
79	6.58
80	6.82
81	7.08
82	7.38
83	7.71
84	8.08
85	8.51
86	8.99
87	9.55
88	10.21
89	10.99
90	11.92
91	13.06
92	14.49

Age	Minimum Withdrawal %
93	16.34
94	18.79
95 or older	20.00

If an annuitant has an RRIF when he or she is under the age of 71, the minimum payout is determined by the formula $1/(90 - Y)$ where Y equals the annuitant's age at the beginning of that year.

Example

John is 70 years of age at the beginning of the year and he has $375,000 in his RRIF. John must withdraw 5% of this amount. Therefore, he must withdraw at least $18,750 from his plan. This amount will be added to John's taxable income and will qualify for the pension income tax credit.

Profit Sharing Plans

Profit sharing plans can be defined as plans whereby amounts paid to or for the benefit of the employees are calculated by reference to the employer's profits. Profit sharing plans are designed to reward good performance and to instill a sense of partnership between the employer and each participating employee. It is anticipated that the plan will lead to increased productivity and increased profits. The intention is to establish a common interest for employees, management, and shareholders.

Profit sharing plans can be established to provide immediate or deferred benefits.

Cash Profit Sharing

The immediate distribution or cash profit sharing plan is the simplest to establish and administer. As long as the regular wage or salary is reasonable and competitive, a cash profit sharing plan should provide the desired incentive to employees. Such arrangements may also be used in lieu of a portion of regular compensation where employers and employees partner in an attempt to turn company operations around.

A profit sharing bonus tends to be used immediately to raise the current standard of living. For this reason, they are not usually intended as a retirement income vehicle.

The amounts received by the employees, either as cash or company stock, whether on an annual or more frequent basis, are taxed as ordinary income in the year received. The company can deduct them from its taxable income as though they were wages.

Profit Sharing with Deferred Benefits

Under the deferred payment type of profit sharing plan, a share of the company's profits is allocated to the employees and set aside in a trust fund each year instead of being paid out immediately. A separate account is maintained for each employee and credited with interest until such time as the account is paid out, usually on the employee's death, retirement, permanent disability, or termination of employment.

A profit sharing plan that is intended to provide retirement income for employees has certain disadvantages in addition to the limitations imposed by the ITA. The plan is indefinite as to the ultimate amount of retirement income that the employees will receive, depending as it does on future profits, the investment yield of the trust, and the price at which annuities may be purchased.

Profit sharing plans with deferred benefits may be divided into three main types determined largely by which provisions of the ITA apply. These are:

- Registered Profit Sharing Pension Plans;
- Deferred Profit Sharing Plans; and
- Employees Profit Sharing Plans.

Registered Profit Sharing Pension Plans

A Registered Profit Sharing Pension Plan is an RPP and is subject to the ITA and pension standards legislation. As discussed in Chapter 1, it constitutes a type of capital accumulation plan, distinguished merely by the fact that the company contributions are related to profits. As with other RPPs, employees may not withdraw their funds from the plan while in service, nor may they have their benfits paid as a lump sum in cash upon retirement.

As with other defined contribution RPPs, both employee and employer contributions are tax deductible and the maximum contribution rules are the same. The interest income of the trust fund is free of tax while it remains in the plan, but all benefits are taxable to the employee when paid out.

Deferred Profit Sharing Plans

A Deferred Profit Sharing Plan or DPSP is an arrangement whereby the employer contributes to the plan a share of the company's profits. The share of profits may be calculated by "reference to the employer's profits" (or profits from a related corporation) or paid "out of profits" from the employer's business. Contributions made by "reference to profits" are expressed as a percentage of profits for the year (*i.e.*, 5% of profits per year). The employer can base these contributions on its own profits for the year or on the combined profits for it and a related corporation. As a result, if there are no profits in the year, no contributions will be made. Alternatively, if contributions are paid "out of profits", they can be calculated using various formulae (including formulae not related to profits), and paid from profits for the year or undistributed profits from previous years. The formulae for contribution calculations may be based on such factors as a fixed dollar amount per employee or a percentage of the employee's salary, and can vary from one employee to the next.

Depending on the terms of the plan, the share of the profits contributed to the plan may be determined on a discretionary basis or contingent upon a criterion such as employee performance and with no minimum contributions required. The absence of a mandatory relationship between profits and contributions often results in a DPSP being more of a savings plan than a profit sharing plan.

The contributions are paid to a trustee who holds and invests them on behalf of the employees. The trustee under a DPSP is usually a Canadian trust or life insurance company, which will charge fees to the employer for the administration of the plan.

Allocations to an employee's account must vest immediately if the employee has completed 24 months of DPSP membership. Amounts forfeited due to employees terminating before they are fully vested must either be paid to the employer or be reallocated to the beneficiaries under the plan on or before the end of the calendar year immediately following the calendar year in which the amount is forfeited.

DPSPs are frequently used as a retirement income vehicle on a stand-alone or supplementary basis. One of the major differences between DPSPs and RPPs is that lump-sum distributions of all or a portion of the employee's DPSP account are allowed before terminating employment. Some people consider this flexibility to be an important advantage of DPSPs. Further, DPSPs are not subject to the detailed minimum pension standards legislation, including locked-in requirements. RPPs, however, offer higher tax-deductible contribution limits and, therefore, a greater degree of tax deferral.

Prior to 1991, a DPSP also permitted voluntary or mandatory employee contributions, which were not tax deductible. However, any earnings on such contributions accumulated on a tax-deferred basis in the plan. For 1991 and thereafter, employee contributions are not permitted.

Tax-deductible employer contributions to a DPSP (when added to any reallocated forfeitures) cannot exceed a maximum contribution per employee that is limited to the lesser of:

- one-half of the money purchase pension plan limit for the year; and
- 18% of the compensation for the year.

The following table outlines the maximum dollar limit for DPSP contributions:

Year	Maximum DPSP Contribution
2009	$11,000
2010	$11,225
2011	$11,485
2012	$11,910
2013	$12,135
2014	$12,465
2015	$12,685
2016	$13,005
2017	indexed in accordance with the growth in the average industrial wage

As noted in Chapter 8, the overall contribution limits apply to the total of employer and employee contributions to defined contribution RPPs, RRSPs, and DPSPs. Thus, the maximum employer contribution to a DPSP may be reduced as a result of contributions to other registered arrangements. The converse is also true.

The employer contribution is deductible to the extent it is paid in accordance with the plan as registered, and it must be made in the taxation year or within 120 days after the end of the taxation year.

Benefits received by employees or their beneficiaries are subject to income tax, except for the return of their own contributions. (Before 1991, non-deductible employee contributions were permitted, to a maximum of $5,500 a year.) All amounts vested in the employee (or his or her beneficiary or estate upon death) must become payable no later than the earliest of the following times:

- The end of the year in which the beneficiary turns 71 years of age; or
- 90 days after the earliest of the following dates:
- the date of the employee's death,
- the date the employee ceases to be employed by the employer, or
- the date of winding-up of the plan.

There are also a number of options available with respect to the form of such payments. The payment may be received as a lump sum. However, if the plan permits, all or part of the amount payable can be paid in instalments. These instalments must be paid at least annually, but can be paid more frequently for up to 10 years from the date on which the amount becomes payable. Additionally, if the employee so chooses, an annuity can be purchased. The annuity payments must begin on or before the end of the calendar year in which the employee turns age 71. If the employee does select an annuity, the amount used to purchase the annuity will not be immediately included in income. Instead, the annuity payments will be included in income as they are received. To qualify for registration, a DPSP must satisfy several other registration requirements, including the following:

- All payments into the trust and the investment returns must be allocated to plan members each year;
- Employees may not borrow from the fund, nor surrender nor assign their interests;
- Trustees must be resident in Canada;
- Trustees must inform all new beneficiaries of their rights; and
- The plan must provide that all income received, capital gains made, and capital losses sustained by the trust be allocated to the beneficiaries within 90 days after the end of the trust, unless previously allocated.

There is also a tax penalty if the DPSP fund is not invested in Qualified Investments as defined in paragraph 204 of the ITA. The investment limitations are broadly comparable to those contained in pension standards legislation, although there is no 10% limit on the investment in one security. Hence, the plan may invest heavily in the employer's own common stock, although not in the employer's notes or bonds.

The tax on acquisition of non-qualified investments is equal to 100% of the cost of the non-qualified investment. On sale of a non-qualified investment, a tax refund equal to the lesser of the tax paid or the proceeds of sale is available.

To prevent the abuse of DPSPs by an employer who might arrange for large amounts of forfeitures to be transferred into the accounts of a few chosen employees, the Canada Revenue Agency (CRA) has prohibited significant shareholders and their family members from participating in the plans. Further, a special tax applies when the DPSP transfers property to a taxpayer at less than fair market value or acquires property from a taxpayer at greater than fair market value.

In addition to the specific requirements of the ITA, DPSPs must comply with the rules in CRA Information Circular 77-1R5.

Employee's Profit Sharing Plans

Employee's Profit Sharing Plans (EPSPs) are governed by section 144 of the ITA and tend to operate either as profit sharing bonus plans or long-term savings or thrift plans. Employee access to their account varies widely from plan to plan, ranging from virtually immediate vesting to vesting deferred until death, termination of employment or retirement. Cash withdrawals by employees in service are allowed.

The funds may be invested in shares of the employer, as these plans have the advantage of not being subject to investment restrictions. Moreover, there is no limit on the amount of deductible employer contributions.

The employer's contributions to the plan are required to be computed by reference to the employer's profits from its business, or by reference to its profits and the profits from the business of a corporation not dealing at arm's length with the employer. Contributions that are made by reference to profits are subject to a minimum employer contribution rate of 1% of the current year's profits.

As an alternative, the plan may specify that employer contributions are made "out of profits". The contributions may be made out of profits for the year or out of accumulated undistributed profits from previous years, but cannot include profits from another corporation not dealing at arm's length with the employer, unless that corporation is also a participating employer in the EPSP. If contributions are made "out of profits", the employer is required to make contributions in accordance with the plan's formula when a profit exists, and such payments are limited by the level of profits. Some examples of "out of profit" formulae are:

- a percentage (must be at least 1%) of employees' salaries or wages;
- a matching amount of employees' contributions (minimum of 1% of each employee's salary or wages);
- a fixed dollar amount of at least $100 per employee per year.

The disadvantage of EPSPs is that the employees must pay tax on all amounts allocated to their individual accounts each year, excluding their own contributions, which come from after-tax income. All income of the trust must be allocated to individual employees either absolutely or contingently, and this income includes the company's profit sharing payment to the plan, the investment income from trust property, and realized capital gains or losses, in addition to the employee's own contributions. Realized capital gains of the trust fund must be allocated to employees and are taxed as capital gains of the employees. When dividends from taxable Canadian corporations are included, however, the benefit of the dividend tax credit is passed on to the employees. It should be noted that interest income is deemed to be employment income.

The allocation is usually in proportion to the employee's earnings or length of service or such other equitable formula as may be adopted. An EPSP may also be used for individual profit sharing allocations that exceed what can be deposited into an employee's DPSP account each year.

Because all input is taxed, payments out of the plan when actually received (usually in a lump sum) will not be included in the employee's taxable income.

Serious inequities are possible under EPSPs, because the employee who is taxed on amounts contingently allocated to him or her may never receive those amounts due to his or her failure to qualify for benefits under the plan's rules. Amounts allocated to an employee, but forfeited on termination of service without full vesting will normally be reallocated to other employees and subject to tax in their hands. Relief is provided by the ITA, in that any employee who ceases to be a beneficiary under an EPSP is allowed to deduct an amount equal to the amount on which he or she paid tax but cannot receive, less certain adjustments.

Introduced in 2012 to prevent the abuse of EPSPs by non-arm's-length employees who might avoid CPP and EI premiums by arranging for profit to be transferred into their accounts in lieu of receiving a salary, the ITA limits the contributions that may be made for significant shareholders and their family members to 20% of their salary or wages from the employer. A special tax applies to EPSP contributions that exceed this amount.

Communication to Employees

Communication is particularly important to the success of a profit sharing plan. Management must show that it believes in the principle of profit sharing. It must encourage employees to participate with management in a spirit of mutual trust and confidence. The announcement and explanation of the plan to employees should clearly set out the principles and philosophy of profit sharing. The plan features must be defined so that all employees understand precisely the purpose of the plan, what they will receive and what is expected of them.

The communication of the plan must be pursued on a regular and continuing basis to keep employees enthusiastic and aware of their interest in the success of the corporate enterprise. Some employers believe that there should be employee representation on whatever body is established to administer the plan.

Other Savings Plans and Deferred Compensation Arrangements

Tax-Free Savings Accounts

In the 2008 federal Budget, the government announced the establishment of the TFSA as a new tax-assisted savings vehicle for Canadians, beginning in 2009. TFSAs are similar in many respects to RRSPs, with two important distinctions: contributions are not tax-deductible and withdrawals are not subject to tax. The distinctive features of the TFSA are as follows:

- Every individual age 18 and over can contribute up to $5,000 each year to a TFSA beginning in 2009, and, unlike RRSPs, there are no earnings-related limits;

- The $5,000 limit will increase with inflation, subject to $500 increments (the limit for 2015 only was increased to $10,000);

- Unused TFSA room accumulates;

- Investment income earned on deposits is not subject to tax;

- Withdrawals are not subject to tax;

- TFSAs can exist until the death of the owner (*i.e.*, there is no set maturity date, etc.);

- Withdrawals are not considered to be income in respect of federal means-tested benefits (*e.g.*, Old Age Security, Guaranteed Income Supplements, and Employment Insurance benefits);

- Withdrawals (of contributions and investment income) are added to the next year's TFSA room; and

- There are no attribution rules on contributions made to a spouse's TFSA, and spousal contributions do not affect an individual's TFSA room.

The list of permitted investments for TFSAs is defined under the ITA and includes investments in cash, guaranteed income certficiates, government and corporate bonds, mutual funds, and securities listed on a designated exchange ("qualified investments"). Although TFSAs are generally considered tax-free, taxes become payable if the assets are invested in "non-qualified" investments or non-arm's-length securities or transactions. Taxes also become payable if the owner makes contributions while he or she is a non-resident of Canada.

Comparison Between a Registered Retirement Savings Plan and a Tax-Free Savings Account

	RRSP	TFSA
Annual Contribution Maximum	$23,820 in 2013 $24,270 in 2014 $24,930 in 2015 $25,370 in 2016 $26,010 in 2017 and indexed thereafter	$5,500 in 2013 $5,500 in 2014 $10,000 in 2015 $5,500 in 2016 and indexed thereafter (rounded to nearest $500)
Unused room carried forward?	Yes	Yes
Are contributions deductible?	Yes	No
Are withdrawals taxable?	Yes	No
Are earnings taxable?	Yes, when withdrawn	No
Date plan must be closed	Convert to annuity, RRIF, or take as cash by December 31st of the year the individual turns 71	Death of the individual
Are spousal contributions permitted?	Yes, subject to contributor's contribution room	Yes, subject to spouse's contribution room
Withdrawals affect means-tested benefits?	Yes	No

The TFSA is primarily a savings vehicle and is not designed specifically for retirement savings. However, given its tax advantages, it may be preferred over an RRSP in some situations. For example, because an individual may continue to contribute to a TFSA until death, Canadians who are 71 years of age or older who are ineligible to contribute to an RRSP may save and earn tax-free investment income by using a TFSA. This represents a significant benefit to older Canadians who previously did not receive any tax assistance for saving once they attained age 71.

Because a withdrawal from a TFSA does not affect means-tested benefits, the TFSA may be a preferred savings vehicle to lower income Canadians who expect to depend mostly on government pension support during retirement. The TFSA allows low income Canadians to save additional sums without reducing their Old Age Security and Guaranteed

Income Supplement, something that may happen when using an RRSP to save.

The TFSA may also be preferred by Canadians who expect to retire in a higher tax bracket than their current bracket. For example, students and part-time workers are most likely currently in a lower tax bracket than the bracket they will be in at retirement. By saving in a TFSA, these individuals will pay less tax on their contribution than they would pay with an RRSP, although the tax is paid immediately and not deferred. This demonstrates that a TFSA may have some advantage as a tax planning vehicle as well as a savings vehicle.

Investment options for the TFSA are similar to the options available to an RRSP. However, any assets held in a TFSA may be used to secure a loan without first being removed. Money held in an RRSP cannot be used in such a manner as it is intended for retirement. This represents a difference in the reasoning behind the two vehicles; the RRSP is a retirement savings vehicle and money in it should used for retirement, while the TFSA is a savings vehicle and any money held in it can be used for any reason.[5]

Pooled Registered Pension Plans

PRPPs are designed to target the self-employed and small to medium-sized businesses that have no employer-sponsored pension plan. An alternative to group RRSPs and group TFSAs, these plans are intended to be low-cost defined contribution plans that are administered by regulated financial institutions rather than by employers. The participating employers will be able to make tax-deductible contributions directly to a PRPP set up for their employees. Employees will also be able to make tax-deductible contributions, will not be taxed on employer contributions or the investment income earned thereon, and upon retirement will be able to draw annual income directly from the PRPP rather than having to roll the money into a LIF or RRIF.

As of January 1, 2013, individuals who are employed (or self-employed) in the Northwest Territories, Nunavut, or Yukon, or who work for a federally regulated employer who has agreed to participate in a PRPP, or who live in a province that has enabling legislation in place, may participate in a PRPP. Although some characteristics of the PRPP will depend on each provincial legislation, the highlights of the PRPP are as follows:

---

[5]   See Chapter 8 for more information about TFSAs.

- Employer contributions to an employee's PRPP account are not included in employment income, and, therefore, they do not generate payroll taxes as do employer contributions to group RRSPs;

- Annual employer contributions to an employee's PRPP account are limited to the employee's maximum RRSP dollar limit for that year, unless the employee directs otherwise;

- Employees may make tax-deductible voluntary contributions as long as they have remaining RRSP room after taking into consideration employer contributions, and they may continute to make contributions after they have left employment as long as they have RRSP room;

- No employer-employee relationship is required to participate in a PRPP, so there is no requirement to transfer out PRPP balances upon termination of employment;

- Employer contributions are subject to immediate vesting;

- General investment rules (similar to RPPs) apply to ensure that investments are reasonably diversified;

- Transfers between registered plans (*e.g.*, RRSP to PRPP, defined contribution to PRPP, and vice versa) are permitted;

- Decumulation options (*i.e.*, ways to withdraw money from a PRPP in retirement) include the possibility of RRIF-type payments from within the PRPP, which is currently not possible with RRSPs, as an account holder must transfer funds to a RRIF from age 71;

- A deceased PRPP member's spouse can become a successor PRPP member, or transfer the fund to his or her own account;

- Administrators of PRPPs must be regulated financial institutions, including trust companies, insurance companies, and other financial institutions with a trust subsidiary;

- The administrator has a fiduciary duty to plan members; and

- The creation of special PRPPs (designated pooled pension plans) that have fewer than 10 participating employers, or where more than half the participants work for a single employer, are contemplated by the tax rules.

Other than as mentioned above, the availability of PRPPs is subject to each jurisdiction introducing enabling legislation to implement PRPPs.[6]

---

[6]   See Chapter 30 for further discussion of PRPPs.

Employee Savings Plans

A variety of plans have been developed to assist and encourage employees to save. Savings plans are generally needed to prepare for exceptional expenditures, emergencies, periods of reduced income, or to supplement retirement income.

Savings plans may be classified according to whether the employees have an immediate entitlement to the company's contributions, or whether entitlement depends on a vesting qualification. In the latter case, the savings plan may suffer from unfavourable tax treatment, especially if it is taxed under section 144 of the ITA as an EPSP (described earlier in this chapter). In savings plans with immediate vesting, the company's allocations are ordinary income of the employee and as such are taxable. The investment income and capital gain or loss in the employee's savings account are taxed like the returns from any other investments the employee may have.

Savings plans may offer a variety of investments. Some companies encourage their employees to hold stock in the company and become shareholders in its success. In some savings plans, employees acquire unissued stock of the company and in others the company's stock is bought in the market. The plan may also make other investments available — frequently the employer will make a number of the trustee's investment funds available.

Savings plans, often called Thrift Plans, are similar to simple CAPs in the sense that contributions by an employee and by the employer are credited to an individual account, together with accumulated interest.

In a typical savings plan, the company may pay 50 cents into the savings fund for every dollar put into the fund by the employees. The employees are allowed to contribute up to a certain maximum amount. The employer's contributions vest completely in the employee in the case of death, total disability, or retirement. In the case of termination of employment, vesting may take place after a fixed number of years or on a graduated basis, depending on the employee's years of service. If the employee leaves without full vesting, the employer contributions on his or her behalf are forfeited and reallocated among remaining members.

Some savings plans provide for automatic payment out of the fund of both employer and employee contributions plus investment earnings after a fixed term of years. In nearly all savings plans, cash withdrawals are permitted at any time, up to the amount that has vested in the employee's account. Where forfeitures are reallocated, many employees elect to leave their money in the fund as long as possible so as to obtain the most benefit of such forfeitures. Distribution is made to the employee in the event of retirement or termination of employment and to the estate in the event of death.

As noted above, the tax treatment of unregistered savings plans is not particularly favourable. Many of the plans in existence are extensions of U.S. designs, adopted by Canadian subsidiaries of U.S. companies although the tax rules are different in the two countries. To improve the tax situation, some companies have registered their plans as DPSPs or have established group RRSPs or group TFSAs.

Many employers with another type of savings plan may switch to a group TFSA for the tax advantages of such plans. However, as with group RRSPs, "employer contributions" will be notional only and will, in effect, immediately vest to the employee.

Salary Deferral Arrangements

A Salary Deferral Arrangement (SDA) is defined in subsection 248(1) of the ITA as any arrangement, whether funded or not, one of the main purposes of which is the deferral of receipt of remuneration that would otherwise have been paid to an employee for services rendered in the year or in a preceding year.

Under the income tax rules, the amount of deferred salary or wages under an SDA is included in the employee's income in the year it is earned, not the year it is received. Any interest or other additional amount accrued in the year to which the employee is legally entitled under the terms of the plan is also taxable to the employee as it is earned. Amounts the employer is legally obligated to pay to the employee are tax deductible in the same year they are taxable to the employee.

The SDA rules essentially apply to current remuneration; that is, to salary, wages, or bonuses that the employee would have received for services rendered in the year but under the arrangement are paid in a subsequent year. However, there are two special exceptions to the SDA rules — one for bonus plans where employees receive their bonuses within three years after the end of the year for which the bonus is payable, and one for sabbatical leave plans. Amounts for which payment is deferred under these plans are included in the employee's income in the year it is received.

Additionally, the ITA also specifically excludes the following as SDAs:

- A registered pension plan;
- A pooled registered pension plan;
- A disability or income maintenance insurance plan under a policy with an insurance corporation;
- A deferred profit sharing plan;

- An employees profit sharing plan;
- An employee trust;
- An employee life and health trust;
- A group sickness or accident insurance plan;
- A supplementary unemployment benefit plan;
- A vacation pay trust;
- A plan or arrangement, the sole purpose of which is to provide education or training for employees of an employer to improve their work or work-related skills and abilities;
- A plan or arrangement established for the purpose of deferring the salary or wages of a professional athlete for the services of the athlete as such with a team that participates in a league having regularly scheduled games; and
- Deferred Share Units pursuant to paragraph 6801(d) of the Income Tax Act Regulations.

Prior to the introduction of the SDA rules, an Employee Benefit Plan was sometimes used to defer salary. An Employee Benefit Plan is a trust to which an employer can contribute for the benefit of employees, but which does not provide any immediate tax shelter. Non-taxable and tax-exempt employers, unconcerned by the lack of an immediate tax deduction for company contributions to the Employee Benefit Plan, used the plan as a salary deferral vehicle for their employees. The use of Employee Benefit Plans in this way has effectively been eliminated by the SDA rules.

Stock Purchase Plans

Stock purchase plans are designed to encourage a group of employees to save and invest in their company's stock. Participation is often open to the majority of employees, but can be tailor-made for executives only. The savings feature of these plans is promoted by the convenience of payroll deductions.

Participation in stock purchase plans is voluntary. A maximum is placed on the number of shares a member may buy or, more often, on the amount of money that may be applied to share purchase each month. The maximum is often related to the employee's earnings. The administrator purchases the appropriate number of shares for the account of each participating employee, usually at the current market price of the company stock. If the subscription price of the shares is less than the fair market value of the shares, the employee must pay tax on the difference. It is deemed to be a benefit by virtue of employment and is therefore taxed in the same manner as the employee's salary. The amount of the taxable benefit is added to the adjusted cost base of the shares. Once the shares have been purchased, the dividends are taxable and realized appreciation or depreciation will be treated for tax purposes in the same way as other capital gains or losses.

Some companies grant low-interest or interest-free loans to employees so that they may buy shares under the stock purchase plan. The ITA provides that if the loan is interest-free, or bears interest at a rate below a prescribed rate, the difference will be a taxable benefit. However, this taxable benefit can be offset in the case of a share purchase loan, because the employee can deduct the imputed interest expense on money borrowed for investment purposes.

Stock Option Plans

Companies grant stock options for three main reasons:

- As incentives for employees to increase the company's profitability and thus raise the price of its shares;
- As a method to retain key employees by creating an opportunity cost if they were to leave employment (assuming the proper vesting conditions, *i.e.*, the right to exercise the optioned shares at, for example, 20% per year); and
- As a method of compensating employees that is more tax-effective than straight salary increases.

Because stock options provide employees with some of the satisfaction derived from ownership of the company (the opportunity of capital gains, dividends and voting rights), they are often established to attract the talent needed by the company, hold experienced staff, or serve as production incentives for senior or middle management.

Under a stock option plan, eligible employees are given options to buy specified amounts of the capital stock of a company (or an affiliated company) at a price fixed on the day the option is granted. The employee is usually given a period of up to 10 years during which the option may be exercised. For publicly traded corporations, the exercise price may not be lower than the market price of the share on the day the option is granted. Alternatively, a reasonable pre-determined formula, based on a weighted average trading price, or an average of daily high and low board lot trading prices for a short period of time prior to the time of grant is acceptable.

The employee obviously gains if, during the period before he or she exercises the option, the company's stock increases in value. The terms of the stock option plan will define the number of shares to be optioned, the class of employees eligible, the last date for exercising the options, the exercise price, and other details. The board of directors or a committee appointed by the board will award the options to individual employees.

Specific approval of the company's shareholders may be required to implement a stock option plan. The board of directors may have the right, under the company's articles of incorporation, to sell or option unissued capital stock without such approval. However, because the exercise of stock options results in a dilution of shareholders' equity, prior approval of the shareholders is often necessary. Applicable securities legislation and stock exchange requirements must also be considered.

Phantom Stock Plans

Phantom stock plans or Deferred Share Unit (DSU) plans under paragraph 6801(d) of the ITA Regulations are bonus or incentive plans where the amount of the bonus is determined by reference to the value of the company's stock. Under a phantom stock plan, the account of each participant is credited with a specific number of notional shares, although no share transaction actually takes place. The account may also be credited with amounts equivalent to the dividends paid and the capital appreciation on the notional holding of company stock. The value of the member's account is either paid out in cash currently or accumulated until death, termination, or retirement.

The main advantage of a phantom stock plan is that the executive is taxed and the company can take a tax deduction when the benefit is actually paid.

The disadvantage of such a plan is that the executive does not obtain capital gains treatment, nor can the executive take advantage of fluctuations in the market by trading the "stock". The disadvantage to the company is that if the stock increases in value quickly, the benefit can be very expensive, since it will be paid in cash rather than being absorbed by the market.

A share appreciation right plan is similar to a stock option plan except that the value of the phantom shares is paid after a specified time and not at the executive's discretion when shares are vested.

Like a stock option plan, a share appreciation right plan provides access to participate in increases in the value of the shares of the corporation.

Restricted Shares and Performance Shares

As stock option plans have been increasingly criticized by shareholder groups, many companies have started to grant restricted shares in lieu of stock options or in combination with smaller stock option grants.

Under restricted share plans, companies grant a certain number of company shares to the executive usually with a two-year vesting period. The rationale for such plan is that the executive then shares the same risks and opportunities as other shareholders. In contrast, stock options provide potential gains to the executive with no downside risk.

A common criticism of restricted shares is that the executive receives the full value of the restricted shares after two years even if the shareholders' return during that period is unsatisfactory, non-existent, or negative.

An alternative to the restricted share is the performance share, which is the same except that the number of shares allocated to the executive or the vesting of these shares depends upon the achievement of certain corporate or individual objectives.

Chapter 15

WINDING UP A PENSION PLAN

Executive Summary[1]

"Winding up" of a pension plan means the disposition of all pension liabilities through either the purchase of annuities, lump-sum transfers, or surplus withdrawals by the employer/sponsor. Pension plans (subject to collective bargaining) may be wound up voluntarily by an employer, and the wind-up may involve all or only part of the pension plan ("partial wind-up"). Regulatory authorities may, under prescribed circumstances, order the wind-up of a pension plan in whole or in part, and may appoint a replacement administrator to complete the process. Plan beneficiaries affected by the wind-up may enjoy certain statutory rights such as grow-in or surplus entitlement, and the wind-up may result in new funding obligations on the employer/plan sponsor. Where a plan sponsor is insolvent and the pension plan is underfunded, a wind-up may result in plan members receiving reduced benefits. Some jurisdictions have special provisions (e.g., the Pension Benefits Guarantee Fund in Ontario and the Retraite transfer in Quebec) that may ameliorate underfunding for plan members.

Introduction

The terms "plan termination" and "wind-up" are often used interchangeably. However, their technical meaning is distinct. The termination of a pension plan results in members ceasing to accrue further pension benefits. The wind-up process involves the disposition of the pension fund assets, including the settlement of pension benefits for the members, former members and other persons, such as beneficiaries who have entitlements under the plan.

---

[1] For more information on pension plan wind-ups, please consult the multi-jurisdictional charts in the *Canadian Employment Benefits & Pension Guide*. Morneau Shepell, *Canadian Employment Benefits & Pension Guide*, loose-leaf (Toronto: LexisNexis Canada, 2003). The table of contents for these charts appears at the back of this Handbook.

The termination and winding up of a pension plan is a complex process subject to a myriad of legislative requirements. The wind-up of a defined benefit pension plan involving the ownership and distribution of any surplus assets can be an especially complex and lengthy process. If a pension plan that is being wound up faces a deficit, the sponsoring employer will be required to fund it. If the sponsoring employer is insolvent, members and pensioners may have to contend with reduced benefits.

A pension plan may be wound up voluntarily by an employer, or in some circumstances the plan administrator, or by order of the regulator under whose jurisdiction the plan is registered. Once the initial decision or order to wind-up the pension plan has been made, the wind-up process is broadly the same in the various jurisdictions.

A pension plan is not considered to be fully wound up until the employer, plan sponsor, regulator, or regulator-appointed administrator has satisfied all of the legislative requirements, received approval from the applicable regulatory authority, where relevant, and has disposed of all of the pension fund assets, including the settlement of pension benefits to plan members.

This chapter explores the various scenarios under which a plan wind-up may be initiated, the process for wind-up, member entitlements, and employer and plan administrator obligations.

Statutory

Although the terms "plan termination" and "wind-up" are often used interchangeably, the technical meaning under the pension legislation in various jurisdictions can be quite distinct.

In Ontario, a "wind-up" is defined as the "termination of a pension plan and the distribution of assets of the pension fund." New Brunswick and Nova Scotia have similar, if not exact, definitions. In other jurisdictions, such as the federal jurisdiction, Alberta, British Columbia, and Newfoundland and Labrador, the terms "termination" and "wind-up" are defined separately. A pension plan may be considered "terminated" in certain circumstances, such as when the plan's registration is revoked, there is a cessation of the crediting of benefits, or the regulator declares a termination. In these jurisdictions, a "winding up" is said to occur when there is a distribution of the assets of a plan that is terminated.

Manitoba uses the terms "termination" and "winding up" interchangeably. Saskatchewan, on the other hand, simply refers to plan terminations.

Partial Plan Wind-Up

A pension plan can be partially terminated. The partial termination of a pension plan involves the settlement of the pension benefits of a specific group of plan members.

Partial pension plan terminations are normally the result of the sale or discontinuance of a part of the employer's business operations or a significant reduction in plan membership resulting from employee terminations and lay-offs.

All jurisdictions, except Quebec (as of January 1, 2001), Prince Edward Island (to be proclaimed), Ontario (as of July 1, 2012), Alberta (as of September 1, 2014) and British Columbia (as of September 30, 2015) permit partial plan terminations. Under federal pension legislation, employers are not permitted to declare partial plan terminations.

In Nova Scotia, a "partial wind-up" means the termination of a part of a pension plan and the distribution of the assets of the pension fund related to that part of the plan. With certain exceptions, those jurisdictions that permit partial terminations provide that the same rights be given to affected members as would have been given under a full plan wind-up.

Who Can Terminate a Pension Plan?

Employer Initiated Wind-Up

Pension legislation in all jurisdictions generally permits an employer to declare the wind-up of a pension plan. Legislation does not require that specific grounds or reasons exist for such a declaration to be made. This unrestricted discretion is, of course, subject to any obligations under a collective agreement governing the pension plan or any contractual obligation stemming from a corporate transaction in which the continuation of the pension plan for a certain period of time is a requirement. In addition, the documents that create and support the pension plan, such as the plan text, must specifically provide that the plan sponsor, usually through the board of directors, has the right to terminate the plan.

An employer may initiate a wind-up for a number of reasons, including where they are a party to a purchase or sale of a business and the purchaser does not provide a pension plan or refuses to take on the existing pension obligation, or they have undertaken an internal reorganization under which the pension plan is no longer a priority, or the plan has significant surplus that the plan sponsor is looking to distribute.

Administrator Initiated Wind-Up

In the case of a multi-employer pension plan (MEPP), the plan administrator has the right to wind-up a pension plan. In the case of jointly sponsored pension plans (JPSP), whether they are MEPPs or not, the plan administrator has the authority to wind-up the pension plan unless the documents that create and support the plan authorize another person or entity to do so.[2]

Under federal legislation, a plan administrator also has the right to terminate a single employer pension plan. In Alberta, British Columbia, and Saskatchewan, the right to declare a plan termination or wind-up is specifically conferred on the plan administrator.

Regulator Initiated Wind-Up

Pension legislation in all Canadian jurisdictions provides the relevant regulatory authority with the ability to order the wind-up of a pension plan, in whole, and sometimes in part (in jurisdictions where a partial wind-up is permitted), in a number of prescribed circumstances. These circumstances include:

- Cessation or suspension of employer contributions (all jurisdictions);
- Cessation of accrual (New Brunswick, Ontario)
- Discontinuance of all or a part of the business of the employer (all jurisdictions);
- Failure to meet prescribed solvency tests (Manitoba, Newfoundland and Labrador, and federal only);
- Employer bankruptcy (New Brunswick, Newfoundland and Labrador, Nova Scotia, and Ontario only);
- Failure to comply with pension legislation (Manitoba, New Brunswick, and Quebec only);
- Sale of the business to an employer who does not provide a pension plan for the affected employees (Alberta, New Brunswick, Newfoundland and Labrador, Nova Scotia, Ontario, and Saskatchewan only); and
- Where a wind-up is in the best interests of members (Alberta and British Columbia).

---

[2]   The wind-up of a MEPP or JPSP is addressed in Chapter 11.

Ontario also permits the Superintendent of Financial Services to order a wind-up where "the liability of the Guarantee Fund is likely to be substantially increased unless the pension plan is wound up". The Pension Benefits Guarantee Fund is discussed in greater detail below. The Ontario Superintendent may also order a wind-up where there are no active members.

The most common reason for the issuance of a regulator-initiated partial wind-up order has been the discontinuance of a significant part of the employer's business, and the most common reason for the issue of a full wind-up order has been the bankruptcy of the employer/plan sponsor. Employee groups have traditionally demanded that regulators issue partial wind-up orders in circumstances where pension plans have significant surplus and a partial wind-up would require the distribution of a negotiated portion of that surplus to the affected members. British Columbia and Alberta have recently joined Ontario and Quebec in eliminating partial wind-ups. If other provinces follow suit, partial wind-up orders should become relatively rare. However, Nova Scotia, in its recent updating of pension legislation, has decided to continue to allow partial wind-ups.

Where a wind-up order is issued on the initiative of the regulator, the administrator of the pension plan or the employer (if the employer is the administrator) is required to wind-up the plan in the same way as in an employer-initiated wind-up.

Member Initiated Wind-Up

In light of the Supreme Court of Canada's decision in *Rogers Communications Inc. v. Buschau*, it is generally understood that employees, as members/beneficiaries of a pension plan, cannot initiate a pension plan wind-up based on general trust law principles. Consequently, if the desire of members is to be acted upon, they will inevitably have to convince the plan sponsor or, where appropriate, the administrator or regulator that there are reasons or grounds for a wind-up as described above.

Wind-Up Process

Introduction

While the decision to initiate a plan wind-up may be made by an employer or, in the case of a MEPP or JPSP the plan administrator, the entity or person charged with executing the wind-up process is typically the plan administrator, whether it be, in the case of single employer pension plans, the employer in its capacity as plan administrator or, in the case of a MEPP or JPSP, the same entity that made the initial decision.

Replacement Administrator

In some circumstances the employer is either unwilling or incapable of completing the wind-up that has been ordered by the regulator (or more specifically, the "Superintendent"). Pension legislation in all jurisdictions provides that the Superintendent may either act as the replacement administrator or (more commonly) appoint a replacement administrator. In most jurisdictions, the appointment of a replacement administrator can only be made in circumstances where the pension plan is to be wound up, although some jurisdictions (e.g., Alberta) provide for temporary replacement administrators of on-going plans if it is in the best interests of the members and the other persons entitled or potentially entitled to benefits.

The regulatory filings that a replacement administrator must make are essentially the same as those that must be made under an employer-initiated wind-up (e.g., application for a wind-up order, filing of a wind-up valuation, etc.). Most jurisdictions (for example, Ontario and Manitoba) prohibit the making of payments from a pension plan where the Superintendent has ordered the wind-up of the plan until the Superintendent has approved the wind-up order, other than ongoing pension payments, without the approval of the Superintendent. Because wind-ups undertaken with a replacement administrator typically take significantly longer to complete than employer-initiated wind-ups, replacement administrators will typically request the approval of the Superintendent to start new pensions pending the filing and approval of the wind-up report.

Replacement administrators are typically appointed in circumstances where the employer is either bankrupt under the *Bankruptcy and Insolvency Act* or has obtained protection from its creditors under the *Companies' Creditors Arrangement Act* and it appears unlikely that the pension plan will be maintained. The steps undertaken by the replacement administrator will depend on whether the pension plan being wound up is in a surplus or a deficit position. If the plan is in surplus, then the replacement administrator will be required to determine surplus entitlement and enable the employer (or the estate of the employer, if bankrupt) to initiate a surplus sharing agreement with plan beneficiaries, as appropriate depending on the surplus rules applicable in the province or jurisdiction.

The recent Supreme Court of Canada decision in *Indalex Ltd. (Re)*[3] indicates that there may be circumstances where the employer as administrator of an on-going plan finds itself in a conflict of interest, suggesting that in such circumstances an independent replacement administrator may be appropriate.

Wind-Up Date

A pension plan that is being wound up, in whole or in part, must have an "effective wind-up date". In the case of a regulator initiated wind-up, the regulator will determine the wind-up date, usually based on a recommendation made by the appointed administrator.

In the case of an employer or administrator initiated wind-up, subject to certain requirements, the effective date is left to the discretion of the appropriate entity. In Ontario, New Brunswick, Nova Scotia, and Quebec, the effective date of a wind-up, in the case of a contributory plan, cannot be earlier than the date member contributions cease to be deducted. In Ontario, New Brunswick, and Nova Scotia, the effective date for non-contributory plans is not earlier than the date notice is given to members. In Quebec, for non-contributory plans, the effective date cannot be more than 30 days before the date on which the notice of termination is given to the active members. Generally speaking, the regulator retains the authority to change the effective date of the wind-up if the regulator is of the opinion that there are reasonable grounds for the change.

In the federal jurisdiction, Alberta, British Columbia, Manitoba, and Newfoundland and Labrador, the employer or administrator also has discretion to set the effective date of plan termination or winding up subject to certain jurisdiction-specific notification requirements, which may affect the date that is ultimately chosen. Under federal pension legislation, the Superintendent must be advised of the termination or winding up no less than 60 days and not more than 180 days before the effective date. In Alberta and British Columbia, the administrator must notify the appropriate regulator at least 60 days before the intended termination or commencement of winding up or, if the intended date is within 60 days of the decision, immediately after the decision has been made. In Manitoba, the effective date of the termination or wind-up cannot be earlier than the date the regulator is advised of the intention. In Newfoundland and Labrador, the regulator must be advised at least 60 days prior to the date of termination and the wind-up of the plan is to

---

3   [2013] S.C.J. No. 6, 2013 SCC 6 (S.C.C.).

commence immediately after the date of termination unless the regulator provides written approval to postpone the commencement of the wind-up.

Saskatchewan is unique in that while the administrator also has discretion to declare a plan termination, there are no specific time requirements for when the regulator must be notified apart from the fact that the notice must be provided immediately after the decision has been made.

Wind-Up Period

As noted earlier in this chapter, partial plan wind-ups or terminations involve the settlement of pension benefits for a specific group of plan members and are normally the result of a particular employer activity that occurs over a period of time, such as a sale or discontinuance or a significant reduction in plan membership. Consequently, in addition to a wind-up date, a partial plan wind-up, and at times a full wind-up, necessitates the determination of a wind-up period — a period that has a commencement date and an end date. The commencement date is generally the date on which the particular employer activity that triggers the partial or full plan wind-up begins; this date may be discernible from public announcements made by the employer in regards to the reorganization or restructuring, discontinuance, or other activity. Other indicators may be the date of a board resolution that approves the commencement of an activity or the date the employer actually initiates certain actions, such as significant lay-offs, in order to give effect to the intended activity. The end date will typically be the date on which the activity comes to a close. In the case of a full wind-up, the end date may be the date of bankruptcy or insolvency, when the attempted restructuring is unsuccessful.

Wind-Up Notice

All jurisdictions require that written notice of the wind-up, full or partial, must be given by employers or plan administrators to a number of parties including, as the jurisdiction requires, members, former members, unions that represent members, other plan beneficiaries or any other person entitled to payment from the plan, plan advisory committees, if any, and, as alluded to above, the appropriate regulator. The chart below summarizes the requirements by jurisdiction.

Jurisdiction	Who Should Receive Notice
Alberta	Members, former members, deceased members' survivors, pension partners or designated beneficiary, trade unions representing the members, and the regulator.
British Columbia	Members, former members, the union representing members, other plan beneficiaries and any other person entitled to payment from the plan, and the regulator.
Manitoba	Members, former members, other plan beneficiaries and any other person entitled to payment from the plan, and the regulator within 60 days of the decision.
New Brunswick	Members, former members, the union representing members, other plan beneficiaries and any other person entitled to payment from the plan, the plan advisory committee, and the regulator.
Newfoundland and Labrador	The regulator and any other person or body affected by the proposed wind-up.
Nova Scotia	Members, former members, the union representing members, other plan beneficiaries and any other person entitled to payment from the plan, any plan advisory committee, and the regulator. But, notice of proposal of partial wind-up is not required for those who will not be affected.
Ontario	Members, former members, retired members (as of July 1, 2012), the union representing members, other plan beneficiaries and any other person entitled to payment from the plan, any plan advisory committee, and the regulator.
Quebec	Members, former members, the union representing members, other plan beneficiaries and any other person entitled to payment from the plan, the regulator, the pension administration committee, and insurer (where applicable).

Jurisdiction	Who Should Receive Notice
Saskatchewan	Members, former members, and the regulator.
Federal	Members, former members and their spouses and common-law partners, and the regulator. Notice to members, former members, and their spouses and common-law partners is required within 30 days.

The content of a wind-up notice will vary by jurisdiction and must be provided regardless of whether the wind-up is employer or administrator-initiated or by order of the regulator. In Ontario, for example, the wind-up notice must include the name of the plan and its provincial registration number; the proposed wind-up date; a statement that each member, former member, or any other person entitled to a pension, deferred pension, any other benefit, or a refund will be provided with an individual statement setting out entitlements and options under the pension plan; and where a plan provides contributory benefits, a notice of the member's right to make contributions in respect of the period of notice of termination of employment required under the *Employment Standards Act*.

New Brunswick, Newfoundland and Labrador, and Nova Scotia are similar to Ontario in what they require to be included in a wind-up notice. In addition, in New Brunswick, the notice must also advise that a wind-up report will be filed with the regulator and be available for viewing and comment 30 days before any disbursement of funds is approved.

In British Columbia, Alberta and Manitoba, the wind-up notice must simply give the effective date of termination or start of the winding up. In Saskatchewan, the notice must advise of the intention to terminate the plan and the proposed date of the termination.

In Ontario, when the Superintendent has issued a Notice of Intended Decision to require the wind-up of a pension plan, such decision together with written reasons must be served upon the plan administrator and employer, and the Superintendent may require the administrator to transmit a copy of the Notice and reasons to such persons (usually the plan members or a representative union) as specified in the Notice.

Wind-Up Report

In all jurisdictions, when a pension plan is wound up, in whole or in part, the plan administrator will be required to file a wind-up report, typically prepared by an actuary, with the appropriate regulator. In certain circumstances, such as if the plan is a defined contribution pension plan or fully insured, the federal jurisdiction as well as British Columbia, Alberta, Saskatchewan, Ontario, Quebec, and Nova Scotia allow certain designated individuals to prepare the wind-up report.

A wind-up report must reflect the terms of the pension plan as well as the pension legislation that governs the plan. Pension legislation specifically identifies what must be included in the report. Generally, all jurisdictions require that a wind-up report indicate the nature of the benefits to be provided to members, former members, retired members, and other persons, the assets and liabilities of the plan, the method(s) for allocation and distribution of plan assets, and the priorities for determining payment of benefits. Depending upon the jurisdiction, additional information may be required as prescribed in the regulations to the pension legislation or as mandated by the appropriate regulator. In addition to the legislative requirements summarized above, each regulator may require additional information as stipulated in their respective policies and guidelines.

If a wind-up report discloses a surplus, the administrator will be required to indicate how the surplus will be dealt with. If this is not provided, a regulator may require a supplemental report dealing specifically with the surplus assets.

The timing for the filing of a wind-up report by jurisdiction is summarized below.

Jurisdiction	Timing of Filing
Alberta & British Columbia	• Within 60 days of the effective date of the wind-up, if the plan does not contain any benefit formula provisions, and within 120 days otherwise.
Manitoba	• Within 6 months of the termination of the plan
New Brunswick	• Within 6 months after effective date of wind-up.
Newfoundland and Labrador	• Within 6 months after the effective date of wind-up.

Jurisdiction	Timing of Filing
Nova Scotia	• Within 6 months after the effective date of wind-up.
Ontario	• Within 6 months after the effective date of wind-up.
Quebec	• Within 90 days of receipt of the regulator's decision to terminate the plan or a decision relating to a notice of termination.
Saskatchewan	• Within 60 days after termination of the plan or within any longer period of time that may be fixed by the regulator.
Federal	• On the termination of the plan or part of the plan.

A regulator has the authority to refuse to approve a wind-up report that fails to comply with the pension legislation that governs the plan. A regulator also has the power to require that a new report be prepared. Generally speaking, if a regulator refuses to approve a wind-up report or to approve a report against the objections of employees, the administrator, employees, or any other affected party, may have the decision of the regulator reviewed by a tribunal or other adjudicative body as the respective pension legislation permits.

Wind-Up Statement

As a general rule, all Canadian jurisdictions require that plan administrators give each employee entitled to a pension, deferred pension, refund of contributions, or other benefit payable upon the wind-up of the pension plan, a statement that contains the same information as required in a retirement or termination statement, as applicable, under the applicable pension legislation. This information would include the employee's entitlement under the plan and the options available to the employee.

In Alberta, British Columbia, New Brunswick, Newfoundland and Labrador, Nova Scotia, Ontario, and Saskatchewan, the statement must provide information on the reduction of benefits due to a funding deficiency or disposition of surplus, if applicable. In Alberta, the statement must also include information on any other rights and options the member or former member may have. The regulations in Ontario and Quebec provide very specific requirements as to what must be contained in the member statements, which are beyond the scope of this chapter. Under federal pension legislation, the statement of member's pension and other benefits must be in a form prescribed under the regulations.

If an employee is entitled or required to make an election in relation to his or her pension benefits, that election must be made within a specified period of time. In Ontario, Nova Scotia, and New Brunswick, for example, the employee must inform the administrator of the election within 90 days after receiving the wind-up statement.

In turn, a plan administrator is required to act on the election made by the employee and make the necessary pension payment within a specified period of time. Again, in Ontario, New Brunswick and Nova Scotia, the administrator must discharge the benefits within 60 days after the later of the date that the administrator receives the employee's election and the date the administrator receives notice that the regulator has approved the wind-up report. In Ontario, if the employee does not make an election, the administration must discharge the benefits by annuity purchase within 60 days from the date the employee was deemed to have made the election.

Wind-Up Comes to an End

The process that must be undertaken to wind-up a pension plan comes to an end when all plan assets have been distributed from the pension fund and the plan administrator has, in writing, advised the appropriate regulator and the Canada Revenue Agency of this fact.

Member Entitlements

When a partial or full plan wind-up occurs, affected plan members gain special rights by virtue of the applicable pension legislation. This section of the chapter highlights the various aspects of member entitlement.

Partial Plan Wind-Ups

Except for Quebec, Ontario, British Columbia, Alberta and Prince Edward Island, where partial plan wind-ups are not permitted, all jurisdictions specifically provide that plan members affected by a partial plan wind-up are entitled to the same rights and benefits as if a full wind-up had occurred on the effective date of the partial wind-up. In Manitoba, this general rule does not apply to a multi-unit pension plan.

Immediate Vesting

Most jurisdictions generally require that members be fully vested in their pension benefits accrued to the termination or wind-up date regardless of age, service, or length of membership or the vesting provisions provided under the individual pension plan. As a consequence, an employee will become entitled to a deferred pension. This protection is of no consequence in the federal jurisdiction, Manitoba, Quebec, Ontario, and Nova Scotia where vesting is immediate upon initial plan membership.

Portability

Alberta, British Columbia, New Brunswick, Newfoundland and Labrador, Nova Scotia, Ontario, and Saskatchewan specifically provide, subject to certain restrictions, for active members to transfer the commuted value of their pension benefits on the termination or wind-up of a pension plan to a locked-in vehicle. The same transfer options are provided that are available for locked-in funds upon an individual member's termination, as described in Chapter 9. Furthermore, in the context of a wind-up or termination, these portability rights are also available to a member who is eligible for the receipt of an immediate pension.

Other than in Quebec, pensioners are not entitled to portability. In this case, the plan administrator must purchase a life annuity that represents the amount of the pension from an insurance company. In Quebec, pensioners have the option to take a lump-sum transfer or have an annuity purchased to provide their pension benefits.

50 Per cent Rule

As noted in Chapter 9, the 50% rule is a standard applicable to contributory defined benefit pension plans. In jurisdictions other than New Brunswick, the rule states that the employer must pay for at least 50% of a member's pension entitlement. In New Brunswick, the plan may set a percentage different than 50%. The 50% rule applies when the plan is ongoing and when the plan is terminated or wound up.

Grow-In

The legislation in some jurisdictions includes provisions relating to early retirement in the context of a plan wind-up. Legislation in Nova Scotia and Ontario also requires that certain members be given "grow-in" rights. Eligible members are those whose age plus years of employment equal 55 or more. They are entitled to receive the following:

- An immediate pension in accordance with the terms of the pension plan, if eligible under the plan;

- A pension in accordance with the terms of the plan to begin at the earlier of:

- o   The plan's normal retirement date, or
- o   The date the member would have been entitled to an actuarially unreduced pension if the plan had not wound up and if membership had continued; and
- • An actuarially reduced pension in the amount payable under the plan and commencing on the date the member would have been entitled to a reduced pension, if the member's membership had continued to that date.

These "grow-in" rights are significant for pension plans that provide generous early retirement benefits, such as an unreduced pension at a specified age prior to normal retirement age. Eligible members also grow into bridge benefits, if they have at least 10 years of employment or plan membership at the date of the plan wind-up.

It should also be noted that the federal regulator, OSFI, interprets the provisions of the *Pension Benefits Standards Act, 1985*, and in particular the definition of "pensionable age", to require a form of grow-in as well.

Distribution of Plan Assets

A regulator must approve a wind-up report before any distribution of plan assets can occur. This requirement is especially important where the pension plan that is being terminated or wound up has insufficient assets to fully cover all plan benefits. That being said, regulators will generally permit pensions or any other benefits that were in-pay before the notice of proposal to wind-up the pension plan to continue to be paid pending the approval of the wind-up report.

Furthermore, despite the restriction, regulators do have the discretion to approve a payment prior to the approval of the wind-up report.

Surplus

Where a defined benefit pension plan is fully terminated, there may be surplus assets in the pension fund. When a plan is fully terminated, surplus represents the value of any excess pension fund assets, i.e., assets not needed to pay or settle all benefits. For partial plan terminations, pension standards legislation requires that the surplus attributable to the part of the plan being terminated be identified in the wind-up valuation report.

The Supreme Court of Canada in *Monsanto* decided that, under Ontario pension legislation, surplus must be distributed when a partial wind-up occurs. Note that the *Monsanto* case was decided before Ontario eliminated partial wind-ups but may still be applicable to partial wind-ups in Ontario that occurred before July 1, 2012, and to partial wind-ups in jurisdictions that permit them and have surplus entitlement language similar to that contained in Ontario's legislation.

The full termination of a pension plan that is in a surplus position will require the assessment of surplus rights in order for the assets to be fully distributed. It is always possible for the employer to pay surplus to members, either as benefit improvements (subject to maximums imposed by the *Income Tax Act*) or as cash payments, provided that the plan contains provisions that specify how this will be done (or is amended to so provide). If the employer wishes to withdraw the surplus, the consent of the regulatory authority is required. Generally this consent cannot be given unless the employer is entitled to withdraw the surplus according to the plan terms, but some jurisdictions permit the employer and the members in the plan to reach an agreement as to how the surplus will be distributed, despite the plan provisions.[4]

Multi-Jurisdictional Plans

Pension plans with members in more than one Canadian jurisdiction can pose unique challenges in the context of a wind-up or termination particularly because the rights available to employees typically vary by jurisdiction. For example, Ontario members have the protection of the Pension Benefits Guarantee Fund where the plan has insufficient assets to pay benefits in full. Furthermore, only Ontario and Nova Scotia offer grow-in to their members. In addition, the right to a distribution of surplus on partial plan wind-up is not available in all jurisdictions.

Since 1968, the regulatory authorities across Canada operated under the Memorandum of Reciprocal Agreement (Memorandum). This Memorandum provided that a plan was to be registered in the jurisdiction where it had a plurality of active membership. While the laws of that jurisdiction were viewed as applying to the operation of the plan, member benefit entitlements were determined according to the member's jurisdiction of employment. However, if a member worked in several jurisdictions during their membership in the plan, there was an ongoing debate over whether the member's benefit entitlement should be based on the member's last jurisdiction of employment (called the "final location approach") or on distinct periods of service in different jurisdictions (called the "checkerboard" approach). Under the final location approach, the laws of the jurisdiction in which the member terminated employment

---

[4]   For further discussion respecting surplus issues, please refer to Chapter 9.

applied to all pension credits earned throughout the employee's career with the employer. Under the checkerboard approach on termination of employment, each period during which pension credits were earned would be subject to the jurisdiction in which the employee reported to work at the time. Whereas most jurisdictions favoured the final location approach, Ontario favoured the checkerboard approach.

In 2008, the Canadian Association of Pension Supervisory Authorities (CAPSA) released a draft agreement, called the Agreement Respecting Multi-Jurisdictional Pension Plans (MJPP Agreement), which had the unanimous support of the pension regulators. Upon adoption by each jurisdiction, the MJPP Agreement would replace the Memorandum. Amongst other things, the MJPP Agreement formally adopts the final location approach for the determination of benefits. In addition, it defines rules for the allocation of assets among jurisdictions. For example, in the event of a plan wind-up, the assets would be allocated among jurisdictions based on rules that set out an order of priority. In general terms, the order of priority, from highest to lowest, would be:

- Voluntary or optional contributions;
- Core liabilities (lifetime benefits including related death benefits and indexation);
- All other benefits that are required to be funded by legislation;
- All other benefits that are not required to be funded; and
- Any remaining assets.

Once assets have been allocated among jurisdictions, the distribution to each individual member would be in accordance with the pension legislation in that member's jurisdiction.

Ontario, Quebec, British Columbia, Nova Scotia and Saskatchewan all signed the MJPP Agreement and, as of July 1, 2012, its terms applied to the extent that the plan is registered in one of these provinces and the plan has members in at least two of these provinces. If a plan was registered in a jurisdiction that had not yet signed the MJPP Agreement, but had members in jurisdictions that had signed the MJPP Agreement, the MJPP Agreement would not apply. If a plan is registered in a jurisdiction that had signed the MJPP Agreement, but it had members in a jurisdiction that had not, the MJPP Agreement would not apply to the non-signing jurisdiction. Where the MJPP Agreement did not apply, the Memorandum would have continued to apply.

On June 2, 2016, CAPSA announced that representatives of the governments of British Columbia, Nova Scotia, Ontario, Quebec and Saskatchewan had signed a new interim Agreement Respecting Multi-Jurisdictional Pension Plans, which came into effect for these jurisdictions on July 1, 2016 (2016 MJPP Agreement). This 2016 MJPP Agreement will be effective in these jurisdictions until a further revised version is released by CAPSA sometime after 2018, and then signed by applicable Canadian pension jurisdictions.

According to CAPSA, the 2016 MJPP Agreement was negotiated as an interim measure while CAPSA coordinates amendments to the agreement that will address the changing solvency funding regimes across Canadian pension jurisdictions. After CAPSA conducts a public consultation, Canadian pension jurisdictions are expected to enter into a further revised agreement. In the meantime, the Memorandum will remain in effect for those provinces which have not signed the 2016 MJPP Agreement, and all similar bilateral federal-provincial agreements will continue in effect.

Employer's Liability on Wind-Up

All jurisdictions in Canada, except Saskatchewan, now require the employer, in circumstances where a pension plan is wound up and there are insufficient funds to fully provide all member benefits, to fund any deficiency over a period of no more than five years. Saskatchewan requires that the employer fund all payments required under its pension legislation or the plan that have accrued to the date of wind-up (whether or not due) including all amounts that are due from the employer but not yet paid, like most of the other jurisdictions. However, only if the plan terminates during the temporary three-year solvency relief period, and there is a solvency deficiency identified in the termination report, will the employer be required to pay the solvency deficiency in a lump sum or for a period not more than five years from the review date. There are some circumstances in which this requirement does not apply.

Underfunded Plans

Where a plan does not have sufficient assets to pay all pensions, deferred pensions, or ancillary benefits, replacement administrators will undertake a review of the funded status of the plan and reduce benefits to a level that the plan can sustain.

The general rule for the payment of pension benefits in the event a pension plan is terminated while underfunded is that payments are made in the following order:

- All member contributions (whether required, voluntary, or transferred in from another plan) are paid first;

- All accrued benefits for which there is no remaining unfunded liability are paid next; and then
- All accrued benefits for which there is a remaining unfunded liability are paid.

A number of jurisdictions (New Brunswick, Nova Scotia, Ontario, and Quebec) provide that Additional Voluntary Contributions are refunded first. Subject to the above priorities, most jurisdictions specify that remaining benefits are to be paid *pro rata* depending on the funded status of the plan; however, British Columbia permits plans to specify the priority in which benefits are paid (e.g., paid to retirees first, then to deferred members) in the event the plan has insufficient assets to pay all benefits. Ontario provides that, in circumstances where the Pension Benefits Guarantee Fund (PBGF) applies to a plan, all prospective indexation increases are eliminated unless all non-indexed benefits are fully funded.

Quebec provides that benefit improvements made within five years of the date of termination are only paid to the extent that they have been funded by special payments. Quebec further provides that lay-off-related benefits are only paid if all other benefits are fully funded.

Pension Benefits Guarantee Fund

Ontario is the only Canadian jurisdiction that maintains a guarantee fund in the event that a pension plan is terminated and there are insufficient assets to fund accrued benefits.

The PBGF was established in Ontario in 1980 and is administered by the Superintendent of Financial Services. It is funded by a levy imposed on employers with pension plans whose members are subject to the PBGF guarantee. There are two components to the PBGF levy. The "basic" levy is a flat $5 per eligible beneficiary — this was increased effective January 1, 2012, from a flat $1 levy per Ontario employee. The "risk" component of the levy is a percentage of the plan's last reported solvency deficiency — which is 0.5% of any solvency deficiency between 90% and 100%, 1% of any deficiency between 80%-90%, and 1.5% of any deficiency under 80%. The maximum levy can be no greater than $300 per member.

Grossly simplified, the PBGF guarantees the first $1,000 per month in pension benefits that were earned in respect of employment in Ontario. The level of the benefit guarantee has remained unchanged since 1980.

As an example, if a plan is 60% funded, a member either receiving or entitled to receive a pension of $2,000 per month will receive $1,200 per month from the pension plan, but will receive an additional $400 per month from the PBGF to reflect the fact that he or she is receiving only 60% of the first $1,000 of his or her entitlement from the plan.

The PBGF applies fully to all pensioners and to all deferred or active members whose age plus service equals 60, and partially applies to those whose age plus service exceeds 50. Members whose age plus years of service are less than 50 receive no coverage. Certain benefits are not subject to the PBGF guarantee, including benefit improvements granted within the last five years, and prospective indexation increases (which, as noted above, are eliminated for Ontario service when the PBGF applies to a plan).[5]

Insolvent Wind-Ups — Quebec

Quebec has instituted rules that enable those plan retirees receiving a pension as of the wind-up date from the underfunded pension plans of bankrupt or insolvent employers to transfer their pension entitlement to the custody of Retraite Québec. The Retraite will continue to pay pensions at the same reduced funded ratio as was supported by the plan and invest the money in a portfolio that includes a level of risk (i.e., by investing in equities or accepting liability mismatches). The Retraite Québec will hold these funds for up to ten years and, if there is sufficient excess investment income, increase pension payments. When first introduced, the legislation provided that if there are investment losses, pensions would not be reduced and the Province of Quebec would make up any shortfall, however recent changes eliminate the guarantee against pension reductions in the event of poor investment experience. After ten years, the Retraite Québec will settle retiree benefits.

Claims Against the Bankrupt Estate of the Employer

Pension legislation in all Canadian jurisdictions provides that the employer is liable to fully fund pension benefits on plan wind-up. As such, the appointed administrator of an underfunded pension plan that is being wound up has a claim against the estate of a bankrupt or insolvent employer for an amount needed to fully fund pension benefits.

The *Bankruptcy and Insolvency Act* provides a priority claim (i.e., a claim that ranks ahead of the estate's unsecured creditors) for unremitted member contributions, as well as for unremitted current service cost payments that were past due as of the date of insolvency. Unremitted special payments and any future payments required are not granted priority status.

A number of jurisdictions (for example, Alberta, Manitoba, and Ontario) provide that any pension contributions collected by employers from employees but not yet remitted to the pension plan are deemed to be held in trust for the pension plan. Manitoba also makes corporate directors of an employer personally liable for unremitted member contributions. Alberta and Manitoba specify that *employer* pension contributions that are due but not yet paid are also deemed to be held in trust.

Some jurisdictions (e.g., Ontario and Manitoba) provide the administrator of a pension plan with a lien over the assets of the employer for "any amount of money equal to employer contributions accrued to the date of the wind-up but not yet due under the plan or regulations"[5] and deem any such funds owing to be held in trust for the pension plan. In Manitoba, the Superintendent also has a lien against the personal property of corporate directors where there are unremitted employee contributions. Ontario's *Pension Benefits Act* further provides that the Superintendent has a lien over the assets of the employer equal to any amounts paid into the pension plan out of the PBGF.

The status of these statutory liens and deemed trusts in the context of employer insolvency has been frequently litigated, and in many cases the lien or deemed trust has been held to have no priority over other claims against the estate of the bankrupt employer. The Supreme Court of Canada's decision in *Indalex Ltd. (Re)*, is the latest case to consider the effect of the deemed trust provision in Ontario's legislation. The Court ruled that deemed trust provisions do not prevail over the super-priority granted by the CCAA court to a debtor-in-possession, or DIP, lender, although it did clarify that the deemed trust provision applied to the entire wind-up deficiency of a plan, There will likely be further cases regarding the status of deemed trusts and statutory liens in the context of an underfunded pension wind-up.[6]

---

5   Ontario *Pension Benefits Act*, subsections 57(4) and (5).
6   See Chapter 10 for further discussion of the *Indalex* case history.

PART II

EMPLOYEE BENEFITS

Chapter 16

OVERVIEW OF EMPLOYEE BENEFITS

Executive Summary

Increasingly complex forces are impacting upon benefit plans today, including the changing landscape and increasing risk associated with prescription drugs, absence management, and the increasing burden of chronic illness (such as mental illness and diabetes). At no other time has the benefit plan been buffeted as much by change, threat, and opportunity as is the case currently. The opportunities afforded through new plan designs, product offerings, member engagement, and health management will engage and challenge the practitioner in the upcoming years.

Part II of the *Handbook* provides an explanation and discussion of each major benefit category and addresses the variations and trends within each benefit. From a strategic perspective, it summarizes the administrative and financial considerations necessary for human resources professionals and financial officers to understand and manage the next generation of their benefits programs.

Background

For most plan members, benefits are a valued component of the compensation provided by their employer or organization as plan sponsor. In the context of the *Handbook*, we will refer to these as employee benefits and will include discussions on traditional core coverages such as life and disability, medical and dental care, to benefits that are typically voluntary, such as critical illness, and sometimes to newer benefits, such as second medical opinion and health system navigation services.

Employee benefits have evolved over the years, largely to supplement the basic protection offered by various government programs and in response to changes in demand as expressed both through both collective bargaining and the need to attract and retain talent.

During the post-war years, federal and provincial governments gradually introduced basic levels of protection including medical care, occupational disability coverage, employment insurance, and other social security benefits. In parallel with the trend in the United States, unions bargained for benefits as a complement to cash compensation and organizations were willing to enhance coverages to attract and retain members.

During periods of recession, particularly during times of wage freezes, benefits were often added or expanded in lieu of wage increases. Benefits came to be viewed as separate from cash compensation and were generally perceived to be of lower economic value; however, employee benefits now comprise a large and increasing component of compensation. Certainly, in no sense is the old moniker of "fringe benefits" appropriate today. Favourable tax treatment has also been a contributing factor to the expansion of benefit plans and this is covered elsewhere in the Handbook.

While the benefit plan itself and the covered items are not significantly dissimilar from years past, the complexity of managing the plan has increased considerably for a number of reasons in recent years.

In years past, the delivery of benefits was generally transactional in nature. For example, was the claim for a legally prescribed drug? If yes, reimbursement proceeded. Was an individual "totally disabled" to the extent of their "own occupation"? If yes, then disability payments would proceed. Interventions were often late, weak, and/or limited to contractual assessments and Canada Pension Plan approvals. Costs were driven by aging and increasing rates of disease. This was also the time of the more traditional "blockbuster" drugs, the main driver of costs in the medical plan at the time.

Present Day

The landscape continues to evolve. Due to improvements in technology and information management capabilities, benefit delivery has moved well beyond the transactional past by employing new methods and relationship/partnering models. These innovations are resulting in significant changes to the benefits plan, related services, as well as interactions with sponsors and their members. We are experiencing a period of fundamental change as the need for member engagement, the continued escalation of benefit plan costs, as well as legislative and accounting standards changes, have led to renewed focus on benefit plans. This has also led to an increased awareness of the need for benefit plan governance, similar to that of pension plans. This is not a legislated requirement, but stems from the need to address continuing, exponential increases to employee benefits spend, an amount that has started to surpass that of some pension plans.

Drugs — A Cost Driver with New Management Attention

Following a few years of reprieve from escalating drug costs, industry studies show that the trend is picking up. Overall spending on prescription drugs in private plans increased by 3.9% from 2014 to 2015.[1] This amount is expected to double by 2018. The typical cost drivers in the benefits plan of the past are being replaced by newer, high cost therapies. With traditional blockbuster brand name medications regularly substituted with generic drugs due to patent expiry (the so-called Patent Cliff), many of those blockbuster drugs are no longer driving huge profits for the pharmaceutical industry or costs for the benefits plans. It has been estimated that the Patent Cliff resulted in $120 billion of lost sales worldwide between 2009 and 2014.[2] In fact, reform in the pricing regime through provincial legislation has reduced the costs of many of these generic products to (generally) 25% of the brand-name product. In an alliance of provinces and recently the federal government as well, the Pan-Canadian Phamaceutical Alliance (pCPA) has been successful in reaching agreement whereby 18 (at the time of writing) of the most commonly used generics are priced at 18% of the reference brand, this pricing being available to all, government, private sector and consumers. There are a number of other initiatives underway by the pCPA; at present it is unclear whether the private payer will benefit through other of their ongoing negotiations.

The replacement for the revenue lost during the Patent Cliff has emerged in the form of biologics and other specialty drugs, with use of these products surging to 29.9% of the spend on all drug claims in 2015 from an already alarming 26.5% in 2014.[3] Generally, these specialty drugs offer superior therapeutic benefits for some of today's most insidious diseases, and lead to healthier working individuals. Where this is the case, such vaccines and therapies will serve to mitigate other costs, such as productivity, lost time, Long Term Disability benefits, etc.

At present, it is reported that there are an estimated 21,000 products in clinical trials.[4] At the end of 2015, there were approximately 1000 drugs in Phase III clinical trials, and just under 500 submitted to the U.S. FDA for approval.[5] Many are specialty and/or biologics and in line with what we have seen in recent years, the largest numbers in development are

---

[1]   2015 Express Scripts Canada *Drug Trend Report*.
[2]   World Preview 2015, Outlook to 2020 8th Edition, June 2015, EvaluatePharmatm.
[3]   2015 Express Scripts *Canada Drug Trend Report*.
[4]   New Drug Pipeline Monitor 7th Edition, December 2015, NDPUIS, Canada.
[5]   *Ibid.*

treatments for oncology, infectious diseases, and the central nervous system. Further, there is ongoing expansion of the indications approved for treatments already on the market. According to World Preview 2015, Outlook to 2020, June 2015 by EvaluatePharma™ : "If there was any doubt that the pharmaceutical industry is entering a period of sustained growth it should be put to rest by this year's World Preview 2015 showing prescription drug sales are set to advance at almost 5% a yearuntil 2020…the patent cliff is firmly in the rearview mirror."[6]

Stakeholders are taking notice of the cost pressures and risks they face. Pharmacy Benefits Managers, for example, are adopting strategies to address the changes, including:

- Formularies, claims features and services aimed at reducing the cost of traditional drugs and at mitigating waste (including non-adherence to therapy) to free these dollars so as to be available to fund the important new therapies.

- Initiatives aimed at controlling the previously unchecked usage and cost of biologics and specialty products, such as:
    - stricter more sophisticated prior authorization protocols;
    - case management and integrating services with manufactuers' patient assistance programs, addressing lifestyle issues, adherence, etc.;
    - utilizing step therapy approaches with respect to approval of individual cases;
    - use of bio-similars as another alternative to the prior approval process (for new patients generally);
    - terminating the practice of automatic listing of all products receiving Notice of Compliance on their open formularies;
    - introduction of stricter contract language;
    - manufacturer negotiations;
    - preferred provider agreements;
    - differentiating between products types;
    - development of new formularies;

---

[6] World Preview 2015, Outlook to 2020 8th Edition, June 2015, EvaluatePharmatm.

o   high cost drug management that mirrors long term disability case management, with compliance conditions for plan members to continue to receive benefits payments.

At the Same Time Comes Risk

For plan sponsors and insurers, the result is a shifting of the value equation to ever increasing sums concentrated in the treatment of few individuals. A related issue is the increasing cost and availability of individual large amount pooling. Individual large amount pooling fees and thresholds are being driven skyward and, for many insurers, the response is recourse to experience rating and the use of pricing differentiation between standard and sub-standard risk pools. Portability for those plans not fully insured is at issue and some sponsors, primarily small employers, are resorting to capping drugs (and similar methods) to control costs. The methods, costs and benefits of pooling are dealt with in greater detail in Chapter 25, including a review of the Canadian Drug Insurance Pooling Corporation (CDPC).

For all of these reasons, and because needed drugs are inaccessible for a portion of Canadians, discussions, academic and white papers, and press calling for a national drug plan (catastrophic or otherwise) are once again at the fore; it is fair to say that this part of the benefits plan is in a state of upheaval.

Paramedical Services

A newer and related discussion centres around paramedical benefits as an example of a benefit cost that is escalating at a very significant ongoing rate as more practitioners and added specialties are sought by members. Some of these treatments may not have proven efficacy to the necessary standard and may not be sustainable in the future if difficult choices become necessary, as seems likely. At the same time, paramedical services are highly valued by the membership, many of whom are net contributors to the extended health plan.

Employee benefits represent a cost that continues to escalate well in excess of increases in wages for a number of reasons, even beyond expensive new treatments. As the population ages, and with increasing incidence of chronic disease, comes increasing frequency and durations of disability, resulting in increasing usage of items and services offered by benefit plans. At the same time, there is a somewhat unheralded but ongoing cost-shifting from provincial governments. Their own budget woes are causing them to, for example, fail to list or delay approvals of new products, creating the demand for the private plans to assume responsibility.

We've talked about prescription drugs. It can be reasonably expected that we will see more disputes in future than has been the case in the past. The conditions giving rise to dispute may result when a claimant is not approved for the medication prescribed or when the treatment is not offered by the plan (or the public system) at all. For example, a recent insurance carrier's declination of drug claims that were purchased for offlabel use, for the right indication but for dependent children less than age 18 for whom clinical trials are not normally done. On a self-insured basis, while the insurance carrier is willing to make the exception at the organization's instructions, the insurance carrier has also excluded payment of the drug from the stop loss provision in addition to requiring that the organization indemnify them in writing from any harmful outcomes resulting from the offlabel use of the dependent child. We touched briefly above on the subject of new contract language. Plan sponsors are advised to understand their contract with the insurer or administrator and the related risk distribution, including dispute risk. They would also do well to be diligent in respect of contract language and of any materials or means that communicate benefit provisions. Communication to members should improve; it should be clear as to coverage limitations and communications should be accurate.

Member Engagement

Surveys show that members are answering more and more of their family's security needs through their organizations' services. To attract and retain members, many employers already provide access to many voluntary benefits, such as home and auto coverage, savings vehicles, retirement planning, second medical opinion, and expanded employee and family assistance program (EFAP) services. It has been demonstrated that flexibility is preferred. To engage members, organizations will need to communicate the value of their offerings to specific plan member segments, as well as engage with members in new ways and with careful, convenient, attractive, and interactive communication methods. As discussed in this chapter, cost pressures are increasing and those members who are not high claimants will demand value in these plans. The most recent entrants into the Canadian workforce are much more diverse; they are demanding innovative, flexible benefits plans along with convenient mobile device and social media avenues for information and service.

New integrated information and modelling capabilities have the ability to demonstrate the return that comes from engaged and healthy members.

In this decade, there will be increasing focus on improving the mental health, engagement, and productivity of members. Organizations' abilities will be tested to provide appropriate policies, workplace environments, treatments, services, and interventions to the significant segment of the Canadian population and workforce that suffers from chronic stress and mental health issues.

Case management is more sophisticated, specialized and customized than in the past. Best practice case management is going upstream to determine the root cause of absence and facilitate appropriate individual services very early and even before absence commences. Stay-at-work programs are gaining attention. Insurers and employers alike are starting to realize the return on this upstream investment, which involves studying the burden of illness that their working population carries. Case management has been utilized in the disability management spectrum for years, but has only recently come to be understood as a preventative technique for disabilities. An increasing trend as well is the use of advocates, not just with the appeal of declined Canada Pension Plan claims, but even with initial applications as these have proven to increase the approval rates resulting in favourable impact on reserves, and therefore, LTD premium rates.

New Benefits Program Delivery Models

The increasing globalization of companies is resulting in an added complexity for organizations in finding the most efficient and economical way to provide coverage while meeting the needs of the local market, as applicable, and maintaining compliance with local regulations. Multi-national pooling and captive arrangements are gaining in popularity. Consideration of these arrangements include limited choice of insurance companies due to the multi-national pooling networks available in countries of operation and the willingness of participating countries to change insurers. In the case of captive arrangements, the capital required in investing to meet regulatory requirements could be a daunting consideration.

There is an increasing trend in every market segment towards consortium and volume purchasing plans. Starting with the provincial health care sector, this trend has since expanded into the provincial education sector in various provinces across Canada. These sorts of plans tend to innovate, to increase the flexibility, and improve the plan or the sponsor's branding and communication, while at the same time, reducing administration and cost generally.

New approaches to product distribution altogether are developing — generally made possible through improvements in technology.

Organizations that bundle insurance and other products together in new convenient packages and online marketplaces (following on the success of U.S.-style exchanges) offering attractive products to retirees and others, are just examples of the newer methods in which people and business will access the insurance market. Retiree offerings online seem to be an ideal beginning for this type of distribution. For retirees in particular there is a great need for health and travel benefits, with employers having exited the space for the most part and with limited coverage available to seniors in some provinces.

All of the factors discussed in this overview are expanded upon in subsequent chapters. The issues highlight the value to be found in managing and communicating this important investment in plan member health, engagement, and productivity. Newer methods improve health and member engagement, while at the same time reducing cost trend; these opportunities will be at the forefront of the most progressive plan sponsors' minds. The ability to capitalize on these opportunities will also depend on organizations' ability to mine and analyze data available through, not only plan members' lagging indicators (health and disability claims), but also predictive indicators (resilience and coping skills). Now that technology has afforded big data to organizations and individiuals alike, our future will depend on how well we integrate this data and help predict the future to quantify the cost of doing nothing and the impact of program changes being contemplated to help stave off further increasing cost pressures.

Chapter 17

PROVINCIAL HOSPITAL AND MEDICAL INSURANCE PLANS

Executive Summary

Canadians receive basic hospital and medical care through a system of provincial government plans. The federal government is an unequal partner in today's health care system, as the role of coordination becomes increasingly difficult, and as federal funding becomes increasingly scarce.

This chapter deals primarily with the mechanics and historical context of government involvement in health care. Fiscal realities of increasing cost and decreasing funds are forcing governments, both provincial and federal, to make difficult decisions. The pace of change in the area of government health care is anticipated to increase significantly given these present challenges.

In more recent times, this has resulted in restructuring the health care delivery model, which considers adopting a risk management model translating to reducing and/or eliminating non-essential/non-critical services, while struggling to reduce wait times.

The integration of private clinics and services into the Canadian health care system is an interesting area of development. Already in some provinces, private coverage is utilized by the public system and, of course, residents have the choice to seek treatment through the private system.

Legislation

Today, the administration and delivery of health care falls under provincial jurisdiction. However, in the late 1970s, the federal government became concerned that some of the basic conditions and standards governing provincial health plans were being seriously eroded and were inconsistent from province to province. On the basic principle that access to health care should not depend on the wealth of the patient, the federal government strongly objected to the user fees charged by hospitals and the extra billing by doctors that were allowed by some provinces.

The federal *Canada Health Act* became effective on April 1, 1984, replacing both the *Hospital Insurance and Diagnostic Services Act* (July

1, 1958) and the Medical Care Act (July 1, 1968). In the *Canada Health Act*, the federal government gave itself the power to impose financial penalties on provinces that do not allow reasonable access to essential health services. The *Canada Health Act* defines the primary objective of Canadian health care policy as "to protect, promote and restore the physical and mental well being of residents of Canada and to facilitate reasonable access to health services without financial or other barriers".

In the 1990s, the provinces faced cuts in federal transfer payments. Provinces responded by scaling down their health care programs, which in turn shifts costs to employer health plans and individuals. The provincial health care programs most likely to be trimmed are those that will not compromise federal funding under the *Canada Health Act*.

Canada Health Act Criteria

The *Canada Health Act* sets out the criteria and conditions that a provincial health program must meet to be eligible for unreduced federal funding. The conditions for federal assistance, as established in the *Canada Health Act*, are:

1. Public Administration: The program must be administered on a non-profit basis by a public authority, appointed by and accountable to the provincial government.

2. *Comprehensiveness*: The program must cover all necessary hospital and medical services. An extensive list of medically necessary services includes standard ward accommodation, physician expenses, services of other health care practitioners while confined to hospital, surgical-dental services rendered in hospital, and many associated supplies and services. Provinces are encouraged to include additional extended health care services, although the provision of extended health care services has no impact on the federal funding eligibility.

3. *Universality*: All eligible residents must be covered for insured health services.

4. *Portability*: Coverage must be portable from one province to another. The waiting period for new residents must not exceed three months. The portability provision does not entitle residents to seek treatment in other provinces, but is intended to cover emergency care.

5. *Accessibility*: Insured services must be provided on uniform terms and conditions for all residents. Reasonable access to insured services must not be precluded or impeded, either directly or indirectly, by charges or other mechanisms. Finan-

cial impediments, such as deductibles, for essential medical services are viewed as a breach of the criteria at the federal level and the funding reduction can be equal to the value of the deductible.

While the provincial plans have some coverage differences between them, all programs must provide the insured health services as defined by the *Canada Health Act* for coverage such as hospital services and physician services, which are described in detail below.

Scope of Coverage

Hospital Services

Prior to the *Canada Health Act*, many provinces allowed "user fees" to be charged by hospitals for standard ward accommodation and outpatient services. User fees were abolished under the *Canada Health Act*. The Act allows provinces to charge a user fee if the hospitalization is for chronic care (in the opinion of the attending physician) and the individual is more or less permanently resident in the hospital. For chronic or extended care hospital stays, approximately half of the jurisdictions levy a user fee.

Medically necessary health care services performed in a hospital are considered insured health services and fall under the hospital global budget. Examples of insured health care services include:

- Accommodation at the ward level;
- Nursing care provided in a hospital;
- Drugs administered in a hospital;
- Operating room and anaesthetic facilities;
- Laboratory and diagnostic services performed in a hospital;
- Radiotherapy and physiotherapy performed in a hospital;
- Outpatient services for emergencies; and
- Medically necessary physician services.

There is no limit on the length of stay in the hospital, other than that the stay must be medically necessary for active treatment. Some provinces also cover medically required surgical services and anaesthetics, X-rays, diagnostic and laboratory tests, and some oral surgical procedures when performed in a hospital setting as part of an outpatient program.

Some associated hospital fees, such as ambulance fees, occupational speech and therapy, psychiatric care, renal dialysis, and rehabilitation services may or may not be covered under the hospital program. Provincial health plans do not cover elective services such as private duty nursing, semi-private or private room accommodation, cosmetic surgery, or drugs to be taken home from the hospital.

Medical Services

To comply with the *Canada Health Act*, physicians participating in the provincial health plan cannot charge the patient anything above what the physician receives from the provincial plan.

In some provinces, a physician may choose not to participate in the provincial plan, in which case the patient pays the physician as billed and the patient submits a claim to the provincial plan for consideration. However, most provinces limit any reimbursement to their applicable provincial or territorial fee schedule, and Quebec will not reimburse any services by a physician who is a non-participating physician.

Supplementary Benefits

Many provinces have expanded their health plan coverage beyond the required in-patient hospital care, physician services, and medical services. Common benefit enhancements include dental care for children, annual eye examinations, and coverage for prescription drugs for specific populations, such as residents age 65 and over or residents in receipt of social assistance.

While some provinces provide limited coverage for paramedical practitioners, the majority of the cost for these types of professionals, such as chiropractors, physiotherapists, osteopaths, podiatrists, registered massage therapists, psychologists, and optometrists, are not covered by provincial programs. Medical supplies required outside of a hospital, such as hearing aids, crutches, and wheelchairs, are also typically not eligible under a provincial program. In many instances, provinces provide some coverage for medical supplies for at least some populations through government programs, such as Ontario's Assistive Devices Program.

As jurisdictions look for ways to reduce their medical care costs, it is often these expanded health benefits that are scrutinized for potential savings. Delisting of services is a common way for a jurisdiction to save money and there are several examples of services such as chiropractor and physiotherapy being delisted in various jurisdictions. As a result of the delisting, these costs often shift from the provincial program to employer sponsored programs or as out of pocket costs for patients.

In addition, jurisdictions may apply user fees to help offset the provincial medical plan costs in addition to the taxes described later in this chapter.

Drug coverage benefits for drugs other than those administered in a hospital vary from province to province. Each province has a formulary, which is a list of drugs that are covered under its respective program. Increasingly, the provincial plans are looking to fees (such as co-payments and deductibles) to curtail the increasing costs without compromising the level of access to basic necessities. British Columbia, Manitoba, and Saskatchewan provide an income-tested drug program for eligible residents. Other provinces, such as Alberta, Ontario, Newfoundland & Labrador, and New Brunswick provide coverage for social assistance recipients and seniors.

The eligibility and reimbursement criteria of plans for seniors, non-seniors, and social assistance recipients differ widely across the country. Thus, the amount patients must pay for a given prescription is unequal across provinces. Given the rising cost of prescription medications, the inequities challenge one of the guiding principles of the *Canada Health Act* — that all Canadians should have similar levels of access to health care benefits. Many provinces are under pressure to provide some government coverage for new high cost specialty drugs but adequate funding for such coverage is a challenge.

There has been periodic media attention on the prospect of a universal pharmacare program in Canada to provide standardized prescription drug coverage to all citizens. Critics of the current system argue adopting a nationwide standard level of coverage should be a priority and that there would be significant savings through economies of scale in adopting a universal drug approach. However, implementing a universal program would be a political challenge.

The federal government announced in early 2016 that it will will join the provinces and territories already participating in the pan-Canadian Pharmaceutical Alliance (pCPA), which facilitates joint negotiation of prescription drug prices. The federal government has said that it is reviewing other ways of reducing prescription drug costs as well. A working group will be formed by provincial and territorial health ministers to discuss a national pharmaceutical strategy.

According to data from the Canadian Institute for Health Information, spending on prescription drugs was forecasted to total $29.2 billion in 2015. Of this, $12.6 billion was paid for by public plans. The remaining $16.6 billion represents private payers, of which approximately 60% is paid by private health insurance (such as employer-sponsored group benefit plans) and 40% is comprised of out-of-pocket payments by individuals.

In Quebec, effective January 1, 1997 (effective August 1, 1996 for seniors and social assistance recipients), the Quebec government introduced a new universal drug plan through the Régie d'assurance-maladie du Québec (RAMQ). This program was an original concept in Canada, as it stipulated that all Quebec residents must either be covered by the plan or by a private group insurance program.

Most provinces cover some form of vision care (usually an annual eye exam) for children and seniors, or for those with a medical necessity.

Out-of-Province Benefits

For out-of-province medical services, all jurisdictions, except for Quebec, have a reciprocal fee arrangement. Under this arrangement, each jurisdiction agrees to pay for the medical services provided in the other jurisdiction. The jurisdiction that provided the service will automatically bill the medical plan of the jurisdiction in which the person who received medical services resides. As a general rule, non-residents who receive services in Quebec must pay the service provider and then seek reimbursement from their own medical plan. The same is true for Quebec residents who require services in other provinces.

Most plans cover unexpected and unforeseen emergency hospital and medical costs arising outside Canada, but only up to the amount that would have been paid if the service had been performed in the province of residence, or up to a pre-set limit per day. Subject to prior approval of the province, some non-emergency, elective services provided outside Canada may be covered, however, there is typically a requirement to demonstrate that the service is medically necessary and that an acceptable equivalent is not available within the province. Some private plans also provide coverage for such services, subject to prior approval.

Private Clinics and Wait Times

Today, most provinces prohibit residents from seeking reimbursement for services provided by the public plan through private clinics. In Quebec, however, as a result of the *Chaoulli* Supreme Court of Canada decision, it is permissible for residents of Quebec to seek treatment in private clinics for pre-determined and approved services when reasonable wait times cannot be met through the public plan. In these cases, the public plan is responsible to pay for such services. The Supreme Court of Canada determined in Chaoulli that excessive waiting for medical services violated the *Quebec Charter of Rights and Freedoms*.

Wait times for surgeries and emergency rooms remains a contentious issue across the country and there is an ongoing debate regarding the privatization of at least some health care services.

Challenges

Health care is a perennial political issue both federally and provincially. The overall cost and proportion of the provincial budget of health care continue to rise year after year. Two issues in particular seem poised to continue this challenge in the years ahead: prescription drug costs and demographics. As noted previously, each province has a different arrangement for prescription drugs. New, high cost specialty drugs are expected to be introduced to the market at an increasing rate and there will be pressure for public plans to cover many of these drugs as the cost can be prohibitive for individuals. The "baby boomers" are now reaching an age which puts a significant strain on the health care system. Provinces are being affected differently as the age profile of residents differs by jurisdiction.

Financing

Federal

The federal and provincial governments once shared the cost of health care on an approximately equal basis. In recent years, however, the federal portion of the health care bill has fallen to below half. Notwithstanding its decreasing share of the budget, the federal government can still impose financial penalties on any province failing to meet any of the conditions specified in the *Canada Health Act*. The Canada Health and Social Transfer (CHST), implemented in 1995, was a federal transfer to provinces and territories, providing them with cash payments and tax transfers in support of health care, post-secondary education, social assistance, and social services. The problem with such block transfers is that it is difficult to determine how the money being transferred is spent. In 2004, the CHST was separated into the Canada Health Transfer and the Canada Social Transfer to improve transparency. In 2011, the federal government confirmed that the Canada Health Transfer would increase by six percent per year until 2016-2017 at which point the increase would be based on a three year moving average of gross domestic product (GDP) growth with a minimum of 3% per year. This change would likely result in a significant decrease to provincial transfers though the current federal government has committed to renegotiate a new health care accord with the provinces. The proportion of costs borne by different levels of government remains a contentious issue.

The federal government also finances health care programs for certain groups of individuals who fall outside the jurisdiction of the provincial plans, including the Armed Forces, the Royal Canadian Mounted Police, various programs for First Nations and Inuit populations, federal inmates, and refugees.

Provincial

Provincial hospital and medical plans that meet the criteria of the *Canada Health Act* continue to be financed in part from the federal government through transfer payments.

Each province and territory has established a method of financing the balance of the costs not covered by federal funding. Three provinces (British Columbia, Ontario, and Quebec) require direct cost sharing by residents and employers. In British Columbia, the maximum monthly premiums as at January 2016 were $75 for a single person, $136 for a family of two, and $150 for a family of three or more. As of January 1, 2017, British Columbia has announced that there will be no premiums for children under 19 years of age amongst other changes. Ontario's and Quebec' health premiums are based on income level; the highest annual premium, $900 in Ontario and $1,000 in Quebec, is collected via income tax. Quebec has announced that individual premiums will be gradually eliminated.

Other provinces levy a payroll tax on employers. The rates of payroll tax payable by employers as of 2016 are:

Province	Cost
Manitoba	2.15% to 4.3% of payroll
Newfoundland and Labrador	2% of payroll
Ontario	0.98% to 1.95% of payroll
Quebec	2.7% to 4.26% of payroll

Quebec has announced that the payroll tax will be gradually reduced beginning in 2017. There are various adjustments to these payroll taxes, including for the size or annual revenue of the employer. For example, in Ontario, the payroll tax rate of 1.95% only applies to employers with

$400,000 or more in gross annual payroll. For some smaller or non-eligible employers, the rate ranges from 0.98% to 1.95%.

The remaining provinces and territories raise funds for health care through general revenue.

Additional provincial funding has been generated through the taxation of group insurance plans. Group benefit plan premiums attract a retail sales tax of 8% in Ontario, 9% in Quebec, and 7% in Manitoba (on certain benefits).

Taxation

The *Income Tax Act* (ITA) does not permit the deduction of premium payments to a provincial health services plan from individual taxpayer income. Further, if the employer pays any portion of the provincial health premium on behalf of an individual, the contribution is taxable as income to the individual.

For 1988 and subsequent taxation years, an individual may claim medical expenses, paid in the 12-month income tax year, as a non-refundable tax credit, if total medical expenses were more than 3% of net income, or a fixed dollar amount that varies. For 2016, the federal threshold is $2,237.

There is also a refundable tax credit for working individuals with low incomes and high medical expenses under the refundable medical expense supplement.

Most employer health and dental plans are constructed and administered in accordance with the definition of a private health services plan as described in the ITA. Except in Quebec, employer contributions to a private health services plan do not give rise to taxable benefits for income tax purposes.

Chapter 18

WORKERS' COMPENSATION

Executive Summary[1]

Workers' Compensation programs have been established by legislation in each of the provinces and territories to provide benefits to employees who are injured at work. These programs are a form of no- fault insurance that guarantees benefits to injured employees and protects employers from the risk of being sued for negligence.

The programs are financed by contributions from employers that vary according to the risk associated with each industry, and may also be adjusted to reflect the experience of individual employers. The contributions are a tax-deductible business expense that is not considered a taxable benefit to employees.

The benefits provided include medical expenses, wage replacement benefits, rehabilitation, and survivor benefits. The benefits are not taxable to employees.

Background

The beginning of the twentieth century was a period of increasing industrialization. At the same time, the incidence of workplace accidents outpaced the ability of the legal system to provide fair and equitable recourse for injured employees. Both employer and labour groups were putting increasing pressure on the government to address the situation.

In 1910, Mr. Justice Meredith was appointed by the Premier of Ontario to head a Royal Commission to study Workers' Compensation schemes that were being developed or implemented in other countries. Meredith completed his study in 1913. The Ontario Workers'

---

[1] For more information on pension benefit accrual during periods when in receipt of Workers' Compensation, please consult the multi-jurisdictional charts in the *Canadian Employment Benefits & Pension Guide*. Morneau Shepell, *Canadian Employment Benefits & Pension Guide*, loose-leaf (Toronto: LexisNexis Canada, 2003). The table of contents for these charts appears at the back of this Handbook.

Compensation Board and the Ontario Workers' Compensation Act came into force on January 1, 1915. The other provinces implemented their own Acts and Regulations by 1950, joined by the Yukon and Northwest Territories by 1977.

The underlying principle behind a Workers' Compensation system is no-fault insurance. An injured employee is guaranteed benefits for injury, disease, or death "arising out of and in the course of employment", in exchange for which the employee forfeits the right to sue the employer for negligence.

Compensation to which an employee is entitled under the Acts replaces the right of legal action against the employer for damages or injuries sustained in the course of employment. With some exceptions, this extends to potential legal action against any other covered employer or employee.

The injured employee is entitled to prompt medical and rehabilitation treatment and reasonable compensation for lost earnings. An injured employee may have a choice of taking action against third parties for negligence or of claiming Workers' Compensation benefits. If the injured employee claims Workers' Compensation benefits, the right to sue the responsible party is acquired by the Workers' Compensation Board (WCB). Generally, the WCB is still responsible for seeking all potential remedies for the injured employee, which may result in compensation in excess of the benefits payable under the Act.

An objective appeal mechanism is integral to the Workers' Compensation system. Appeals may be initiated by the employer or by the injured employee.

Over time, the scope of benefits and services provided under Workers' Compensation has expanded well beyond compensation for lost earnings and medical treatment for workplace accidents. A wide range of health care, disability benefits, rehabilitation services, and survivor benefits are paid through the WCB.

Eligibility

Workers' Compensation coverage is generally mandatory for all employees in industrial occupations. In some provinces, domestic employees, casual employees, employees in certain service industries, and employees in the "knowledge" industries, such as finance and insurance, are exempt from mandatory coverage. Employee groups exempt from mandatory coverage may still be covered for Workers' Compensation on application by the employer.

Sole proprietors and executive officers are not subject to mandatory coverage, but may elect to be covered as employees. Voluntary coverage from a private insurer may be preferable for executives and proprietors to provide benefits commensurate with earnings.

Assessment Basis

The Workers' Compensation system is funded solely by assessments paid by covered employers. Contributions from employees are not permitted. Assessments are based on either individual liability or collective liability.

Individual liability is the assessment basis frequently used for government or public agencies, Crown corporations, and large public transportation organizations (i.e., shipping, airlines, and railways). Each employer is self-insured, or individually liable for accident and sickness costs as they occur. The annual assessments that are paid to the WCB reflect the actual costs of accident and sickness occurrences, plus the WCB's administration expenses in adjudicating and managing the claims. Generally, the costs are assessed on a pay-as-you-go basis. In some jurisdictions, deposits are required to cover the capitalized value of costs.

The vast majority of industries in Canada are assessed on the basis of collective liability. Employers are divided into industry classes and/or rate groups according to similar business activity and inherent accident and hazard risks. Every year assessment rates, expressed as a percentage of payroll, are determined based on the cost experience of each class or rate group. Collectively, the assessment rates are intended to provide enough revenue to cover:

- Expected costs of current and future benefit claims;
- Administration expenses, cost of accident prevention programs/ agencies, and other statutory obligations; and
- Any necessary adjustments to meet funding requirements established by policy or legislation.

The employers' assessments vary within each province and across provinces. The assessment rate is applied to the annual payroll of the covered employees, up to an assessable earnings maximum. The maximum varies significantly by jurisdiction, and changes every calendar year in most jurisdictions.

Accountability

To manage the cost of workplace accidents, and to encourage employers to participate in accident prevention and early return to work initiatives, all jurisdictions, except Yukon, currently offer an experience rating program for employers subject to collective liability. There are two common types of experience rating methods that serve to link assessments and actual experience for an employer:

- Prospective – the average industry assessment rate is adjusted for an employer by applying discounts or surcharges to the rate for the current year, based on the experience of the employer in past years.

- Retrospective – assessments are adjusted after the year has passed, by providing refunds or surcharges based on the actual experience of the employer for the year (or years).

Manitoba, Nova Scotia, Prince Edward Island, and Saskatchewan use only the prospective method. Newfoundland and Labrador, the Northwest Territories, and Nunavut use only the retrospective method. Alberta, British Columbia, New Brunswick, Ontario, and Quebec use both prospective and retrospective experience rating methods. Quebec also allows employers to create mutual groups for the purposes of determining the experience rating adjustment.

Taxation

The tax situation regarding Workers' Compensation may be summarized as follows:

- The employer contribution is a tax-deductible operating expense;
- The employer contribution is not a taxable benefit for employees; and
- Payments to injured employees are not subject to tax.

Benefits

Workers' Compensation benefits can be discussed in five broad categories:

- Health Care;
- Short-Term Disability (STD) ;
- Long-Term Disability (LTD);
- Rehabilitation; and

- Survivor.

Money that is paid to the employee to compensate for financial loss goes beyond income replacement to include health care, rehabilitation services, and survivor benefits. STD and LTD benefits are expressed as a percentage of wages, up to an annual compensable maximum, except in Manitoba where there is no maximum for claims incurred on after January 1, 2006. In all of the jurisdictions, the annual compensable maximum is equal to the assessable earnings maximum on which assessments are based.

Health Care

All medical expenses incurred as a result of a workplace accident or disease are paid by the Workers' Compensation system. Covered medical expenses include hospital charges and physician and surgeon fees normally covered by the provincial health care schemes, as well as the cost of drugs and ancillary services usually covered by private medical insurance plans. Transportation costs for treatment, clothing allowances, and long-term care allowances are also covered under the system.

Short-Term Disability

STD benefits are payable to the disabled employee until the employee has recovered and is capable of returning to the pre-accident occupation or, having gone through a rehabilitation program, is estimated capable of earning at the same level as prior to the accident. The percentage of earnings used to calculate the benefit amounts vary from jurisdiction to jurisdiction; however, it usually ranges from 75% to 90% of net earnings, with one jurisdiction at 75% of gross earnings.

A disabled employee who cannot return to work, or who is incapable of replacing pre-accident earnings becomes eligible for LTD benefits.

Long-Term Disability

A severe injury may cause the employee to be disabled beyond the STD period. Prior to implementing wage-loss systems, compensation for a permanent impairment fell under two different categories of benefits:

- permanent partial disability, and
- permanent total disability. Under these programs, an injured employee would have received a benefit linked to the nature and extent of the injury or disease and this benefit was payable for life.

During the 1980s and 1990s, several Canadian jurisdictions changed their permanent disability award systems to allow for a "dual award system". This dual award system is both a monthly benefit based on an earnings loss system (usually calculated as a percentage, such as 90% of net loss of income), which is usually paid out until age 65, and a lump-sum payment awarded for the non-economic impacts of the permanent impairment. An injured worker entitled to LTD benefits may have the benefit reduced to reflect estimated capable or actual post-accident earnings, Canada Pension Plan disability pension, or other sources of income. These reductions are reviewed either annually or at specific dates depending on the jurisdiction. In addition, most jurisdictions provide for some form of pension for injured workers after age 65. The benefit ranges from a defined pension, to the accumulation of a retirement account with fixed contributions, to a benefit based on demonstrated loss of pension.

As disability benefits vary from province to province, it is important to review the specific details for each jurisdiction. The Association of Workers' Compensation Boards of Canada (AWCBC) publishes an annual summary of benefits information entitled *Workers' Compensation Benefit Comparison*.[2] Additionally, in the majority of jurisdictions, the various WCBs have websites that explain in basic terms the types of awards provided to injured or diseased workers.

LTD benefits under Workers' Compensation are adjusted for cost-of-living increases. In all jurisdictions, the payments are indexed annually, although the level of increase varies by jurisdiction.

Rehabilitation

To facilitate a return to work, the injured employee may participate in a medical or vocational rehabilitation program funded by the WCB. A variety of rehabilitation programs exist, and a determination of what programs are available to be used by the employee must be made on a jurisdiction-by-jurisdiction basis. Examples of some services provided include counseling, job search assistance, ergonomic modifications, tuition, homemaker assistance, and on-the-job training. Some jurisdictions also provide relocation assistance, self-employment, and legal services.

---

[2]   To review a summary of publications published by the AWCBC, visit their website at http://www.awcbc.org/en.

Survivor Benefits

- In the event that an employee dies as a result of a workplace injury or disease incurred in the course of employment, all jurisdictions provide survivor benefits. In addition, all jurisdictions pay a lump-sum benefit for burial expenses, and a certain amount for transportation of the employee's body.

- The benefits for the spouse range from a relatively short-term pension with a larger lump-sum payment to benefits payable to age 65 or for life with or without a smaller lump-sum payment. The amounts paid to the surviving spouse may be dependent upon the spouse's age, the number and ages of the dependent children, and whether or not the spouse is disabled.

- The benefits for dependent children are in the form of a monthly allowance and generally terminate at age 18, but may be extended if the child is disabled or attending school.

Emerging Legislation

Workers' Compensation Board perspectives on chronic stress claims:

The majority of provinces have generally restricted consideration of mental disorders to those associated to occupational injury or illness. The acceptance of an occupational relationship generally required a traumatic brain injury, reaction to surgery, prolonged disability or a clearly acute, singular traumatic event. Occupational relationships were not considered from cumulative stress. The provincial boards did not have legislation, policy, or ability to delineate cumulative occupational stress.

British Columbia

In 2012, the British Columbia government passed Bill 14, which revised the *Workers Compensation Act* provisions relating to mental disorders. The new legislation introduced support for compensation for a traumatic mental event, allowing that a cumulative series of stressors arising out of, and in the course of employment, could now be considered for compensation.

Ontario

The Ontario *Workers' Compensation Act*, prior to 1998, contained no reference to chronic stress, neither including nor excluding such claims. Nor did the Board have any formal written policy concerning chronic stress. The Board, in practice, tended to deny any claims for chronic stress, citing the need for an event that was "sudden, shocking or life threatening in nature".[3] As of June of 2016 there remains no specific policy regarding a method of acceptance of chronic mental stress claims that are not a reaction to an acute event.

Recent changes to the Ontario compensation legislation now allow for post-traumatic stress with stipulations specific to first responders. Other provinces are being confronted with appeals focussed upon Constitutional challenges of discrimination. The premise of these challenges relate to the differential treatment between organic and non-organic injuries; organic injuries are accepted from cumulative stress as a disablement arising out of the employment, whereas mental disability has exlusions prohibiting this consideration.

Nova Scotia

As of June of 2016 there is an active case with the Workers' Compensation Appeal Tribunal that relates to over a decade of claimed harassment in the workplace. The case involves a constitutional challenge that section 2 of the legislation requiring a traumatic event offends the *Charter of Rights and Freedoms*. The Tribunal held that the claimed traumatic event of being physically assaulted was not established in evidence. However, the harassment would constitute, more likely than not, a disablement arising out of and in the course of employment. But for the exclusions of the traumatic mental stress legislation, the claim would be allowed.

This case is subsequent to *Dale v. N.S.*,[4] where the Tribunal was authorized to rule on whether entitlement would be granted "but for" the exclusions of section 2 requiring a single traumatic event. The appeal may very well result in changes to the legislation and policy, broadening the acceptance of mental disabilities that can be reasonably associated with occupational exposures.

---

[3]   Decision No. 262/99I2, 1999 CanLII 16185 (ON WSIAT).
[4]   *Dale v. Nova Scotia (Workers' Compensation Appeals Tribunal)*, [2015] N.S.J. No. 311, 2015 NSCA 71 (N.S.C.A.).

Chapter 19

EMPLOYMENT INSURANCE

Executive Summary[1]

Employment insurance (EI) provides individuals with temporary income replacement as a result of employment interruptions due to work shortages, sickness, non-occupational accidents, maternity leave, parental leave, adoption leave, and for those with family members who are seriously ill with a significant risk of death. It also promotes "active" re-employment assistance to help unemployed workers to find and create jobs.

This chapter provides an overview of the various benefits available within the EI program as well as eligibility criteria, amount and duration of benefits, an overview of the EI Premium Reduction Program, and information about supplemental plans that employers can provide to their employees.[2]

Quebec is currently the only province with its own parental insurance plan. A summary of this program is also included in this chapter.[3]

History

The *Unemployment Insurance Act* was first introduced in Canada as an amendment to the *British North America Act* in 1940 and exclusive jurisdiction in matters pertaining to employment insurance was conferred on the federal government. This contrasts with welfare assistance, which is a provincial responsibility.

---

[1] For more information on pension benefit accrual during maternity, parental, and other leaves, please consult the multi-jurisdictional charts in the *Canadian Employment Benefits & Pension Guide*. Morneau Shepell, *Canadian Employment Benefits & Pension Guide*, loose-leaf (Toronto: LexisNexis Canada, 2003). The table of contents for these charts appears at the back of this Handbook.

[2] Further details on these various sections can be accessed by visiting www.servicecanada.gc.ca.

[3] Further details on this program can be accessed by visiting www.rqap.gouv.qc.ca.

Governing Legislation

Through the passage of Bill C-12, the *Unemployment Insurance Act* was replaced by the *Employment Insurance Act*, which received Royal Assent on June 20, 1996.

Changes to the Act in 1996 were intended to bring together, in a single statute, all provisions for income support and employment assistance for eligible unemployed persons in a manner that better accommodated the variety of work arrangements in today's labour market. The *Employment Insurance Act* provides self-employment assistance to help claimants start their own enterprises and job creation programs. All prior references to "unemployment insurance" were replaced by "employment insurance".

Since 2005, all EI benefits are delivered by Service Canada on behalf of Human Resources and Skills Development Canada (HRSDC).

In 2010, the *Employment Insurance Act* was amended to establish a new EI Operating Account.

The 2016 Federal Budget proposed changes to improve the EI program. This includes making changes to the eligibility rules for new entrants and re-entrants, temporarily enhancing benefits in certain regions, and investing in improved service delivery. In addition, starting in 2017, the waiting period for benefits will be reduced to one week. This chapter assumes that these changes will be enacted.

The Government of Canada and the existing EI Commission continue to have full responsibility related to EI benefits and program delivery, including eligibility and benefit levels.

Regular Benefits

Regular benefits are payable to individuals who become unemployed due to loss of work, through no fault of their own. The claimant must be ready, willing, and capable of working each day and actively looking for work. With the 2012 Federal Budget, the Government announced tighter rules for payouts to the unemployed, requiring jobless workers to be willing to accept jobs at lower pay or commute farther for work if they want to collect EI benefits. The changes to the EI rules mean that frequent claimants, for example, seasonal workers, must be willing to take any job in their region for which they are qualified after receiving EI benefits for seven weeks, even if taking the job means substantially lower wages. The 2016 Federal Budget proposed changes to these rules to simplify job search responsibilities for EI claimants. Claimants would continue to be required to conduct job search activities and accept suitable employment, but requirements to accept work at lower pay and with longer commuting times would be eliminated.

Individuals who leave jobs voluntarily without just cause, or who lose jobs due to misconduct, do not qualify for EI benefits. Benefits also will not be paid to a claimant who is out of work because he or she is directly participating in a labour dispute (*i.e.*, a strike, lockout, or other type of dispute).

An exception to the disqualification of claimants who leave their jobs voluntarily is available under the Work Force Reduction program. Under this program, workers who agree to leave their jobs to preserve their co-workers' jobs may receive regular EI benefits, as long as they meet the other eligibility requirements.

Qualifying Period

In order to be eligible for benefits, the hours of insurable employment that are used to calculate the benefit period must have been accumulated during the qualifying period.

The qualifying period is the shorter of:

- The 52-week period immediately before the start date of a claim; or
- The period from the start of a previous benefit period to the start of the new benefit period, if the claimant applied for benefits earlier and his or her application was approved in the last 52 weeks.

Only the insurable hours that fall within the qualifying period are used to start a benefit period. However, the qualifying period may be extended to 104 weeks if the claimant was not employed in insurable employment or if they were not receiving EI benefits.

Most claimants will need between 420 and 700 insurable hours of work in their qualifying period to qualify, depending on the unemployment rate in their region at the time of filing their claim for benefits.

The following table outlines the number of hours of insurable employment required to qualify for benefits:

Insurable Hours Required	
Regional Unemployment Rate	**Hours of Work Needed to Qualify for Benefits**
6.0% and under	700
6.1% to 7.0%	665
7.1% to 8.0%	630
8.1% to 9.0%	595
9.1% to 10.0%	560
10.1% to 11.0%	525
11.1% to 12.0%	490
12.1% to 13.0%	455
13.1% and over	420

In some instances, a minimum of 910 hours in the qualifying period may be needed to qualify (*i.e.*, for new entrants and those re-entering the workforce after two years) or a minimum of 600 hours (*i.e.*, for sickness, maternity, parental, compassionate care, or parents of critical ill children benefits).

It should be noted that the 2016 Federal Budget proposed the elimination of the 910 hours requirement. This would be replaced with a regional labour market threshold. With these changes, new entrants and re-entrants will face the same eligibility requirements as other claimants in the region where they live. This measure is proposed to take effect in July 2016.

Duration of Benefits

The period for which benefits are payable to a claimant is determined by the number of hours of insurable employment during the qualifying period and the rate of unemployment in the region in which the individual resides. The maximum benefit payment period for regular benefits is 45 weeks.

The 2016 Federal Budget proposed the duration of EI regular benefits be extended by five weeks, up to a maximum of 50 weeks of benefits, but only for eligible claimants in the 12 economic regions with the sharpest increases in unemployment. Extended benefits will be available for one year starting in July 2016, with the measure being applied retroactively to all eligible claims as of January 4, 2015.

The 2016 Federal Budget also proposed temporary measures to offer up to an additional 20 weeks of EI regular benefits to long-tenured workers in the same 12 EI economic regions, up to a maximum of 70 weeks of benefits.

Extended benefits for long-tenured workers will be available for one year starting in July 2016, with the measure being applied retroactively to all eligible claims as of January 4, 2015.

Special Benefits

Special benefits are also paid to individuals who are not working because of pregnancy, parental leave to care for a newborn or adopted child, sickness, or compassionate care leave to care for a gravely ill family member. An eligible employee who becomes legitimately unable to work for any of these specified reasons may claim EI benefits.

Each type of special benefits has an individual maximum number of weeks payable in one benefit period. Individual maximums are:

- 15 weeks for maternity benefits;
- 35 weeks for parental benefits;
- 15 weeks for sickness benefits;
- 26 weeks for compassionate care benefits; and
- 35 weeks for parents of critically ill children benefits.

Special benefits may be paid in any combination during a benefit period, provided the claimant proves entitlement for each type of benefit claimed. A maximum of 50 weeks of special benefits can be paid in the initial benefit period, when regular and special benefits are combined. However, a maximum of 102 weeks of combined special benefits may be payable, and the initial benefit period extended to a maximum of 104 weeks.

Greater detail on each of the special benefits is provided below.

Maternity Benefits

Maternity benefits are payable for a maximum of 15 weeks to the biological mother, including surrogate mothers, who cannot work because they are pregnant or have recently given birth. To receive maternity benefits, the claimant is required to have worked for 600 hours in the last 52 weeks or since the last claim. The mother can start collecting maternity benefits either up to eight weeks before she is expected to give birth or at the week she gives birth. Maternity benefits can be collected within 17 weeks of the actual or expected week of birth, whichever is later.

Parental Benefits

Parental benefits are payable only to the biological, adoptive, or legally recognized parents while they are caring for their newborn or newly adopted child. Parental benefits are payable to a maximum of 35 weeks. To receive parental benefits, the claimant is required to have worked for 600 hours in the last 52 weeks or since the last claim.

For biological parents, EI parental benefits can be paid starting from the child's date of birth. For adoptive parents, parental benefits can be paid starting from the date the child is placed with them for adoption.

Parental benefits can be claimed by one parent or shared between the two partners but cannot exceed a combined maximum of 35 weeks.

The number of weeks for EI maternity or parental benefits entitlement does not change for multiple births (twins, triplets, etc.) or if more than one child is adopted at the same time.

For natural or adoptive parents, the period during which maternity and parental benefits may be claimed may be extended by the number of weeks during which a child is hospitalized.

The province of Quebec has established its own program that offers maternity, paternity, parental, and adoption benefits, the Quebec Parental Insurance Plan (QPIP). More information on this provincial program is provided at the end of this chapter.

Sickness Benefits

Sickness benefits may be paid up to 15 weeks to an individual who is unable to work because of sickness, injury, or quarantine, but who would otherwise be available for work if not for their incapacity due to medical reasons.

To receive sickness benefits, the claimant is required to have worked for 600 hours in the last 52 weeks or since the last claim and your normal weekly earnings have been reduced by more than 40%.

Compassionate Care Benefits

Compassionate care benefits may be paid up to a maximum of six weeks to an individual who has to be absent from work to provide care or support to a gravely ill family member at risk of dying within 26 weeks. To be eligible for compassionate care benefits, the individual must show a decrease of more than 40% of regular weekly earnings from work and an accumulation of 600 insured hours in the last 52 weeks or since the start of the individual's last claim.

Unemployed individuals already receiving EI benefits can also apply for compassionate care benefits.

Family members can share the six weeks of compassionate care benefits. Each family member must apply for and be eligible for these benefits. Each family member can claim the benefits at any time during the 26-week period, either at the same time or at different times.

Parents of Critically Ill Children (PCIC) Benefits

Critically Ill Children Benefits may be paid up to a maximum of 35 weeks to either parent (or can be shared between them) who must be away from work to provide care or support to a critically ill or injured child.

To be eligible to establish a claim for the PCIC benefit, you must be able to show that:

- your regular weekly earnings from work have decreased by more than 40% because you need to provide care or support;
- you have accumulated 600 insured hours of work in the 52 weeks prior to the start of your claim, or since the start of your last claim, whichever is shorter;
- you are the parent of the child who is critically ill or injured; and
- your child is under 18 years of age at the time the 52-week window opens.

The *52-week window* begins on the day the medical certificate is issued; or, if the claim is made before the certificate is issued, from the date the specialist medical doctor certifies that your child is critically ill or injured.

Employment Insurance Special Benefits for Self-Employed People

Self-employed Canadians can apply for EI special benefits (maternity, parental, sickness, and compassionate care benefits) if they are registered for access to the EI program.

Waiting Period

For regular benefits and for any of the special benefits listed above, a two-week waiting period applies before EI benefits are payable. In the case of EI parental benefits being shared by both parents, a single waiting period may apply. It should be noted that the 2016 Federal Budget proposed the EI waiting period be reduced to one week effective in 2017.

Benefit Amount

For regular benefits and for any of the special benefits listed above, the basic benefit rate is 55% of the individual's average insured weekly earnings up to the maximum amount. In 2016, the maximum yearly insurable earnings are $50,800. This means that the maximum amount is $537 per week.

The benefit rate is based on the claimant's total earnings before deductions during the "best weeks" in the qualifying period (52 week period prior to the start of the EI claim).

In regions of Canada with the highest rates of unemployment, the best 14 weeks will be used; in regions with the lowest rates of unemployment, the best 22 weeks will be used. In other regions, the number of weeks used to calculate benefits will be somewhere between 14 and 22, depending on the unemployment rate in those regions as illustrated in the chart below.

The total earnings for the claimant's best weeks are divided by the corresponding divisor to obtain an average. This number is then multiplied by 55% to obtain the amount of weekly benefit up to the maximum of $537 per week.

Regional Rate of Unemployment	Required Weeks/Divisor
6% and under	22
6.1% to 7%	21
7.1% to 8%	20
8.1% to 9%	19
9.1% to 10%	18
10.1% to 11%	17
11.1% to 12%	16
12.1% to 13%	15
13.1% and over	14

EXAMPLE:

Meghan Vallis worked for 50 of the past 52 weeks. She lives in a region where the unemployment rate is 9.5% (therefore a divisor of 18). During her best 18 weeks of work Meghan earned a total of $17,000.

Step 1:

Calculate average weekly earnings $17,000/18 = $944.44

Step 2:

Calculate weekly benefit

$944.44 X 55% = $519.44

If certain conditions are met, claimants are entitled to exclude "small weeks" — in which the claimant earned $225 or less — in calculating their weekly benefit rate.

Family Supplement

The Family Supplement provides additional benefits to low-income families with children. A claimant does not have to apply for this supplement; it is automatically added to his or her EI payment. Only those individuals who receive the Canada Child Tax Benefits, a program administered by the Canada Revenue Agency, will be entitled to benefits.

The Family Supplement may increase an individual's benefit rate to as high as 80% of his or her average insurable earnings and is based on the family net income up to a maximum of $25,921 and the number of children in the family and their ages. However, maximum weekly benefit is still $537.

If an individual and their spouse both claim EI benefits at the same time, only one individual can receive the family supplement. It is generally better for the spouse with the lower benefit rate to receive the supplement.

The family supplement benefit gradually decreases as income level increases, so that when the maximum income of $25,921 is reached, no supplement is payable.

Working While Receiving Employment Insurance Benefits

A Pilot Project allows individuals receiving EI benefits (except maternity or sickness benefits) to work part-time and keep 50 cents of his EI benefits for every dollar earn, up to 90% of the weekly insurable earnings that was used to calculate EI benefit entitlement.

If an individual does work while receiving maternity or sickness benefits, earnings will be deducted dollar for dollar from the EI benefits paid.

Earnings or allowances payable to a claimant for attending a course of instruction, training to which there was a referral, from employment on a Job Creation Partnership, or from employment under a Self-Employment agreement are not deducted from unemployment benefits payable under specific circumstances.

Employers and their employees facing a temporary reduction in the normal level of business activity can participate in a Work-Sharing agreement with Service Canada in order to avoid layoffs. Earnings received in any week by an employee from the Work-Sharing employer shall not be deducted from the Work-Sharing benefits payable. Earnings received from other sources will be deducted from the employee's weekly Work-Sharing benefits.

Contributions

The Maximum Insurable Earnings (MIE) is the income level up to which EI premiums are paid, and it determines the maximum rate of weekly benefits paid. The MIE for 2016 is $50,800.

The EI program is financed from employee and employer contributions, with certain special programs and benefits funded by the federal government. The employer contribution rate is 1.4 times the employee's rate. The rates are set each year.

The following table outlines the rates and maximums for 2016:

	All provinces except Quebec		Province of Quebec*	
	Rates	Annual Maximum	Rates	Annual Maximum
Employee	1.88%	$955.04	1.52%	$722.16
Employer	2.63%	$1,337.06	2.13%	$1,081.02

*The rate for Quebec is lower due to the province offering its own parental benefits.

Under the *Employment Insurance Act*, employers and employees base contributions on all insurable earnings, up to the MIE. Employees earning less than $2,000 are entitled to a refund of contributions. No refund is provided for employers in respect of employees earning less than $2,000.

Employers with an approved wage loss replacement plan qualify for a rate reduction.

Employment Insurance Premium Reduction Program

An employer plan is deemed to be the "first payer" and EI is deemed to be the "second payer" of disability benefits. Any payment received from a short-term disability plan reduces the EI benefit paid for the same week. As a result, the cost to the EI fund is reduced if the employer operates a short-term disability plan for employees.

In recognition, employer EI premiums are reduced if a short-term disability plan is approved by and registered with HRSDC. Weekly indemnity plans and Cumulative Paid Sick Leave Plans are short-term disability plans that can qualify for an EI premium reduction. The amount of the reduction depends on the type of plan. At least 5/12 of the premium reduction must be returned, directly or indirectly, to the employees. Such sharing can be achieved through the following examples of acceptable arrangements:

- A written mutual agreement on how the savings will be returned to the employees;
- A cash rebate equal to 5/12 of the savings divided amongst the employees, which is treated as employment income subject to source deductions (*i.e.*, EI, CPP/QPP); and
- Providing new or increased benefits, including upgrading existing benefits, or providing more holidays or time off work.

For each calendar year, the rates of premium reduction are determined based on four categories of qualified plans, with a different rate for each category.

To qualify for EI premium reduction, a short-term disability plan must provide disability benefits that are at least equal to the EI benefits in terms of benefit amount, duration, and contract provisions. The employer must have a formal written commitment to provide disability benefits after service of no more than three months of continuous employment.

Minimum requirements to qualify for EI premium reduction include:

- Disability benefits that are at least equal to the EI sickness benefits (*i.e.*, 55% of insurable earnings);

- Payment of benefits starting on or before the 15th day of disability (or 8th day starting in 2017);
- In the case of weekly indemnity plans, payment of benefits for at least 15 weeks for each disability occurrence;
- Eligibility to claim benefits within three months of continuous employment;
- 24-hour coverage;
- Designation of the plan as the first payer (preventing plan benefits from being integrated and/or coordinated with EI benefits); and
- In the case of weekly indemnity plans, reinstatement of full disability coverage after a disability within one month of return to work for future disabilities not related to the initial disability cause, and within three months of return to work for a recurrence of the initial disability cause.

Supplemental Plans

Employers may provide supplemental benefits through a supplemental plan to increase an employee's income while in receipt of maternity, parental, or compassionate care benefits. Supplemental payments are not deducted from EI benefits provided that:

- The payment when added to the employee's EI weekly benefits, does not exceed the employee's normal weekly wage earnings (100% of gross salary); and
- The payment is not used to reduce other accumulated employment benefits such as banked sick leave, vacation leave credits, or severance pay.

Such supplement can be paid during the EI waiting period without affecting the start of the EI benefits. Employers do not have to register supplemental plans; however, special reporting requirements must be followed. Payments from a non-registered supplemental plan are not considered as insurable earnings; therefore, EI premiums are not deducted from supplemental plan payments.

Another type of supplemental plan employers may provide is a Supplemental Unemployment Benefits (SUB) plan. The purpose of a SUB plan is to provide supplemental payments to EI, training, or disability.[4] A SUB plan must be registered with Service Canada in order that payments

---

[4]   SUB Plans to EI sickness benefits are discussed in Chapter 21.

from registered plans are not deducted from the employee's EI benefits nor EI premiums deducted from SUB payments.

Income Tax on Employment Insurance

The tax situation regarding EI benefits may be summarized as follows:

- EI premiums paid by the employer are a tax-deductible expense to the employer and do not give rise to taxable income for the employee.
- Premiums paid by the employee give rise to a tax credit, which reduces the amount of income tax. The tax credit is 15% of EI premiums for federal tax purposes.
- EI benefits are taxable income to the recipient.
- Benefit repayments are possible under the "clawback" measure. The intent is to discourage individuals with higher annual incomes from repeatedly collecting benefits. The following rules apply regarding the repayment of EI benefits for individuals whose income exceeds a certain amount:
  o All first-time claimants (defined as those who were paid regular benefits for less than one week in the 10 taxation years before the current taxation year) are exempted from benefit repayment since they are not, by definition, repeat claimants;
  o All those who receive special benefits (maternity, parental, sickness, and compassionate care) will no longer have to repay any of those benefits; parents who stay at home with their newborn/newly adopted children or workers who are too sick to work are not penalized; and
  o If the claimant's net income exceeds $63,500, he or she will be required to repay 30% of the lesser of (a) his or her net income in excess of $63,500, or (b) the total regular benefits paid in the taxation year.

Quebec Parental Insurance Plan

On January 1, 2006, the Province of Quebec established its own parental insurance plan. It provides maternity, paternity, parental and adoption benefits to Quebec residents as defined in an *Act respecting parental insurance*.

The QPIP is an independent insurance organization. The Conseil de gestion de l'assurance parentale acts as the manager and trustee of the Parental Insurance Fund. The administration of benefit and client relationships is provided by the Ministry of Employment and Social Solidarity of Quebec.

To be eligible, a Quebec resident who has a biological or adopted child needs to have at least $2,000 in insurable income during the reference period (usually the last 52 weeks) and must have stopped working or have seen a reduction of at least 40% in his or her usual employment income. Self-employed workers are also eligible.

Benefits could be as high as 75% of average weekly income (AWI) starting without a waiting period. The maximum insurable income is $71,500 in 2016. A particular aspect of the program is the choice between two options, which differ in terms of duration and level of benefit.

The following table summarizes the options:

Type of Benefits	Basic Plan		Special Plan	
	Max. number of benefit weeks	% of AWI	Max. number of benefit weeks	% of AWI
Maternity	18	70%	15	75%
Paternity	5	70%	3	75%
Parental*	7 25	70% 55%	25	75%
Adoption*	12 25	70% 55%	28	75%

* Parental and adoption benefits may be shared between parents.

If the net family income is under $25,921, an increase in benefits may be granted.

The QPIP is financed by employees, employers, and self-employed workers. Premiums are collected by Revenu Quebec. For 2016, the employee premium rate is 0.548% of earnings up to a maximum of $391.82, the employer premium rate is 0.767% up to a maximum of $548.41, and the self-employed workers rate is 0.973% up to a maximum of $695.70. In consideration of this plan, EI premiums for Quebec residents are reduced.

Chapter 20

EXTENDED HEALTH AND DENTAL CARE PLANS

Executive Summary

Extended health care (EHC) plans and dental care plans are types of group accident and sickness insurance that provide employees with coverage for a variety of medical and dental services, treatments, and supplies. EHC plans generally operate as second payer to provincial medical programs, and payment under an EHC plan is limited to medically necessary expenses not paid by provincial insurance and within the eligibility requirements of the group contract or plan document. Under an EHC plan, the major coverage categories are prescription drugs, hospital accommodation above ward level, medical services and supplies, a variety of health care practitioners, emergency out-of-province expenses, and vision care. Under a dental plan, the major coverage categories reflect the type and complexity of services, i.e., basic services, including diagnostic, preventive, and restorative dental services; supplementary basic services, which add specific surgical, endodontic and periodontic treatments; major services, covering significant dental work such as crowns; and orthodontic services. This chapter provides detailed information on the various services and treatments covered under the different categories of EHC and dental plans. It also explains significant administrative features, such as payment methods, coinsurance, and coordination with provincial insurance,[1] with particular attention to cost-containment measures. There is also an explanation of Health Care Spending Accounts (HCSAs), which supplement EHC and dental care benefits, and the taxation of these plans.

---

[1] See Chapter 17 for a detailed discussion of provincial hospital and medical insurance plans.

Attributes

Employee

Coverage under EHC and dental plans generally includes employees and their eligible dependants. The definition of an employee generally means an active, full-time employee. However, some plan sponsors also include part-time employees and retirees in the definition.

Dependants

Dependants generally include legally married or common-law spouses (including same-sex) and dependent children under the age of 18. The age limit for dependent children is often increased to age 25 for full-time students, and waived for children who have a severe physical or mental disability.

Deductible

With a deductible, the employee is required to pay the first fixed dollar amount of incurred out-of-pocket expenses before the plan will consider the remaining expenses for reimbursement. For example, a $100 per person calendar year deductible requires an individual to pay the first $100 of eligible expenses incurred during the year before the EHC or dental plan reimburses any additional expenses. Deductibles can be expressed as a flat dollar amount per calendar year or as a flat dollar amount per claim (for example, $2 per prescription). The deductible may also vary depending on whether the employee has single, couple, or family coverage.

Coinsurance

A coinsurance provision refers to the percentage of an eligible expense that will be paid by the plan; the remaining percentage will be paid by the claimant. If, for example, the coinsurance factor is 80%, the plan will pay for 80% of eligible expenses with the claimant paying the remaining 20%.

Cost Sharing

The cost of EHC and dental plans may be shared with employees in a variety of ways. The most direct method is to have the employee pay a portion of the monthly plan premiums through payroll deduction. However, employees can also pay for a portion of the plan cost through a deductible or a coinsurance provision.

Extended Health Care Plans

Each province, under the direction of the *Canada Health Act*, provides residents with coverage for hospital accommodation at the ward level, and for basic medical expenses including physician visits. Prior to the establishment of provincial medical programs, costs related to prevention and treatment were the responsibility of each individual. EHC plans (also referred to as Supplementary Health and Major Medical) were introduced to supplement the provincial medical programs and provide reimbursement of expenses for services not covered by these plans.

As a general rule, EHC plans operate as second payer to the provincial medical programs. Consideration for payment under the EHC plan is limited to medically necessary expenses not paid by the provincial programs, and within the provisions of the insurance contract or plan document.

EHC plans vary in structure. The most common structure is to have all eligible medical expenses covered under one benefit plan; however, these plans can generally be separated into the following categories:

- Prescription drugs;
- Hospital;
- Medical services and supplies;
- Emergency out-of-province; and
- Vision care.

Prescription Drugs

Coverage of drugs under EHC plans varies considerably. These differences are due to the definition of drugs eligible under the plan, the reimbursement level, and the method used to pay claims. The most prevalent definition of eligible drugs is a "prescription drug" plan that covers only those drugs that legally require a prescription.

Non-prescription life sustaining drugs, such as insulin for diabetes, are generally also covered.

By comparison, a "prescribed" plan is much more liberal, and covers any drugs dispensed by a pharmacist and prescribed by a physician, whether or not a prescription is legally required. This includes medicines that are otherwise available over-the-counter (OTC), without payment of a dispensing fee.

The growing prevalence of specialty drugs for common conditions is having a significant impact on EHC plans. Specialty drugs are usually expensive, require special handling and often involve more complex administration (i.e. infusion or injection). Many specialty drugs are biologic drugs that are synthesized from living entities, such as cells and tissues, rather than a chemical process, and considerable research is required for their development. The annual cost for biologics for one claimant can often exceed $10,000 and can be as high as $500,000. Additionally, the unique manufacturing process associated with these drugs means that generic substitutes are difficult to create. However, the impending emergence of Subsequent Entry Biologics (SEB's) or "biosimiliars", while not identical to the original biologic drug, may provide similar therapeutic outcomes at a lower cost. The number of claims submitted for biologics is low but increasing each year and the dollar impact on a plan can be significant. Countering the impact of biologics is the fact that several brand name drugs have had their patent protection expire recently, allowing lower cost generic versions to be produced. In addition, the pan-Canadian Pharmaceutical Alliance negotiates on behalf of all provinces and terrirories as well as the federal government to reduce the cost of brand and generic drugs. Despite these efforts, higher dispensing fees and markups at the pharmacy mitigate the savings to plan sponsors.

Currently, some drugs claimed under EHC plans are processed on a reimbursement, or pay and submit basis. The individual pays the pharmacist in full at the time the prescription is filled and files a claim for reimbursement. The claims administrator, usually an insurance company, adjudicates the relevant information at the time the claim is processed. Along with the reimbursement cheque, the employee receives an explanation of benefits statement that indicates the amount submitted, the amount eligible, and whether deductible and coinsurance were applicable.

At the other end of the spectrum, the pay-direct method combines paperless data processing with online real-time claim adjudication. Under a pay-direct method, the individual presents a pay-direct drug card at the time the prescription is filled. The claim is adjudicated for price and eligibility through electronic transmission, directly between the claims administrator and the pharmacist. The pharmacist is able to advise the employee immediately whether the medication is eligible, and what amount the plan will pay. If the medication is eligible, the individual only pays the pharmacist any required plan deductible or coinsurance.

The convenience of a pay-direct card generally results in cost increases for the first two years primarily associated with increased utilization. However, the cost-control opportunities of pay-direct and real-time electronic adjudication relative to manual adjudication may outweigh the cost increase over time.

A hybrid method of the paper-based reimbursement and the pay-direct drug card is the deferred payment method, but this option is less prevalent. Under this arrangement, an employee pays the pharmacist directly for the full amount of the expense and provides a card to the pharmacist to electronically submit the claim to the insurer directly rather than completing a paper claim form. Reimbursement of any eligible expenses is provided back to the employee directly.

Mandatory Prescription Drug Coverage in Quebec

In Quebec, it is mandatory for every resident to have coverage for prescription drugs. If a resident is eligible for prescription drug coverage through their employer or an association, this coverage is mandatory unless already covered under another private health plan for prescription drugs. If coverage is not available through an employer or association, residents must register for the public plan provided through Régie de l'assurance maladie du Quebec (RAMQ).

Employers providing group coverage to their employees for accident, illness, or disability must also provide a prescription drug plan at a level at least equal to that provided by RAMQ. RAMQ's prescription drug deductible, effective July 1, 2016, is $18.85 per month and the coinsurance level provided is 66% The maximum annual contribution of deductible and coinsurance combined for residents in $1,046. Private plans must cover all drugs that appear on RAMQ's List of Medications, which is updated frequently. Group plans with less than 250 covered individuals must also include stop loss coverage.

Employees who decline coverage under their employer's plan because they have coverage elsewhere are required to provide proof of this coverage to their employer. The employer must retain this documentation on file in case RAMQ requests a copy. Effective April 11, 2007, plan sponsors are also responsible for notifying RAMQ if the plan will not be renewing, if an employee's coverage is cancelled due to failure to pay premiums, or if the plan sponsor is terminating the plan for all employees. If coverage is cancelled under a private plan and coverage cannot be secured under another private plan, it is the employee's responsibility to register him or herself and his or her family under RAMQ.

At age 65, all Quebec citizens are automatically registered for the prescription drug plan, even if they have coverage through their employer's plan. Employees age 65 and over may continue to be covered by their employer's plan; however, they must contact RAMQ to terminate coverage under the public plan. In practice, the increase in premium demanded by the insurer for employees age 65 and over forces the employee to subscribe to RAMQ. Some employers have chosen to modify their plan for employees over age 65 to act as a "top-up" to the RAMQ plan, providing the employee with equivalent coverage to employees under age 65 while keeping the cost of the private plan at a reasonable level.

Hospital

Provincial medical programs in Canada pay for hospital accommodation limited to ward level, unless semi-private or private accommodation is deemed essential for medical reasons. Supplemental hospital plans were designed to cover the additional cost of semi-private or private hospital accommodation.

Medically necessary services rendered in hospital are also covered by provincial medical programs and include physician services, nursing care, in-hospital lab tests, drugs administered in-hospital, outpatient emergency services, operating rooms, surgical equipment, and supplies.

Although the number of EHC plans that cover unlimited private accommodation is decreasing, many still cover the full cost of semi-private for an unlimited period of hospital confinement. The hospital benefit can be provided as a separate benefit or as part of the EHC plan. In either case, the hospital benefit can be subject to, or exempt from, any deductible and coinsurance provisions applicable to other medical expenses.

In most cases, the claimant assigns payment to the hospital and the hospital submits the claim for reimbursement. The patient seldom sees the bill from the hospital. Most providers make payments directly to the hospital, eliminating advance payment by the individual other than for incidental costs not covered by the plan, such as telephone and television services.

The average length of stay in hospital has decreased over time but the average per diem rates charged by hospitals have increased dramatically. The net result is an overall cost increase associated with providing hospital coverage under an EHC plan.

Medical Services and Supplies

There is a wide range of medical services and supplies that are typically covered under the EHC benefit. These include:

- Paramedical practitioners (e.g., chiropractors, registered massage therapists, physiotherapists, and podiatrists);
- Prosthetic appliances and durable medical equipment (e.g., hearing aids, crutches, and orthotics);
- Private duty nursing;
- Ambulance services; and
- Accidental dental.

The EHC plan covers reasonable and customary charges for these services and supplies when medically necessary, and when prescribed, ordered, or referred by a physician. However, coinsurance, deductibles, and/or individual maximums for specific services and supplies may apply when calculating the eligible amount may be compulsory depending on the terms of the plan. Individual maximums for specific services and supplies may be in the form of a dollar limit and/or time frequency (e.g., one every three or five years). For example, hearing aids may be eligible based on a maximum of $500 every five years.

Paramedical services under EHC plans are typically performed by licensed practitioners such as chiropractors, physiotherapists, massage therapists, and naturopaths. The utilization of these services continues to grow as employees search for alternative forms of medical therapy and paramedical services become more generally acceptable and easily accessible. The cost of these services can escalate very quickly, particularly when they are not being covered under provincial government health care plans and there are no annual limits in the EHC plan.

While many have focused on dealing with their prescription drug program, managing the cost of paramedical services, particularly massage therapy and physiotherapy, should not be ignored as these claims have increased significantly higher than both the general inflation rate (i.e., the Consumer Price Index (CPI)) as well as the utilization/inflation trend factor typically used for EHC plans by major insurers, and have become a much larger component of the overall extended health care cost.

Emergency Out-of-Province

Most provincial medical programs provide coverage for residents in need of emergency care and treatment while temporarily absent from their province and/or country. However, the level of coverage is very limited and will typically not reimburse the full cost, particularly in the United States where the cost of health care services is significantly greater.

The EHC plan covers these additional medical costs up to reasonable and customary charges. Most plans do not apply a deductible or coinsurance to emergency out-of-province claims; however, there are usually limitations in the number of days covered for travel (e.g., 90 days) and a fixed dollar maximum.

Vision Care

Most provincial medical programs cover the costs of professional fees for basic eye examinations and testing for certain residents. Due to reductions in federal transfer payments and health-cost pressures, most provincial plans have limited coverage for children and seniors only. Most provinces cover medically necessary eye exams. Reimbursement for eye examinations can be provided under an EHC plan, and may be coordinated with the provincial medical plan.

Because eyeglasses and elective contact lenses are not covered under provincial medical plans for the working population, coverage can be provided as a benefit under an EHC plan.

Reimbursement of eyeglasses and contacts is typically based on a maximum reimbursement of $150 to $250 in any 12- or 24-month period. For contact lenses required to bring an individual's visual acuity to a medically acceptable level, a higher maximum is usually provided. The objective is to provide corrective eyewear, not to provide a fashion statement. Even so, vision deficits often require corrective lenses substantially more expensive than the benefit provided under the EHC plan. While laser eye surgery has become a popular and accessible procedure, the cost is not typically covered under EHC plans. When it is covered under an EHC plan, laser eye surgery may have a separate maximum or be subject to the vision care maximum set in the plan.

Vision care benefits tend to be expressed as 100% coinsurance up to a fixed dollar maximum. This fixed dollar limit is usually less than the cost of an average pair of adult glasses, and offers the plan some protection against inflation.

To stretch the value of the benefit dollar, some insurance companies participate in a preferred provider network of vision care retailers. These retailers offer discounts of 10% to 20% to their preferred customers. This feature is provided as part of an EHC plan at no extra cost, and serves to reduce the amount that the employee would otherwise pay out-of-pocket above the plan maximum.

Managing Rising Extended Health Care Costs

Although the rising cost of health services has stabilized in recent years, the factors affecting EHC plans continue to average well over the annual rate of inflation as measured by the CPI. Some of the main cost drivers behind these increases are:

- *Prescription drug costs* — The rising cost of drugs continues to be the primary factor influencing extended health costs. Contributing to this is the increase in average pharmacy fees, the quantity of drugs being dispensed per claimant, and the introduction of new, more expensive specialty drugs being developed for more common conditions. Drugs prescribed for mental health issues often represent the highest percentage of drug costs for a plan sponsor. The aging of the Canadian population also impacts prescription drug costs as older employees will typically require more frequent and more expensive prescription drugs.

- *Paramedical costs* — As employees look for alternatives for managing their health issues, the demand for paramedical practitions such as massage therapists, physiotherapists, chiropractors, naturopaths and acupuncturists has increased steadily over the last several years and is often the second largest component of an extended health plan's claims costs. Demand has also increased due to more awareness of the availability of these services due to advertising by these types of practitioners

- *Obesity* — While the rise of obesity levels has slowed in recent year, a survey released in 2014 by the Organisation for Economic Co-operation and Development (OECD) found that more than 50% of the Canadian population was overweight or obese. The Government of Canada reports that rates of obesity in children and youth have nearly tripled in the last 30 years. The cost to treat obesity and related illnesses is substantial and many organizations have developed wellness strategies in order to proactively assist employees in making positive lifestyle choices.

- *Changing demographics* — The working and general population is aging. On average, older people take more prescriptions and claim for medications that are generally more expensive. In addition, people are living longer as a result of modern medical therapies. A combination of these factors results in higher plan utilization, which impacts ongoing plan costs.

- *Government cost-shifting* — With reductions in federal transfer payments, provincial government plans are reducing and/or eliminating coverage. The impact of this is to transfer health care responsibilities and costs to private EHC plans. Shorter hospital stays also shift costs from government plans to private health plans as drugs and services that would be covered while the employee is in hospital are now shifted to the private plan sooner.

In response to these cost pressures, EHC plans are being modified to incorporate cost-containment measures and/or promote prevention measures. The objective is to balance the comprehensive protection of the plan against the need for affordable benefits.

Increasing Deductibles and Coinsurance

While many plans still have relatively low deductibles, some plans are designed to cover more catastrophic events, leaving the individual responsible for routine expenses. In addition, many plans have some level of coinsurance in place. For example, the deductible may be $250 per person per year or more, with 80% coinsurance over the deductible. In most cases, the coinsurance reverts to 100% after the individual has satisfied the deductible, and incurred out-of-pocket expenses of some fixed dollar amount per year. The objective of this design is to promote partnering with individuals through cost-sharing, while still providing financial safeguards for the employee against unexpected large expenses.

Modification to Drug Program

There are a number of measures plan sponsors can take to control and manage prescription drug costs, particularly in conjunction with a pay-direct drug card. Such measures include the following:

Generic Substitution

Generic drugs contain the same active ingredients and strength as brand name drugs that are no longer protected by patent. The difference is usually a lower cost (as much as 60% savings can be achieved through generic drug utilization). Most provinces, including Ontario, have mandated generic substitution unless expressly prohibited by the physician. EHC plans using a pay-direct basis allow for the enforcement of uniform application of generic substitution.

Lowest Cost Alternatives

Instead of limiting the medications available under the plan, this feature limits reimbursement. Payment is based on the price of the lowest-cost drug that contains the same active ingredients and the same strength. This may also apply to the coverage of many new medications on the market, such as time-release capsules, that represent a more convenient form of an existing lower cost medication. Pharmaceutical companies often provide rebate cards via physicians or obtained online that pay for all or a portion of the difference in cost between the brand name and generic drug in an effort to maintain market share.

Therapeutic Substitutions

This feature involves the substitution of a less expensive drug within the same therapeutic classification but with different active ingredients than the prescribed drug. The intent is to move the patient through a medically accepted protocol of treatment for the condition, generally moving from least to most expensive medication in sequence.

Lifestyle Drugs

Some plan sponsors choose to limit certain drugs on the basis that usage is related to lifestyle, and as such, not considered medically necessary under the plan. Examples of drugs include smoking cessation, sexual dysfunction, fertility, anti-obesity, and oral contraceptives.

Managed Care Formularies

A formulary covers a specific list of eligible drugs that are updated periodically (e.g., quarterly). Some formularies mirror the provincial drug programs available to seniors and those on social assistance. In this case, as the provincial plans delist drugs, the EHC plan would also remove these drugs as an eligible expense. Other formularies may be based on the provincial plan plus selected drugs, or, less often, a specific list of drugs tailored to an employee population. Under this scenario, formularies are designed and managed by the insurance company or claims administrator and typically include the most cost-effective drugs that have proven to have comparative efficacy. A viable formulary is not static and requires regular review of new medication to evaluate comparative efficacy and cost relative to the current list of eligible drugs. The goal of the formulary is to provide patients with required medications in a manner that is both cost-effective and high quality.

Tiered Copayments

Under a tiered copayment program, the amount reimbursed is determined by the type of medication or the employee's choice. If a drug is available in a generic formulation it is up to the employee to choose either the brand name drug or the generic version. For example, the first tier, could be for the generic drugs, and pay 100% under the EHC plan, the second tier could be set at 80% for brand name drugs with no available generic, and the third tier, could be for brand name drugs where there is a generic available. Under the third tier, if the employee wishes to have the brand name drug, the amount paid by the EHC plan could be equivalent to the cost of the generic drug. Most insurance companies and claims administrators have tiered plan options available as a method of cost containment and plan sustainability.

Change Management

When the decision is made to manage prescription drug costs using a modified drug plan, the success of the change may be impacted by how and when it is communicated to employees. Having a strategy in place prior to making any modifications is crucial to ensure employees are comfortable with the changes and understand how to modify their behaviours in obtaining drug coverage. Failure to do this may result in employee frustration and dissatisfaction with the EHC plan and employer.

Integrated Approach to Evaluating Costs

Plan sponsors are starting to take a holistic approach to managing overall health benefit costs. In this scenario, data is analyzed by disease state across various benefit programs such as the extended health plan (including prescription drugs), health risk assessments, employee assistance, and absence and disability, for example. When examined in an integrated fashion, the plan sponsor is provided with a comprehensive picture of health within an organization and health risks can be identified ahead of trend. This enables evidence-based decisions to be made to alter the course of those trends and mitigate future costs and risks. Going forward, analyzing data in this way can also assist with tracking the impact of program design changes a plan sponsor makes (e.g. preventive health and wellness or cost-control features), or help validate the rationale for modifications to existing programs the plan sponsor is considering for the future. Based on the analysis of the data collected, this may mean that use of the EHC benefit is promoted to reduce larger costs such as absence and disability.

Health Care Spending Accounts

An HCSA is an individual employee account that involves the allocation of a fixed dollar amount by the employer. The account allows for maximum flexibility with the dollars so designated, because individual choice is made at the level of service. Some of the advantages to employees and employers of an HCSA are:

- An HCSA allows more choice to the employees without requiring a major overhaul of the plan;
- An HCSA utilizes the defined contribution concept versus the defined benefit approach;
- An HCSA is easier to administer than a complete flexible benefit plan; and
- There is better communication of the value of benefits as part of employees' total compensation package.

Most employers offering an HCSA use it to supplement the EHC and/or dental care benefits. To qualify for tax-favoured treatment, an HCSA needs to be structured as a private health services plan as defined by the Canada Revenue Agency (CRA). Unused credits or incurred expenses not reimbursed may be rolled forward up to 24 months, at which time any remaining credits or expenses will be forfeit. The plan sponsor must decide between rolling over credits or expenses and cannot choose both. Payment of eligible expenses is deductible by the employer and is not taxable (except in the province of Quebec) to the employee.

Coordination of Benefits

Coordination of Benefits (COB) guidelines were developed by the Canadian Life and Health Insurance Association (CLHIA) and apply to all group insurance providers in Canada. The purpose of COB is to eliminate overpayments by plan sponsors, and maximize reimbursement to employees. These guidelines provide the sequence in which an expense will be adjudicated if there are two private health plans involved, and identify the primary plan and the secondary plan. Most commonly, COB applies to an employee who has a spouse with coverage under a group plan. In this case, the employee would submit his or her own expenses to his or her own plan first, and then submit the unpaid balance to the spouse's plan. The spouse would submit expenses to his or her own plan first. Expenses for dependent children are submitted to the plan of the parent whose birthday falls first in the calendar year. If the parents' birthdays are on the same date, the expenses should be submitted under the plan of the parent whose first name comes earliest in the alphabet.

There are also rules for coordination of dependent child claims that accommodate those employees who are divorced, legally separated, have remarried, or are in a common-law relationship. In these cases, expenses for dependent children should first be submitted under the plan of the parent with custody of the children and then under the plan of the spouse of the parent with custody. The claim can then be submitted under the plan of the parent without custody and then under the plan of the spouse of the parent without custody. If the parents have joint custody, the birthday rule as described previously should be applied.

Dental Plans

Dental plans were first introduced in the late 1960s as a result of collective bargaining and the absence of any public programs. The majority of employee benefit programs now include dental coverage, which generally represents the largest component of a plan sponsor's total employee benefit costs.

The Canadian Dental Association, which represents dentists on national issues, prepares procedure codes for dental services. In addition, each province has a dental association (except Alberta) that selects the procedure codes to be included in the provincial fee guide, and also assigns the suggested cost for each code. At the end of each year, provincial dental associations publish the suggested changes to the fee guide for the upcoming calendar year; however, there is no formal agreement binding dental practitioners to the fee guide. The purpose of the fee guide is to provide guidance as to the reasonable and fair charges for dental services. Claims administrators like insurance companies, for example, often rely on the fee guides to determine the amount eligible for reimbursement based on the service provided.

The dental association in the Province of Alberta no longer provides a dental fee guide; rather, it provides dentists with a range of fees for procedure codes. The range of fees is based on an annual survey conducted by the association of its members regarding the fees charged for the majority of the dental services performed. Insurers use their own claims data to determine appropriate maximum reimbursement levels for various services. However, dentists set their own rates, creating much more variance amongst dentists than in other provinces.

Categories of Dental Services

Dental plans can be broadly categorized into four major areas of coverage that relate to the type of service, the general frequency, and the financial severity of the service.

1. *Basic services* — diagnostic (i.e., exams, X-rays), preventive (i.e., tooth sealants), and restorative (i.e., fillings).

2. *Supplementary basic services* —endodontics (i.e., root canals), periodontics (i.e., gum surgery), and some surgical procedures, relining and rebasing of dentures.

3. *Major services* — crowns, removable prosthodontics (i.e., partial and complete dentures), and fixed prosthodontics (i.e., bridges).

4. *Orthodontics* — braces to correct misaligned teeth.

Generally, plan sponsors introducing dental plans will limit the plan to basic services (including supplementary basic services), and may require a minimum service period for eligibility. In smaller plans, coverage may be limited to natural teeth that are present at the time the adult individual becomes eligible under the plan.

Typically, dental plans provide the highest coinsurance for basic services, and are set at a lower percentage for major services and orthodontics. Annual dollar limits usually apply to basic and major services (sometimes combined) on a per person basis. Orthodontic service limits are usually expressed as a flat-dollar amount per lifetime and are sometimes limited to dependent children only. Any deductible is expressed as a flat-dollar amount per covered person or per family per calendar year.

Adjudication of eligible expenses under dental plans is typically limited to the maximum suggested fee specified for general practitioners in the current Dental Fee Guide of the employee's province of residence. Some dental plans do allow for adjudication based on a specialist fee guide, such as a periodontist. Plan sponsors can also elect to have the dental claims reimbursed on a current fee guide, or a fee guide from a prior year (lagged fee guide).

Predetermination of Benefits

When significant expenses are anticipated (i.e., greater than $500), dentists can file a statement of proposed services and fees, known as a pre-treatment review. The pre-treatment review determines what portion of the total expense will be reimbursed by the plan, thus avoiding misunderstandings or misgivings before the work is done.

Alternate Benefit Clause

Where there is a choice of dental services that an individual may receive, some plans will limit payment to the least costly, professionally acceptable alternative. For example, there may be a choice of replacing missing teeth with a bridge or with a less costly partial denture. If the plan features an Alternate Benefit Clause, the employee may still receive a more costly treatment but would be reimbursed on the lower cost option and required to pay for the additional cost out-of-pocket.

Assignment of Benefits

The standard dental claim form allows the employee to authorize payment directly to the dentist. The assignment of benefits reduces the employee's initial cash outlay, but the employee is still financially responsible for any portion not reimbursed by the plan. Most dental plans allow assignment of benefits; however, some dental offices, as well as some Dental Associations oppose this practice and some plan sponsors are restricting this feature out of concern that assignment leads to higher costs because the employee will have no incentive to verify services and fees stated on the claim form. Although several insurance companies have attempted to prove or disprove this conjecture, results have been inconclusive.

Electronic Data Interchange and Online Claim Submission

Electronic data interchange (EDI) is the electronic transmission of claim data from the point of service — such as the dental or pharmacy office — to the claim payer. The transmission alerts the service provider to verify coverage under the EHC or dental plan while the patient waits for confirmation of the amount covered. Completing a paper claim form is not required when using EDI. The majority of dental claims are now submitted electronically since most dental offices are connected to the Canadian Dental Association network and claims administrators are capable of adjudicating claims online and in real time. Prescription drug claims are processed in a similar fashion for plans with pay-direct drug cards, and advances in claims administrator systems has made it possible for most paramedical practitioners or the employee to submit claim online.

Cost Management

As with EHC, cost increases have forced plan sponsors to consider cost management strategies. The most common approach is "tweaking" the dental plan by decreasing coinsurance and benefit maximums and increasing deductibles. Other strategies include reducing the frequency of recall examination coverage for adults from 6 to 9 or 12 months, and lowering periodontal coinsurance or placing limits on the units of periodontal service covered per person per year.

While these options provide an immediate impact on cost, they are generally perceived as short-term solutions as dental costs will continue to rise due to inflation and utilization. Some plan sponsors have taken a more pragmatic approach by making the cost of benefits more explicit through employee cost sharing or the introduction of defined contribution concepts like flexible benefit plans and HCSAs.

Income Tax on Health Plans

The following is an overview of the current income tax treatment of private health services plans, including employer-sponsored EHC and dental plans:

- If the plan is contributory, the premiums paid by the employee are not directly deductible from income for tax purposes. However, the employee contribution may be included in the calculation of the individual's medical expense tax credit (paragraph 118.2(2)(*q*) of the *Income Tax Act*).

- Employer contributions can be charged as an operating expense of the employer for tax purposes.

- Employer contributions to a private health services plan are not added to employee income for tax purposes, with one exception. In Quebec, employer contributions (as defined in the provincial regulations) are included as a taxable benefit for the purposes of calculating provincial income tax payable. The amount of the taxable benefit may be included in the calculation of the individual medical expense tax credit.

- If an employer pays, in whole or in part, the employee contributions under any provincial hospital or medical plan, the payment is deemed to be taxable income in the hands of the employee.

- For 1988 and subsequent tax years, an individual may claim a non-refundable, non-transferable tax credit for medical expenses. The amount of the medical expense tax credit is equal to qualifying medical expenses paid within any 12-month period ending in the taxation year, in excess of the lesser of $2,237 (for the 2016 tax year), or 3% of net income for the year.

Medical expenses that have been reimbursed, or are eligible expenses for reimbursement, are not eligible expenses for tax purposes. Similarly, premiums paid to provincial hospital or medical insurance plans are not eligible expenses in the calculation of the medical expense tax credit.

The federal government announced in its 2010 Budget that cosmetic surgical and non-surgical procedures for purely aesthetic reasons are not an eligible expense for the medical tax credit. The CRA provides a listing of eligible and ineligible expenses with regards to the medical tax credit on their website. This list is updated on a regular basis and should be referenced when determining eligible expenses for this credit.

Chapter 21

DISABILITY BENEFITS AND INCOME PROGRAMS

Executive Summary

Most employers provide employees with some level of disability benefits or income replacement coverage in the event of absence from work due to illness or accident, whether or not the cause is related to work. The range of contingencies addressed by disability benefits and income plans begin with occasional absences, through to short-term and on to serious disabilities that result in long-term absences from work.

This chapter explores the sources of disability benefits and income protection plans that may be broadly classified into the following major categories:

- Short-term disability (STD) plans;
- Long-term disability (LTD) plans; and
- Critical illness plans.[1]

This chapter also provides detailed discussions of plan designs, case management and the treatment of tax as it relates to employee disability benefits and income programs.

---

[1] Various government plans, such as Employment Insurance (EI), the Canada and Quebec Pension Plans (CPP/QPP), Workers' Compensation, and provincial automobile insurance plans provide disability benefits. See Chapter 19 for information about EI, Chapter 2 for information about the CPP/QPP, and Chapter 18 for information about Workers' Compensation. Some form of disability income may also be provided under group and individual life insurance plans, individual disability plans, and credit and automobile insurance plans.

Short-Term Disability Plans

Sick Leave Plans

Sick leave is a term used interchangeably with salary continuance to describe short-term income replacement plans. Sick leave plans are generally self-insured. In the past, many were adjudicated and administered by the employer. With the advent of privacy legislation and the evolving complexity of disability claims adjudication, employers have started looking outside of their organizations for assistance with the adjudication of disability claims. Benefits are normally paid directly from payroll, and as such, are subject to all the normal taxes and payroll deductions. Taxes and payroll deductions typically include income and payroll taxes, union dues, pension and insurance contributions, Canada and Quebec Pension Plan (CPP/QPP) contributions and Employment Insurance (EI) premiums. Employer contributions for CPP/QPP, EI, and Workers' Compensation, and any provincial health taxes on payroll also generally apply. Benefits paid through a Health and Welfare Trust will not be subject to all of the same payroll taxes and contributions. Contributions made to the trust will, however, attract premium tax and sales tax in some provinces.

A sick leave plan can be either formal or informal. Under an informal plan, there is no set policy regarding the payment of sick leave benefits. There has been a decrease in the number of such plans, most likely as a result of employers' fear of claims of discrimination. Under a formal plan, the payment is usually the full amount of the employee's salary or a defined percentage of salary, minus the normal deductions. The employee's length of service can be associated with the level of payment he or she will receive. Under a sick leave bank, the employer must decide the number of days of sick leave granted, whether the sick leave can accumulate, and whether sick leave credits are earned gradually during periods of active work or allocated at the beginning of a reference period. For example, the plan might credit 20 sick days at the beginning of each year, with unused sick leave days carried forward for use in future years. In general, most sick leave banks pay 100% of salary. A common concern with sick leave banks is that some employees who become genuinely disabled will not have sufficient sick leave days accumulated to carry them through to the commencement of long-term disability benefits.

Under some sick leave banks, employers "buy back" excess sick leave days by paying out a cash bonus at the end of the year. The buy back is a percentage of value of the days that would have been lost if the employee had been absent. Buy backs and other awards and incentives for good work attendance are mechanisms employers can use to decrease employee absenteeism.

According to accounting rules,[2] compensated absences should be accounted for in the reporting period in which the employee has rendered service, rather than in the future, after the employee begins to receive benefits.

Whether or not sick leave banks will be subject to these accounting requirements depends upon whether or not the benefits "vest" or "accumulate". If the benefit vests or accumulates, accounting rules will apply. Basically, vesting occurs if after a specific or determinable date, the employee's entitlement to the benefit is no longer dependent upon the employee being employed by the employer. If, for example, the unused sick leave credits are vested, with employees receiving all or part of their unused sick leave in a lump sum when they retire or terminate employment, these benefits will have to be accounted for on an accrual basis. A benefit accumulates if the employee can carry it forward to one or more periods after the period in which it was earned, even though there may be a limit with respect to the amount that can be carried forward. In general, any benefits that vary with the amount of additional service performed by the employee are benefits that accumulate. If, for example, the employer buys back sick leave days, accounting rules would not apply, as the benefit is not carried forward into the next period.

Other non-accounting issues arise with respect to a vested sick leave plan. For example, it may encourage employees to develop a sense of entitlement such that the benefit has been earned and can be used for discretionary absences, including those unrelated to illness or injury. Additionally, an employee may accrue sick leave at a low rate of pay (in the early years of employment) but have it paid out at a relatively high rate of pay (during the later years of employment), compounding the unfunded liability associated with vested sick leave plans.

As employers began to realize the potential liability that can accumulate, especially with accumulating plans, there was and has been an increased interest in eliminating sick leave banks. The introduction of accounting rules has only added fuel to the fire.

There are other reasons why sick leave plans pose significant risk, one being the significant liability that may be accrued for unused sick days. This can be addressed by prohibiting carry over from year to year, however, such a limitation typically results in insufficient accumulation of sick days to carry through until the LTD threshold (typically set at 17

---

[2]   See Chapter 14.

weeks or six months from the first day of absence). For sick leave plans that allow for accumulation, employees without sufficient accumulation of days may not be covered for a period of time between the end of sick leave days and the start of LTD. EI may be used to bridge this period, but it is possible there will be a gap in income.

Salary continuance provides continuation of full salary during sick leave absence. Such plans typically lack clear accountability for both the employee and the employer. The employee receives full salary and may not have any clear role or requirement for the salary continuation. However, employers may easily lose track of employees and the cost of absence. This issue can be addressed with formal disability management processes, and by a proactive provider who gets involved to validate entitlement to salary continuation and also manages the process of return to work preparation and any barriers to work.

Weekly Indemnity (or Short-Term Disability Plans)

Weekly indemnity and STD are terms used to describe an income replacement plan that may be self-insured or insured, and in which claims are generally adjudicated by a third party. The main distinction between sick leave plans and STD plans is the involvement of a third party in claims adjudication.

Self-insured plans often use the services of an outside provider to perform specific services such as adjudicating and paying claims. The employer may retain some administrative responsibilities, or may subcontract the administration to the third party. Where the provider is an insurance company, the arrangement is described as an Administrative Services Only (ASO) arrangement to indicate that the employer remains fully responsible for the financial risk.[3]

Self-insured STD plans are typically funded through the payroll system. Benefits paid to disabled employees through payroll are subject to CPP/QPP, EI, and Workers' Compensation contributions in addition to income tax deduction and payroll taxes. A third party arrangement can be structured to establish an arm's length relationship for claims adjudication. Benefits paid under an arm's length arrangement historically have not been subject to payroll tax or CPP/QPP, EI, and Workers' Compensation contributions, but would be subject to income tax for the recipient; premium tax and sales tax will apply to such arrangements in some

---

[3]   For more information on ASO arrangements, see Chapter 25.

provinces. On December 15, 2011, Bill C-13, *Keeping Canada's Economy and Jobs Growing Act* (the Act) received Royal Assent.

The most pertinent impact for group insurance programs is that employers who provide employer-funded wage loss replacement plans (WLRPs) on a self-insured basis must deduct CPP contributions from those benefits.

The amendment makes the CPP Act consistent with the *Employment Insurance Act* as a result of the Federal Court of Appeal decision in 2003 requiring that EI premiums be paid on uninsured disability benefits.

This change applies to CPP and does not impact the Québec Pension Plan (QPP), as it is related only to the reversing of the TTC court decision with respect to CPP.

It was later clarified that employees receiving CPP disability benefits are exempt from this change. However, the requirements for EI deductions and remittances remain.

Plans Not Affected by the Legislation

Trusts or insured STD/LTD programs

Employers do not have to make CPP and EI deductions under an insurance policy or a trust that meets CRA guidelines. The term "insurance policy" would extend to experience-rated, refund arrangements.

Salary continuance/sick bank arrangements: Employers offering these programs should already be making employee and employer contributions for CPP/QPP and EI premiums.

Non-taxable ASO disability plans: Non-taxable plans continue to be exempted and therefore do not need to deduct CPP contributions (both employer and employee) from benefits provided under these plans.

Benefits are generally expressed as a percentage of pay and may vary by length of service. For example, the STD benefit may be a lower percentage of earnings for employees in their first year of service. Benefits are usually paid from the first day, for a maximum duration such as 15 or 26 weeks. The benefit duration is chosen to dovetail with the commencement of LTD benefits.

STD plans may provide a percentage of pay ranging between 55% and 85% of gross weekly earnings or more, and may vary based on the employee's seniority and may change as the disability absence reaches certain timeline thresholds, for example, 75% for the first 12 weeks, reducing to 60% thereafter.

STD amounts may be integrated with other disability benefits to ensure that employee income during a period of disability does not exceed income while actively working. Other disability benefits include CPP/QPP, Workers' Compensation, automobile insurance, and any other disability benefit that may be payable to the employee. EI benefits are not offset against weekly indemnity benefits, as the employer plan is first payer. However, in carve-out plans, STD payments may be suspended while the employee is eligible to receive EI benefits.

Benefits typically begin on the first day of absence if the disability is caused by a non-work related accident or if the employee is hospitalized, and on the eighth day (shorter and longer waiting periods sometimes also occur) for absence related to illness. The waiting period for illness is intended to discourage casual absences. The maximum benefit period is usually in the range of 15 to 26 weeks, but in very rare cases may be as high as 104 weeks.

Benefits received by the employee are taxable income, unless the premiums have been entirely paid by employee deduction. CPP/QPP and EI contributions, and other employer and employee payroll taxes are not applicable if the weekly indemnity plan is insured or administered by a third party at arm's length from the employer, but such arrangements would attract premium taxes and sales taxes in some provinces.

Supplemental Unemployment Benefits Plans

A Supplemental Unemployment Benefits (SUB) plan, as the name implies, tops up or supplements EI disability benefits. SUB plans are a form of self-insured income replacement that can be structured to pay benefits during periods of unemployment due to temporary stoppage of work, training, illness, injury, quarantine, or periods while receiving maternity or parental benefits. SUBs are different, in that unlike other forms of employment income or disability benefits received by the employee, they will not reduce the amount of EI benefits payable.

Benefits under EI are payable for up to 15 weeks in the event of maternity leave and 35 weeks for parental leave.[4] EI benefits are often lower than the disability income benefits provided by the employer. Two well-known court decisions, *Brooks v. Canada Safeway Ltd.,*[5] and *Alberta*

---

[4]   For more information on EI see Chapter 19.

[5]   *Brooks v. Canada Safeway Ltd.*, [1989] S.C.J. No. 42, [1989] 1 S.C.R. 1219 (S.C.C.).

Hospital Association v. Parcels,[6] stipulated that disability coverage should be maintained during a period of maternity leave, and that all pregnancies have some period of disability related to delivery (usually deemed six weeks). SUB plans are commonly used to "top up" the EI benefit to make total disability benefits equivalent to the employer plan. Since the inception of the Quebec Parental Insurance Plan in 2006, which provides more generous benefits than those paid by EI, SUB plans are not as commonly utilized in Quebec as they used to be.

As distinct from other SUB plan applications, SUB plan registration for maternity or parental supplements is not required. It is necessary to formally document the program in order to ensure eligibility of SUB plan status under EI benefits. SUB plans for sickness, quarantine, and layoff still require annual registration with Human Resources and Social Development Canada.

Maternity and parental SUB plans can supplement up to 100% of earnings. All other SUB plans can supplement up to 95% of earnings.

Long-Term Disability Plans

LTD payments commence after a qualifying disability period that typically coincides with the end of the sick leave, STD or a weekly indemnity plan. Because of the financial impact associated with long-term liabilities and potentially significant monthly benefits, LTD benefits tend to be insured. The employer is responsible for making certain that the insurance contract fully reflects the benefit provisions communicated to employees.

LTD plans are designed to reflect continuous disability. Many insurance contracts allow for short periods of active employment during the qualifying disability period, to avoid a negative incentive for employers and employees to attempt partial or early return to work. LTD benefits are expressed as a percentage of pay, ranging from 50% to 70% of gross income.

LTD benefits are integrated with other sources of disability income such as Workers' Compensation, CPP/QPP and other employer and government sources. The objective of integrating disability income from other sources is to limit the disability income received from all sources to a reasonable percentage of pre-disability earnings, thus providing adequate income while maintaining an incentive for the employee to

---

[6]   *Alberta Hospital Association v. Parcels*, [1992] A.J. No. 320, 1 Alta. L.R. (3d) 332 (Alta. Q.B.).

return to work. Methods of integration range from a direct offset, or reduction in the amount of LTD benefit payable for every dollar paid under government sponsored benefits programs, to an offset only after disability income from all sources exceeds a fixed percentage of the pre-disability earnings of the employee.

LTD payments generally continue for as long as the employee remains disabled, as defined in the contract, but generally not past the age of 65. Criteria for disability are carefully defined in the plan and benefits are paid only when an employee meets the "definition of disability" test, as defined in the plan contract.

It is in the best interest of all parties to have the LTD plan provide financial encouragement for the employee to try to return to work. Typically, the incentive would be a rehabilitation benefit that would allow the employee to earn an income and still receive LTD benefits.

The LTD plan may offset only 50% of the income earned under an approved rehabilitation program, or it may not reduce the LTD benefit until the individual's total income reaches 100% of earnings prior to disability. Some LTD plans support rehabilitation during the STD period by not extending the qualifying period for LTD for the period during which the individual was engaged in approved rehabilitation employment.

Benefits are not taxable on receipt if the entire premium, for all employees, was paid by the employee from after-tax dollars. Employer contributions are not taxable, but render the benefit taxable on receipt. The relative merits of taxable and non-taxable LTD plans for a particular group depend on a number of factors, including the income levels of the employees in the group.

Design Issues

When designing a disability income plan, several fundamental issues must be taken into account. These issues are discussed below.

Definition of Disability

The definition of disability establishes the criteria that will be applied to determine whether a compensable disability exists, and therefore whether benefits will be paid. Usually, the definition is segmented into two phases, an "own occupation" phase and an "any occupation" phase.

The own occupation phase is most often the STD period, plus the first two years of the LTD claim. The any occupation phase follows until the maximum LTD benefit period is reached. Claimants are considered disabled if the illness or injury prevents the employee from performing the essential duties of either their own or any occupation during the corresponding phases of the definition. Caution should be exercised in the own occupation phase of the definition as the disability could be related to the occupation of the claimant rather than to his current job, depending on the wording of the definition. For example, a chef working on a cruise ship who develops a serious case of sea-sickness may be considered disabled under an "own job" definition but not under an "own occupation" definition.

Evaluation of disability can be made more objective by quantifying the test. For example, the employee might be considered disabled if unable to perform at least 80% of normal duties during the own occupation phase. During the any occupation phase, the employee may be considered disabled if he or she is unable to perform a job that pays at least 67% of his or her pre-disability earnings. The percentage can be changed to make the criteria less or more stringent, and there are differences among insurance companies. Education, training, age, and experience would be taken into consideration, particularly in the adjudication of the any occupation definition of disability.

Pre-Existing Conditions Limitation

Some insurers limit their liability by restricting coverage for medical conditions that existed before the employee became insured. For example, the pre-existing condition clause may state that if an employee was receiving medical treatment for a condition that existed during the three-month period immediately prior to being covered, disability benefits would not be payable for that specific condition until the employee had been covered under the program and working for 12 months, or until after a 90-day period, during which the employee received no medical care for the pre-existing condition. Disability coverage in respect of unrelated causes would not be affected. Restrictions are more common in small groups or in industries with a high turnover rate.

Exclusions

Most STD and LTD plans specify circumstances under which no disability benefits will be paid to the employee. Examples of some standard exclusions include:

- Disabilities arising from an attempted suicide, or self-inflicted injuries;[7]
- Injuries incurred as a result of war;
- Disabilities incurred as a result of the commission of a criminal offence;
- Benefits will not be paid if the employee is in prison; and
- Any period in which the employee is not under the care of a licensed physician.

Replacement Ratios

Taking income from all sources into account, an LTD replacement ratio in the range of 80% to 85% of pre-disability income balances the employee objective of income security against the employer objective of a reasonable benefit with some room for financial motivation to return to work. For STD plans, a higher replacement rate may be acceptable to the employer.

EI Premium Reductions

Employers whose sick leave, weekly indemnity, or STD plans match or exceed EI disability benefits are eligible for EI premium reduction. Five-twelfths of this reduction must be shared, directly or indirectly, with the employees covered under the plan. The employer may provide a cash rebate (which is taxable income), new employee benefits, or increased existing benefits.[8]

The Management of Disability Claim Issues

The management of disability claims is becoming increasingly complex. Relative to other employee benefits, the non-financial needs and service expectations of the claimant have considerable impact on the outcome of disability income claims.

---

[7]   This is more typical in LTD policies, but may be included in some STD polices.
[8]   More information regarding this topic may be found in Chapter 19.

Measuring the Cost of Absences

Disability income plans represent a substantial financial liability for the employer. These costs have been growing over the last decade.

An employer has limited control over many of the factors influencing cost; however, cost is influenced by the disability claims adjudication process. Early intervention, progressive return to work policies, and support of rehabilitation programs have reduced disability costs for a number of employers.

In support of early intervention:

- Every LTD claim originates as an STD claim;

- Early intervention means early in the disability, not early in the LTD claim;

- The likelihood of return to work from disability is less than 50% after six months of absence.

In addition to the disability benefits paid to the disabled employee, there are other costs associated with an employee's absence from work. The employer generally assumes the cost of continuing life insurance, health, and pension benefits. Measuring the cost of absence also takes into account the cost of replacement workers or overtime costs for existing workers, and the physical and emotional strain on co-workers and supervisors who must absorb the extra work. Prevention and active management of disability claims have helped employers control the costs associated with employee absence.

Managing Disability Income Plans

Attendance management programs focus primarily on handling occasional absences (*i.e.*, those lasting only one or two days or no more than a week). Employers have developed many different programs to improve attendance. The range of programs includes disciplinary action for inappropriate behaviour, providing no income during casual absence, and incentives for perfect attendance. An increasingly large number are also putting in place programs to accommodate work and family responsibilities. The most effective attendance management for an organization will depend on a number of factors, including the levels of absence, the industry, and the corporate culture.

After a period of absence of approximately one week, the focus moves from absence management to disability management. In the past, employers and insurers generally thought of two distinct categories of disability benefits: short-term and long-term. This distinction led to an awkward transition of the claim from the short-term plan to the long-term plan. Although administration and claims documentation may be different for short-term and long-term plans, the focus today is to manage all disability claims with the intent of getting the employee back to work as soon as possible, even if in a reduced capacity.

The focus on early intervention and early return to work applies equally to both non-occupational and occupational disabilities. The likelihood of a successful return to full-time employment reduces with each day that the person remains absent from work.

Claims management reduces the cost of disability plans, the number of claims initially approved, or their duration through the use of contractual limitations or stringent adjudication guidelines. Claims management remains important for cost control, but the impact of human rights legislation and changing societal philosophies and values requires a shift beyond managing the claim to managing the disability.

Managing disabilities results in the lowering of the cost of disability and disabled employees receiving much-needed additional assistance. The emphasis shifts from a focus on lost abilities to identifying residual capacities.

Disability management programs, whether administered by an insurance carrier or a disability management firm, operate during both the short- and long-term phases of disability. Features of a disability management program include prevention, early intervention, case management, rehabilitation, and support by the employer.

Prevention

Employers should consider taking preventative steps to effectively decrease the number of disability claims. Such steps include creating workplace wellness programs and Employee Assistance Programs (EAPs).[9] Workplace wellness can be viewed as having two key elements: organizational wellness and employee wellness. Organizational wellness involves managing business functions and employee well-being in a manner that allows the organization to be more resistant to environmental pressure. Employee wellness involves managing both psychological and

---

[9]   See Chapter 27 for more information on EAPs.

physical issues in response to environmental stress, including one's work environment. EAPs offer a confidential and professional consulting service to help employees and their families identify and resolve a wide range of personal difficulties and work-related problems. Their primary focus is to provide assessment and referral services, as well as short-term counselling to employees and their families. EAPs have evolved to become proactive in their approach and are increasingly looked upon as a means to promote well-being, good health, and issue resolution.

Early Intervention

Early intervention is timely and proactive disability management. In early intervention, the employee is contacted shortly after the onset of a medical absence (usually within five days) to determine whether he or she is a candidate for a return to work, or whether various interventions are needed to promote the return to work.

Case Management

Action plans are of little value unless implementation and accountability are assigned to an individual or a team. In most insurance companies, a case manager is assigned to coordinate the activities of the plan and work in liaison with all caregivers, the claimant, the employer, and any other stakeholders. The case manager may be the adjudicator, the rehabilitation consultant, or someone specifically designated by the insurance company or disability management provider. The case managers are able to intervene and to assist in the employee's reintegration into the workplace before problems are too big to be resolved.

Rehabilitation

There are two distinct types of rehabilitation: medical rehabilitation and vocation rehabilitation. Medical rehabilitation deals with medical recovery and the restoration of function. Medical professionals, including doctors, nurses, physiotherapists, and others control this process. Vocational rehabilitation deals with the re-establishment of employment at the prior job, or through retraining. Vocational rehabilitation is conducted by specialists in this field. The case manager generally coordinates all of these functions.

Support of the Employee

All parties gain when an individual returns to full or partial function after a disability. The employer often needs to make accommodations to facilitate early return to work. Light or modified duties, special equipment or modifications to the work site may be necessary. The cost and inconvenience of the accommodation are usually outweighed by the value of returning the employee to work. This duty to accommodate the employee, which has been confirmed by the courts, extends to the point of undue hardship on the employer, a notion still not well-defined. At a minimum, the employer has to demonstrate that an analysis has taken place regarding the necessary modifications to reintegrate the employee.

Challenges of New and Emerging Illnesses

New and emerging illnesses present tremendous medical and vocational rehabilitation challenges to employers, insurers, and health care practitioners. Incidence of new disability claims has been on the rise for a number of years with the proportion of new claims related to stress and mental and nervous disorders increasing each year. At the same time, there has been a sharp rise in the number of disability claims attributed to new diagnoses such as fibromyalgia, multiple chemical sensitivity, environmental diseases, repetitive strain injury, and chronic fatigue syndrome.

Successful recovery from physical and mental disabilities requires a multi-disciplinary approach, addressing the emotional and psychological needs of the claimant, as well as the medical condition and symptoms. The chances of success are increased with a supportive employer and suitable workplace accommodations available during the recovery phase.

Current and Continuing Cost Drivers

Mental Health Conditions

Since the early 1990s, mental health conditions have been a significant driver of disability claims incidence and duration. It is estimated 20% to 33% of STD claims are directly related to a mental health condition. It is also estimated that 33% to 50% of LTD claims are directly related to a mental health condition. Additionally, another 30% to 40% of claims are thought to have mental health issues as a factor that contributes to the complexity and length of a physical disability claim.

Mental health claims are typically complex for several reasons. One is the difficulty in confirming a clear diagnosis, given the heterogeneous causes and presentation of most mental health conditions. As well, mental health medications are generally metabolized differently for different people, which makes a medication match more difficult.

Issues of workplace stigma and the probability of disrupted workplace relationships during the pre-disability period, when symptoms first start to show, make return to work more difficult in many cases. As well, the nature of many mental health conditions impact employees' self-confidence, which may present as a factor in return to work readiness.

Musculoskeletal Conditions

Musculoskeletal conditions are also a major cost driver. This is largely due to an aging workforce and increasingly sedentary work.

Mental health is a factor in pain tolerance, accident proneness, self-care during recovery, and vascular constriction, all of which are complicating factors in musculoskeletal recovery and return to work.

Role of Health Care Providers and Insurance Carriers in Adjudication

The physician was traditionally expected to provide answers that would satisfy the competing interests of the patient, the employer, and the insurer. More recently, it is being recognized that responsibility for adjudication of disability benefits rests with the insurer, not the physician. The trend is not to ask the physician whether the employee is "disabled". The physician is being asked to identify restrictions and limitations, and provide objective findings that describe the condition. The insurer uses factual information from the physician to draw a conclusion on the presence and degree of disability and impairment.

There is growing recognition of the need for a multi-disciplinary model of health care in treating most mental and physical impairments. Employers and insurers are beginning to involve other health care practitioners in the assessment and treatment of disabling conditions.

Burden of Proof

Under an income replacement plan, the burden of proof is on the claimant to provide evidence of disability in order to receive payment. The adjudicator requires objective and medical support to evaluate whether the requirements for disability are met under the terms of the contract. For example, where the plan requires inability to perform the essential duties of the job, and a slight change in duties would keep the employee at work, the employee would not be considered disabled.

After a disability is admitted as a claim, the burden of proof effectively shifts to the insurer. It is relatively difficult to show cause for benefit termination once payments have commenced. Most insurers are relatively stringent in their initial adjudication.

The ability to defend an objective decision made by a professionally qualified claim examiner leads many employers to retain third-party services for disability claim management.

Subrogation

The purpose of subrogation (the substitution of one party for another as creditor) is to make certain that the right party pays and that a claimant does not get paid twice for the same loss. Subrogation is a right that exists under common law. Most disability plans include an explicit subrogation clause in the policy wording. Under civil law in Quebec, subrogation is not an automatic contractual right. An explicit contract provision must detail how and when subrogation terms will be applied.

Accounting

STD and LTD plans are also encompassed in the accounting standards provided for under various accounting standards. Where the post-employment benefits and compensated absences do not vest or accumulate, the cost is recognized when a situation occurs that requires the employer to provide a benefit. As a result, if the STD or LTD benefits are not related to service, then the cost is recognized when the employee becomes entitled to receive the STD or LTD benefit. Most STD and LTD plans are not service-related. If, however, in the rare circumstance that the STD or LTD benefits were service-related, the liability would be accounted for on an accrual basis. It is important to note that if the risk of liability has been transferred to an insurance company, the liability would be limited to any outstanding premiums at that time.

Tax Issues

The tax treatment of various disability benefits is somewhat complex. The following are a few general rules associated with disability plans:

- Employer-paid contributions or premiums to disability plans are deductible business expenses for the employer.

- Employee-paid contributions or premiums to disability plans are not eligible income tax deductions or credits in the year they are paid; cumulative contributions can be deducted from taxable disability benefits when received, if they were not used elsewhere to lower taxable income.

- Employer-paid contributions or premiums to disability plans are not taxable benefits to employees.

- Disability benefits received by a disabled employee are generally taxable income. The main exceptions to this are Workers' Compensation and employer-sponsored disability plans that are fully funded by employee contributions. Interpretation Bulletin IT-428 states that the onus is on the employer to clearly establish that the plan is an "Employee Pay-All Plan". As a result, to avoid the possibility of benefits being taxed, the plan should be documented at the time it is established as an employee-paid plan.

- Canadian employers who self-insure disability plans are required to remit CPP for disabled employees. The rationale considered by the Canada Revenue Agency is that self-insured benefits are income from an employer, and should have the same deduction requirement. Disability benefits from an insured plan are considered differently, and do not have this requirement. Bill C-13 impacts both the disabled employees, who are given a new deduction, and employers, in terms of matching that deduction, when a self-insured disability plan is in place. Certain self-insured multi-employer plans may be exempt; however, each of these situations will be considered on a case by case basis.

Group Critical Illness Insurance

Critical illness insurance is a relatively new product, offered in Canada by a few carriers since the mid-1990s, and designed to fill needs where gaps exist between life insurance and disability insurance. Group critical illness insurance first became available in 1997, and is often described by insurers as a tax-free, lump-sum payment, which is usually paid out within 30 days of diagnosis of a critical condition. A critical condition may cover such items as a heart attack, stroke, cancer, bypass surgery, kidney failure, blindness, deafness, organ transplants, multiple sclerosis, and paralysis. With advances in medical science, people now survive many illnesses that might previously have been fatal. However, people who survive can place added burdens, including financial ones, on their caregivers. Critical illness insurance differs from disability insurance, and should not be taken as a replacement of disability insurance. Cost is one of the main reasons why employers are unwilling to provide critical illness insurance as a benefit. However, if it is offered as an optional benefit or as part of a flexible benefits plan, such concerns should be eliminated.

Effective January 1, 2013, critical illness insurance is considered differently from a tax perspective. Group critical illness insurance is now considered under the *Income Tax Act* in the same manner as "group sickness or accident insurance plans". As such, employer-paid premiums are taxable to the employee.

Chapter 22

WORKPLACE HEALTH MANAGEMENT

Executive Summary

At its most simplistic workplace health management is about the impact of work on health and health on work. While seemingly straightforward, workplace health management addresses the complex question of how the work environment influences employee health and in turn how individual and collective employee health influences work and productivity.

Workplace health management has evolved significantly from its humble start 130 years ago, when the sole focus was the reduction of workplace deaths and injuries as part of the larger labour movement. Learning from the past, Canada has redefined health, examined the impacts on both the individual and the organization, updated the legal and regulatory landscape, and determined with more clarity than ever before that health is a shared responsibility. Today, workplace health management is an integrated framework of shared accountability addressing health awareness, prevention, intervention, and recovery.

Definition of Health

There has been considerable advancement in the definition of health. Over time we have moved through the traditional disease approach where biology dictates health to the biopsychosocial model that includes biological, psychological (thoughts, emotions, and behaviours), and social factors as determinants of health, to the current view that health is dynamic and includes all of the above with a focus on optimal functioning and resiliency. Looking forward, the concept of "brain health" continues to evolve and promises yet another foray into the definition of health.

Definition of Workplace Health

The definition of workplace health is also evolving and, depending on one's perspective, workplace health may mean different things. The traditional safety model defines workplace health as preventing the injury and illness of employees. Operationally, workplace health refers to the strategies, policies, programs, and practices found in the workplace that provide benefits to improve the health of employees. The healthy workplace perspective defines workplace health as a collaboration between employees and managers focused on continual improvement to protect and promote the health, safety, and well-being of employees and the sustainability of the workplace. A more business oriented definition of workplace health speaks to an ongoing process of understanding and fine-tuning the employee-employer relationship to satisfy the mutual interests of individual and corporate well-being and prosperity.

Strategic Pillars of Workplace Health Management

To fully address the impact of work on health and health on work, consideration must be given to the four strategic pillars that influence outcomes: leadership and management, the employee, the environment, and the workplace.

Leadership and Management

One of the most pivotal roles of leadership is to embed health management into the "DNA" of the organization. To do that effectively requires a supportive environment and creation of a "health culture". A health culture addresses:

- Organizational norms — "how things get done around here";
- Values — beliefs about what is important;
- Peer support — assisting colleagues to achieve health goals;
- Organizational support — policies, procedures, communication, etc.; and
- Climate — the sense of community and shared vision.

With the creation of a health culture comes the understanding that workplace health management is more than a "nice to have" for organizations; it is a business imperative.

Leadership is often seen as the holder of the "purse strings", which it often is. However, leadership's role is much more robust. Leadership and management support are critical to building and sustaining successful workplace health management initiatives. This goes beyond simple endorsement of programs and involves active and visible participation in the following activities:

- Creating the vision (*e.g.*, mission statement);
- Committing to the vision;

- Connecting the vision to organizational values, strategy, and goals;
- Gaining budget and resource commitment;
- Educating and engaging people leaders about workplace health management;
- Communicating and sharing the vision with employees;
- Serving as a role model (*i.e.*, walking the talk);
- Creating accountability and responsibility (*e.g.*, making it a key performance indicator for people leaders);
- Enabling feedback and continuous evaluation (*e.g.*, employee engagement surveys, metrics); and
- Acknowledging and rewarding successes (*e.g.*, incentives, public recognition).

Do leadership and management impact outcomes? Management-related factors have been shown to contribute more to the success of health management programs than the content of the actual workplace health intervention.[1]

Throughout the development process and once health management is built into the DNA of the organization, ongoing evaluation is needed. It is important to measure program outcomes, impact, return on investment, and return on experience. To keep the health management program relevant and fluid it is just as important to also assess the workplace itself to see if there have been changes to the workplace environment and culture that could influence the effectiveness of different strategies.

Healthy Employee

A fundamental premise in workplace health management is the understanding that workplace health management is something organizations do "with" and "for" employees not something that is done "to" employees. The distinction is critical. Workplace health management is not about the programs, it is about the end-user, the employee, hence the importance of employee participation and buy-in to workplace health initiatives. The best way to promote health and engage employees is to make it personal for them; buy-in occurs more readily because the "what's in it for me" question is answered, often by the employees themselves.

---

[1]   *Best Practice Guidelines: Workplace Health in Australia*, online: Health and Productivity Institute of Australia, http://www.hapia.com.au/Corporate Wellness.html.

Healthy Environment

The impact of the work environment on health was pioneered by the labour movement in its efforts to address worker safety. Safety is and remains a critical element of workplace health management. Considerable gains have been made in the safety landscape resulting in strong internal responsibility systems, metrics, and measurement, etc., mostly driven by occupational health and safety legislation. Historically the focus has been on physical health. Today, when talking about "work on health", addressing the physical work environment is not enough. Factors such as violence in the workplace, harassment, bullying, and mental disorders are front and centre.

The Ontario *Occupational Health and Safety Act* specifically addresses workplace violence and harassment and goes so far as to include the influence of domestic violence on the workplace. As with physical safety, the trend is toward encapsulating mental and psychological health into legislation. The Province of British Columbia has expanded mental disorder coverage under the *Workers Compensation Act* to include cumulative work-related stress, bullying, and harassment.

Healthy Workplace

As no two organizations are the same, there is no fixed formula for what should or should not be included in a workplace health management program. The selection of components or interventions needs to correlate with the objectives and goals of the workplace health management program so that the mutual needs of the individual and organization are satisfied. To foster early adoption, utilization, and credibility, the end-user must be kept in mind. Interventions should be people-oriented, easy to navigate, sustainable, evidence based (*e.g.*, based on reputable studies or interventions), and include follow-up.

Workplace health management interventions typically fall into two categories: core components and voluntary components. In the Canadian landscape, core components typically include drug and health benefit plans, employee assistance programs, Workers' Compensation, absence and disability management programs (*i.e.*, short-term disability or sick leave benefits), and, depending on the industry, components such as pre-employment medicals and health surveillance.

The spectrum of voluntary components can be quite broad and is predicated by organizational culture, the health management objectives, and budgetary constraints. Common voluntary interventions include health risk assessments, health coaching, wellness seminars and workshops, biometric screening, weight loss programs, and vaccination programs. Increasingly, more attention is also being placed on mental health. Interventions such as mental health education, risk factor awareness, and resiliency training are newer entries into the health management spectrum.

Given the importance of employee health to an organization's bottom line, there is a growing trend toward inserting some voluntary interventions, such as health risk assessments, into the core category. Health risk assessments, as an example, are commonly utilized in the benefit enrolment process on the premise that an employee who is better informed about his or her risk factors is more likely to select benefit options that support a healthier lifestyle.

The Mental Health Commission of Canada, in January of 2013, launched the *National Standard of Canada for Psychological Health and Safety (PHS) in the Workplace*, CSA Z1003/BNQ 9700-803-7. The PHS standard is voluntary and is intended to assist companies in creating an environment that encourages mental health. It is also intended to align with other related standards such as Healthy Enterprise (BNQ 9700-800), Occupational Health and Safety Management (CAN/CSA-Z1000), and Occupational health and safety - Hazard identification and elimination and risk assessment and control (CSA Z1002), as well as other accepted standards on management systems. It is hoped that the aspects outlined in the PHS will aid in changing the way mental health and illness is addressed in the workplace.

Intervention and Program Principles

From research efforts and review of organizational successes and failures in the health management field, key intervention and program factors that enhance effectiveness, success, and participation have been identified. The findings are as follows:

- An integrated approach is more effective than single elements alone. While a single element approach can be effective, returns on health are multiplied with an integrated approach. Siloed approaches may lead to a fragmentation or redundancy of effort.

- A participatory or collaborative approach that includes managers, employees, and providers is more effective simply because it builds ownership.

- Multidisciplinary approaches offer the most promising results. Health is complex and interventions are not one-size-fits-all. Addressing the health issue from more than one viewpoint provides a holistic orientation, allows for a more tailored experience, and heightens the probability that one of the approaches will resonate with an individual.

- Multifaceted safety campaigns are more effective at reducing non-fatal injuries. For example, a safety campaign that focused on both promoting positive attitudes toward safety and the behavioural aspects of safety at work resulted in a reduction in the number of injuries resulting from accidents.[2]

- Employee participation in decision-making is a key psychosocial factor that contributes to a healthy workplace.

- Health promotion success factors include the participation of employees in planning, implementation, and evaluation of changes.

- A combination of individual and organizational approaches to workplace stress and psychological health is the most effective.

- Staying active and returning to ordinary activities as early as possible enhances the recovery process.

- Health management programs that utilize a "stages of change" approach to individualize the intervention to the individual employee's characteristics are more effective.

- Work-related exercise programs were found effective in reducing workplace injuries, preventing musculoskeletal disorders, and reducing fatigue and exhaustion.

- It is essential to rigorously evaluate programs and communicate successful outcomes to key stakeholders.

- Going beyond the legal or regulatory minimums have significant, positive impacts on worker health, and also on the health and sustainability of the enterprise.

The Changing Workplace and New Challenges to Health Management

As we push forward towards the third decade of the new millennium — which begs the question as to whether it can still be referred to as the new millennium — there are a whole host of changes and challenges that face the modern work environment. Whether it is changes in societal norms, human rights, or medical advancements, there are tangible impacts to the modern workplace that need to be navigated when considering Health Management approaches and best practices.

---

[2]   *Interventions to prevent injuries in construction workers,* van der Molen et al, (December 2012) 10.1002/14651858.CD006251.pub3.

Some of the more prevalent changes and challenges in today's workplace are:

- mental health in the workplace; awareness, de-stigmatization, illness prevention and accommodation;
- prolongation of employee careers and delayed retirement;
- recessions and downsizing — maintaining engagement and health in an economic downturn;
- gender identity and equality in the work place, human rights space; and
- legalization and use of medical marijuana as a mainstream treatment modality.

Mental Health in the Workplace

Mental health and mental illness is an evolving workplace consideration — gaining awareness in the medical community, in the mainstream media, and in the public eye. With increased awareness comes the increase of publicity, increased medical attention, increased incidence of diagnosis and treatment, and increased potential for workplace absence or impact due to mental health concerns.

There is a delicate balance to be struck between the acknowledgment and effective treatment of mental illness and the reactive medicalization of stress, grief, and other normal emotional responses. Awareness can be powerful, but awareness without education, training, and adequate support can result in increased lost time and potential stigmatization in the workplace.

Organizations should look to adopt a multi-faceted Mental Health strategy in the workplace, incorporating:

- access to information and increased awareness about the signs and symptoms of mental illness;
- attention to the needs of employees expressing concerns, or requesting help — and making those requests acceptable and taken seriously;
- provision of sensitivity training to all employees, and support (counseling) for employees in distress, in a safe and confidential environment that protects the privacy of each participant;[3] and

---

[3]   Employee & Family Assistance Programs (EAP/EFAP) can be particularly effective in this regard, please see Chapter 27 for further information.

- structured and supported approaches to reintegrating all employees back to work from medical absence. It is critical that this type of support be extended to all returning employees, so that it is not exclusively provided to employees with mental health concerns — thereby identifying them as such.

Research clearly shows that supportive and inclusive work environments will promote continued attendance at work, better employee engagement, and fewer lost-time days due to mental health illness. Employees should also be encouraged (where appropriate) to remain at work in a suitable capacity even during times of mental health challenge — to maintain social contact and support, maintain engagement in meaningful work, and to decrease the isolation of persons suffering from mental health issues.

Prolongation of Careers and Delayed Retirement

The prolongation of careers — as Canadians live longer, work longer, and retire later in life — introduces the potential for increased health and wellness issues associated with age: degenerative musculoskeletal conditions, circulatory and cardiopulmonary conditions, diabetes, and increased access to health and wellness benefits. While the lives of people in general are getting longer, that doesn't necessarily equate to prolonged ability to manage the rigors of daily work, which can result in increased lost time hours.

Employers need to be cognizant of the challenges that face older workers, and the potential that employees may look to stay in the workforce longer to support themselves or their families amidst increasing costs of living. Investment in education, and preventative measures to minimize the potential for repetitive strain issues, ergonomic challenges, and excessive strain on their workers will help organizations to promote continued health during the prolonged working careers of their employees.

Recessions and Downsizing

The age of technology and increased efficiency has brought about staggering changes across the broad landscape of industry. Businesses operate more quickly, and more efficiently than ever before, making competition and viability in the global market that much more difficult. Many organizations are forced to make difficult decisions, including reductions of their workforces, consolidation of duties, and restructuring to ensure efficient operations and maximum return on financial investment. These changes, brought on by recessions in the market or intense competitive pressure, make it very difficult to maintain positive engagement and employee health — especially in an economic downturn.

Based on our own support of large-sized organizations from the industrial sector, we have identified three key strategies that have proven to be effective in managing recession-related organizational changes, and minimizing the impact of those changes on the workforce from an absence and disability management perspective:

1. Having a clear and thorough understanding of the STD and LTD policies that support employees through medically-supported absences.

2. Having a clear and thorough understanding of where employees may be limited in their abilities, but more importantly — what employees are able to do, if affected by long-term or permanent disabilities, and how those abilities can be leveraged in the workplace.

3. Having a solid suite of employee and employer support services to supplement the typical resources available within the workplace, or through the public health system.

The employ of these three strategies can benefit organizations on many levels. Not only will the three strategies help to ensure that organizational absence and disability is managed effectively, they will also show the organization's investment in their employees' wellbeing, and reinforce an accountability and participation in the recovery process from both sides.

Gender Identity and Human Rights Equality

"Gender identity" is not defined in any human rights Act, but the Ontario Human Rights Commission defines it as follows:[4]

> "Gender identity is each person's internal and individual experience of gender. It is their sense of being a woman, a man, both, neither, or anywhere along the gender spectrum. A person's gender identity may be the same as or different from their birth-assigned sex. Gender identity is fundamentally different from a person's sexual orientation." Gender identity can become a complicating factor in the workplace in situations where an employee's behaviour or practices may not align with expectations

---

4   Ontario Human Rights Commission, "Policy on preventing discrimination because of gender identity and gender expression", approved January 31, 2014. See http://www.ohrc.on.ca/en/policy-preventing-discrimination-because-gender -identity-and-gender-expression.

of the larger work community. Areas of particular conflict in recent years have been around use of segregated (men's and women's) washroom facilities based on gender identity as opposed to birth-assigned gender (male/female), or sexual orientation. Other areas may include requests for special consideration through accommodation, or absenteeism due to specific gender needs.

Generally speaking, all employees, regardless of gender, race, ethnicity, secular beliefs, or sexual orientation are expected to be treated with equality and fairness, and should not be discriminated against on the basis of any of the above differentiating characteristics or beliefs. In employment situations, all employees should be expected to comply with performance and behavioural guidelines, regardless of personal characteristics or beliefs, and should promote an inclusive and positive working environment for all.

Persons whose birth-assigned sex does not conform to their gender identity should be provided with the same opportunities as those whose birth-assigned sex and gender identity does conform. Opportunities for special accommodation or special needs at work should be reviewed and awarded based on the same factors and considerations for every employee, with merits being considered on a case-by-case basis, regardless of their unique characteristics, and in a way that promotes a fair and equal approach for all.

Legalization and use of Medical Marijuana

With the growing trend towards medical marijuana prescription and usage, and pending legalization of marijuana in Canada (2017), employers have to rethink and reformulate their corporate drug and alcohol policies to allow for the use of medical marijuana as a mainstream medical treatment modality.

Health Canada currently has two defined categories of patients considered eligible for access to medical marijuana under the *Marihuana Medical Access Regulations:*[5]

Category 1:   Symptoms being treated within the context of providing compassionate end-of-life care, OR at least one of the symptoms associated with:

• Severe pain and/or persistent muscle spasms from multiple sclerosis, a spinal cord injury, or spinal cord disease;

---

[5]   http://www.laws-lois.justice.gc.ca/eng/regulations/SOR-2013-119/.

- Severe pain, cachexia, anorexia, weight loss, and/or severe nausea from HIV/AIDS infection;
- Severe pain from severe forms of arthritis; and/or
- Seizures from epilepsy.

Category 2:   Debilitating symptom(s) of medical condition(s) other than those described in Category 1.

The application of eligible patients must be supported by a medical practitioner and the applicant and their medical practitioner must both declare that conventional treatment(s) for the Category 1 or 2 symptoms described above have been tried or considered, and have been found to be ineffective or medically inappropriate.

In the context of the workplace, complications due to medical marijuana usage and consumption during work hours can arise in the following areas:

- Ingestion through smoking, and providing employees with an accessible location to smoke according to their prescribed schedule. Consideration needs to be given to other employees, similar to that given to cigarette smoking, understanding that individuals may choose or prefer not to be exposed to marijuana smoke — including those who smoke cigarettes or occupy designated cigarette smoking areas.
- Consideration for the impairing effects of medical marijuana, and what acceptable thresholds exist in the workplace as it relates to full and effective performance of the job. This is particularly important in roles that require operation of machinery, vehicles, or other equipment where safety may be a factor. Risks need to be understood and treated carefully to ensure that no degree of impairment could result in workplace accident or injury — either to the impaired employee, or others whose safety may be secondarily compromised.
- Ability to prevent and regulate abuse, sale, or trafficking of substances within the workplace under the guise of prescribed medical use.

For employers, it is essential that policies are revised and kept current, and that changes are clearly communicated to the employee group to ensure understanding and compliance.

Use of a health management or disability management program can be very effective to ensure that employees using medical marijuana are able to confidentially supply the necessary proof of prescription and medical support for the prescription to validate the need for medical marijuana use, and to assess the role that this form of medication (or any other medication for that matter) may play in the employee's ability to effectively and safely do their job.

Where concerns for use and employee safety may exist, employers are encouraged to discuss their concerns with their employee, offer safe alternatives for continued work, and to encourage participation in a review process to ensure that use is appropriate, regulated, and that the potential risks are quantified, or ruled out as appropriate.

Big Data Analytics

Big data analytics is a combination of two concepts — big data and analytics. The two combine to enable an emerging information management technology that has the ability to examine large quantities of data and provide insights to address various issues and answer many questions. Within the context of health management, it provides stakeholders with new insights that have the potential to advance personalized care, improve outcomes, and avoid unnecessary costs.[6]

The tools for measuring health, engagement, and productivity are often disconnected, making it difficult to see the overall picture and determine the best strategy for driving improved results. The opportunity to utilize big data analytics is emerging in many areas, including health management solutions. Organizations are increasingly seeking assistance from service providers in analyzing the effectiveness of their health management programs, to assist in determining if their investment or "spend" is being effectively allocated.

For example, Morneau Shepell has developed a family of data analytics solutions branded the "Total Health Index (THI)". By implementing a THI solution, employers are able to benchmark their current risks and opportunities for the health, engagement, and productivity of their workforce. Employees complete a confidential self-assessment that measures their engagement level, gauges physical and psychological health, and determines their ability to cope with stress. Employees receive their own results along with ideas and resources on how they can make the most of their work, health, and life. Aggregate workforce data is shared with the employer. This aides employers in developing better strategies to improve outcomes for both their employees and the organization itself.

Using big data analytics can provide insight into the employees' life, physical and psychological health, and work metrics. Employers are able

---

[6]   Big Data Analytics in Health White Paper, Canada Health Infoway, April 2013.

to gain knowledge of the impact of coping skills on employees' productivity, health, and engagement which can assist them in aligning their health management investment in health and wellness programs for better outcomes.

Chapter 23

GROUP LIFE AND ACCIDENT INSURANCE

Executive Summary

Group life insurance was one of the earliest benefits offered to employees and remains one of the most common group benefits in Canada. Group life and Accidental Death and Dismemberment (AD&D) coverage provides tax-effective compensation to an employee and the employee's family in the event of the employee's or dependent's death or accidental injury resulting in a traumatic loss. Plan costs are low compared to the relatively high coverage amounts. The coverage is provided in addition to any government or legislated death or dismemberment benefits.

As plans have evolved over the last 30 plus years, there is much more flexibility in types of coverage available. Employees can supplement employer-sponsored group life coverage with additional coverage purchased on an optional basis to meet their own specific needs and utilize payroll deduction to pay the premiums. When employment terminates, there is portability of the coverage through the group contract's conversion provisions.

This chapter describes the various types of group life and AD&D coverage available and how the coverage is structured, and provides a general overview of what affects plan costs.

Background

Life insurance was one of the earliest employee benefits offered to employees and remains one of the most common group benefits in Canada. Although there are different types of group life, the most common type is group term insurance, which is one-year term insurance, typically renewable each year but not having a guaranteed renewal rate. Group term life insurance represents pure life insurance coverage, and does not include any element of investment or savings. It provides a lump-sum death benefit payable to the employee's designated beneficiary(ies) in the event of the employee's death from any cause while insured.

AD&D coverage pays a benefit if an employee dies or suffers a traumatic injury as the result of an accident. AD&D coverage is relatively inexpensive and is frequently offered in a principal sum amount equal to the group term life insurance coverage.

Both the life and AD&D benefits are generally offered as basic mandatory benefits by an employer on the premise that, should the employee have an accident or should the employee die while employed, there is some financial support for his or her family. These benefits are independent of any death benefits payable under any government plan or Workers' Compensation legislation.

Basic Group Term Life Insurance

Schedule of Insurance

The level of insurance provided under an employer-sponsored group insurance plan reflects affordability, competitive pressures, the level of paternalism, and, where applicable, the outcome of collective bargaining. Generally, basic group life insurance is paid by the employer and coverage is mandatory. The schedule of benefits for a class of employees defines the amount of life insurance payable.

The amount of employer-paid life insurance takes into account all other sources of employer-sponsored death benefits. Such benefits may be payable under registered pension plans, profit-sharing plans, survivor income provisions, optional life insurance, and other plans.

The amount of life insurance protection provided can be nominal or very substantial. In cases where the basic life benefit is low, the trend with employers is to supplement the amount of basic mandatory life insurance with employee-paid optional life insurance, which is discussed later in the chapter under "Additional Group Life Insurance Plans and Provisions".

Eligibility and Participation

It is not mandatory to offer group life insurance to all employees of an employer, but the group eligible for coverage must be well-defined. (See "Governing Guidelines".) For example, if certain part-time employees are eligible for insurance, eligibility can be based on the number of hours worked per week. Written communication should specify the minimum service requirements and any other conditions for eligibility.

Group life plans that are fully employer-paid generally have 100% participation by all eligible employees. Where employee contributions are required, insurers generally require participation of at least 75% of the eligible group to avoid adverse selection (i.e., enrolment weighted to those employees most at risk). If participation is less than the stated minimum, coverage is usually subject to the approval of medical evidence of insurability. Lower participation may be allowed for certain large groups without evidence of insurability requirements.

A paramount feature of group life contracts is that coverage is issued with a limited requirement for providing evidence of the employee's good health. Contracts are issued with an overall maximum on the amount of insurance per life insured, and a non-medical maximum per life insured. The non-medical maximum is less than or equal to the overall maximum. All eligible employees in the group can be insured up to the non-medical maximum, without submitting any health evidence. Amounts in excess of the non-medical maximum must be approved by the insurance company based on the medical evidence submitted by each employee. In the case of very small groups of 10 employees or less, all amounts of coverage may be subject to evidence of good health.

Rating a Basic Group Life Plan

Basic group term life insurance is issued at a rate per $1,000 of coverage based on the demographics (ages, gender mix and volume of coverage) of all employees at the time the contract is initiated with the insurer. The contract is renewable each year, subject to the right of the insurance company to adjust the rates based on changes in the demographics of the group and the insurer's mortality/morbidity tables. In general, the rate tends to remain stable over the years as young employees continually enter the group to replace retiring employees and to offset the gradual aging of the remaining employees.[1]

- *Mortality* – The number of deaths in a group of people, usually expressed as deaths per thousand. The age and sex of the insured are normally part of the mortality element.

- *Morbidity* – The incidence and severity of sicknesses and accidents in a well-defined class or classes or persons.

The renewal rates for a small group are generally not affected by the group's mortality and morbidity experience as this experience is "pooled" by the insurance company with other groups of similar size. It is the insurance company's mortality and morbidity experience of its total pool of small group life insurance contracts that will affect the overall rating of its small group life insurance contracts. In the case of a very large group, however, the renewal rates are affected less by the insurance company's overall experience than by the experience of the actual group itself. In large groups, the employer's cost is often determined entirely by the mortality and morbidity experience of the group.

---

[1]   The mortality and morbidity experience refers to the mortality and morbidity that actually occurs to a group of insured employees of a given insurance company, in contrast to expected mortality and morbidity.

Group insurance premiums are typically lower than individual premiums because the marketing and administrative costs for each individual are lower and the risk is spread over a greater number of people.

Waiver of Premium

A waiver of premium provision is commonly included in group life insurance contracts. Under a waiver of premium provision, the premiums for basic life insurance coverage are no longer required when an employee becomes totally disabled before age 65. The insurance company continues the life coverage during the period of total disability but not usually beyond age 65.

If the group plan terminates while the employee is considered totally disabled, coverage remains with the current insurer until the employee is no longer disabled. If the termination of the group plan is a result of a transfer of coverage to a new insurance company, the new insurer is not responsible for the life insurance coverage until the employee returns to active employment, at which time premiums will once again become payable.

There are differences among insurance contracts with respect to the criteria for total disability.

Employers may choose not to insure the waiver of premium provision. Under policies with no premium waiver provision, the ongoing premium rate may be fractionally lower; however, premium payments must be continued during periods of disability in order to maintain the life insurance coverage. If the plan is transferred to another insurer, arrangements must be made with the new insurer regarding the assumption of the disabled risk and the amount of premium necessary to continue coverage.

Living Benefits (also known as Compassionate Assistance)

Payment of life insurance proceeds to terminally ill individuals was a concept introduced in the late 1980s to provide necessary income for the employee. Proceeds from the basic group life insurance benefit are paid out to the employee in the case where the medical prognosis indicates death is imminent for the insured individual. The advance payment is typically limited to one-half of the insurance amount (usually up to a maximum of $100,000). Insurers will require the written consent of irrevocable beneficiaries.

The payment is administratively treated as a loan and interest is charged. Principal and total interest are deducted from the remaining death benefit before payment is made to the beneficiary upon the employee's death.

Conversion Privilege

The Canadian Life and Health Insurance Association (CLHIA) guidelines require group life contracts to provide employees with an opportunity to convert group life insurance within 31 days of termination of coverage. Conversion allows the employee to purchase an individual insurance policy from the insurance company at standard individual rates without any medical evidence of insurability. Death within 31 days of termination of group life coverage is treated as if the individual had exercised the conversion privilege. The employer is responsible for advising the terminated employee of the conversion features.

The employee may convert all or part of the amount for which the employee was insured up to a maximum of $200,000 under the group life contract. The employee usually has the choice of a one-year term contract, a term-to-age-65 contract, or a permanent life contract. An employee selecting a one-year term contract must convert the coverage at the end of the first year to a term to age 65 or a permanent life insurance contract if they wish the coverage to continue beyond the first year. The converted policy will not include any disability provisions.

The conversion privilege was designed to protect employees in poor health who would otherwise be unable to purchase insurance at a reasonable price, if at all. Employees in good health have the option of purchasing a variety of individual insurance plans at more competitive prices in the individual marketplace.

Instalment Disability

Under an instalment disability provision, an employee who becomes totally and permanently disabled receives the amount of life insurance, paid in monthly instalments, until the total amount is paid out. This benefit attempts to use the group life insurance to pay LTD benefits in addition to death benefits.

With the commonality of long-term disability (LTD) benefits, the instalment disability benefit has become relatively uncommon. It can be found in some older contracts subject to collective bargaining, particularly in the absence of LTD benefits. The insurance community has developed more flexible alternatives for advancing death benefit proceeds to provide financial assistance to the terminally ill, as noted under "Living Benefits" above.

Accidental Death and Dismemberment

Basic Accidental Death and Dismemberment

AD&D benefits typically provide 24-hour coverage, both on and off the job. AD&D benefits are offered to provide financial protection to an employee and the employee's family in the event of the employee's accidental death or dismemberment as a result of an accident. Dismemberment usually includes loss of limbs, fingers, senses such as sight and hearing, or loss of use of limbs, or permanent paralysis. The payment generally depends on the severity of the injury and the principal sum is typically tied to the basic life insurance amount. For example, most AD&D plans pay 200% of the principal value for paralysis.

With the changing global economy and more international travel, AD&D benefits have become more comprehensive. Additional benefits, such as rehabilitation, repatriation of the deceased, family transportation, spousal occupational training, home alteration, and vehicle modification are commonplace to AD&D plans. Other common modifications include day care benefits, continuation of coverage, conversion privileges, and waiver of premium.

AD&D policies usually exclude payment of benefits in the event of death as the result of war, riot, or other hostilities, self-inflicted injury, commission of a crime, air travel while acting as a pilot, and other like conditions. Additional coverage is often provided in the event of an employee's accidental death while travelling on the business of the employer. This business travel coverage is limited to business travel and does not provide coverage off the job.

Optional Accident Death and Dismemberment

Many employers offer AD&D on an optional, fully employee-paid basis. Optional programs can be designed to allow employees to purchase AD&D coverage for themselves and/or their family in amounts that reflect the additional income perceived necessary in the event of accidental death or dismemberment. Coverage amounts are usually available in units of $10,000 or $25,000 for the employee with dependent family benefits being a percentage of the employee's elected amount of coverage.

Rating an Accidental Death and Dismemberment Plan

AD&D coverage is relatively inexpensive and is frequently offered in a principal sum amount equal to group life insurance, and is expressed as a rate per $1,000 of coverage. AD&D rates also renew each year and, while the basic life insurance rates are impacted by the demographics of the employee population, the AD&D rates are most often based on the insurer's block of business with adjustments for higher risk industries. Rates tend to remain stable over the years. Basic AD&D plans are most commonly employer-paid.

While group insurers offer an AD&D product, there are also special risk carriers in the market that offer AD&D as their niche product. Special risk carriers tend to be lower in cost and they offer more comprehensive coverage, through the addition of modifications such as those outlined above.

Accidental Death and Dismemberment Waiver of Premium

A waiver of premium provision is commonly included in AD&D insurance contracts. Under a waiver of premium provision, if an employee becomes disabled before age 65, the insurance company continues the AD&D coverage during the period of total disability with no further premium payment. If the policy with the insurer is terminated most insurance plans will not continue the waivers. The new insurance company must agree to insure the waivers.

Additional Group Life Insurance Plans and Provisions

Dependant Group Life Insurance

Some employers provide nominal amounts of dependant group life (DGL) coverage as part of the basic benefit package for employees. The principle behind DGL insurance is to pay for funeral expenses upon the death of a spouse or dependent child. Some plans offer DGL insurance on an optional basis, with the employee paying for the chosen level of coverage.

The coverage amounts are generally expressed as a nominal flat amount, such as $10,000 for a spouse[2] and $5,000 for a dependent child; however, the amounts can vary depending upon the schedule selected by the employer.

---

[2]   See Chapter 26 for a more in-depth discussion of domestic partner benefits.

DGL is usually not available to retirees. Coverage for the spouse may include a conversion privilege on the employee's death or termination of employment. There is no conversion provision for the dependent child benefit.

There is usually a waiver of premium provision to continue the DGL insurance without further premium payment in the event that the employee qualifies for waiver of premium under the basic life insurance plan.

Premium rates for basic DGL are expressed as a flat monthly rate per family unit, irrespective of the actual ages or number of insured dependants.

Optional Group Life Insurance Plans

Employee, spousal, and child optional life (OL) plans allow employees to supplement basic group life insurance based on individual need. Coverage can be offered in multiples of salary or multiples of any flat dollar unit, with a maximum amount of coverage dictated by the insurance company. Employees can choose the amount of OL insurance based on personal circumstances, including the income required by the family, personal debt, investments, and other sources of income. OL insurance provides employees with the advantage of lower rates and the convenience of payroll deduction. For some employees, OL premiums are competitive with the cost of an individual policy; however, for other employees, an individual policy may be less expensive given the competitive marketplace for preferred risks. Employees need to consider the required duration of any life insurance coverage as the OL plans are based on continued employment with the employer and, on termination of employment, are subject to the overall conversion maximum of $200,000 under most group insurance contracts.

Optional life insurance usually requires medical evidence of insurability. For larger groups, coverage may be offered on a guaranteed issue basis during the initial enrolment and at the time employees first become eligible.

Most optional life rates are age-related based on five-year age bands. Increasingly, rates reflect not only age, but also gender and smoker/non-smoker status. Rates based on age or smoker/non-smoker status encourage higher participation, as younger employees are not subsidizing older employees, and non-smokers are not subsidizing smokers.

Waiver of Premium under Optional Life Insurance

A waiver of premium provision is commonly included in optional life insurance contracts. Under a waiver of premium provision, if an employee becomes disabled before age 65, the insurance company continues the life coverage during the period of total disability with no further premium payment. If the policy with the insurer is terminated, the insurance coverage with the original insurer remains in force for the disabled employee. There are differences among insurance contracts with respect to the criteria for total disability.

Survivor Income Benefits

Survivor income benefits describe a rarely used form of employee life insurance under which the proceeds at death are paid as an annuity to the surviving family/beneficiary. The annuity is commonly a percentage of salary for the spouse and an additional benefit for each child. No survivor income benefit would be paid on the death of an employee with no spouse and no dependent children. Benefits may or may not be integrated with survivor benefits payable under the Canada Pension Plan or Quebec Pension Plan (CPP/QPP).

Payments to the spouse are normally for life, while those for children generally cease at a fixed age, such as 21, or 25 (26 in Quebec) if enrolled in school. Annuitizing the death benefit provides a steady flow of income and assists with the financial obligations of the family. In recent years, most survivor income plans have been converted to the equivalent life insurance amounts.

Tax Issues

The following are some general rules regarding the tax treatment of group life and AD&D insurance:

- An employer may deduct premiums paid to a group life insurance policy, for income tax purposes, as taxation guidelines dictate. The same applies to premiums for survivor income, dependant life, and AD&D insurance.
- Employees may not deduct their own contributions to a group life, survivor income, dependant life, or AD&D plan from their incomes for tax purposes.
- Life insurance premiums are subject to premium tax and, in the provinces of Ontario and Quebec, to retail sales tax. Premium tax varies by province and territory (in 2012, the insured rate ranges from 2% to 4%).

- An employee is taxed on employer contributions for employee and dependant group life insurance, including any related premium and retail sales tax.

- Since 2013, employees are taxed on employer contributions for AD&D and critical illness insurance.

- Death benefits paid to beneficiaries under group life, dependant life, or AD&D policies are not taxable as income. Any interest paid by the insurer is taxable to the beneficiary.

- An employer may make direct payments of death benefits to the spouse or common-law partner of a deceased employee in recognition of his or her service. Under the *Income Tax Act*, the first $10,000 of such death benefits are received tax-free. A beneficiary other than the surviving spouse or common-law partner is also eligible to receive a tax-free death benefit, to the extent that the $10,000 amount is not fully utilized by the surviving spouse/common-law partner. The definition of death benefit was amended in 2001 and subsequent taxation years to refer to a surviving spouse or common-law partner. This has the effect of recognizing same-sex common-law partners. As a transitional rule, persons who would have qualified as common-law partners in either 1998, 1999, or 2000 are allowed to make a retroactive joint election to be treated as common-law partners for those years.

Governing Guidelines

There is no specific legislation governing group life insurance in Canada. The CLHIA has drafted guidelines with respect to group insurance, replacing guidelines previously issued by the Association of the Provincial Superintendents of Insurance. The CLHIA guidelines provide minimum standards of practice for life insurance companies with respect to:

- Provision and contents of plan descriptions made available to employees;
- The life insurance conversion privilege;
- Continuation of coverage when the life contract terminates; and
- Assumption of risk in a change of carrier situation.
- By and large, group benefit insurers in Canada comply with these guidelines.

The Canadian Constitution, the *Canadian Charter of Rights and Freedoms* and associated federal and provincial human rights legislation prohibit discrimination on enumerated grounds. The significance of the human rights legislation to benefit plans is that the criteria for coverage eligibility must be common for all employees in a class. Group plans cannot discriminate in terms of eligibility requirements or amount of coverage provided on the basis of a variety of personal characteristics, including age, sex, sexual orientation or marital status. Premiums, however, may be structured to reflect actuarially supportable risk characteristics.

The major impact of various employment standards legislation on group life insurance is to provide benefit continuation during the statutory termination notice period and to ensure information on conversion privileges is made available to the employee.

Death Benefits Under Government Plans

The CPP/QPP provide death and survivor benefits. The lump-sum death benefit is a modest amount (maximum in 2016 is $2,500) that is intended to cover immediate cash needs. A survivor benefit is an ongoing benefit payable to a spouse or common-law partner (which includes same-sex partners) and dependent children who meet the requirements specified under the CPP/QPP.

Workers' Compensation plans also provide an immediate lump-sum death benefit to defray immediate costs resulting from the employee's death, and ongoing pensions to the survivor and dependent children. Benefit amounts vary by province and territory.

Chapter 24

POST-RETIREMENT AND POST-EMPLOYMENT BENEFITS

Executive Summary

Employers provide post-retirement and post-employment benefits for many reasons, and employees have come to expect or may have an entitlement to these benefits. In this chapter, we define post-retirement benefits as benefits received after employment during retirement. These benefits may include different types of insurance coverage as well as discounted services and products. Post-employment benefits, such as self-insured Workers' Compensation benefits, continuation of health and dental benefits for long-term disability recipients, or accumulating sick leave banks, differ from post-retirement benefits as they are triggered by an employment-specific event that does not necessarily satisfy the eligibility criteria for retirement. Nevertheless, both types of benefits are subject to specific accounting standards, and cost issues are playing an increasingly significant role in the employer's assessment of these benefits.

Post-retirement benefits are generally accrued over the service period of the employee. Post-employment benefits liabilities that accumulate over a service period are also accrued over that service period. However, post-employment benefits that do not accumulate are accounted for when the event takes place ("event-driven benefits").

Numerous factors are influencing the higher costs, and, as a consequence, cost containment strategies have become increasingly important. This chapter identifies the main types of post-retirement and post-employment benefits, provides a detailed discussion of the major cost and cost-containment issues, and highlights some of the legal issues arising from changing the terms of post-retirement plans. In addition, taxation, accounting, and funding aspects of post-retirement and post-employment benefits are explained.

Background

In addition to pensions, many Canadian employers provide other post-retirement and post-employment benefits to retired and former employees.

Post-retirement benefits may include:

- Life insurance during retirement;
- Extended health and dental coverage during retirement;
- Payment of provincial health insurance premiums during retirement (*e.g.*, B.C. Medical Services Plan premiums);
- Retirement gifts; and
- Subsidized purchases.

Post-employment benefits may include:

- Continuation of extended health and dental coverage during disability;
- Sick leave programs that accumulate or vest.
- Self-insured long-term disability (LTD) income benefits;
- Self-insured Workers' Compensation benefits;
- Accumulated vacation days payable upon termination, retirement, or death;
- Lump sum retirement allowance; and
- Negotiated severance arrangements or buyout agreements.

Employers have provided and continue to provide retiree benefits for a number of reasons:

- *Paternalism* — The employer may accept an obligation to take care of, or to reward, long-service employees.
- *Extension of active employee benefits* — Retiree benefits may be considered a natural extension of the active employee benefits.
- *Competitiveness* — Retiree benefits may help employers to attract and retain employees, particularly employees with longer experience.
- *Negotiation* — Retiree benefits are often part of a union-negotiated package.
- *Employee Entitlement/Employer Precedent* — The providing of post-retirement or post-employment benefits may be influenced by both the employees' expectations of having such a benefit in place and the expectations that such benefit entitlements will continue in the future. The employer may also continue the coverage simply because they have always done so.
- *Cost Deferral* — With the implementation of accrual accounting, this rationale is no longer applicable. Previously an employer could have provided benefits in lieu of other compensation. The employer would view the benefits, based on an active employee group — particularly a relatively young one — with a reasonably

small retiree population, as a cost that could be deferred indefinitely in the future. The accounting changes under the various accounting bodies — CPA Canada Handbook — Accounting (CPA Canada), Public Sector Accounting Board (PSAB), Financial Accounting Standards Board (FASB), and International Financial Reporting Standards (IFRS) — have negated this strategy.

Post-retirement and post-employment benefits were once considered a low-cost ancillary benefit because cost was reflected on the company balance sheet on a pay-as-you-go basis and there were generally fewer retirees than active employees.

Since the introduction of the various accounting rules under CPA Canada, FASB, PSAB, and IFRS, post-retirement benefits and post-employment benefits that accumulate must be accounted for on an accrual basis in the period in which the employee provides services to the employer, rather than when the employee retires or terminates and receives the benefit. This method requires an employer to recognize the cost of providing these benefits much earlier than under the pay-as-you-go basis.

As for other significant non-accumulating or event-driven post-employment benefits, the employer must recognize the full present value of the benefit provided when the event occurs.

Cost Issues

The cost issues facing Canadian employers regarding post-retirement benefits can be summarized as follows:

- The number of retirees is growing. The baby-boom generation, born in 1945 to 1960, has started to attain retirement age. There are also more early retirements than in the past, meaning more people are receiving post-retirement benefits sooner.

- With progress in medicine, life expectancy continues to increase. Because people are not retiring at later ages, this increases the number of years in retirement, and thus the duration of future benefit cash flows.

- Benefit cost inflation continues to outpace price inflation and wage indices. Contributing factors include higher utilization and introduction of new technology, new drugs, such as biologic and specialty drugs, and new services with substantially higher prices.

- Government-sponsored benefits continue to be reduced. Examples are the introduction of retiree premiums, increased deductibles, reduction of the list of drugs covered, and restrictions to certain services such as chiropractor services or physiotherapy. Unless employer plans are worded with specific limitations for adding new services, the benefits removed from provincial Medicare plans may automatically be covered by employer plans.

- For a national employer, differences between provincial Medicare plans can be material. The challenge is to develop a sustainable and equitable approach to post-retirement benefit coverage for retirees across Canada. For example, Ontario provides seniors over age 65 with prescription drug coverage through the Ontario Drug Benefit plan (ODB), while drug coverage is only provided to seniors with a low level of income in New Brunswick and Newfoundland and Labrador. On an ongoing basis, a national employer needs a strategy to respond to continuous changes in provincial health care coverage.

- An individual's use of most medical benefits increases with age. Accordingly, as the retiree population grows and ages, utilization of these medical benefits also increases.

- A sustained low interest rate environment has resulted in a reduction in discount rates. This in turn is increasing the cost of providing these benefits, as a greater liability must be established on a present-value basis to cover future benefit cash flows.

- With the changes in accounting practices hitting the bottom line on financial statements, financial analysts and investors have put more focus on these costs and liabilities. As a result, many employers are reviewing the benefit promise to retirees and the corresponding financial obligations.

Types of Post-Retirement Benefits

Life Insurance

Retiree life insurance is typically in one of the following forms:

- A flat amount (*i.e.*, $5,000 or $10,000); or
- An amount related to earnings at retirement (*i.e.*, 25% or 50% of earnings), which may reduce in the following years to a typically flat ultimate amount.

Coverage is usually for the life of the retiree although some plans will have age limitations, such as age 75, or will terminate early retiree coverage at age 65. Typically employers pay 100% of the cost of this coverage. Optional life insurance and dependant life insurance benefits usually cease at retirement.

Medical Care

The retiree medical plan often mirrors the active employee medical plan (including coverage for spouses, if applicable), possibly with lower internal limits and the inclusion of (or reduced) lifetime maximums. Historically, most employers did not require retiree contributions, but this is becoming more common. Coverage is typically for the life of the retiree although some plans only provide coverage for early retirees to age 65, or for a specified period after retirement (*e.g.*, 15 years).

Medical benefits are valuable to retirees. Utilization of medical services such as prescription drugs, hospital services, and private-duty nursing care increases with age. Ancillary benefits, such as out-of-country coverage and paramedical services, are also meaningful to the retiree.

From age 65, Medicare, in most provinces, at least partially covers the cost of prescription drugs. Usually, coverage for prescription drugs under private plans either stops or is integrated with Medicare coverage at age 65.

Dental Care

Dental care is less commonly included with retiree benefits. The plan design often mirrors the benefits provided to active employees, possibly with lower annual benefit amounts and without orthodontia.

Provincial Health Insurance Premiums

Certain provinces (*e.g.*, British Columbia) charge monthly premiums to residents covered under the provincial health insurance program. Some employers pay part or all of these premiums on behalf of employees, and may continue to do so during retirement.

Other Post-Retirement Benefits

Some companies provide products or services to their retirees at no cost to the retiree, or at a discount. Examples include: reduced transportation fares, subsidized fitness memberships, and discounts on merchandise.

Post-Employment Benefits

There are various benefits that are provided upon termination of employment, leave, or disability that do not fall under the scope of what we have defined as post-retirement benefits. The various guidelines refer to these benefits as "post-employment" benefits, because they are triggered following a specific event that is not necessarily retirement. These benefits are also subject to similar scrutiny under the various accounting standards.

Accumulating Benefits

Post-employment benefits that accumulate (for example, a sick bank that pays the unused balance at termination of employment) will be subject to the same accrual accounting required of benefits provided after retirement.

Examples of accumulating post-employment benefits are:

- Sick leave programs that accumulate and are payable ("vested") upon termination, death, and/or retirement;
- Accumulated vacation or overtime days payable upon termination, retirement, and/or death;
- Lump sum retirement allowance; and
- Negotiated severance arrangements.

Event-Driven Benefits

As for event-driven benefits, post-employment benefits that do not accumulate, a liability will need to be calculated and accounted for only when the event takes place.

Examples of event-driven post-employment benefits are:

- Continuation of extended health and dental coverage during LTD;
- Self-insured LTD income benefits; and
- Self-insured Workers' Compensation benefits.

Post-Retirement Benefit Cost Containment Strategies

Mechanisms for reducing the cost of post-retirement benefits have become particularly important since the applicable accounting standards came into effect. Employers have turned to a variety of cost-containment strategies including:

- Establishing or increasing existing employee eligibility requirements (for example, post-retirement benefits could be limited to those employees who have completed a minimum number of years of service with the employer, or who were hired before a certain date);
- Increasing user fees through higher deductibles and coinsurance;

- Implementing cost ceilings on certain benefits in the form of annual and lifetime plan maximums;
- Reviewing and benchmarking design of benefit programs with the goal of looking for cost-savings that can be realized through plan design changes;
- Greater efficiencies in the management of the benefit plan such as carrier consolidations and alternate funding arrangements;
- Sharing increased cost, with members contributing a higher share of the premiums; and
- Re-pricing plan costs, separating retiree experience from active experience to ensure that the retirees' premiums are exclusive of any subsidization from the active employees' plan experience.
- Some of the more recent strategies that have been adopted by employers include:
- Replacing medical and dental coverage with a Health Care Spending Account (HCSA), which controls costs by setting a limit on the amount of benefits that can be claimed in a year;
- Providing medical and dental coverage through retiree exchanges or marketplaces: under this approach, the employer provides a fixed contribution (similar to an HCSA allocation) but also arranges access to a retiree exchange or marketplace that allows retirees to purchase individual insurance coverage at a discount and genrally without providing medical evidence; and
- Eliminating retiree benefits: this is typically done only for future retirees. In such a case, it is possible for employers to negotiate a conversion option with their medical benefits, whereby the retirees can convert their group policy to an individual policy without providing evidence of insurability. See "Legal Issues" below.

Changing the Terms of Post-Retirement Plans — Legal Issues

As described above, employers are facing increasing retiree benefit costs and many employers are attempting to contain such costs. Cost-containment measures may include significant changes such as completely overhauling the plan or even terminating the plan. Termination of the plan may involve a lump sum settlement to members at some percentage of their expected future liability to the employer. Alternately, it may involve minor changes, such as increasing deductibles or coinsurance. In making such changes, employers need to be aware of the potential legal ramifications of altering or terminating employee benefit plans.

The employer will encounter greater legal difficulties in reducing or terminating current retiree benefits as opposed to reducing or terminating entitlement to future retiree benefits for currently active employees. Both scenarios need to be thought out carefully. Although the crystallization of the post-retirement retiree benefit promise is not as clear-cut as it is for pensions, case law in Canada and the United States has advanced a generally accepted principle that a promise of retiree benefits vests at retirement.

With respect to retiree benefits in the unionized context, it is important to note the 1993 decision of *Dayco (Canada) Ltd. v. The National Automobile Aerospace and Agriculture Implement Workers Union of Canada.*[1] In that case, the Supreme Court of Canada held that retiree benefits are capable of vesting at the time of retirement, and therefore could be grieved after the expiry of a collective agreement. The case involved an attempt to terminate post-retirement medical benefits for retirees already in receipt of the benefits. Similarly, the 1995 decision of the Newfoundland Supreme Court in *Kennedy v. Canadian Saltfish Corp.,*[2] considered in a non-unionized environment, also concluded that a retiree has a vested right in the benefits provided at the time of retirement.

Since the Supreme Court ruled on the principle of vested benefit rights at retirement, numerous cases involving the reduction of post-retirement benefits have come before the courts. Many but not all of these cases are structured as class action lawsuits, where the claims of potentially thousands of retirees are consolidated into a single law-suit.[3]

There are several retiree challenges to changes in private benefit plans that have been certified as class actions. Although some of these more recent challenges have not been heard on their merits, it is interesting to note which reductions are being challenged and being allowed to proceed. In the case of *Acreman v. Memorial University of Newfoundland,*[4] the retirees challenged the University's decision to stop paying 100% of premiums for employee health benefits and instead impose a 50% contribution from employees. The court has approved the certification of the class action, stating that there is an identifiable class of retirees that are affected by the University's decision, and that the retirees' individual claims are sufficiently similar to be classified as a class action.

---

[1]   *Dayco (Canada) Ltd. v. The National Automobile Aerospace and Agriculture Implement Workers Union of Canada*, [1993] S.C.J. No. 53, 102 D.L.R. (4th) 609.

[2]   *Kennedy v. Canadian Saltfish Corp.*, [1995] N.J. No. 368, 11 C.C.P.B. 103 (N.L.T.D.).

[3]   For a discussion of pension class action lawsuits, see Chapter 9.

[4]   *Acreman v. Memorial University of Newfoundland*, [2010] N.J. No. 443, 2011 NLCA 55 (N.L.C.A.).

In *Dell'Aniello v. Vivendi Canada Inc.*,[5] the retirees challenged a plan change that increased the annual deductible and imposed a $15,000 lifetime cap on coverage. In this case, the Quebec Superior Court declined to certify the challenge as a class action, citing insufficient common issues among the plaintiffs in the proposed class. However, the Court of Appeal and Supreme Court reversed this ruling and ultimately certified the case as a class action.

In the class action case of *O'Neill v. General Motors of Canada Ltd.*,[6] the Superior Court of Justice (Ontario) released its decision in July 2013 in favour of the retirees. GM had reduced health and life insurance benefits to certain non-union salaried retirees. The ruling was largely based on communications from GM to employees that included a Reservation of Rights Clause ("ROR Clause") to reduce benefits. It was determined that the ROR Clauses in various communications to employees were not clear and unambiguous. For example, the ROR Clause only made specific reference to active benefits and not retiree benefits. Furthermore, the retiree health and life insurance benefits were part of the employment contract and benefits documentation provided for a reasonable assurance of retirement security. Interestingly, the court ruled against a sub-set of the retiree class that were executives, as the ROR Clause clearly and unambiguously allowed for the reduction of benefits.

Often when challenges to the reduction of post-retirement benefits are mounted as class actions, the parties settle the action without going to trial. For instance, in the case of *Smith v. Labatt Brewing Co.*,[7] the employer made significant changes to retiree benefits. These changes included reducing the unlimited lifetime coverage for drugs and most other medical benefits to a lifetime cap of $50,000, reducing the lifetime maximum out-of-country emergency coverage from $1 million to $50,000, and dramatically increasing the annual deductibles for individual members and their families. In approving the settlement, the court noted that the criteria for certification of the class had been satisfied. The settlement increased the out-of-country emergency coverage from a $50,000 to $200,000 cap, maintained coverage for catastrophic health costs, and increased the annual deductibles of $25 for a single person and $50 for a family to $350 and $750, respectively. The court approved the settlement as "fair, reasonable and in the best interests of the class as a whole", largely because it maintained coverage for future catastrophic health costs.

---

5   *Dell'Aniello v. Vivendi Canada Inc.*, [2012] J.Q. no 1611, 2012 QCCA 384
     (Que. C.A.).
6   *O'Neill v. General Motors of Canada Ltd.*, [2013] O.J. No. 3239, 2013 ONSC
     4654 (Ont. S.C.).
7   *Smith v. Labatt Brewing Co.*, [2009] O.J. No. 117 (Ont. S.C.J.).

Several cases have come before the courts in the form of individual retiree claims (rather than a class action) opposing a change in retiree benefits. In the case of *Gustavson v. TimberWest Forest Corp.*,[8] the retiree's agreement with the employer promised the retiree and his dependants employer-paid basic medical, extended health care and out-of-province emergency coverage. The agreement also gave the employer the right to amend or discontinue any part of the benefit package, but also stated that the retiree benefits "shall not be substantially less than those provided for in the agreement". The court ruled that the employer's decision to remove out-of-province emergency coverage from the retiree's benefit package constituted a change that resulted in a benefit package that was "substantially less" than what was provided in the agreement.

In *Lacey v. Weyerhaeuser Co.*,[9] the retirees were promised "fully funded" health benefits for their lifetime. The employer later decided that it would only contribute 50% of the cost of coverage, with the retirees responsible for the other 50%. Four retirees challenged this change to their benefits scheme. The court ruled that the employer's communication with employees indicated the employee benefits were a form of deferred compensation, rather than gratuitous benefits. Although this communication also reserved a right on behalf of the employer to make changes to the benefits scheme from time to time, the court found that the 50/50 cost share effectively terminated (rather than changed) benefits for those retirees who could not afford it. The Supreme Court of Canada denied the appeal of the ruling.

On the other hand, when objections have been made to changes in public "statutory" plans, the courts have treated retirees less favourably. For example, in *B.C. Nurses' Union v. Municipal Pension Board of Trustees*,[10] the retirees challenged a reduction in subsidized premiums for their benefits, along with a reduction in health and dental coverage. The court maintained that whether retirees had a vested interest in benefits at the time of retirement had to be determined by an examination of the legislative intent behind these "statutory" plans.[11] The court ruled that these changes were acceptable, concluding that the legislative intent behind this public "statutory" plan revealed no vested interest for the retirees. Similarly, in *Bennett v. British Columbia*,[12] the court ruled that

---

[8]   *Gustavson v. TimberWest Forest Corp.*, [2011] B.C.J. No. 1943, 2011 BCPC 272.

[9]   *Lacey v. Weyerhaeuser Co.*, [2012] B.C.J. No. 481, 2012 BCSC 353 (B.C.S.C.).

[10]   B.C. Nurses' Union v. Municipal Pension Board of Trustees, [2006] B.C.J. No. 156, 2006 BCSC 132 (B.C.S.C.).

[11]   In contrast, an examination of the intention of the contracting parties is entered into for private plans.

[12]   *Bennett v. British Columbia*, [2012] B.C.J. No. 497, 2012 BCCA 115 (B.C.C.A.).

the legislative intent behind the "statutory" plan did not create a vested interest in premium-free benefits for retirees. The court determined that had this been the legislative intent, it would have been explicitly included in the "statutory" plan. As a result, the change initiated by the employer, requiring partial payment by retirees for continued coverage, was deemed acceptable.

Taxation of Post-Retirement and Post-Employment Benefits

Taxation rules affecting retiree benefits can be summarized as follows:

- For income tax purposes, an employer may deduct premiums to post-retirement life, medical, or dental plans for current retirees in the same way as wages or other operating expenses;

- A retiree is taxed on employer contributions for post-retirement life insurance, including any related premium and sales tax. Paid-up life insurance premiums are taxable to the retiree in the year of purchase, except in Quebec, where the premium is amortized over the expected lifetime of the retiree;

- A retiree is taxed on employer contributions for provincial health insurance premiums;

- Except in Quebec, the retiree is not taxed on the employer's contribution to the medical or dental plan. In Quebec, since May 21, 1993, employer contributions are included as a taxable benefit for the purposes of calculating provincial income tax payable. The amount of the taxable benefit can be included in the calculation of the individual medical expense tax credit;

- All provinces charge premium tax on all group insurance premiums, and in some jurisdictions (namely Ontario, Quebec, and Newfoundland and Labrador), contributions to self-insured health and dental plans are subject to the premium tax. Premium tax varies by province and by territory (in 2016, it ranges from 2% to 4%). Insurance premiums are also subject to retail sales tax in Ontario (8%) and Quebec (9%). In Manitoba, group life insurance, accidental death and dismemberment, disability, and critical illness premiums only are subject to an 8% retail sales tax; and

- Lump sum payments (e.g., retirement allowance, vested sick leave) are taxed as income in the year in which the payment is received.

Accounting of Post-Retirement and Post-Employment Benefits

Historically, accounting for post-retirement and post-employment benefits was handled on a pay-as-you-go basis, which means that the cost was reflected in the financial statements as the benefits were actually paid to members and companies had no obligations on their balance sheet for future benefits.

The various accounting standards, such as CPA Canada (Section 3462 for private entities, Section 3463 for not-for-profits, and PS 3250/3255 for public entities), FASB (ASC 715), and IFRS (IAS 19), require companies to recognize:

- On the income statement, the cost of post-retirement and accumulating post-employment benefits over the working lifetimes of the employees;
- On the income statement, the cost of event-driven post-employment benefits in the year the triggering event occurs; and
- On the balance sheet, an accrued liability for the future costs of retiree benefits for active members and current retirees.

The accrual accounting method of accounting for the post-retirement benefits and for post-employment benefits that accumulate reflects the benefit value over the active working career of the employee. It is similar to the methodology for expense and liability recognition under pension plans.

Funding of Post-Retirement Benefits

Life Insurance

There are several funding alternatives for retiree life insurance benefits. The simplest and most common funding method is to purchase one-year renewable group term insurance, usually in conjunction with a one-year renewable term insurance for the active employee benefit plan. In some cases, the active and retiree benefit experience is combined into one policy and a blended rate is charged.

Alternatively, the retiree and active rates are separate, reflecting the experience and demographics of each group.

Employers who want to show the true cost of the retiree life benefit to their retirees will tend to adopt a separate retiree rate. Considering that employer contributions to life insurance coverage is a taxable benefit, that decision will significantly increase the taxable benefit to retirees while reducing the actives' taxable benefit.

Another funding method for retiree life insurance is for the employer to self-insure the first $10,000 of benefit payable in the event of the member's death. Under current tax regulations, an employer can pay a member's beneficiary up to $10,000 without it being taxable income in the beneficiary hands. Because death benefits in excess of $10,000 are considered taxable income to the recipient if paid by the employer, life insurance above $10,000 tends to be insured.

A third funding method is to pre-fund the cost of retiree benefits. The retiree life insurance can be purchased from an insurance company on a single premium, paid-up basis. The advantage of this method is that the obligation relating to the life insurance benefit can be settled at the time of retirement. The main disadvantage is the relatively expensive price, since group insurance companies maintain margins for adverse deviations when quoting paid-up premiums. The end result is usually a paid-up premium that is significantly higher than the actuarial obligation that the employer would otherwise have on the books. Another disadvantage is the large taxable benefit that the retiree will face in the year of purchase (except in Quebec).

Medical and Dental Care

The employer's promise to pay health and dental care benefits is not generally pre-funded and most benefits are paid at the time that they occur. There is no financial or tax incentive, at present, for employers seeking to pre-fund the post-retirement medical or dental care liability. Effective tax-sheltered vehicles, such as those that have encouraged the growth of pension plan funds, do not exist. Until such vehicles are available, pre-funding retiree benefits represents a significant challenge.

Trust Legislation

The Employee Life and Health Trust (ELHT) is a relatively new vehicle created by the Canadian Federal government in 2010 for the delivery of life, disability, health, and dental programs for both active and retired employees and their dependents. One of the main advantages of the ELHT is the ability to allow employers to pre-fund employee and retiree health and welfare benefits and receive staggered tax deductions for current service contributions.

The ELHT has been of particular interest for employers looking to wind up their retiree health and dental programs, as this vehicle provides an option to move the financial obligations of these programs to a third party (*i.e.*, independent trust) in a tax-effective manner once settlement funds are paid in full. This was a major motivator for employers such as General Motors and Chrysler during their recent negotiations with the Canadian Auto Workers, and the creation of the ELHT was a partial condition in receiving government financial assistance during the 2008 economic crisis.

However, uptake on ELHTs has been relatively limited to date:

- While ELHTs do allow for some tax deferral, tax treatment is not as favourable as it is for pension plans;

- Not all post-retirement and post-employment benefits may be covered under an ELHT;

- Since an ELHT requires the establishment of a separate trust, the ongoing administrative commitment is considerable; and

- Upon wind up or reorganization of an ELHT, any surplus trust assets may not be distributed to the employer.

Chapter 25

FINANCIAL MANAGEMENT AND ADMINISTRATION OF EMPLOYEE BENEFIT PLANS

Executive Summary

This chapter addresses the financial aspects of benefit plan stewardship, administration arrangements, and the many alternatives available to plan sponsors.

Under financial management, in a typical group insurance contract, the insurance company agrees to insure specific group benefits that are payable to the individuals eligible under the plan. The plan sponsor[1] agrees to pay the premiums to maintain the contract in good standing for the year, and to provide the insurance company with necessary records to administer the benefit. In the case of a self-insured benefit, the insurance company would provide Administrative Services Only (ASO) and the plan sponsor would contractually accept the financial liability for all claim payments and administration charges.

Administering employee benefits involves a wide variety of tasks with the purpose of applying the plan provisions in favour of the plan's beneficiaries. Administration's most important output is employee records, which form the basis of claims payments and other services. Obtaining member consent to the collection, use, and disclosure of the personal information in these records has become a key concern of administration in the context of legislated protection of personal information. Plan sponsors can choose from a wide range of administrative arrangements, including in-house administration, but the clear trend has been to outsource administration to an insurer or a specialized third-party administrator.

---

[1] The plan sponsor is typically an employer, but can also be a union, a health and welfare trust, or an association that has been formed other than for the purpose of obtaining insurance.

Renewal Process

Group insurance policies and related agreements are generally written on a one-year renewable basis. The annual cycle lends itself to a review of all aspects of the relationship between the insurance company and the plan sponsor at least once a year. As part of the annual renewal process, the insurance company has the right to adjust its premium rates, expenses, and reserves for the upcoming year. Conversely, the plan sponsor has the right to renew the contract or to seek alternatives in the marketplace. While a one year renewal is the norm, it is not a contractual requirement. Most contracts can be terminated with relatively short notice, typically 30 days.

Cost continues to be a key factor in the evaluation of the insurer relationship. The definition of cost will depend on whether the plan sponsor has purchased insurance (either fully pooled or with risk-sharing financial arrangements, such as retention or refund accounting) or whether the plan sponsor self-insures using only the administrative services of the insurance company.

Premium defines the gross cost of the benefit in insured arrangements. The premium is calculated at the beginning of the year by the insurance company. The premium calculation may take into account prior claims experience, demographics, risk distribution, occupations within the group, geographic location, interest charges, taxes, and plan design. In this context, claims experience would include actual paid claims as well as the insurer's reserve and administrative expenses, pooling charges, and projected inflation and anticipated utilization. Unless the plan sponsor is participating in some form of retention accounting, or the benefit is self-insured, the premium represents the cost of providing the benefit. Negotiating the lowest sustainable cost, therefore, is generally in the best interest of the plan sponsor and the employees, while keeping in mind the financial stability of the plan over the medium to long term.

Net cost is gross cost less any experience refunds the plan sponsor is entitled to receive. The net cost is calculated as the paid claims, plus the insurance company expense charges, reserves, taxes, and any interest adjustments. The definition of net cost applies to retention accounting and to self-insured benefits that are administered by the insurance company on an ASO basis.

Underwriting Considerations

Plan sponsors select from a continuum of risk arrangements or underwriting options that allocate the risk between the insurance company and the plan sponsor. Risk is defined as the potential for loss or gain resulting from the variance between premiums (projected cost) and actual cost.

At one extreme, benefits are underwritten on a fully pooled basis, with the insurance company assuming the full risk in the event that actual costs exceed premiums. The insurance company retains any profit arising if premiums exceed claims plus all other expenses including reserves, interest, and taxes.

The liability of the plan sponsor is limited to the premium paid. At the other extreme, the plan sponsor self-insures the risk, regardless of the actual claims level. The role of the insurance company is strictly to perform the administrative and claims adjudication services.

The underwriting option most appropriate for a plan sponsor depends on the benefit under consideration, the number of employees in the group, employee turnover in the group, and the risk tolerance of the plan sponsor. The terms being offered by the insurance company may also impact on the decision of the plan sponsor.

Each benefit has unique attributes that define its inherent risk. Two key attributes of the benefit are the magnitude of potential claims and the frequency of claims. Large amount claims occurring with a low incidence will lead to a high degree of volatility in annual costs. For example, Accidental Death and Dismemberment (AD&D) claims are relatively infrequent and each claim represents several thousand dollars. The combination of infrequent incidence and a large amount for each occurrence increases the risk of fluctuation in expected claims year-to-year. Conversely, vision care claims, for example, occur more frequently, and the benefit schedule usually limits the dollar amount of any one claim.

Relative to AD&D insurance, the combination of high incidence and low dollars per claim reduces the potential underwriting risk. The number of individuals covered in a group is a commonly used measure of claims stability. As the number of employees increases, it becomes more likely that future claims can be projected based on the past claims of the group. The term "credibility" is used to denote the likelihood that past experience can be used reliably to project future claims. If the credibility is low, either because the group is small or the experience has been volatile, the insurance company will rely on its standard rate tables to determine the premium. If the credibility is high, the insurance company is more likely to base the premiums on the claims experience of the group, and the plan sponsor may be more likely to consider some form of risk sharing.

Some organizations are more inclined towards fully pooled or pure insurance. Others have a higher tolerance for risk sharing and wish to negotiate risk-sharing arrangements with the insurer. The same is true for plan sponsor preferences in underwriting options for the benefit plans.

The insurance community has responded to plan sponsor needs by offering a wide range of underwriting options.

Underwriting Options

Fully Pooled

Under this arrangement, the insurance company assumes the full risk of a deficit in the event that actual costs exceed premiums. Conversely, the insurance company profits from any surplus.

There is no annual financial accounting under a fully pooled arrangement, but the insurance company will prepare a renewal report and will normally disclose the experience of the group. Many insurers, however, have implemented strict internal policies that prohibit the disclosure of a group's detailed claims experience due to privacy concerns. Therefore, it will likely be more difficult in the future for smaller plan sponsors (i.e., under 25 plan members) to view their own claims history other than premium and claims paid on an annual basis. The renewal may reflect the overall experience of the insurance company for groups with similar characteristics. However, in most cases, the experience of the group will be factored into the renewal analysis.

A Pooled funding arrangement is suitable for small groups to minimize year-to-year cost fluctuations. In addition, pooled funding is generally appropriate for benefits with highly volatile costs, such as AD&D, where a single claim can represent several years of premium. It is appropriate that many plan sponsors of smaller groups elect pooled funding for group life and long-term disability (LTD) benefits as these usually involve relatively large amounts of insurance and a low claim incidence.

Retention Accounting (also known as Refund Accounting)

Typically in a retention accounting situation, the employer receives from the insurance company an annual financial accounting of the plan, as well as access to some or all of the surplus arising if claims were lower than expected. The specific terms governing each refund account depend on the terms of the underwriting agreement negotiated between the insurance company and the plan sponsor.

The financial accounting takes into account the premiums paid to the insurance company, claims paid by the insurance company, changes in the reserves, administrative expenses, taxes, and the interest earned or charged. When premiums exceed the charges against the account, the insurance company declares a surplus. Depending on the terms of the underwriting agreement the surplus may be released to the plan sponsor, held by the insurance company on behalf of the employer in a Claims Fluctuation Reserve (CFR) or Rate Stabilization Fund (RSF) used to buffer future volatility, applied against prior deficits under the account or left on deposit with the insurance company.

Deficits arise when the premium is not sufficient to cover the charges against the account for a given year. While the policy remains in force with the insurance company, the plan sponsor usually accepts that any future surplus will be applied to reduce or eliminate the deficit. In addition, specific repayment options may be negotiated between the parties. The ultimate liability for the deficit remains with the insurance company, unless liability for deficit on termination is specifically written into the terms of the underwriting agreement.

Retention Charges

Retention charges are the charges made by the insurance company against the account for policy administration, claims adjudication, profit, and risk. Other charges may be passed through the plan such as charges of third parties used by the insurer (for example, the cost of independent medical exams and outside rehabilitation counsellors used in the adjudication of disability claims) and a charge for the insurer's cost of capital or return on equity.

These latter charges were introduced in conjunction with the government's solvency Minimum Continuing Capital and Surplus Requirements (MCCSR)[2] and as a result of demutualization and the insurer's desire to produce a return on equity for their shareholders.

Pooling

Pooling is an insured arrangement whereby, in return for a pooling charge, plan sponsors who have their group benefit plans underwritten on a retention accounting or ASO (see ASO section below) basis, are protected in situations where an individual claim exceeds a specified amount, or the total claims paid out under the group benefits plan exceed a specified

---

[2] The MCCSR measures the insurer's capital adequacy to meet its obligations to policyholders. The MCCSR ratio is expressed as a percentage of the minimum requirement. An MCCSR of 100% means that a company has adequate capital to meet its obligations to policyholders.

amount. A plan sponsor buys this protection from an insurer. There are three common types of pooling arrangements:

- *Large amount pooling* (LAP)— provides the plan sponsor with financial protection in the event of large catastrophic claims exceeding the specified LAP limit. If a plan member's healthcare and prescription drug claims exceed the pooling limit, the excess is absorbed by the insurer and not charged in the financial accounting. At renewal, excess claims are typically removed from the underwriting analysis unless they are expected to recur. LAP normally applies to health and group life benefits, but it is also occasionally used for LTD benefits;

- *Duration pooling* — is a variation of LAP. It is commonly used in LTD accounting and it protects the plan from individual claims that exceed a fixed duration (e.g., two years or five years, regardless of the monthly benefit payable); and

- *Aggregate stop loss pooling* — provides the plan sponsor with financial protection in the event of an unexpected surge in the number of claims during the accounting period. The protection level is generally defined in terms of a percentage of the annual premium (e.g., 125% of premium).

Administrative Service Only (ASO)

A plan sponsor choosing to self-insure a benefit foregoes the risk transfer offered by insurance companies. Depending on the benefit, it may remain strategically more efficient to use the administrative services of the insurance company rather than replicate the necessary infrastructure to manage claim data and adjudicate claims. The insurance company is compensated for its services, either on a percentage of paid claims or on a per transaction basis.

Some plan sponsors favour pooling protection combined with their ASO arrangements, and this is generally considered to be best practice. The same pooling options are available under an ASO plan as under a retention accounting plan, allowing the plan sponsor to choose to protect the plan from claims exceeding their acceptable level of risk.

By definition, a self-insured plan does not involve premiums. The plan sponsor has a range of payment options to replace the monthly premium flow.

Some plan sponsors may choose to mirror an insured arrangement, remitting monthly deposits to the insurance company based on projected claims. Deposit rates reduce the month-to-month fluctuation, but require annual reconciliation against actual cost and may require a lump-sum payment should there be a shortfall.

Alternatively, the insurance company will invoice the plan sponsor based on the prior month's claims plus expenses. Monthly costs will fluctuate, but most insurance companies are prepared to offer some form of equalization to avoid excessive variation in cost from month to month. No annual reconciliation is required because of the "pay-as-you-go" arrangement.

A third option for a self-insured plan is to create a debit arrangement between the plan sponsor and the insurance company. The insurance company is authorized, on a daily or weekly basis, to withdraw funds equivalent to claims plus expenses from a designated account established by the plan sponsor. The insurer must then report to the plan sponsor and provide the reconciliation.

Underwriting Disability Benefits

Disability benefits present unique risk management challenges for plan sponsors and warrant further discussion with respect to the underwriting of these programs.

Plan sponsors commonly self-insure short-term disability (STD) plans without pre-funding. The maximum exposure on any one claim, however, is limited for the most part by the benefit duration. Over time, the claims experience of most groups shows a reasonable element of predictability. Insured coverage is available for smaller groups, or for plan sponsors with a lower tolerance for risk.

LTD plans represent a significantly different risk-management challenge. A typical example of the present value of an LTD benefit that provides a 66¾% benefit to age 65 for a 40-year-old employee with annual earnings of $45,000 could be close to $350,000. Many organizations are not large enough to assume a risk of this magnitude without some form of protection. Not surprisingly, LTD benefits are generally insured. For larger groups, plan sponsors may choose to insure the LTD benefits with some form of retention accounting. It is prudent to add some form of pooling to mitigate against experience fluctuation. Pooling is also generally available to those plan sponsors who prefer to self-insure the LTD plan.

Self-insured disability plans in the private sector are now under government scrutiny following the bankruptcy of several high visibility corporations that used self-insured disability programs.

Elements of Financial Accounting

With risk-sharing arrangements such as retention accounting, the insurance company will prepare an annual financial accounting. The overall financial position of the plan identifies premiums paid to the insurance company as well as paid claims and related reserves, expenses, interest, and taxes. Recognizing most contracts of insurance involve obligations that may extend beyond the end of the accounting period, reserves are established by the insurance company to provide for obligations for these future liabilities. It is important to remember that the ownership and accountability of each type of reserve is a matter to be negotiated between the insurance company and the plan sponsor, and documented in the underwriting agreement.

Incurred But Not Reported Reserve

Incurred But Not Reported (IBNR) claim reserves reflect liability for claims that are incurred during the contract year and submitted after the close of the contract year but are payable from the premiums collected during the accounting period.

The level of the IBNR reflects the claim reporting pattern associated with the benefit. For example, the IBNR for group life insurance tends to reflect a reporting lag of roughly one month between the date of death and the date the claim is filed with the insurance company. By contrast, the IBNR under an LTD contract with a six-month elimination period would be in the order of 50% to 60% of the premium.

The IBNR requirement under a healthcare, drug or dental benefit has undergone a significant reduction in the last decade due to point-of-sale transactions and the ability for the practitioner (e.g., dentist or pharmacist) or the plan member to remit claims electronically.

The insurance company may be willing to reduce the IBNR requirements or eliminate the reserve from the annual accounting if the plan sponsor is willing to delay the financial reconciliation to allow the late-reported claims to flow through the account. In some cases, an insurer may allow the plan sponsor to enter into an agreement to take over the responsibility of the IBNR entirely.

Waiver of Premium Reserve

Waiver of premium reserves are held under group life insurance contracts in which the plan sponsor has insured the continuation of coverage for disabled lives without future payment of premium.

Despite the term "waiver of premium", the reserve is not based on the future value of the premiums being waived on behalf of the disabled individual. Rather, the waiver of premium reserve is based on the discounted value of the death claim, taking into account the probability of recovery, termination, or death and discounting the face amount of the claim for projected interest earnings.

The insurance company remains liable for the death benefit for approved waiver of premium claims beyond the termination of the contract, usually through to age 65. The waiver of premium reserve allows the insurance company to reflect this obligation in the financial accounting before the death claim occurs.

The plan sponsor may choose not to insure the waiver of premium provision, in which case benefit continuation for disabled employees would be conditional on premium continuation. Self-insuring the waiver of premium provision renders the plan sponsor responsible for arranging continued coverage for the disabled individuals in the event the group life insurance contract is transferred to another insurance company.

A sponsor must weigh the cost savings against the potential liability of the continuing premium payment for disabled employees.

Disabled Life Reserve

Under an income-replacement benefit, Disabled Life Reserves (DLR) reflect the obligation of the insurance company for benefit continuation beyond policy termination. Once a claim is admitted and payments commence, the insurance company becomes liable for future benefit payments, usually through to age 65, provided the individual continues to qualify under the terms of the benefit plan. The reserve reflects the present value of future benefit payments and claim-related expenses, adjusted for mortality and recovery assumptions, and discounted for projected interest earnings.

Pending Claim Reserve

The pending claim reserve reflects the present value of disability claims that were submitted before the end of the accounting period but have not yet been approved for payment. The insurer generally multiplies the DLR for these pending claims by a percentage factor to reflect the uncertainty around approval of the claim.

Claims Fluctuation Reserve

Claims Fluctuation Reserves (CFR), also known as Rate Stabilization Fund (RSF), reflect funds that are established typically from surpluses arising from the financial accounting of the plan and held by the insurance company. By withholding a portion of the surplus against future deficits, the insurance company is protecting itself against the contingency the plan sponsor will terminate the relationship while the account is in a deficit position. In consideration of a CFR, the plan sponsor should expect a reduction in any risk and cost of capital/return on equity charges levied by the insurance company. Amounts held may vary depending on the insurance company but are usually limited to no more than 25% of annual premium for tax reasons.

Administration of Employee Benefit Plans

Background

Accurate and efficient administration is fundamental to the successful operation of an employee benefit plan. Although administration is not directly visible to the employee, its most important output is the employee records, which, in turn, run the premium and claims payment processes. Because it results in the records that result in claims payments and other member services, administration directly impacts the quality and accuracy of service experienced by membership. Secondly, in an increasingly complex and litigious environment, quality and efficient administration reduce the legal risk to the plan sponsor that results from the offer of benefits.

Plan sponsors can select from a wide range of administrative arrangements, each with a different level of resource involvement and costs for the employer. The most appropriate administration arrangement will depend on the corporate culture, the internal resources of the employer, the technology available, the number of divisions, and level of decentralization and member self-service that is considered appropriate.

Outsourcing

There are several reasons why there has been a growing trend towards outsourcing the administration of group benefits. First of all, to be competitive, many employers are focusing on their core businesses and expertise. This may lead to strategic alliances or the outsourcing of some generic functions. In the case of pensions and benefits, employers will often outsource some functions of administration and communication, while retaining control of the strategic components that are most important to the individual employee-employer relationships. Another reason for outsourcing is the growing complexity of administration and increased exposure to litigation. Employers will not want, or cannot afford, to retain sufficient expertise in-house. Additionally, the increasing cost of investments in technology to administer benefits means that more employers will not be able to justify the investment for in-house use only.

A plan sponsor has the option of outsourcing either to its insurer or to a third-party administrator. A third-party administrator (TPA) is an organization that specializes in benefit administration. The use of TPAs has been growing in Canada, due to the fact that they not only provide expertise in benefit administration, but plan sponsors also find it advantageous to house their enrolment data on an administration platform that does not belong to one specific insurance company in the event there is a change in carriers. Many TPA's have become competitive in this space as they have invested in the required technology.

Privacy Issues

The federal *Personal Information Protection and Electronic Documents Act* (PIPEDA) came into force on January 1, 2001, and was amended in 2010. Any organization covered by PIPEDA must obtain the consent of an individual before they collect, use, or disclose the personal information of that individual. PIPEDA was phased in over a three-year period and as of January 1, 2004, applies to all organizations regarding the collection, use, and disclosure of personal information in the course of "commercial activity" within a province, unless the province has adopted "substantially similar" privacy legislation. All provinces now have similar types of legislation.

Personal information, as defined in the Act, includes information, both factual and subjective, about an individual. It includes information such as age, identification numbers, income, blood type, evaluations and disciplinary actions, credit records, and medical records.

Personal information does not, however, include such things as a person's name, title, or business address. Personal health information is described as an individual's mental or physical health information, and that includes information regarding health services provided, and tests and examinations.

For those involved in benefit administration, the most important provision in PIPEDA is the requirement to obtain an individual's consent before collecting, using, or disclosing information. The intent behind this provision is to ensure that the information is only used for the purpose for which it was collected. If an organization is going to use it for another purpose, consent must be obtained again. An employee cannot be reprimanded for refusing to provide consent. For employers and insurers, concerns remain due to the fact that some issues are not expressly addressed: What type of consent is required? Written or oral consent? Expressed or deemed consent? Will a general consent signed by an employee be acceptable? Another provision specifies that information must be appropriately safeguarded. Employees should be assured that their information will be protected by specific security measures, including measures such as locked cabinets, computer passwords, or encryption. It is also essential that those who work with this information understand their obligations under PIPEDA, to ensure that employees' personal information is properly secured and is properly disposed of when no longer necessary for the purpose for which consent was given.

Key Administration Tasks

Maintaining Employee Data Records

Much of the employee data necessary for benefit purposes can be gathered during the enrolment process. The employee provides basic information at the time of enrolment, including his or her full name, gender, and date of birth. The employer adds the date of hire, salary, or insurable earnings and an identification number. The identification number assigned by the employer may be the same as the Social Insurance Number (SIN), in which case an authorization to use the SIN should be part of the enrolment form. This is not recommended as the federal *Income Tax Act* (ITA) specifically states that an employer is not to communicate an individual's SIN without the individual's written consent. The most commonly used identification number is either a payroll number or an individual employee number that is unique to the employee.

In Quebec, specific authorization is necessary to permit the employer to use personal information for the administration of the plan. For further information regarding consent and other privacy issues in Canada, see the discussion above on "Privacy Issues".

For medical and dental benefits, the employee will need to indicate whether coverage is required for the employee alone, or for his or her dependants, as well. If family coverage is selected, the employee will also need to indicate if his or her dependants have coverage available through another plan in order to properly apply the coordination of benefits.

Additionally, benefit enrolment forms typically include the beneficiary designation for life and accidental death insurance benefits. As well, the process must prompt collection of any evidence of insurability that is required. Smoker status for the employee and/or spouse is required in many cases for optional life coverage premium calculations.

Having gathered all of the necessary information, the benefit administrator will either enter the information in the administration system, or relay the information to the insurance company or TPA, either online or through an electronic feed.

Alternatively, employee online self-service is now readily available. It includes employee enrolment, and plan selections in the case of flex plans.

Changes in employee data are inevitable, and may range from a change in the dependant information, to a change in the status of the employee for benefit coverage. The employer remains responsible for maintaining accurate records and for protecting the confidentiality of personal information of the employee.

Premium Billing

Premiums, or, in the case of self-insured plans, deposit rates, are based on employee data. The exact data vary by benefit. For life and AD&D insurance, premiums are typically based on the insured volumes.

Disability premiums are based on either the monthly benefit or the monthly insured payroll. Health and dental premiums are typically based on the number of employees covered, and by single, couple and family status. Alternatively, some plans offer a tier structure based on the number of people covered, such as employee, employee + 1 and employee + 2+.

The monthly billing can be prepared by the insurance company, a TPA, or by the plan sponsor.

In the case of the insurance company or TPA preparing the billing statement, the plan sponsor notifies the insurance company of any changes in employee data since the prior billing period. The plan sponsor may produce the billing statement itself using an internal administration system that keeps track of the employee data. Alternatively, the administration system may be developed by the employer or purchased from a vendor.

Administering Employee Contributions

Many benefit administration systems are designed to automatically calculate any employee contributions required, provided the system has current data and current rates.

The interface between the benefit administration system and the payroll system may be electronic, or may require human intervention to transfer the information each pay period. In some cases, the employer relies on the payroll system to calculate and administer deductions, and maintains a separate administration system for benefit records.

Alternative procedures will generally be necessary to administer employee contributions for employees not on the active payroll system. Postdated cheques or pre-authorized debit can be arranged for employee contributions due during unpaid leave, maternity leave, retirement, or for employees in receipt of disability benefits.

In Quebec, employee contributions for medical and dental plans can be included in the tax credit for medical expenses, and should be recorded separately from other employee contributions.

Claim Payment

When an employee submits a claim, the claim must be adjudicated to determine whether the claimed item is covered, and the amount of reimbursement to be paid. The objective is to pay the claim accurately and as promptly as possible. Most medical and dental claims are handled by an insurance company or TPA. With the exception of short-term salary continuance, claims are rarely handled by the employer. Insurance company or TPA adjudication, including validation of an employee's eligibility, streamlines the process and provides the employee with a greater sense of confidentiality. The trend towards insurance company or TPA validation is reinforced by the rapidly growing use of electronic data interchange in adjudicating claims at point of purchase. To re-emphasize, it is because the benefits administration process determines the accuracy of the claims function itself that the process must be executed with a very high degree of care.

Management Reports

Reporting capabilities by all parties have improved significantly in recent years. Such capabilities are an important benefits management tool for the employer and should be given high priority.

Obviously, the insurance company or TPA should be readily able to produce a wide range of financial and claims management reports for each benefit. Interpretation of the information provided by the insurance company or TPA may require supplementary data from the benefit administration system.

Benefits that are self-insured and self-administered rely solely on internal systems to develop the analytical tools essential to govern the plan. It may be necessary to integrate data from several sources, including the benefit administration, attendance systems, and payroll systems.

The benefit administration system stores information on the employee population, which can in turn be compared to the claimant demographics for plan review and pricing. Demographic profiling is particularly important in terms of pricing for flexible benefits.

Lastly, it is good practice to audit the accuracy of all of the records and outputs of the benefits administration process. As a starting point, reconciliation can be conducted by comparing data files between parties and/or by performing an audit on the premises of the insurance company or TPA.

Quality Control and Audit

Regardless of who completes administrative tasks, the employer must ensure that there is a very high level of quality and accuracy. With respect to those aspects completed in-house, one way to review quality is through a peer review process or sampling of a certain number of transactions on a regular basis.

Because of the increasing complexity and the related risks associated with the performance of the obligation, a growing number of plans will conduct regular audits of the benefits administration processes and outcomes themselves.

This project will generally have the following objectives:

- Reduce the risks related to the provision and administration of employment benefits;
- Identify where additional controls or interfaces would improve results;
- Identify opportunities to streamline processes and, where possible, improve services to membership; and
- Identify and quantify the resources employed in relation to the benefit plans and determine if they are appropriate.

Administration in a Collective Bargaining Environment

At a minimum, administration of benefits in a union environment requires the ability both to segregate the employees by coverage classification and to administer more than one distinct set of plan rules. Often, there are several collective bargaining units that may negotiate benefits and wages at different times.

Negotiated benefit changes may be retroactive, placing additional stress on the administration system. Some benefit administration systems have not automated the ability to implement plan-wide retroactive changes, and require adjustment at the individual record level.

Tools and Trends in Benefits Administration

Administration Systems

As employers develop benefit plans that respond to diversity and changing needs, the ability to provide effective administrative solutions becomes critical to the success of the plan design. Human resource and benefit administration systems can be bought, adapted, or created internally, depending on the employer's needs and resources. The resources and budget required to create a full human resource system are beyond the means of most employers.

An administration system purchased by an employer for in-house use should take into account the corporate methodologies in terms of technology, architecture, and supported solutions. The ability to maintain the system with internal resources allows the employer to keep the system responsive to a changing environment. In addition, the employer may be able to add or build additional modules that are not dependent upon outside proprietary databases.

Benefit administration can be addressed as a separate stand-alone system or as a module of a complete human resource administration system. Administration packages are available with a wide range of features and functions.

Full-service software providers deliver a significant degree of custom design, performed in partnership between the vendor and the employer. The product is ready to be installed when delivered to the employer. By contrast, tool-kit or shelf-ware applications are developed by the vendor, with the employer assuming all responsibility for the costs of customization, construction of interfaces, testing, and ongoing maintenance. Some vendors in both categories will provide additional support using their technical personnel on a fee-for-service or contract basis.

Implementing benefit guidelines on a consistent and timely basis has always been a challenge to human resource professionals and benefit administrators. Rules-based or table-driven applications use the administration system itself to manage policy guidelines, reducing the incidence of *ad hoc* changes required. For example, eligibility rules can include a screening process to ensure that only eligible employees participate in selected benefits or options. Rules-based applications can also initiate benefit changes automatically upon certain life events, including a change in marital status or a change in employee status.

Administration packages and systems vary in the level of flexibility, compatibility, and ease of implementation. The more rigid systems essentially force the employer to adapt to a rigid set of predefined codes. A more versatile system allows the employer to define the codes to match their own.

To be able to manage retroactive adjustments, the administration system must accommodate not only all changes predating the current deduction period, but also the discrete periods in which these changes were in effect. Employee premiums and taxable benefits at both federal and provincial levels can be addressed within a well-designed benefit administration system to avoid the need for manual calculation. The need to administer multiple concurrent changes will depend on the plan design, but will definitely increase with the number of employees in the group and the frequency of changes allowed under the plan.

Flexible Benefits

A flexible benefit environment will affect the enrolment process and the maintenance of employee data. In addition to the information noted above, the employer will need to record the benefit options chosen by the employees. There are typically credits or contributions that need to be calculated to reflect not only the benefit option chosen, but also the date of entry into the plan.

In a flexible benefit plan, the employee may have discretion over the allocation of credits. Some benefit elections will have no taxable benefit implications. Others will give rise to a taxable benefit just as if the employer had contributed directly to the premiums. The order in which credits are applied is an essential consideration of the administration system and the taxable benefit calculation.

In-house administration systems are not the only solutions for employers. As technology continues to progress, many employers find themselves continuously updating their software. This can be costly for the employer in terms of money expended for the upgrades and employee hours spent ensuring proper implementation of the software. As a solution, some plan sponsors are turning to Application Service Providers (ASPs). An ASP is a third party that manages and distributes software-based services. Basically, ASPs provide another method of software delivery. Rather than purchasing and upgrading software, the employer accesses the ASP software via the Internet. Ongoing support from the ASP is available. Typically, this type of solution offers regular upgrades and a high degree of flexibility.

Member Self-Service

A rapidly growing area in benefits administration is that of member self-service websites for employees. Not only can employees obtain information about their benefits via the Internet, but they can also update and enroll in their plan, particularly flexible benefits plans. Employees are able to print off forms and information that they require. Beneficiary designations are printed off, signed, and submitted for the completion of a proper record and a legally valid designation.

Also of great advantage to employees are benefits modelling tools, as they make the educational and administrative stages of the system more streamlined. Using a flexible benefits modelling tool, the employee is able to consider the different options available and the costs and taxable benefits at different levels of coverage.

Another advantage of online enrolment is the ability to ensure that the employee completes all of the necessary information. When the employee fails to enter the required information, or the information is incorrect, the employee will be notified of the error and will be unable to proceed until the necessary information is provided. In the paper-based environment, the errors are not detected until they are processed, causing administrative delays. Another advantage of self-service websites is the ability to provide access 24 hours a day. Participants can access the website in the evenings, on weekends, or at whatever time is convenient for them. Not only can information regarding the company's benefits be accessed online, but information and links can be provided as a useful source of reference material. A new trend is the development of rollout of applications for mobile devices such as smartphones and tablets. These apps give the flexibility to employees to access their benefit information from almost anywhere and even process some transactions without having to use a computer.

From the employer's perspective, self-service benefits can save costs, promote increased efficiency and accuracy, and eliminate paperwork.

Provision of a high quality, engaging experience can even tie in with other Human Resources programs and enhance the corporate image.

Employers have some legitimate concerns, however. Security is probably the most pressing concern for employers and employees when dealing with confidential information over the Internet. To address this, it is necessary that the site be encrypted. Each employee will need a secure personal identification number and a password. If appropriate steps are taken, security concerns should be allayed.

Contact Centres

Another recent trend observed in the administration of employee benefits is the outsourcing of contact centre support to a TPA. As a natural extension to the employer's human resources department, the contact centre acts as the front-line support for employees who have questions on their benefits plan. Employees can call a toll-free number to speak with benefits specialists who are trained to help them on various aspects of their benefits plan administration, such as the enrolment process, beneficiary designation changes, coverage changes, etc. As an alternative approach and with the growing use of online tools, some contact centres have recently started to offer the possibility to initiate chat sessions and interact online with benefits specialists.

A service report, produced on a regular basis (quarterly, semi-annually, or annually), is usually provided by the TPA to highlight the activities for a given period. This report typically includes a section on call activities with key observations, typical questions per type of call, sample comments from employees and retirees, as well as any formal complaints received. The report usually also includes a section on the self-service (website) and processing activities, and a section on recommended actions to address process issues and complaints. This report gives employers a very good indicator of their benefits plan administration, helping them to better address problems and align their communication strategy. It can become the principal source of information for assessing employees' perception of the benefits plan.

Insurance Companies

Selecting an Insurance Company

Whether the role of the insurance company is to insure the benefit or to pay claims on an ASO basis, the selection of the right insurance company and the establishment of a good ongoing relationship is a factor in the success of the benefit plan. The same applies if retaining more than one insurance company, either for different benefits or for different employee groups. Similar principles apply in the selection of a TPA other than an insurance company.

A plan sponsor may have one reason, or a combination of reasons, for inviting proposals from other insurance companies. Periodically marketing a benefit program allows the plan sponsor to determine whether the costs charged by the insurance company are competitive, and to confirm that the services offered by the insurance company meet with current needs and expectations. Reasons for marketing a benefit plan may include:

- Evidence of uncompetitive rates and/or expense costs;
- Merger or acquisition;
- Consolidating two or more benefit programs;
- Introduction of a new program such as flexible benefits or plan redesign;
- Lack of responsiveness and flexibility;
- Poor claims service by the current insurance company;
- Inability to reach agreement on financial elements such as deficit recovery;
- Disability claims management issues;
- Review of the marketplace of new technology and innovative services (e.g., management of prescription drug costs, administration systems, mobile applications); and
- Ensuring good governance and due diligence of the benefit program
- Mandatory tendering policy.

The reason for marketing will influence the criteria for selecting the successful proposal. Clearly articulated and prioritized selection criteria serve to streamline the analysis of quotations. Selection criteria may address any problems the plan sponsor seeks to resolve through the marketing, as well as all positive aspects of the relationship with the incumbent insurance company. Cost is generally high on the list of criteria, but it is seldom the only factor in the evaluation.

In some cases, it is readily apparent from the analysis that a single insurance company will best meet all of the selection criteria. Alternatively, it may be necessary to prioritize criteria, as several candidates excel on a few criteria, but no one candidate scores top marks on all.

Request for Proposal

The request for proposal (RFP) provides the insurance company underwriters with sufficient data to assess the risk and to establish the premium required to operate the plans on a sustainable basis. It also establishes the information to be provided in the quotation for the plan sponsor or its broker/consultant to assess the competitiveness of the quotation. Information obtained as part of the proposal may be relevant in the years following to ensure the insurance company complies with commitments made in their proposal.

All of the information necessary to prepare the quotation should be included in the request for proposal or specifications. Plan design, employee data, open claim lists, and premium, claim, and rates histories are important elements of the evaluation by the insurance company.

Within the request for proposal, the plan sponsor will often raise a series of questions to arrive at the non-financial evaluation of the proposals. Questions can be used to clarify the financial aspects, particularly when retention accounting is involved. The structure of the questions may influence the insurer response and the relative evaluation between insurance companies.

The quoted premiums or costs are usually compared using consistent assumptions of the insurance volume and the expected claims. Cost analysis includes both the gross cost and the net cost.

Service capabilities and commitments can also be compared and evaluated against the selection criteria. For example, if consistent and timely processing of short and long term disability claims were important selection criteria, the analysis may focus on the adjudication systems, the quality assurance programs, and the experience and knowledge of the candidates.

Cost analysis will generally narrow the number of contenders to a few finalists. Interviews with finalists may be useful to probe the qualitative criteria and the acceptability of the proposed service team. Finalist interviews allow more in-depth assessment of insurance company administration and underwriting capabilities, and allow the plan sponsor to query any weak aspects of the proposal.

Change of Providers

If the outcome of the marketing suggests a change of insurance companies, a checklist of transition issues, and a timetable with roles and responsibilities for each task will ensure that all important details are appropriately handled in the transition. It can be helpful to develop the transition plan with the new insurance company. Important transition issues vary by benefit, but may include the following:

- For all benefits, notice of termination will need to be provided to the prior insurance company(ies) as required in the policy.

- For all benefits, but particularly for group life and disability benefits, all employees who are not actively at work on the transition date will need to be reported to both the old and the new insurance companies no later than 31 days after the effective date of the new policy. The Canadian Life and Health Insurance Association (CLHIA) Guidelines[3] outline the protection of group life insurance benefits for all plan members on transfer of insurance company.

- The change of insurance companies will need to be effectively communicated to employees. Under an insured underwriting basis, claims that occur prior to the termination date remain the liability of the prior insurance company. Employees will need to know where to submit new claims and whether benefits are affected by the transition.

- Copies of the old policies, confirmation of any benefit plan design changes, and, most importantly, individual claim histories for those benefits having annual or lifetime limits and deductibles can be provided to the new insurance company. This may facilitate duplication of existing benefits.

In a change of providers, identification cards and employee booklets will need to be reissued. For group life and AD&D benefits, the new insurance company should accept existing beneficiary designations; however, this is the time to encourage employees to update the beneficiary and dependant information on their files.

Partnering with an Insurance Company

An insurance company may be hired to perform any combination of the following functions relative to the management of the benefit plan:

- Adjudication, management, and payment of claims;

- Administration of premiums;

- Determination of eligibility for claim purposes;

---

[3]   CLHIA was established in 1984 and is an association of life and health insurance companies in Canada. The CLHIA sets out guidelines on various matters and members generally abide by such guidelines.

- Issuing of various documents (e.g., contracts, booklets, and enrolment cards);
- Underwriting of the plan (including plan design and funding) and premium rate setting; and
- Day-to-day communication with employees.

As plan sponsors streamline their internal processes and resources, insurance companies are expected to provide a wider range of services and to show a greater degree of adaptability. Plan sponsors are becoming more demanding and informed consumers. Insurance companies are delivering more innovative and varied responses to meet the diverse and sophisticated expectations of plan sponsors and their constituents.

Underwriting Agreements

The financial terms and conditions governing a retention accounting plan are commonly documented in an underwriting agreement. For relatively uncomplicated arrangements, an informal letter of agreement may suffice. A more formal and explicit agreement is more common when the plan sponsor is accepting part of the liability normally held by the insurance company, usually in exchange for lower risk charges or for a reduction in the reserves normally required.

Performance Standards Agreements

A performance standards agreement outlines specific time and quality commitments that the insurance company promises for the payment of claims, processing of employee coverage updates, and responding to queries from the benefit administrator and/or plan members. There may be monetary penalties for the insurance company for failing to meet the performance standards or rewards for exceeding the performance standards.

The performance standards agreement may be documented in correspondence with the insurer, or addressed within the underwriting agreement. Where the group is very large, or where service problems have been difficult to resolve, a separate written agreement may be appropriate.

Multi-Employer Plans

A multi-employer plan covers employees of two or more financially unrelated employers and uses a common fund to accumulate contributions and pay benefits to eligible employees. Multi-employer plans often provide benefits for employees of a specific industry.

The advantage to covered employees is the consistency and continuity of benefit coverage in the event of change of employers within the industry. These benefit plans are usually, but not always, provided through a health and welfare trust.

Health and welfare trusts are not specifically mentioned in the ITA; however, Interpretation Bulletin IT-85R2 "Health and Welfare Trusts for Employees" does attempt to explain the Canada Revenue Agency's (CRA) opinion as to the tax treatment of such trusts. The Bulletin stipulates the following requirements in order for a trust to qualify for treatment as a health and welfare trust:

- The funds of the trust cannot revert to the employer or be used for any purpose other than providing health and welfare benefits for which the contributions are made;
- The employer's contributions to the fund must not exceed the amounts required to provide these benefits; and
- Payments made by the employer cannot be made on a voluntary or gratuitous basis. They must be enforceable by the trustees.

The CRA requires an annual tax return be filed; however, unlike pension plans, registration is not required. The trust agreement establishes the mandate of the board of trustees. The agreement includes:

- A description of the purpose for creation of the trust fund;
- Identification of the parties to the trust agreement, the number of trustees, and method of their appointment;
- The powers, duties, and responsibilities of the trustees including their powers for establishment and collection of contributions and requirements for the use of professional advisers;
- The trustees' liability and indemnification; and
- The rules for amendment and termination of the trust fund.

Trustees are usually elected or appointed, and may be employee/union only, employer only, or include representation from both the union and the participating employers. If the trust is created pursuant to a collective agreement, the trustees will be responsible for managing the benefits in accordance with the terms of the collective agreement. The collective agreement usually establishes the cost sharing of contributions and the benefits to be provided and often specifies either the applicable contribution rates or benefits levels, but not usually both. If the collective agreement specifies the level of benefits to be provided, the trustees are responsible for making certain the contributions are set at an adequate level. If the collective agreement specifies the applicable contribution rates, the trustees are responsible for establishing the level of benefits, usually in a formal plan document.

Decision-making and management decisions are generally within the purview of the board of trustees, who are responsible for ensuring good governance. The trustees' fiduciary responsibilities require them to act solely for the benefit of the trust and not for their own self-interest, to exercise their duties with integrity and due standard of care, to make every effort to educate themselves and seek expert opinion where necessary, to act impartially between beneficiaries, and to attend trustee meetings.

The day-to-day administration of the trust fund, including premium remittance, may involve individual employers but more often involves the administrators of the plan on behalf of the trust.

Hour-Bank Plans

In industries where employees may work for many different participating employers at the same time or sequentially, an hour-bank system is commonly used to keep track of member eligibility. Hour-bank plans are common in the construction trades. In an hour-bank system, the trust defines the number of hours per month required to qualify for coverage in the following month. The administrator is responsible for recording the number of hours worked each month to the hour bank and debiting the monthly benefit charge from the hour bank, for each plan member. A member can often increase the hours credited to the hour bank by working overtime or working additional shifts. The additional hours fund periods of shorter employment when the member is not working a full week, such as temporary layoff, short weeks, or vacation.

In a typical hour-bank plan, a new employee must work the equivalent of two or more months of target hours and be a union member to achieve eligibility. When a covered employee ceases employment with a participating employer, benefit coverage may be continued based on the terms of the agreement and the number of hours remaining in the hour bank and/or on a voluntary self-pay basis, depending on plan rules.

Chapter 26

FLEXIBLE BENEFITS

Executive Summary

The successful implementation of a flexible benefits plan can only be achieved through the well-balanced interaction of design, pricing, administration, and communication. Core plus options plans with credits and Health Care Spending Accounts (HCSAs) are the most popular plans and are ideal to help organizations achieve their cost containment objectives while contributing to plan members' satisfaction. Most organizations fear that anti-selection, intrinsic to any flexible benefits plan, would increase their costs, but this can be greatly reduced with simple design, pricing, and communication strategies. Initial objectives setting and involving key stakeholders early in the flex project are also essential to achieve results aligned to each plan sponsor's objectives.

Background

Flexible benefits are a natural choice for organizations seeking to partner with plan members in managing the cost of the benefit plan, to reposition benefits as part of the overall compensation package, and to meet the diversified needs of the workforce. This chapter reviews the evolution of flexible benefits, provides an overview of design, and discusses implementation steps, pricing and tax considerations.

History and Evolution

Flexible benefits first appeared in the United States in the late 1970s. The first flexible benefits plan in Canada was introduced in 1983.

In the early years, flexible benefit administrative requirements were often an afterthought — and too often a barrier. For many employers, the cost associated with administration outweighed the advantages they would achieve with greater flexibility. Until the advent of affordable administration technology, flexible benefits were primarily the domain of large organizations.

Flexible benefits plans have become more commonplace since the 1990s. A variety of factors have led to the resurgence of the "flex benefits" popularity. One of the main reasons for the success of flexible benefits plans is the diverse employee population, whose changing needs in various stages of life or in differing family circumstances have prompted a desire for more variation in the coverage. Additionally, these plans are seen as a mechanism for maximizing the cost-effectiveness of the organization's expenses for plan member benefits, as rising costs became a concern for organizations. In the province of Quebec, unlike the rest of Canada, employer-paid premiums for Health and Dental benefits are taxable. As such, it became particularly important in Quebec that plan members saw value for the taxable benefits conferred by the employer-paid premiums; choice of coverage that best suits plan member needs became paramount. Finally, the lowering of the technology barrier has meant that more organizations can offer some form of flexible benefits on a cost-effective basis. Some benefits providers have lowered the threshold for availing of flexible benefits programs to as small as five to 75 lives with appropriate anti-selection mechanisms built into the program.

Canadian flexible benefits plans are now at a more mature stage, having benefited from the experience of earlier approaches. The primary problem with these earlier designs was the multitude of choices offered under various flexible benefits plan structures, which caused communication, administrative, and pricing issues. Also, some organizations introduced flexible benefits to shift a significant and increasing portion of the cost to plan members. This resulted in rapidly increasing out-of-pocket expenditures for plan members, which were not sustainable over the long term even with the use of HCSAs. In some cases, offering a choice between taxable and non-taxable Long Term Disability (LTD) benefits plans has also proven to be problematic as the non-taxable plans tend to represent a smaller group and see significant renewal increases from year to year, jeopardizing the viability of the plan. Flexible benefits plans now have a more streamlined, tax-effective type of design that better meets the needs of the plan members.

Elements of Flexible Benefits

A traditional benefits plan provides the same benefits and the same level of coverage for all employees in the same class. There is little opportunity for a plan member to take more or less of any benefit based on individual circumstance or preference. Plan design tends to reflect the needs of the "average" plan member, and the willingness of the organization to pay for the benefits.

Flexible benefits plan, or "flex", is now a common term for benefit practitioners. A flexible benefits plan is commonly defined as one that allows plan members to choose some or all of their benefits in order to meet their own personal needs. Flex plans may use the common cost-sharing mechanism of identifying the level of contributions required from plan members based on a percentage split as you would with a traditional plan. Another attractive feature of flex plans is the ability to introduce the defined contribution approach whereby the commitment of the organization becomes the level of contribution versus the continuing provision of the same level of benefits year after year — this is through a mechanism called "flex credit structure". Typically, in order to allow plan members to choose their coverage levels, credits are given to plan members to help them pay for coverage levels they choose depending on the price tag of each option. Where a plan member's choice of coverage levels have price tags that are less than flex credits allocated, plan members may choose to transfer the credits on a dollar-for-dollar basis into various vehicles. There are tax-effective options such as an HCSA, a Tax Free Savings Account (TFSA) and a Registered Retirement Savings Plan (RRSP), as well as taxable options such as a Personal Spending Account (PSA) or a cash-out option. Taxation of credits varies with the use of credits. The price tag of an option is the price plan members have to pay to buy this option. Where a plan member's choice of coverage levels have price tags that are greater than flex credits allocated, the amount in excess of the flex credits is then paid for via payroll deduction. It is important to distinguish the price tag of an option from the premium for an option. The premium is the cost that the insurer charges to the plan sponsor to provide coverage under an option while the price tag is what is assessed as chargeable to the plan members for the options they choose. The two are not necessarily one and the same depending on the plan sponsor's objectives for the flex plan.

In general terms, most flexible benefits plans are designed within three major design themes:

- Modular plans;
- Core plus options plans; and
- Cafeteria plans.

All of these designs could include an HCSA component.

Modular Plans

Under a modular plan, the plan member may choose from a selection of pre-packaged benefit options. Medical and dental benefits are typically packaged together; sometimes life and disability options are included in modules. The primary advantage of a modular plan is administrative simplicity and ease of understanding. It can also help mitigate the effects of anti-selection, especially for smaller groups of plan members. For risk-averse organizations, this option would be the most prudent design to start with.

However, from the plan member's perspective, this approach may not be as appealing as other flexible benefits plan designs. Modular plans restrict the flexibility to choose coverage under specific benefit lines. In designing a modular plan, the plan sponsor may want to focus on providing coverage for specific groups of plan members (e.g., younger/older, plan member only/with dependents) or to offer various levels of coverage (e.g., basic/enhanced). This may lead to modules that are not appealing to all plan members. For example, a plan member's need for life insurance may have nothing to do with his or her dental needs, and yet the plan member must take a high level of life coverage to obtain a high level of dental coverage, if that is how the modular plan is designed.

	Module A	Module B	Module C
Life insurance	$10,000	1 × salary	2×x salary
LTD	50%	60%	70%
AD&D	$10,000	1 × salary	2 × salary
Medical care	Option 1	Option 2	Option 3
Dental care	No coverage	Option 1	Option 2
Employee contribution	None	None	Yes
HCSA	Yes	None	None

Core Plus Options Plans

Core plus options is the most commonly used approach for flex plans. There are three structural elements in a core plus options plan: core, credits, and options.

The core is the minimum level of benefits that the plan sponsor requires a plan member to have. It may include a minimum level of life, disability, and health coverage. The scope of the core will depend on the culture of the organization. It is increasingly common to include an Employee and Family Assistance Program (EFAP) within the core benefit. With increasing awareness of mental health issues, organizations find value in investing in EFAP to mitigate disability and drug claims related to mental health. Expanding services within the EFAP, such as health coaching, also help contribute towards organizational health and wellness objectives. Health system navigation support services have also become popular given increasing chronic health issues and greater demand on our health system. Service examples include finding the best health care provider or diagnostic lab in the plan member's local area, within Canada, or around the world, as well as second-opinion services that include reviewing pathologies from tests already conducted. These services have resulted in meaningful change in diagnosis and/or change in course of treatment.

Beyond the core, a number of benefit options are offered. Each option has a price tag. Under a flex credit structure, flex credits are allocated to plan members to purchase options. Credits that remain unused following the purchase of the desired coverage options may then be allocated to various alternatives. For example, employees may be allowed to allocate their credits to tax-effective vehicles such as HCSA, RRSP, TFSA or taxable options such as cash or PSA.

Options available under a flex plan are limited only by the imagination and the ability to administer them. Options will generally include some choices within the traditional benefits, including medical, dental, life insurance, and accidental death and dismemberment (AD&D) insurance. In addition, the opportunity to purchase critical illness (CI) insurance, vacation days, home and auto as well as pet insurance, or fitness and wellness options could be included.

The core plus options structure allows the plan sponsor to better manage costs while giving plan members a wider range of choice. It is then no wonder that the core plus options design is the most popular in Canada today. However, the administration, communication and education requirements for a core plus options plan is substantially more complex than a modular plan given the greater degree of choices.

Cafeteria Plans

A plan with no core coverage and the ability to mix and match coverage levels by line of benefit is called a "cafeteria" plan. This design is not typically used in Canada. Most organizations are uncomfortable with a cafeteria plan because it affords the plan member an opportunity to remain without coverage. In addition, the greater the degree of choice, the greater the risk of adverse selection as well as the communication and education needs. This concept is discussed later in the chapter.

Credits

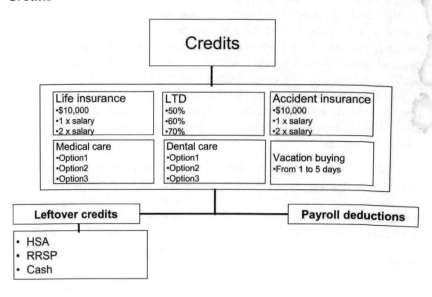

Health Care Spending Accounts

Each of the flex designs discussed above may include an HCSA. An HCSA is an individual plan member account into which unused flex credits are allocated on a pre-tax basis (subject to provincial taxes and administrative fees for Quebec residents). To be tax effective, the HCSA must be funded by plan sponsor contributions alone. The account allows for maximum flexibility with the credits so designated, because these can be used for any expense deemed eligible under the Medical Expense Tax Credit of the *Income Tax Act* (ITA). The plan member submits his or her eligible medical and dental expenses and is reimbursed tax-free (other than plan members who reside in Quebec) from the HCSA.

Coverage under an HCSA must be "in respect of hospital care or expense or medical care or expense which normally would otherwise have qualified as a medical expense under the provisions of subsection 118.2(2) of the ITA related to the determination of the medical expense tax credit".[1]

To ensure that the payments made out of the account will be classified as non-taxable income for plan members (other than Quebec residents), the HCSA must be established as a Private Health Services Plan (PHSP). This means that the plan must contain the following basic elements:

- An undertaking by one person;
- To indemnify another person;
- For an agreed consideration;
- From a loss or liability in respect of an event;
- The happening of which is uncertain.

In order to satisfy the above requirements, the credits allocated to the HCSA must be made at the beginning of the plan year, at which time they are locked in. The basic principle behind a contract of insurance is the element of risk. Thus, a "use it or lose it" provision applies. Tax rules allow the employer to specify that either the HCSA balance or the unpaid benefit year expenses can be carried forward for one additional benefit year (up to two years with advance tax ruling) before they are "lost". Insurance companies provide reporting to identify credits that are subject to forfeiture to allow plan sponsors to communicate with their plan members in accordance with their objectives.

An increasing trend in flex plans is providing extra HCSA credits when plan members participate in health and wellness initiatives. This could be as simple as completing a Health Risk Assessment (HRA) at the time of enrollment, or participating in online health challenges, e.g., meeting minimum requirements for nutritious eating, exercise, sleep, and/or mental health breaks.

How to Implement a Flexible Benefit Plan

The process of implementing a flexible benefits plan is fundamentally the same process that an employer would apply to any major decision.

---

[1]   Canada Revenue Agency, Interpretation Bulletin IT-339R2, Meaning of *"Private Health Services Plan"* (1 January 1995).

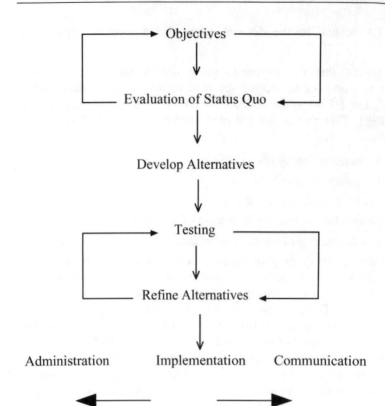

Objectives

Implementing a flex plan represents a substantial investment of time, and becomes an integral part of the organization's brand, total compensation strategy and culture. As such, it is essential that objectives be clearly articulated, quantified, and prioritized at the outset.

The benefit plan objectives must be aligned to business objectives so that senior management can fully support the initiative from conception to implementation. Flex benefits cross many disciplines and affect many individuals. Hence, it is prudent to seek input from the key stakeholders at the outset, and to use them as a sounding board at various stages of the process.

Although objectives may vary from organization to organization, the following five are common situations in which a flex plan may be considered:

- The organization is faced with a diverse workforce with dissimilar benefits needs;

- There is a mandate to help plan members shift from entitlement to a greater sharing of accountability, and to shift corporate culture towards viewing benefits as an element of total compensation;

- After a number of mergers and acquisitions, benefit plans across the organization are being consolidated and harmonized;

- The plan sponsor is struggling with low plan member appreciation of a high-cost benefit plan;

- The organization needs to reinforce its image as a responsive and progressive organization; and

- Competitive pressure for talent (*e.g.*, most financial institutions and insurance companies now offer flex plans).

Evaluation of Status Quo

Evaluation of the *status quo* should include the current administration and delivery systems. Where internal recordkeeping systems and payroll interfaces cannot support the transition to flex, it may be necessary to revise the plan design, the timetable, or the budget to allow for required programming or upgrades. The effectiveness of current communication channels will also affect the communication strategy associated with the new plan.

Develop Alternatives

A road map should begin to emerge of where the current plans are, and where they need to be relative to the business plan and the benefit objectives. Designing the alternatives requires attention to detail and an understanding of underwriting fundamentals. Organization senior leadership needs to endorse both the objectives and the evaluation to avoid expensive and frustrating surprises at any later stage of the process.

Testing

The degree of change from the current plan will guide the timing and the level of testing required. Most organizations will test the prototypes against the plan objectives, looking for improvement over the current plan. An assessment of winners and losers is also paramount to manage expectations and inform decision on plan design tweaks that may be required.

Each plan member will judge the new plan from the perspective of "What is in it for me?" Plan sponsors often conduct the testing with plan members through focus groups. Employee testing provides the plan sponsor with an opportunity to "test drive" the new plan, and to be able to better position the pricing strategy based on projected enrolment distribution.

Administration

Flex benefits require additional administration on top of the basic administration requirements of a traditional plan. The additional administration functions include annual (or biennial) enrolment, re-enrolment after a qualifying "life event", and ongoing administration related to new hires, terminations, premium calculations, and administration of HCSAs, PSAs, RRSPs and TFSAs. As flex plans mature and movement amongst different options becomes less frequent, biennial re-enrollment is becoming increasingly popular to mitigate the time and effort required for these events. Advancements in technology, such as Decision Support Tools that provide modeling of insurance needs to help plan members make informed choices, have also started to emerge.

Re-enrolment requires the updating of price tags and flex credits, as well as communication support to help plan members review their choices. An enrolment package is typically developed for the re-enrolment period and plan member selections are recorded and verified for the upcoming policy year.

Throughout the year, changes to annual benefit selections are permitted only as a result of a life event. Life events typically include, but are not limited to:

- Birth of the first child;
- Marital status change; and
- Obtaining/losing coverage under another plan, such as a spouse's plan.

Administration of an HCSA requires recording each employee's credit level; to complete year-end processing allowing plan members to carry forward and/or forfeit unused HCSA credits; and for residents in Quebec, to report claims and expenses by the plan member for tax purposes. Insurers are able to manage these accounts cost effectively on behalf of the plan sponsor.

Most Canadian insurers are able to administer flex plans. As an alternative and for more complex flex plans, there are also third party administrators (TPAs) that could be considered for this purpose. The advantage of TPAs is that administration of these programs are their core competency. Changes in benefits providers would not necessitate re-enrollment as the TPAs are responsible for plan member record keeping, thus avoiding disruptions typically associated with a change in benefits provider.

The payroll files also need to be updated following the annual enrolment process, as well as throughout the year for new employees or employees who have changed coverage.

Communication

The successful introduction of a new flex plan requires effective communication. Plan members need to be informed of the options available, as well as the consequences of their decisions. As mentioned earlier, some benefits administrators provide Decision Support Tools that provide modelling of insurance needs to help plan members decide which options to choose. In addition, many plan members will be faced with new terminology and concepts that are quite unfamiliar to them. As a result, it is essential that plain language be used in preparing communication materials, and that technical and legal jargon be avoided wherever possible. Timeliness is also an integral component of a successful communication strategy. Disseminating information in a timely manner assists in containing and eliminating negative plan member speculations, which can sometimes jeopardize the acceptance of the plan.

Plan members have a broad range of communication media available to them for the introduction of a flex plan. Combining two or more of these methods will reinforce the message, as individuals absorb information in different ways. Examples of approaches that could be used when introducing employee choice or making design changes include:

- *Direct contact*: general employee meetings, and individual employee meetings;
- *Print*: newsletters, posters, booklets, workbooks, and question and answer (Q&A) sheets; and
- *Electronic*: software programs, web-based technology, company intranet, and video. Emerging trends also include the use of mobile devices and social media.

Each plan sponsor's objectives are unique, as is the setting and environment in which the communication takes place.

Face-to-face meetings continue to be the most effective means of delivering the strategic message accompanying the benefit change, as it provides plan members with the opportunity to ask questions. Smaller groups present better environments in which to facilitate discussion regarding the impending changes.

With the changing technology as well as the advent of "virtual workforce", the method of flex benefits communication has also evolved. While paper communication may continue to play a role in the process, web-based, mobile device and social media technology is becoming increasingly popular. Computers and mobile devices can be used for enrolment and for online access to relevant documentation. Software programs have been written that allow employees to examine their options using "what if" scenarios, which helps to increase plan members' comfort with their decisions. The ability to share information with dependants is enhanced if the Internet is used. Additionally, web and mobile device-based technology is a very efficient method of distributing information to all plan members, no matter where they are located.

Although some plan sponsors may question the feasibility of using such media, the reality is that computers and mobile devices are increasingly becoming part of the fabric of our society. Statistics regarding mobile device usage by teens clearly shows that the younger generation of workers is much more computer literate, and that the barriers that may apply to certain classes of older workers regarding computer usage may effectively be eliminated in the workforce of the future.[2]

Pricing

Overall cost objectives, set by the organization, drive the pricing strategy. Where plan members are presented with coverage options, the relative pricing between options must "make sense" to the plan member making the choices. Strategic pricing may also involve the creation of an incentive to encourage plan members to choose a particular option over another to support the underlying objectives of the flex plan. Pricing may involve a deliberate investment in the first few years of the plan in order to gain control of the cost curve in future years.

Medical and dental pricing require reliable claims data. Preferably, for each component of the medical and dental plans, the claims data will be available by individual — whether plan member, spouse, or dependent child. Claims data is used to develop a realistic price tag for each option, sometimes partly adjusted to take into account the tendency of high-end users to select the more liberal benefit options.

---

[2]   Communication is also discussed in Chapter 29.

For those plans with flex credit structures, the credit formula is as important to the pricing strategy as the determination of the price tags for each benefit option. The credit formula for medical and dental benefits tends to be a flat amount per employee, often varying by category and coverage level. Alternatively, credits for salary-related coverage such as Life and LTD are typically earnings related. Credits linked to service may be a consideration where rewarding employees with long service forms a key objective for the benefit plan.

Pricing requires a balance between plan sponsor objectives and plan member perception. Many plan sponsors use partial or temporary subsidies either directly or across plan options. A common example is to strategically lower the opt-out credit value for those who waive coverage in order to stabilize the pricing of the overall plan. This serves as a disincentive to simply opt for the cash value and encourages seriously assessing true insurance needs.

Cost management and plan member satisfaction are common objectives of organizations considering flex benefits. It is usually possible to balance these objectives, provided the real objective is cost management, not cost reduction. Where the objective is cost reduction, it is extremely difficult to achieve plan member satisfaction simultaneously. It is prudent to include in the pricing not only the first-year costs, but also a three-year or five-year projection to fully understand the financial impact of the flex plan relative to the current plan. A mid-term projection also helps to avoid surprises for the plan sponsor and for the plan members.

Anti-Selection

In a flex plan, where plan members make benefit choices, there is always potential for anti-selection. Anti-selection occurs when plan members can anticipate their need for benefits and choose the option that provides the most coverage at the least cost. For example, employee plan member is advised that extensive dental work is required — the plan member then selects the highest dental option and subsequently has all of the dental work performed during the period coverage is at the highest level.

The potential for anti-selection can be controlled through design and pricing of the flex plan while still providing freedom of choice. Design and pricing strategies may include:

- A step-up or step-down rule, which prevents plan members from moving from the lowest level of coverage to the highest after being advised of a condition that may require treatment or vice versa, by limiting them to move up or down only one level at a time at each re-enrollment;

- A lock-in provision, which restricts the plan member's ability to change his or her selection for a specific period (*e.g.*, minimum three years for an option that provides orthodontic coverage in order to ensure injection of premium into that option to sustain significant claims during the first year of enrollment);

- Providing incentives to select lower coverage options;

- Providing less than a full-value rebate to employees waiving coverage;

- Grouping coverage of more predictable expenses with unpredictable expenses, for example, including vision care with health benefits;

- Encouraging use of the HCSA as an alternative to insuring more predictable expenses, such as vision care and paramedical treatment; and

- Requiring proof of insurability for certain changes such as increases in life or LTD coverage levels.

Tax Issues

Income tax considerations are an important factor in the selection of benefits and in the design of the overall plan. In choosing his or her benefits, a plan member is encouraged to consider which benefits are taxable upon receipt, which employer-paid premiums are considered taxable income, and which plan member-paid premiums and/or expenses are tax deductible. These considerations are especially necessary in the case of a dual-income family, where both spouses have group coverage and have the opportunity to coordinate benefits. Fortunately, many enrolment tools now incorporate programming that allocates credits and payroll deductions automatically to the most tax effective arrangement.

There is no existing definition of a flex plan under the ITA. However on February 20, 1998, Interpretation Bulletin IT-529, "Flexible Employee Benefit Plans" was released by the Canada Revenue Agency (CRA). Although it does not have the force of law, IT-529 does provide the CRA's position regarding the taxation of flex benefits. The following commentary touches upon some of the information provided in the Bulletin. Although the ITA does not contain provisions that apply specifically to a flex plan as a whole, the design of the plan must satisfy certain conditions in order to avoid adverse tax consequences for "all" of the benefits provided for under the plan. The Bulletin has categorized flex plans into two types:

- Under the first type, the plan sponsor allocates a notional amount of flex credits to each eligible plan member. Prior to the beginning of the plan year, the plan members allocate their credits to various benefits available under the flex plan. Some of these benefits may or may not result in a taxable benefit to the plan member. The plan sponsor is then obligated to provide the plan member with the benefits selected.

- Under the second type, the plan members are able to select a level of coverage for each benefit available under the plan ranging from no coverage to a premium level of coverage. A standard level of coverage is set out by the plan sponsor for each benefit and a dollar value is assigned to each level of coverage above or below the standard. The cost of any coverage above the standard will be withheld from the plan member's salary and the difference between the standard level of coverage and the cost of coverage below the standard will be credited to the plan member's account.

The plan sponsor's allocation of credits annually to its plan members represents the plan sponsor's contribution to benefits. In the second type of flex plan, as outlined above, the contributions by the plan sponsor are determined by the true cost of benefits provided less plan member contributions.

According to the Bulletin, where one part of the plan is a salary deferral arrangement, a retirement compensation arrangement, an employee benefit plan, or an employee trust, the ITA sections relating to those arrangements will apply to the entire flexible plan. However, if the plan members are allowed to select the benefits and how such benefits will be funded prior to the plan year, the flexible plan will be segregated. As a result, the taxable benefits will not, in effect, taint the non-taxable benefits.

If the plan member is allowed to choose their benefits, that decision is irrevocable for the plan year unless:

- There is a "life event", such as birth or death of a dependant, a change in marital status, or loss of spousal benefits; or
- There is a change in employment status that changes the amount of flex credits, e.g., moving from part-time to full-time employment, promotion from a salaried class to an Executive class, etc.

The change cannot be retroactive.

If an employee's negotiated salary is converted to flex credits, such converted amount will be included in the employee's taxable income.

However, once the employment contract expires and the contract is renegotiated, the salary can be decreased and the new contract can include additional flex credits. These additional credits will not be included in the employee's income as part of his or her salary and wages.

Regarding HCSAs, the Bulletin states there is no advantage to having the HCSA funded through payroll deductions. To be tax-effective, it must be funded by the plan sponsor contributions alone. If the HCSA meets the requirements of a PHSP, payments made out of the account will not be taxable income to the plan member (except for residents in Quebec for whom it is nevertheless taxable). However, if it does not qualify as a PHSP, the amount of any benefit received out of the plan will be taxable to the plan member. See the discussion regarding HCSAs at the beginning of this chapter for further information.

Regarding disability insurance offered under a flex plan, unless the entire plan is funded "solely" from plan member payroll deductions, any resulting benefit paid out of the plan will be taxable in the hands of the plan member. As flex credits are considered plan sponsor monies, use of such credits to obtain coverage will result in the plan member being taxed when any benefit is received if disabled. However, if the plan sponsor has two separate disability plans, one paid for solely through plan member contributions and the other through solely plan sponsor contributions, benefits received out of the plan with premiums paid solely by payroll deductions will not be taxable income. In such cases, there can be no cross-subsidization between the plan sponsor-paid plan and the plan member-paid plan.

The Bulletin also refers to vacation buying and selling. When a plan member buys additional vacation days with flex credits, the plan member must use the vacation days in the year in which it was purchased. If the vacation is carried forward to the following plan year, the arrangement may be considered to be a salary deferral arrangement. When a plan member forfeits vacation days to which he or she is entitled in exchange for additional flex credits, the value of the vacation forgone is considered taxable income. In this situation, the plan member is considered to have purchased the extra benefits by way of additional services rendered. It is not the flex credits obtained, but rather it is the trading of vacation entitlement by the plan member that triggers a taxable event.

Chapter 27

EMPLOYEE ASSISTANCE PROGRAMS AND OTHER EMPLOYEE BENEFITS

Executive Summary

Change is a common theme in the current working environment. Employers have seen considerable change in the make-up of the workforce in the past few decades and this is having an effect on the way they view traditional employee benefit offerings.

The most notable transition is the shift in employee demographics. The baby boomer generation continues to retire, leaving employers with the challenge of attracting and retaining employees from younger generations, and what Generation X and Generation Y employees are looking for in an employer is typically not the same as what their baby boomer counterparts looked for. The present day workplace is also subject to new challenges arising from such factors as evolving technology, immigration, globalization, and re-structuring due to merger or acquisition activity. In response to these new expectations, employers are considering the merits of non-traditional benefits and are redesigning their total rewards strategy to meet these diverse needs.

This chapter covers many benefits that may be offered to employees, including employee assistance programs. The chapter also includes information on perquisites in the new working environment. Although not addressed in this chapter, taxation is an issue to be considered in the provision of non-traditional employee benefits and perquisites.

Employee Assistance Programs — Overview

History and Recent Developments

Employee assistance plans were originally introduced into the workplace in the 1950s to deal with employee alcohol and drug abuse problems. Over time, these plans have evolved into Employee Assistance Programs (EAPs), also known as Employee and Family Assistance Programs (EFAPs), and their scope of coverage has expanded to include a variety of issues. EAPs are an employer-sponsored benefit offering confidential services to eligible employees and family members to support myriad aspects of physical and mental well-being whether the issue originated in or outside of the workplace.

The demographics of the Canadian workforce have been changing substantially over the past three decades. There are more dual-income families, more single-parent and same-sex parent families, and the baby boomers are retiring. These changes and other life factors create additional stress on working individuals and their families, many of whom are struggling to maintain a suitable work-life balance. EAPs offer confidential and professional services to help employees and their families identify and resolve a wide range of personal difficulties and work-related concerns. While EAPs have typically been turned to for assistance during difficult times, they are increasingly offering services that proactively support employee health and wellness.

Purpose of EAP

As a business, an EAP has two clients to serve: the organizational client who purchases the service for its own employees and the end-user client who confidentially uses the service as part of his or her benefits program.[1] The objective of the EAP then is twofold: the EAP must provide meaningful support and services to end-user clients that enable them to effectively navigate their issues to their own satisfaction, while at the same time, the EAP must serve the organizational client with programs that demonstrate the value of EAP by correlating employee health and productivity with the success of the organization itself.

Cornerstone of Success: Confidentiality

EAPs can play this dual role due to the cornerstone of EAP success: confidentiality. For an organization new to EAPs, it may at first seem strange to agree to purchase a service and also agree to not know who is using it. However, it is exactly that perceived paradox that allows EAPs to thrive and be successful with both the organizational and end-user clients. EAPs take confidentiality (and privacy) seriously, as it is vital to client access: employees use the EAP because they know their request for service and the details surrounding it are confidential.

---

[1]   Throughout the segment of this chapter that focuses on EAPs, the term "client" refers to the end-user of EAP services who is either the eligible employee or eligible family member. The term "organizational client" refers to the employer providing the EAP services to its employees.

In EAPs, as with other health care fields, there are legal limits to confidentiality such as when a risk of harm to self or others is identified. An EAP should explain the legal limits to confidentiality to clients when services are accessed and in writing, such as on the corporate website. In some cases, such as mandated counselling for substance abuse referrals, collaboration with the workplace or other mental health professionals is possible, but only if an employee consents to counselling appointment dates being shared.

EAPs offer confidentiality but clients do not access the services anonymously. Aggregate data (containing no identifying information) is available to the organizational client regarding overall program usage.

Benefits to the Business and the Employee

The business case for implementing an EAP is simple: providing access to effective support services reduces the financial impact of personal and family problems on employee productivity, absence rates, and turnover levels. Organizations benefit from EAP services that offer both at-work and return-to-work programs that cover all aspects of the employee lifecycle. Having an EAP in place can reduce the emotional impact of an employee's personal issues at work.

Recent studies suggest EAP programs typically provide a $5-$10 return on investment for every dollar spent.[2]

Access to EAP is valued by employees and is an integral component of the rewards package expected by today's changing employee demographic. A competitive rewards package often supports an organization's staff recruitment and retention strategy. Many companies find that providing EAP to staff is complementary to their own core organizational values.

The benefit of an EAP to employees and their eligible family members can be profound as any EAP that collects client feedback can attest to. An EAP allows clients to get assistance when they need it and take a proactive and holistic approach to their own wellness. Using the confidential and professional services offered through an EAP helps clients through a variety of life events ranging from the mildly stressful to

---

[2]   Attridge, M. (2013). The Business Value of Employee Assistance: A Review of the Art and Science of ROI. Keynote address at the meeting of the Employee Assistance Professionals Association, Phoenix, AZ.
Attridge, M. (2010). 20 years of EAP cost benefit research: Taking the productivity path to ROI. Part 3 of 3. Journal of Employee Assistance, 40(4), 8-11.

the devastating, and receiving this support can have a positive effect on their personal and professional lives. EAP services are available to clients free of charge and with few administrative details to attend to, which makes getting help simpler and less complicated than processing services (such as seeing a therapist or dietitian) through an insurance model.

Whether the benefit is to the organizational client or the end-user client, EAPs should be able to provide some evidence of benefits through statistical measures, such as client satisfaction survey data or usage reports. Anecdotal evidence, such as client testimonials, is also useful to document and can complement statistical data, which together may provide a clearer idea of the impact the EAP can have on individuals and, in turn, their organization.

Choosing an EAP

Two things are essential for an EAP to be successful: a private and confidential service and a multidisciplinary network of professionals to provide the services. These two elements cannot generally be provided using internal resources alone and because of this, employers find that outsourcing the EAP service offers a more satisfactory solution.

EAP provider selection reflects the employer's priorities. Written specifications are distributed to a number of pre-qualified vendors and an objective evaluation of EAP providers takes into account:

- How access to treatment is facilitated;
- How quality service is assured;
- How confidentially is maintained;
- How client satisfaction is assessed;
- How plan costs are set in the first and subsequent years;
- The EAP delivery model offered;
- The provider's ability to service areas where the employee population resides; and
- Accreditation.

For detailed information on choosing an EAP, readers may wish to consult the resources available through EASNA,[3] a tri-national employee assistance trade association.

---

[3]   www.easna.org.

Accessing EAP

Standard Eligibility

Eligibility for EAP services can vary but typically, those eligible for EAP services include the employee, spouse or common-law partner, and dependants up to 21 years old or, if the dependant is engaged in full-time studies, up to 25 years old. Eligibility requirements are defined by the organizational client but many choose to conform to standard EAP eligibility. In some cases, depending on the needs of the organizational client, other groups may be eligible for services including volunteers, associates, and members, etc.

EAP will generally use a presumptive eligibility system followed by screening to ensure that individuals accessing the service are are, in fact, eligible for EAP services. With skilled intake staff, it is fairly easy to determine eligibility in a way that does not make a client uneasy and that protects confidentiality. Some organizational clients request that eligibility is verified through employee lists they send to their EAP provider, which requires ongoing maintenance from both the organizational client and the EAP. This approach adds complexity to the intake process, especially when eligible employees are not found on the eligibility list and may well cause a delay in providing service. Organizational clients considering the employee eligibility list are advised to review their goals and determine if an eligibility list would actually facilitate reaching those objectives. EAPs find that the number of EAP users who do not fulfill eligibility requirements is negligible. Individuals contacting the EAP who are not eligible and not at risk may be provided with information for an external community resource. Individuals contacting the EAP who are not eligible, but who are at risk, should still be triaged to a clinician immediately for care and containment of the situation as the safety of the caller is first priority. The individual in question can then be provided with an external community resource appropriate to their needs.

Accessing Service

In the past, clients have primarily made their first contact with an EAP through the telephone, but this has changed. The EAP industry is evolving to meet the technological demands of clients by providing intake options online and through mobile devices in addition to the telephone intake option. As technology changes quickly and often, EAPs should expect continued innovation to influence their strategy for reaching clients. As many EAPs have global clients and operations, any intake process should also be accessible to clients around the globe.

Clients contacting an EAP are asked to provide information such as their name and the company they have access to the EAP through. This may be followed by some voluntary demographic questions used in aggregate data reports.

As part of the intake process, clients are typically screened for risk and then communicate (via phone, online, or mobile chat) with an intake staff about the help they need. Details of the service(s) booked should be reviewed for the client by the end of the intake process. Clients are transferred immediately to a clinician in the following situations: distress that requires immediate clinical support, disclosure that a child is being harmed or neglected, or disclosure that the client is considering causing harm to self or others. This immediate transfer to a clinician for a risk assessment is important from a safety and service point of view.

Call Centre Support

Though clients access EAPs via several modalities, for most cases the EAP call centre continues to be the client-service hub. As EAPs provide crisis response, an EAP call centre should provide a live answer multi-lingual response 24 hours a day, 365 days a year, which can include clinical support. However, 24/7 availability is not just for clients at risk. This assures that all clients, no matter their time zone or work schedule, can access the EAP at their convenience and in the official language of choice. To accommodate clients uncomfortable in English or French, or the hearing impaired, EAPs typically use a telephonic translation service or TTY (Text Telephone) to communicate with these clients.

Intake staff respond to client inquiries, arrange services, and provide callers with the information they need to access the service or support required. EAPs providing access through online or mobile services that are not necessarily accompanied by 24-hour live support should ensure these online or mobile programs refer to the call centre number at each stage so clients always know where to go for immediate and live support. An EAP that provides service 24 hours a day, 365 days a year should have resilient infrastructure and formal disaster recovery protocols in place, for their call centres in particular, to mitigate the risks of outages caused by technological, grid, or emergency issues.

EAP Counselling Services

EAPs typically offer a variety of counselling services across several modalities to ensure that their suite of services is flexible enough to offer the right fit to any and all clients accessing services.

EAP Counselling Services	Modalities of Service
• Individual • Family • Couple • Crisis • Career & resiliency • Fitness coaching • Mandated & specialized counselling services	• In-person • Telephonic • Online • Video • Chat • Self-directed learning

Counselling Options

For the most part, EAPs provide solution-focused, short-term counselling, though some may offer enhanced support for depression, trauma, and addiction cases. As solution-focused therapy fosters client self-reliance and responsibility, this model is most appropriate for clients who have a well-defined concern, are able to quickly establish a therapeutic alliance with their counsellor, and are prepared to work actively toward an identified solution. EAPs do not provide long-term counselling or specialized treatment programs (*e.g.*, eating disorder management) but where clinically indicated, counsellors may case manage clients to one or more appropriate public or private resources that offer longer term or specialized services.

As a clinical, ethical, and legal best practice, EAPs should use carefully crafted screening methods for all clients who initiate contact, regardless of the presenting issue. Best practice includes screening for depression, alcohol and drug use, and risk of harm to self or others. Depression screening uses a standard tool such as the Major Depression Inventory (MDI-10), a self-report mood questionnaire developed to screen for depression. Preferred screening tools align to the ICD-10 or DSM-V-TR diagnoses of depression and provide an estimate of symptom severity. Screening for drug and alcohol use involves the client completing a questionnaire about current alcohol and drug use (both frequency of use and quantity).

Determining whether there is a risk of harm to self or others through mandatory questions is another screening tool often employed to assure the safety of the client. EAPs should have protocols in place to address assessments that indicate abuse, imminent risk of harm to self or others, or in situations where serious deterioration in mental status or functioning is present.

Depending on the situation of those involved, several types of counselling are generally offered to cater to the needs of clients, including individual, couple, and family counselling, as well as some specialized or mandatory sessions, which are described below.

Individual Counselling

In individual counselling, the professional counsellor acts as a facilitator to help the client address issues and concerns in a focused manner. The counsellor and client explore feelings, behaviours, relationships, choices, and the client's current situation, and then identify techniques and strategies the client can use to move closer to his or her goals.

Couple Counselling

Couple counselling typically involves two people attending sessions together to discuss specific issues within the context of their relationship. EAP best practices generally include guidelines about counsellors not seeing couples and individual partners concurrently to prevent a perceived bias.

A couple can expect questions from their counsellor about the couple's roles, patterns, rules, goals, and beliefs, which gives the counsellor an understanding of how the couple relates to one another. The counsellor then works with the couple to help them understand what they can do to communicate better with each other and work together effectively to address their concerns.

Counselling can support both the mending of a relationship and the process of ending a relationship. Couples in the midst of a separation use counselling to find common ground as they negotiate interpersonal issues and child custody.

Family Counselling

Counsellors can help family members find constructive ways to relate to each other and explore solutions for moving forward beyond the presenting issue.

Counsellors support change within the individual and support each participant in the context of their particular relationship and place within the family so that all involved in the counselling can benefit. Issues addressed in family counselling include; relationship difficulties, blended families, sickness or death, eldercare, building parenting skills, adoption, and extended family relationships.

Online Group Counselling

In keeping with today's technological advancements and employees' lifestyles, EAPs may offer services via online group sessions where multiple participants discuss their similar issue(s) with a counsellor in a private and secure online setting. Group interactions allow participants to build relationships, receive feedback on how to meet goals and overcome challenges, and gain encouragement from others in working towards a common goal.

Crisis Counselling

EAP infrastructure is built so that when crisis situations are identified through a standard risk assessment, the client in crisis can be offered immediate support by a counsellor. Typically, the first support a client receives is from a clinician at the EAP call centre, whether over the phone or through online chat.[4] This first intervention deescalates risk to assure the client is safe. Follow-up services are arranged for the client and 24/7 support is typically available between sessions should the need arise.

Further to individual crisis support, EAPs are in a position to provide community support in times of need. When disasters of any magnitude occur, entire communities are displaced and/or immobilized; homes are destroyed; workplaces and school systems shut down; local emergency response units are over-taxed; local counsellors are caught in the turmoil and are often as impacted as the rest of their community. In order to meet the elevated need for support, EAPs can provide on-the-ground support services where they are needed most by bringing additional support staff to the affected area and employing mobile units in areas where offices may be inaccessible.

Career Counselling

Career counselling helps people identify career direction and choices, assess their interests and skill sets, and develop and use strategies that enhance work engagement and performance. Career counsellors use a variety of career management tools, resources, approaches, and support to help clients make more informed career decisions and better manage career transitions.

Career counselling gives clients the opportunity to take a proactive approach to improving, changing, or planning their career. EAP career

---

[4]   See explanation of chat counselling later in this chapter.

counselling services generally include career management and planning, resiliency coaching, and pre-retirement planning. Through these services, clients become better equipped to manage career paths, maximize strengths, improve job performance and engagement, and enhance their contribution to their organization. Clients have the opportunity to assess their interests and skill sets and learn how to more skillfully handle organizational change and role expectations. Resiliency programs help clients become better able to perceive, process, and respond to stressful situations and learn how to make adjustments to their coping strategies where needed. Pre-retirement sessions offer clients practical tips and tools to assess lifestyle goals and how they fit into their upcoming retirement, while supporting the client as they get used to the idea of their lifestyle shift. Whatever the career issue, it is a hands-on experience for clients that allows for self-reflection and discovery related to their professional life and an opportunity for developing increased resiliency and focus at work.

Fitness Coaching

As the link between physical and mental health is well known, many EAPs are promoting wellness through the provision of physical fitness information and programs that offer a coaching element. Much like counselling, coaching is about client goals and giving clients the tools they need to achieve them.

Mandated and Specialized Counselling

To complement personal and career counselling services, an EAP may also offer more specialized services to address the needs of employees and organizational clients affected by mental health or addiction issues that are impeding performance or attendance at work. These services would typically be available for the employee eligible for EAP, not the employee's spouse or dependents. Designed as part of an early intervention strategy, these programs address situations that are beyond short-term EAP support or are part of a disability case management treatment plan. These specialized programs include employee performance management, substance abuse management and relapse prevention, depression, post-trauma, anxiety or anger management, and support for return-to-work plans in situations where a mental health issue is a factor in an absence from the workplace. These programs can be used independently or together if clinically appropriate.

Some of these programs are employer-referred with the EAP providing confirmation to the employer that the employee is seeking help and following the treatment plan. Clients sign a waiver consenting to this information being shared with their employer. The objective of these types of programs is to prevent or manage workplace performance issues, absence, and disability through clinical interventions addressing issues requiring longer-term, more specialized, or more intensive levels of care. Successful management of these issues provides significant benefit to both the client and organizational client, including increased productivity.

An EAP may also provide health management services.[5]

Modalities of Support

EAPs have evolved to include more options in terms of how clients receive support from a counselling professional. Technological advancements, along with a focus on individual learning and lifestyle needs, have given rise to expanded EAP offerings that may now include professional counselling services via the telephone, online, video, chat, and self-learning tools. Clients benefit as they are able to access a service that delivers the right fit for them each time a request is made.

The modalities typically offered through EAPs are outlined below, along with some indications as to when and under what circumstances the modalities are the best fit for the client. Standard service levels are in place when it comes to offering appointments to clients. For most situations, clients are offered an appointment that will take place within three to five business days. This time frame gives clients time to make arrangements to accommodate the appointment (such as childminding). For clients in situations assessed as urgent or even life-threatening, appointments within 24-48 hours are offered, and when a client is in a life-threatening situation, immediate clinical support is provided to make sure the client is safe and the risk is appropriately contained.

EAPs recognize that counselling is no longer a one-size-fits-all endeavour and strive to meet the needs of their clients by offering multiple options for accessesing and receiving service.

In-Person Counselling

In-person counselling is most beneficial for clients whose issues necessitate a higher touch or level of direct intervention such as in cases of addictions, child welfare, domestic violence, or work-assisted referrals, and for clients who feel best supported by face-to-face interaction with their counsellor.

---

[5]   See Chapter 22 for information on this subject.

Telecounselling

Telecounselling is suitable for most client issues and may be most beneficial for clients who have physical mobility issues or geographical constraints, who desire the increased anonymity of telecounselling, or who appreciate the convenience of saving travel time.

E-Counselling

E-counselling is conducted on a secure website where clients consult with a counsellor via asynchronous (time-delayed) exchanges using text-based narrative therapy. E-counselling appeals to clients who prefer not to travel, appreciate a greater sense of anonymity, and are most comfortable expressing themselves in writing. This type of counselling offers clients the additional benefits of engaging in counselling without an appointment and within the privacy of their own space.

Video Counselling

Video counselling is conducted on a secure platform where clients consult with a counsellor via webcam. It is ideal for clients who cannot travel to a counselling office, are comfortable with webcam technology, and prefer to engage in counselling within the privacy of their own space. As with telephone and e-counselling, video counselling is an effective way to address the challenges of serving clients in small and/or remote locations. Video counselling allows for couple and family counselling when participants are in different geographical locations.

Online Counselling: Chat and Group

Chat is a synchronous, live counselling option used to provide clients with immediate clinical support on a secure platform. It is an immediate clinical consultation for clients who prefer a chat option. This service is relatively new to the EAP market and demonstrates the evolution of EAPs as they embrace new technologies and accommodate client communication preferences.

Group counselling, typically associated with recovery programs like Alcoholics Anonymous, is well-known because it works. In an EAP setting, group counselling can be done online. This maintains confidentiality (through online avatars) and it provides two main benefits for clients: group and counsellor support coupled with getting that support from the comfort of their own space.

Self-Directed Learning

To address the needs of clients who contact the EAP looking for support but who prefer not to interact with a counsellor, EAPs may choose to provide self-directed learning opportunities through educational tool kits on various topics. Typically, tool kits offer research-oriented information to visual learners and an information-based approach to problem assessment, understanding, and resolution, which is a clinically sound option for those who do not want to participate in live counselling right away or at all.

Complementary Programs and Services

To support work-life balance, EAPs typically offer complementary services to support matters pertaining to the family, legal and financial queries, physical health, and nutrition. Some of these services are described below.

Family Support Services

When it comes to family matters from birth to palliative care, there is a lot of information to navigate. The average client does not have the time or expertise to do this research while in the midst of handling a potentially difficult family situation. EAPs should offer information and referral services relating to family matters, which are generally broken into two broad categories: eldercare and child care.

Child care inquiries include; childminding and daycare options, new parenting programs, information on learning disabilities and assessments, special needs programs, summer camps, and private schools.

Eldercare inquiries include; senior housing options, government financial support for seniors, home and palliative care, caregiver support, physical and mental ailments affecting seniors, and information on making homes accessible.

Increasingly, EAP clients are finding themselves in the "sandwich generation", caring for both young children and aging parents. Within the EAP, clients may be able to receive a consultation with a family support specialist who offers specific referral options and general information. Tipsheets and information brochures are often sent to the client to help give them a holistic picture of the matter they are inquiring about.

The cost of any program or service referred to is typically the client's responsibility.

Legal Services

EAPs may connect clients with experienced and credentialed lawyers who provide confidential legal guidance and/or representation. Legal consultations would typically focus on family law, criminal law, wills and estates, civil litigation, real estate, and landlord and tenant matters. Legal consultations on immigration law, employment disputes, corporate law, tax law, or legal matters outside of Canada are typically not provided by an EAP legal service. Telephonic consultation services may be available for clients with general questions about a particular area of law, looking for specific answers to legal questions, or seeking advice from a lawyer on the best course of action.

EAPs may also provide a referral service for clients wishing to retain the services of a lawyer. By accessing legal support through their EAP, clients may be offered a discount on the lawyer's fees and/or a free time-limited consultation.

Financial Services

An EAP financial consultation service can allow clients to connect with an experienced financial professional through telephonic or in-person sessions, along with a growing number of online programs. Financial consultations may be available on a wide variety of topics including; debt and credit counselling, retirement, tax, mortgage and real estate planning, divorce settlements, terminations, bankruptcy, general budgeting, and life insurance.

Nutritional and Naturopathic Services

EAPs may provide nutritional and/or naturopathic services through a registered dietitian or naturopathic doctor depending on the type of nutritional information and support the client is looking for. Consultations may be provided over the phone or in person, depending on the situation, and take place in the context of short-term, solution-focused support. Online health programs and health packages designed for the self-directed learner are also options for clients seeking support for their physical health. Over the course of the consultations, the client can ask questions and receive clarity on the next steps for improving or maintaining their physical health. Often times, the client is given resources to review and homework (*e.g.*, a nutrition log) that is reviewed by the dietitian or naturopath during a follow-up session.

Services for Client Organizations and On-Site Support

EAPs may offer services to support clients and organizations in times of change or crisis or to address issues and events that occur outside of regular day-to-day business or to provide specialized services to organizations with a global workforce. These services are described in the sections below.

Trauma Interventions

EAP trauma services can address an organization's need to provide support to managers and employees affected by traumatic events and get back to business. Whether it's the death of an employee, serious injury to a colleague, or a threat to safety, employees may experience stress and anxiety symptoms and a decrease in productivity at work. Trauma counsellors trained in critical incident debriefing, community crisis response, and general trauma interventions conduct risk assessments and follow-up, which can minimize the likelihood of post-traumatic stress and deterioration of an employee's well-being to a degree where absences are likely.

Organizations that employ first responders — for example, police, fire and EMS — may have additional cause to use trauma intervention services to address the cumulative effects of trauma exposure on these specialized teams.

EAP trauma services can help organizations and their employees cope successfully with situations that may hinder an employee's ability to function normally including:

- Restructuring or major change in the workplace;
- Accidents;
- Violent behaviour in the workplace;
- Sudden or violent death;
- Workplace robbery;
- Terrorism;
- Natural disasters; and
- Situations of fraud and the surrounding inquiry.

On-site defusing and debriefing meetings with staff are designed to normalize reactions and, when possible, minimize post-traumatic stress, enabling most members to resume normal functioning. Trauma services may also include individual trauma counselling, post-traumatic stress support, training in critical incident stress management, response protocols and trauma symptom warning signs, development of peer teams for the organization, and, in the case of natural disasters, on the ground mobile response units.

Intercultural Solutions

EAPs may also provide intercultural programs designed to enhance individual and organizational effectiveness on a local and global scale through cross-cultural training programs. These programs raise awareness of cultural nuances, and give people the skills they need to work and live effectively in their new setting. Additionally, they enable the strategic development of global competencies across organizations regardless of country location, training objectives, population size, and time.

A company's global workforce may include expatriates, short-term assignees, multicultural domestic and international teams, local national employees, international permanent hires, international business travellers, and global virtual teams, and intercultural training solutions address these emerging needs.

Services provided for intercultural companies and their employees may include:

- Selection and preparation services for the employee and family;
- Cross-cultural training for the expatriate and family;
- Executive coaching and training for the short-term assignee or business traveller;
- Destination services including orientation assistance, assistance with home searches, settling in, schooling, lease renewal, and departure and disconnect services;
- Repatriation services;
- Online support tools;
- In-person or virtual group business training for teams working within a multicultural setting; and
- Corporate social responsibility training.

Organizational Health and Training

EAPs may offer comprehensive organizational health and training solutions that contribute to the development of healthy workplaces. By first understanding unique workplace challenges and opportunities, a successful workplace wellness strategy can be developed and implemented. Typically, services offered include:

- Wellness seminars and workshops delivered by adult educators on topics such as workplace violence prevention, stress, trauma, and change;
- Support and consultation on long-range initiatives;
- Prevention-focused consultations on such topics as pandemic planning and workplace violence prevention;
- Occupational health promotion services;
- Assistance with organizational compliance to new legislation;
- Workplace coaching to build management, communication, and/or behaviour competencies and facilitate smooth workplace relationships and effective leadership;
- Workplace assessments to analyze organizational function (or dysfunction), identify what is working well and what is not, and recommend solutions to address underlying issues; and
- Workplace mediation to support a culture of fairness and equity while supporting existing human resources policy in the areas of conflict resolution and performance management.

Organizational health and training solutions aim to meet the objectives of organizational clients who seek support for a variety of issues including reducing workplace conflict, turnover, and absenteeism and/or presenteeism while learning how to provide a safe, diverse, and harassment-free workplace within the context of their own existing policies. By taking a proactive approach to wellness at an organizational level, financial objectives may also be realized through reduction of short and long-term disability claims and prevention of legal action and turnover as a result of poorly managed conflict.

On-Site Health Screening

Please refer to Chapter 22 for information about this service.

Account Management Support

Account management should offer ongoing support for organizational clients. Generally, a client organization has an EAP account manager who serves as a primary contact and relationship manager. Through this relationship, a partnership develops between the organizational client and the EAP, which can help the organization meet the strategic objectives of having an EAP in place. Account managers should monitor the quality and efficacy of EAP program deliverables and interpret statistical data provided to the organizational client. Account managers should also provide strategy and communication expertise to the organization about how to best engage employees and people leaders at the organization to support EAP usage. Where a strong relationship exists, an account manager is well-placed to make recommendations to the organizational client about using the EAP to make the greatest impact on employee wellness and engagement. The account manager is typically the point of contact for EAP manager orientations, EAP promotional materials, and quality assurance management and investigations. Account managers may also be invited to participate in an organization's internal committees, such as a joint health and safety committee and wellness or EAP committees. In environments with unionized and non-unionized staff, an account manager sitting in on a committee can promote the EAP as a neutral third party that works collaboratively to meet the needs of all employees eligible for EAP services.

Management Consultations

Management consultations are discussions requested by a manager, supervisor, or human resources representative regarding workplace issues or workplace management situations that are negatively impacting employee work performance. These situations include disruptive behaviour, threats of violence, substance abuse, relationship difficulties, medical, financial, and/or legal concerns, and may lead to an employee's mandatory referral to the EAP if the employee does not independently address the issue. The purpose of management consultations is to help managers set clear boundaries with employees, to intervene early and quickly, and maximize the likelihood of resolution with staff.

Aggregate Data Compilation

With each service offered through an EAP comes the opportunity to collect and mine data. EAPs should collect data to monitor internal functioning, provide statistical data to client organizations, and support industry research. These aggregate statistics must be anonymous and must not contain any information that could identify any individual client. Aggregate data and statistical reports should be prepared for the organizational client on a regular basis and typically cover utilization rates, statistical demographic data, presenting issues and trends, types of services being used by clients, and client satisfaction rates. These reports can show the value the organizational client receives from its EAP and demonstrate how the EAP is measuring up to the service levels agreed upon. Trends in EAP usage may also be used by the organizational client to proactively identify and address trends within their own organization.

Health Risk Assessments

Aggregate data can be used to understand behavior and health behavior change, and some EAPs now offer health risk assessment (HRA) tools to their organizational clients. HRAs can be used to identify health risks on an individual level, but big data analysis can also uncover organizational health trends. Organizations can use HRA analysis to identify issues and solutions to employee health and wellness.

Research and Expertise in the Marketplace

As clients accessing services change and evolve, so too must the EAP. EAPs must stay current on challenges, such as the multi-generational workforce and explosive use of social media, which have increasing implications on how people seek support, how companies manage their workforce, and which elevate employee relations to a new level.

To remain viable and relevant in today's ever-changing world, to maintain and improve upon clinical best practices, to enhance their expertise in the field, and to continue to support clients effectively, EAPs must stay abreast of current research and trends in the areas of counselling, client benefits, clinical services, user demographics, and technological developments. EAPs would also do well to contribute to collective industry knowledge through internal program research, conference presentations, and market publications.

Quality Management and Improvement Programs

This chapter has thus far explored the capacity of an EAP's services to support the client and/or organizational client. This section will now focus on the internal programs an EAP should have in place to assure quality and better serve its clients.

Credentialing and Professional Requirements

EAPs employ a significant number of mental health professionals licensed through their respective professional associations. To maintain the integrity of the organization and protect clients, an EAP should have a strong verification system in place to ensure all counsellors maintain their professional credentials. This can be accomplished through the ongoing collection of documentation and credentials, including liability insurance, evidence of membership with a professional licensing body, copy of a relevant degree, and resume or curriculum vitae. Having valid and up-to-date documentation is a contractual obligation of any counsellor employed by an EAP.

The minimum educational requirement for a counsellor is the successful completion of a Master's Degree in counselling, psychology, or social work. Further to education, EAPs typically look for counsellors with the following experience and professional qualifications:

- a minimum of five years of post-graduate counselling experience;
- EAP industry experience and knowledge of workplace issues;
- the ability to clinically manage high-risk crises;
- the ability to work with individuals, couples, and families;
- a customer service focus and approach;
- substance abuse assessment and counselling experience; and
- professional registration with a mental health licensing body.

Training and Development

Providing internal training and development programs lets EAPs fuel a prepared and knowledgeable workforce, better serve clients, and build a culture of learning. A training department supports the strategic goals of the EAP by assessing the training and development needs of internal employees and then delivering programs that address those needs to ultimately benefit the EAP's clients and client organizations. Internal training offered to EAP staff includes new hire orientation and continuous learning programs, and covers technical, service, and/or clinically related topics, depending on the audience. Training professionals create and deliver customized content in English and in French, which meets language law requirements if an EAP is operational in Quebec.

Training professionals should adhere to best practices in training methodology and follow training competency architecture such as that published by the Canadian Society for Training and Development. As such, training programs should be offered in a variety of modalities to increase learner engagement and support all styles of learning. These include in-classroom, telephonic, e-learning, blended, and multimedia presentations, as well as access to material for independent learning.

EAPs with a robust internal training program experience cost benefits versus hiring outside consultants and are better equipped to be agile when it comes to aligning programs to the needs of the business. Another advantage of internal programs is having training professionals who understand the language and the culture of the EAP in which they work.

Complaint and Compliment Management

As with any business focused on meeting the needs of its clients, EAPs must have programs in place to measure client satisfaction from both the end-user client and organizational client point of view. From a big picture perspective, broad categories including effectiveness, appropriateness, accessibility, and provider competence are used to determine whether an EAP is meeting its objectives. The mechanisms used for monitoring success metrics may vary and can include satisfaction survey data, quality monitoring and evaluation of staff, audits, utilization rates, and complaint documentation and investigation.

A program that documents and investigates complaints is a useful way for an EAP to address individual concerns and use analysis to uncover systemic issues negatively impacting the client. Complaint management programs build trust on an individual client and organizational level as they demonstrate a commitment to listening to client concerns and following up with them appropriately. With this type of program, an EAP must also build a culture where employees understand the importance of documenting client concerns and submitting them to the complaint management team.

At the other end of the spectrum rests client feedback in the form of compliments. A robust program will also have a mechanism for officially documenting complimentary feedback from clients. Due to the nature of services provided by EAPs, complimentary feedback can be a powerful reminder of the role the EAP plays in supporting the health and well-being of its clients and can provide a window into the quality of the service being offered. Highlighting client compliments to their own staff in a way that maintains client confidentiality is a tool that EAPs can use to increase employee engagement and foster a shared sense of purpose.

Continuous Improvement

As part of a holistic approach to business success, an EAP may employ a form of continuous improvement program. Quality and service improvements are the cumulative effect of many small improvements made daily at every level in the organization, and a continuous improvement program provides a mechanism for implementing process improvement, process redesign, and new design. Stronger processes and protocols result in reduced waste and errors and quicker response or cycle time.

A continuous improvement program should ask these key questions:

- How can it be done better or easier?

- Are we doing the right things?
- Does this process or task provide value to the business and to the customer?

Implementing a continuous improvement program and fostering a continuous improvement culture in an EAP setting provides many benefits including:

- Increased employee success and satisfaction;
- Improved client and customer service experience and satisfaction; and
- Increased efficiency, effectiveness, and quality.

In a competitive marketplace, EAPs may find that applying a continuous improvement approach as part of their overall business strategy provides a strong foundation for sustainability and innovation.

Accreditation

Though not required, some EAPs choose to go through the accreditation process with the Council on Accreditation (COA), which has developed an EAP-specific accreditation program. According to EASNA, becoming accredited distinguishes an EAP and suggests the "organization has met the highest possible international standards for quality management and service delivery".[6]

Digital and Social Media

The emergence and popularity of social media has changed the way many organizations do business and EAP is no exception to that. To complement the various online solutions that are available, EAPs are also delving into the social media realm to reach more people and develop a strong online presence and remain relevant in the digital world. Channels for digital communication include the web, blogs, videos, podcasts, smartphone and tablet applications (or "apps"), instant messaging, Search Engine Marketing (SEM), quick response codes, and viral elements. EAPs are developing and implementing digital strategies to interact with and engage clients in a way that suits their lifestyle and takes digital trends into account.

---

[6]   "Overview", EASNA, online: http://www.easna.org/accreditation/accreditation -overview.

Employee Wellness

Wellness Programs

Employers are increasingly making the link between productivity and wellness and, as a result, are seeking out wellness programs in larger numbers. Wellness programs may be adopted by employers to support the promotion of good health through education and the facilitation of improved health and fitness. Typically, such programs are funded by the employer, but can be offered on an optional basis with employees bearing some of the cost.

The scope of wellness programs varies. A comprehensive program might encompass stress management, weight management, smoking cessation, nutritional counselling, ergonomic assessments, and other preventive care programs, such as annual flu clinics. Employer-sponsored programs may include in-house fitness facilities, subsidized gym memberships, or may simply provide easy access to community options.

A wide range of services and delivery methods makes it possible to tailor the program to the objectives, resources, and budget of the employer. Government agencies or public organizations may be available to assist employers in promoting wellness.

Usually, the employer is seeking to reduce absence or health care costs or to improve productivity. As with any employee benefit, quantifiable objectives are necessary to build and manage a sustainable program.

Fitness Club Memberships

Fitness club memberships may be offered by employers as either a stand-alone benefit, or as a component of a wellness program. Wholly subsidized membership is usually offered to executives, while partial subsidization or discounted rates are more commonly offered to non-executive employees. Fitness club memberships provide access and eliminate the financial barriers to formal fitness organizations.

Recreational Facilities

Workplace recreational facilities are one way for employers to enhance the health and team building relationships of its employees. Depending upon the budget and objective, there are a variety of options available. Employers with a large concentration of employees at one location may find it feasible to install an on-site fitness centre with basic exercise equipment. This benefits those who would otherwise not have the opportunity to exercise, considering their work schedule, commuting time, and family responsibilities. The centre may be used for fitness classes during lunchtime or outside regular work hours. Fitness instructors can be hired or chosen from qualified volunteers in the employee population.

Workplace recreational facilities can also be provided to allow employees the opportunity to relax at the end of a workday or to relieve stress by having the opportunity for a midday break. Recreational facilities may include game tables (e.g., ping-pong, air hockey), cards, and board games — options that offer employees the opportunity to socialize with colleagues outside their daily work group, thereby helping to build interdepartmental relationships.

Costs for the facilities can be funded by the employer alone or in combination with fees paid by employees. Employer contributions representing a substantial portion of the costs are recommended, as much as possible, so as not to financially discourage participation and use of the facilities.

Work Environment and Work-Life Balance

Alternative Work Arrangements

As society moves further into the information age, the nature of work, the workplace, and workers is evolving. Technology has irreversibly and inescapably changed how and where people work. Employees are rethinking and reprioritizing what they expect from their employers. Employers, in their quest to maintain job satisfaction and attract and retain employees, have introduced measures and policies aimed at reducing work-related stress and increasing employee engagement. Alternative workplace arrangements are being implemented in an attempt to promote a more satisfactory work environment.

Telecommuting

Telecommuting is one of a number of alternative workplace arrangements. Although the details of telecommuting (also referred to as teleworking) may vary from employer to employer, the common principle noted in most definitions is that the employee is working at a remote site away from the normal office location.

Without a doubt, the popularity of this arrangement is growing and there are well over one million telecommuters in Canada today. Many businesses are able to accommodate employees, realizing that getting the work done well is more important than where the work is done. For example, transaction-based data processing can be managed as easily from a home in rural British Columbia as from an office tower in downtown Montreal.

There are a variety of advantages associated with telecommuting. Some of these potential advantages are:

- increased employee productivity;
- office space savings;
- improvement in employee job satisfaction;
- eliminated or reduced commuting time;
- reduced absenteeism; and
- recruitment and retention tool.

Nonetheless, planning is absolutely necessary to reduce the impact of potential disadvantages, including isolation, reduced sense of belonging and team spirit, boredom, and career or promotion concerns.

Job-Sharing

Job-sharing is where two people voluntarily share the responsibilities of one full-time job, dividing the pay, holidays, and other benefits between them, according to the number of hours worked. Demographic changes are forcing employers to examine potential qualified employees required in full-time positions but available only on a part-time basis because of lifestyle choices, family responsibilities, or other physical or personal constraints.

Phased Retirement

As they approach retirement age, employees may be interested in gradually phasing into retirement over a period of time rather than transitioning directly from full-time employment to full-time retirement. Phased retirement allows employees to gradually prepare for retirement and benefits employers by retaining experienced employees for a time, which creates the opportunity for smoother transitions to the next generation.

In December 2007, the Income Tax Act was amended to allow registered pension plans to permit members who are at least 60 years old or at least 55 years old and eligible to retire with an unreduced pension benefit, to receive an annual pension of up to 60% of their accrued pension while continuing to work and to accumulate additional years of credited service.

Phased retirement is not mandatory. Plan sponsors may offer phased retirement at their discretion if permitted under the applicable pension standards legislation. The legislation in most jurisdictions allows phased retirement agreements in line with the Income Tax Act standards for defined benefit plans. Given the potential cost associated with such benefits, plan sponsors should carefully assess the potential cost implications of phased retirement and other alternatives before introducing them.

Flexible Hours

As today's employers face new challenges attracting and retaining the best employees in their field, flexible working hours are another enticing mechanism that a company can use to attract potential employees. "Flextime" is when the employee works longer hours on some days and shorter hours on others. There are two common types of flextime: flex hours and the compressed workweek.

Under flex hours, the employer establishes the core hours required during the workweek. Once this is set, the flextime is then organized around the core day. For example, the core hours may be from 9 a.m. to 3 p.m. The employee then has the option of starting anytime prior to 9 a.m. and finishing at any time after 3 p.m., so long as his or her full working hours are completed.

In a compressed workweek arrangement, the employee must still complete the working hours specified by his or her employment agreement. However, the compressed workweek arrangement allows the employee to work those hours in less than five days by working longer hours over four or four-and-one-half days.

Workplace Dress Code

Organizations that have traditionally enforced formal business attire are relaxing their dress codes to "business casual" dress codes, which have become the norm throughout many workplaces. In its general application, employees are permitted to forego the business suit and dress shoes, provided their business casual clothes are presentable and appropriate in a business environment. Many employers have adopted a workplace dress code policy, going so far as to list those items of clothing and footwear that are acceptable and those that are not. Often included are items that can be worn occasionally in a "casual dress" environment, at the employer's discretion, such as denim. To maintain an appearance of professionalism when appropriate for business needs, an employer's workplace dress code policy can include a requirement for formal business attire when meeting with external clients.

Dependant Care

Eldercare

The senior population in Canada is increasing. Seniors are living longer, hospital stays are shorter, and seniors are experiencing more difficulty obtaining suitable accommodations (*e.g.*, retirement or nursing homes). As a result, the responsibility for the seniors' well-being frequently rests on the shoulders of their children, many of whom are full-time employees. While it is clearly not the responsibility of the employer to look after the parents of their employees, employers are certainly becoming more aware of the impact that this issue is having on productivity in the workplace. In fact, there are a variety of potential problems that might arise as a result of eldercare responsibilities, including: absenteeism, tardiness, frequent distractions, depression, inability to work overtime, and turnover.

There are a number of approaches that employers can take to provide eldercare assistance to employees who are caregivers. It may include direct assistance (e.g., financial assistance) or indirect assistance, such as allowing for flexible work arrangements and providing EAP services.

Child Care

The increasing number of single-parent households and those where both parents work outside the home leads to additional challenges for the employer. Child care is becoming an increasingly valuable benefit for employees with children, particularly those who are required to travel as part of their job.

Some employers have been able to accommodate on-site child care centres. More often, for those organizations offering assistance, the employer will provide daycare subsidies to employees to defray the cost of child care expenses. Further creative solutions are beginning to emerge. To provide for the contingency of sick children, a few property and casualty insurers have added "child-sitting" services to their standard homeowner and tenant policies. Another innovative response brings temporary childminding services to the home as part of a service subscribed to by the employer. Employers may also help employees find affordable daycare solutions from reliable sources that suit work schedules through referral services offered through their EAP or otherwise.

Domestic Partner Benefits

Today's family bears little resemblance to the traditional family of a few decades ago. It is no longer composed of the working father, stay-at-home mother, and 2.5 children. In fact, the traditional model only applies to a relatively small percentage of today's society. We now see a variety of familial relationships, ranging from single-parent families to blended families to grandparents raising grandchildren. As a result of the Supreme Court decision in *M. v. H.*,[7] same-sex partnerships have also been added to the contemporary definition of family. Domestic partner benefits have arisen out of the need to accommodate unmarried opposite-sex and same-sex partners, and to put them on the same footing as married spouses.

By 1999, all federal and provincial human rights legislation had been voluntarily amended, and governments included sexual orientation as a protected ground. Employers are required to provide domestic partners with coverage or risk claims of discrimination.

Employers will have to determine how they are going to define who is eligible for domestic partner benefits. Unlike a marriage, there is no specific and universal definition of domestic partnerships. However, certain elements are normally included in most definitions. Basically the partners, either opposite or same-sex, must reside together in a committed relationship. Employers need to establish criteria that domestic partners need to meet in order to be eligible for benefits, and such criteria typically include cohabitation for a specific period of time (usually one to three years).

Some employers have required documentation of cohabitation and/or certification from the employee that the person named as his or her domestic partner actually meets the eligibility requirements as set out by the company; however, this practice is no longer commonplace.

---

[7]   *M. v. H.*, [1999] S.C.J. No. 23, [1999] 2 S.C.R. 3 (S.C.C.).

Training and Development

Training Programs (Internal/External)

Job training or skills enhancement training, now more than ever, constitute a business imperative. For an organization to remain competitive in delivering leading edge products and services, and in recruiting and retaining top talent, training and development is very much a part of the total reward strategy of progressive organizations.

Professional Association Memberships

These memberships are generally provided to professional employees (*e.g.*, actuary, accountant, human resource professional). Membership dues are considered a necessary part of doing business, and allow professionals to develop and maintain their key competencies, thus contributing to the success of the organization.

Tuition Reimbursements

In general, employers combine educational leaves (see "Paid and Unpaid Leaves") with tuition refund programs, which reimburse employees for course fees. Supplementary expenses for textbooks and other course materials may or may not be paid by the employer. Some employers will pay course-related fees in advance, while others may require successful completion before fees are reimbursed.

Employer paid or reimbursed tuition for courses that primarily benefit the employer will not result in a taxable employment benefit when it is reasonable to assume the employee will continue employment for a reasonable period of time after the completion of the training.

Paid and Unpaid Leaves

In an effort to reduce unscheduled days of absence, and to improve productivity by helping employees to achieve work-life balance, today's employers offer a variety of options for leave from the workplace.

Educational Leaves

A leave of absence for educational purposes can either be short-term or long-term in duration. In general, such leaves can benefit both the individual employee and the employer. A short-term leave enables employees to successfully complete courses for continuing education programs approved by the employer. This enables employees to take ongoing, part-time studies towards completion of a certification or degree while maintaining their jobs. Educational leaves can also be longer in duration, allowing employees to pursue advanced, post-graduate education that will have a direct benefit to their job and the employer. Full-time education is often taken in the form of extended leaves of absence from work, and can be an unpaid leave, or the employee can be paid through a salary deferral arrangement.

Ordinarily, employers combine these leave arrangements with tuition refund programs, which reimburse employees for course fees.

Personal Care Days

Personal care days are to be used by employees for commitments (scheduled or unexpected) that occur during the workday, such as personal or family appointments, child care or eldercare needs, as well as emergencies. Personal care days are typically renewed on an annual basis, and are offered on a paid-time basis. Employers may or may not permit personal care days to be carried over from one year to the next. The number of days offered by employers varies from two to five days per employee per year and, once those days are used, employees may be required to use vacation days or request unpaid time off to attend to personal or family matters. Upon termination, unused personal care days must be forfeited and do not form part of the employee's final payment.

Bereavement Leave

Paid time off is frequently offered to employees who have experienced the death of an immediate family member, such as a spouse, child, parent, or sibling. An employer's formal policy may also be extended to include other family members (*e.g.*, aunt, uncle, cousin, niece, and nephew) and/or the immediate family members of a spouse. The length of paid time off can vary from one day to five days.

Sabbaticals

Sabbaticals, as a form of alternative work arrangement, were traditionally associated with the academic environment. Other employers are considering sabbaticals and periods of unpaid leave as a mechanism to regenerate those in "mid-career" and to motivate employees in general. Outside of the academic environment, sabbaticals are not typically funded by the employer. Some employers allow employees to budget for a sabbatical by voluntarily reducing salary for a fixed period to accrue income for the sabbatical period.

Paid Maternity/Paternity Leaves

See Chapter 19 and Chapter 21 for information about this topic.

Vacation

The most common form of vacation accumulation is based on an employee's years of service. As the length of tenure increases, the number of days of annual vacation also increases for the employee. It is still prevalent to award increased vacation time based on predetermined service anniversary years. For example, many employers offer two or three weeks' vacation after the completion of one year of service, and an additional week of vacation thereafter at the 5-, 10-, 20-, and/or 25-year service anniversaries. New employees by and large will receive prorated vacation entitlement equal to:

first year of service vacation entitlement/12 × #of months worked in the first year.

Employers may also reward management or executives with additional paid vacation time, in recognition of the increased demands placed on these employees as a result of career advancement.

Employers and/or employees' immediate supervisors may determine when vacation is taken, e.g., in off-peak seasons, operation shutdown, or in coordination with other department members.

Employers may still allow vacation carryover, to a predefined maximum number of weeks. However, a carryover policy has a financial impact to an employer due to the requirement to account for this accrued obligation. As well, an employee's saved vacation may be earned at a lesser compensation level than when it is taken in the following year (when compensation may be higher). To address these issues, employers are increasingly demanding that vacation be taken in the year it is earned. Such a policy serves to eliminate the financial impact to the employer, and to ensure employees receive time away from work to rejuvenate and restore well-being.

Employers may also allow the buying of additional paid vacation time, or the selling of unwanted paid vacation time, as part of a flexible benefits design.[8]

Additional Benefits

Critical Illness Benefit

First introduced in the United Kingdom, South Africa, and Australia, critical illness coverage pays the insured a tax-free lump-sum payment if he or she survives a minimum number of days (usually 30 days) after he or she is diagnosed with a covered critical illness. Payment is not dependent on inability to work and the money can be used in any way the insured sees fit.[9]

Long-Term Care

Long-term care insurance is a relatively new benefit offered to employees by only a few employers in Canada. Long-term care expenses are often unexpected, costly and, depending on the type of care required, an individual's finances can be substantially affected. Factors such as a changing health care system, an aging population, and the rising cost of home care services, have prompted insurers to develop a product to address this need. Long-term care insurance provides a benefit when someone suffers from a severe cognitive impairment, or needs help performing activities of daily living, such as dressing, bathing, going to the bathroom, eating, or moving about.

While the government provides many important medical services, long-term care is not considered medical, but rather custodial, which is not fully covered by the government. The reality is that individuals and families often have to pay a significant portion of the cost when long-term care is necessary. Long-term care is not limited to the sick or elderly and may also be required as part of a recovery from an accident, or as a result of an extended period of disability. A long-term care insurance plan can protect assets and lifestyle by providing the resources to obtain care and by allowing an individual to make choices about their own care.

Many Canadian insurers have developed individual long-term care products in amounts to cover various levels of risk, depending on the

---

8   Please see Chapter 26 for a discussion on this topic.
9   Please see Chapter 16 for information about this benefit.

needs of the applicant. Several group products are emerging, with many more still in the development stage. In either case, at this time, most long-term care programs require that the applicant provide evidence of good health.

Group Legal Insurance

The spread of group legal plans in Canada as an employee benefit has been limited and those plans that do exist are most often a negotiated benefit found in a union setting. Group legal plans provide a specified range of legal services that do not compromise the relationship between the employer and the employee. Services generally include the following:

- Purchase or sale of residential housing;
- Landlord and tenant issues;
- Motor vehicle offences;
- Separation;
- Adoption;
- Divorce; and
- Wills and estate issues.

The employer may contract with those who provide the legal services, either a closed group of qualified lawyers or internal counsel, to provide the services for a fixed annual fee per person. Alternatively, the employer may agree to pay a fixed amount towards the cost of the specified services, allowing the employee to choose the lawyer.

With the lack of growth of group legal plans, an increasing number of EAP providers include legal referral services as a component of the overall service package. A referral to qualified lawyers may meet the needs of most employees.

Second Opinion and Medical Care Navigation Services

Two options for employee benefit programs are services that either facilitate access to a second opinion of a medical diagnosis or provide assistance navigating the medical system (both public and private).

Second Opinion — Providers work collaboratively with a network of international physicians and medical facilities to review diagnostic information and facilitate a second opinion. Various ancillary services may be provided as required.

Navigation Services — Provide assistance navigating public and private medical services through personalized case management. This is usually done through one-on-one telephonic counselling and could include an explanation of tests and treatment plans, specialized advice, emotional support, or information on how to access other services.

Second Opinion and Medical Care Navigation Services have become mainstream; many insurance carriers offer these services as part of their health care benefit or standard group program offering.

Perquisites

Over and above the traditional benefits provided to employees, a number of organizations provide additional non-cash benefits.

As with all benefits, perquisites assist in attracting and retaining key people. Appropriately designed benefits can reinforce the value system of the organization. While certain perquisites are for the benefit of all employees, others are exclusively for executives, and still other perquisites may extend to professionals, sales and marketing staff, or middle management.

Some perquisites may be required because of market practices. Others are offered by organizations wishing to distinguish themselves from their competitors, to foster a unique corporate culture, or to attract a specific type of employee.

Although tax consequences are no longer the primary rationale for providing non-cash compensation, taxation remains an issue to be considered in evaluating the alternatives.

The following are some of the principal reasons why organizations provide perquisites, and the corresponding benefits that meet the objectives:

- *Business needs* — Certain perquisites are provided to increase productivity, facilitate client service, and reinforce client relationships. These additional benefits are seen to contribute to the success of the organization, and include:
    - Company cars;
    - Business club memberships;
    - Conferences;
    - Expense accounts;
    - Home Internet connections;
    - Mobile devices (smartphones, tablets, etc.); and
    - Personal computers for home use.

- *Wellness* — Perquisites provided to promote fitness and good health, ensure the ongoing productivity of employees and executives, and prevent health problems that could, in the case of executives, have significant adverse impact on the organization. They include:

  o   Annual medical examinations; and

  o   Fitness club memberships.

- *Recognition* — These benefits are generally provided to all employees and are designed to recognize employees for their commitment and contributions to the organization. They include:

  o   Company-sponsored events;

  o   Discount on employer products and services;

  o   Recreational facilities;

  o   Referral bonuses;

  o   Service awards; and

  o   Service excellence rewards.

- *Financial planning* — Financial benefits are intended to allow executives, in particular, to focus on the company business and avoid situations that could distract them from their corporate responsibilities. Formal guarantees of compensation arrangements with regard to termination following a merger, acquisition, or any other "change of control" (*i.e.*, "golden parachutes") may also assist the executives in focusing on these corporate transactions without being unduly concerned about the impact on their own personal situation. Such perquisites include:

  o   Employment contracts;

  o   Financial/tax planning;

  o   Golden parachutes;

  o   Home security systems;

  o   Legal counselling;

  o   Personal loans;

  o   Scholarships for family members; and

  o   Tax preparation services.

- *Status* — Benefits provided generally to senior management, as status symbols, are to reinforce the perceived contribution of the individuals to the organization. They include:

o   Company cars;

o   Company paid parking;

o   Concierge services;

o   First-class travel;

o   Personal assistants;

o   Reserved parking; and

o   Spouse travel expenses.

Company Cars

Vehicle benefits compensate employees for using a vehicle for business purposes. Company cars can also be provided as a status and recognition benefit.

Company owned or leased vehicles are provided if there is a business justification. It is common for senior management, marketing, and sales people to have access to company cars. Licensing fees, insurance premiums, and variable costs incurred for business purposes, are generally paid by the employer. Variable costs incurred for personal reasons are generally paid by the employer for senior management positions but can be paid by the employees in other positions.

Another common practice is to compensate employees for the use of a vehicle for business purposes using one of the following approaches:

- Cents per kilometre driven;
- Monthly reimbursement of operating expenses;
- Monthly car allowance;
- Monthly car allowance plus cents per kilometre driven;
- Monthly car allowance plus partial operating costs (*e.g.*, fuel); or
- Monthly car allowance plus all operating costs.

Vehicle benefits are no longer considered to be significant tax advantages. Nevertheless, the preferred approach to providing such benefits will generally depend on their tax-effectiveness considering the distances driven each year and the portion of the kilometres driven for business purposes as opposed to personal reasons.

Financial and Retirement Planning

In the past, individual financial counselling was provided primarily to highly compensated executives in the belief that advice on large capital accumulation, investments, tax, and estate planning applied only to them. Increasingly, employers are aware that there are consequences for all employees if they do not plan properly for retirement.

Employers are now turning to individual financial planning for employees who are close to retirement and for those who are being offered termination packages.

The trend towards a broader audience for individual financial planning reflects the increasing use of defined contribution pension plans, savings plans, flexible benefit plans, downsizings, and early retirements.

In addition to financial counselling, many employers offer retirement counselling for employees approaching retirement. Retirement counselling sessions can be conducted for individuals or on a group basis. These sessions help the individual anticipate the lifestyle changes associated with retirement, and the decisions that may need to be made about retirement income.[10]

From a tax position, the fees paid by an employer for retirement counselling, or re-employment counselling, do not produce taxable income for the employee. However, other employer-provided benefits related to financial counselling do constitute taxable income to the employee.

---

[10]   See Chapter 28 for a detailed discussion of these topics.

PART III

DEVELOPING AREAS

Chapter 28

RETIREMENT PLANNING

Executive Summary

As a result of the baby boom generation nearing retirement and the general aging of the Canadian population, the need for retirement planning has become more apparent to employers and professionals in human resources. In turn, retirement planning is becoming a vital part of an employee's benefit package, as well as an effective means of communicating and promoting employer-provided retirement benefits.

This chapter outlines, in detail, the key considerations that employers should keep in mind before hosting a valuable and informative retirement planning program, including:

- The reasons for and against choosing to deliver information about retirement planning;
- Employees' needs and which topics to cover (e.g., should topics focus on financial matters such as sources of retirement income, budgeting, and investments, or should they feature the "softer" topics of lifestyle planning and health issues during retirement?);
- The most effective format for communicating information (i.e., print, online, or in-person seminars), and the pros and cons of each; and
- Understanding the target audience and how their needs change depending on the stage of their career.

Introduction

Employer pension plans are designed to supplement, not replace, government benefits and personal savings. Younger employees are often unaware of this arrangement and generally tend to think that having an employer-provided pension plan means that their retirement plans are taken care of. However, around the age of 40, employees begin to show more awareness of the need to take control of their retirement plans.

Employees typically have difficulty comprehending the defined benefit plan, while the capital accumulation arrangement is more easily understood. But what is it employees recognize?

Prior to retirement, employees have a tendency to think of capital accumulation — or the lump sum that he or she will receive upon retirement. Rather than focusing on a pension benefit, employees are often associating their pension with their personal Registered Retirement Savings Plan (RRSP).

However, as employees approach retirement, this relationship is reversed, and the predictable monthly income delivered by a defined benefit plan becomes better appreciated. In fact, the lump sum delivered by a capital accumulation arrangement often causes more questions, such as: How do I invest this money? Will it be enough? How long will it last?

For the benefit of younger employees as well as those nearing retirement, employers are providing financial counselling and/or retirement planning as an effective means of communicating employer-provided retirement benefits. These services help motivate employees to start thinking about estate planning, budgeting, changes in lifestyle, and health issues.

Before providing retirement planning information to employees, employers must consider the reasons for and against delivering such information, and their employees' needs. Other considerations that employers need to factor include the format and content for presenting information, the target audience, alternate providers, and how to pay for any associated costs.

Objectives

There are many reasons for employers to provide retirement planning seminars for employees, but the common thread is the aging population. As the segment of the population known as the "baby boom" (i.e., those born between 1946 and 1966) nears retirement, many human resources professionals are noticing a significant increase in the number of questions from employees related to retirement planning. Employees' concerns are not limited to questions about their pension plan provisions and requests for retirement estimates, they also extend to government plans, personal savings vehicles and investments, and lifestyle and health-related issues.

The aging population results in an increased need for retirement planning information from the perspective of both the employee and the employer.

The Employee's Perspective

Many plan sponsors are taking steps to inform employees of their responsibility to understand their pension plan and to prepare for retirement. As employees become more aware of this responsibility, they become more aware of their financial uncertainty. For many employees, even if they understand that they need to plan for retirement, there's a fear of the unknown — after all, it is hard for an individual to get started on a personal savings plan if the individual is unsure how to invest his or her money.

Most individuals are aware of increases in life expectancy. In general, they realize that they can expect to live longer than their parents, and certainly longer than their grandparents. In particular, over the last 90 years, life expectancy has increased by 22 years for women and 20 years for men. The following table sets out life expectancies at birth, according to Statistics Canada:

Year of Birth	Males	Females
1920	59	61
1950	66	71
1980	72	79
2005	78	83
2010	79	83

In addition, the average age at retirement remains low, currently at approximately age 63. As a result, employees will be spending more years in retirement. Not only will people be living longer on their savings, but healthier lifestyles will result in more active retirement years for many. All these factors combine to increase the importance of planning for retirement.

Employees also experience psychological uncertainty regarding the transition to retirement. A 2004 Morneau Shepell 60-second survey found that only 27% of individuals over the age of 55 cited financial security as the main factor in deciding when they would retire. This compares to 62.5% of individuals under age 45. For those over age 55, 66% indicated they will retire when they reach a target age or when they no longer enjoy working. As employees approach retirement eligibility, the decision to retire becomes about so much more than just the financial side — employees need to prepare for the lifestyle changes that go hand-in-hand with retirement to ensure a smooth and successful retirement transition.

Left to their own devices, many employees start planning too late.

The Employer's Perspective

Employees approaching retirement are often very anxious about planning their "golden years". This often results in an increase in the number of questions to human resources representatives and a greater workload for these professionals. In turn, offering comprehensive information about retirement planning is often appreciated by employees.

However, providing retirement planning information also has several benefits for employers, including:

- Increased appreciation of employer-provided benefits — The increased awareness and understanding of employer-provided benefits as one of the pillars of the employee's retirement plan means that he or she better appreciates those benefits.

- *A more self-reliant workforce* — Employees who understand their own responsibilities for their future welfare can plan ahead for themselves. Retirement planning information is another way to communicate to employees what is an employer's responsibility, and perhaps most importantly, what is theirs.

- *Workforce planning* — As mentioned above, employees approaching retirement often find that concerns over psychological and lifestyle transitions are greater than financial concerns. This can result in a disengaged workforce of employees who no longer want to work, but are not psychologically ready to retire. Retirement planning information can assist employees in considering the options in advance, encouraging a smooth transition to retirement.

- *Improved governance* — For pension plans, governance is synonymous with the CAP and CAPSA guidelines. The CAP guidelines indicate that in order to decide which types of information and decision-making tools to provide to CAP members, the CAP sponsor should consider:
  - The purpose of the plan;
  - What types of decisions members must make;
  - The cost of the information and decision-making tools;
  - The location, diversity, and demographics of the members; and
  - The members' access to computers and the Internet.

The CAP guidelines go on to state that, "for example, members of a retirement plan should be provided with information and tools that focus on retirement planning".

The CAPSA guidelines are less explicit with respect to retirement planning information, but state that the plan administrator should consider both its fiduciary and other responsibilities when deciding what to disclose, the manner and form of disclosure, and to whom the information will be disclosed. In addition, the plan administrator should consider providing members with information on the benefits, risks, and responsibilities inherent in membership in the plan, and should provide members with sufficient information to make informed decisions about their options under the pension plan.

Despite CAP and CAPSA guidelines, there are no legal requirements to provide retirement planning information to employees. The provision of such information does not provide the plan sponsor with a "safe harbour" as provided under ERISA in the U.S. It is yet to be determined whether a Canadian employer providing retirement planning information is still vulnerable to litigation relating to communication of their pension plan. However, it is widely believed that compliance with industry best practices (i.e., compliance with the CAP and CAPSA guidelines) will go far in proving to the courts that an employer has fulfilled its fiduciary duty.[1]

Reasons Against

There are several reasons for an employer to choose not to provide retirement planning information:

- *No obligation* — For example, through an Employee Assistance Program, an employer might provide assistance in finding a doctor, but would not provide the doctor. Perhaps an employer's fiduciary duty in providing retirement planning information is met by providing a list of local retirement planners.

- *Concern regarding providing advice* — Canadian courts have not yet dealt with the issue of plan sponsor liability for providing or making available poor financial advice to a plan member. However, there is a fine line in providing retirement planning information for employees. Employers may choose to provide information to help fulfill their fiduciary obligations, but employers must ensure that the information provided does not add to their liability.

- *Uncompetitive pension plan* — Employers with less generous pension plans may be reluctant to draw attention to the arrangement, especially if employees are not voicing any

---

[1]   For further discussion on these guidelines please see Chapter 4.

concerns. Others feel that it is not only important to communicate what employees have through their employer arrangements, but also what they don't have.

- *Too many employees retiring* — Some employers are beginning to experience labour shortages, and many are concerned over possible future shortages. If employees are remaining at work, and are fully engaged in their work, an employer may be less likely to provide retirement planning information that may cause an increase in retirements.

Each employer must explore its own reasons for and against providing retirement planning information, as well as the goals of providing such information, target audience, and topics to be covered.

Format

Retirement planning information can take many different forms. In general, the best approach is to provide information in as many ways as possible, allowing employees to choose the format best suited to them. Employers should consider what combination of the following delivery formats will best reach the majority of their target audience, within budget restrictions.

Retirement Planning Booklets

Booklets typically require a larger initial investment than other options, but are more easily updated. This format provides written material for employees to review at their convenience, and requires no other tools, such as computer or Internet access. However, there is no guarantee that employees will read the booklets, and employees may require a contact to address further questions.

A thorough retirement planning booklet will include content related to the financial (including government, employer-provided, and individual sources of income), psychological, and health transitions in retirement, as well as worksheets and/or spreadsheets and references for further information.

E-Learning

Many employers use e-learning tools with great success for purposes of job-related training for employees; making use of this format is a natural option to explore for retirement planning information. This can be an effective format for employees who are accustomed to receiving information online and in smaller chunks, and is an excellent way to reach a geographically dispersed employee base.

E-learning is typically used in situations where an employer requires proof that an employee has completed modules of job-related training, achieving a minimum level of knowledge when tested. For some employees, gaining retirement planning knowledge in smaller modules with regular interactive quizzes for reinforcement is appropriate. However, some employees find the regular testing approach to be too stringent for topics related to personal development.

Retirement Planning Tools and Mobile Apps

Tools and apps continue to be an area of rapid expansion . All of the major banks provide readily available retirement planning tools, and the federal government provides the Canadian Retirement Income Calculator.[2]

In addition, many third-party pension administrators and insurance companies offer retirement planning tools and mobile apps as a standard or additional feature of their services. The advantage of this option for retirement planning tools is the ability for members to access information tailored to their employer pension plan, drawing on personal information, capital accumulation account balances, and/or projecting their defined benefit pension at various commencement dates.

Retirement planning tools should include calculators as well as written information and links to additional information. The tools should assist individuals in estimating not only their retirement income, but also their retirement budget. The ability to save various scenarios is a valuable feature, as is the ability to include household income (rather than just the employee's individual sources of retirement income).

While retirement planning tools are valuable in assisting employees with their retirement planning, employees are often reluctant to use them without some encouragement, therefore, demonstration sessions can be effective. As a result, providing employees with the option to work with online tools and/or participate in retirement planning seminars may be the most beneficial approach.

---

[2]   The Canadian Retirement Income Calculator is available at http://www.esdc.gc.ca/en/cpp/cric.page.

Retirement Planning Seminars

Retirement planning seminars are perhaps the most effective way of providing information to employees where geographical dispersion permits. For employers intent on providing information to all employees, seminars could be offered on a mandatory basis, during paid work-time. However, most employers choose to offer seminars on a voluntary basis.

Consideration should be given to the appropriate length of seminars. While a three-hour delivery format can work for a live presentation, this is too long for a web seminar delivery. If possible, seminars should be provided in a series of 1.5 to 2-hour sessions spread over a period of weeks or months.

In some cases, employers choose to offer retirement planning seminars in a one- or two-day format. This approach is typically reserved for employees very close to retirement who are willing to dedicate a full day (or perhaps a weekend) to gaining retirement planning knowledge. While this is an excellent format to encourage spouses to attend, this is a tiring format for attendees and may result in lower retention of information.

Consideration should also be given to the delivery format. Generally, face-to-face communication is the most effective way to communicate with a group. The presenter can immediately see who the audience is, and adapt their strategy to fit audience needs. In addition, participants typically share stories or news articles that can be verified or disproved by the presenter. Where there is a mix of participants in different geographical locations, webcast sessions are a good solution. They limit the cost of travel, while allowing the speaker to have "live" access to their audience.

A webcast involving video streaming of the presenter, allowing participants to see the presenter in real-time, can be effective. However, this is a more expensive delivery method, typically reserved for larger organizations or presentations, such as at an Annual General Meeting, where participants are located around the globe.

A challenge in offering retirement planning seminars is encouraging employees to attend. A particular problem can be failure to attend by employees who previously registered. There are several ways to encourage attendance:

- Offer seminars during paid work-time;
- Offer a choice of seminar times;
- Provide food;
- Offer incentives such as a draw for all participants;

- Require employees to pay a portion (or all) of the cost; or
- Use reverse billing (i.e., if an employee does not attend the session they registered for, they are required to pay a fee and will not be eligible to attend future sessions).

Recorded Seminars

Due to the lack of face-to-face interaction, and production costs, recorded seminars should be used only as an alternative to live seminars when all or most of the following conditions are met:

- Employees are geographically dispersed;
- Work conditions do not permit seminars to be offered during paid work-time and employees are reluctant to attend seminars on their own time;
- Employees are unlikely to read information; and
- Employees do not have access to computers or the Internet.

Ideally, recorded seminars should be taped in small modules lasting no more than 30 minutes. However, some employers choose to record a longer live seminar. Employees unable to attend the live seminar would then be able to view the recording at their own convenience.

Gamification

Many employers, banks and insurance companies are looking to gamification (i.e., the application of game playing elements, such as points scoring, competition, rules of play) to engage employees in retirement planning.

Of course, planning for retirement is not a game — yet the techniques of gamification make a serious topic far more approachable. In fact, many employers are looking to gamification to engage employees in retirement planning and to help motivate them to plan for their future.

Gamification techniques include:

- Implementing a contest that sets up different locations or work teams against each other to see which group can increase their knowledge of retirement best practices;
- Mobile apps or online features that enable participants to visualize different scenarios for retirement, based on their savings and investing activity; and
- Leveraging online calculators that use gaming techniques — such as a retirement "number" or "score" — to motivate employees to

save more, invest appropriately, and achieve higher levels of success.

Target Audience

The information needs of younger employees in the early- to mid-career stages differ significantly from those of employees approaching retirement. Depending on the goals and budget of the plan sponsor, several approaches for delivering information to employee groups are common:

- *Target particular groups*: Priority for receiving information could be given to certain groups of members — for example, members over a certain age, or members of particular divisions, full-time members versus part-time. This approach is typically used where an employer has a limited budget, and/or a large number of employees who are very close to retirement. This approach is also useful where an early retirement window or downsizing program is driving the employer's interest in providing retirement planning information. Targeting a particular group allows the employer to tailor the information provided to the needs of that audience.

- *Waves of invitations*: To provide seminars on a cost-effective basis, some employers elect to invite only those members above a certain age in the first year. The age limit may be decreased gradually from one year to the next, in order to stagger the audience and ensure that priority is given to those closest to retirement. This approach is also effective where there is a limited budget available.

- *Waves of information*: Some employers begin with providing general information useful to employees of all ages and career stages, with successive waves of information gradually targeting those closer to retirement. This approach has the advantage of reaching the maximum number of employees in the shortest time, perhaps maximizing compliance with governance objectives.
  - An alternate approach is to provide information targeted towards those close to retirement first, with future waves of information targeted towards younger employee groups.

- *Open invitation*: The majority of employers choose to provide the same information to all employees at the same time. By clearly defining the target audience and topics to be covered, employees can decide for themselves whether or not it would be beneficial for them to attend.

Regardless of target audience, if retirement planning information is delivered to employees in information sessions or seminars, consideration should be given to inviting spouses to attend. While this invitation is typically greatly appreciated by members, it is usually a low-cost option due to low take-up rates. If desired, a fee could be charged for spouses attending a seminar.

Most information sessions are given in English and/or French. If there are members who speak a first language other than English or French, it can sometimes be useful to invite adult children to attend as they are often responsible for helping parents navigate their way through the Canadian retirement system.

Providers

There are many providers of retirement planning information and services. The following table outlines several alternatives, along with the advantages and disadvantages of each.

OPTION	PROs	CONs	COST
Organization's own HR representatives	• Low cost, Accessible • No actual or perceived bias - not affiliated with any company that sells financial products • Knowledge of typical member questions	• May need to be trained • May need to research and develop information • Not perceived to be "experts" in retirement planning (regardless of background or education)	• N/A • May be cost related to developing content
Financial Planners	• Low/no cost • Experts in financial side of retirement planning • Often willing to do one-on-one financial counselling sessions	• Actual or perceived bias — may try to sell financial products or further services • Potential implied endorsement of financial planner for individual services • Ability to focus only on financial issues • Not experts in registered pension plans	• Likely low or no cost

OPTION	PROs	CONs	COST
Insurance company representatives	• Low/no cost • Experts in financial side of retirement planning	• Actual or perceived bias - may try to sell financial or insurance products	• Likely low or no cost
Pension and benefit consultants, employee assistance program providers	• Experts in subject matter • Coverage of financial and non-financial retirement planning topics, if desired • No actual or perceived bias - not affiliated with any company that sells financial products • Knowledge of typical member questions • Employee assistance program providers may also provide information related to psychological and health transitions in retirement	• Higher cost	• Fee for service, typically charging by the hour

Who Pays

In many cases, the employer or plan sponsor takes responsibility for the cost of providing retirement planning information. However, in some situations the cost may be shared or paid for entirely by employees or trade unions. Capital accumulation-type pension arrangements may already require regular monthly or annual fees from members. A portion of this fee may be allocated to employee communications, including retirement planning booklets, seminars, or software.

It should also be noted that pension legislation allows for payment of fees associated with the administration of a registered pension plan from the pension fund. In determining whether it is appropriate to pay for retirement planning information from the pension fund, it is important for the plan administrator to consider what types or topics of retirement planning information may be considered to be "associated with the administration" of the plan. For example, while most would agree that coverage of the terms of the pension plan are clearly associated with the administration of the plan, does this extend to coverage of government pensions or individual savings? Should information pertaining to lifestyle transitions be paid for from the plan?

From a governance perspective, the prudent plan sponsor should document the reasons for, and goals of, providing retirement planning information. In addition, any committee discussion leading to a decision regarding payment of fees associated with providing retirement planning information from the fund should also be documented.

Content

Many employers focus first on the financial side of planning for retirement. Where improved governance is the primary reason for providing retirement planning information, this is likely sufficient. However, once employees have taken care of the financial components of planning for retirement, the decision to retire becomes about more than money — a complete and successful transition to retirement involves consideration of lifestyle, health, and even legal concerns. Indeed, for the employer concerned with workforce planning, inclusion of non-financial topics is certainly appropriate.

From the employee's perspective, the level of interest in retirement planning topics is largely age-dependent. For younger employees who are early in their career, a brief description focusing on establishing and reaching savings targets is likely sufficient. As employees approach retirement eligibility, they become more interested in the details of both financial and non-financial plans for retirement.

The following provides a summary of the financial and non-financial topics that could be included in a complete retirement planning offering, broken down by career stage:

Early- to Mid-Career

- *Planning and saving*: Information at this level needs to put the retirement planning exercise in context. Employees should be guided through an overview of the key elements required to build a successful financial strategy. Topics could include:
  - The importance of planning;
  - Life expectancy and retirement income;

- o Rules of thumb for establishing and reaching retirement savings goals at different career stages;

- o Earning benefits while employed: government benefits and employer-sponsored programs;

- o A summary of the employer's pension plan(s);

- o How to use retirement planning tools available, if any; and

- o Choosing a financial adviser.

- *Investment topics*: Members of capital accumulation-type arrangements typically have investment information available to them through administration or investment manager websites. However, this information is often written assuming a basic understanding of investment terminology. Many employees do not have this basic understanding, and therefore need introductory level information to provide an unbiased view of investment concepts.

- Information at this level should be designed to simplify terminology and increase comfort with investment decisions, to help plan members understand and work with the forces that drive the markets. Many employers find that offering basic investment information increases the number of plan members making investment choices under their capital accumulation arrangement, thereby decreasing the number invested in the default fund offering. Investment topics could include:

- o Asset classes;

- o Investor profile and risk tolerance;

- o The importance of asset allocation and how to choose an appropriate mix;

- o Overview of pension plan investment options under the employer plan, if any;

- o Investment strategy and expected returns;

- o The impact of investment management fees;

- o Reviewing the investment strategy; and

- o Seeking professional advice.

Mid- to Late-Career

Between ages 40 and 55, employees become more willing to spend time planning for retirement, and more willing to take responsibility for retirement planning. Retirement planning information is typically well-received at this stage, and a wide variety of topics can be introduced to employees.

- *Sources of retirement income*: Retirement income can be paid in many forms, each with its own rules, advantages and restrictions. Information should provide employees with details with respect to the various sources of retirement income — government and employer-provided, as well as individual savings. Information might also include:
  - o   Forms of pension, transfer options, and descriptions of LIFs, LIRAs, and annuities;
  - o   Estimating benefit amounts;
  - o   Eligibility for benefits, tax issues and death benefits;
  - o   Other sources of income (assets, post-employment careers); and
  - o   Information for those who choose to retire outside of Canada.
- *Budgeting for retirement*: Early in an employee's career, it is likely sufficient (and likely all the employee will have energy for) to establish retirement savings targets based on rules of thumb, such as the typical 70% replacement ratio. However, as employees get closer to retirement, it is important to refine this estimate. Topics could include:
  - o   Guidance through the process of budgeting for the various phases of retirement by preparing a real budget;
  - o   How and when to budget for retirement;
  - o   Consideration of how changes in lifestyle will impact expenses;
  - o   Budgeting exercises;
  - o   Information with respect to typical expenses and expected lifetimes;
  - o   Impact of taxes and inflation; and
  - o   Where to get help.
- *Legal issues at retirement*: Retirement is a good time for employees to review their legal affairs, as this life transition can cause changes in needs. Topics could include:
  - o   Estate planning;
  - o   Wills and intestacy rules;
  - o   Beneficiary designations;
  - o   Insurance and taxes;
  - o   Gifts;
  - o   Trusts and guardianship;
  - o   Personal planning;

- ○ Powers of attorney;
- ○ Living wills;
- ○ Travel insurance;
- ○ Impact of life changes such as death of spouse, divorce, remarriage, or illness; and
- ○ Where to get help.

- *Benefits protection*: Income protection, financial security and housing needs also change at retirement. Employees need to plan for their benefit and insurance needs at retirement and review available options and decision factors. Information could include:
  - ○ Life and health insurance needs (options, sources, typical costs);
  - ○ Employer-sponsored group benefits at retirement, if any;
  - ○ Government-provided benefits and health programs;
  - ○ Residential care options and costs;
  - ○ Sources of support and information services; and
  - ○ How to choose an insurance agent.

- *Lifestyle planning*: The "softer" side of planning for retirement also becomes relevant to employees at this stage of their career. Information can help employees create a vision of a meaningful and fulfilling future as they emotionally prepare for retirement. An exploration of changes in work, attitudes, relationships, and leisure as employees move towards retirement can assist in a smooth transition, and an engaged workforce. Topics could include:
  - ○ Consideration of retirement transition models (e.g., phased retirement versus the traditional view of retirement as an event);
  - ○ Trends, flexible work options, and finding the right fit;
  - ○ Relationships (i.e., building and maintaining supports, changing relationships, larger community);
  - ○ Exploring options with respect to leisure time and incorporating choices; and
  - ○ Approach to life and attitudes that sustain optimal health.

- *Health issues*: To complete the retirement planning offering and take the opportunity to encourage a healthy workforce, information can also be provided to increase awareness and understanding of age-relevant health issues by providing a list of key considerations for lifelong healthy living. Topics may include:

- o   Consideration of typical physiological changes (e.g., normal aging versus disease);
- o   Wellness topics by decade, to encourage employees to make healthy choices now that will result in healthier retirement years;
- o   The yearly physical (what to ask for);
- o   Nutrition and weight management;
- o   Stress; and
- o   Exercise.

Late-Career

- *Review of transition topics*: Employees in the final approach to retirement may need a review of topics previously covered, to give them detailed information to assist in completing forms and choosing between options at retirement. Information could include:
  - o   Tangible and intangible factors in the decision to retire;
  - o   Changing their mind;
  - o   Options (i.e., part-time work, phased retirement);
  - o   How and when to transfer funds and claim various sources of income;
  - o   Commencing pension payments;
  - o   Forms of pension for defined benefit arrangements, and how to choose between them;
  - o   Transfer options and considerations for defined contribution arrangements;
  - o   Drug benefit coverage;
  - o   Investment strategy; and
  - o   Choosing an advisor.

Governance Considerations

The delivery of retirement planning information to employees has many advantages for both employees and employers. While the employer may have many reasons for providing retirement planning information, improved governance is a significant consideration. From a governance perspective, employers should give consideration to how to monitor the usage and effectiveness of the information provided. In addition, copies of the invitations to the seminars or sessions and information provided should be archived, along with employee attendance and feedback received.

Chapter 29

COMMUNICATING BENEFITS AND RETIREMENT SAVINGS PLANS

Executive Summary[1]

Well-designed and carefully planned communication is essential to increase employees' understanding and appreciation of benefits and retirement savings plans and, therefore, maximize the return on the organization's investments.

There are seven steps to the development of a successful communication strategy, from setting objectives to measuring success. Key steps include knowing your audiences, developing key messages and selecting the right media.

Communicating benefits and retirement savings plans is also subject to specific laws, regulations, and guidelines that every plan sponsor needs to carefully consider.

Why Effective Communication Is So Important

When dealing with benefits and retirement savings plans, chances are a "quick memo" will be insufficient in generating the positive perception the organization is hoping for among employees. Many employees may simply never see or notice this single communication in the mountains of documents that hit their desks, inboxes, and homes every day. Many others may not understand how the pension or benefits plans work and may require a lot more information. And — worst case — employees may perceive the communication as bad news because of a lack of background information or poor understanding of basic notions.

---

[1] For more information on required member communications related to pension plans, please consult the multi-jurisdictional charts in the *Canadian Employment Benefits & Pension Guide*. Morneau Shepell, *Canadian Employment Benefits & Pension Guide*, loose-leaf (Toronto: LexisNexis Canada, 2003). The table of contents for these charts appears at the back of this Handbook.

This may sound a bit drastic, but this is a surprisingly common experience among organizations that approach employee communication as an afterthought. Organizations that are successful at engaging employees in understanding the full scope of their "total company rewards" and in the rationale for change are often those that have the highest employee satisfaction and retention. Successfully engaging employees is best achieved through a well-thought-out and thorough communication strategy.

Successful organizations invest time, effort, and money in communication for the same reasons they offer benefits and retirement savings plans in the first place: to attract, retain, and engage their employees. Benefits and retirement savings plans are important components of the total rewards package, and ensuring they are well understood and appreciated by employees is the best way to maximize the return on investment.

There are many more immediate reasons for effective communication of benefits and retirement savings plans:

- Improving employees' awareness and understanding of both the plans and their value;
- Complying with legal requirements;
- Ensuring employees manage their plans well and use the available tools effectively;
- Helping employees manage their own health effectively; and
- Helping employees make important insurance and retirement decisions.

Working toward these goals through a well-designed communication strategy will naturally lead to increased employee appreciation and buy-in. In addition, it will encourage greater ownership and responsibility among employees for their individual health and retirement planning.

The Strategic Communication Process

Effective employee communication begins with a well-crafted strategy and careful planning. Whether the purpose is to create permanent reference material on benefits and retirement savings plans, introduce a new plan, communicate small changes to an existing plan, or provide ongoing education about benefits and savings, the overall process is the same. Typically, designing any communication strategy follows a seven-step process:

Following this process will focus the communication efforts and ensure they meet both the organization's and employees' needs. Let's look at each of these steps in more detail.

Setting Objectives

The first step in designing a successful communication strategy is setting the overall objectives, as they will help focus the required communication effort and will strongly influence the whole strategy. The communication objectives should be clear, well-articulated, and measurable at the end of the process.

Common objectives in communicating benefits and retirement savings plans include:

Awareness objectives	Understanding objectives	Acceptance objectives
Ensure employees are aware of: • Plan offerings • Benefits changes • Enrolment/ reenrolment process • Available tools and resources	Increase employees' understanding of: • Benefits and savings issues • How the plans work • Rationale for change • Employee responsibilities • Benefits value	Ensure employees: • Enrol on time and without error • Accept and support change • Adopt new behaviours • Make sound benefits choices and decisions

A successful communication strategy will typically include a mix of awareness, understanding and acceptance objectives.

If employees need to make important benefits choices or decisions at any point during their participation in the organization's benefits and retirement savings plans, this will also have significant influence on the communication strategy. In these situations, employees need to understand the cost-benefit equation of each decision they make and the risks attached to each option. They also need clear and complete information, as well as tools and education to help them make their decisions. This clearly calls for more sophisticated media and personalized information.

In today's environment, the prevailing message for employees is that plan participation requires shared accountability and not just passive entitlement. This is not only true for defined contribution pension arrangements and flexible group insurance programs, where the biggest challenge is motivating employees to take ownership of their plans and related decisions, but even more so in the case of the more recent "shared risk" type of pension plans, whereby member benefits can be affected by the plan's financial situation. In that context, members need to be even more engaged in the monitoring of their plan's situation in order to promptly readjust their retirement planning strategy — if there is a need to do so — to ensure they remain on the right track in view of their retirement.

Employees need to be self-reliant and actively plan for their well-being and financial security, and this sharing of responsibilities needs to be supported by well-designed communication and education programs. Plan sponsors need to provide sufficient education to help employees make informed decisions about their insurance coverage and their savings and investments. The best way to deepen employees' knowledge and appreciation of their benefits is to communicate with them year round, not just during specific time windows such as open enrollment. Regular, short communication that focuses on the specific actions and behaviors plan sponsors want to encourage is a best practice for engaging employees. However, plan sponsors must not cross the line between information and advice if they want to avoid legal liability.

Analyzing the Audience

Next to articulating clear objectives, defining and understanding the various audiences that have a stake in the benefits and retirement savings plans is key to designing a successful communication program.

The audiences can include a number of different employee segments:

- Front line, sales, and head office;
- Union, non-union, hourly, and salaried;
- Administrators, managers, and executives;
- Full-time, part-time, and temporary; or
- Active employees, retirees, and individuals on leave.

They can also include several subsets of employees, who may require different and/or additional communication to support their roles in assisting employees. These might include:

- Human resources professionals, as the perceived "owners" of the benefits and retirement savings plans or "experts" supporting the organization on these matters;

- People managers, given their front-line role in answering their employees' questions and concerns; and
- Senior executives, as they often need to understand the business and operational impact of changes to the employee offer.

While these groups are certainly key, the objective should not be to make them into benefits experts. Rather, they need to be informed in advance of any communication coming to their employees and be comfortable conveying key messages related to the benefits and retirement savings plans. They can also be important influencers of opinion and buy-in during major change, so it is important to be aware of and support their roles.

Once all audiences have been identified, it is important to clarify what it is they each need to think, say, or do with regard to the benefits and savings programs. With this information, it is easier to understand the transition or actions that the audiences need to take and the supporting tools and information they will need to do so.

It is also important to be sensitive to the current state of employee morale. Communicating at times when employees are discontented with an organization must be very different from times when employees are positive and supportive of the organization. Understanding the other changes that might be going on in the organization, as well as each audience's specific needs and concerns, will help gauge the audiences' expected reactions to the communications and plan them in a way that addresses audience concerns directly and sets a positive tone.

Demographics, such as location, language, age, comprehension level, education, tenure, and online sophistication, may also play a large factor in the communication planning.

For example, considering generational differences is key to preparing more targeted communication, especially as interest in retirement planning and health care varies greatly with age. Communication targeted to a younger demographic could use language that is a bit more relaxed, focus on the first steps toward financial wellness and rely on media channels that are more popular among a younger audience to grab their attention. By comparison, communication for members belonging to an older demographic could use language that is a bit more formal, focus on financial security and key retirement decisions and reflect an older audience's reading needs. Ideally, communicating by demographic implies that there could be several iterations of the same booklet, website, email, etc., to reflect the different information needs and learning styles of the audience. If that is not possible, generational differences should at least be taken into consideration in the drafting of the generic communications pieces.

New hires are another audience with special needs. They need short, simple, and heavily branded communication that will make a good lasting first impression and help them make sense of complex benefits plans at a time when they are overloaded with new information.

Audience analysis can also take into account the life stage of the employee within the organization. From a work perspective, employees who switch from a temporary to a regular employment status, for example, will have specific communication needs (i.e., benefits they are now eligible for and the actions they need to take). From a personal perspective, employees going on maternity or parental leave, sick leave, getting married or divorced will require customized communication to guide them during these particular life events. Given the huge amounts of personal employee information contained in the HR databases of mid to large organizations, it is possible to harness the data available to provide employees with the information they need, when they need it.

When dealing with sensitive issues, such as major benefits changes, some organizations will want to test the water with employees before finalizing the plan design or the communication plan. This can be achieved through individual interviews, surveys, focus groups, or a mix of all these methods. Collecting employee input and anticipating their reactions is essential when introducing or communicating a plan that is supposed to be based on employee needs, such as a flexible group benefits program. Engaging employees in plan design is extremely useful in developing a program that fits better with employees' needs, in reducing the risks of failure or negative reaction, and in delivering effective communication. In some cases, employee consultation can be a decisive factor in securing employee buy-in and can greatly contribute to enhancing the employer's image and brand. However, consultation must be conducted with expert care to ensure employees' expectations are managed appropriately.

Developing a Content Inventory

The next step in designing an effective communication strategy is to clearly define the subject matter and make a list of topics that will need to be covered. Benefits and retirement savings communication usually goes beyond basic plan details to address common employee questions and concerns. It is often useful and even necessary to provide a broader picture of relevant benefits and retirement savings issues to increase understanding and appreciation.

Typical topics that may be included in a benefits and retirement savings communication plan include:

- The rationale for change and how/if it fits into the broader organizational and/or human resources objectives;
- How the plans work and detailed plan provisions;
- Basic group benefits plan principles and explaining what drives group benefits costs and technical plan terms like deductibles, maximums, and limitations;
- Basic investment principles and concepts like risk tolerance, diversification, and fund volatility;
- General retirement planning issues, such as how to create an appropriate retirement savings plan and how to recognize and address shortfalls in retirement savings;
- General health care issues, such as why health care costs are increasing so rapidly and why prevention and wellness are important;
- How to make benefits choices and decisions;
- Administrative procedures, including how to enroll/make changes, how to submit claims, how to transfer current or change future allocations in defined contribution plans, and what is required to take early retirement and start a pension benefit;
- The cost of benefits and retirement savings plans and, more specifically, the cost sharing between the employer and the employees;
- The full value of the employer's investment in its employees — including the value of benefits and retirement savings plans — in a broader total rewards framework;
- An explanation of what benefits are taxable and when;
- Plan member responsibilities; and
- Government plans, how they evolve, and the implications the changes have for members.

In developing a content inventory, it is important to constantly refer back to the audiences' needs and concerns to ensure they are addressed. It is also important to remember that benefits and retirement savings communication may be subject to provincial and/or federal regulatory requirements, such as pension legislation requirements and the Capital Accumulation Plan (CAP) Guidelines.

Branding and Key Messages

Creating a specific brand for the communication program and articulating the key messages is another strategic communication step. Ideally, branding and key messages should align with the broader organizational and human resources values, objectives, and image. As with every step in the communication design process, key messages in particular should also take into account the audiences' needs, issues, and concerns.

Identifying the key messages will ensure important messages are communicated with clarity, consistency, and maximum impact across all media. Key messages typically address basic questions such as:

- What is the purpose of the plan?
- What are the advantages of the plan?
- What is changing and why?
- What is the impact of the changes on employees?
- What is the cost sharing?

Branding and key messages should be reviewed and approved by all relevant program stakeholders before developing any communication material.

Evaluating and Selecting Media

More than ever, communicators have an expansive range of communication channels at their disposal. The challenge is not in finding a channel — it is in recognizing which channel(s) will be the most effective for each audience and message. Adult learning patterns are quite diverse. Some people will typically prefer face-to-face communication, while others will learn more efficiently by reading. Increasingly, younger employees want information delivered in short, digestible bites — typically through the online and mobile communication channels they use most.

Moreover, repetition and reinforcement greatly increase comprehension. Studies repeatedly show that people retain information best when it is provided to them in a number of different ways. For all these reasons, a successful communication strategy will likely integrate many different channels or media.

The selected media should match the communication objectives, the characteristics of the audiences, the messages being communicated, and the nature of the organization. For example, it is unlikely that a large manufacturing facility will successfully communicate its programs if it relies entirely on electronic channels. Conversely, print distribution may be ineffective for a highly mobile workforce, such as a national sales organization. Production and distribution requirements may also influence these choices. Other factors such as the culture of the organization, the environment, budget constraints, or a requirement for frequent updates may narrow the options to be considered as well.

Below are some considerations on the typical communication channels used for communicating benefits and retirement savings plans.

Electronic

In this era of rapidly proliferating electronic devices, applications, and tools, electronic channels of all shapes and sizes are increasingly becoming an essential part of most organizations' internal communication planning tool kit. Electronic media that organizations currently use include:

- Internet and intranet sites and portals;
- Decision support and modelling tools;
- Email;
- Narrated online demos, tutorials, and videos; and
- E-magazines.

Internet and Intranet Sites and Portals

A benefits website allows employees to find the information they need anywhere and anytime. It is probably the most important investment an organization can make in their benefits communication as a website will live on, well after costly enrollment guides are forgotten or dense pension booklets are thrown away.

Current trends in benefits website include making them available on the Internet rather than the intranet so that employees and their families can have easy access to the information, and making them responsive, that is, adaptable to the device they are accessed on. This way, users can see the website in the most optimal layout whether it is accessed from a laptop, a tablet or a mobile phone.

Decision Support and Modelling Tools

Decision support tools aimed at helping employees make informed decisions about their benefits — during open enrollment, for example — or their savings in view of their retirement are increasingly popular. They are extremely powerful when developed with a strong end-user perspective in mind and with plain language help tips.

Email

Email is certainly one of the most used channels for benefits communication. To stand out in the sea of emails that employees receive each day, subject lines must be enticing to grab the reader's attention and message content must be kept short, ideally one subject and action per email, with links to full details. A banner and some visual elements can also make the email more attractive.

Narrated Online Demos, Tutorials and Videos

These types of recorded communications are a good alternative for audiences who prefer to "see and hear" rather than to read, and for groups of employees who may not be able to attend a live and/or face-to-face information session. When used efficiently (i.e., when the content does not last more than two minutes and the language used is carefully chosen to convey simple messages), they can be a powerful communication tool.

E-Magazines

E-magazines are powerful communication tools to generate excitement around a new program or initiative or to explain changes being made to a program. E-magazines combine the capabilities and features of several media into a single platform that can be accessed electronically, via email, or hosted on a web site. E-magazines are usually menu-driven and contain hyperlinks to other websites or documents. Content is animated, like in PowerPoint presentations, with high quality graphics. They also allow for the integration of video clips. E-magazines are highly effective in motivating employees to take action and in promoting new initiatives.

When computers or other electronic devices are not readily accessible to employees at work, organizations are also employing innovative solutions to address the problem, such as providing on-site, self-service kiosks.

Electronic communication media have many advantages: they are available around the clock, they are easily updated, they enable easy research of information, they facilitate personalized communication and powerful interactive tools, and they are "green".

Electronic media are clearly the norm for benefits and retirement savings plan administration, and communication solutions can often be efficiently integrated into these tools. They allow for an employee self-service model, where tools and information are made available to employees electronically to access when they need them.

Face-to-Face

Face-to-face communication includes group information sessions, individual meetings, and information booths. Face-to-face communication remains one of the most effective means of delivering messages and engaging employees because it is the only channel that is truly two-way and interactive. Surveys regularly show that employees prefer to receive information on benefits and retirement savings plans in small group meetings, where they can direct questions to the speaker/specialists. Face-to-face communication also provides an opportunity to gather feedback on what employees understand or appreciate in their benefits and retirement savings plans.

When the strategy includes objectives such as educating employees on complex benefits issues or helping them making important decisions, face-to-face communication is essential. Face-to-face communication is also key when communicating major changes or introducing benefits to new employees.

Webcasts/Webinars

Webcasts and webinars are becoming increasingly popular within organizations that need to communicate with employees across different/remote geographic locations. They are a good alternative to face-to-face meetings or training sessions, as they can either be interactive, allowing employees to ask questions and obtain immediate answers, or pre-recorded, allowing employees to listen to the presentation during or after office hours, submit their questions online, and obtain answers within a given period of time.

Social Media

In the 15th edition of this Handbook published in 2012, we reported that organizations were starting to look at ever more cutting-edge communication delivery methods — such as Facebook, LinkedIn, Twitter, YouTube, blogs, online chat, and RSS feeds — to communicate with employees at all levels, but particularly with the growing Generation Y workforce.

Since then, surveys conducted in the United States and Canada indicate that organizations having used social media for benefits communication remain solidly in the minority. Top reasons provided for not using social media include lack of time, staff and resources to devote to launching and maintaining social media and lack of executive buy-in about social media's effectiveness for benefits communication.

From an employee perspective, survey results also indicate that employees are not comfortable with the idea of hearing from their employer through social media tools such as Facebook — a platform most commonly used to stay in touch with friends, relatives and families — which survey respondents feel are more closely associated with their private lives than their work lives.

This does not mean that all social media tools are inappropriate for benefits communication. When used appropriately, as part of an integrated communication strategy and as a complement to traditional channels, the social media tools listed below can contribute to engage employees in their health and financial decisions, especially younger ones, to communicate with them and their family more frequently, and to gather real-time feedback.

Ultimately, we must learn from social media and apply what is known to work best to the more traditional communication channels in order to communicate more effectively with the younger generation.

Most relevant social media tools for benefits communication		
Media	**What it is**	**When to use it**
Blog	Website consisting of posts displayed in reverse chronological order (most recent post appears first). A blog can be informational or more personal. Majority of blogs allow visitors to leave comments.	• To educate on a year-round basis • To increase awareness through discussion around an interesting topic • To obtain feedback
Microblog	Message limited to a set number of characters (i.e. currently 140 for Twitter). A micbroblog can be displayed as text message on mobile phones (at user's discretion). Feeds can also be pulled into websites.	• To promote (i.e. new website, new blog, new tool) • To provide factual info (i.e. important dates or deadlines, reminders and tips)
Podcast	Audio clip that can be downloaded and listened to at a later time.	• To educate

Print

Print communication includes newsletters, posters, decision and enrolment guides, booklets, personalized statements, question and answer documents, and an infinite variety of other printed material. Print is the traditional, and still widely used, medium for benefits and retirement savings communication, but it is losing ground to electronic media.

Print has the following advantages: it pushes information, it is highly portable, and it is the most appropriate medium for comprehending lengthy and detailed information. Plan sponsors often believe their plan members feel reassured by the tangibility of a booklet or a regular newsletter, and they are often right. For reference material, electronic media are sometimes simply the method highlighting brief key messages or for distributing content that employees will ultimately print and read.

One of the most powerful media for benefits and retirement savings communication is personalized print. The reason for its impact rests in its ability to address the quintessential communication challenge — "what's in it for me?" Providing a compelling and personalized answer to this question ensures the success of every communication effort. Personalized communication is also often used when employees have to make important personal decisions, such as choosing between two different types of pension plans or choosing benefit options that best fit their personal situations. Moreover, personalized pension statements are required by law.

Employers also use personalized communications to educate employees on the full value of their employment relationship through total rewards statements, which outline the costs of the total employment offering for both the employee and the employer, as well as any additional perquisites and offers employers may provide to their employees. While total rewards statements can be offered online as well, the most common delivery method is still print.

Contact Centres

Contact centre solutions include information hotlines (using toll-free numbers), call centres, interactive voice response systems, and online chat/response. Contact centre solutions are very effective for ongoing day-to-day questions and transactions and individual support in situations such as the introduction of a new plan or an enrolment campaign. They also provide a level of confidentiality that is essential to more personal questions.

Planning and Executing

Planning and executing effective benefits and retirement savings communication requires significant time and dedicated resources. After the objectives are set, the content and messages defined, and the media chosen, the planning and execution begin. Execution typically includes the following steps and requires strong communication and project management skills:

- Research and writing;
- Peer and technical reviews and revisions;
- Translation, when necessary;
- Testing of material with decision-makers and a representative sample of employees;
- More revisions;
- Graphic design, layout, and production; and
- Distribution.

The importance of pension and benefits experts conducting a "technical review" of all communication cannot be emphasized enough. The project plan should always include sufficient lead time for these reviews and their subsequent revisions.

One of the biggest challenges of communicating about complex benefits and retirement savings plans is writing content that is clear, simple, and free of jargon. This is particularly important when communicating limitations or exclusions, because these restrictions will not be enforceable if their explanations cannot be understood by the average plan member.

Measuring Success

To truly understand if the communication strategy is successful and having the desired impact, it needs to be measured and evaluated. It is critical to collect employee feedback and assess what was successful about the strategy and where improvements need to be made and to weave that information back into the evolving strategy for future communication. This feedback can be gathered in a variety of ways, including surveys, focus groups, interviews, or informal discussions.

The impact of communication is also observable and measurable through the actions and reactions of employees — such as questions asked during meetings, plan enrolment statistics, number of views of an e-magazine/webinar/video and usage patterns of the benefits and retirement savings plan website(s), if applicable. If there is a call centre, a look at the question log is also a good way to see what has been understood and not understood. People managers and supervisors are also a good source for understanding what employees are thinking.

Typically, measurement is the most often overlooked element of a benefits and retirement savings plan communication strategy. Remember, if it is not measured, it can't be managed. Thus, identifying "what success will look like" and how it will be measured during the communication strategy design will help identify the next steps, build on the successes, and avoid repeating the mistakes. For example, surveying employees' comprehension of key messages can help identify knowledge gaps early and reduce potential liability of "negligent misrepresentation" (see "Implications of Plan Member Communications" later in this chapter).

Finally, understanding the return on the communication investment in quantifiable terms can be helpful in budget discussions with the Chief Financial Officer.

Legal Aspects of Benefits and Retirement Savings Plans Communication

This next section summarizes the main aspects of legislation and regulations that have a direct or indirect influence on benefits and retirement savings plans communication.[2]

Pension Legislation Requirements

Currently, most pension standards legislation requires employers or plan sponsors to provide plan members numerous communications, including:

- A written description of the plan;
- A personalized printed annual statement; and
- A statement when an employee retires or "terminates" membership in a pension plan.

Additional statements or advance notices may also be required in particular situations, such as wind-ups, asset transfer applications, marriage breakdown, plan amendments, or surplus sharing applications.

An important consideration for plan sponsors is that these communications must be easily accessible and available to all plan members.

---

[2]   See Chapter 9 for more detailed information about pension legislation requirements related to communication.

In Quebec, the law also requires that a plan member meeting be held annually.

Electronic communication is discussed in a later section, "Electronic Communication and Guidelines".

Written Plan Description

Pension standards legislation across Canada requires the employer, plan sponsor, or plan administrator to ensure every plan member and eligible employee receives an explanation of how the plan works and a description of plan members' rights and responsibilities. In federally registered plans, the spouse of a plan member must also receive a copy of this information.

Simply distributing the official plan text is not a solution and may even be a dangerous way to handle this requirement for the plan sponsor. In Quebec, the law specifically states that the plan description must be a distinct printed document, written in plain language.

Usually, plan members receive this information as a summary of main plan provisions in booklet form. Unfortunately, writers of these booklets are often hesitant to stray far beyond the legal terms and jargon of the pension industry and, consequently, many of these booklets remain unread or misunderstood.

Taking the time and effort to write a plain language plan booklet is worth the investment. Being introduced to complex provisions and formulas in a straightforward, easy-to-read way can help a plan member extract meaning from the official plan documentation.

All plan amendments must also be explained to plan members in writing. Current legislation outlining when this information must be communicated varies from jurisdiction to jurisdiction.

Individual Annual Statement

In most jurisdictions, active plan members must receive a printed annual statement within six months (nine months in Quebec and New Brunswick) of the plan's year end. In Quebec, these statements must also be provided to non-active members.

The information required on these statements varies by jurisdiction but generally includes personal data, contribution amounts, service and benefit accruals, and retirement dates. For defined benefit plans, some jurisdictions also require the statement to include information about the plan's current financial status.

With the advent of shared risk pension plans in provinces such as New Brunswick, communication obligations are enhanced as the plan's situation could influence whether members' benefits are increased or decreased. Under article 20(4) of the New Brunswick Shared Risk Plan Regulation 2012-75, the administrator has the obligation to disclose specific information to the employer, members, former members and the trade union that represents the members within 12 months after the review date of each actuarial valuation report. Such information includes the open group funded ratio and termination value funded ratio of the plan; the investment performance of the fund; the administrator's assessment of the need to reduce benefits or the opportunity to increase benefits, including a description of the risk factors affecting the plan.

Statement When Plan Membership Ends

Current pension legislation requires that active plan members who end their membership in the plan or retire from the organization must receive a statement within 30 to 90 days of this event, depending on the jurisdiction. If a court order or domestic contract requires the division of pension benefits as a result of marriage breakdown, the spouse or former spouse of the member may also be entitled to a copy of this statement.

This statement must outline the deferred pension at retirement, as well as any opportunity for early or postponed retirement and the impact of either of these actions on the pension benefit. If a plan member can transfer funds out of the plan, the transfer value, options, and any restrictions related to a solvency deficiency must also be explained. In the case of plan wind-up, additional information concerning the wind-up and funded status of the plan may be required.

In the event of the death of a plan member, generally the spouse, common-law partner, beneficiary, or estate must receive a written statement that outlines any pension benefits payable from the plan.

Access to Information and Documentation

Current pension legislation ensures that plan members are entitled to view a variety of plan documents at least once a year. These documents may include the plan text, actuarial reports about the plan, as well as annual information returns and financial statements of the pension fund. Plan members can view this information at their employers' premises or at the provincial regulator's office. Since January 1, 2012, Ontario entitles members to electronic access to various plan documents. In a number of jurisdictions, this access is also available to an authorized agent of the plan member or the member's spouse.[3]

Guidelines for Capital Accumulation Plans

In 2004, the Joint Forum of Financial Market Regulators published the *Guidelines for Capital Accumulation Plans*.[4] These Guidelines set out rights and responsibilities for sponsors of capital accumulation plans such as defined contribution registered pension plans, group Registered Retirement Savings Plans, group Registered Education Savings Plans, and Deferred Profit Sharing Plans. These Guidelines reflect the expectations of all Canadian pension, insurance, and securities regulators. They do not replace legal requirements but, rather, supplement them.

Among other aspects, the Guidelines also provide guidance on communications for capital accumulation plans. More precisely, they define the responsibilities of plan sponsors in ensuring that employees have access to the necessary information and decision-making tools and receive regular statements and reports regarding the plan and the plan investment options. The Guidelines clearly stipulate that even if a service provider is used, the plan sponsor is still responsible for ensuring that this provider fulfills the obligations under the Guidelines.

Electronic Communication Guidelines

Although many issues surrounding electronic communications remain to be resolved, electronic communication channels continue to evolve and play an increasingly more dominant role in retirement savings plans. In February 2002, Canadian Association of Pension Supervisory Authorities (CAPSA) released its *Guideline No. 2 — Electronic Communication in the Pension Industry*. In the Guideline, CAPSA states that the benefits of electronic communication are readily identifiable, namely reduced administrative costs, improved service for members, and enhanced fiduciary monitoring. As stated in the introduction, the intent of the Guideline is to help administrators and members "apply the provisions of applicable electronic commerce legislation to pension communications required under the pension benefits legislation in each jurisdiction". Furthermore, CAPSA states that the Guideline only applies to

---

[3]   See Chapter 9 for further information about access to information and documentation.

[4]   See Chapter 4 for further discussion of the CAP Guidelines.

communications between the administrator and members and is not meant to apply to other forms of pension communication.

According to the Guideline, where the applicable pension benefits standard legislation requires a written document to be provided to a member or vice versa, such communication can be achieved through electronic means. An electronic document must be accessible by the recipient and capable of being retained so that it can be used for subsequent review.

In addition, all jurisdictions in Canada have e-commerce legislation, which is intended to make the law media neutral. In other words, many documents that previously could only be communicated in paper format will be permitted in electronic form. A common theme running through e-commerce legislation and the CAPSA Guideline is that no one should be required to communicate or to receive communications electronically. This is necessary, as some employers and plan members may not want to communicate electronically and some simply may not be able to communicate electronically.

Legislative clarification regarding the status of electronic pension plan communications has resolved some of the uncertainty, thereby enabling administrators to forge ahead and make use of a more efficient communication medium. The Ontario Electronic Commerce Act, 2000, for example, specifies what the Act does not apply to, including wills and codicils, powers of attorney, agreements of purchase and sale, any documents that create or transfer interests in land, negotiable instruments, and documents that are prescribed by regulation. Pension documents are not mentioned. However, a beneficiary designation must still be signed in writing as a document akin to a will.

The Financial Services Commission of Ontario (FSCO) released Policy A300-805: Electronic Communication Between Plan Administrators and Plan Beneficiaries, providing some guidance to Ontario administrators. FSCO's Policy confirms that electronic communication between administrators and beneficiaries required under the Pension Benefits Act is acceptable as long as the communication complies with the Pension Benefits Act, Ontario's e-commerce legislation, and the CAPSA Guideline.

In some situations, documents that are communicated must be signed, and this leads to the use of electronic or digital signatures. There are special legal issues, such as validity of signatures and adequacy of communications, to consider when an administrator intends to use electronic signatures for matters such as making or changing beneficiary designations or spousal waivers. According to Ontario's e-commerce legislation, an "electronic signature" is defined as "electronic information that a person creates or adopts in order to sign a document and that is in, attached to or associated with the document". This definition is fairly universal, with slight variations from jurisdiction to jurisdiction. According to the CAPSA Guideline, an electronic signature must reliably identify the plan member and be associated with the relevant document in light of all the circumstances. However, administrators continue to require written signatures for beneficiary designations and spousal waivers and consent.

So far, pension plan administrators and service providers have been cautious in using electronic communications. Generally, important notices and member statements continue to be delivered in print, although some secondary documents such as plan booklets and investment information in defined contribution plans are often provided through electronic means. Print versions are made available upon request. Nevertheless, there have been developments in electronic communications. For example, since July 1, 2012, the Ontario *Pension Benefits Act* authorizes administrators to electronically send certain notices, statements, and other plan records to members, former members, retired members, and other plan beneficiaries.

Regulators have gradually accepted the electronic filing of some pension documents. The federal Office of the Superintendent of Financial Institutions requires Annual Information Returns and Certified Financial Statements to be filed either by disk or electronic transfer for federally regulated pension plans, and has produced detailed specifications of such submissions. On January 1, 2011, the Alberta Superintendent of Pensions also provided the option to electronically file Annual Information Returns. Some regulators are requiring electronic filing. The British Columbia Superintendent of Pensions has required electronic filing of Annual Information Returns since December 31, 2010. Similarly, since January 1, 2013, FSCO has made electronic filing of documents, including Annual Information Returns, mandatory.

A related aspect of electronic communication of interest to plan administrators is electronic document storage. Even documents signed by hand, such as beneficiary designations and spousal waivers, can be permanently and cheaply stored. Electronic commerce legislation and the CAPSA Guideline require that such electronic documents be held securely and in a way that identifies their origin and prevents tampering.

Electronic communication in the benefits and retirement savings industry will continue to be a topic of discussion in the future. Further clarification is still required from legislators to provide administrators with the certainty that they need to continue moving forward in the evolving electronic age.

Legal Implications of Plan Member Communications

Employers are becoming increasingly concerned and increasingly aware of the liabilities that can occur as a result of poor pension plan communication to members. This liability has been further brought to the forefront and exposed by many court decisions. Clear and accurate information is an absolute necessity, and implementing preventative measures will provide the groundwork for avoiding future liability.

While there are a variety of regulatory obligations placed upon employers and administrators to communicate information to employees, the common law implications must not be overlooked when considering the legal ramifications of employee pension plan communications. Actions have been brought on the basis of negligent misrepresentation and breach of contract. The following discussion is an overview of a number of cases that have examined negligent misrepresentation and breach of contract in a pension context. Full citation for cases discussed in this chapter can be found in the Case Table.

Negligent Misrepresentation

For employees to succeed in a claim based upon negligent misrepresentation, the following five requirements must be met:

1. There must be a duty of care between the administrator/employer and employee/beneficiary based upon a "special relationship";

2. The representation made must be "untrue, inaccurate, or misleading";

3. The administrator/employer must have acted negligently in making the representation;

4. The employee/beneficiary must have reasonably relied upon the misrepresentation; and

5. The reliance must have been detrimental to the employee/beneficiary, in that damages must have resulted.

After reviewing the list of requirements, one might think that the employer or administrator must actively mislead employees by actual statements to establish negligent misrepresentation, but this is not so. Failure to disclose pertinent information and available options to employees, or providing information in a confusing way, can also be categorized as negligent misrepresentation.

The case of *Spinks v. Canada*,[5] illustrates how an omission, a failure to fully inform the employee, can lead to employer liability on the grounds of negligent misrepresentation. In this case, Mr. Spinks had worked for the Australian Atomic Energy Commission for approximately 20 years prior to emigrating to Canada to take a position with Atomic Energy of Canada Ltd. On his first day of work, he attended a sign-on interview, which was designed to inform new employees about their employment and provide them with information regarding their pension plan. Mr. Spinks was also provided with a pension administration screening form. On this form, an employee could elect to count previous employment elsewhere as pensionable service under the federal government plan. Mr. Spinks returned the form without having completed the section regarding previous employment. Some years later, he was shocked to learn a colleague who had previously been employed in England had bought back his years of English service. Ultimately, it was held that it was the duty of the staffing officer to advise Mr. Spinks competently and to take care in providing that advice, regardless of whether there was a request for advice. In addition, although the screening form referred to other forms of employment, it did not refer to employment with foreign governments. This lack of information, which Mr. Spinks had relied on, led him to erroneously conclude that he could not buy back his Australian service.

Providing clear and accurate information is an absolute necessity if the employer or administrator wishes to avoid liability. Even relying upon a form prescribed by legislation will not necessarily spare the employer or administrator from resulting liability. In *Deraps v. Labourer's Pension Fund of Central and Eastern Canada*,[6] Mrs. Deraps was seeking damages representing the survival benefits she would have otherwise received had she not signed a spousal waiver form for her husband's disability pension. Her husband was diagnosed with cancer at the time he applied for disability benefits under his union's pension plan. They met with a union pension counsellor, who was hired by the union to provide information to members regarding the terms and conditions of their pension plan. Mrs. Deraps stated that she and her husband were not given advice nor much information beyond what was on the forms. The forms contained two options: Mr. Deraps could receive a full pension, with Mrs. Deraps to receive 60% of his benefits after he died, or Mr. Deraps could receive a full pension with Mrs. Deraps receiving nothing after his death. The Deraps chose the second option and Mrs. Deraps signed a spousal waiver. She stated that she believed that signing the waiver would mean a reduced

---

5   [1996] F.C.J. No. 352, 134 D.L.R. (4th) 223 (F.C.A.).
6   [1999] O.J. No. 3281, 21 C.C.P.B. 304 (Ont. C.A.).

survivor pension upon her husband's death — not a complete disentitlement to a pension.

The Ontario Court of Appeal concluded that the union pension counsellor, as agent for the administrator, had been retained to provide information to union members regarding the terms and conditions of the pension plan. As an agent with specialized knowledge, skill and expertise, she had a duty to advise plan members and their spouses about the nature of the options available to them under the plan. Therefore, by failing to provide complete and clear information to Mrs. Deraps, the pension counselor breached her duty of care and this amounted to negligent misrepresentation. In its decision, the Court of Appeal stated that, as a result of her personal circumstances and the "highly confusing language in the waiver," it was reasonable to conclude that Mrs. Deraps did not understand that she was signing away her entitlement.

It appears as if the *Deraps* case is taking the administrator's duty to a higher level — ensuring that correct information is disseminated does not suffice. Administrators must actually ensure that the information is understood by the recipient. All consequences of the recipient's decisions, both positive and negative, must be brought forth to the recipient and any applicable spouse.

In addition to failing to provide employees with the information they require to make informed decisions, the employer or administrator cannot avoid liability by simply advising employees to obtain independent advice. In *Allison v. Noranda Inc.*,[7] the employer provided Mr. Allison with a letter informing him of two separation pay options. Under both options, the total amount of severance monies remained the same. One option was a lump-sum option and the other was an instalment option. What the letter and the employer did not explain was that the separation pay option that Mr. Allison had selected would significantly affect the amount of pension benefits that he received at age 55. However, the employer did advise Mr. Allison to seek independent advice, which he did.

Upon reaching age 55, Mr. Allison applied for his pension benefits and, at this point, became aware of the consequences of his selection. The New Brunswick Court of Appeal stated that the employer was under a duty to disclose to the employee material information relating to the pension consequences that would occur as a result of his selection of the separation pay option. Such failure constituted a negligent misrepresentation that misled Mr. Allison into believing that his selection

---

[7]   [2001] N.B.J. No. 241, 28 C.C.P.B. 1 (N.B.C.A.).

would not impact upon his pension benefits. Stating that the employee should receive independent advice does not relieve the employer from its liability if material facts are not disclosed.

As always, honesty is the best policy and, without a doubt, deceptive practices will open the employer or administrator to liability. In *Ford v. Laidlaw Carriers Inc.*,[8] Laidlaw had made an early retirement offer to its employees. The president of Laidlaw spoke to the trustee of its employees' benefit plans to find out how the employees' shares in the retirement plans would be valued for payout to an employee who accepted an early retirement offer. The trust company provided inaccurate advice to the president, which the president discovered upon reviewing the plans. However, despite this knowledge, the president conveyed the inaccurate information to the employees. The court held that Laidlaw's misrepresentation constituted a term of the retirement offer. The employees were therefore entitled to receive from Laidlaw the difference between the amount of money each of them actually received from their retirement plans and what they were told they would receive if they submitted their early notice of retirement.

When the plan administrator misleads or fails to provide relevant information to a plan member or beneficiary, the courts will generally assume that the member or beneficiary relied on the administrator's advice to the member's or beneficiary's detriment. In *Smith v. Canadian National Railway Co.*,[9] the plan member commenced a common-law relationship one month before retiring under the plan. Under the terms of the pension plan, the spouse was entitled to a survivorship pension only if the common-law relationship commenced at least one year before the retirement date. After retirement, the plan member and his common-law spouse were erroneously advised that a spousal pension was payable. The plan administrator discovered the error after the plan member died and withdrew the spousal pension. The spouse sued, and the judge required the administrator to pay a spousal pension even though the misrepresentation took place after the member retired and there was nothing the member or spouse could have done to become eligible for a spousal pension. The judge found that the spouse would have made alternative arrangements for her retirement, such as asking the member to provide for her in his will, had she known she was ineligible for a spousal pension. Thus, where a plan administrator negligently misleads a member and does not correct the error within a short period of time, and if the court finds that the member was damaged by the misrepresentation, the member will be entitled to compensation.

---

[8]   [1994] O.J. No. 2663, 12 C.C.P.B. 179 (Ont. C.A.).

[9]   [2002] N.S.J. No. 262, 2002 NSSC 148 (N.S.S.C.).

Breach of Contract

An employer or administrator who intends to rely on formal documentation to prevent liability, while simultaneously leveraging less formal means of plan communication, cannot assume that the terms of the formal plan documents will always prevail and that they will thus be shielded from legal liability. The employer/administrator can actually amend the terms of the employment contract and create new obligations for itself by simply communicating a different version of the formal documentation to employees. It is also important to keep in mind the *contra proferentem* rule, which provides that ambiguous provisions in a written document will be construed against the person who drafted the document.

In *Lawrie v. Deloro*,[10] Deloro was acquiring the employees' company. The surplus in the acquired company's pension plan was owned by the employee plan members. The pension plan was replaced by a new pension plan. Under the terms of the new plan, the surplus was to belong to Deloro. Following the acquisition of the assets of the acquired company, Deloro sent the employees a letter that promised to provide benefits that were at least as favourable as the benefits they previously had. The court held that this letter written by Deloro to the employees created a special arrangement between Deloro and the employees and, as a result, the employees were entitled to the surplus.

In *Schmidt v. Air Products Canada Ltd.*,[11] the Supreme Court of Canada dealt with another issue of surplus entitlement. Air Products had distributed a booklet to its employees, which contained a statement that any remaining surplus would be paid to the employees. However, the booklet's influence on surplus entitlement was doubtful, since it specifically stated that the plan would be subject to amendment from time to time. The Supreme Court of Canada stated that the statement regarding surplus contained in the booklet could not, in this case, form the basis for an estoppel preventing the company from now claiming the surplus for itself. However, the Supreme Court left the door open for future cases to rely on plan booklets and other communications by making the following statement:

> Documents not normally considered to have legal effect may nonetheless form part of the legal matrix within which the rights of employers and employees participating in a pension plan must be determined. Whether they do so will depend upon the wording of

---

[10]   [1993] O.J. No. 42, 99 D.L.R. (4th) 679 (Ont. C.A.).

[11]   [1994] S.C.J. No. 48, [1994] 2 S.C.R. 611 (S.C.C.).

the documents, the circumstances in which they were produced, and the effect which they had on the parties, particularly the employees[12]

In *Hembruff v. Ontario (Municipal Employees Retirement Board)*,[13] the Ontario Court of Appeal concluded that potential plan changes under consideration do not have to be announced until they are officially implemented. The plaintiffs were members of the Ontario Municipal Employees Retirement System (OMERS). In 1998, these members resigned employment and elected to receive commuted value payments, before knowing the plan would be amended to provide benefit enhancements effective January 1, 1999. The plaintiffs argued that, given the OMERS Board's track record with the government, it was likely that the Board's recommendation for benefit enhancements would be adopted. Consequently, they believed the Board had an obligation to inform members when the Board's decision to recommend benefit enhancements was "almost certain" or "highly likely". The court concluded that the Board's process was done in good faith and that imposing an obligation to disclose plan changes under consideration would result in an unmanageable burden for administrators. Nevertheless, this case highlights the need for administrators to establish appropriate policies for disclosure and communication.

---

[12] *Ibid.*

[13] [2005] O.J. No. 4667, 78 O.R. (3d) 561 (Ont. C.A.).

Chapter 30

EMERGING TRENDS

Executive Summary

This chapter charts the emerging major trends and themes that affect pensions and benefits by scanning a broad spectrum of significant issues for employers, benefit plan sponsors, and the various stakeholders who need to be alert to the changing environment. A focus on pensions includes the expansion of CPP, which will have a significant impact on the Canadian retirement income system, the on-going financial challenges of a low interest environment and increasing longevity, the continued decline of defined benefit (DB) employer-sponsored pension plans, despite plan innovations designed to better balance risks between employers and employees, and the potential for a redesign of the Ontario pension regulator.

Other pension themes meriting discussion are; the issues of sustainability, particularly in public sector plans; the continued and increasing attractiveness of defined contribution (DC) plans; the increasing popularity of TFSAs coupled with the introduction of PRPPs; and the continuing development of the concept of responsible investing.

The focus on benefit plans highlights the impact of the increasingly important search for cost savings, the sources of some major drivers of costs, and the issue of managing the benefits of a diverse workforce.

Other significant benefit themes include; drug reform, with the lower costs of generics now being offset by the increasing popularity (and cost) of biologics, speciality drugs and biosimilars; the shared accountability model approach taken by some progressive employers; increased awareness and sensitivity towards mental illness in the workplace, including the National Standard; medical marijuana in the workplace; retiree benefit exchanges which offer an alternative approach to reducing employer liability and administration; and big data analytics.

Major Trends in Pensions

Some of the biggest pension trends include the following:

- The proposed expansion of CPP from a benefit rate of 25% of covered earnings to 33% is arguably the biggest pension development in Canada in half a century.

- Pension reform has resulted in the continued flourishing of DC plans, and the end of a potential comeback for DB plans in the private sector.

- Hybrid plans, which offer a better balancing of risks between employers and employees in employer-sponsored pension plans.

- Increased life expectancy continues to grow the pressure to retire later in life.

- The slow adoption of PRPPs by provincial governments has stalled their acceptance, except perhaps for Quebec's version, the VRSP.

- The issue of sustainability of public sector plans has gone off the radar, in the face of robust pension returns, but may re-emerge in the not-too-distant future.

- The continued growth in popularity of retirement vehicles that have only minimal employer involvement, in particular TFSAs.

- Efforts to harmonize pension plan regulations across provinces continue, with five provinces signing on to a Revised Multi-jurisdictional Pension Plan Agreement.

- The proposed replacement of FSCO and DICO with the Financial Services Regulatory Authority.

- The legislated requirement in Ontario to disclose whether ESG factors (environmental, social and governance) are incorporated in pension investment decision making.

- Specific to DC plans:
  - A greater focus on retirement income has resulted in higher contribution formulas and a rise in auto-enrollment and mandatory participation programs.
  - Member decision-making support continues to evolve to aide members in understand the impact of their decisions on their retirement income.
  - As part of the above bullets, the number of DC investment options is trending lower, in the hopes of simplifying the decision making process for members.

CPP Expansion

What is arguably the biggest development in Canada's retirement income system in the last half century is about to unfold. In June of 2016, the provinces and the federal government agreed to an expansion of the benefit rate from 25% of covered earnings to 33%.

This expansion is significant in that it signals a shift in government thinking as to the purpose of public pensions. Rather than simply provide a subsistence level of retirement income, governments are now intent on closing the pension gap for the many middle-income earners who do not currently have workplace pension coverage. While there will still be a role for Pillar 3 (workplace pension plans and RRSPs), we can expect to see some shrinkage in pension coverage in the years to come, the same as occurred after 1976 once the CPP was fully phased in. Contributions to RRSPs will also be affected.

This is not to say that Pillar 3 will wither away. Total assets in workplace plans and RRSPs will continue to grow in absolute terms as will contributions to TFSAs. Nevertheless, there will be a de-emphasis of individual responsibility for retirement saving and a reduction in the role played by employers as pension plan sponsors.

Pension Reform

The CPP expansion will also affect the evolution of pension standards reform. Apart from hybrid pension plans (see below), we can now consider that the pension reform initiative that commenced in Ontario in 2007 with the Arthurs Commission is essentially dead. There is no longer any hope that DB pension plans will stage a comeback in the private sector. As it is, only 10% of employees in the private sector are still participating in DB pension plans and that percentage is certain to shrink as over half of existing DB plans are closed to new hires with virtually no new DB plans being established. DC plans, on the other hand, are still flourishing (see Defined Contribution Trends below) and have become the new hotbed of innovation as plan sponsors and third party administrators are continuing to make such plans more effective for participants.

Hybrid Plans

Hybrid plans are pension plans that have both DB and DC characteristics. The main type of hybrid plan is the Shared Risk Pension Plan (SRPP) which Morneau Shepell had a key part in developing for the New Brunswick government in 2012. The SRPP is actually a more general form of the better known hybrid, the Target Benefit Pension Plan (TBP).

In 2013, it appeared that hybrid plans held great promise. They provided greater certainty of benefits for participants with minimal risk for employers and they practically eliminated the problem of individual longevity risk that exists in DC plans. Hybrid plans have, however, made very little progress in the interim. Governments have been slow to draft regulations to enable such plans to be implemented and the problem of transitioning from a DB plan to a hybrid has not been completely resolved. Moreover, it is clear that such plans are not appropriate for smaller groups. It is still expected that hybrid plans will eventually become more popular but will do little to improve the low participation rate in workplace pension plans in the private sector. One possible catalyst will be a large government, such as the federal government, converting the existing public sector plans under its jurisdiction to hybrid plans.

Retirement Age

Canada continues to be one of the very few countries in the developed world that has chosen to ignore the implications of improving longevity on retirement age. The OECD publishes a bi-annual report of pensions in the OECD and G20 nations called "Pensions at a Glance". In their 2015 report, they note, "67 has indeed become the new 65 and several countries are going even further towards ages closer to 70". Canada, if anything, is going backwards in this regard, as the steps taken by the former Conservative government to move the commencement age for OAS and GIS from 65 to 67 have been reversed by the new Liberal government.

Nevertheless, change is inevitable. In the mid-1960s, the average life expectancy for males as measured from birth was 68.75 while the average retirement age was 67.5. Based on the 2011 Canada life tables, male life expectancy has increased to 79.3 (it would be higher again in 2016), while the average retirement age is 63. In the 1960s there were six workers for every retiree; today there are four, and within 25 years it will be just a little more than two workers per retiree.

Pooled Registered Pension Plans (PRPPs)

PRPPs are defined contribution vehicles that are very similar to group RRSPs and defined contribution pension plans. They were the creation of the previous Conservative government and were intended to be a private-sector approach to improving workplace pension plan coverage by making it easier for employers to provide a plan and by auto-enrolling employees.

Employees would contribute to a PRPP by payroll deduction. Apart from selecting the PRPP provider and remitting the amounts contributed by employees, the employer has virtually no other responsibility or liability. The employer could contribute to PRPPs as well, but most of the contributions are expected to be made by the employees themselves.

The initial enthusiasm for PRPPs eventually fizzled out in most provinces as governments were slow to pass enabling legislation and regulations governing PRPPs and when they did, they made PRPPs voluntary on the part of employers. Given that workplace pension plans are already voluntary, it is not surprising that there were few takers of PRPPs as most employers who thought workplace pension coverage was a good idea (or affordable) already offered a plan.

The one exception is Quebec which embraced PRPPs (which they labeled VRSPs) and made access to a VRSP mandatory for every employer with five or more employees (this is still being phased in at the time of writing). It is too early to tell whether VRSPs will be successful in improving pension plan coverage in Quebec and indeed, the experiment may be cut short depending on the impact of the CPP expansion.

Consequently, what started out five years ago as a promising way to offer easy access to most employees of a low-cost vehicle looks destined to be relegated to the periphery of Pillar 3.

Sustainability

After the Great Recession of 2008-2009, a very major concern in pension circles was the sustainability of DB pension plans. The economic conditions at the time created a perfect storm of significant investment losses within pension funds, plunging interest rates that made pension promises more expensive, and reduced tax revenues to fund the pension promises. This was primarily a public sector issue as most private sector employers either do not maintain a DB pension plan or have closed their plan to new hires.

For the most part, the public sector pension plans attempted to improve sustainability by reducing or eliminating early retirement subsidies, making post-retirement indexation of pensions conditional on the funded status of the plan and raising employee and employer contributions. New Brunswick went one major step beyond this by converting a number of its public sector plans to SRPPs. To date, no other province has followed New Brunswick's lead. Unless the federal government takes action, it is unlikely that SRPPs will proliferate in the public sector in the absence of another economic crisis.

In recent years, the sustainability of public sector plans is an issue that has gone off the radar. That is pension returns have been robust and the country has been able to avoid a recession. While the sense of urgency has passed, sustainability remains an issue that may re-emerge in the not-too-distant future. Actuaries have continued to assume real returns on pension fund assets of 4% or more which may prove to be unachievable if interest rates remain low (which is expected for many years to come). What may trigger a new crisis is a recession that squeezes tax revenues and triggers investment losses at the same time.

Tax-Free Savings Accounts (TFSAs)

Since their introduction in 2009, TFSAs have become enormously popular. Of approximately 28 million Canadians age 20 and up (this includes retirees), approximately 11 million have opened a TFSA. By contrast, the take-up rate of RRSPs in the late 1950s and 1960s was extremely low (in 1965 for example, only 29,190 new RRSPs were registered, representing 0.3% of the labour force).

Not all moneys saved in TFSAs will be used to produce retirement income, but it is expected that a significant amount will.

Revised Multi-Jurisdictional Pension Plan Agreement (MJPPA)

Five provinces (Ontario, Quebec, B.C., Alberta, and Nova Scotia) have signed a revised MJPPA, replacing a MJPPA that was signed by Ontario and Quebec in 2011 and also a MJPPA that was signed by all provinces except for PEI back in 1968. Those who are hopeful that the provinces will co-ordinate their efforts to regulate pension plans in a way that lessens the frustration for national plan sponsors would do well to remember George Santayana's quote: "Those who cannot remember the past are condemned to repeat it." Efforts to harmonize pension plan regulation across provinces (and the federal jurisdictions) go back at least to 1964, with little progress to show for it.

Proposed Creation of the Financial Services Regulatory Authority

On November 4, 2015, an Expert Review Panel (Panel) appointed by the Ontario Ministry of Finance to review the mandates of the Financial Services Commission of Ontario (FSCO), the Financial Services Tribunal (FST), and the Deposit Insurance Corporation of Ontario (DICO) released a Preliminary Position Paper (Paper). Among the Paper's 37 recommendations is the establishment of a new regulatory agency called the Financial Services Regulatory Authority (FSRA). The FSRA would replace both FSCO and DICO.

Key features of the proposed FSRA include:

- A governance structure comprised of an independent expert board of directors to oversee FSRA operations, and a Chief Executive Officer that reports to the board;

- A self-funded FSRA that operates outside of the Ontario Public Service as a way to support operational independence, and to improve the FSRA's ability to recruit professionals and industry expertise;

- The FSRA would operate as an integrated regulator of financial services with distinct market conduct, pensions, and prudential regulatory functions organized by divisions;

- Each FSRA division would be led by a Superintendent. For instance, the Superintendent of Pensions would be operationally accountable to the CEO;

- The FSRA would have the authority to levy administrative monetary penalties in the pension and other sectors it regulates;

- The FSRA board would be required to meet with the sectors it oversees at least once a year;

- The FSRA would create a separate "Office of the Consumer" to consider the perspective of consumers in all of its policy-making and actions; and

- The Pension Benefits Guarantee Fund (PBGF) would be administered and overseen by an entity that is separate from, but accountable to, the FSRA.

In addition, highlights of recommendations concerning the FST included:

- The FST would operate separately from FSRA, with its own budget;

- The FST would have the power to recruit professional resources with experience in the regulated sectors;

- A mechanism would be established to appropriately allow and encourage policy-level discourse between the FST and FSRA's board; and

- Legislative or other means should be implemented to ensure that the courts give deference to the FST on policy or matters within its subject-matter expertise.

On March 31, 2016, following a review of nearly 50 submissions from various stakeholders, the Panel released their Final Report, with little substantive change from the recommendations made in the Paper.

The proposed changes in Ontario are intended to provide operational flexibility to regulators, encourage a flexible and consumer-oriented regulatory approach and clarify and streamline the regulator's mandate. The proposal to authorize the new financial regulator to impose administrative penalties (*i.e.*, levy fines without mounting a prosecution in the courts) would be a significant expansion of authority.

It is uncertain at this time if these recommendations will come to fruition, and if so, the time frame involved. Similar previous recommendations, such as the proposed merger of FSCO and the Ontario Securities Commission (circa 2000), have been made and subsequently languished or fallen out of favor. It remains to be seen if the recommended creation of FSRA will similarly fall by the wayside.

Use of ESG Factors in Investment Decision-Making

Effective January 1, 2016, Ontario plan administrators are required to disclose in their Statements of Investment Policies and Procedures (SIPPs) whether they consider environmental, social and governance (ESG) factors in their investment decision making, and, if so, how. Specific disclosure respecting this will also be required on annual plan member statements issued after July 1, 2016. This requirement follows a recommendation made by Harry Arthurs in the 2008 Report of the Expert Commission on Pensions in Ontario. This development may signal a trend worth watching. Many similar concepts have come before, *e.g.*, "ethical" investing, ethical screens, responsible investing, socially responsible investing, *etc.* The United Nations Principles for Responsible Investment suggest that there is growing recognition that effective research, analysis and management of ESG issues is a fundamental part of assessing the value and performance of an investment over the short, medium and long term.

Defined Contribution (DC) Trends

There are quite a few distinct trends related to DC plans, including:

- As capital accumulation plans (CAPs), including registered DC pension plans, continue to grow (both in terms of assets and member participation) and mature, an increased focus on retirement income can be expected, which in turn will lead to advancements in contribution features, member decision-making support, investment options, decumulation options, and governance practices.

- The wide variety of vehicles that have become available in the last few years, including TFSAs, PRPPs, VRSPs, and most recently the announcement by the Federal government of the proposed CPP expansion, has begun to raise questions about the optimal group plan design. We expect this will spark discussion about original plan design objectives and the circumstances under which they were conceived and whether design frameworks need to be challenged in today's evolving landscape.

- As those design frameworks are challenged, the definition of plan objectives and the need to monitor the plan's achievement of them will become more specifically articulated. Sponsors will consider whether and how to monitor their plan's success and where needed to modify their arrangements to maximize the value of their programs, deliver the most efficient retirement outcomes for members and maintain their competitive edge in the attraction and retention of employees.

Contributions

Contribution levels play a critical role in the accumulation of CAP assets to provide sufficient retirement income. As the industry has moved to focus members on their retirement income needs and the levels of retirement income projected to arise from their participation in these programs, plan sponsors have been reviewing and will continue to review their program design features from this perspective as well. We have seen and expect we will continue to see a rise in auto-enrolment or mandatory participation programs (to ensure all members participate in their available programs). Greater focus is being placed on contribution formulas that target company spend appropriately to meet business goals while at the same time encourage higher combined employee and employer levels of contribution. These levels may be higher than what might have been the norm in the past, but are now considered reasonable, to achieve with greater probability the levels of savings necessary to fund retirement income goals.

Member Decision-Making Support

Consistent with the focus on providing retirement income, we will continue to see member decision-making support evolve to help members understand the impact of their decisions — including contribution levels, investment strategy and decumulation strategy — on their expected level of retirement income. For example, next-generation DC tools have arrived that now help members to understand the leap from accumulating assets to structuring a retirement income. These tools will also allow members to model the impact of their contribution behaviour (*e.g.*, reflecting any matching contributions or changes in the level of match over time) on their projected retirement income.

Today's decision support tools for DC members have become much more robust than they were even five years ago, helping members to understand the linkage between their investment choices and expected retirement income and the "undefined" nature of it by providing a range of outcomes under various economic scenarios and the associated probabilities of achieving them. Increased rigour and methodology employed in retirement projection analysis and modeling tools will continue to assist employees in understanding the outcomes that can be anticipated and the variables that can impact them with greater reliability.

Investment Options

There has been a continuing trend observed of reducing the number of investment strategies available in fund lineups to simplify the decision-making process for members. As part of this trend, there has been an increased focus on offering "ready-made" investment porfolios made up of defined mixes of different asset classes, such as target date and/or target risk funds. We expect this trend to continue to evolve as sponsors move away from offering a "variety" of funds and towards more packaged comprehensive portfolio solutions, thereby allowing the member to spend more time focused on understanding their retirement goals, timeline, and risk tolerance level (with the appropriate investment selection being a natural outcome).

To accommodate more sophisticated members who wish to take a more active role in the design of their portfolios and who wish to select from a-la-carte fund lineups, there has been an increasing trend towards strategies managed by institutional investment managers that employ greater sophistication and diversification in the selection of securities than has been observed in the past or in the retail investment market. Strategies that include consideration of non-traditional investments such as emerging market equity, real estate and global fixed income products, an expanding breadth of passively managed approaches, and strategies that focus on absolute return objectives or low volatility, to name a few, are expected to continue to attract greater attention. However, plans sponsors should bear in mind that CAP programs are generally intended for a diverse employee group. Consequently, it may be better to limit non-traditional investments to being components within pre-defined portfolios rather than offering them on an a-la-carte basis.

Decumulation

Traditionally, members have been faced with the choice of self-managing or annuitizing their accumulated assets to provide retirement income, usually on a retail basis and outside the benefits of a group plan. As CAPs mature, more decision-making support for members approaching retirement as well as additional options for converting assets into retirement income can be expected. These options will need to reflect a variety of lifestyle choices, retirement needs (*e.g.*, phased retirement), and tolerance for risk. Sponsors are beginning to consider the advantages of offering group sponsored decumulation vehicles like Group LIFs and Group RRIFs or where permissible, the paying of variable pension-like payments directly out of their pension programs. These options can provide members with dramatic fee savings and consequently larger retirement incomes. We expect more sponsors will begin to offer their members group sponsored decumulation vehicles to assist them in the conversion of their accumulated savings into a retirement income and that this will be a continuing trend.

Governance

Finally, with more members dependent on CAPs as a significant source of retirement income, an increased focus on plan governance, both on the part of plan sponsors and regulatory bodies, can be expected. Particular areas of focus will include member communication and decision-making support, clarification of member and plan sponsor roles and responsibilities, decumulation options, suitability of investment options and reasonableness, transparency and disclosure of fees paid by members, particularly any undisclosed fees or operating expenses. One should also expect greater focus on any conflicts of interest among service providers — particularly in the common situation where the recordkeeper is offering proprietary investment products, or receives undisclosed remuneration from investment mangers.

Major Trends in Benefits

Some of the biggest benefits trends include the following:

- Drug reform is now complete, so the positive wave of lower drug pricing for generics has now plateaued.
- Specialty drugs continue to be released in the marketplace, with very positive results for the patient, but at significant cost. Both insurers and employers struggle to find the appropriate approach.

- The top two cost drivers for employers are mental illness and musculoskeletal conditions.

- In January 2013, Canada became the first country in the world to release a voluntary standard to promote and facilitate a psychologically safe workplace, the National Standard for Psychological Health and Safety in the Workplace.

- In the current environment of low salary increases, progressive employers have focused on their benefits programs and are looking at ensuring their philosophy aligns with their business model.

- Progressive employers also focus on designing programs that reinforce joint accountability of health with employees. Through smarter data analytics and technology, employers can engage their workforce in changing behaviors.

- Given the increase in prescriptions, employers need to focus on medical marijuana and how it is addressed under their benefits programs and policies.

- Employee program flexibility is still key, as well as offering more employee paid benefit options to enhance the overall package.

- Retiree benefits continue to be transitioned out of many employer packages. Canada's first retiree exchange was introduced in 2016 and offers employers an alternative approach for reducing employer liability and administration.

- Big Data analytics is an emerging area providing insights that have the potential to advance personalized care, improve outcomes, and avoid unnecessary costs.

Drug Reform

Over the past few years employers have enjoyed a reduction in their drug spend. Savings were realized from two factors: generic drug pricing reform & several brand name drugs coming off patent.

Several years ago legislation was passed to lower the cost of generic drugs to 25%-35% of the brand name cost (percentage varies by province) with a further reduction to 18% of the brand name cost for certain medications (those used to treat high cholesterol, acid reflux, and certain mental illness conditions).

The lower costs for generic drugs, combined with several high cost brand name drugs coming off patent from 2012 to 2014 (what we call a "patent cliff"), worked together to reduce drug spend for employers.

The positive pricing effects of these changes, however, have now materialized; the savings have plateaued and drug cost has started to increase.

Biologic Drugs, Specialty Drugs and Biosimilars

At the same time that any potential savings for drug plans have plateaued as a result of drug reform and the patent cliff, new high cost biologic and specialty drugs continue to enter the marketplace. These new mediations have significantly increased the drug cost in benefit programs.

Biologics are drugs that are made from living organisms that require special maintenance, administration and management. Specialty drugs are traditional medications that have a high cost and are developed from highly complex molecules. Both biologics and specialty drugs are highly effective, however the costs to purchase these drugs can range from $10,000 to $100,000 a year for treatment for one individual.

Additionally, biologic and specialty drugs are being developed for more maintenance conditions such as high cholesterol and asthma which have the potential to impact a large segment of the population. New hepatitis therapies such as Sovaldi and Harvoni have entered the market place. While these medications can cure hepatitis, Sovaldi can cost up to $80,000 per person for three months of treatment.

Due to the complex nature of these therapies there will never be true generic drug substitutions. Cost relief for these drugs may come from the introduction of biosimilars (also called subsequent entry biologics). While a generic drug has the same active ingredients as a brand name drug, biosimilars have similar therapeutic effects but are not completely interchangeable. Biosimilars will have a smaller price tag compared to traditional biologic or specialty drugs, but they will still have a high cost.

The best way to manage the substantial increase in cost, as well as who should pay for these drugs (the employer, employee or government), remain areas for debate. Without any drug intervention programs in place group benefit plans are covering these costs for employees as well as an employee's dependents.

Cost Drivers — Mental Illness and Musculoskeletal Conditions

Increased awareness and sensitivity towards mental illness in the workplace, as well as initiatives to de-stigmatize the idea that mental illness is "bad", have increased prescriptions for mental illness related medications. Consequently this has resulted in an increase to drug spend (and disability spend) as more claims for mental illness are being submitted and reimbursed.

Increases in the cost and amount of claims for musculoskeletal medications such as rheumatoid arthritis have also increased total drug and disability spend.

Medical Marijuana

As medical marijuana prescriptions become more popular employers are faced with the dilemma of a duty to accommodate for employees taking this type of medication. Employers are encouraged to have a policy in place in the event that an employee may be required to use medical marijuana while on the job. Updating drug and alcohol policies to include language around medical marijuana is encouraged.

The medical marijuana landscape is still changing. To date medical marijuana does not have a Drug Identification Number (DIN) and therefore is not typically eligible as a drug to be reimbursed through a group benefit program.

The National Standard of Canada: Psychological Health and Safety in the Workplace

The Standard was commissioned by the Mental Health Commission of Canada in 2013 and is the first standard of its kind in the world. The Standard is voluntary, adoption is not legally required, and it outlines a systematic approach to develop and sustain a psychologically healthy and safe workplace. It focuses on mental illness prevention and mental health promotion, and provides a set of guidelines, tools and resources focused on promoting employees' psychological health and preventing psychological harm due to workplace factors.

The Standard outlines thirteen workplace factors impacting psychological health, and provides a process to implement a management system. The Standard has been adopted by several leading organizations, and continues to gain the interest of employers.

An Employer's Role with Employee Well-Being

As employers grapple with the cost pressures on their benefits program, progressive organizations have started to take a more focused approach. They realize that they have a limited budget to spend, but are looking more holistically beyond just the cost of their benefit program (or individually at each component, like drugs, disability, etc.). The organizations have worked to start integrating the data to determine the message that is uncovered. Additionally, as they look at their workforces, they may have concerns with an aging population, and/or with finding the right talent to be productive.

Once they have determined their employee health cost drivers, and set the objectives for their benefit program, they will likely find themselves realizing that they, as the employer, cannot do this alone. They can provide the tools (support) for their employees, but the employee also has a role — the shared accountability model.

Diverse Workforces Need Diverse Benefit Options — those that reinforce shared health accountability with employees

Four generations are represented in the Canadian workforce. With this diversity of age and lifestyle comes diversity in healthcare needs. Many employers are being challenged to simultaneously accommodate the needs of the veterans and baby boom generations (many of whom have chronic conditions) and Generation X, who tend to start families later and change careers more frequently than did their older co-workers. The millennials continue to grow in the workforce, and will represent more than 75% by the year 2020. These employees expect corporate employers to provide benefits.

Cost pressures on today's benefit programs call for employers, employees and all other stakeholders, to play an active role in finding a path forward. Leading organizations continue to look to flexible benefits programs as a way to define their contribution to these programs, and provide the options that employees want. Employers are now able to provide many tools to help employees assess their current health, and also to help them improve it. Providing sustainable programs over the long term will require most organizations to employ some combination of modifications to cost sharing, reductions in benefits, and radical innovations in plan design. The leading innovations in plan design incent employees to take online health assessments, and employ real-time coaching to help them set a plan. They are able to set goals on their smartphone/tablet/laptop and are able to track their progress via linkages with their device. Additionally, they can participate in a corporate fitness challenge, or set up teams to compete in physical activities with other corporate teams.

Beyond focusing on fitness, which can improve many chronic health conditions (or slow or prevent the onset), many employers are determining that mental illness may be the leading cost driver within their organization. On the same shared accountability model, employers are implementing mental health strategies as part of their overall framework, or establishing a separate strategy. As employers look to their employees, what is now emerging is the acknowledgement that beyond what has been done to date, helping employees through the coping crisis may be the best support they can provide. As the workforce continues to change, improving how an employer can help employees cope may pay the largest dividends.

Voluntary Benefits

With the rising costs of benefit plans employers are always looking for ways to save money. Historically employees have viewed their benefit program as a right — something they are entitled to without much involvement from them, outside of any cost sharing or deductibles. Employers are more and more attempting to change this mindset; to partner with their employees to help them understand the costs associated with providing benefits.

The concept of consumerism promotes the ideology that employees should be cost conscious about their benefit program, and look for lower cost services and products when submitting claims to help maintain the financial strength of the program.

At the same time as employees are becoming more responsible for the cost of their benefits, they also want more choice, freedom and flexibility to have the benefits they want. Employers (and employees) spending money on benefits an employee may not need does not create a lot of value for that individual. It also creates unnecessary cost. Additionally, if an employee doesn't feel like they're getting the benefits they want they may not be invested in the program. Furthermore they may not be the best consumer (looking for the best prices) which can create additional spending waste within the program.

In order to strike the balance between giving employees choice, and at the same time keeping costs down, many employers are shifting their benefit program to include more voluntary benefits and removing core coverage. Voluntary benefits such as Optional Life (for employees, spouses and dependent children), Optional Accidental Death & Dismemberment and Optional Critical Illness are becoming more prevalent while benefits such as Basic Dependent Life and Basic Accidental Death & Dismemberment are becoming less popular.

These voluntary benefits are 100% employee paid. The only cost to a plan sponsor is to help administer the plan — set up payroll deductions, answer questions from employees and assist with processing any claims (some of these costs may even be picked up by the insurer). Removing Basic Coverage and replacing it with Voluntary Coverage allows employees the freedom to purchase the coverage they want at a low cost, while saving the employer money on providing benefits for people who may not want them.

Some plan sponsors are promoting Voluntary Retiree Benefits as an option for their retiring workforce. Voluntary Retiree Benefits such as health and dental can provide security for employees and can be purchased by either an individual retiring or by an employee at a much lower cost than the employer insuring its own retiree benefit program (this can also eliminate any Other Post-Employment Benefit valuation requirements).

Looking to the future, voluntary benefits is an area that may grow to provide more choice than it does today. Universal and term life insurance, hospital coverage, home insurance and pet insurance may be on the horizon as options for employees to purchase on a group basis through traditional benefit programs.

Retiree Marketplace Exchange

Traditional group retiree benefits are becoming less prevalent than they used to be. In an effort to control and contain costs employers are no longer sponsoring these programs. This leaves a gap for employees who may be retiring soon — how and where will they get insurance?

Morneau Shepell, has recently announced a new voluntary Retiree Marketplace Exchange. Individuals can access the marketplace and customize a retiree benefit program that meets their needs. Insurance can be underwritten by one of a few select insurance carriers that are participating in the exchange. This presents choice for the individual to purchase what is important to them at a lower cost than individual health benefit products.

It also brings a low cost solution for employers — they can choose to allow employees to use the marketplace exchange, and the benefits can be paid for directly by the retiree. The employer's liability is reduced and retirees can have a level of financial security for when they leave the workforce.

Big Data Analytics

Big Data analytics is a combination of two concepts — big data and analytics. The two combine to enable an emerging information management technology that has the ability to examine large quantities of data and provide insights to address various issues and answer many questions. Within the context of health management, it provides stakeholders with new insights that have the potential to advance personalized care, improve outcomes and avoid unnecessary costs.

The tools for measuring health, engagement, and productivity are often disconnected, making it difficult to see the overall picture and determine the best strategy for driving improved results. The opportunity to utilize Big Data analytics is emerging in many areas, including health management solutions. Organizations are increasingly seeking assistance from service providers in analyzing the effectiveness of their health management programs, to assist in determining if their investment or "spend" is being effectively allocated.

Using Big Data analytics can provide insight into the employees' life, physical and psychological health, and work metrics. Employers are able to gain knowledge of the impact of coping skills on employees' productivity, health and engagement which can assist them in aligning their health management investment in health and wellness programs for better outcomes.

TABLE OF CASES

WEBSITES

Government and Non-Government Organizations Referred to in Pension Handbook

Organization	Role/Stated Objectives	Website Address
Statistics Canada	Statistics Canada provides Canadian social and economic statistics and products	www.statcan.gc.ca
Canada Revenue Agency (CRA)	CRA regulates compliance with Canada's tax legislation	www.cra-arc.gc.ca
Employment and Social Development Canada (ESDC)	Develops, manages and delivers social programs such as EI, CPP, OAS, and GIS	www.esdc.gc.ca
Retraite Québec	Retraite Quebec ensures that Québec registered pension plans are administered in accordance with the *Supplemental Pension Plans Act.*	http://www.retraitequebec.gouv.qc.ca/
CPP Investment Board	Crown Corporation responsible for managing CPP funds.	www.cppib.ca
Canadian Association of Pension Supervisory Authorities (CAPSA)	A national interjurisdictional association of pension regulators whose mission is to facilitate an efficient and effective pension regulatory system in Canada	www.capsa-acor.org

Organization	Role/Stated Objectives	Website Address
Association of Canadian Pension Management (ACPM)	ACPM acts as the informed voice of plan sponsors, administrators and their service providers in advocating for improvement to the Canadian retirement income system.	www.acpm.com
Canadian Institute of Actuaries (CIA)	National organization of the Canadian actuarial profession, which promotes advancement of actuarial sciences and sponsors programs for the education and qualification of members and prospective members.	http://www.cia-ica.ca/
Association of Workers' Compensation Boards of Canada	National not-for-profit organization, which facilitates the exchange of information between Workers' Compensation Boards and Commissions, plays a leadership role in providing safe and healthy workplaces.	www.awcbc.org
Chartered Professional Accountants Canada (CPA)	CPA represents Chartered Professional Accountants in Canada. It conducts research into current and emerging business issues and sets accounting and assurance standards for business, not-for-profit organizations, and government	https://www.cpacanada.ca/

Organization	Role/Stated Objectives	Website Address
Financial Reporting and Assurance Standards Canada	A public website which houses news and information on the financial reporting and assurance standards boards and oversight councils and the work that they do.	www.frascanada.ca
Canadian Life and Health Insurance Association (CLHIA)	CLHIA is a voluntary trade association that represents the collective interests of its member life and health insurers	www.clhia.ca
CFA Institute	A global, not-for-profit organization of investment professionals from over 100 countries worldwide	www.cfainstitute.org
Morneau Shepell	Morneau Shepell is a human resource and technology company	www.morneaushepell.com
Social Investment Organization	The Canadian Association for socially responsible investment	www.socialinvestment.ca
Willis Towers Watson (Canada)	Willis Towers Watson is a global advisory, broking and solutions company.	www.towerswatson.com/en-CA
World Economic Forum	The World Economic Forum is an independent international organization committed to improving the state of the world	www.weforum.org
FEDERAL AND PROVINCIAL PENSION REGULATORS		
Federal	Office of the Superintendent of Financial Institutions	www.osfi-bsif.gc.ca

Organization	Role/Stated Objectives	Website Address
Alberta	Alberta Treasury Board and Finance – Pensions	http://www.finance.alberta.ca/business/pensions/
British Columbia	Financial Institutions Commission – Pensions Division	www.fic.gov.bc.ca
Manitoba	Labour and Immigration – Office of the Superintendent of the Pension Commission	www.gov.mb.ca/ labour / pension
New Brunswick	Financial and Consumer Services Commission – Pension Division	http://www.fcnb.ca/industry-pensions.html
Newfoundland and Labrador	Pension Administration and General Insurance Division	http://www.fin.gov.nl.ca/fin/department/branches/divisions/pensions_adminstration.html
Nova Scotia	Department of Finance – Pension Regulation Division	http://www.novascotia.ca/finance/en/home/pensions/default.aspx
Ontario	Financial Services Commission of Ontario	http://www.fsco.gov.on.ca/en/pensions/Pages/Default.aspx
Quebec	Retraite Québec	http://www.retraitequebec.gouv.qc.ca/en/Pages/accueil.aspx
Saskatchewan	Financial and Consumer Affairs Authority - Pensions Division	http://www.fcaa.gov.sk.ca/pensions

TABLE OF CONTENTS FOR THE MORNEAU SHEPELL PENSION CHARTS IN THE CANADIAN EMPLOYMENT BENEFITS & PENSION GUIDE

INDEX